Science, Class and Society is the first systematic attempt to compare classical sociology and historical materialism—the respective and rival traditions founded by Comte, Durkheim, Weber and Pareto on the one hand, and Marx and Engels on the other. Therborn starts with a critique of four major recent 'self-reflective' accounts of sociology from within the modern discipline itself—those of Talcott Parsons, Wright Mills, Alvin Gouldner and Robert Friedrichs. He then turns to the history of the discipline which preceded sociology—the emergent 'economics' in the age of Enlightenment, and furnishes a compelling account of its material and social background, from Smith and Ricardo to Jevons to Keynes. Situated against the ascent of classical economics, sociology is interpreted as the product of a subsequent 'age between two revolutions'—a system of thought that emerged in the aftermath of the French Revolution, and matured on the eve of the proletarian revolution in Russia, in the work of Durkheim, Weber and the 'elite theorists' from Michels to Pareto. The purpose of the new discipline of sociology, Therborn argues, was to cope with the increasing problems of class conflict and industrial unrest in Europe as the 19th century progressed towards its hour of reckoning in the First World War. Therborn locates the major intellectual achievement of this tradition in the discovery of what he calls the 'ideological community' as an object of legitimate scientific enquiry, comparable with the 'market' of classical economics. In doing so, he throws new light on the work of Durkheim and Weber in particular. The book ends with an analysis of the conditions of formation—social and theoretical—of Marxism itself. Written in an urbane and lively style, *Science, Class and Society* promises to become a classic for sociology students and readers, socialist and non-socialist alike.

Göran Therborn

Verso

Science, Class and Society

On the Formation of Sociology and Historical Materialism

First published by NLB, 1976
© Göran Therborn, 1976
Second impression, 1977
Third impression, 1980

Verso Edition first published, 1980
© Göran Therborn, 1980

NLB and Verso Editions, 7 Carlisle Street, London W1

Printed and bound in Great Britain by
Redwood Burn Ltd
Trowbridge and Esher

ISBN 0 902308 09 2 (cloth)
ISBN 0 86091 724 X (paper)

Contents

Preface

The present study is an attempt to grasp certain fundamental aspects of the social sciences – sociology, historical materialism and more briefly, for comparative purposes, economics – both as activities in society and as specific discourses on society. It is concerned with the social and theoretical formation of social science. An analysis of this kind has its own formation: it is part of a situation in the social disciplines that is characterized mainly by crisis, by reappraisals and reorientations, by contradictions and conflicts. In such situations, where old footholds no longer seem firm, classical assumptions are brought into question and submitted to new investigations and interpretations. Such undertakings are always adventurous and hazardous; in the opinion of some, no doubt, impetuous and even pretentious. Nevertheless, they are made; and for some at least, they are necessary.

This conjuncture within the social disciplines is fundamentally related to the conjuncture in the world at large: the crisis and defeats of imperialism, the new economic problems of advanced capitalism, the conflicts that have attended the development of the educational system, the sharp escalation of the class struggle in the Western countries and so on. How does this contradictory world really function? How should it be dealt with? How preserved, or how transformed? Such questions have become insistent, and press heavily on those disciplines that aim at a scientific study of the social world.

It is one of the main theses of this book that the same society and the same social conjuncture are lived and experienced differently by people in different social positions. I have lived and continue to live the situation indicated above in commitment to the working class and the labour movement. The lessons of the latter's experiences and struggles have been a decisive social component in the formation of my own work, even in the field of abstract social theory. Theoretically, I have been formed by a number of years of work on the classical tradition of sociology and on that of Marx; a central element of this formation has been the contribution of Louis Althusser to the analysis of concepts and discourses. The combined lessons of the labour movement and Marxist theory have drawn my attention to the specific characteristics of the social disciplines as social activities and as conceptual systems.

This study has benefited from the comments of a number of persons, teachers, colleagues and friends. My text has been carefully edited and retyped. My Scandinavianisms have been corrected. Quotations in German, French and Italian have been translated into English. Among the many people to whom I am deeply indebted, two must be singled out: Gunnar Olofsson, colleague and friend, who read the first version of my manuscript in its entirety, and with whom I have had innumerable stimulating discussions; and my editor and friend Perry Anderson, who has accompanied this effort throughout with encouragement and constructive criticism.

With debts of gratitude to many, the author is now alone with his reader.

Göran Therborn
Göteborg, September 1975.

Chapter One

Sociology of Sociology, Marxism of Marxism

The social sciences make up an important part of the world we live in today. We find them in social administration, corporate calculation, and military intervention, in the running of hospitals and prisons, enterprises and schools, of educated families and mass media. If we look carefully, we will also find something perhaps more deserving of the name of social science, not in the hands of the rich and ruling, but in the organizations of the downtrodden, oppressed and exploited.

The social sciences are in the world to say something about it. Increasingly they provide the lenses through which we perceive the world we live in. Unevenly but significantly, their frames of reference replace the unreflected ether of ancient tradition, the revelations of religion, the scales of inherent morality, and the sublimities of literary culture. These changes are to be seen most obviously, perhaps, in the curricula of educational systems and the contents of radical journals.

Robing themselves in the mantle of science, the social sciences claim to be not just one way of experiencing and talking about the world, but something that yields systematic knowledge of it. They are, at the same time, part of the world, and, as such, related to the sufferings, joys and struggles of its peoples, and to different societies and social classes.

The truth of a science and its social place and function are mutually irreducible; but at the same time, the relation between *what* is produced and *where* it is produced is never merely contingent. This holds for all scientific enterprises, and is, of course, particularly important in the case of those disciplines whose very object is the social world of which they themselves are a part. The contemporary crisis of the social disciplines has been initiated by social developments which question, more or less seriously, both their truth and their relationship with the various social classes and institutions.

The 'development of underdevelopment' (Gunder Frank's apt expression[1]) and the present condition of advanced capitalism, combining unprecedented inflation with high levels of unemployment, have undermined some of the central tenets of liberal economics. The latter development has shattered the smug complacency of Keynesian crisis-management, prompting even the metropolitan bourgeoisies to question the usefulness of liberal economics. The social upheavals of the Western world – the anti-war movement, the student revolt and the desublimated malaise of the middle strata – have shaken the fragile edifice of sociology to its foundations. Social value-integration has been torn apart both within society at large and within the little academic universe of sociology itself. Nor have the ironies of history spared the science of historical materialism. Marxism has had to cope with both its successes and its failures – the Stalinist holocaust, the Sino-Soviet split, the failure to date of proletarian revolutions in the advanced capitalist countries, and the rise of new movements of rebellion, among women, students and others.

The advance in recent decades of discourses on society claiming scientific superiority to other discourses was, then, a process that contained within itself certain contradictions, which have now been laid bare in the present crisis of the social sciences. It is in this conjuncture of growth, contradiction and crisis that the present study is located. Its objective is to contribute to a resolution of the crisis, social as well as scientific. However, this volume does not aim at a study of the current situation as such, but rather to elucidate certain entities enmeshed in it: the social disciplines and their constitutive relationships to different social forces. In this way, it is hoped to ascertain clearly what is at stake in the current crisis, and thus to identify a point from which rational positions can be adopted and new moves made.

The study attempts to examine the formation of scientific discourses on society, their formation as systems of concepts, propositions and investigations, and the relations between this practice and other social practices. While centred on sociology and historical materialism, it starts from an overview of the first social science, economics, and attempts also to suggest the pertinence of the analysis proposed to so-called political science. The study advances analytically from two areas that have already been explored in recent reassessments and re-analyses of sociology and historical materialism – initiatives parallelled in contemporary discussions of theoretical economics by the neo-Ricardian critique of marginalism.

I. The Lacunae of the Sociology of Sociology

As an ambitious upstart discipline with unsettled tastes, after a wandering childhood in many different homes and belonging to no solid family lineage, sociology has always been rent by controversy over fundamentals. In its rapid growth over the last decade it has even taken on the aspect of an entire society in miniature. It has itself become a subject of sociological investigation, in the new discipline of the sociology of sociology.[2] The American Sociological Association bears a certain resemblance to the general political scene in the USA: a ruling liberal establishment – 'corporate liberal' as left-wing critics say – overwhelmingly financed by foundation grants and government contracts[3]; a militant opposition of students and young academics, the Sociology Liberation Movement (later split into two loose factions, a Radical Caucus and a Socialist Caucus); a women's liberation movement, Sociologists for Women in Society; Black and Chicano movements, the National Caucus of Black Sociologists and the Junta de Sociólogos Chicanos, respectively. At least two of the opposition groups have journals of their own; the Radical Caucus publishes *The Insurgent Sociologist* and the sws its *Newsletter*.

There are, then, in the history of sociology, many more or less

[2] The sociology of sociology was first introduced as a special session at the annual meeting of the American Sociological Association in 1967. An interesting contribution to the genre, apart from the works considered below, is the collection of articles edited by Larry and Janice Reynolds. *The Sociology of Sociology*, New York, 1970. For a bibliographical survey, see, for example, Elizabeth Crawford, 'The Sociology of the Social Sciences', *Current Sociology*, XIX, 2, 1971, actually published in 1973.

[3] R. Friedrichs, *A Sociology of Sociology*, New York, 1970, p. 120.

agonizing attempts at reappraisal. Four of these, however, are of special importance, and it is with these that the present endeavour will primarily be concerned. The major works with which this contribution must risk comparison are Talcott Parsons' *The Structure of Social Action* (1937), C. Wright Mills' *The Sociological Imagination* (1959), Alvin Gouldner's *The Coming Crisis of Western Sociology* (1970), and Robert Friedrichs' *A Sociology of Sociology* (1970).[4]

For good or for ill, Parsons is probably the most important postclassical sociological theorist. *The Structure of Social Action* is Parsons' first and, in the opinion of many, best major work. It was of great significance in establishing an official sociological genealogy among the very diverse currents of sociological thought, bringing into focus the key role of Emile Durkheim and Max Weber in the formation of classical sociology. In a subtle analysis of previous social thought, Parsons laid the foundations for his own sociological theory, which he presented as a systematic elaboration and further development of the classical heritage. This theory was expounded above all in two volumes published in 1951, *The Social System* and *Towards a General Theory of Action* (with Edward Shils and others), and in *Economy and Society* (1956, with Neil Smelser). Known as structural-functional analysis or, for short, functionalism, this theory was dominant in sociological thought from about the late forties until the middle sixties. Even thereafter Parsons has remained very much in the centre of sociological debate, but now more often as a central target of criticism.

Mills' *The Sociological Imagination* and Gouldner's *The Coming Crisis of Western Sociology* are without doubt the most distinguished modern attempts at a critical reassessment of the formation, achievements and tasks of sociology. In both, Parsons is a main object of attack. Mills, the author of, among other things, *The Power Elite in USA*, tried to keep up a tradition of progressively committed sociological craftsmanship in a world of Cold War machination and massification. Though his radicalism dates further back, Gouldner's work, on the other hand, is written with an eye to the

---

[4] Another important and completely different re-analysis of sociology should be now signalled: Herman and Julia Schwendinger's *Sociologists of the Chair*, New York, 1974, which unfortunately cannot be treated here. This book is a large-scale, hardhitting Marxist *Ideologiekritik* of classical US sociology, that also relates the latter to its European sources of inspiration.

student movement of the late 1960's, and apparently expresses some of its moods. It has given rise to intensive discussion among sociologists.[5]

Whether Robert Friedrichs' *A Sociology of Sociology* should be numbered with the others is perhaps debatable. It can hardly be said to be as central to the mainstream of sociological self-analysis as the other three, and might well be replaced by some other work. But nevertheless, as a serious and, it seems, fairly widely respected – even acclaimed – contribution to an analytical sociology of sociology, it is at least worthy of consideration.

1. The Dialectic of Talcott Parsons

Parsons' *The Structure of Social Action* laid the foundation of what was, from about the late forties to the middle sixties, the dominant sociological theory, usually, but not quite accurately called functionalism. Written during the Depression, it dealt with the treatment of capitalism by four authors of the late 19th and early 20th centuries, the British economist Alfred Marshall, the French sociologist Emile Durkheim, the Italian engineer turned economist and sociologist Vilfredo Pareto, and the German historian, economist and sociologist Max Weber. In nearly 800 pages of serene and subtle analysis, neither the Depression nor any other mundane feature of capitalism play any overt role. But the links with concrete worldly concerns remain, as will be shown below. In fact the critical thrust of Parsons' work was obvious to any American intellectual from the first page of the first chapter. Having quoted from the more established upper-class Harvard intellectual Crane Brinton, he begins: 'Spencer is dead. But who killed him and how? This is the problem.' To most of us today, it might seem rather trivial to issue an intellectual death certificate for Herbert Spencer.[6] But the 19th century English Social Darwinist was the man who 'dominated the

[5] In the *American Journal of Sociology*, for example, Gouldner's *Crisis* has been the subject of a review symposium (vol. 77, 1971, pp. 312–23) and the focus of a special issue on 'Varieties of Political Experience' (vol. 78, no. 1, July 1972), which led to a violent polemic, above all between Gouldner and S. M. Lipset (vol. 78, no. 5, no. 6, vol. 79, no. 1, March, May, July 1973).

[6] There are, however, some valiant knights trying to resurrect old Spencer. See the Foreword by Ronald Fletcher and the introductory essay by Stanislav Andreski to the latter's selection of Spencer, *Herbert Spencer*, London, 1971.

thought of the average American – especially the middle-class American – during the half-century after Appomattox'.[7] He was the man whose works sold 368,755 copies in America from the 1860's to 1903,[8] the man to whom the cream of American society, scientists, politicians, writers and tycoons, paid homage at a princely banquet at the New York Delmonico Hotel in 1882.[9]

Parsons' theory, particularly as embodied in *The Social System* – a monumental but dated postwar work – has been harshly criticized for its inability to deal with change, especially change resulting from internal contradictions.[10] But *The Structure of Social Action* is, precisely, a study of change: the emergence of a new social theory. Here, in fact, Parsons uses a dialectical conception of change, with internal contradictions and triadic schemas of thesis-antithesis-synthesis. Parsons' starting-point was his 'theory of action', a framework that posited ends, means, conditions, and guiding norms as the essential elements of an analysis of human acts.[11] His main antagonist was utilitarianism, an important variant of the theory of action embodied in a powerful Anglo-Saxon tradition that included Hobbes, Locke, classical liberal economics and in its later phase, Spencer himself. Now utilitarianism was, according to Parsons, an inherently unstable theory of action, basically because it implicitly postulated that the ends men sought were random. It tended to break down, either into 'radical rationalistic positivism' for which ends were governed by the scientifically valid knowledge held by the actors, or into 'radical anti-intellectualistic positivism' in which men were driven by forces unknown to the actors themselves, who dwelt in ignorance, error, and illusion. This instability Parsons called 'the utilitarian dilemma' – 'dilemma' being the word used in *The Structure of Social Action* for 'contradiction'.[12]

Parsons' main achievement was to show that there was a solution to this dilemma in the emergence of a new, voluntaristic, theory of action, in the works of Marshall (partially), Durkheim, Pareto, and

[7] H. S. Commager, *The American Mind*, New Haven, 1961, p. 89.

[8] R. Hofstadter, *Social Darwinism in American Thought*, Boston, 1955, p. 34.

[9] Hofstadter, op. cit., p. 48.

[10] A famous example of such a criticism is R. Dahrendorf, 'Out of Utopia: Toward a Re-Orientation of Sociological Analysis', *American Journal of Sociology*, 64 (1958), pp. 115–27, several times reprinted elsewhere.

[11] T. Parsons, *The Structure of Social Action*, New York, 1968, ch. II.

[12] Ibid., ch. III.

Weber. The crucial innovation was the systematic inclusion of normative elements in theory: men's actions were determined not merely by self-interest, whether rationalistic or instinctual, but primarily by social norms. Since normative elements had originally been negated in the alternative variants of radical positivism, the rise of the voluntaristic theory of action could be seen as a kind of 'negation of the negation'. In contrast to the other three authors, however, Weber had come not from the utilitarian and positivistic tradition but from the idealistic tradition, which had ignored the factual, conditional elements in the analysis of action. Weber's work thus represented another example of synthesis and the negation of the negation. For Parsons, Marx was basically a utilitarian. The Marxian view was then negated by Werner Sombart, to whom capitalism was the manifestation of a particular *Geist*. This idealistic negation was in turn negated by Weber, who, Parsons argued, transcended 'the Marx-Sombart dilemma' by incorporating both normative and non-normative elements in his theory of action.[13]

This grand dialectical schema is one of two aspects that give Parsons' analysis its persuasive force. The new theory becomes the Synthesis in which all previous contradictions are *aufgehoben*. But the efficacy of this dialectic rests above all on Parsons' choice of starting-point, his decision to treat social theory as a theory of action. With another starting-point the dialectic of action schema would be of limited relevance. Parsons is aware of other possibilities, but does not confront them. He seems to be thinking primarily of behaviourist psychology.[14] In interpreting Marx as a kind of collectivist utilitarian, Parsons was merely repeating a widespread opinion, not frontally and vigorously challenged until the work of Louis Althusser appeared in the 1960's – if we discount the various Hegelian and/or Feuerbachian versions of the 'young Marx'.

Parsons' dialectic was not meant to be pure theory only. The grand Synthesis also had explicit political implications. Sociology, in Parsons' view, effected a transcendence of the acute contradictions and struggles of the period, of 'the individualism-socialism dilemma'. In his preface the author pointed out: 'The basis on which the four writers were brought together for study was rather empirical. It was the fact that all of them in different ways were

---

[13] Ibid., p. 499.
[14] Ibid., pp. 69, 77f.

concerned with the range of empirical problems involved in the interpretation of some of the main features of the modern economic order, or "Capitalism", "free enterprise", "economic individualism", as it has been variously called.'[15] The overwhelming emphasis in *The Structure of Social Action* is on the conceptualization of action and not on the interpretation of capitalism. But its lesson is not hidden: 'It is particularly significant that . . . Durkheim's preoccupation with socialism was very early, antedating the *Division of Labor*, although he did not come to a systematic exposition of his view until later. In particular, one of the main reasons why he ventured into the unknown paths of sociology was raised by the theory of laissez-faire individualism. From Durkheim's point of view, as from that of Pareto and Weber, socialism and laissez-faire individualism are of the same piece – they both leave out of account certain basic social factors with which all three are concerned.'[16]

The second reason for the persuasive force of *The Structure of Social Action* is the genuine theoretical achievement on which its just claim to intellectual brilliance rests. With great penetration, it

[15] Ibid., p. xxii.

[16] Ibid., p. 341. It is particularly significant that Parsons' assertion about the background of Durkheim's sociology is supported neither by available evidence nor by Parsons' own reference, Marcel Mauss' introduction to the posthumous publication of Durkheim's *Socialism*, New York, 1958 (1st ed., 1925). What Mauss in fact says is that Durkheim's dissertation *The Division of Labour in Society* was originally planned 'quite abstractly and philosophically under the title: The Relationship of Individualism to Socialism', and that Durkheim soon came to see his philosophical problem in terms of sociology (p. 32). Durkheim's very first publication, published in 1885 and written the preceding year, was a review of the German organicist economist and sociologist Schaeffle, *Revue Philosophique*, XIX, 1885, pp. 84–101. From Durkheim's early writings we can infer that he came to sociology above all through the works of Comte, Espinas, Spencer, and the German ethical economists. In these writings no abandonment of socialist economics can be discerned. See above all the review article 'Les études de science sociale', *Revue Philosophique*, XXII (1886), pp. 61–80. It is also significant that in these years Durkheim refers to Comte alone and not, as he did later, to Saint-Simon too. See further his 'Cours de science sociale' (from 1888), included, with the former text, in J. C. Filloux (ed.), E. Durkheim, *La science sociale et l'action*, Paris, 1970, pp. 77–110. The 'socialist economics', which Durkheim did study thoroughly in these years was that of the German *Kathedersozialisten*, but their ethical economics was carried over into Durkheim's own sociological enterprise. See further ch. 5 below. Parsons' unsubstantiated claim indicates the political passion and objective behind his intricate theoretical analysis.

discerned systematic theoretical convergences in the works of authors hitherto usually regarded as very different and unrelated. In the terms of his theory of action, Parsons concluded that sociology was to be defined as 'the science which attempts to develop an analytical theory of social action systems in so far as these systems can be understood in terms of the property of common-value integration'.[17] With this result of Parsons' analysis, the convergence on common values, we have little quarrel. His historical analysis and explanation of the emergence of sociology, and, above all, his assessment of its specific contribution to a science of society, are significantly less compelling.

2. Wright Mills Against Abnormal Forms of the Sociological Division of Labour

C. Wright Mills was not primarily a theoretician: his most important contribution to the discussion of sociology and the social sciences is concerned not with social theory but with 'the sociological imagination'. Mills himself has given us some very fine examples of this, for instance the following: '. . . those [social analysts] who have been imaginatively aware of the promise of their work have consistently asked three sorts of questions: (1) What is the structure of this particular society as a whole? . . . (2) Where does this society stand in history? . . . (3) What varieties of men and women now prevail in this society and in this period?'[18] The immediate social background of Mills' work is not, as it was for Parsons, capitalism, but what Mills calls the post-modern 'Fourth Epoch', the post-World War II period of big inhuman bureaucracies, the power elite, the Cold War, and the Bomb.[19] To explain the unease and indifference of this age, increasingly that of the 'Cheerful Robot', is the primary task of the sociological imagination.[20]

At present, however, sociology and the social sciences are unfit for their great task. Mills' vision of the development of sociology recalls the characteristic themes of a nostalgic populism. Once upon a time there was a classical age of free sociological craftsmen, who were independent, moral and concerned with substantive issues. In

[17] Parsons, *The Structure of Social Action*, p. 768.
[18] C. W. Mills, *The Sociological Imagination*, London, 1967, pp. 6f.
[19] Ibid., pp. 11f, 165f.
[20] Ibid., pp. 13, 171–76.

the same distant glow Mills sees Comte and Weber, Spencer and Durkheim, Veblen and Schumpeter, Sombart and 'all that is intellectually excellent in Karl Marx'.[21] Then came the high-brow intellectuals with the abstract verbiage of 'Grand Theory' (Parsons being the archetype) and the bureaucrats with their 'Abstracted Empiricism' (Paul Lazarsfeld and lesser minds),[22] who represented the dissociation of theory and research, previously held together by a moral commitment to, so to speak, the concrete empiricism of substantive social issues. After the fall, the two parts underwent a separate, distorted overdevelopment.

Mills is concerned to re-establish the sociological craft, now that the grotesque effects of the excessive division of labour during the industrialization of sociology have become apparent.[23] Mills was indeed an admirable craftsman – admirable for his courage in a period of severe Cold War pressure as well as for his skills as an imaginative social analyst and writer. But like a good populist he gives no indication of how free craftsmanship can become 'the signal feature' of cultural life in a world marked by the 'Fourth Epoch':[24] he merely affirms that it ought to be so. Unlike the Hegelian Parsons, Mills identifies no inherent contradictions in Grand Theory and Abstracted Empiricism, and heralds no new external forces. He gives us his book and his own example. That is at least a great deal more than nothing.

3. Social Theory and Personal Experience: The World of Alvin Gouldner

Hegel's *Phenomenology of Mind* was punctuated by the guns of the battle of Jena, in which Napoleon routed the feudal Prussian army. The *Phenomenology* contains a chapter on the French revolution, and Hegel saw and supported Napoleon as its fulfilment; but the battle itself and Hegel's personal reactions to it are not to be found in its pages. Hegel is indeed one of the most formidably abstract of theorists; and the personal life of the theorist has never been much displayed in the tomes of classical scholarship.[25]

---

[21] Ibid., pp. 6, 165; ch. 6 passim.
[22] Ibid., chs. 2–3.
[23] Ibid., see particularly Appendix.
[24] Ibid., p. 14.
[25] Hegel finished the *Phenomenology* on the night of October 12th–13th 1806,

The very different style of progressive theorists in the American 1960's is significantly marked by the populist and expressive culture that became widespread among students and middle strata in that decade. In Alvin Gouldner's *The Coming Crisis of Western Sociology* we find theory explicitly located in the personal experience of its author. In the first two lines of his preface we are already told that 'Social theorists today work within a crumbling social matrix of paralyzed urban centres and battered campuses'.

In a later polemic[26] Gouldner has formulated the central tenet of his book: 'Every social theory has both political and personal relevance, which, according to the technical canons of social theory, it is not supposed to have.'[27] The objective of the book is to contribute to a sociology of social theory or, better, a theory about social theorists.[28] Gouldner's intended sociology of sociology has a specific orientation; it is a 'Reflexive Sociology' whose goal is the deepening of the sociologist's awareness of who he is, not just in his public role as a sociologist but as a man in a particular society and, above all, in particular immediate surroundings.[29] Reflexive Sociology is both an end in itself and, in guiding the critique of prevailing sociology, a means of releasing the socially liberating potential of sociology from conservative and repressive constraints.[30]

---

and Napoleon occupied Jena on the 13th. Hegel saw him and wrote to his friend Niethammer: 'It is a marvellous feeling to see such a personality, concentrated in one point, dominating the entire world from horseback. It is impossible not to admire him.' The famous Preface, however, was not written until January 1807, and there Hegel explicitly rejects any personal situating of a philosophical work. He points to the dawning of a new era: 'It is surely not difficult to see that our time is a time of birth and transition to a new period.' But: 'The very attempt to determine the relationship of a philosophical work to other efforts concerning the same subject introduces an alien and irrelevant interest which obscures precisely that which matters for the recognition of the truth.' The Preface is quoted in the translation by Walter Kaufmann in his excellent *Hegel*, London, 1966, pp. 380 and 370. On Hegel and the battle of Jena, see Kaufmann, p. 111f and Shlomo Avineri, *Hegel's Theory of the Modern State*, Cambridge, 1972, p. 63f, from which Hegel's letter to Niethammer is cited.

[26] A. Gouldner, 'For Sociology: "Varieties of Political Experience" Revisited', *American Journal of Sociology*, 78 (1973), pp. 1063–93, p. 1081.

[27] A. Gouldner, *The Coming Crisis of Western Sociology*, London, 1971, p. 41.

[28] Ibid., pp. vii, 483.

[29] Ibid., ch. 13.

[30] Ibid., pp. 442f, 510. 'For Sociology: "Varieties of Political Experience" Revisited,' p. 1081.

Gouldner's work has a bold historical sweep and is itself presented as one of a projected series; his very interesting book on Plato has already appeared (*Enter Plato*), and future volumes are promised on the 19th century Romantic movement and on a generalized theory of social theories. The broad historical canvas that Gouldner paints is structured in a way that combines elements of both Parsons and Mills. As in Mills there is an original unity, which is then split in two, with the unfortunate consequences of one-sided development. There is, however, no invocation of the ideals of the classical golden age. Instead, as in Parsons, there is a process of internal contradiction, convergence and synthesis (though in this case the latter is not yet achieved). In Gouldner's analysis, the originality unity is that of Western Sociology, which splits after the death of its founder, Saint-Simon. With Comte and Marx, it divides into Academic Sociology and Marxism. The latter goes east from Western Europe, to Russia; the former goes west to the USA (by the 1960's the centre of Academic Sociology had moved as far as Berkeley on the American West Coast). But now both are in crisis and tending to converge.

Despite its arresting title, the book really refers to a problem situated on a somewhat lower level of historical generality than the above-mentioned master plan. The crisis of Western Sociology with which Gouldner deals is mainly the crisis of Parsonian functionalist dominance in American sociology – expressed in drifts towards Marxism, the internal disintegration of the Functionalist school, and the rise of new types of theory and research. The analytical core of Gouldner's study is devoted to the work of one sociologist, Talcott Parsons. Gouldner's basic methodological conception is that all social theory rests on an 'infrastructure' of background assumptions – primarily about a particular domain, such as that of man and society, but also more general 'world hypotheses' and sentiments.[31] His thorough and imaginative analysis of Parsons is focused on the manifestations of domain assumptions and sentiments in Parsons' sociological theory.

Sociological changes in general, and in particular the crisis with which Gouldner is concerned, have been instigated, not by the progress of scientific inquiry, but rather by changes in the cultural infrastructure of society and in other external social aspects of life.

[31] Gouldner, *The Coming Crisis of Western Sociology*, ch. 2.

The crisis of functionalism has been provoked above all by the emergence of a new culture among students from the middle strata, and by the rise of the 'welfare state', with its demand for a sociology usable in various types of state intervention.[32] Gouldner's briefer explanation of the crisis of Soviet Marxism is similar. The basis for a theory of order and restraint (such as functionalism) was provided by a social layer whose object was to consolidate and enjoy the fruits of past achievements.[33] In the wake of economic reform, there arose the need to legitimate a relaxation of public authority; one way of achieving this was to incorporate into Marxism the functionalist emphasis on system interdependence.[34]

The methodological model for Gouldner's sociology of social theory is obviously inspired by the Marxist infrastructure-super-structure dichotomy. There is the not unimportant difference, of course, that Gouldner's infrastructure of sub-theoretical assumptions and sentiments would be located by Marxists in the ideological superstructure. A further difference is that Gouldner's 'super-structure' of social theory does not possess the autonomy and specific efficacy that characterize its Marxist namesake. It is true that, warning against 'the danger of . . . a primitivistic regression to an orthodox, if not vulgar Marxism', Gouldner protests against the belief 'that Academic Sociology has accomplished absolutely nothing at all in the last thirty years'.[35] But these accomplishments are not taken into account in his explanation of sociological change. On the contrary, we are emphatically told that 'there is really no evidence that the changes that Functionalism has already manifested and promises to further undergo . . . have anything whatsoever to do with the researches and findings these have produced, either within or outside the framework of Functional theory.'[36] Now, while internal theoretical developments may indeed have played a rather negligible role in the process Gouldner describes, the problem of the specificity of the theoretical 'superstructure' remains. Gouldner is at his best, which is highly impressive, in his analysis of subtheoretical assumptions about man and society – in Parsons, in Plato, to whom Parsons is related, and in the relationship

[32] Ibid., chs. 9–10.
[33] Ibid., p. 458.
[34] Ibid., p. 469.
[35] Ibid., p. 441.
[36] Ibid., p. 370. Cf. the *resumé* of causal forces on p. 410.

between the sociological world of Erving Goffman and the ideological world of the new American middle strata. But his refusal to acknowledge the specificity of the theoretical level leads him to juxtapose a host of different theories in a manner that is at best trivializing, and at worst, grotesque. Subtheoretical quips are not infrequently substituted for theoretical analysis. This is related to and aggravated by what might be called an unhappy love of Marxism, which leads the author to see its image in the most unexpected authors.[37]

4. The Sociological Ego in a World of Conversation

Gouldner's *Coming Crisis of Western Sociology* and Robert Friedrichs' *Sociology of Sociology* are not only contemporaries, but also, apparently, intellectual siblings. After the event the two authors have mutually complimented each other.[38] Although less flamboyant and less analytical than Gouldner's, Friedrichs' volume is no less ambitious in scope and is more even and careful in its treatment. Less daring in sweep, it is nevertheless more comprehensive in its coverage of the field, discussing a greater number and variety of authors – including some, like Sartre and Husserl, not usually treated in studies of this type.

Like Gouldner, Friedrichs is above all concerned with the sociologist's images of man, including first and foremost images of themselves. The organizing machinery of the text is taken from Thomas Kuhn's *The Structure of Scientific Revolutions*; 'paradigm' is a central concept, used by Friedrichs in the rather loose sense of 'dominant view'. In a striking echo of Gouldner's distinction between a theoretical superstructure and a determining sub-theoretical infrastructure, Friedrichs distinguishes between first- and second-order paradigms.[39] The determinant first-order paradigm is 'the grounding image the social scientist has of himself as scientific agent' (emphasis omitted), whereas the discipline's 'image . . . of its subject matter' is the second-order paradigm.

---

[37] These accusations should not detract from the great value of a book that has suffered a whole barrage of adverse criticism with very few direct hits.

[38] A. Gouldner, 'For Sociology: "Varieties of Political Experience" Revisited', p. 1085. Gouldner there also quotes Friedrichs on Gouldner from the *Louisiana State University Journal of Sociology*.

[39] Friedrichs, *A Sociology of Sociology*, p. 55.

The self-image of the social scientist is, the reader will remember, only a part of Gouldner's infrastructure. It is of little value in analyzing ideological content, and Friedrichs himself uses it mainly to present a dichotomy. On the one hand there are the sociologists with a good self-image, the 'prophets', whose line runs from Comte (as he practised though not as he preached) to C. Wright Mills; the majority of pre-World War II American sociologists represent the 'prophetical mode'.[40] On the other hand there are those with a bad self-image, the 'priests' hiding under their 'cloak of neutrality', practising a 'priestly mode' of sociology inaugurated by Max Weber and dominating American sociology from World War II till about 1960.[41]

In the 1960's new prophets are emerging. The pivot of Friedrich's argument is that this is not a temporary deviation from the inexorable ascent of the priests. The probably enduring recovery of the prophetic mode is not, as in Parsons' scheme, the outcome of scientific evolution; nor is it due to the needs of the epoch, as Mills implies; nor, as in Gouldner's perspective, the result of the rise of a prophetic self-image in society at large. The reason why virtue can be confident of lasting recompense is mainly that the full implications of the image of man expressed in the priestly mode of science cut 'dramatically against the grain of the humane image of man that has been the West's heritage from its Hebraic and Greek forebears'.[42] Once revealed, these implications will repel decent Western men and reinforce the position of the prophets.

The vocabulary used in this presentation – good, bad, virtue, decent and the like – should not be interpreted as simply ironic. It is an adaptation at a distance to the curiously moralistic and theological style of the author, who is greatly concerned with the reaffirmation of the high values of the Judaeo-Christian and Hebraic-Greek tradition.[43] His pivotal thesis is in fact both a fine piece of scholarly analysis, and an elegant *tour de force*. Instead of starting from a presumably scientific theory in order to reveal the underlying subtheoretical images of man and society that subtend it, Friedrichs creates a philosophy of man as an extrapolation of the cognitive assumptions of natural science and elicits its ugly implica-

[40] Ibid., ch. 3.
[41] Ibid., chs. 4–5.
[42] Ibid., p. 259.
[43] See, e.g., ibid., pp. 64f, 220, 248, 268, 274, 276, 286, 312, 314.

tion: a depersonalized, deterministic, relativistic and instrumentalist view of man.[44] He also gives examples of how these implications tend to materialize in works of sociology.

For Friedrichs, as for Parsons, Mills and Gouldner, the world has more or less tragically split into two, and it is the concern of the writer to restore some kind of unity. For Parsons the synthesis, basically between positivism and idealism, was already there and waiting only to be discovered. In Mills' eyes, the solution was to return to the classic ideals that reigned before the split into Grand Theory and Abstracted Empiricism. Gouldner saw the prospect of a convergence in the internal crises of both off-shoots of Western Sociology, Academic Sociology and Marxism. Friedrichs' two poles are much wider apart than those of the other authors. On the one hand, there is the world as an object of scientific knowledge – intersubjective, recurrent, relational; on the other hand, Man's *Existenz* – intrasubjective, unique, existential experience.[45] The implications of a scientistic metaphysic are the denial and attempted suppression of the latter.

Within this broad perspective, Friedrichs is able to locate Marxism much more correctly than most Western academics. He is well aware of the difference between the young and the mature Marx.[46] On the latter, and on Engels and Lenin, Friedrichs says: 'There is absolutely no doubt that one can document the rigid and dogmatic nature of their political style. But what the larger scientific community in the West has failed to realize . . . is that an equally compelling case may be made that the basic stance taken by the founding fathers of dialectical materialism is in the best tradition of social science. . . . Their commitment as social scientists was not to any particular vision of the future, but to the epistemology that characterized natural science in general. As political activists they were of course dogmatic; but as scholars they both professed and documented an openmindedness that was to be closed only by empirical facts.'[47] These comments on Marxist science are, however, no more complimentary than those on Marxist politics. Friedrichs' purpose is to show that Marxism cannot directly be used

[44] Ibid., ch. 10. The ugly consequences, in Friedrichs' view, result from a 'reification' of the current epistemological stance of science (p. 224).

[45] Ibid., p. 298f.

[46] Ibid., p. 283f.

[47] Ibid., p. 264.

as a basis for a 'prophetic mode' of sociology. Indeed, he regards Marx's writing of *Capital* as equivalent to an adherence to fascism. In the words of the author himself: 'Indeed to turn for one's compass to *Existenz* exclusively could prove at least as tragic as the opposite recourse, the reification of the intersubjective assumptions of science, as may be illustrated by the early Heidegger's dramatic plea to the German people to follow their *Fuhrer*, on the one hand, and the later Marx's identification with the materialism of science, on the other.'[48] The solution, then, is basically to regard the scientific and existentialist perspectives as two lenses, both contained within the human eye.[49] This means in particular the acknowledgment of a personal dimension in the science of sociology.[50]

The second-order paradigm of sociology, its image of its subject matter, is in Friedrichs' view the idea of 'the system'. It was established as a dominant image after World War II by Parsons.[51] In the past the system paradigm was related to the priestly first-order paradigm, and the most challenging recent competitor with the former, the conflict paradigm, was connected with the prophets. In the future, however, this might not be necessarily so, and indeed Friedrichs argues rather convincingly that system must take precedence over conflict, if sociology is to be a nomothetic science not merely concerned with unique cases.[52] The fundamental weakness of the thesis of the system paradigm, which testifies to the author's scant concern for the problems of scientific theory, is of course its empty generality. Friedrichs begs the question of the systematicity of the system of sociology as distinguished from that of, say, economics, biology, or cosmology.

After all his strong words about prophecy, priestcraft, science, and cloaks of neutrality, Friedrichs consigns the reader to an idyllic 'dialogal' pluralism of prophets and priests, system- and conflict-images, where the liberating and the ordering callings of sociology are fused in a conception of the sociologist as '*witness* to the profoundly social dialogue that is man'.[53] That is, man's world is after

48 Ibid., p. 315.
49 Ibid., p. 298f.
50 Ibid., p. 315.
51 Ibid., ch. 2, esp. 14f.
52 Ibid., p. 293.
53 Ibid., p. 328.

all an intellectual conversation, far removed from the world of hunger, filth, exertion, and combat in which materialist scientists and dogmatic politicians immerse themselves.

5. The Absent Society of an American Ideology

Although mutually distinct in many obvious and important ways, all these four works share two lacunae which, for the purpose of the present study, it is essential to note: *society* and *science*. The question of society has two relevant aspects. First, the role of society as subject-matter for the theoretical enterprise; and second, society as the context of social theorizing. In the works of Parsons and Mills the decisive presence of society in its first aspect is emphasized on a large historical scale. Parsons brings his four authors together to analyze their interpretation of 'some of the main features of the modern economic order', that is, capitalism or 'free enterprise'. It is in their interpretation of this phenomenon that the new theory of action emerges. Mills sets out to summon sociologists to the task of analyzing and interpreting the 'substantive problems' of the present historical era, the 'Fourth Epoch'.

Now, the question of society as a subject-matter for social science immediately raises the problem of the scientific appropriation of society as distinct from, say, its ideological or artistic appropriation – that is, the problem of science. Only in relation to this can the adequacy of Parsons' and Mills' attention to the subject-matter of social science be evaluated. Here, as was indicated above, we shall find a lacuna. But their focus on society at large as subject-matter distinguishes both the liberal Parsons and the radical Mills from the contemporary prophets and radicals Friedrichs and Gouldner.

Of his own brand of sociology, Gouldner writes: 'The core of a Reflexive Sociology, then, is the attitude it fosters towards those parts of the social world *closest* to the sociologist – his own profession and its associations, his professional role, and importantly, his students and himself – rather than toward only the remote parts of his social surround.'[54] Gouldner himself notes the difference between this conception and that of the classical sociology of knowledge, which was concerned mainly with the importance of class and other extra-academic social forces.[55] The shift in emphasis is

[54] Gouldner, *The Coming Crisis of Western Sociology*, p. 505.
[55] Ibid., p. 512.

certainly made for the noblest of moral reasons. But it is noteworthy that Reflexive Sociology is more concerned with guiding the personal morality of the social scientist than with the social contradictions and forces of social change he discerns; the problem is how he can himself relate to those forces. We have already seen that, for all his sympathy with sociology as prophecy, Friedrichs' main demand is not for prophetic judgments about the present economic order and its substantive problems, but for more attention to *Existenz* and to the sustenance of 'the values that the West derives from its Hellenic and Hebraic roots'.

The absence or near-absence of society from these four reassessments of sociology concerns above all society as a context, as a determinant of sociology and social science. This social vacuum is most evident in the case of Parsons. The dialectical schema of *The Structure of Social Action* is emphatically an intrascientific dialectic. The author says: 'The central interest of the study is in the development of a particular coherent theoretical system, as an example of the general process of "immanent" development of science itself.'[56] The extremely detailed analyses of Parsons' huge book are overwhelmingly pure conceptual analysis.

Mills is certainly explicit about the impact of society upon social science. He points for instance to the influence of the 'liberal practicality' of piecemeal reform and the 'illiberal practicality' of bureaucratic administration upon American sociology.[57] But in Mills' exposition, on the whole, only the fallen are socially determined. The virtuous – as is evident already in the ecumenical amalgamation of Comte, Spencer, Marx, Weber, and Durkheim – are not. What is determined, in its relationship to types of practicality, is the tradition of empirical study of contemporary social facts. But the classical tradition oriented towards a theory of history, to which Mills himself pledges allegiance, is not.[58] Classical economics is bluntly identified by Mills as 'the major ideology of capitalism as a system of power', and in a rapid historical survey of the social and ideological roots of various disciplines, he even indicts demography (in relation to Malthus); but there is not a single word on the roots of classical sociology.[59] Classical sociology is related to ideological

[56] Parsons, *The Structure of Social Action*, p. 12.
[57] Mills, *The Sociological Imagination*, ch. 4.
[58] Ibid., pp. 21–3.
[59] Ibid., pp. 81–4.

legitimation only from the other side, not as the ailing patient but as the unaffected clinician.[60]

Gouldner's view of how social theory develops is designed as an antidote to Parsons' conception of immanent development. Both as man and as political agent, the theorist is seen as playing a crucial role in the development of theory. In Gouldner's grand historical model of the development of sociology the different phases of the latter are connected with various social forces.[61] Thus, one of the basic causes of the crises in academic sociology and Marxism is held to be the changing role of the state in east and west. Society is there, but it is in fact strategically subordinated to a suprasocietal cultural determinism. It is not so much man and his politics as man and his culture whose importance Gouldner is concerned to demonstrate. Sociology, for Gouldner, is primarily related to utilitarian culture,[62] and we are told that middle-class society began with utilitarian culture,[63] not with, say, the emancipation of Western European towns, textile manufacturing, enclosures, colonial robbery, and other forms of 'primitive accumulation'. The author is at pains to stress that Functionalism, the hitherto dominant form of post-classical Academic Sociology, is not inherently related to either capitalist or socialist society.[64] The primary affiliation of Function-alism is with Platonic Philosophy, with which it shares a common cultural infrastructure of subtheoretical assumptions and senti-ments.[65] It is in terms of this infrastructure that Gouldner dissects Parsonian Functionalism. Ancient slavery, feudalism, capitalism, socialism have all so far left this 'essentially conservative' culture basically unaffected. But this does not mean, the author points out, that it is perennial.[66] For a structure that has withstood two thousands years of economic and political upheaval is now at last beginning to crack under pressure from the 'swinging' middle strata and New Left students of the American 1960's![67]

Friedrichs is no more a believer in the socially immaculate con-

[60] Ibid., p. 36.
[61] Gouldner, *The Coming Crisis of Western Sociology*, ch. 4.
[62] Gouldner, ibid., ch. 3.
[63] Ibid., p. 88.
[64] Ibid., p. 331.
[65] Ibid., ch. 11.
[66] Ibid., p. 436.
[67] Ibid., pp. 378–410.

ception of sociology than is Gouldner. For instance, he attributes the consolidation of the system paradigm in sociology largely to the conformist climate of the 1950's.[68] But again, as with Gouldner, economic and political arrangements and their structuring of classes of people have little weight in comparison with suprasocietal values. The two authors differ mainly in their evaluation of these values: to Gouldner they are essentially, though not in all circumstances, conservative; to Friedrichs, who always adds 'Hebraic' to Hellenic values, they are above all 'humane' (and left unspecified). The decisive argument for regarding the dominance of the priestly mode of sociology as transitory is that it can be shown to cut against the grain of the humane Hebraic and Greek image of man.[69] When this is revealed, as it is in Friedrichs' book, its fate is sealed.

We have already noted the discrepancy between the self-image of the social role of the sociologists of sociology and their actual social location, between the presented task and the proposed solution. Gouldner evokes a crumbling society, a vast historical panorama, and wants to relate the sociologist to all this. But he ends up with his eyes focused on the university classroom. Friedrichs invokes the Hebraic prophets, who thundered against the venality and treachery of the rich and mighty of their time, only to arrive at a conception of the sociologist as witness to human dialogue. The same type of discrepancy occurs in Parsons, who is concerned with the problem of the modern economic order and believes that the voluntaristic theory of action and the professions constitute a 'path out of the individualism-socialism dilemma' (in other words, the solution to the economic, political, and ideological struggles between labour and capital). Mills' ambitions for his brand of sociology are scarcely more modest. In spite of the power elite, the Bomb, and the predominantly non-imaginative character of the contemporary social sciences, Mills professes: 'The sociological imagination is becoming, I believe, the major common denominator of our cultural life and its signal feature.'[70]

There is in all four authors a tendency to present social revolutions as sociological revolutions, to turn economic and political struggles and transformations into questions of culture and

---

[68] Friedrichs, *A Sociology of Sociology*, p. 17.

[69] Ibid., pp. 221, 258.

[70] Mills, *The Sociological Imagination*, p. 14.

morality. It was this tendency that, according to Marx and Engels, characterized the 'German Ideology', the ideology of both German liberalism and socialism, in contrast with the real economic and political achievements of liberals and socialists in England and France. The overdevelopment of philosophy in Germany they regarded as corresponding to the underdevelopment of modern classes and class contradictions.[71] All four authors are Americans, and I would suggest, without advancing further evidence here, that the tendency described is rather common among both liberal and radical American intellectuals. One can speak of an American Ideology in roughly the same sense as of the German Ideology which Marx and Engels decisively abandoned in the middle of the 1840's.

Leaving aside for the moment the question of 'the American Ideology', I will simply say, as a preliminary, that in contrast to the subsocial, immanent conceptions of Parsons and (in a crucial respect) Mills, and to the basically suprasocial, culturalist views of Friedrichs and Gouldner, the present study is intended to analyze social science in its real social context.

6. Empirical Sociology on the Academic Market

There is within the discipline of sociology a growing interest in its own historical and social roots, springing from a source quite different from that of the concerns of its theoreticians and *engagé* intellectuals. For a number of years now, Paul Lazarsfeld, one of the foremost positivist methodologists of sociology – in Mills' eyes, a leading and sophisticated spokesman of Abstracted Empiricism – has been directing an international research programme on the history of social research and empirical sociology. Centred on the concept of institutionalization, successful or failed, and considerably inspired by Joseph Ben-David's studies of the emergence of new disciplines[72] – such as bacteriology, psychoanalysis, experimental psychology – and of different national university structures,[73] this

---

[71] K. Marx and F. Engels, *The German Ideology*, Moscow, 1964, esp. pp. 206f, and 501f, *Marx–Engels–Werke*, Berlin, 1956 (MEW), vol. 3, pp. 176f, 441f.

[72] J. Ben-David and R. Collins, 'Social Factors in the Origins of a New Science', *American Sociological Review*, vol. 31 (1966), pp. 451–66.

[73] J. Ben-David and A. Zlozcover, 'Universities and Academic Systems in

effort has yielded works both empirically meticulous and of broad interest. The major figure in this school has been Anthony Oberschall, who has edited the most important volume so far, *The Establishment of Empirical Sociology* (1972). Oberschall has also written a monograph on *Empirical Social Research in Germany, 1848–1914* (1965) and to the former book he has contributed an introductory theoretical model and the strategic chapter on the rise and institutionalization of sociology in the United States.

Ben-David focuses primarily on the academic establishment – or alternatively the blocked establishment – of new intellectual specialities. His essentially intra-academic model emphasizes the role of academic competition, analyzing for instance the preconditions necessary to draw talented, status-competing academicians into new branches of science. Oberschall has extended this model considerably and conceptualized it into an explicit supply and demand schema. He particularly stresses that the establishment of a new discipline is dependent on the maintenance of both supply and demand by 'fairly cohesive, large, and identifiable groups':[74] its institutionalized supply must be supported by a powerful lobby, and there must be an effective and resourceful demand.

This is all very well, but there seem to be two significant weaknesses in the argument. One of them follows from the market model, the other from the research programme envisaged by Lazarsfeld and his associates. The market model does not include a systematic analysis of the social determination of the forces active in demanding and supplying sociology. The empirical investigations identify a number of groups, organizations, and individuals, and locate them within a supply and demand mechanism. But the relation between these and the structure and functioning of society is usually specified only in *ad hoc*, though sometimes very perceptive, *aperçus*. It is not linked to a theory of social development.

Concentrating on empirical sociology, the research programme is designed as a corrective to the common type of history of sociology, which is exclusively interested in the history of social theory. The result so far has been that the inner connection between theory and

Modern Society', *Archives Européennes de Sociologie*, vol. 3 (1962), pp. 45–84; J. Ben-David, 'The Scientific Role: The Conditions of Its Establishment in Europe', *Minerva*, vol. 4 (1965), pp. 15–54.

[74] A. Oberschall (ed.), *The Establishment of Empirical Sociology*, New York, 1972, p. 5.

empirical research has been left unclarified. Oberschall distinguishes between social research and sociology. The demands for these were originally largely separate and distinct, and it was only in the Sociology Department of the University of Chicago in the 1920's that the supply of both was finally institutionalized as a unity.[75] The problem here is that 'sociology', as distinct from social research, is left unspecified. It seems to refer to a body of social theory, but what kind of theory is not discussed. In consonance with Lazarsfeld's positivistic conception of social science, theory is seen mainly as something that makes empirical studies cumulative and generalizing. Little interest, if any, is taken in theory as the production of concepts defining an object of investigation. The unity of sociology and social research is characteristically framed in terms of the academic establishment of cumulative research – not in terms of the union of a particular conceptual system with empirical studies.[76]

This weakness in the historiography of empirical sociology points to the second lacuna in the four great reappraisals of sociology with which we have already dealt: the problem of sociology as a science. Before turning to this problem, we will note one more point about Lazarsfeld's historical project: because of its primary concern with empirical research and, probably even more, because of its view of theory, it too, like Parsons and the others, leaves social theory socially undetermined.

7. The Unreflected Self-Assurance of Sociological Scientificity

Parsons does discuss the scientific status of the social sciences and the specificity of sociology in relation to other disciplines. By way of summary it can be said that Parsons founds the non-natural empirical sciences in a kind of philosophical anthropology, in which disciplines are distinguished by their relation to the schema of human action. Technologies of different sorts involve only means and given ends, and are already present at the most elementary level, the single act. With a system of acts there emerges the problem of economic rationality – the adaptation of ends that are no longer given to scarce means – and to deal with it, economics. With the

---

[75] Ibid., p. 6f.

[76] A. Oberschall, 'The Institutionalization of American Sociology', ibid., pp. 187–251.

emergence of a plurality of actors two new problems announce themselves, power among the actors, and their integration. This provides the bases of politics and sociology, respectively.[77]

But apart from the dangers of empiricism, from which he sharply distinguishes his own position,[78] the scientificity of the sciences of action is basically unproblematic to Parsons. Indeed, the analytical focus itself is unproblematic: he quite legitimately chooses to concentrate exclusively on the action schema, without denying the possibility of other models. His starting-point is doubly unproblematic. In the first place, the action model, with its means-end way of thinking, is regarded as rooted in the common-sense experiences of everyday life. In the second, as a central component of liberal economics,[79] whose origins and scientificity Parsons takes for granted, the action model is, from the outset, located within the domain of science.[80] The point of arrival, the voluntaristic theory of action, is not in fact a new, previously unknown territory either. It is defined by its inclusion of all the factors in the various antecedent theories of action, which comprised differently arranged, incomplete combinations of factors.[81]

At one level Mills' *The Sociological Imagination* seems to be devoted to (social) science – its promise, its perversions and uses; its philosophies of science, its subject-matter, and its methods and techniques. The discourse on this level is, however, built over a theoretical void. We are told that the subject matter of social science is human variety, 'all the social worlds in which men have lived, are living, and might live',[82] and are referred to the study of history, of biography, and of their intersection in social structure. But the basic problems of a science of history, social structures and the types of men and women they contain, are never discussed. The chapter on

[77] Parsons, *The Structure of Social Action*, pp. 765f. Psychology is here regarded as concerned with the variables of action deriving from the hereditary basis of personality.

[78] Ibid., p. 728f.

[79] Max Weber took his concept of action from his conception of (marginalist) economic theory. See further, ch. 5, below.

[80] See, e.g., Parsons, *The Structure of Social Action*, pp. 99, 129f. On the other hand, Parsons was greatly concerned with the relationship of the phenomena analyzed by economics to the extra-economic social order.

[81] This is clear from Parsons' definition of the theories of action in terms of mathematical functions, ibid., p. 78f.

[82] Mills, *The Sociological Imagination*, p. 132.

philosophies of science is basically on work ethics and practices, and the discussion of method is mainly about techniques of sociological craftsmanship. The knotty problems of a science of history and society, such as causality and determination, time, periodization and so on, are, on the whole, left aside. For a discussion of problems of that sort, Mills substitutes a largely unreflective faith: 'In brief, I believe that what may be called classic social analysis is a definable and usable set of traditions; that its essential feature is the concern with historical social structures; and that its problems are of direct relevance to urgent public issues and insistent human troubles.'[83] But since this so-called classic analysis is an aggregate of vastly different, mutually contradictory epistemological and substantive theoretical positions, Mills' faith must inevitably beg many questions. The idealism of Sombart or the positivism of Spencer? The social science of Comte, of Marx, or of Weber? Or perhaps some kind of synthesis or reshuffling of positions?

Friedrichs devotes himself to a substantial and sophisticated discussion of basic problems of science. He is principally interested in two things, the necessary dilemmas of choice in all scientific research and the cognitive assumptions underlying science. The latter are three: the subject matter of science is accessible to intersubjective experience, that is, it is empirical; it has recurrent features, thus making possible a nomothetic discourse; these features are linked in determinate relationships and are therefore open to systematic investigation.[84] But as we have seen above, Friedrichs' discussion is not geared to analyzing the scientific problems of a science of society, but rather to staking out the morally acceptable limits of such a science. This overriding concern leads Friedrichs to accept a fundamentally unspecified idea of system as the 'paradigm' of a scientific sociology, an idea that would at most take us to the threshold of a science of the particular system that human society is.

For his part, Gouldner is perfectly explicit: 'I do not intend to focus on sociology as a science, or on its "method".'[85] The rationale of this intention is an epistemological position that might be dubbed positivism in reverse. For Gouldner, as for the positivists,[86] the

[83] Ibid., p. 21.
[84] Friedrichs, *A Sociology of Sociology*, ch. 9.
[85] Gouldner, *The Coming Crisis of Western Sociology*, p. 27.
[86] I have tried to analyze the different views of scientific knowledge of positiv-

problem of the production of scientific knowledge is above all a question of method, of reliable techniques of empirical research. Besides scientific method there are values, which the positivists think should be suppressed as bias, and in actual scientific practice are suppressed, but which Gouldner thinks are and should be active as guides to work.[87] In both cases the specific theoretical questions of science are implicitly denied or brushed aside. Gouldner's some-times rather comical discoveries of 'Marxist' influences in anthropology and sociology are one consequence of this conception of science.

Parsons and Mills feel themselves to be securely located within the experiences and problems of everyday life, and the existing scientificities of liberal (classical and marginalist) economics and classical sociology, respectively. With the wisdom of hindsight, we can say that these positions cancel each other out: Parsons illuminates the internal contradictions of Mills' classical family, while Mills denounces classical economics as an ideology of capitalism. Friedrichs and Gouldner, on the other hand, rest confidently on the extrascientific foundations of individual experience and social values. Forswearing the apparent security of both the intrascientific and the infrascientific, the present study will hazard a social scientific discourse on the foundations of social science. This does not mean that the disciplines examined will be summoned to court to have their scientificity proved or disproved. It means, more modestly, that the foundations upon which they base their claim to scientificity will be treated not as something self-evident, but as historical products, and that their production and structure will themselves be taken as objects of investigation.

II. Philosophy or History? Problems of a Marxism of Marxism

Marxism claims to be both a science and a guide to socialist action: as a historical phenomenon, Marxism is not simply a theoretical

---

ism, historicism, and Marxism in the title essay of a book, *Vad är bra värderingar värda?* (What is the Value of Good Values?), Staffanstorp, 1973.

[87] Gouldner, *The Coming Crisis of Western Sociology*, p. 27f. Cf. p. 412 for 'scientific technostructure'.

corpus claiming the allegiance and attention of a certain group of intellectuals, but rather a *union of a historical materialist theory and a revolutionary movement*, primarily but by no means exclusively *proletarian* in character. This relationship, which has taken various forms, has always been complicated. But for good or for ill (depending on one's position), it provides a key to the history of the world in this century – a history that includes the rise of mass proletarian parties and of national liberation movements led or influenced by Marxism, the October Revolution and the ascent of the Soviet Union, the rise and fall of German and Italian fascism, revolution in China, Cuba and Indo-China, and now, as the century moves into its last quarter, the spectre of revolution in South-Western Europe.

The historical significance of Marxism is thus overwhelmingly greater than that of sociology or economics. It is all the more surprising, then, that there is no Marxism of Marxism to match the flourishing sociology of sociology. This absence is hardly warranted by the history of Marxism, which has in no sense been a success-story free from blockages and reversals. Fundamental aspects of Marxist theory have been called into question both by its historic defeats, so far, in North America and Western Europe, and by the aftermath of its successes – Stalinism, the Sino-Soviet split, the present social and political condition of that third of the world claiming to be governed by Marxist theory. These and other contradictory and often unexpected developments of the union of Marxist theory and practice make it possible to speak also of a crisis of Marxism.

Paradoxically, however, while the sociology of sociology is sustained by the crisis of sociology, the crisis of Marxism is expressed, above all, in the *absence* of a comparable effort of auto-analysis. In the last decade there has been a revival of high-quality Marxist analysis: of imperialism and under-development, of contemporary metropolitan capitalism, of fascism, of the social and political structures of individual countries. These are all strategic subjects, and in renewing its investigation of them, Marxist theory testifies to its own vitality. But although the history of Marxism itself is of equal and perhaps greater importance, many Marxists still tend to shrink from it. However, this odd circumstance – the lack of a Marxism of Marxism – can itself be explained by Marxist analysis. The reasons for it are to be sought in the trajectory of the class struggle and the way in which the union of Marxist theory and practice has developed within it.

One noteworthy aspect of that union is that the landmarks of theory have, virtually without exception, been established by thinkers who were also political leaders: Marx and Engels (leaders of the League of Communists and of the First International), Lenin, Gramsci, Mao Tse Tung. This fusion of theoretical and political activity reached its zenith with the Bolsheviks; nearly all their leading politicians – Stalin, Trotsky and Bukharin, perhaps the most intellectual of them all – made significant contributions to theory and social analysis. This formidable record is just one expression of the enormous fertility and significance of the union of theory and practice in revolutionary Marxism. Nevertheless, not many are ever equipped lucidly to analyze their own experiences, their own mistakes, the real effects of their own intentions. Attempts to do so very often err towards either triumphalism or factionalist denunciation (exemplified in different ways in Trotsky's writings on the theory and politics of his enemy, Stalin, and in current Mao-inspired Chinese writings on the Soviet Union). Thus, the problems of a Marxism of Marxism lead directly to the question of the relationship between the Marxist intelligentsia and the revolutionary movement.

An intelligentsia is wedded to its class by the cohesive power of a common interest that binds together more or less divergent experiences, practices and problems; as such, the relationship is never simple or without complication. The fact that a union of theory and practice has been achieved in the history of Marxism is a remarkable historical achievement, but Marxism has not been spared the difficulties inherent in it. In brief and crude summary of a long and tragic story, it can be said that since the late 1920's at least – when Marxism had to adjust itself, in one way or another, to the unexpected strength of its enemies, in spite of the new depression – the relationship between the Marxist intelligentsia and the Marxist labour movement has been characterized by either a total submersion of the former in the latter, or a grave attenuation of the link between them. In the first case, Marxist analysis was subordinated to the immediate practical needs of an embattled and, for a long time, profoundly authoritarian leadership. In this situation, very important contributions could sometimes be made by the leadership itself, as is shown by Mao's writings from the thirties and forties. But a more characteristic product is probably the distorted and triumphalist *Short History of the Communist Party of the Soviet Union*, which served hundreds of thousands of militants as an introduction to a Marxism of Marxism. The other case, typified principally in the tradition of 'Western Marxism', has become more and more widespread in the Soviet Union and Eastern Europe since Stalin's death, often at very high intellectual levels. Here, scientific analysis became divorced from strategic political problems, or confronted them only as they occurred in other epochs or on other continents. The role of a Marxism of Marxism was assumed by a *philosophy of Marxism*, a series of subtle and esoteric discussions of methodology and epistemology, in which intellectuals fought historic political battles *sotto voce*.

For reasons which have yet to be explained, this situation of polarization, involving a loss of either intellectual perspective or experiential connection, has not been fundamentally altered by the 20th Congress of the CPSU or the Chinese Cultural Revolution, or by the recent social upheavals in the West – movements of anti-imperialist solidarity, the resurgence of mass working-class militancy, revolutionary movements of students and women. The ideological crisis of metropolitan capitalism has been fought out largely in the terms of betrayed bourgeois and petty-bourgeois ideals. In this conjuncture, Marxism has been courted by virtually every conceivable non-Marxist ideology: by existentialism, phenomenology, critical academic sociology, and by several variants of theology. To raise the question of a Marxism of Marxism is to take a resolute stand against all attempts to capture and exploit Marx for non-Marxist purposes; and to adopt as a guiding principle (whose foundations and development are themselves to be investigated) the claim that Marx himself made for his work: that Marxism is a specific science, related to the working class as a guide to socialist revolution.

For the present, we are concerned only with the earliest stage of a Marxism of Marxism, an analysis of the formation of Marxism by Marx and Engels. This involves the double task of elucidating the bases of the claim of historical materialism to scientificity, and of relating its production to the class struggles in which Marx and Engels participated. Anticipating the epistemological position adopted below, we may define the first task as an attempt to account for the *object* of historical materialism as a science: that is, to discover what it is that historical materialism studies scientifically, in its

pursuit of a genuine knowledge of society and its history. Furthermore, an investigation of the scientific foundation of historical
materialism entails another responsibility. Historical materialism
claims not only to be a science among others, but also to employ *a
particular mode of scientific analysis and explanation*, a particular way
of treating its object. Thus, the basic meaning of *dialectics* must also
be clarified.

Even though there is little in the field of Marxism to correspond
to the sociology of sociology, a Marxism of Marxism is not obliged
to start from nowhere. It will be indebted to the immense existing
literature on Marx, to biographies and to specialized treatments of
Marxist concepts, theories and methods. In particular, a Marxism
of the formation of Marxism will have to attend to earlier, chiefly
philosophical efforts, begun from the same premises, to grasp the
essential properties of historical materialism.

Among the major efforts at elucidation of the scientific basis of
historical materialism are three, all recent, which deserve special
consideration: two from Western Europe, by Galvano Della Volpe
and Louis Althusser, and one from the Eastern sector, by Jindřich
Zelený. These bodies of work have created important 'schools' of
Marxism in their respective countries, Italy, France and Czechoslovakia; and Zelený's mode of analysis has, perhaps above all, been
crucial to the development of a significant school in West Germany.
They all explicitly locate themselves in the Marxist-Leninist
tradition, and all made their contributions as members of their
national Communist Parties – though, unlike the major Bolshevik
theoreticians, all three were politically peripheral. Their common
effort has been to defend, clarify and develop the scientificity of
Marxism: Della Volpe (d. 1968) was concerned in particular to
resist the incursions of strong native idealist and historico-philo-
sophical traditions, descended from Vico and Croce, into Italian
Marxism, while Althusser has combatted the numerous attempts to
exploit Marx's early writings for the purpose of transmuting
Marxism into a philosophy of man. Althusser, Della Volpe and
Zelený are philosophers, and their projects, therefore, differ in focus
from the present study. They are not, then, so much rival discourses
(in the same sense as the various sociologies of sociology) as different
possible starting-points for an analysis of this kind. This study
draws mainly on the work of Louis Althusser; and it is proper,
therefore, to explain this choice, and to give a brief account of the

range and results of the chosen work. The immediate task, then, is to relate this study to those of Althusser, Della Volpe and Zelený – not to make a comparative analysis of their conceptions of Marxism, which, although it would certainly be valuable, is beyond the scope of the present study. It will not be possible here to convey the full richness of these *oeuvres*, which will be analyzed only in their direct bearing on the problems of a Marxist analysis of the formation of Marxism.

1. The Hour of Methodology

Della Volpe and Zelený both belong to that important and versatile tradition of Marxist self-analysis which centres on the method of historical materialism. 'Method' in this tradition does not refer to research techniques but rather to explanatory logic, to the formal character of concepts and modes of explanation. One of the focal questions of this tradition is that of the significance of Hegel's logic and dialectic. In this respect, Della Volpe and Zelený represent opposite poles. Juxtaposed, their works may thus indicate some of the common problems of the methodological approach.

Della Volpe is an anti-Hegelian, implacably inimical to all speculative, non-scientific philosophy. The objective of his main work, tellingly entitled *Logic as a Positive Science*, is the emancipation of thought from all aprioristic speculation and metaphysics, and the establishment of logic and the theory of knowledge as a science. The only knowledge worthy of the name is scientific knowledge. There is no particular philosophical logic or method of producing knowledge. There is only one method and one logic, that of the modern experimental sciences.[88] In this perspective, Della Volpe

[88] Galvano Della Volpe, *Logica come Scienza Positiva*, Messina, 1956, p. 198f and passim. A more accessible introduction to and overview of Della Volpe's work is the French edition of his posthumous *Rousseau et Marx et autres essais de critique matérialiste*, Paris, 1974, which besides the title essay (which recapitulates the basic themes of the former work but not its very detailed philosophical analyses of Aristotle, Kant, Hegel and Galileo), includes three important essays on Marxist method, and a valuable general introduction by Robert Paris. It should be noted that Della Volpe's conception of 'logic' was broad, including not only formal analyses of thought but also considerations on the relationship between thought and reality. In his *Logica* he sometimes uses logic and gnoseology synonymously, as for instance in the programmatic preface. This was one of the positions from which he criticized the formalism of the logical positivists (see

defines Marx's critique of Hegel as the third major step in the development of a nondogmatic, scientific logic, the first being Aristotle's critique (in his political philosophy, for instance) of Plato's classification of concrete species, the second being Galileo's critique of scholastic conceptions of the fabric of the world.[89] The common core of these critiques is their attack on *a priori* reasoning, the philosophical foreclosure of the empirical world. They did not, however, dictate a simple return to empirical investigation. Della Volpe is concerned above all with a new type of concept that replaces philosophical abstractions. These new concepts, and the scientific method allied to them, are 'determinate abstractions'.[90] The decisive flaw of the concepts of speculative philosophy is not their vacuity, but on the contrary their 'vicious plenitude'. The critique of such concepts is primarily a critique of hypostatization, of a substantification of abstract, generic concepts that fills them with particular, unassimilated and unexplained empirical contents. Hegel's philosophy of the State, for example, consisted in the generalization of the state of a particular epoch into an undifferentiated essence of the State. Thus, the Marxian critique of political economy is a critique of the indeterminate abstractions of the economists, in which historically specific forms of production and property are volatilized into concepts of production in general and property in general.[91]

The scientific logic of historical materialism involves an historical 'mise-au-point' of concepts, achieved by means of the methodological circle concrete-abstract-concrete – or, as Della Volpe also terms it, the method of induction-deduction. Scientific investigation begins with the historico-material concrete of experience. The subsequent process of abstraction and analysis is based on the

---

Rousseau et Marx, p. 309). Della Volpe's conception of the oneness and scientificity of logic is also explicitly directed against Engels' postulation of laws peculiar to dialectics (*Logica come Scienza Positiva*, pp. 178–9).

[89] *Rousseau et Marx*, p. 261f.

[90] 'Thus, that *determinate abstraction*, [Marx's] method of economic science, is the same as the specific connection or method of the philosophical sciences, is demonstrated by the fact that they have in common the premise of a materialist rejection of apriorism and that they each resolve themselves into sociology (the critique of political economy is none other than a materialist economic sociology) or, in other words, history-science or (materialist) science of history . . .', *Logica come Scienza Positiva*, p. 211.

[91] *Rousseau et Marx*, pp. 197–277; *Logica come Scienza Positiva*, pp. 113f, 185f.

problems and self-criticism of present-day society.[92] 'It is thus a question of using these abstractions to assess historical *antecedents* in their theoretical connection with the *consequences* or present and problematic historical phenomena which must be resolved.'[93] Moreover, it is necessary to elucidate the ideal logical structure of present-day society without losing the essential historical determinacy of the concepts. Thirdly, these determinate abstractions are hypothetical, not categorical and absolute, and must be verified in social and economic practice. With this return to the concrete, now grasped as a totality of multiple determinations, the methodological circle is closed. The abstractions are in this way rigorously and repeatedly 'mises au point', experimentally and historically.[94]

Della Volpe has described the logic or method of historical materialism as a 'moral galileism'. 'Moral' refers to the 'moral' or human sciences, and 'galileism' is employed 'to distinguish the method of historical materialism not merely from the idealist method, with its hypostases, but also from the positivist method, with its idolatry of "facts", and its distrust (traditional since Bacon) of hypotheses or ideas'.[95] The term 'moral galileism' is a succinct expression of certain significant aspects of Della Volpe's conception of Marxist method. Although he later pointed out, rather too hastily it seems, that the abstractions of the human or moral sciences differ from those of the natural sciences in that the former 'involve no element of repeatability', because what is historical never repeats itself,[96] he conceived of science (and scientific method) as one.[97] More important, however, than the negation of the fundamental distinction between natural and human sciences – which Della Volpe shared with Marx and Engels – was that the characterization of historical materialism as a 'moral galileism' implied a denial of any basic distinction between mechanical and dialectical thought. Della Volpe retained the term 'dialectic' to denote a thought which, like historical materialism, 'reproduces' or grasps the objective con-

---

[92] *Rousseau et Marx*, p. 246f.
[93] Ibid., p. 250.
[94] Ibid., p. 251f, 293f.
[95] Ibid., p. 269.
[96] Ibid., p. 295. The third, posthumous edition of the *Logica* (Rome, 1969) was, in accordance with the author's wishes, re-entitled *Logica come Scienza Storica* (Logic as historical science).
[97] Ibid., pp. 294, 295n.

tradictions of the real world. This contradictory world is not, as in the Hegelian dialectic, an original unity that has developed into a unity of opposites, but a permanent unity of multiple, diverse contradictions or oppositions. The dialectic is thus subsumed into the method of determinate abstraction with which historical materialism studies society and its objective contradictions: 'In short, the dialectic works in and through determinate abstraction, which thus discovers or "reproduces", and thereby progressively masters, objective contradictions.'[98]

Zelený's work, like that of Della Volpe, starts from a preoccupation with the logical and epistemological problems of the classical Western tradition in philosophy.[99] Their concerns, however, are very different. Della Volpe approached historical materialism from the perspective of the logical rupture of empirical science from metaphysics and speculative philosophy. Zelený, on the other hand, is interested in the contribution made by the new science of historical materialism to the existing, already scientific logic of science: in short, in the difference between dialectical and non-dialectical empirical sciences. His reading of Marxism is one of those designed to elicit its specifically dialectical character, its *differentia specifica* with respect to mechanical materialism. In this tradition, the Czech philosopher is perhaps the most important representative so far of an approach that sees the Marxist dialectic as a *scientific* mode of analysis and explanation, in sharp contrast with the lineage, extending from the Lukács of *History and Class Consciousness* to Marcuse, for which the dialectic is a non-scientific (and for the latter at least, *anti*-scientific), 'totalitarian' and all-encompassing philosophy of history.[100]

[98] Ibid., p. 299. Lucio Colletti, Della Volpe's most important follower, has later made a sharp distinction between Marx the scientist and Marx the dialectician (with a positive evaluation of both). See below, chapter 6. Colletti has made a number of important and controversial contributions to Marxist philosophy and social theory, criticizing the 'idealist reaction against science' – in traditional philosophy, in interpretations of Marx (by Lukács and the Frankfurt School) and in subjectivist sociology – and also in the positivist Marxist of the Second International and the conception of dialectical materialism developed by Engels, Plekhanov and Lenin. See his *Marxism and Hegel*, London, 1973, and *From Rousseau to Lenin*, London, 1972.

[99] This discussion is confined to Zelený's main work, *Die Wissenschaftslogik und 'Das Kapital'* (The Logic of Science and *Capital*), Frankfurt, 1968. This German edition is an enlarged second edition; the first was published in Czech in 1962.

[100] See further, ch. 6, below.

Whereas Della Volpe based his analyses mainly on Marx's methodological writings, Zelený uses the economic analyses of *Capital* to make a careful comparison of its logical structures with those of Ricardo. He distinguishes three types of relation: 'relationships of surface appearances, especially quantitative relationships', 'inner, substantial relationships'; and 'relationships between essence and surface appearance'.[101] The first type is analyzed by both Marx and Ricardo according to the logic of Galilean-Newtonian mechanics – in Marx, for instance, in the case of the rate of circulation of money, or of the effects of changes in the productivity of labour on exchange-value.[102] The novelty of Marx's work hinges on its distinctive treatment of the other two types of relation.

In Marx's investigation of capitalism, the mechanical mode of analysis of systems is subordinate to a new kind of deduction and scientific determinism, developed out of, and in critique of, Hegel's dialectic. The second of the types of relation listed above is of little interest to Ricardo who, in conformity with the mechanical mode of thought, conceives 'essence' as something 'qualitatively fixed and undifferentiated' (Zelený's category of 'essence', derived from the metaphysical tradition, might here be translated as a set of concepts explaining the operations of a system, or, anticipating our later analysis, as a 'pattern of determination'), whereas Marx sees 'essence' as 'a contradictory process, that has successive phases of development and distinct levels of depth'.[103] Marx's study of capitalism is not primarily concerned with what happens in a fixed system of market exchange when the values of the variables of the system (productivity, the availability of land, for example) change, but rather with the laws of development and change of the system itself.

In order to grasp the world as a structured unity in auto-development through its inner contradictions, Marx utilizes forms of causal relationship and deduction logically different from those of axiomatic science. Zelený analyzes the logical character of Marx's dialectical derivation, in the first chapter of *Capital*, of the money form of value from the substance of value, where the aim is to trace neither the simple logical connections among concepts nor simply the historical genesis of the money form, but rather the inner

[101] Zelený, p. 36.
[102] Ibid., pp. 113f, 124.
[103] Ibid., p. 36.

necessity, the logical connections in its historical genesis.[104] This new analytic logic is derived from Hegel, but involves also a materialist critique of Hegel for the purposes of empirical science, in which the dialectical deduction is based on three preconditions: first, a thorough empirical knowledge of the object of dialectical analysis; second, a knowledge of its limits, that is, of its relationship with the actual, not dialectically deducible historical reality; and third, the premise that the phenomenon whose development is to be revealed in its inner necessity by dialectical deduction has in fact reached a certain level of maturation.[105] Here as elsewhere, Zelený makes no attempt to evaluate the import of dialectical procedure. The new conception of causality on which Zelený focuses involves an interpenetration of cause and effect, which undergo interversion in the development of the social totality and its immanent contradictions. Again, this is illustrated in Marx's analysis of the genesis of money and capital.[106]

Ricardo and Marx also differ decisively in their manner of relating the essence to the immediate reality, the 'surface appearance'. For Ricardo straightforwardly identifies phenomena as instances of the working of a law. Marx, on the other hand, discovered that laws are as a rule effective only through a chain of 'mediations' which relate the phenomenon (say, the market price of commodities) to the law (the labour theory of value), which rules despite apparent contradictions between itself and the phenomena that it explains. Here is a kind of scientific determinism different from that of classical mechanics.

The best contributions of the methodological tradition of Marx-analysis are of great importance for the understanding and further development of historical materialism, and the works of Della Volpe and Zelený are undoubtedly among the very best. Zelený's logical investigation is particularly valuable in any attempt to define the specificity of historical materialism. However, for the purposes of a study of the formation of Marxist social theory, there seems to be a radical flaw in the methodological approach. The hour of methodology, so to speak, strikes either too early or too late. The methodologist tends to find either a scientific programme, a commitment to a scientific method, or a method at work in a developed discourse.

[104] Ibid., ch. 6.
[105] Ibid., pp. 92–3.
[106] Ibid., 9, 117f.

Della Volpe can be said to represent the former tendency, and Zelený the latter. But a study of the formation of a science must be concerned above all with what happens in between, with the way in which the new scientific discourse emerges and develops.

Della Volpe locates Marx's decisive break with speculative philosophy in the critique of Hegel's philosophy of the State (1843), where the latter's aprioristic dialectic is denounced. *The Economic-Philosophical Manuscripts* of 1844 are seen basically as a continuation of the earlier critique of Hegel from the standpoint of a commitment to empirical science, though here Della Volpe also notes the appearance of the 'polemico-critical' concept of alienated labour. With the critique of Proudhon in *The Poverty of Philosophy*, the problem of a new 'scientific dialectic' is posed. In the *Introduction* of 1857 (included in the *Grundrisse*) where Marx expounds the method later used in *Capital*, the problem is finally solved.[107]

This analysis is devoted entirely to the question of scientific programmes, and, even in that respect, its treatment is unbalanced: it deals only with Marx's divergence from Hegel and not at all with his divergence from the scientific ideal derived from classical mechanics, which appears to have been the main reason why, in spite of everything, Marx retained the dialectic, in his own transformed version. But what became of these programmes? In what concrete theoretical developments did they actually operate? Della Volpe's analysis illustrates the methodological approach in its 'premature' form, with its resultant blindness to the really critical moments in the formation of historical materialism. As we shall see in chapter six, there occurred many important changes in Marx's view of society and social theory between the critique of Hegel's philosophy of the State and *The Poverty of Philosophy*, changes made manifest in *The German Ideology* (1845–6), which are overlooked by Della Volpe. Marx's conceptions of the economy and of the working class changed, and so too did his view of utilitarianism, Feuerbach and 'mechanical materialism', of political economy and of politics. In the formation of historical materialism as a scientific discourse on society, these changes were indubitably pivotal events. But even in retrospect from *The Poverty of Philosophy*, Della Volpe fails to explore them.

---

[107] *Rousseau et Marx*, pp. 197–258. Cf. *Logica come Scienza Positiva*, pp. 113f, 185f.

Zelený, for his part, deals with the intricacies of the Marxian dialectic in the ostensibly finished form of *Capital*. In the second part of his book, he does in fact study the basic stages of Marx's critique of Hegel, and finds the decisive rupture in *The German Ideology*.[108] However, the procedure he employs illustrates anew the limitations of methodological analysis. In Zelený's exposition, a work of considerable philosophical erudition and subtlety, *The German Ideology* is seen as representing a break with Marx's prior 'teleological-eschatalogical' critique of human alienation with its concomitant conception of history and communism as man's transcendence of his alienation, in favour of an attention to the practical, empirical history of mankind, and of a critical method and political conception 'freed from teleological-eschatalogical elements'.[109] Thus, we are left once again with a hiatus between Marx's adoption of a scientific programme, and the method applied when the new discourse has actually been developed.

The fatal consequence of this gap in methodological analysis is not simply that it leaves an unexplained void: rather, to borrow a phrase from Della Volpe, it is its 'vicious plenitude', unconsciously filled with an unassimilated, unanalyzed reality. The methodological reading hides the *empiricist* assumption that the subject-matter and methods of study of a science are fundamentally unproblematic. This is implied when Della Volpe characterized historical materialism as a *moral* galileism, thus assuming that Marxism is unproblematically a scientific successor to moral philosophy; and when historical materialism is analyzed as a non-hypostatized (Della Volpe) or dialectical (Zelený) political economy. But can it be assumed that Marxism is just a new conception of political economy? What of the materialist conception of history? Where would *The Eighteenth Brumaire*, *The Civil War in France* and *Anti-Dühring* (in fact written jointly by Marx and Engels) fit in, if that were the case? What is the object of a discourse that includes both very detailed theoretical economic analyses (of value, commodities, the movement of capital and so on) and social and political historiography?[110] How did this use of scientific dialectic method emerge?

[108] Zelený, p. 281.

[109] Ibid., pp. 205f, 213f.

[110] The problem cannot be solved simply by describing historical materialism as a 'sociology' (see n. 90 above), or even, more precisely, as a materialist sociology: utilitarian and other non-Marxist varieties of materialism have explicitly pre-

2. From a Philosophy of Theoretical Practice to the Threshold of a Marxism of Marxism

The work of Louis Althusser also belongs to the philosophy of Marxism.[111] But there are two ways in which it differs decisively from previous efforts in this field. First, Althusser's philosophical investigation of Marx has focused sharply and deliberately on the emergence of historical materialism as a new scientific discourse. It emphasizes the theoretical rupture that brought Marx's new scientific object into being, and, analyzes the specificity of the Marxian conceptions of contradiction and causality, its new mode of explanation. In this way, Althusser escapes the limbo of the methodological approach. Second, in the development and revision of his own conception of Marxist philosophy, Althusser has come to believe that the study of the formation of historical materialism cannot be philosophical, but must, of necessity, be itself historical-materialist. After a decade of philosophical elaboration, Althusser has explicitly posed the problem of a Marxism of Marxism, and while apparently having no intention of contributing directly himself, has provided important epistemological tools for that purpose. In a sense, then, Althusser's work has reached the limits of the philosophy of Marxism, in so far as the latter has served as a substitute for a Marxism of Marxism. This is not to say that Althusser signals the end of Marxist philosophy. It means rather that philosophy cannot continue to usurp the role of an ongoing practice of historical materialism and Marxist politics, but must henceforth seek a proper relationship with the latter. Given its importance for the present study, some attempt at an overview and critical-analytical summary of the controversial Althusserian *oeuvre* seems fitting. It should be borne in mind that the latter will be examined here only in so far as it bears upon the study of the formation of

---

sented themselves as 'sociology'. See further, chs. 4, 5, and 7 below. However, for an interesting Della Volpean discussion of 'Marxism as Sociology', see Lucio Colletti, *From Rousseau to Lenin*, pp. 3–44.

[111] Virtually all Althusser's major published works are now available in excellent English editions (London: NLB, except *For Marx*, published by Allen Lane): *For Marx* (1970), *Reading Capital* (1970), *Lenin and Philosophy and Other Essays* (1971), *Politics and History* (1972), *Reply to John Lewis* (1976, forthcoming). Among those of his works not yet translated are *Philosophie et philosophie spontanée des savants*, Paris, 1974, and *Eléments d'une autocritique*, Paris, 1974.

historical materialism. No general evaluation, philosophical or political, is intended.

It was in 1960 that Althusser published the first of a series of essays that was to be collected in *For Marx*, his first major work. This same year saw the appearance of Jean-Paul Sartre's lengthy *Critique de la Raison Dialectique*. Though hardly noticeable at the time, it was a year of beginnings – the beginning of one period and, for another, the beginning of an end. Written in the late 1950's, Sartre's work recalls the years of defensiveness and disillusion within Marxism and the labour movement, the arid era of the 'personality cult' – more apparent after the fascist threat and the early post-war hopes had receded – the Twentieth Party Congress and the upheavals in Eastern Europe. Althusser's essays, on the other hand, point forward to the renaissance of Marxism-Leninism among the young generation in the later 1960's and to the growing – and increasingly ambiguous – intellectual influence of the Chinese Revolution. Althusser was, in 1962, one of the first Europeans to read Mao Tse tung as an important dialectician.[112]

Sartre's *Critique* is undeniably a great intellectual achievement and represents, in the author's personal way, an intransigent left-wing position in a difficult political situation. It therefore constitutes an excellent pole of reference against which to distinguish the specific characteristics of Althusser's work. This collocation of the two men is not merely an arbitrary literary device. It is clear that *Critique de la Raison Dialectique* and *For Marx* were written as different reactions to an experience that was in many ways common to both. Althusser even makes a number of direct references to Sartre – always critical and dissentient, but not without personal respect[113] – and several points and distinctions underlined by him should certainly be read with Sartre in mind.

The common experience, though differently lived, was of course the period of Stalinism (theoretical and political) in the European labour movement, East and West. It was the period of dogmatism, when analysis was reduced to 'simple ceremony' (Sartre)[114] and

---

[112] L. Althusser, 'Contradiction and Overdetermination', in *For Marx*.

[113] For explicit references to Sartre by Althusser, see, e.g., *For Marx*, pp. 27, 125, 127, 203; *Reading Capital*, pp. 131, 135f; *Réponse à John Lewis*, Paris, 1973, pp. 43f, 73.

[114] J-P. Sartre, *The Problem of Method*, London, 1963, p. 27. This text forms the introduction to the *Critique*, as yet untranslated into English.

'slight idiosyncracies in . . . using the Famous Quotations' (Althusser).[115] It was the period of mechanical reductionism: of the theoretical to the political, of the political and ideological to the economic, of the building of a whole new society to the master-concept of economic development.[116] In a certain sense the two philosophers even seem to see their task in somewhat the same way. For the organized Communist Althusser, a rigorous commitment to Marxism does not simply mean the re-establishment of the Marxist-Leninist *status quo ante* before Stalin's deviation. 'The end of dogmatism puts us face to face with this reality: that Marxist philosophy . . . has still largely to be constituted, since as Lenin said, only the corner-stones have been laid down.'[117] To the non-organized Existentialist Sartre, Marxism is not a condemned or senile and obsolete doctrine: 'Far from being exhausted, Marxism is still very young, almost in its infancy; it has hardly begun to develop. It remains, therefore, the philosophy of our time.'[118] Marxism has so far developed 'directive principles, indications of tasks and problems' but not an established body of knowledge: 'We must find the method and constitute the science.'[119]

Even their definitions of the specific philosophical task in front of them sound similar. Althusser refers to the 'necessity . . . for a theory which defines itself dialectically, not merely as a science of history (historical materialism) but also and simultaneously as a philosophy . . . therefore capable of accounting for itself', of taking itself and its scientificity as an object.[120] This Marxist 'accounting for itself' is the object of Althusser's philosophical effort, in *For Marx*, in *Reading Capital*, and, reformulated, in *Lenin and Philosophy* and *Reply to John Lewis*. In Sartre's work, '*critique*' is meant in the Kantian sense of the determination of the scope of its object, not as an attack on it. 'Its aim is simply to discover and found dialectical rationality,'[121] and since the experience of the dialectic is itself dialectical, this entails showing how dialectical reason

---

[115] Althusser, *For Marx*, p. 27.
[116] Sartre, *The Problem of Method*, pp. 22, 35f, 178. Althusser, *For Marx*, pp. 105–16, *Réponse à John Lewis*, ch. 3.
[117] Althusser, *For Marx*, pp. 30–31.
[118] Sartre, *The Problem of Method*, p. 30.
[119] Ibid., p. 35.
[120] Althusser, *For Marx*, p. 39. Emphasis omitted.
[121] Sartre, *Critique de la Raison dialectique*, Paris, 1960, p. 134.

accounts for itself and its own intelligibility.[122]

At the political level too there are similarities, which are not confined to their comparable attacks on the economism rampant in current Marxist theory and practice. In the adverse situation of European Communism in the fifties and sixties, the post-Stalin thaw led to a strong upsurge of outspoken revisionism and reformism, to tendencies of accommodation to the booming capitalist world. Althusser's theoretical *recommencement* of Marxism and Marxism-Leninism was the first clear indication of a left-wing road from the Stalinist deviation. While not pointing directly to that road, Sartre's work also took up a left-wing position, and was in no way representative of an accommodating reformism.

In the end, however, these similarities serve only to illuminate the fundamental differences between the two men. What Sartre offers is a philosophical anthropology, 'the intelligible foundations of a structural anthropology', the 'basis of a "prolegomenon to all future anthropology"'.[123] His aim is explicitly metaphysical: 'our object is not to reinstate the real history of the human species, but rather to establish the truth of history'.[124] Althusser, in contrast, firmly reasserts a commitment to empirical science in a milieu which, unlike the dominant intellectual traditions of Scandinavia and the Anglo-Saxon countries, is permeated by various kinds of philosophizing about Man, History and the like. In order to emphasize its scientific aspect as strongly and provocatively as possible, Althusser has described Marxism as a 'theoretical anti-humanism', humanism being a non-scientific ideology, bourgeois in character.[125] 'Simply put, the recourse to ethics so deeply inscribed in every humanist ideology may play the part of an imaginary treatment of real problems. Once *known*, these problems are posed in precise terms; they are organizational problems of the forms of economic life, political life and individual life. To pose these problems correctly and to resolve them in reality, they must be called by their names, their *scientific names*.'[126] Instead of trying to lay an extra-scientific

[122] Ibid., pp. 133, 137.
[123] Ibid., pp. 156, 153.
[124] Ibid., p. 142. Emphasis omitted.
[125] Althusser, *For Marx*, esp. Part Seven.
[126] Ibid., p. 246. Cf. *Réponse à John Lewis*, pp. 67–8. Like Sartre, Althusser refers to problems of individual life. For humanistic readings of Marx at the time of Althusser's intervention, see, for example, J.-Y. Calvez, *La Pensée de Karl*

foundation for it, Althusser's philosophy sets out to discover what is involved in the constitution of historical materialism as a science, and to determine how a Marxist philosophy should be related to this science, not as its founder or substitute, but as its servant.

Many of Althusser's sharpest formulations should certainly be read as intended to emphasize this complete difference of direction. It is in opposition to the 'founding' efforts of philosophical anthropology that Althusser dares to characterize Marxism as an anti-humanism. It is in opposition to the attempts of Sartre and others to establish *the* truth of history in a process of 'totalizations', starting from the singular individual and based on the assumption of 'the fundamental identity of a single life and human history',[127] that Althusser affirms that history is a process having neither 'subject(s) nor end(s)',[128] and that all analysis confronts 'the ever pre-givenness of a structured complex unity'.[129] It is in opposition to Sartre's definition of Marxism as 'History itself taking consciousness of itself',[130] and others like it, that Althusser contends that Marxism is no historicism and emphasizes the specificity of scientific practice.[131]

Marx, Paris, 1956, E. Fromm, *Marx's Concept of Man*, New York, 1961, E. Kamenka, *The Ethical Foundations of Marxism*, London, 1962, E. Thier, *Das Menschenbild des jungen Marx*, Gottingen, 1957. Sartre is another example, of course.

[127] Sartre, *Critique de la Raison dialectique*, p. 156.
[128] Althusser, *Réponse à John Lewis*, p. 69f.
[129] Althusser, *For Marx*, p. 199.
[130] Sartre, *Critique de la Raison dialectique*, p. 134.
[131] Althusser, *Reading Capital*, p. 199f. By 'historicism' Althusser means the body of thought which arose under this label in the late nineteenth century in German and Italian epistemology and philosophy of history. The works of Dilthey, Rickert, Windelband, and Croce are central to this tradition. A crucial problem raised by it concerns historical relativity and its significance to the adequacy and truth of scientific concepts and propositions. Historicism has had its effect on Marxism through the early works of Gramsci, Korsch, and Lukács. In sociology it has left its imprint via Weber, Simmel, and Mannheim. For a relatively short exposition, glowingly enthusiastic, of historicism see K. Mannheim, 'Der Historismus', *Archiv für Sozialwissenschaft und Sozialpolitik*, vol. 54 (1924), pp. 1–66. Virtually all the main ideas presented there by Mannheim have been central targets of Althusserian attack: the unfolding central subject of history, the circular, expressive social totality, the particular truth of the epoch, the substitution of *Weltanschauung* for science, and so on. In the contemporary Anglo-Saxon and Scandinavian world 'historicism' is usually thought of as the target of Karl Popper's attack, *The Poverty of Historicism*, London, 1957. Popper

3. Science and Philosophy: Four Problems and Two Stages

What is Althusser's main achievement, and how is the present study of Marxist social theory related to his work? Althusser's fundamental project is to constitute the specificity of Marxist philosophy, which is already present in the classical works of Marxism, but in an unsystematized, untheorized, mainly 'practical' state.[132] This philosophical project is indissolubly wedded to an elucidation of Marxism as science. There are three basic reasons for this double reading of Marx. The first is the general link between science and philosophy, a link whose character Althusser has formulated in two very different ways (we shall return to this question later). The second is the thesis retained throughout his successive conceptions of philosophy and its relationship with science – that there occur simultaneously in Marx's career decisive changes in his views of history and of philosophy.[133] This simultaneity brings with it the risk of confusion and a reduction of science to philosophy, or vice versa, and therefore necessitates clarification of the links between science and philosophy in Marxism.[134] Thirdly, the attempt to determine the specificity of Marxism in relation to the philosophies of Hegel and Feuerbach, from which Marx had to start out, necessarily entails consideration of Marx's claim to have substituted a science for the 'German Ideology'. Given the imbrication of science and philosophy both in the general history of science and in the Marxian system, Althusser is led to demarcate four distinct problems: (1) the specificity of the Marxist theory of society (historical materialism) as a *science*; (2) the specificity of historical materialism as *a* science, among others; (3) the specificity of Marxism as a *philosophy* (dialectical materialism), as distinct from science, politics, and ideology; (4) the specificity of Marxism as *a* philosophy, among others.

---

utilizes a personal definition of the traditional concept in order to contrast the objective of historical prediction with his own idea of science as 'social engineering'. Croce, Dilthey, Rickert and Windelband are not even mentioned by Popper, who on the other hand deals, among others, with Comte and J. S. Mill, who belonged rather to the tradition that the classical historicists attacked. The further question of the differences and similarities in Popper's and Althusser's critiques of 'historicism' must be left aside in this context.

[132] Althusser, *For Marx*, pp. 167–82.
[133] Ibid., p. 33, *Réponse à John Lewis*, p. 56.
[134] See, e.g., *For Marx*, pp. 28–30, 33.

Althusser has devoted himself primarily to (1) and (4), each in turn constituting the main theme of the two periods into which Althusser's work so far can be divided. The specificity of Marxism as a science, its 'epistemological break' or rupture with preceding conceptions of history and society, is the focus of *For Marx* and *Reading Capital*, both published in 1965, the first a collection of essays written between 1960 and 1965, the second a joint product of a seminar directed by Althusser at the Ecole Normale Supérieure in 1964–5 (in addition to those of Althusser and Balibar, the first edition of *Reading Capital* contained several contributions by other hands, which have been excluded from subsequent editions). These works are also concerned with questions of Marxist philosophy, but in a form that subsumes them into the commanding problem of science. Philosophy figures here as a kind of epistemological science of science. In the second phase of his work, which can be dated from the autumn of 1967 (indicated in the Preface to the second edition of *For Marx*), Althusser departs from his earlier conception of philosophy, above all by relating Marxist philosophy to politics and to science, and by elaborating the difference between philosophy and science. (This new phase in Althusser's thought was initiated after heated philosophical and political debates on his positions both inside and outside the French Communist Party, and in the wake of the Cultural Revolution). To this period belong *Lenin and Philosophy* (1968), *Reply to John Lewis* (1972) and *Elements of Self-Criticism* (1974). The difference between philosophy and science is treated at some length in a course of lectures given in the autumn of 1967 but not published until 1974, *Philosophie et Philosophie Spontanée des Savants*. In the present context, Althusser's treatment of (1) and (2) above are most immediately relevant; but his conceptions of philosophy, which bear upon his conception of the relationship between science and society, are also pertinent. One of the major constants of the entire Althusserian *oeuvre* has been its insistence on the scientificity of Marx's analysis of society and history and, concomitantly, on an anti-empiricist conception of science. In Althusser's work, Lenin's critique of spontaneism and his dictum that 'without revolutionary theory, there can be no revolutionary movement' have been introduced directly into epistemology. Thus, the aim of *For Marx* was to show the 'epistemological break' – located in the *Theses on Feuerbach* and *The German Ideology* – between Marx and the Young Marx, between Marx the scientist and Marx the Hegelian-Feuerbachian social philosopher, and to contribute to the development of a theory of scientific and other theoretical practices. In a retrospective summation, Althusser has written: 'If I were asked for a brief summary of the essential *Thesis* I have been trying to defend in my philosophical essays, I should say: Marx founded a new science: the science of History.'[135]

Althusser's studies of the emergence of Marxist science appear to have been based firstly on his intimate knowledge, as editor and translator, of the work of Feuerbach, Marx's most immediate philosophical starting-point, and secondly, on a well-developed French tradition of anti-empiricist epistemology and history of science. The crucial figure in that tradition is Gaston Bachelard, the philosopher of science, whose main works appeared in the 1930's and 1940's.[136]

It was from Bachelard that Althusser borrowed his concept of 'epistemological break', which denotes the passage from a pre-scientific to a scientific theoretical problematic.[137] Bachelard was a militant anti-empiricist, and his concept of epistemological break[138] is related to his much more developed idea of 'epistemological obstacles'. The epistemological obstacles to the production of scientific knowledge are firstly, the initial or immediate experience,

---

[135] *Eléments d'une autocritique*, p. 105. For an English translation of the essay quoted from, see 'The Conditions of Marx' Scientific Discovery', *Theoretical Practice*, 7/8 (1973).

[136] An overview of this tradition is provided by the essays by Dominique Lecourt on Bachelard, Canguilhem, and Foucault in *Marxism and Epistemology*, London, 1975. The very strong influence of that tradition on Althusser's original conception of his philosophical project is indicated by his presentation of the 'Théorie' series, of which his own works have formed the major part, on the back cover of the first editions of *Pour Marx* and *Lire le Capital*. There it is stated: 'The "Théorie" series aspires to take heed of the *de facto* encounter that is happening before our eyes between, on the one hand, the conceptual development of the philosophical principles contained in Marx's discovery, and on the other hand, certain works in the fields of epistemology, the history of ideologies and of knowledge and in scientific research.'

[137] Althusser, *For Marx*, p. 32. For a definition of the concept of epistemological break and related concepts, see M. Pecheux and E. Balibar, 'Definitions', in M. Fichant and M. Pecheux, *Sur l'histoire des sciences*, Paris, 1969, pp. 8–12.

[138] To my knowledge Bachelard used the expression 'epistemological rupture' only once, and that of 'epistemological break' [coupure] not at all. See Lecourt, *Marxism and Epistemology*, pp. 114–16, which is an index of Bachelard's key concepts. Althusser used the term 'epistemological break' in order to give Bachelard's idea 'tout son tranchant'. *Eléments d'une autocritique*, p. 31.

and secondly, generalizations from initial experience.[139] After a long exposition of bizarre ideas in 17th and 18th century natural 'science' (including the taste of electricity and the maladies and sex of metals) Bachelard concludes: 'In my opinion, epistemology must accept the following postulate: the object cannot be designated as an immediate "objective"; in other words, a progress toward the object is not initially an objective one. One must therefore accept that there is a real break [*rupture*] between perceptual knowledge and scientific knowledge.'[140] This tradition also includes the logician Jean Cavaillès, who ended a book on logic containing, among other things, a critique of Husserl, by saying: 'It is not a philosophy of consciousness [*de la conscience*], but a philosophy of the concept that may provide a theory of science.'[141] Another figure in this tradition is Georges Canguilhem, the author of a renowned study of the concept of reflex, and a proponent of a strongly discontinuist conception of the history of science, who has written: 'Complacently investigating, finding and celebrating forerunners is the clearest symptom of ineptness in epistemological criticism . . . In any coherent knowledge each concept is related to all others. Aristarchus of Samos is not a forerunner of Copernicus for having put forward a heliocentric theory, even if Copernicus referred to him as an authority.'[142] Althusser also refers to the works of Alexandre Koyré, another great historian of science and the biographer of Galileo, and to contemporary works by Michel Foucault on the 'archaeology' of discourses.

One of the fundamental analytical concepts of the first period of Althusser's treatment of the emergence of Marxist science is that of *problematic*. This concept can be found in Bachelard, though Althusser has acknowledged another source. [144] It bears a certain resemblance to Kuhn's now rather modish concept of 'paradigm'.

[139] G. Bachelard, *La formation de l'esprit scientifique*, 5th ed., Paris, 1967, p. 14f.

[140] Ibid., p. 239. Cf. idem, *Le rationalisme appliqué*, Paris, 1949, pp. 102–5.

[141] J. Cavaillès, *Sur la logique*, Paris, 1960, p. 78. This book was written in 1942, the year in which Cavaillès joined the Resistance. He was killed by the Nazis in 1944.

[142] G. Canguilhem, *Etudes d'histoire et de philosophie des sciences*, Paris, 1968, p. 21.

[143] Althusser, *Reading Capital*, pp. 16 n, 44 n.

[144] To Jacques Martin. *For Marx*, pp. 32, 62f. For Bachelard, see Lecourt, *Marxism and Epistemology*, p. 91.

Both are designed to think discontinuities in the history of science. But they are not synonymous. Kuhn's concept includes a sociological component, referring to the 'disciplinary matrix', to what is shared by a particular scientific community at a particular time.[145] The concept of problematic is used exclusively in the analysis of discourses. It denotes the specific unity of a theoretical complex, scientific or not, and serves to conceptualize and delimit 'all the possible thoughts' of such a complex. That is, the problematic of a given thought is a knowledge that must be produced by analysis and cannot simply be collected by inspection. The concept of 'problematic' is the centre-piece of an anti-empiricist study of discourses. It is precisely to the problematic, or system of questions, in Marx's work that Althusser's thesis of 'the epistemological break' refers. This thesis does not necessarily imply, as has sometimes been inferred by critics, that a word such as 'alienation' cannot be found in the pages of Marx's mature works.[146]

'All the lines of demarcation that philosophy traces can be reduced to modalities of a single fundamental line: that between the scientific and the ideological,' writes Althusser.[147] But nevertheless, he has always evaded the crucial question of what precisely it is that constitutes scientificity.[148] On the whole, it seems, the jurisdictional authority of the philosophy of science is very weak: this is vividly illustrated in the present condition of Anglo-Saxon philosophy of science, following the collapse of the ambitious claims of Karl Popper under the cumulative (though internally divided) attack of Kuhn, Feyerabend, Lakatos and others.[149] It is, however, possible

[145] T. Kuhn, 'Reflections on My Critics', in I. Lakatos and A. Musgrave (eds.), *Criticism and the Growth of Knowledge*, p. 271f.

[146] Althusser has clarified this distinction and admitted the occurrence of notions of Hegelian and Feuerbachian origin in Marx's later works (*Lenin and Philosophy and Other Essays*, p. 90). Furthermore he has even come to think that the notion of alienation might do 'provisional service' in the new Marxist discourse, in which it is subordinated to the concepts of exploitation and surplus-value, helping to avoid a purely accounting conception of the latter, *Réponse à John Lewis*, p. 58 n.

[147] *Philosophie*, p. 50.

[148] *Reading Capital*, p. 68; *Philosophie*, p. 27.

[149] Karl Popper's view of science is set forth above all in *The Logic of Scientific Discovery*, 1959 (1st ed., in German, 1934). The recent debate in Anglo-Saxon philosophy of science took off with Thomas Kuhn's *The Structure of Scientific Revolutions*, Chicago, 1962. An overview of the debate can be gained from I. Lakatos and A. Musgrave (eds.), *Criticism and the Growth of Knowledge*, Cam-

to isolate the Althusserian conception of science, and to summarize it, briefly and crudely, in five points.[150] (1) There exists an external world independent of men's conceptions of it, of which science tries to gain knowledge, and which provides science with its real object. (Materialist postulate). (2) What science studies is not external reality as it appears to everyday sense perceptions, but a theoretically defined object, by means of which it strives to grasp the real world. (Anti-empiricist thesis).[151] These conceptual objects are incessantly worked upon and transformed in the scientific production of knowledge. (3) The rise of a new science, then, means above all the discovery-production of a new system of concepts defining an object of systematic investigation. This entails a break with previous conceptualizations. (Discontinuist thesis of the history of science). Without such a defined object there can be no scientific knowledge (there are 'technical practices', however, which produce various sorts of technological know-how: the social-psychological, the administrative, the political, and so on). (4) A basic difference between science and ideology is that the former is an open system of questions asked of its object, the answers to which are not prejudged. Ideology, on the other hand, is characterized by posing problems whose solutions are pre-ordained, produced outside the cognitive process. Ideological questions constitute a mirror in which the ideological subject can recognize its own ideological solutions. (This Experiential thesis corresponds to the criterion of testability or refutability in Anglo-Saxon philosophy of science. In common with the latter it must be said to have a weak discriminatory power.) (5) No external proof of the truth of a science can be given. The verification of scientific propositions is itself part of scientific practice. (Anti-pragmatic thesis.)[152] On one occasion, in a brief

---

bridge, 1970; the individual contributions provide further references. In Swedish there is a recent very valuable dissertation on the subject, Ingvar Johansson, *Kritik av den popperianska metodologin* (Göteborg: Dept. of Theoretical Philosophy, mimeo, 1973. English edition forthcoming).

[150] Althusser's conception of science is developed above all in *Reading Capital*, particularly pp. 34–69, 83–90, 119–44, and 145–57; and *Philosophie*, pp. 36f, 100f. Cf. further *For Marx*, pp. 62f; *Lenin and Philosophy and Other Essays*, pp. 42f, 71f; *Eléments d'une autocritique*, pp. 19–52.

[151] That is, what natural science studies is not nature as it appears to the layman, but as it is grasped by conceptual objects, such as those of classical mechanics and relativity theory.

[152] That what can be observed and measured, relevant to a scientific theory, is

formulation that emphasizes materialist versus idealist rather than empiricist versus anti-empiricist conceptions of science, Althusser lists three constitutive elements of a science: a materially existing object, a theory and a method.[153] Althusser's stress has always fallen on theory rather than method; and by 'theory' he means a body of 'objective, verified and verifiable' knowledge.[154]

Althusser's discussions of science have never explored the problems of verification or empirical validation posed by his conception of scientific theory as a body of objective knowledge. How then does this very general conception of science function as a measure of the scientificity of historical materialism? Althusser sets out to establish this not by inquiring whether the developed corpus of historical materialism meets the conditions of science in general, but by using his conception of scientificity to elucidate the kind of break that Marx made with his own theoretical pre-history in 1845. He does not provide any epistemological guarantees of the scientificity of Marxism, but rather demonstrates the occurrence of a break *of a scientific character* with pre-existing philosophies of history. With this aim, he has contrasted historical materialism with the latter in terms of their conceptual content and mode of functioning: 'Their conceptual content. I showed that Marx had replaced the old basic concepts (which I called notions) of the Philosophies of History with absolutely new, unprecedented concepts . . . Where the Philosophies of History spoke of man, economic subject, need, system of needs, civil society, alienation, theft, injustice, mind, freedom – where they even spoke of "society" – Marx began to speak of production, productive forces, relations of production, social formation, infrastructure, superstructure, ideologies, classes, class struggle, etc. I concluded that there was not a relationship of continuity (even in the case of Classical Political Economy) between the system of Marxist concepts and the system of pre-Marxist notions. . . . Their mode of functioning. I showed that in *practice* Marxist theory functioned quite differently from the old pre-Marxist conceptions. It was clear to me that the basic system of

---

a matter for the scientists in question to determine seems to be a well-established tenet in the Popperian and post-Popperian tradition. Cf. Johansson, op. cit., p. 53 (referring to Popper and Agassi and stating that it is unaffected by the critique of Popperian methodology).

[153] *Philosophie et philosophie spontanée des savants*, p. 103.
[154] *Eléments d'une autocritique*, p. 38.

concepts of Marxist theory functioned in the mode of the "theory" of a science, as the "basic" conceptual apparatus opening onto the "infinity" of its object (Lenin), i.e., destined endlessly to pose and confront problems so as to produce new knowledges. Let us say: as a provisional *truth for* the (infinite) conquest of new knowledges, themselves capable (in certain conjunctures) of renewing this first truth. By comparison, it was clear to me that the basic theory of the old conceptions, far from functioning as a (provisional) *truth for* the production of new knowledges, presented itself practically, on the contrary, as the *truth of* History, as exhaustive, definitive and absolute knowledge of it, in short as a system closed in itself, without any development because without any object in the scientific sense of the term, and only ever finding in the real its own mirror reflection.'[155] This approach, with its focus on the formative event, seems promising for a study of the scientific formation of historical materialism. Moreover, this focus on the specificity of historical materialism with respect to preceding philosophies of history has also led to the clarification and elaboration of certain basic Marxist concepts and their mode of functioning in a novel type of analysis and explanation: contradiction and political conjuncture,[156] the temporalities and form of causality involved in the explanatory metaphor of base and superstructure,[157] ideology,[158] to name several.

There is, however, a notable imbalance in Althusser's treatment of historical materialism. He has never really attempted to explore the second aspect of his quadripartite distinction, that of the specificity of historical materialism as *one* science *among others*. Characteristically, Althusser has assembled Marx's predecessors under the rubric of 'Philosophies of History'. This is hardly satisfactory. Before Marx, there was not only the German Ideology, which is fairly adequately covered by Althusser's designation, but also political historiography (particularly in post-revolutionary France), political theory[159] and classical political economy.

[155] Ibid., pp. 110–11; 'The Conditions of Marx' Scientific Discovery', *Theoretical Practice*, 7/8 (1973), p. 6.

[156] *For Marx*, pp. 89–128, 193–218.

[157] *Reading Capital*, pp. 73–198.

[158] 'Ideology and Ideological State Apparatuses', *Lenin and Philosophy and Other Essays*.

[159] Prior to his studies of Marx, Althusser himself wrote a brilliant study of Montesquieu and his initiation of the scientific treatment of politics and history,

Althusser does not endorse Marx's attribution of scientificity to political economy, because of the underlying anthropological problematic that it shares with Feuerbach – the latter speaking of man and his alienation, the former of his needs and his 'propensity to truck, barter and exchange'.[160] But his 'symptomatic' reading of Marx, a very elaborate examination of the structure of enunciations and silences of *Capital*, is accompanied by an *immediate* reading of liberal economics. Apart from some of Marx's comments on the classical economists, Althusser's only basis is the definition of economics given by A. Lalande in a Philosophical Dictionary.[161] On the assumption (which inspection suggests is warranted) that Lalande's definition is not grossly biased, and given Althusser's immediate concern, which is to show that in Marx there is an object of analysis radically different from that of the received economic tradition, this mode of argument is not illegitimate. But it is manifestly illegitimate, in Althusser's own terms, as a judgment of the scientific claims of economics itself. Althusser also dismisses the later non-Marxist social disciplines: lacking a theoretical base that relates them to a real object of their own, they are not real sciences, but rather, 'by-products' of various technical-administrative activities, ideological techniques of social adaptation and re-adaptation.[162] To non-Marxist practitioners of what they themselves regard as social science, these assertions are of course outrageous. But their reaction is understandable; and Althusser would probably be content to leave it at that. However, as long as the specificity of historical materialism as one scientific pursuit among others remains undetermined, the Althusserian approach to the study of the scientificity of Marxism remains seriously deficient. This failing has gone unremedied primarily because Althusser's approach refrains from installing itself as an epistemological legislator of scientific and non-scientific behaviour, preferring to observe the operations of scientificity in an ongoing scientific practice of break and polemic with rival theories. It is clear, however, that the character and value of the scientificity of historical material-

---

Montesquieu. La politique et l'histoire, Paris, 1959. This text is published in the English collection, *Politics and History*, NLB, 1972.

[160] *Reading Capital*, pp. 84, 158f; *For Marx*, p. 228f.

[161] *Reading Capital*, p. 162.

[162] *For Marx*, p. 172 n; *Philosophie et philosophie spontanée des savants*, pp. 36, 46f.

ism must be analyzed not only in relation to the German Ideology but also in relation to other discourses on society; and furthermore, that these discourses be subjected to analyses of equal systematicity and rigour. Similarly, their profundity and insight notwithstanding, Althusser's studies of the relationship between Marx and Hegel have been unbalanced by their author's neglect of the specificity of Marxism as one science among others.[163] For as Zelený and others have pointed out, Marx's elaboration of a model of science distinct from that derived from classical mechanics was significantly indebted to Hegel.[164]

Althusser's excursions into the problematic area of Marxist philosophy are relevant here only in so far as they concern the relationship of historical materialism, as a science, with society. Within sociology, this question has been discussed in terms of the relationship between science and values. For Althusser, it has to do with the status of philosophy. In his original project, it was by means of a Marxist philosophy, not of a sociology, that Marxism was to account for itself. The existence of such a philosophy – as yet in a mainly practical, unelaborated theoretical form in Marxist-Leninist scientific and political practice – distinct from historical materialism, was to prevent positivist deformations of the latter.[165] Althusser conceived of this philosophy, dialectical materialism, as a Theory of practice in general, and, in its relationship with science, as a Theory of theoretical practice. Analogously with Lenin's conception of theory in *What is to be Done?*, this theory was to guard against the intrusions of spontaneous ideology into scientific practice. Thus the emphasis in Althusser's first philosophical period was on the distinction between ideology in society and the specificity of science. Philosophy related the two in the negative sense of demarcating their respective territories, itself functioning as a kind of science of this demarcation. In the second period of Althusser's thought, the problem of ideology in general gives way to that of the different ideologies of different social classes. The relationship of science to society is now more complex: the problem is no longer simply that of a series of intrusions and expulsions of ideology, but

[163] See the essay 'Lenin before Hegel' included in *Lenin and Philosophy and Other Essays*, and 'Marx's relation to Hegel' in *Politics and History*.

[164] Althusser's reading of Marx focused not on Hegel but on Spinoza, 'Marx's only direct ancestor, from the philosophical standpoint', *Reading Capital*, p. 102.

[165] *For Marx*, pp. 26f, 39; ch. 6.

rather of a differentiated relationship to the ideological class struggle. In keeping with this new conception of the relationship between science and society, philosophy too appears in a new light. No longer a science of the demarcation of theoretical practice, it becomes 'in the last instance class struggle in theory'.[166] Unlike those of science, the enunciations of philosophy are not propositions, true or false. Philosophy is a mode of intervention in the theoretical area inhabited by sciences, philosophy and theoretical ideologies, by way of theses which are 'juste ou non' and whose main effect is to separate the scientific from the ideological.[167] This intervention is determined, in the last instance, by the class struggle, and the theses advanced express different class positions, materialist or idealist.

In Althusser's first formulation, it was clear what was meant by philosophy, although dialectical materialism itself tended to be subsumed under Bachelardian epistemology. In the second formulation the distinctive quality of Marxist philosophy is clearly marked (it expresses a materialist, proletarian position in philosophy), but the specific theoretical content of philosophical interventions, determined by but irreducible to the class struggle, remains somewhat obscure.[168] More important for present purposes, however, are the consequences of this new formulation for the study of the formation and development of historical materialism. Marx's break with his past is seen no longer as an epistemological *coupure* of science from ideology but as an abandonment of bourgeois ideologies induced as an effect of the political and theoretical class struggle. Marx's political evolution and his relationship with the working class become determinant in his scientific development. His changes of political position led him to abandon the idealism of the German Ideology and to adopt a materialist, proletarian philosophical position from which his new scientific work could begin. 'Without the politics nothing would have happened; but without the philosophy, the politics would not have found its theoretical expression, indispensable to the scientific expression of its object.'[169]

---

[166] For Althusser's latest definition of philosophy, see *Eléments d'une autocritique*, pp. 85–101.

[167] *Philosophie et philosophie spontanée des savants*, p. 13f.

[168] Althusser has admitted this, *Réponse à John Lewis*, pp. 41–3 n; *Eléments d'une autocritique*, p. 88.

[169] *Eléments d'une autocritique*, p. 124; 'The Conditions of Marx' Scientific Discovery', p. 10. Cf. *Réponse à John Lewis*, p. 56f, and the anticipation of the

To those critics who have contested his thesis (retained but reformulated in his later works) of the rupture in Marx on the grounds that 'what the Althusserians never consider satisfactorily is what led Marx to exchange ideology for science',[170] Althusser has given his reply: not the idea of man's alienation, but the encounter with working-class politics. Thus, a philosophy of science and ideology makes way for a historical materialist study of the class struggle and the ideological superstructure. The itinerary of Althusser's philosophical self-criticism leads us to the threshold of something other than a philosophy of Marxism: to a Marxism of Marxism.[171]

The present work is related to that of Althusser in three ways. First, it is deeply indebted to Althusser's conception of science and to the manner in which he has brought it to bear on the analysis of the constitution of historical materialism. Second, it will attempt to adjust the imbalance in his work, by showing the specificity of historical materialism not only in relation to preceding philosophies of history but also in relation to other developed social disciplines with scientific intentions. Third, it will attempt to cross that threshold, to undertake the task whose elements Althusser has so clearly indicated: the social-scientific study of Marxism as a social science. Before proceeding to this, however, we shall have to state, in general terms, the conceptions of 'science' and 'society' that will be used in this study.

III. What is Science and What is Society?

It is not sufficient simply to establish our point of departure, and subsequent bearings. We must also decide the procedure to be followed: it is necessary to prepare certain instruments of analysis. We are going to investigate the study of society as a science in society. Without claiming any special competence in the philosophy of science, we must have some conception, however provisional, of the character of science, if we are to plot the course of our own analysis successfully.

new Althusserian conception in the discussion of Marx's encounter with the realities behind the German Ideology in *For Marx*, p. 74f.

[170] P. Walton and A. Gamble, *From Alienation to Surplus Value*, London, 1972, p. 142.

[171] *Eléments d'une autocritique*, p. 115; 'The Conditions of Marx' Scientific Discovery', p. 7.

1. The Elusive Object of the Philosophy of Science

Now, the distribution of scientificity and non-scientificity to different but equally ambitious discourses is a hazardous business even for philosophers of science, who are sometimes apparently led to substitute an amusing gamesmanship for the grave intellectual austerity of epistemology. We might, for example, mention Thomas Kuhn, who can proudly state that his own view of science provides for a 'far surer and more direct' dismissal of the scientific claims of Marxism and psychoanalysis than Popper's, and then, 'to avoid irrelevant contemporary controversies', choose to consider, of all things, astrology.[172] Or, we can discern the utter crudity with which Mario Bunge dismisses psychoanalysis as a pseudoscience by simply comparing his own picture of psychoanalysis – in terms of racial memory, *ad hominem* replies to critics, etc. – with a serious exposition of the discipline such as David Rapaport's *The Structure of Psychoanalytical Theory*.[173] We can follow the meandering logic of Sir Karl Popper's philosophical contribution to counter-insurgency, as it struggles against the 'historicism' of revolutionary Marxism on behalf of reformist 'piecemeal social engineering'.[174] Within the covers of the same book we are told, on the one hand, that by questioning psychologism, Marx opened the way to a penetrating conception of a specific realm of sociological law and that he rightly

[172] Thomas Kuhn, 'Logic of Discovery or Psychology of Research?', in Lakatos and Musgrave, op. cit., p. 7.

[173] M. Bunge, *Scientific Research*, New York, 1967, vol. I, p. 40 f.

[174] According to Popper himself, his concern for the demarcation between science and non-science grew out of his encounters with Marxism, psychoanalysis and psychology in the summer of 1919, against a background of the receding enthusiasm of a revolutionary period – and, one might add, in the midst of a counter-revolutionary tide. (By the summer of 1919, attempts at a proletarian revolution in Austria had been effectively stifled, and in Hungary and in Germany the shortlived Soviet republics had all been suppressed.) See *Conjectures and Refutations* (4th ed.), London, 1972, p. 34f. In another context, Popper has recalled the decisive political experience that turned the teenage Marxist into an anti-Marxist. In 1919 in Vienna, Popper witnessed an unarmed workers' demonstration being shot down by the police. One possible reaction to that might have been hatred of the bourgeois state apparatus. The lesson Popper drew was that the revolutionary tendencies in the labour movement must be combated, as instigators of sharp class struggle. See a TV programme from Radio Bavaria, the text of which has been published as *Revolution oder Reform? Herbert Marcuse und Karl Popper, Eine Konfrontation*, Munchen, 1971, p. 9.

predicted the transformation of 'unrestrained capitalism' through the class struggle; and on the other, in words that still echoed two decades later, in the debates about the young Marx in the 1960's: '"Scientific" Marxism is dead. Its feeling of social responsibility and its love for freedom must survive.'[175] Against Marx the 'historicist', the philosopher of science concludes: 'Indeed it is necessary to recognize as one of the principles of any unprejudiced view of politics that everything is possible in human affairs.'[176] Advocating a technological approach to society, against both 'historicism' and the laissez-faire economics of Von Hayek, the same guardian of science is anxious to point out that 'it is one of the most characteristic tasks of any technology to point out what cannot be achieved'.[177] In the many dismissals of Freud, or of Marxism, as a 'historicism' or a 'providential design' called 'dialectic' (Toulmin and Goodfield),[178] we can in fact observe the operation of double standards. No one would dare – and Toulmin and Goodfield do not – to banish Isaac Newton from the domains of science for his belief that nature was created by God and that God occasionally intervened to set the motions of the planets right.[179] Nor do Toulmin and Goodfield deny scientific credentials to the French 19th century physiologist Claude Bernard for believing that: 'In every germ is a *creative idea* which unfolds and exhibits itself through organization. Here – as everywhere – everything is derived from the idea, which alone creates and guides.'[180] The social disciplines certainly fall far short of the natural sciences in scientific development, but in neither case should we forget that: 'In the whole history of science there has been scarcely a man who saw and accepted the full implications of his own intellectual innovation.'[181]

The most readily available criterion of scientificity is, of course,

---

[175] K. Popper, *The Open Society and Its Enemies*, London, 1966, vol. II, pp. 88, 193, 211. Popper has later withdrawn most of his rather condescending admiration for the ethical aims of dead Marxism, referring to Leopold Schwarzschild's virulently anti-Marxian biography *The Red Prussian*, ibid., p. 396.

[176] Popper, ibid., p. 197.

[177] K. Popper, *The Poverty of Historicism*, London, 1961, p. 61.

[178] S. Toulmin and J. Goodfield, *The Discovery of Time*, London, 1965, p. 235.

[179] For the story of Newton, see for example Charles Gillespie, *The Edge of Objectivity*, Princeton, 1961, p. 265.

[180] S. Toulmin and J. Goodfield, *The Architecture of Matter*, New York, 1962, p. 335.

[181] Ibid., p. 334.

'scientific method'. J. D. Bernal, for instance, whose vast *Science in History* also deals with the social disciplines, writes of the latter: 'All these studies can be classed as sciences only insofar as they employ the scientific methods used in the natural sciences, that is, insofar as they rest on a material basis and their accuracy can be checked by successful prediction and practical use.'[182] It is certainly true that no discipline not oriented to systematic empirical questioning and demonstration could be called a science of the factual world. But Bernal's rather technocratic conception of science does not take us very far. Whatever else is to be admitted, everyone agrees that science includes first of all the disciplines of nature developed since the 16th century. There is little controversy either over the rights of men like Copernicus, Galileo, and Newton, Lavoisier and Dalton, Bernard, Virchow, Darwin and Mendel, to name only a few, to be ranked among the foremost contributors to what we call science, together with such 20th century giants as Einstein and Rutherford. What did these men do? To say that they applied the scientific method is scarcely to provide a very illuminating answer.

If we examine the way in which the contributions of these scientific masters are presented in general histories of science – for example, such deservedly respected volumes as Herbert Butterfield's *The Origins of Modern Science*, Charles Gillespie's *The Edge of Objectivity*, or Stephen Toulmin's and June Goodfield's series *The Fabric of Heavens, The Architecture of Matter*, and *The Discovery of Time*, as well as the work of Bernal – we may find some usable idea of what counts as a work of science. Here, the outstanding landmarks in the development of science are discoveries of *patterns of determination*. The cosmological pattern of motion of celestial bodies, the determinants of the mechanics of bodies in motion, the unification of cosmology and terrestrial mechanics on the basis of the law of gravity – the development of physics by Copernicus, Galileo, and Newton might thus be summarized in a few words. The pattern of determination of Newtonian mechanics was later superseded by the development, from about the turn of the last century onwards, of sub-atomic quantum mechanics and relativity theory. The emergence of chemistry as an independent science – in the late 18th and early 19th centuries – out of questions previously suspended between physics and medicine, follows the

[182] J. Bernal, *Science in History*, London, 1972, vol. 4, p. 1019.

same course. The decisive steps were the discovery of elements, compounds and mixtures – involving the demolition of phlogiston theory by Lavoisier – and the establishment of the determinants of chemical composition, in the atomic theory first presented by Dalton.

The decisive contributions to the rise of the biological sciences in the 19th century were of a similar character. Bernard's demonstration of regulatory mechanisms in the living body, Virchow's theory of the determination of cell formation (by division of pre-existing cells), Darwin's principle of natural selection, Mendel's demonstration of the mechanism of heredity, are all examples of discoveries of patterns of determination.

It is freely conceded that this reading of the founding history of modern science is incomplete even as the briefest summary. It does not adequately cover the development of taxonomic disciplines like botany and zoology, with the fundamental contributions of Linné and Cuvier respectively. We might perhaps concur with Charles Gillespie, who says: 'Taxonomy little tempts the historian of scientific ideas. The problems were fussy and practical, but the question whether classifications are natural or artificial did not ultimately prove interesting.'[183] Whatever the temptations of historians, however, it seems highly improbable that the study of society can be conceived as a taxonomic project. This has not been a primary concern of either economics, sociology, historical materialism, politics, or anthropology – though it has been given specific attention in the last-mentioned discipline.[184]

It is a thesis of the present study that the problem of the social disciplines as sciences can fruitfully be analyzed in terms of a search for *patterns of societal determination*. We have already seen that the history of the more developed natural sciences is most revealingly to be read as just such a search. Support for this conception of science can also be found in the philosophy of science. Mario Bunge, for example, writes: 'In short, there is no science proper unless the scientific method is applied to the attainment of the goal of science: the building of theoretical images of reality, and essentially of its web of laws. Scientific research is, in short, the search for pattern.'[185] It is neither assumed nor claimed that the patterns we may find in

[183] Gillespie, *The Edge of Objectivity*, p. 170.
[184] In connection with the setting up of the Human Relations Areas Files.
[185] Bunge, *Scientific Research*, vol. I, p. 28.

the social disciplines are, in the rigour of their determination, on a par with those of the natural sciences. It *is* assumed and claimed that if there exist any sciences of society – or at least, attempts to constitute such sciences – they will by definition be centrally concerned with the discovery of social determinants and the study of their operation (unless they have an overwhelmingly taxonomic aim). The 'pattern of determination' is a theoretical system discovered – produced by a scientific practice and held to account for the behaviour of phenomena of the extratheoretical world. As such, in my opinion, it corresponds to and is rather more precise than the concept of 'scientific object' in the French tradition of anti-empiricist epistemology. It remains rather vague, of course, and the reader is asked to suspend judgment on it until its heuristic usefulness can be evaluated from its application as a guiding thread in the analysis below.

It is further claimed here that human 'society', as something exhibiting some kind of immanent order, governed by certain regularities that can be discovered by systematic empirical investigation and analysis, is not a self-evident conception among human beings. Society as a possible object of science, and the social determinants at work in it, had to be discovered, just as did oxygen and the mechanism of chemical combination, or the evolution of plants and animals and the principle of natural selection governing that process. Though little attention is given in histories of the social disciplines to the discovery of society, it would be imprudent to claim that it has been of less importance than the opening up of nature to scientific investigation.

The proper object of study of a social *science* is not simply social action or social institutions, but the operation and effects of a social pattern of determination in a particular area, which may be that of a particular institution or of certain systems of social action. The empirical study of, say, political institutions is no more the sufficient condition of a real political science than the observation of birds with binoculars is of the science of ornithology, even where the bird-watcher is attached to an institution called a 'university'.

We have been speaking here of society, social determinants, and a science of society. But Althusser, following Marx, has characterized the Marxian oeuvre as having founded a science of history.[186]

---

[186] Althusser sometimes talks metaphorically of history as a 'theoretical continent' opened up by Marx, comparable to two other such continents,

There is in fact no substantial difference between the two expressions. What Althusser refers to is obviously the history of human society, not the history of coral reefs or of finches – to take two famous examples from the concerns of Charles Darwin. As a study of history, Marxism is primarily a study of the development of social patterns, of modes of production and class relations, not a narrative of unique events. Its contribution to historiography is its elucidation of a pattern of social determination which bears upon events – in places of material work as well as cabinets of state and within the covers of books. The historical perspective of historical materialism pertains to its focus on a social determinant with a specifically temporal dimension. As we have seen, it is the pattern of social determination – for example the concepts of social totality and of social contradiction – and the concept of time in historical materialism, that Althusser has highlighted in his analysis of the Marxist theory of history.

2. One Concept of Society

Social sciences in society – what, then, do we mean when we speak of 'society'? That there is more than one answer to this question is precisely one of the themes of the book. But in order to write about the answers we have first to adopt one – at least temporarily. It is possible to write as many reasonable scientific treatises on science in society as there are scientific approaches to the study of society. Only one such approach will be used here. Though it is the conviction of the author that it is by far the most fruitful one, only two claims are made for it here: 1. It is *one* fruitful approach to the study of how the pursuit of scientific knowledge and other social phenomena are articulated, making possible distinctions between different types of articulation and demonstrations of how directly to address the problems with which the social disciplines are grappling; 2. Compared with the other major approaches to a science of society that have been developed so far, it provides the best basis for further

mathematics, opened up by the Greeks, and physics, opened up by Galileo and his successors, which includes, as a 'regional science', chemistry and, with the development of molecular biology, biology. See, for example, *Lenin and Philosophy*, p. 42. Whether that view is fruitful, or might become so, I am not sure, but if so, then it would be logical to expect the possibility of other regional sciences working on the continent of history as well as historical materialism.

scientific development. The approach in question is *historical materialism*.

To speak of society, then, is to speak of social arrangements determined in the last instance by a specific combination of forces and relations of production. These concepts will be examined in proper detail in a later chapter; for the present, certain general guide-lines must suffice. On the one hand, we must consider the processes of labour, the arrangements organizing a certain degree of productivity in men's appropriation of nature; and on the other, the system of relations involving the distribution of the means of production, the objective of production, and the relations between the performance of physical labour and the appropriation of the fruits of that labour. The former constitute the forces of production and the latter, the relations of production. Since the varying forms of the latter are of primary importance in distinguishing different types of society, it is on these that we should concentrate.

It should be added that the economic structure defined by the relations and forces of production is necessarily linked to specific juridical, political and ideological structures. Usually, it is the political framework that provides the unit of analysis (for example: what type of society was 11th century China or 17th century Britain? What type of society is the Soviet Union today?).

Among types of society, or modes of production, we shall be particularly concerned with the capitalist one. Capitalist relations of production can be characterized roughly as follows. The means of production are distributed among those who dispose of liquid monetary resources. Labour is performed by people without means of production who sell their labour power to those who possess such means and who appropriate the products of their labour. Production is geared to the accumulation of capital: products are sold for profit, the decisive part of which is invested again to yield new profits, and so on. Capitalist society must be distinguished not only from the notion of 'industrial society', which connotes purely technological conditions found also in post-capitalist societies, but also from that of 'market society'. A market economy, in which production is carried out by labourers who possess means of production and who sell their products on the market to secure their own consumption – as in commercial peasant agriculture or post-guild handicrafts – is distinct from the capitalist mode of production, and in Marxist terms is defined as petty commodity production.

Social science cannot, in a historical materialist perspective, be regarded as society becoming conscious of itself. It is not sufficient to speak simply of 'society': scientific inquiry must analyze the actual situation of human beings living in concrete societies, which are not undifferentiated. Because of their different roles in the structure and functioning of society, human beings can be grouped in different categories. Where the relations of production entail a separation of production and the appropriation of what is produced (above what is necessary for the survival and reproduction of the immediate producers), Marxism sees men as divided into *classes*. This separation is characteristic of all past societies except very primitive, 'tribal' societies – but there are in our own time societies in which the building of a classless communist society has begun. Grounded in the distinction between labour and the appropriation of the product of labour, the relationship between classes in such a mode of production is fundamentally antagonistic and takes the form of class struggle (economic, political and ideological), of widely varying intensity.

The two classes of the capitalist mode of production are the bourgeoisie (the capitalists, who possess the means of production, appropriate the surplus product, and gear production to the accumulation of capital) and the proletariat (the class of workers, who sell their labour-power to the bourgeoisie). Since they usually contain more than one mode of production, actual historical societies also contain more than two classes. Petty commodity production, which has never constituted the mode of production of a whole society (which would in that case have been classless), is regularly found in societies dominated by capitalism. In contrast with the classes of the capitalist mode, those who execute the roles defined by petty-commodity relations of production form the *petty* bourgeoisie.[187]

It follows from the Marxist thesis of the determinant role of the economy that classes defined principally by relations of production (though not exclusively: they are affected also by the juridical-

---

[187] What is said here about the Marxist concept of class is summarized from an analysis of it in G. Therborn, *Klasser och ekonomiska system* (Classes and Economic Systems), Staffenstorp, 1971, pp. 297–328. I have also applied it in an empirical study of Sweden, *Om Klasserna: Sverige 1930–70* (2nd ed.), Lund, 1973, which will appear, in abbreviated form, in R. Scase (ed.), *Readings on Swedish Class Structure*, London, 1975, forthcoming.

political and ideological structures linked to the relations of production), are the decisive human groupings in (class) society. There are other groupings, also comprised of people having certain roles in the mode of production, which are not defined by the relations of production. But, while they possess a certain autonomy, neither these roles nor their occupants are in any sense free-floating or unattached to the economic and social structure. Of these categories, the most obviously relevant to an analysis of science in society is, of course, the *intelligentsia*. The elaboration of a social science – or indeed, of any generalized discourse – requires special intellectual skills formed within a certain division of labour. In what social milieu have the intellectual skills of the social disciplines been developed? What is the character of the intelligentsia that has produced these disciplines?

Sociology of sociology, Marxism of Marxism, pattern of social determination, type of society (mode of production), class, intelligentsia: the stage is set. Enter *dramatis personae*.

Chapter Two

The Economy and the Economics of Capitalism

Even the most abstract theoretical discourses and scientific endeavours are the product of particular societies in a particular historical period. As human beings live in societies and as these societies – like the rest of the universe – have a temporal dimension, the products of the human mind always have some kind of social and historical anchorage. Dirk Struik has admirably shown how this applies even to the purest of pure thoughts, the development of mathematics.[1]

1. The Economy and the Polity of Political Economy

Economics is, of course, no exception to this social rootedness. It constitutes, however, a very special and probably unique case in the history of scientific practice. Economic discourse emerged as a concomitant of the rise of what this discourse was about: the capitalist economy. This should be understood in a strong sense. The discipline of economics – as it is conceived in the Western countries in our time – did not emerge as a penetration into previously unknown territory discovered by new scientific instruments, like sub-atomic physics and molecular biology. Neither should the emergence of economics be understood mainly as a result of the economy emerging from its earlier implication in kin, religious, legal, political, and other non-economical relationships – even though this was important.[2] The rise of economics was directly related to the rise of a new type of economy.

[1] D. Struik, *A Concise History of Mathematics*, London, 1963.
[2] This theme is central to Karl Polanyi and his 'substantivist' conception of the economy. See, for example, his famous essay 'Aristotle Discovers the Economy', in the posthumous collection *Primitive and Modern Economies*, Garden City, 1968.

The titles of the works of classical economists compared with those of their predecessors already reveal that they were going to talk of something rather new. In 17th century England these works were usually published as 'discourses of trade', in 18th century France often as *éléments de commerce*. Lest too much be made of this, two qualifications should be noticed. 'Trade' in 17th century English not only meant commerce; it also meant occupation, primarily of an artisan character. But what these economic writers chiefly had in mind was the buying and selling of goods.[4]

A focus on trade and commerce obviously implies a change from the autarchic ideal of Aristotle and from the basic self-sufficiency of the feudal manor. But trade can be carried out in different ways and need not necessarily be market trade for the accumulation of capital. It could be an administered procurement of supplies, an exchange of gifts or a form of armed robbery, for instance.[5]

There was trade both in the Ancient world of city states and empires, and in the Middle Ages of feudal Europe. But this trade differed in important aspects from that of commercial capitalism in which trade was carried out by merchants with a view to buying and selling for profit. Ancient and medieval writings on trade thus differed considerably from the modern discourses on trade.

Aristotle distinguished limited direct exchange for immediate use, from exchange for money and profit and the lending of money for interest. The former he regarded as part of the natural provision of goods and as such to be treated by economics. The latter he considered artificial and belonging to the secondary field of chrematistics.[6] The Roman Empire was later a world both of

[3] J. Schumpeter, *History of Economic Analysis*, New York, 1954, p. 160; W. Letwin, *The Origins of Scientific Economics*, London, 1963, p. 214f.

[4] Letwin, op. cit. The French *commerce* could likewise have different meanings: adopted by the Austrian 18th century cameralist Sonnenfels, it became *Handlung*, 'the science by which the largest number of people may be supplied with occupations' (A. Small, *The Cameralists*, Chicago, 1909, p. 531).

[5] The distinction between different types of trade is worked out theoretically and subjected to empirical investigation by Polanyi and his associates in C. Arensberg, K. Polanyi, and H. Pearson (eds), *Trade and Market in the Early Empires*, New York, 1957.

[6] G. Tozzi, *Economisti greci e romani*, Milan, 1961, p. 143f. The extent of market trade in the Ancient world was the object of an inconclusive discussion at the Second International Conference of Economic History, at Aix-en-Provence in 1962 (see the first volume of its proceedings, *Trade and Politics in the Ancient World*, Paris, 1965). M. J. Finley has recently emphasized the non-market charac-

fabulous fortune-making and considerable trade: but though it gave rise to a highly developed property and contract law, Rome produced neither (full-blown) capitalism nor economics in the modern sense. An attempt to spell out the linkage between these rather non-controversial facts must be left out here. Two short notes may, however, at least give a hint of the special economic pattern involved. The rivalry between Rome and Carthage, resulting in the three Punic Wars of the third and second centuries B.C. was – in its economic aspects – not even primarily a commercial rivalry. The main stake of the First Punic War was tribute (of grain etc.) from Sicily.[7] The most important trade of the Roman Empire was the grain trade to Rome. This trade was also tributary, and after 57 B.C. grain was distributed free to the population.[8] Rome lived on this amassed wealth and on the work of captured slaves of a conquered world. But as an economic historian has strikingly formulated it, 'her only export was Roman law and government'.[9]

Even with the gradual recovery of extralocal trade as the Middle Ages progressed, the predominant concern with trade was different from one formulated in terms of division of labour, expansion of markets, and accumulation of capital. It was centred on securing the supply of food and other necessities of everyday life.[10] A prominent contemporary Italian economic historian, Carlo Cipolla, has tried to convey the atmosphere thus: 'Day-to-day life in a mediaeval city resembled life in a fortress more closely than life in a modern city.'[11]

The ruling ideology, Christian theology, condemned enrichment by trade. Thomas Aquinas and others discussed the 'just' price which ought to be paid for goods, and attacked usury, the lending of money for interest. The 'just' price tended to resemble the traditional, customary price, and it has been pointed out that this focus on the just price was fairly adequate to the conditions pre-

---

ter of the ancient economy in *The Ancient Economy*, Berkeley and Los Angeles, 1973, esp. chs. V–VI.

[7] The Second Punic War was above all about the appropriation of the Spanish gold and silver mines. For a brief economic-historical overview, see, for example, H. Heaton, *Economic History of Europe*, New York, 1948, p. 39f.

[8] Ibid., p. 47.

[9] Ibid., p. 50.

[10] *Cambridge Economic History of Europe*, vol. III, Cambridge, 1963, pp. 328f (England and France), 400 (Italy and Spain).

[11] Ibid., p. 422.

vailing in feudal society. In an overwhelmingly natural economy, little responsive to price fluctuations – both because of its organization and because of difficulties of transport, any considerable change in price would mainly mean windfall gains for a few traders and speculators.[12] The self-regulating market did not exist.

In the 17th and 18th century pamphlets and books on trade there was, however, a different conception of trade, more consonant with the commercial capitalism that had emerged, spearheaded by the big foreign trade merchants. The East India Company director Thomas Mun, in *England's Treasure by Forraign Trade*, argued the case of the merchant and of foreign trade as a means of making profit on 'stock'. The supplier to the Navy Josiah Child, later an East India Company Director, was concerned in his *Discourse About Trade* with the threat to English merchants from the efficient Dutch and others in the field of export of goods and accumulation of bullion. Nicholas Barbon, the most prominent London builder of the late 17th century, stated at the beginning of his *Discourse of Trade*: 'The chief end or business of trade is to make a profitable bargain.'

These people should not be taken as arbitrary examples or special pleaders. They are characteristic and important contributors to the rise of political economy.[13] Their contributions were discourses on trade, more specifically discourses on capitalist trade, a sort of commerce different from that of the dominant Ancient and Mediaeval patterns, which presented its own problems.

The conception of the economic process as one of commodity production (production for sale on a market) and of accumulation of capital is not essentially different among the French 18th century physiocrats, who pleaded the cause of agriculture, or in Adam Smith's criticism of the 'mercantile system'. When Quesnay considers the farmers the only productive class and sees everything that favours agriculture as favourable to the nation, he is not thinking in terms of a natural economy and of provision of sustenance. He is referring to a commercialized agriculture, where agricultural products are sold on a market, and where higher agricultural prices and profits mean that farmers and landlords can afford to spend

[12] E. Roll, *A History of Economic Thought*, London, 1961 (2nd ed.), p. 43.

[13] Letwin, op. cit., chs. 1–2 (on Child and Barbon), p. 92f (Mun); the quotation from Barbon is on p. 215. Cf. Roll, op. cit., pp. 66, 76f; Schumpeter, op. cit., p. 195f.

more on the goods and services of the sterile manufacturing and commercial class.[14] Quesnay emphasizes that the products of the earth do not constitute wealth (*richesses*) unless they are marketable (*commerçable*).[15]

For all his hostility to the mercantile system and the privileges of the big merchant companies, Adam Smith was, of course by no means hostile to commercial society. On the contrary, the division of labour, which Smith regards as the cause of opulence in well-governed societies, is in its turn derived from 'the propensity to truck, barter, and exchange one thing for another'.[16] When the division of labour has been thoroughly established: 'Every man thus lives by exchanging, or becomes in some measure a merchant, and the society itself grows to be what is properly called a commercial society.'[17] Smith is clearly not visualizing a society of individual commodity producers. The division of labour is intimately related to the accumulation of capital, to production for profit by means of paid labour.[18]

In the latter half of the 18th century, particularly but not exclusively in England, political economy began to appear as the title of what is now regarded as economic discourses.[19] In an indirect way the new term also underlined the ties of the new discourse to commercial capitalism. Economy and economics are words of Greek origin, put together from *oikos* and *nomos*, meaning house and law, respectively. To the Greeks, economics meant household management, the running of a dominantly autarchic patriarchal household, worked in Aristotle's time by slave labour. Now it was only the word, not the subject matter, that was taken over when political economy asserted itself in the late 18th and early 19th centuries.

[14] F. Quesnay, *Tableau économique des physiocrates*, Paris, 1969, pp. 45f. 162f, 226.

[15] Quesnay, p. 221.

[16] A. Smith, *The Wealth of Nations*, London, 1970, p. 117.

[17] Ibid., p. 126.

[18] Ibid., Book Two, and p. 271f.

[19] 'Political economy' was used by Smith's countryman Sir James Steuart in 1767, by the Italian Pietro Verri in 1763, by Mirabeau and Du Pont among the physiocrats. See E. Cannan, *A Review of Economic Theory*, London, 1964, p. 39f. Smith regarded the 'inquiry into the nature and causes of the wealth of nations' as synonymous with political economy, *The Wealth of Nations* (Cannan ed.), London, 1961, vol. II, p. 200. Political economy then appeared in the titles of works of Ricardo, James Mill, Malthus and Say.

The change was rather abrupt. In the 1740's Francis Hutcheson, Adam Smith's teacher and predecessor as professor of moral philosophy at Glasgow, still dealt with the following subjects as pertaining to 'Principles of Economics': marriage and divorce, duties of parents and children, the rights of masters and servants.[20]

It is not ancient household management, the Roman writings *de re rustica* (on agriculture), or the feudal concern with the management of manors, to which historians of the early beginnings of political economy and economics pay significant attention – and rightly so. It is rather early conceptions of exchange value, money, interest and such like which are the subject of their study.

The rise of commercial capitalism is one of the two major events of 16th and 17th century Europe which circumscribe the rise of political economy. The new economic system and the discourse on it both emerged in Europe, but both are also closely connected with events outside Europe – that is with colonial expansion, by plunder and by trade. We have already come across a couple of East India Company directors among the contributors to the new theory. In the 16th century the influx into Europe of plundered gold and silver from South America caused traditional 'just' prices to be replaced by market prices in a secular inflation. The French philosopher Jean Bodin secured himself a place in the history of economics for his explanation of the inflation, with a pioneering statement of a quantity theory of money.[21]

The commercial and industrial enterprise and prosperity of Glasgow, Adam Smith's formative milieu, was above all due to colonial trade: the leading trade was the import and re-export of tobacco from America and the West Indies; the main industries made 'hoes and spades for the Negroes of Maryland' and 'saddles and shoes for the plantations'.[22]

The second major event which opened up the vista of political economy, was the destruction of the classical feudal polity of the Middle Ages and the emergence of a new type of state, in a welter

[20] Hutcheson in his *Short Introduction to Moral Philosophy*. See Cannan, op. cit., p. 38. Cf. Finley, *The Ancient Economy*, p. 17f.

[21] Roll, op. cit., p. 59; Schumpeter, op. cit., p. 311f. Schumpeter acknowledges Bodin's achievement but emphasizes the difference between it and what later became established as the quantity theory of money.

[22] J. Viner, Introduction to the new edition of J. Rae, *Life of Adam Smith*, New York, 1965, p. 88f.

of struggles. Commercial capitalism as an economic system could grow 'in the pores' of the old society, and capitalist enterprise could coexist side by side with feudal manors, largely self-sufficient peasant households and guild artisans. But, as regards the polity, the various forces of this age of transition left their imprint on one and the same state. To assess the dominant character of the new centralized states of the 16th–18th centuries is therefore a difficult task and the subject of considerable controversy.[23] In this context we need only take into account a few features immediately pertaining to political economy.

Political economy emerged as a term to denote the management of a state in contrast to the running of a family household.[24] Public finance and taxation was the central preoccupation of both the rulers of the post-mediaeval states with their mercenary armies and incipient central administration, and writers on economic affairs. According to Schumpeter public finance was the central topic around which the continental pre-classical economic literature evolved.[25] It was of great interest also to the British classics. Book V of *The Wealth of Nations* is devoted to taxation and public finance, and the contents of Ricardo's main work justified its title *Principles of Political Economy and Taxation*.

This change in itself testifies to the transformation that had taken place from the period when the economy was hardly more than the economy of the royal household, the yield of royal domains and the various profits of royal justice and administration.[26] Before the modern era in Europe it would have made little sense to inquire into questions of the wealth of *nations*. But this new relationship between state and economy remains much too general as an explanation of the political background to the rise of political economy. We might add that the founders of political economy were involved in the

---

[23] This subject is comprehensively treated by Perry Anderson in one of the most important works of Marxist historical scholarship since the second generation of European Marxism, the age of the Bolsheviks and the pre-war Second International, *Lineages of the Absolutist State*, London, 1974. For references to the debate on the character of feudalism see Anderson, p. 15f; I. Wallerstein, *The Modern World System*, New York, 1974, p. 157f. Also relevant to the issue is the discussion of the seventeenth century 'crisis' in Europe, T. Ashton (ed.), *Crisis in Europe 1560–1660*, London, 1967.

[24] Cannan, op. cit., p. 39f.

[25] Schumpeter, op. cit., p. 200.

[26] *Cambridge Economic History of Europe*, vol. III, p. 293.

struggle for the abolition of the feudal system of taxes. Quesnay, Mirabeau, and the physiocrats, for example, attacked the fiscal system of the *ancien régime*, the immunization of nobles and clergy, and the *corvées* in favour of a single tax on land.[27]

However, the reflections on public finance and taxation that turned out to be of real importance to the new economic theory were those that argued that the state should adapt its measures to the capitalist economic system. The state should behave congruently with the mechanism of the economy. The political aspect of political economy was its theoretical contribution to the struggle for a bourgeois state. Quesnay, Smith and Ricardo based their discussion of taxation on an analysis of the incidence of taxation, i.e. the determination by the forces of the capitalist market of those who were ultimately to pay the taxes. In its taxation and in its management of the national debt the state should base itself on such an analysis and thereby, naturally enough, not hamper or undermine the development of capitalism but favour it. Ricardo was so anxious about the restrictive effects of taxation on the accumulation of capital that he wanted to abolish 'all taxes affecting the transfer of property from the dead to the living'.[28]

These were the principles of taxation that informed the new discipline – albeit not necessarily with the same concrete recommendations for policy as those of Ricardo. This fact stands out in comparison with the simultaneous fading of another system of political economy. From the late 15th century onwards there had developed a literature devoted directly to problems of state finance and state economic administration, a literature chiefly known under its German name Cameralism (*Kameralwissenschaft*), though produced in Italy, Spain and France as well. The name derived from *Kammer*, the princely treasury, and the cameralists were above all concerned with securing a sufficient supply of money to the treasury. This concern was not related to the functioning of capitalism but to princely power. Cameralism produced recipes of administration, but no economic analysis in the sense of the new economics. In the first half of the 19th century it withered away. In Austria a work of the last great cameralist Sonnenfels was the official

[27] Quesnay, op. cit., p. 105f.
[28] D. Ricardo, *Principles of Political Economy and Taxation*, London, 1971, p. 170f.

handbook in economic affairs up to the year of bourgeois revolution of 1848.[29]

A political structure functional to the operation and development of a capitalist economy – in Marxist terms a bourgeois state – was the fundamental political programme of nascent political economy. That is, a bourgeois state but not a night-watchman state. It was the feudal 12th century philosopher John of Salisbury, and not the classical economists, who concluded that the king's office, dealing with punishment, resembled that of an executioner.[30] The principle of laissez-faire from the very beginning meant not state passivity but, basically, acceptance of the economic laws of capitalism.

According to Adam Smith the state had three functions: firstly defence, secondly justice, and thirdly 'the duty of erecting and maintaining certain public works and certain public institutions, which it can never be for the interest of any individual or small number of individuals to erect and maintain; because the profit could never repay the expense to any individual or small number of individuals, though it may frequently do much more than repay it to a great society'.[31] Neither were the physiocrats, who are sometimes singled out as the villains of the piece by latter-day liberal defenders of the British classics,[32] protagonists of a passive guardian state. In the words of Mirabeau 'the first priority of the sovereign's agents' was education; while defence and justice, and fiscal administration were second and third only. What should be taught was above all physiocratic economics, and besides that reading, writing, arithmetic and agricultural art.[33]

This means that there is a fundamental continuity in the political conception of economic theory. From the classics to Keynes the amount of state intervention considered necessary for the successful reproduction of capitalism has certainly increased considerably. *That* such intervention – over and above the guarantees of army and police – was necessary and useful, was part of the theoretical corpus of classicism as well as of mercantilism.

---

[29] Small, *The Cameralists* (this book is summarized in A. Small, *Origins of Sociology*, Chicago, 1924, chs. VIII–IX); Schumpeter, op. cit., p. 161f.

[30] *Cambridge Economic History of Europe*, vol. III, p. 281f.

[31] A. Smith, *Wealth of Nations* (Cannan ed.), vol. II, p. 209.

[32] Such as in L. Robbins, *The Theory of Economic Policy in English Classical Political Economy*, London, 1952.

[33] M. Lutfalla, Preface to Quesnay, op. cit., p. 40.

All such interventions were judged according to the needs of the reproduction of capitalism. This is clear in the principles of taxation, in the conception of public works, and in the main aims of education. The repressive and administrative apparatus of the state was seen from the same economic angle. In his Glasgow lectures, Adam Smith declared 'Till there be property, there can be no government, the very end of which is to secure wealth and defend the rich from the poor'.[34]

The same went for public charity. Because they threatened the accumulation of capital – and made the rich poor but not the poor rich – Ricardo and Malthus campaigned for the repeal of the Poor Laws and of public charity. That the key issue was not laissez-faire principles as such was illustrated by Ricardo, who could think of the well-being of the poor as secured by 'some effort on the part of the legislature . . . to regulate the increase of their number'.[35]

On the basis of a similar view the role of the state, the 'vulgar economist' Nassau Senior could, therefore, say about a decade later of state provisions of relief that 'as far as they can be effected without materially diminishing industry, forethought and (private) charity, it is the impervious duty of government to provide them'. Whereas Ricardo and Malthus thought that poor relief could not be given 'without materially diminishing industry', Senior thought it could be given to chronic invalids and the insane, and even to able-bodied men in some circumstances, on condition that it left them in a substantially inferior position compared to labourers in market employment – in workhouses of a semi-punitive character.[36] On the other hand, Senior was the leading economic opponent of the labour movement's demand for a ten-hour bill on the grounds that it would drastically reduce the profits of the entrepreneurs, all of which were made during the last hours of the day.[37]

Such a perspective on the state is not essentially different in

[34] Smith, *Wealth of Nations* (Cannan ed.), vol. II, p. 236 n.

[35] Ricardo, op. cit., p. 127. Smith was also critical of the Poor Laws but dealt very briefly with them, mainly in terms of their interference with the mobility of labour (the administration of relief fell on the parishes). Smith, op. cit. (Penguin ed.), p. 240f.

[36] Robbins, op. cit., p. 95f.

[37] See, for example, K. Marx, *Capital*, vol. I, Moscow, 1962, chapter IX, section 3, p. 224f. After the labour rebellion of 1830, the Whiggish conservatism of Senior was increasingly motivated by fear of the working class; L. Rogin, *The Meaning and Validity of Economic Theory*, New York, 1956, p. 251.

Keynes, though the lenses he looked through can be said to be much less short-sighted. The utility of more extensive state intervention and the acceptance of a certain amount of equalization of wealth follow from the same logic of capital accumulation, once the problem of effective demand is discovered. The point of Keynes's *General Theory* was that classical economics only produced a special case of the conditions for an efficient reproduction of capitalism. (Ostensibly the theory is about 'employment', purely and simply; in fact it is about employment in a capitalist system, concerned as it is with wage-labour working for, or unemployed by, private entrepreneurs who are guided by their striving for profit.)[38]

Therefore Keynes could logically conclude: 'But if our central controls succeed in establishing an aggregate volume of output corresponding to full employment as nearly as is practicable, the classical theory comes into its own again from this point onwards.'[39] Politically, he declared: 'I defend it (the enlargement of the functions of government) . . . both as the only practical means of avoiding the destruction of economic forms in their entirety and as the condition of the successful functioning of individual initiatives.'[40] To leave no doubt that he adhered to the semantic rules of liberal economic discourse, Keynes added that by 'individual initiative' and 'individualism' he meant the activity of the private entrepreneur. The sentence just quoted is followed by this: 'For if effective demand is deficient, not only is the public scandal of basic resources intolerable, but the individual enterpriser who seeks to bring his resources into action is operating with the odds loaded against him.'

2. The Intellectuals of Ascendant Capitalism

The intellectual and the capitalist are often regarded as an unhappy and incessantly quarrelling couple. Indeed in the major conservative forecast of the doom of capitalism – Joseph Schumpeter's *Capitalism, Socialism and Democracy* – the development of an independent post-clerical intelligentsia is regarded as one of four critical forces undermining capitalism.[41] That picture is mainly a myth, mistaking

---

[38] J. M. Keynes, *General Theory of Employment, Interest and Money*, London, 1936, Book One.

[39] Ibid., p. 378.

[40] Ibid., p. 380.

[41] J. Schumpeter, *Capitalism, Socialism and Democracy* (4th ed.), London,

a part of the intelligentsia – the specialists in mastering symbols and formulating and conveying messages thereby – for the whole. More than a social analysis, it seems to express a surprised irritation that there are *some* people of intellectual standing injurious enough to question the incumbent social order. In fact, of course, the rise of a capitalist economy and a bourgeois state had their great intellectual companions. We might refer to the English natural science and Dutch painting of the 17th century. Here, however, a few words must be said about political economy. It is, by the way, of some interest that in his own gloomy picture of intellectuals, Schumpeter, the author of a monumental history of economics, says nothing about economics and economists.

Many of the important early contributors to the new economic theory were indeed primarily active businessmen. This was the case with most of the distinguished English 17th century writers: Gerald Malynes was a merchant official, Edward Misselden a prominent member of the Merchant Adventurers, Thomas Mun and Josiah Child directors of the East India Company, Nicholas Barbon London's leading builder, Dudley North a director of the Levant Company and the Africa Company.[42] The Irish-Frenchman Richard Cantillon was a banker and the Dutchman Pieter de la Court a manufacturer.[43]

But this is much too narrow a perspective to grasp the intellectual panorama in which political economy in the 18th century emerged as a coherent discipline. Coherent political economy was one of the products of the Enlightenment. Adam Smith was one of the central figures of the Scottish Enlightenment. Both he and his friend David Hume knew the *philosophes* of Paris in person.[44] Quesnay was, as we have seen already, a contributor to the *Encyclopédie*, though the physiocrats were regarded by other *philosophes* as a dogmatic group apart. To them the Neapolitan nobleman and Parisian diplomat Galiani was more congenial – also an outstanding figure in the

---

1961, ch. XIII. The whole argument is summarized in an appended Address, p. 417.

[42] Roll, op. cit., pp. 67, 73; Letwin, op. cit., pp. 26, 49, 186.

[43] Cantillon's biography is included in H. C. Recktenwald (ed.), *Lebensbilder grosser Nationalökonomen*, Köln-Berlin, 1965, pp. 58–71. On de la Court, see Schumpeter, *History of Economic Analysis*, New York, 1954, p. 197 n.

[44] Rae, op. cit., ch. XIV.

history of economics.[45] Theoretically, political economy arose as part of what were perhaps the two most important currents of thought of the emergent bourgeoisie in its ideological struggle against established feudal society – utilitarianism and (mainly in the case of the physiocrats) natural law.[46]

But that the blossoming of political economy was part of a large and sophisticated intellectual movement does not mean that it 'floated freely' above classes and their struggle. This is obvious from the business and political careers of many economists or civil servants. William Petty, whom Marx regarded as the first classical economist,[47] made himself one of the country's biggest landlords in the course of his land survey of Ireland.[48] The philosopher John Locke was secretary to the Council on Trade and Plantations and an investor in the silk and slave trade.[49] David Ricardo made himself an enormous fortune as a stockbroker and contractor of loans during the Napoleonic Wars. He was also a member of Parliament, as an independent, though tending to the Whigs.[50] Before he was invited to a chair of economics, the Marquis Vilfredo Pareto was for about twenty years general manager of an Italian railway company and an unsuccessful liberal politician.[51]

Von Böhm-Bawerk, the distinguished Austrian marginal economist and Marx-critic, was three times Minister of Finance of the Austro-Hungarian empire.[52] His brother-in-law, the equally distinguished baron Von Wieser, became Minister of Commerce in the last years of World War I and of the Empire.[53] For a short time in 1919, in the chaotic days of the new Austrian republic, Schumpeter

[45] On the reputation of Quesnay and Galiani in the French Enlightenment see P. Gay, *The Enlightenment*, vol. II, New York, 1969, p. 348f. Galiani's place in the history of economics might be judged from the fact that he is included, among 28 economists from Quesnay to Walter Eucken, in Recktenwald, op. cit. He made a very important contribution to the theory of value. See Schumpeter, *History of Economic Analysis*, p. 300f.

[46] Cf. Robbins, op. cit.

[47] Marx, op. cit., p. 81 n.

[48] Letwin, op. cit., p. 119f.

[49] Ibid., p. 162f; C. B. McPherson, *The Political Theory of Possessive Individualism*, Oxford, 1964, p. 253 n.

[50] Recktenwald, op. cit., pp. 176–93. A portrait of Ricardo is also included in the Introduction to the Penguin edition of his *Principles*.

[51] Recktenwald, op. cit., p. 390f.

[52] Ibid., p. 40.

[53] J. Schumpeter, *Ten Great Economists*, New York, 1951, p. 298.

was an unsuccessful Minister of Finance; subsequently, before he wholly went into academic life in the middle twenties, he was also President of a small Austrian bank.[54] John Maynard Keynes too was offered a bank directorship twice, but preferred to make his fortune as a jobber in currency, primary commodities, and securities. He was an active member of the Liberal Party and played an important part in many government economic commissions and delegations.[55]

In the main, it appears that the major economists represented a much more direct linkage between theory and practice than is indicated by the usual anecdotes about Knut Wicksell and Adam Smith. (Wicksell was a professor of economics and financial law, but was incapable of doing his yearly income declaration.[56] Adam Smith, the author of the famous propensity to truck, barter and exchange, from which so much good was supposed to be derived, is said to have been obliged to ask a friend to buy his horse corn for him.[57]) The list above could indeed be much extended by today's professors, participating in the shaping of incomes and other policies of the governments of capitalist countries. But it is not only a question of individual economists making their careers in the bourgeois world of business and politics. We should also look at the character of the intellectual society in which political economy was debated and developed.

Virtually alone among the classical economists Adam Smith was an academic, a university professor. The academic world of Glasgow and Edinburgh intermingled with the haute bourgeoisie and the aristocracy in a host of clubs and societies, cultural, political and economic. One such club was founded in Glasgow in the 1740's by one of the city's wealthiest merchants with a view to inquiring into the principles of trade in all its branches. This merchant, Andrew Cochrane, was not only a leading spirit of the merchant community. He was a friend of Adam Smith, one of the latter's informants in his work on *The Wealth of Nations*, and Smith was a member of Cochrane's club, perhaps the first political economy club in the world.[58] In Edinburgh in the 1750's Smith was one of the founders of an

[54] Recktenwald, pp. 510, 516.
[55] R. F. Harrod, *The Life of John Maynard Keynes*, London, 1951. About Keynes's operations as a speculator, see pp. 288–303.
[56] T. Gårdlund, *Knut Wicksell*, Stockholm, 1956, p. 355.
[57] Rae, op. cit., p. 66.
[58] Ibid., p. 90f.

illustrious Select Society, devoted to the debating and promotion of the arts, sciences, and manufactures of Scotland. It contained the cream of Scottish society, intellectuals such as Carlyle, Ferguson, and Hume, earls and businessmen. Topics for discussion were predominantly economic.[59] Such was the milieu in which *The Wealth of Nations* was conceived.

The French physiocrats were in a sense more of an independent intellectual school, with journals and an intellectual *salon* of their own. On the other hand, all this was based on protection from the court and the king. Francois Quesnay was the physician of Mme de Pompadour. Through her he became the king's doctor too, and the salon of the physiocrats was Quesnay's apartment in the palace of Versailles.[60] In spite of these ties to the *ancien régime*, the agricultural orientation of the physiocrats was not of a feudal kind. The physiocrats were the spokesmen of the kulaks, the rich capitalist farmers. Quesnay wrote in the *Encyclopédie*: 'The advantages of agriculture . . . hence depend greatly on the amalgamation of land into large farms, which are most profitably cultivated by rich tenants.' 'We do not envisage the rich tenant-farmer as a worker who labours himself: he is rather an entrepreneur who directs his enterprise and makes it profitable by his intelligence and his wealth.'[61]

By far the most renowned setting of 19th century economics was the London Political Economy Club, of which Ricardo, Malthus, and James Mill were founding members, and to which Senior, McCulloch, J. S. Mill, Jevons, Edgeworth and Marshall sooner or later came to belong.[62] The official account of its foundation might sound to some contemporary readers like a vulgar Marxist oration: 'The Political Economy Club was founded in London in the year 1821, chiefly by the exertions of the late Thomas Tooke, F.R.S. (a City merchant and a historian of prices), to support the principles

[59] Ibid., p. 107f.

[60] Recktenwald, op. cit., pp. 30–43. One of the physiocratic treatises, by Dupont de Nemours, was dedicated to Mme de Pompadour because of her protection of economic science (J. Hollander, 'The Dawn of Economic Science', in the collective volume, *Adam Smith 1776–1926*, Chicago, 1928, p. 17). Another physiocrat, Mercier de la Rivière, was invited to Russia by Catherine the Great (Robbins, op. cit., p. 34f).

[61] Quesnay, op. cit., p. 179f.

[62] *Political Economy Club, Centenary Volume*, London, 1921. All members up to 1921 are listed on p. 358f.

of free trade set forth in the well-known London Merchants' petition of 1820, originated and written by Mr. Tooke.'[63] The Political Economy Club was a gathering of economic intellectuals, business-men, and bourgeois politicians. By 1905 it had had as members seven Chancellors of the Exchequer.[64] Its social character is pin-pointed in its centenary celebration of *The Wealth of Nations*, in 1876. The company at the grand dinner and special discussion included eight Cabinet Ministers, headed by Gladstone as chair-man of the discussion; it was, as a later historian of economics has written, 'representative, in the most distinguished way, of politics, learning, the City, the civil service, and the aristocracy (a duke, two earls, etc)'.[65]

The basic social constant of political economy and mainstream economics is its attachment to the protagonists of commodity production, the bourgeoisie above all, but also, as we have seen, the embourgeoisified aristocracy and, sometimes, the petty bourgeoisie. It has had no ties either to the feudal aristocracy or to the working-class movement.

The classical English and Scottish mixture of bourgeois and aristocrats also characterized the Austrian marginalists, though with a higher proportion of the latter.[66] Léon Walras, the French founder of marginalism and professor at Lausanne, was linked to

[63] Ibid., p. viii.

[64] Ibid., p. 335.

[65] T. W. Hutchison, *A Review of Economic Doctrines 1870–1929* (2nd ed.), Oxford, 1962, p. 1. The splendour of the celebratory evening was above the usual, but it was not unusual in its connections with politics and business. Of the Club's members up to 1921 about a third were civil servants and members of government, and another third businessmen, bankers and landowners. See A. W. and S. E. Coats, 'The Changing Social Composition of the Royal Economic Society 1890–1960 and the Professionalization of British economics', *British Journal of Sociology*, vol. XXIV, 2, June 1973, p. 182.

[66] Carl Menger, the founder of the Austrian School, came from a bourgeois family of lawyers, civil servants and merchant-landowners. He is said to have become devoted to economics by writing market surveys for an official gazette in Vienna (Recktenwald, op. cit., p. 348f). Von Böhm-Bawerk and Von Wieser both belonged to the (recent) nobility. Schumpeter, too, had high aristocratic connec-tions and schooling, through the remarriage of his mother (Recktenwald, pp. 501, 509). The political tendency of the Austrian marginalist school was generally German-Liberal. Von Wieser's liberal anti-feudalism is particularly pungent in his *Rektoratsrede* (Presidential Address) at the Prague University in 1901 (F. von Wieser, *Gesammelte Abhandlungen*, Tübingen, 1929, pp. 346–76).

the traditions and strivings of the French petty bourgeoisie. The faithful son of a professor (an economist and philosopher), a reformist writer who remained true to the spirit of the 1848 revolution under the Second Empire, and for a time director of a cooperative bank, Walras was invited to Lausanne by the local liberal authorities. With a nice sense of the social character of economics he said of his political opinions that he wanted to base himself on both political economy and socialism, i.e. on two wholly different doctrines.[67]

The Englishman in the marginalist trio, Stanley Jevons (the third being the Austrian Menger), came from a manufacturing family gone bankrupt and worked himself back into solid middle-class society as an assayer to the Australian mint; he returned to England for an academic career and as a writer on social affairs. In the latter capacity, he attacked trade unions and the 'delusion' of a 'supposed conflict of labour with capital'.[68]

It is hardly tenable to assert a direct linkage between the rise of marginalism and rentier capitalism, as Bukharin contended in his famous critique.[69] But marginalism, like classical economics, was

[67] Recktenwald, op. cit., p. 315f. Walras's political opinions are best gathered from his *Études d'économie appliquée*, Paris-Lausanne, 1898, and from the excellent edition, by William Jaffé, of *Correspondence of Léon Walras and Related Papers*, Amsterdam, 1965, I–III. Walras was a land reformer, who sought the abolition of rent but the retention of capitalist ownership of the means of production.

[68] S. Jevons, *The State in Relation to Labour*, London, 1882, p. 98. Strictly speaking, Jevons was not wholly against trade unions, which could be a natural means for a body of workers to obtain concessions from an employer. The main point was rather that they should not be class unions, and that sooner or later the workers and their employer should unite in fair competition against other workers-and-employers.

[69] A new English edition of Bukharin's work appeared in 1972: *The Economic Theory of the Leisure Class*, New York and London (1st Russian ed., 1919). In Bukharin's argument, marginalist economics (Bukharin dealt with the Austrian tendency) and the rentiers were only very loosely tied together, mainly by the general theory of imperialism as the decadent, parasitic stage of capitalism. But his linking of privileged strata marginal to the economic process with consumptionist and aesthetic-individualist conceptions of society is thought-provoking. In another context I have tried to show the resemblance between Bukharin's elucidation of subjectivist economics and the social roots and characteristics of present day subjectivist sociology, as presented by Gouldner, op. cit., pp. 380–410; G. Therborn, 'Den förstaende sociologin och rentierens politiska ekonomi' (Verstehende Sociology and the Political Economy of the Rentier), in *Vad är bra värderingar värda?*.

certainly the product of a mainly bourgeois intelligentsia. In time marginalism roughly coincided with the emergence of the working-class as a mass movement – in England with its re-emergence after the defeat of Chartism. None of the prominent representatives of the new economic doctrine was associated with the working-class movement. On the contrary, many were outspoken critics of it, above all of its revolutionary and marxist tendencies; Böhm-Bawerk and Wieser, Pareto, Jevons, Marshall, J. B. Clark.[70] This criticism could rise to the pitch of undisguised, flaming class hatred, as Alfred Marshall's letters on an intransigent strike by engineering workers (chiefly for an 8-hour-day) in 1897 reveal: 'I want these people to be beaten at all costs: the complete destruction of unionism would be as heavy a price as it is possible to conceive, but I think it is not too high a price.'[71] The more academic position of marginalism, as compared to that of classical economics, certainly did not still the passions of class commitment.[72] One of the significant new economists was indeed a disrespectful radical who sympathized with the labour movement, the Swede Knut Wicksell. But he was essentially a petty-bourgeois, belonging like Strindberg to a generation of radicals predating the rise of the working class – known in Sweden as the generation of the 1880's. He was a neo-Malthusian, an anti-clerical, an anti-militarist and an anti-chauvinist, but no socialist.[73]

---

[70] In spite of the author's own main thesis (see n. 72), this is clear even from the overview of Hutchison, op. cit.

[71] *Memorials of Alfred Marshall* (Pigou ed.), London, 1925, p. 400. Like Senior, Marshall rapidly turned from benevolence to fear and hatred, once the working class began to assert itself. Marshall was not against unions on principle, as long as they kept their place, in the shadow. But above all he was concerned with the international competitive position of British capital. His opinion on the engineering strike was expressed in letters to the Master of Balliol College at Oxford, who was in basic agreement but thought Marshall somewhat too virulent (Ibid., pp. 398–403). Cf. A. Petridis, 'Alfred Marshall's Attitudes to the Economic Analysis of Trade Unions', *History of Political Economy*, vol. V, 1, Spring 1973; and R. M. Tullberg, 'Marshall's Tendency to Socialism', *History of Political Economy*, VII, 1, Spring 1975). Marshall came to regard the socialist movement as 'by far the greatest present danger to human well-being' (Marshall, op. cit., p. 462). For Pareto, see below, ch. 4.

[72] Academic specialization and the growing disagreement between economists, on one hand, and businessmen and politicians, on the other, is a theme developed by Hutchison, op. cit.

[73] Gårlund, op. cit. Wicksell also had a petty-bourgeois family background

The Keynesian revolution in 20th century economics also had, as has been mentioned above, a clearly bourgeois location. In contemporary mainstream economics there is little reason to qualify the assertion that no single economist of any prominent standing in his profession in the capitalist countries has been connected with the working-class and the labour movement, or striven for another economic system than that ruled by the bourgeoisie (capitalism).[74] (Social liberal economists, on the other hand, attached to some form of reformed or 'mixed' welfare capitalism and having some connection with labour organizations with the same aim, are no rarity in the wake of the Keynes's 'revolution'.)

Writing about the composition of the British Royal Economic Society in 1960 from the perspective of 'professionalization' – that is, the idea that educated occupations are becoming, or have become, largely independent of outside society and governed by an internal code of their own – two authors have expressed a disarming surprise at the role of businessmen: 'Considering that the R.E.S. was a learned society publishing a purely scholarly journal, the size of the business contingent in the membership (39% of those with known occupations were businessmen, bankers or landowners, another tenth were in accounting) is most surprising, for British businessmen have not usually been noted for their command of scientific and technical expertise or their interest in academic subjects.'[75] The authors even found that the business contingent has increased in recent decades. The latter is not such a reliable finding, however, as the occupation of a third of the members was unknown to the researchers. Not a single worker or trade union official appears in the authors' computations.

The character of economics should not to be interpreted in too narrow a manner. The point is not that economics have been

---

and before his later academic career was an independent popular lecturer.

[74] The assertion holds for all the 28 economists in Recktenwald, op. cit., and for the 13 (including three appended shorter biographical sketches) in Schumpeter, *Ten Great Economists*. Discounting the overlap, this makes 34 in all. The single exception, famous as a critic of political economy, is Karl Marx. It holds also for the 7 Nobel Prize economists of 1969–73, with the possible exception of the Norwegian econometrician, Ragnar Frisch.

[75] Coats and Coats, op. cit., p. 169. The social composition of the R.E.S. is given on p. 170. Businessmen alone comprise 32·9%, teachers of all sorts 35·4%. To what extent businessmen are managers and entrepreneurs is unclear.

'supremely indifferent to the well-being of the working-classes'.[76] That cannot be said in any literal sense of the bourgeois themselves, so why should it be a mark of bourgeois economics? Even Andrew Carnegie and the late 19th century US 'robber barons' were interested in charity.

When Nassau Senior presented his infamous 'last hour' argument against a ten-hour bill at the London Political Economy Club he got little support – Senior argued that all the manufacturer's profits were made in the tenth hour of the day, and therefore that a ten-hour bill together with fluctuations of trade and prices of raw materials, would tend to wipe out profits altogether and paralyze industry. The majority had more sympathies for the views of the factory inspector Francis Horner who had been invited to the club for a discussion and whose reports Marx later made ample use of in *Capital*. Horner pointed out that several of the largest manufacturers had more advanced views on the Factory Bill than Senior. So the club members critical of Senior were thus still in good company.[77]

The class character of economics was rather expressed in the limited horizons of even the most radical economists. There have been respectable economists who could think of supporting another economic system than the prevailing capitalist one. But their alternative has always had a curiously *déjà vu* character: it has invariably turned out to be an idealized picture of the present system.

John Stuart Mill even sympathized with the Chartist movement in the 1830's and 40's but he felt ill at ease with its scant attention to the importance of individualist forethought and self-command. The control of a legislature by the working-class he thought would be horrible.[78] In his *Principles of Political Economy*, he included a chapter 'On the Probable Futurity of the Labouring Classes' which envisaged a society of commodity production by individual co-operative enterprises. Mill also pointed to the way to bring this

[76] As Robbins, op. cit., p. 5, presents, without references, the view he wants to combat.

[77] *Political Economy Club*, op. cit., pp. 273–5. The bill was actually concerned only with child labour, but it was thought that it would have indirect effects on adult labour too. Cf. G. D. H. Cole and R. Postgate, *The Common People*, London, 1963, pp. 259, 311f. In Schumpeter's opinion, by the way, Senior gave the best argument for the thesis of the value-neutrality of economists. Schumpeter, *Economic Doctrine and Method*, London, 1954, p. 82.

[78] J. S. Mill, *The Earlier Letters of J. S. Mill*, Toronto and London, 1963, pp. 533, 641, 643f, 729.

about: workers should free themselves 'not by robbing the capitalists of what they or their predecessors had acquired by labour and preserved by economy, but by honestly acquiring capital for themselves'.[79] Walras was another great supporter of cooperative commodity production, explicitly seeing the task of cooperatives as being 'to make everybody capitalists'.[80] As an ardent neo-Malthusian, Wicksell told the workers that they should not fight the ruling economic system as the principal cause of their miserable situation, but they should instead and above all prudently control their procreation.[81] In his economic policy writings he supported measures of equalization. With all qualifications, however, capitalism – not merely competitive commodity production but exploitation of wage-labour by those owning the means of production – remained for Wicksell, otherwise a blasphemous academic enfant terrible, the best and indeed the only really conceivable mode of production.[82]

The bourgeois view of competition has changed considerably since the last century. When the free marketeers of Austrian marginalism – Von Mises and Von Hayek (the aristocracy played a surprisingly dominant role in Austrian economics) – and their friends in the 1920's were proclaiming that a socialist mode of production was economically impossible, they were fighting a

[79] J. S. Mill, *Principles of Political Economy*, London, 1970, Book IV, ch. 7, p. 133f.

[80] L. Walras, *Economie appliquée*, op. cit., p. 285. Walras here meant what Marxists call petty bourgeois – producers for the market who do not employ wage-labour – but he also regarded capitalist relations of production (i.e. privately owned non-agricultural means of production worked by wage-labour) as just. 'In my ideal conditions of distribution [répartition] and production, *wage-labour* [le salariat], or the contractual sale of labour on the market for services, remains . . .' Ibid., p. 273 (emphasis original). Walras also declared that the 'true solution' of the problem of wages and other working conditions lay 'in the suppression of strikes by means of a rational intervention of the state, with a view to a better functioning of the markets for products and services' (p. 277).

[81] Gårlund, op. cit., p. 92f.

[82] Gårlund, op. cit., p. 234f. The most relevant and explicit of Wicksell's political writings is probably the pamphlet *Socialiststaten och nutidssamhället* (The Socialist State and Contemporary Society), Stockholm, 1905 (on wage-labour, p. 32). By striving for educational opportunity for all and for high taxes on inheritance, the Liberal party, Wicksell concludes, should be able to gather even the socialist labour party under its banner (p. 40). The attitude of another, more respectable, radical economist, Philip Wicksteed, was basically the same. Wicksteed was a not unsympathetic critic of Fabianism from the right (Hutchison, op. cit., p. 95f).

rearguard action.[83] For they based their argument on the principles of competitive capitalism. More congenial today are the theories of 'convergence' developed by, among others, the Nobel-prize winner Jan Tinbergen and John Kenneth Galbraith, both left-of-centre economists.[84] Though formulated not in terms of cooperative competition but in terms of state intervention, 'techno-structure' and the role of management, the convergence thesis of this type of economist is essentially the same as the thesis of Mill, Walras and Wicksell: a definitive, discontinuous break with the capitalist mode of production is impossible and contrary to economic logic.[85]

3. Economics as Science and as Verstehen

What is the contribution of economics to a scientific study of society? Little light on this is provided by the definitions of economics in the work of prominent economists. To Adam Smith and to Malthus economics was 'an enquiry into the nature and causes of the wealth of nations', an orientation they basically shared with the physiocrats. Ricardo held that 'the principal problem in Political Economy' was 'to determine the laws which regulate this distribution (of the produce of the earth among the three classes of landowners, capital owners, and labourers)'. Jevons averred that economic theory 'may, perhaps be described as the mechanics of human interest'.[86] In a well-known meta-economic text of this century we can read that economics is 'the science which studies human behaviour as a relationship between ends and scarce means

[83] F. A. Von Hayek (ed.), *Collectivist Economic Planning*, London, 1935.

[84] J. Tinbergen, 'Do Communist and Free Economies Show a Convergent Pattern?', *Soviet Studies*, vol. XII, April 1961; J. K. Galbraith, *The New Industrial State*, New York, 1967. I have made a critical analysis of Galbraith, of a further development of Tinbergen's argument by the Swedish economist Adler-Karlsson, and of their conception of the economic system, in Therborn, *Klasser och ekonomiska system*, Staffanstorp, 1971, pp. 76–169.

[85] Another Nobel Prize economist, Simon Kuznets, has also argued in his own way that there is only one modern economic system or 'epoch', distinguished by 'the extended application of science to the problems of economic production'. There are variants in the modern epoch, but what Kuznets calls 'the authoritarian states', meaning 'non-business' ones, should not be regarded as 'completely sui generis' (S. Kuznets, *Modern Economic Growth*, New Haven, 1966, p. 8f).

[86] Ricardo, *Principles of Political Economy and Taxation*, Preface; S. Jevons, *Principles of Political Economy*, London, 1871, p. 24.

which have alternative uses'.[87] The most widely used modern text-book of economics teaches its students: 'Economics is the study of how men and society *choose*, with or without the use of money, to employ *scarce* productive resources to produce various commodities over time and distribute them for consumption, now and in the future, among various people and groups in society.'[88]

For our purposes there are two difficulties here. One is the widely divergent character of the statements, even while they pertain to the same object. For all the differences of opinion involved, contemporary economists would, by and large, generally agree that Quesnay, Smith, Malthus, Ricardo, Jevons, Robbins, and Samuelson belong to their tribe and have made contributions to economics, of greater or lesser importance. This disagreement over fundamentals in a context of diffuse general agreement applies also to more specific, highly significant events, such as the meaning of the 'marginal revolution'.

Introducing the special issue of the *History of Political Economy* on the Marginal Revolution, Mark Blaug commented: 'Unfortunately, there appears to be no agreement as to just what the new paradigm was that Jevons, Menger, and Walras put forward.' Having referred to a number of interpretations – an emphasis on demand rather than supply, a subjective theory of value to supplant labour-cost theories, an extension of the maximization principle from firms to households, an interpretation of the consumer rather than the entrepreneur as the epitome of rational action, principle of proportionality of marginal utilities to prices as a condition of consumer equilibrium, general equilibrium analysis, a conscious acknowledgement of constrained maximization as the archetype of all economic reasoning – Blaug concluded: 'Whichever version we adopt, it is difficult to sustain the thesis that Jevons, Menger and Walras were really preoccupied with the same paradigm.'[89]

Keynes, for his part, lumped together Ricardo, though not Malthus, with Marshall, Edgeworth, Pigou and other pre-Keynesian marginalists as representatives of 'classical economics'.[90]

[87] L. Robbins, *Essay on The Nature and Significance of Economic Science* (2nd ed.), London, 1952, p. 16.

[88] P. Samuelson, *Economics* (6th ed.), New York, 1961, p. 6.

[89] M. Blaug, 'Was There a Marginal Revolution?', *History of Political Economy*, vol. 4, 2, Fall 1972, p. 274f.

[90] Keynes, *General Theory of Employment, Interest and Money*, ch. 2.

The second and fatal difficulty is that the definitions do not – with the partial and dubious exception of Jevons' mechanical analogy – say anything about the scientificity of the enquiries and studies in question.

Marx was of the opinion that political economy emerged as a science of its own with the classical economists, from Petty and Boiguillebert to Ricardo and Sismondi.[91] Marx was above all interested in theories of value and surplus-value. But it is not for having discovered the labour theory of value that Boisguillebert and Petty are praised, or that the physiocrats are paid a special homage. It is for their discovery of the 'social form', the 'social process' or the 'form of production', in which labour operates as the source of exchange value.[92]

The classical economists themselves were not aware of the preconditions and limits of this social form – which was one of Marx's main criticisms of them[93] – and Marx himself did not elaborate at great length what he thought they had discovered. From Marx's own analysis it is clear, however, that the exchange value of commodities is an expression of a particular kind of social interdependence – an interdependence between independently producing private producers, an interdependence governed not by deliberate control but by competition adjusting supply and demand.[94] Boisguillebert had shown this competitive social process in his analysis of value, and so, Marx seems to imply, had Petty.[95] Marx emphasized, too, that the physiocrats and their importance could not be understood if one did not see their view of agricultural labour as the only source of value and surplus-value in its connection 'with their proclamation of free competition'.[96]

[91] K. Marx, *A Contribution to the Critique of Political Economy*, London, 1971, p. 52f; *MEW* 13, p. 39f. Cf. *Capital*, vol. I, p. 81 n; *MEW* 23, p. 95 n.

[92] K. Marx, *A Contribution to the Critique of Political Economy*, p. 52f; *MEW* 13, p. 39f. *Theories of Surplus Value*, part 1, Moscow, n.d., ch. 2; *MEW* 26: 1, ch. 2.

[93] *Capital* I, p. 80f. *MEW* 23, p. 95f.

[94] Ibid., p. 72f. Cf. *A Contribution to the Critique of Political Economy*, p. 61f. *MEW* 13, p. 47f.

[95] *A Contribution to the Critique of Political Economy*, p. 54; *MEW* 13, p. 40.

[96] *Theories of Surplus Value*, p. 53; *MEW* 26: 1, p. 23. Marx also mentions here the 'proclamation' of 'the principle of large-scale industry', which in the context seems to be synonymous with 'large-scale enterprise', worked with wage-labour. Cf. also *A Contribution to the Critique of Political Economy*, p. 60f. (*MEW* 13, p. 45f) on free competition and large-scale industry with regard to Ricardo.

What Marx emphasized in his assessment of the scientificity of classical economics was, then, the discovery of a pattern of social determination, something law-bound, not randomly malleable by arbitrary will or violence, divine or human.[97] Marx referred to this in various, rather oblique ways, as a system of private labour and private exchange, as free competition, and so on. It has a common name nowadays, of which Marx and Engels, for no very clear reason, were not very fond: the *market*.[98]

Schumpeter, another eminent historian of economics, adhered to an empiricist and positive conception of science very different from Marx's. But we find in his writings something else too. Schumpeter gives a series of definitions of science, all slight variations pointing to the use of special methods, specialized techniques of fact-finding and analysis. These definitions can be summarized in the following two equivalent sentences: 'science is refined common sense' and 'science is tooled knowledge'.[99] All this seems to be worlds apart from the definitions advanced above, that science is the systematic study of a specific object: that this object has the character of a pattern of determination or of regularities; that the emergence of a science of society, such as economics, involves the discovery of a specific social pattern of determination, the functioning of which it is then the task of science to analyze. Schumpeter's treatise is not informed by such a conception but its author has, in his own way, taken account of it.

Though in fact a panoramic overview, Schumpeter's work is – much as its title suggests – concerned with 'economic analysis', which is clearly distinguished from 'economic thought', or the sum total of opinions on economic subjects.[100] In economic analysis Schumpeter includes economic history, economic statistics and sociology, as well as economic theory. But his actual concern is not with history, statistics, or sociology proper, and he also uses economic analysis and analytic work in a narrower sense.

We are given little explicit elucidation of what economic analysis

---

[97] Its law-bound character is particularly stressed by Marx, for example, in *Theories of Surplus Value*, p. 44 (*MEW* 26: 1, p. 12), and in *Anti-Dühring*, Moscow, 1962, p. 343f. (*MEW* 20, p. 237f.)

[98] In *Anti-Dühring*, for instance, Engels refers to '– "the market" – to adopt Herr Dühring's style for once' (p. 315; *MEW* 20, p. 214).

[99] Schumpeter, *History of Economic Analysis*, p. 7.

[100] Ibid., p. 38f.

in this stricter sense is. But we are given 'an example', if only one: 'from earliest times until today analytic economists have been interested, more or less, in the phenomenon that we call competitive price'.[101] Competitive price is not the same as market, of course. The former is something determined by the latter, which means that an analysis centered on competitive price must be an analysis of the operation of the market as a determinant.

Economics as the study of the operation of the market as a social determinant is defined much more clearly by another historian of the discipline. Mark Blaug writes in the introduction to his analytic-ally focused *Economic Theory in Retrospect*: 'The problem that gave rise to economics in the first place, the "mystery" that fascinated Adam Smith as much as it does a modern economist, is that of market exchange: there is a sense of order in the economic universe, and this order is not imposed from above but is somehow the out-come of the exchange transactions between individuals, each seeking to maximize his own gain. The history of economic thought, there-fore, is nothing but the history of our efforts to understand the workings of an economy based on market transactions.'[102]

If this is true, then we should be able to find the market determin-ant at the centre of all the major stages in the development of economics. This seems indeed to be the case, from the adumbrations of economic theory in the 16th century to Keynesianism and today's codified economic wisdom.

The French 16th century philosopher Jean Bodin won himself a place in the history of economics by refuting the thesis that the price rise of his time was due to the debasement of coin, and by instead explaining it primarily by the increase in the supply of gold and silver.[103] The analytic contribution of the mercantilist writers was in their studies of the market mechanism in the international balance of trade and payments.[104]

The physiocrats discovered the interdependence of a system of production. Though the physiocrats themselves, as we have seen, clearly had a kind of capitalist economy in mind, Quesnay's famous *Tableau* could be taken as a model for an input–output analysis not necessarily concerned with the market. But the analytic use of it

---

[101] Ibid., p. 39.

[102] M. Blaug, *Economic Theory in Retrospect*, London, 1968, p. 6.

[103] Schumpeter, *History of Economic Analysis*, p. 312; Roll, op. cit., p. 59.

[104] Schumpeter, *History of Economic Analysis*, p. 352f.

made by Quesnay himself dealt with the market determinant: from his first 'important observation' of the effect of the demand of the rich landlords on agricultural production to his discussion of two 'economic problems', the effect of an exogenously induced rise in the price of agricultural products, and the effect of indirect taxation.[105]

In Adam Smith we encountered not only the market determinant as the 'invisible hand' linking private and public interest, but also analyses of how the market forces of supply and demand operate to regulate the rates of wages, profits and rents, and profits and wages in different branches.[106] In the classical model there is a distinction between natural price, governed by value, and market price, determined by market demand and supply. The distinction, however, does not mean that it is not the market that determines the functioning of the economy. This is very clear from Ricardo's analysis.

The market not only plays the decisive role in apportioning capital between different branches or in determining the pattern of foreign trade. It operates in the determination of the distribution of the produce into rent, profit and wages, i.e. of what Ricardo regarded as 'the principal problem in Political Economy'.

The rate of profit depends on the rate of wages, which disposes of the question of profit.[107] Wages, in their turn, depend on two factors. One is the demand and supply of labourers, i.e. the population principle: when the market price of labour rises above its natural price, increasing working-class procreation will create an excessive supply, thus bringing down wages again, and vice versa. The second is the price of the necessities of life, basically food, which regulates the natural price of labour.[108] Rent, thirdly, is regulated by the supply and demand of land.[109] The particular problem of Ricardo's model is that fertile land becomes increasingly scarce, leading in the long run to diminishing returns in agriculture, thereby higher rents (for the fertile land), more expensive food and therefore higher wages, lower profits, and consequently stagnation. Given the assumption of diminishing returns in agriculture, the market is still the regulating force in the classical Ricardian

---

[105] Quesnay, op. cit., pp. 59f, 79f, 105f.
[106] Smith, *Wealth of Nations*, Book I, chs. VIII–XI.
[107] Ricardo, *Principles of Political Economy and Taxation*, ch. VI.
[108] Ibid., ch. V.
[109] Ibid., ch. II, esp. p. 93 f.

system.[110]

Little need be said of the market focus of marginalist economics. It is enough to quote Walras, the greatest of them all: '*Pure political economy* is essentially the theory of the determination of price under a hypothetical regime of absolute free competition.'[111] The 'neo-classical' concentration on resource allocation was squarely about market determination. The fact that the market is the common object of both classical and neo-classical economic analysis does not mean, however, that there are no important differences between the two in their conception of the role and operation of the market. In the view of Walras and the other marginalists, the market for factors of production and the market for final goods are analogous, and market interdependence adequately provides the basic unity of the economic system. Ricardian-type models (classical and modern), on the other hand, integrate technological interdependence between different branches of production and extramarket distribution of the population into different classes, thereby differentiating between factor markets and markets for final goods, and limiting the extent of market determination in the former case. In a Ricardian type of analysis, economic equilibrium may be determined in terms of structural necessities of the system and need not be defined in a wholly subjectivist way as the outcome of the free choice of maximizing individual units.

But what of the Keynesian theory of employment, then? Keynes was a critic of the theory of the self-adjusting market economy and a supporter of certain types of state intervention. He used an apparatus of supposedly 'fundamental psychological factors, namely the psychological propensity to consume, the psychological attitude to liquidity and the psychological expectation of future yield from capital-assets'.[112] The gist of Keynes's contribution was, however, a new analysis of how the market functions as a determinant of employment in an economic system like that of Britain in the 1930's. This is most clear in chapter 19 of the *General Theory*, which discusses the effect of a reduction of money wages upon employment. This was *the* practical problem involved in the Depression decade, with its dismal parade of well-meaning and well-off professors of

---

[110] Cf. E. J. Nell, 'Theories of Growth and Theories of Value', in G. C. Harcourt and N. F. Laing (eds.), *Capital and Growth*, London, 1971, pp. 196–210.

[111] L. Walras, *Eléments d'économie politique pure*, Lausanne-Paris, 1900, p. xi.

[112] Keynes, *General Theory of Employment, Interest and Money*, p. 246f.

neo-classical economics proclaiming, with Professor Cannan of LSE in 1932, that unemployment was due to workers 'asking too much'.[113] Keynes exploded their argument, analyzing the effect of a reduction of money wages on aggregate effective demand, given certain plausible assumptions. What he did was to point out that the market functioned as a determinant in a way other than his predecessors had thought. Had he been unable to show *how* the functioning of the market mechanism, given his assumptions, produced less than 'full' employment, there would have certainly been no 'Keynesian revolution' in economic theory.

The market is the basis of 'the grand neo-classical synthesis' that Paul Samuelson has so successfully taught an international body of students for twenty-five years in the seven editions (to date) of his *Economics*. In the words of this enthusiast: 'How is it that nearly 10 million people [in New York] are able to sleep easily at night without living in mortal terror of a breakdown in the elaborate economic processes upon which the city's existence depends? For all this [the solution of the city's basic economic problems] is undertaken without coercion or centralized direction by any conscious body.'[114]

The study of market determination is the core of economic analysis – not only in the study of how prices are set and resources are allocated, or how different markets are related by an equilibrating mechanism. Macroeconomic discussion of trade cycles, growth and government policies is principally about the effects of various forces and policies – monetary policies, taxes, public investment, and so on – upon the market mechanism, and the result of these measures on employment and income when they have, so to speak, waded through the market stream.

Though economists may also make other sorts of analysis – such as input-output analyses, for instance – it is fundamentally upon the discovery of the market as a determinant of regularities in the social world of human beings that the claim of economics to scientificity justly rests. Or, rather, it rests upon the production of

---

[113] E. Cannan, *A Review of Economic Theory*, p. xiv n, quotation originally from an article in *Economic Journal*, vol. XLII, 1932, p. 357. For an interview of wage-cutting economists, see e.g., L. Klein, *The Keynesian Revolution* (2nd ed.), London, 1968, p. 43f.

[114] Samuelson, *Economics*, p. 38.

the market as a conceptual object – frequently attacked by empiricists, from the German historical or ethical school to American institutionalism, for its abstract character – by means of which economists try to grasp what happens in that part of the real world called economic.

We have seen that economics emerged in connection with the rise of capitalism and of the bourgeoisie. Do the three continuities in the history of economics – capitalism, bourgeoisie, market – together mean that economics is adequately described as the science of the capitalist economy, and that, therefore a critique of political economy (economics) must be a critique of the historical limitations of capitalism and the rule of the bourgeoisie? No. For a capitalist economy is not the same thing as a market economy. The market presupposes a number of buyers and sellers with certain maximization tendencies linked in a network of exchange. It does not assume, as does capitalism, the existence of two separate classes of capital-owners and wage-labourers, membership of which is chiefly governed by forces other than the market.

This points to a critical problem, the *articulation of the market* with the rest of the human world. The analysis of market determination must always start from something, and the question of articulation pertains to this something. To a large extent the economic theories of *value* are concerned precisely with the problem of articulation. So far we have virtually bypassed theories of value. Market determination held the stage of economic analysis among the classical labour theorists of value, among the marginal utility theorists of value, and in Keynes who was scarcely at all interested in theories of value.[115] We have not said that it was the discovery of the labour or the marginal theory of value that made political economy into a scientific discourse.

The position taken here thus differs considerably, not from Marx as we have seen, but from the views of distinguished modern Marxist economists. Both to Maurice Dobb and to Ernest Mandel it is the theory of value which puts political economy on a par with

---

[115] Instead of a separate theory of value, Keynes wanted a distinction between a theory of the individual firm or industry and, on the other hand, a theory of output and employment in the whole economy. It was in the latter that he himself was interested. Keynes, *General Theory of Employment, Interest and Money*, p. 292f.

the sciences of chemistry and physics.[116] But what their sharp criticism of the subjective theory of value, of its deficiency compared to the labour theory, amounts to is that the former does not take account of the external framework in which market exchange occurs in a capitalist economy.[117] That is, Dobb and Mandel point to the problem of the articulation of the market with the rest of society. A similar view of the theory of value, but from the other side, is to be found in Frank Knight, an important American liberal economist of the inter-war period: 'The greatest improvement introduced by the marginal utility viewpoint came in the field of distribution theory as a by-product of the changed view of cost. The classical Ricardo-Senior-Mill theory of distribution was utterly unrealistic. It did not consider the problem as one of the valuation of services furnished to production, under competition or monopoly, but as a matter of the successive slicing off of the social income by the three main economic classes found in the society of post-feudal Europe.'[118]

Marx also emphasized the problem of what is here called the articulation of the market with the rest of the world, when he stated the problems of a theory of value: 'Political economy has indeed analyzed, however incompletely, value and its magnitude, and has discovered what lies beneath these forms. But it has never once asked the question why labour is represented by the value of its product and labour-time by the magnitude of that value.' In a footnote to the sentence just quoted Marx says, among other things, 'The value-form of the product of labour is not only the most abstract, but is also the most universal form, taken by the product in bourgeois production, and stamps that production as a particular species of social production, and thereby gives it its special historical character'.[119] Following Franz Petry, Paul Sweezy has referred to the problem of articulation as 'the qualitative value-problem', stressing that in Marx's theory of value it formed a single conceptual framework with 'the quantitative value-problem'.[120]

The market mechanism is part of the functioning of a capitalist economy. But it is only a part and it also extends beyond capitalism

---

[116] M. Dobb, *Political Economy and Capitalism* (2nd ed.), London, 1968, p. 5; E. Mandel, *Marxist Economic Theory*, London, 1968, vol. II, p. 710.

[117] See esp. Dobb, op. cit., pp. 30–33, 182–4; Mandel, op. cit., pp. 714–16.

[118] F. Knight, *The Ethics of Competition and Other Essays*, London, 1935, p. 153.

[119] *Capital*, vol. I, pp. 80–1; *MEW* 23, pp. 94–5.

[120] P. Sweezy, *The Theory of Capitalist Development*, New York, 1964, p. 25.

in the sense that it is the mechanism of another economic system, simple commodity production. The critique of political economy, therefore, is not primarily concerned with the historical limitations of political economy, but with its limitations in accounting for the functioning of capitalism. This critique, then, asserts that the characterization of Western capitalist economies simply as market economies is a grave distortion.[121] It is from this that its historical limitations follow, its inadequacy in the analysis of the evolution of capitalism.

Sociology and historical materialism are both critiques of political economy in this sense, centring on the problem of articulating the market to other patterns of social determination. This is a problem for both theories, and one that pertains above all to the realities of capitalist society, the society in which these theories grew up.

The insertion of the market into a broader pattern of social determination has been mainly an endeavour of the critique of political economy. In the economic tradition – to the extent that economists have been concerned with 'founding' their analyses of the market – the general line has been to link the market to sovereign individual subjects. There have been two different variants of this.

In one of them, the market economy is regarded as deducible from the characteristics of the human psyche and physiology. Adam Smith hinted at man's propensity to trade. But it was with marginal utility theory that psychologistic economics achieved its full and brief bloom, as a utilitarian interpretation of marginalism. Menger and Jevons, who spoke of economics as the 'mechanics of self-interest', held that their theory was deducible from psychology.[122] For a time, the psycho-physical 'Weber-Fechner Law' of the human experience of stimuli of weight, temperature etc., was believed to provide a basis for marginal utility economics.[123] Eventually this turned out to be a myth, and the psychologistic vogue faded

---

[121] I have tried to show this in a critique of a number of liberal textbooks on economic systems, by Gregory Grossman, Georg Halm, William Loucks, and Oxenfeldt–Holubnychy, *Klasser och ekonomiska system*, pp. 31–58. Cf. O. Lange, 'Marxian Economics and Modern Economic Theory', in D. Horowitz (ed.), *Marx and Modern Economics*, New York, 1968, pp. 68–87.

[122] C. Menger, *Untersuchungen über der Methode der Sozialwissenschaften*, Leipzig, 1883, p. 76f; Jevons, *Principles of Political Economy*, p. 24.

[123] The Weber-Fechner Law was treated and criticized by another Weber, Max, the sociologist, 'Die Grenznutzlehre und das psychophysische Grund-

away. In retrospect, it turned out that 'what was important in marginal utility was the adjective rather than the noun'.[124]

The subjectivist constructions of marginalist microeconomics – together with the subjective theory of value – then came to be regarded, not as deductions from psychology and physiology, but as an expression of the meaning of economic phenomena. Marginalist economics made meaningful was a way to understand (or with a loaded German word, *verstehen*) what happened in the market economy. The first systematic exposition of this idea was that of Max Weber, who argued that the economic man was not a finding of psychology but an ideal-typical construct to enable us to understand the regularities of the market. Before he was a sociologist, Weber was an economist and a historian, and out of his interpretation of marginalist economics he was to build his *verstehende* sociology. In economics Weber's argument was particularly followed and further developed by the ultra-liberal, anti-interventionist tendency of Ludwig Von Mises, Lionel Robbins, and others.[125] In this second individualist conception of the foundation of economics, the market economy is seen as based on rational, free human action.

One of the most ambitious and renowned efforts at *Verstehen* in the history of economics is Philip Wicksteed's *Common Sense of Political Economy*. In the words of Lionel Robbins – himself a distinguished spokesman for a *verstehende* economics – who wrote an enthusiastic introduction to a later edition, 'it is . . . the most exhaustive non-mathematical exposition of the technical and philosophical complications of the so-called *marginal* theory of pure economics'.[126] In contrast to Smith and Ricardo, Wicksteed does not begin with labouring man, toiling for the stone-age market for

---

gesetz', *Gesammelte Aufsätze zur Wissenschaftslehre*, Tübingen, 1922.

[124] Blaug, *Economic Theory in Retrospect*, p. 299. The expression is T. W. Hutchison's. The decline and fall of the utility concept in marginalist economics is the subject of one of George Stigler's *Essays in the History of Economics*, Chicago, 1965. The notion of utility has been replaced by the construction of preference scales and principles of maximization behaviour that are at least not explicitly psychological.

[125] Robbins, *An Essay on the Nature and Significance of Economic Science*; L. von Mises, *Human Action*, New Haven, 1949; cf. F. Machlup, *Essays on Economic Semantics*, Englewood Cliffs, 1963, p. 109.

[126] P. Wicksteed, *Common Sense of Political Economy*, London, 1933, vol. I, p. xii.

hunted animals, but with the shopping *mater-familias*.[127] The universality of marginalist exchange is shown by appeals to the common sense of those who were familiar with such interiors of Edwardian England as the following: 'Whether our housewife is apportioning the stuffing of a goose at table, or her housekeeping money in the market, or her time and attention between schemes for getting boarders and the more direct cultivation and furthering of the general tastes and interests of her life; and whether her husband is conducting family prayers, or posting up his books at the office, or weighing the advantages and disadvantages of a partial retirement from business . . . they and all the people they are concerned with are alike engaged in administering resources, in developing opportunities and choosing between alternatives, under the great controlling guidance of the two principles we have been continuously illustrating throughout our investigation.'[128]

A *verstehende* discourse begs the question: understandable to whom? Make sense to whom? Common sense where? A *verstehende* exposition typically tries to explain the unfamiliar by the familiar. It seeks to make something understood by making it meaningful, showing how it makes common sense, in terms of some familiar experiences and values. This is the closed ideological circle of recognition/miscognition, criticised by Althusser. A scientific explanation, on the other hand, explains the familiar by the unfamiliar (discovered by science).[129]

To the class to which economists belong, this economic common sense may be easily understandable. To a class that experiences the capitalist market economy as poverty, oppression, and periodic unemployment, Wicksteed's common sense – or any other attempt to portray the economy as, by and large, based on free and rational human action – may appear preposterous or blatantly apologetic.[130]

[127] Ibid., I, p. 18f.

[128] Ibid., I, p. 159.

[129] This view of scientific explanation is shared, from a quite different philosophical position from Althusser's, by Karl Popper, *Objective Knowledge*, Oxford, 1972, p. 191. Cf. S. Toulmin, *Foresight and Understanding*, New York, 1963, p. 60.

[130] Showing the practical applications of the marginal principle, Wicksteed pointed out, for instance, that one way of removing unemployment was through wage cuts (vol. II, p. 637 f). Workers' hatred of strikebreakers had 'no social justification' and was 'economically unsound' (II, p. 694f). It was Wicksteed who wrote the first marginalist critique of Marx's value theory, correctly perceiving that Marx's theory of surplus-value and exploitation was the main thing to attack.

A good part of economic theory, classical as well as neo-classical, should probably be most properly regarded as attempts at *Verstehen*, at making economic phenomena meaningful by referring to man in the state of nature or to the shopping consumer. The theory of profit has tried to understand it as a recompense for something, for labour and diligence, for abstinence, or risk-taking.[131] It might be argued that the so-called marginal revolution largely pertained to the question of the meaning of the market pattern of determination.

However, a *verstehende* discipline is an ideological discipline, and bourgeois and petty-bourgeois 'common sense' has left its ideological finger-prints on the scientific analyses and intelligible predictions of market regularities. In begging the question – understandable to whom? – this second route to an individualist foundation of market theory is as closed as a psychologistic one.

The problem of the social context of the market has been posed by a recent challenge to the marginalist theory of value and modern microeconomics, and their applicability to the analysis of income distribution, technological development and economic growth. The central figure in this challenge, which differs notably from earlier institutionalist and ideological critiques of marginalism by its very high level of technical rigour and sophistication, has been Piero Sraffa, the Cambridge economist who was once a friend of the famous Italian Marxist Antonio Gramsci. Sraffa's main work is his tightly argued treatise *Production of Commodities by Means of Commodities* (1960); other important contributions have been made by Robinson, Garegnani, Nuti and Pasinetti.[132]

Their collective critique has first of all discredited the marginalist thesis that profits can be understood and explained as determined

(Paper in *Common Sense*, II, pp. 705–33.) Wicksteed's critique was instrumental in converting Bernard Shaw and the Fabians to marginalist economics.

[131] The conception of profit as originally derived from labour and diligence is the classical conception of primitive accumulation, derided and replaced by Marx in the penultimate chapter of *Capital*, vol. I; cf. Smith, *Wealth of Nations*, Book I, ch. VI, Book II, Introduction, ch. I. Senior was a notorious advocate of the abstinence theory (Roll, op. cit., p. 344f). The view of profit as a recompense for risk-taking was developed by Frank Knight, *Risk, Uncertainty and Profit*, Boston and New York, 1921.

[132] An excellent record of the most important interventions, from the defence as well as from the prosecution, is Harcourt and Laing (eds.), *Capital and Growth*, op. cit. Cf. also the anthology of critiques, E. K. Hunt and J. G. Schwartz (eds.), *A Critique of Economic Theory*, London, 1972.

by the marginal productivity of capital (in the non-Marxist sense of means of production – in other words the relationship of producer goods and labour to output). Distribution in a capitalist economy thereby ceases to be underpinned by technology. Sraffa has proved that the relative prices of two commodities will change when the rate of profit changes, even if they are still produced in the same way (because the labour put into the commodities has been put in at different points in time). His conclusion is that 'the reversal in the direction of the movement of relative prices, in the face of unchanged methods of production, cannot be reconciled with *any* notion of capital as a measurable quantity independent of distribution and prices'.[133] If the definition of capital as a homogeneous, measurable quantity is dependent on the system of distribution, then to argue that it is the productivity of capital which determines the share of distribution appropriated by the owners of capital, is an illogical circularity.

Another blow to marginalist economics has been the discovery of the possibility of reswitching of techniques. That is, one technique (with a particular ratio of production goods and labour) may be more profitable than another at one level of profit, then become less profitable with a higher rate of profit, but become more profitable again at a still higher rate of profit. Contrary to marginalist assumptions, it is then impossible to say that when the rate of profit is relatively high the most profitable technique is the one with a relatively low ratio of capital goods per man. There is no necessary relation between the rate of profit and technique, neither a positive nor an inverse relation between 'quantity of capital' and the rate of profit.[134]

One of the most direct implications of all this is that explanations of the rate of profit must refer to determinants outside the free world of utility-maximizing individual choosers. In the distribution of a capitalist society 'it's class that counts', as one of the British Cambridge economists has put it.[135] One who is not a trained

---

[133] P. Sraffa, *Production of Commodities by Means of Commodities*, Cambridge, 1960, p. 38 (italics original).

[134] Ibid., ch. XII. See also L. L. Pasinetti, 'Switches of Technique and the Rate of Return in Capital Theory', in Harcourt and Laing, op. cit., pp. 261–86; and P. Garegnani, 'Heterogenous Capital, the Production Function and the Theory of Distribution', in Hunt and Schwartz, op. cit., pp. 245–91.

[135] Harcourt, in his introduction to Harcourt and Laing, op. cit., p. 24.

economist should not substitute theoretical or other sympathies for real competence in evaluating the validity of these highly technical attacks on the very core of marginalist economics. It is a fact, however, that leading neo-classical theorists have admitted the pertinence of them. The Cambridge critique has taught even Paul Samuelson 'to suspect the simplest neo-classical parables'.[136] Sraffa remains a Ricardian and we cannot deal here with the question of the relation of the Neo-Ricardian critique to the Marxist critique of political economy.[137] In any event, the problem which Marxist theory has traditionally brought into focus, the articulation of market exchange with a wider historical social context and with class struggle, has been taken right to the centre of controversy in contemporary academic economic theory.

---

[136] P. Samuelson, 'A Summing Up', in Harcourt and Laing, op. cit., p. 240. Samuelson concludes, not wrongly but not very persuasively either, 'that scholars are not born to live an easy existence' (p. 250).

[137] On this point, see the excellent article by B. Rowthorn, 'Neo-Classicism, Neo-Ricardianism, and Marxism', *New Left Review* 86 (July–August 1974).

Chapter Three

The Age of Sociology: Between One Revolution and Another

Though not always immediately discernible beneath different theories and conflicting schools, the historical identity and continuity of economics is not too difficult to perceive, because of its limited and relatively explicit focus on the market, and its formalized procedures of analysis. An attempt at situating sociology in social and intellectual time and space is a more hazardous enterprise. Is it at all possible to ascribe such an amorphous congerie of thought-systems to any particular phase of history at all? The framework of our analysis provides us, at least, with a field in which to search for one. By sociology will be meant, not social thought or social science in general, but the specific discipline answering to (because giving itself) the name of sociology. In this respect, sociology is an immediately identifiable empirical phenomenon. Our intention, however, is to study it as an object of scientific analysis – to ascertain whether it is a possible science. Our aim, in other words, is a scientific analysis of the possible emergence of a science by the name of sociology. Now as an object of scientific analysis, sociology is not something immediately given in the discourse of sociologists. A study of the formation of sociology as the emergence of a possible science involves a search for the theoretical discovery or empirical enquiry into specific pattern(s) of social determination in discourses calling themselves sociological. It will then be necessary to consider whether such patterns are related to those of other social discourses, possibly sociological or proto-sociological in content without this designation.

The official or nominal inauguration of sociology can be situated exactly. The term was coined by Auguste Comte in his forty-seventh *Cours* of positive philosophy, which first appeared in 1838. Comte's social writings, from about 1820 on, unquestionably form one of the beginnings of sociology. Since the first of them were written in intimate cooperation with Henri Saint-Simon, the latter is also obviously relevant.

Another obvious pioneer is Herbert Spencer, at one time an enormously influential proponent of sociology, as well as of social evolution, laissez-faire and other causes. Spencer was an English Victorian who for half a century from the 1850's developed his sociology as part of a vast system of 'synthetic philosophy'; but his most important influence was in America.[2] That influence underlines Spencer's considerable role in the history of sociology, as it was in the United States that sociology first acquired a definite and powerful academic position.[3] One of the 'Fathers' of American sociology, who was himself no Spencerian, Charles Cooley, wrote: 'I imagine that nearly all of us who took up sociology between 1870, say, and 1890 did so at the instigation of Spencer.'[4]

Another coordinate by which sociology can be situated is its

[1] A. Comte, *Cours de philosophie positive*, IV, Paris, 1908, p. 132. There is an abridged English edition, translated by Harriet Martineau, *The Positive Philosophy of Comte*, 3 vols., London, 1896.

[2] Spencer's most important sociological works are *Social Statics* (1st ed. 1850), *The Study of Sociology* (1st ed. 1873), and *The Principles of Sociology* (parts I–III 1876, part IV 1879, part V 1882, part VI 1885, parts VII-VIII 1896). In time, the later parts of *Principles* overlap with the classical works of sociology, such as Ferdinand Tönnies, *Gemeinschaft und Gesellschaft* (1887), or Emile Durkheim, *De la division du travail social* (1893), but Spencer and his work are generally regarded as belonging to an earlier generation. An overview of Spencer's work is given by J. Rumney, *Herbert Spencer's Sociology*, London, 1934. There is a recent, perceptive intellectual biography of Spencer, J. D. Y. Peel, *Herbert Spencer, The Evolution of a Sociologist*, New York, 1971. It is most valuable in its portrait and analysis of Spencer's social and intellectual context. The failure of British sociology before 1945, the story of a discipline that never really took off despite repeated attempts, is told up to World War I by P. Abrams, *The Origins of British Sociology*, Chicago, 1968.

[3] See A. Oberschall (ed.), *The Establishment of Empirical Sociology*, New York, 1972, esp. the essay by the editor, 'The institutionalization of American sociology.'

[4] C. H. Cooley, 'Reflections upon the Sociology of Herbert Spencer', in his collection of essays, *Sociological Theory and Social Research*, New York, 1930, p. 203. The sociologies of Comte and Spencer are resumed at length in the first work of the American classics, Lester Ward's *Dynamic Sociology* (1st ed. 1883). Ward presented them thus: 'They alone, of all the thinkers of the world, have the merit of having carried their generalizations from the phenomena of inorganic nature up to those of human action and social life.' Op. cit., New York, 1898, vol. I, p. 142.

classical age – the epoch in which it first achieved intellectual maturity. There can be no doubt that this age was the period from the 1880's to about 1920, the age of Emile Durkheim in France, of George Simmel, Ferdinand Tönnies and Max Weber in Germany, of Vilfredo Pareto, the Italian in Switzerland, and of the American Founding Fathers from Lester Ward to Charles Cooley.[5] In that period, too, sociology became a university subject in France and the USA, and in Germany it was at least an organized academic interest, embodied in the *Deutsche Gesellschaft für Soziologie*.[6] Important sociological journals were launched in the 1890's, the *Revue International de Sociologie* (1893), *American Journal of Sociology* (1895), *Rivista Italiana di Sociologie* (1897). Durkheim started a sociological yearbook, *L'Année Sociologique* (1898). Linked to the first mentioned publication was the *Institut International de Sociologie*, an international organization in which most of the leading sociologists, with the exception of the Durkheimians, were represented.

The rise of sociology, then, is a Western European and North American phenomenon of the 19th century. These coordinates are course, merely geographical space and chronological time. One important implication of them, however, is that sociology – at least as a self-conscious intellectual enterprise – is a post-revolutionary body of thought. Sociology does not belong with the ideas of 1789. It is not part of the Enlightenment and the Age of Reason. It did not develop as part of the struggle of the bourgeoisie against the ruling aristocracy of feudalism and absolutism.

The bourgeois revolution was not, of course, a single event but a historical process of economic, political, juridical, and ideological ruptures between old social institutions and new bourgeois forms. In this revolutionary process a capitalist market emerged, the political power of feudal landowners was defeated and a state

[5] The 'Fathers' of American sociology are generally thought to be Lester Ward, William Graham Sumner, Franklyn Giddings, Albion Small, Edward Ross, Charles Cooley, and (usually though sometimes left out) Thorstein Veblen. A very good exposition of the first six is given by C. Page, *Class and American Sociology*, New York, 1940.

[6] Only in the Weimar Republic, after the fall of the Wilhelmine *Reich*, was sociology acknowledged by German universities. The acceptance was not won without struggle. A brief account of the general political and intellectual background to its introduction is given by F. Ringer, *The Decline of the German Mandarins*, Cambridge, Mass., 1969, p. 228f. Cf. Oberschall, op. cit., p. 9f.

representing the bourgeoisie and furthering the development of capitalism was created, in which feudal privileges were abolished and equality before the law was established. In every country a particular event can normally be singled out as decisive: the independence of Holland from Spain, the settlement of 1688 in England, the French Revolution of 1789, the American Civil War and the defeat of the Southern slaveowners,[7] the national unification of Italy and Germany.[8] These events, however, constituted neither the first nor the last important moments of the bourgeois revolution in each country, as the long persistence of the power of the landowning aristocracy in England, Italy, and Germany makes evident.

Nevertheless, the post-bourgeois revolutionary timing of sociology is rather striking. It is adumbrated in France by Comte and the master of his youth, Saint-Simon, during the Bourbon Restoration after the great revolution. Spencer appeared in England not only after the revolution of 1688 but after the parliamentary reform of 1832 and the repeal of the Corn Laws as well. American, German, and Italian[9] sociology all wholly post-date the decisive events of the respective bourgeois revolutions of their countries.[10]

[7] Cf. B. Moore, *Social Origins of Dictatorship and Democracy*, Boston, 1967, ch. III.

[8] The French revolutionary armies had a shattering impact upon many aspects of the established structure of Germany, even though Germany still remained, economically, socially and politically, behind other Western countries. The impact of the French Revolution also left an important imprint upon German social theory (see below).

[9] From today's perspective, Italian sociology of the classical period is to be found above all in the works of Mosca and Pareto. Historically, as an intellectual activity, Italian sociology was rather different. For an early account see G. Fiamingo, 'Sociology in Italy', *American Journal of Sociology*, vol. I (1895), pp. 335–52. A comprehensive bibliographical essay on the history of Italian sociology is O. Lentini, 'Storiografia della sociologia italiana (1860–1925)', *La Critica Sociologica*, no. 20, Inverno, 1971–2, pp. 116–40.

[10] This should be qualified by noting among the prominent early sociologists a number of Western-oriented or Western-influenced intellectuals in Eastern Europe, like the Austrian Pole Ludwig Gumplowicz, the Czech Thomas Masaryk, and, from the Russian Empire and often in longer or shorter Western emigration, Maxim Kovalevsky, J. Novikov, Evgeni De Roberty (all closely connected with the *Institut* and its review), Edward Westermarck and the subjectivist critic of Spencer and Comte, K. N. Mikhailovsky. Further removed but of similar background were the early Japanese students of Spencer and Comte, like Nagao Aruga and Tongo Takebe (K. Odaka, 'Sociology in Japan: Accommodation of Western Orientation', in H. Becker and A. Boskoff, eds., *Modern Sociological Theory*, New York, 1957, pp. 711–30).

In Western Europe, with the exception of Scotland, the older institutions of higher learning, the universities, were captured by the bourgeoisie only relatively late. In the 19th century they were typically linked to landowners and pre-bourgeois political structures. Oxford and Cambridge in England and the German universities are famous examples. Rather than havens of new ideas, the universities tended to be 'sanctuaries in which exploded systems and obsolete principles found shelter and protection, after they had been hunted out of every other corner of the world'.[11] Sociology consequently emerged outside the universities, as a rather maverick body of thought, much marked by the personal idiosyncracies of the first individual sociologists. We shall see below that it was only considerably later, when the universities became attuned to bourgeois society, that sociology became academically institutionalized and started to develop as a relatively coherent discipline.

It seems unlikely that this relationship between the emergence of a science of society – as sociology claims to be – and the social upheavals designated by the notion of bourgeois revolution should be a mere random coincidence. But how then are the two connected? What was the novelty of sociology within intellectual history?

For it is obvious that the appearance of sociology was not just a first application of scientific methods to social affairs. When sociologists appeared, social science was already being practised, as we have seen. Political economy reached its classical age a full century before sociology. Yet earlier, Hobbes and Montesquieu had set out to analyze society with the methods of the natural sciences in mind.

1. The Bourgeois Revolution and the Conservative Thesis

Sociology might, however, be said to introduce a systematic concern with social order – in a reaction against the individualism of the Enlightenment and the declarations of the Rights of Man. Sociology might be seen as part of or at least intimately connected to a counter-revolutionary conservatism.

In this respect there exists an interesting thesis, argued by conservative as well as by radical critics, that the origins of sociology

[11] Smith, *Wealth of Nations* (Cannan ed.), vol. II, p. 294. Smith's attitude was not mere sour grapes; as a well-established Scottish university professor, he had no need of envy.

were conservative. Its main spokesman is the American sociologist Robert Nisbet, who himself belongs to the former category.[12] He has propounded his thesis for over two decades in a number of essays, culminating in a very fine book, *The Sociological Tradition*. The 'Sociological Tradition' consists of five 'unit-ideas' or foci of concern – community, authority, status, the sacred, and alienation. The tradition developed as response to the problems of order raised by the democratic (French) and industrial revolutions. The gist of Nisbet's argument may be conveyed by the following quotation:

'The paradox of sociology – and it is, as I argue in these pages, a creative paradox – lies in the fact that although it falls, in its objectives and in the political and scientific values of its principal figures, in the mainstream of modernism, its essential concepts and its implicit perspectives place it much closer, generally speaking, to philosophical conservatism. Community, authority, tradition, the sacred: these are primary conservative preoccupations in the age, to be seen vividly in the intellectual line that reaches from Bonald and Haller to Burckhardt and Taine. So are presentiments of alienation, of totalitarian power rising from mass democracy, and of cultural decay. One will look in vain for significant impact of these ideas and presentiments on the serious interests of economists, political scientists, psychologists, and ethnologists in the age. But in sociology they are – transfigured of course, by rationalist or scientific *objectives* of the sociologists – at the very core of the discipline.'[13]

Undoubtedly Nisbet here grasps something of the tenor of sociological discourse, from the blending of industrialism and mediaevalism in Saint-Simon, to Max Weber's cultural despair at the 'iron cage' of developed capitalism (to which he was nevertheless committed because it was an expression of modern rational culture).[14] Nisbet's choice and treatment of his sociological unit-ideas might be questioned. The decisive objection to his and similar conceptions, however, is that they present the scientific objectives

[12] Other authors, of rather different ideological orientation, who have been considerably influenced by Nisbet in this respect, are, L. Bramson, *The Political Context of Sociology*. Princeton, 1961, and I. Zeitlin, *Ideology and the Development of Sociology*, Englewood Cliffs, 1968.

[13] R. Nisbet, *The Sociological Tradition*, London, 1967, p. 17f.

[14] See, for example, the famous ending of Weber's *The Protestant Ethic and the Spirit of Capitalism*.

of sociologists as unproblematic. For our concern here is with the meaning of these objectives and with the achievements they represent – in other words, the contribution of sociology to a science of society.

On the whole, interpretations of the emergence of sociology which counterpose individualism and concern for social order do not take us very far and easily become misleading. Herbert Spencer, for instance, held an organic conception of society, but he was at the same time an arch-individualist, whom it is hardly possible to delete from the annals of sociology.

So far as social order is concerned, even Comte in the days of his letters to Tsar Nicholas and to Reshid Pasha hardly surpassed that pre-sociological theorist of society, Thomas Hobbes,[15] who wrote his *Leviathan* against the background of the Civil War between the monarchy and parliament in the 1640's. There was no doubt a strong individualist current of thought in the Enlightenment and even earlier, in the 17th century. It typically used classical natural law theory to stress natural rights rather than emphasise natural duties.[16] But this form of individualism should not be interpreted in the light of more familiar modern theories. In particular, it should not be seen as a version of nineteenth century liberalism or a kind of classical or neo-classical political economy writ large. The crucial role of Hobbes, a defender of absolutism, in these individualist doctrines of natural law should warn us against any such facile interpretations.[17]

Further, even more telling evidence against the assumption that

[15] Comte's notorious letters to Czar Nicholas and the Grand-Vizier of the Ottoman Empire, offering his doctrine as the best theory of conservatism, are reproduced by the author in the preface to *Système de politique positive*, Paris, 1853, III, pp. xxix–l; *System of Positive Polity*, London, 1876, vol. III, pp. xxiv–xliv.

[16] L. Strauss, *Natural Right and History*, Chicago, 1953, p. 182. Cf. L. Crocker, *Nature and Culture : Ethical Thought in the Enlightenment*, Baltimore, 1963, ch. 1.

[17] Strauss locates the change in Hobbes on the basis of the proposition from which Hobbes deduces his defence of absolutism: 'The finall Cause, End or Designe of men (who naturally love Liberty and Dominion over others) in the introduction of that restraint upon themselves (in which wee see them live in Common-wealths), is the foresight of their own preservation, and of a more contented life thereby.' T. Hobbes, *Leviathan*, London, 1972, p. 223. With shrewd but belated insight, the reactionary university of Oxford condemned Hobbes and his book posthumously in 1683 for this individualism (see the excellent introduction by C. B. McPherson, p. 21).

the Enlightenment was individualist in a liberal sense, is to be found in the virtually universal admiration for classical antiquity among the *philosophes*. The Enlightenment was strongly attracted by tradition and by collectivist traditions at that. It turned to an antique-pagan heritage, instead of a mediaeval-christian heritage such as became important to 19th century conservatism. Marcus Tullius Cicero, the stern politician and philosopher of the Roman Republic, was the 'real favourite' of the *philosophes* who esteemed Ancient culture.[18] The austere public virtues of Sparta, the Roman Republic, and even the Roman Empire at its zenith, were the social ideals of many of the *philosophes*, not a freewheeling individualism.

The classical ideal of a public-spirited community was shared by theorists from one end to the other of the political spectrum. Montesquieu, who was not only an admirer of the English constitution but also a proud defender of the French nobility,[19] emphasized it as much as the Whigs Adam Ferguson and Edward Gibbon, or radicals like Mably and Rousseau.[20]

They differed, however, as to the contemporary relevance of this ideal. A republic governed by virtue was one of the forms of government Montesquieu distinguished in *L'Esprit des Lois*, but though he held that when virtue prevailed in the ancient republics men 'performed actions unusual in our times, and at which our narrow minds are astonished',[21] he regarded the virtuous republic as irredeemably a thing of the past, irrelevant to the present.[22] With some qualifications, the same can be said of Ferguson and Gibbon. Ferguson, living through the first great boom of Scottish capitalism (then thriving on the trade with American plantations), had a

[18] P. Gay, *The Enlightenment I: The Rise of Modern Paganism*, London, 1967, p. 105f, and passim.

[19] Montesquieu's aristocratic stand can be found in Book XXX of *L'Esprit des Lois*. There exists a modern biography of Montesquieu, probably the single most influential writer of the Enlightenment, R. Shackleton's *Montesquieu*, Oxford, 1961.

[20] Ferguson, Gibbon, and Montesquieu all wrote histories of Rome: Gibbon's monumental *The History of the Decline and Fall of the Roman Empire* is still of wide intellectual interest; the *History of the Progress and Termination of the Roman Republic* by Ferguson, and Montesquieu's *Considerations on the Causes of the Greatness of the Romans and their Decline*, are now forgotten.

[21] Montesquieu, *De l'esprit des lois*, Paris, 1970, p. 79; *The Spirit of Laws*, Chicago and London, 1952, Book IV, ch. 2, p. 14.

[22] Shackleton, op. cit., pp. 272–7.

notably clear conception of the reasons for the obsoleteness of ancient virtues: 'We live in societies where men must be rich, in order to be great; where pleasure itself is often pursued from vanity; where the desire of a supposed happiness serves to inflame the worst passions, and is itself the foundation of misery; where public justice, like fetters applied to the body, may, without inspiriting the sentiments of candour and equity, prevent the actual commission of crimes.'[23]

The same reasons which for Ferguson and other well-adjusted intellectuals made Spartan and Roman virtues at most a nostalgic cultural ideal, made them a political necessity for radicals like Rousseau and Mably. The republics of Rome and, above all, Sparta were constantly invoked by Rousseau as standards for damning comparison with contemporary reality. It is from the point of view of Sparta – 'eternal proof of the vanity of science' – that Rousseau in his first Discourse on the Arts and Sciences seeks to defend virtue.[24] In the *Discourse on Inequality* the Spartan lawgiver Lycurgus is presented as the model of a revolutionary politician.[25] Constructing, in *The Social Contract*, the principles of an altogether new society, Rousseau again takes his materials – on constitutions, voting, censorship, dictatorship, and religion – largely from Rome

[23] A. Ferguson, *An Essay on the History of Civil Society*, Edinburgh, 1966, pp. 161–2. Ferguson's politics are discussed in D. Kettler, *The Social and Political Thought of Adam Ferguson*, Ohio, 1965, ch. IV, and p. 258f. Gibbon, who cautiously attributed the decline and fall of Rome partly to Christianity's weakening of the civil and military spirit, considered the Roman experience relevant to current politics in a very special sense: Europeans should learn from Rome to stick together against the non-European savage peoples: 'The savage nations of the globe are the common enemies of civilized society.' Gibbon, op. cit. (Bury ed., London, 1896–1900, in VII vols.), vol. IV, p. 163f.

[24] J.-J. Rousseau, 'Discourse on the Arts and Sciences', in *The Social Contract*, London, 1955, p. 126.

[25] J.-J. Rousseau, 'A Discourse on the Origin of Inequality among Men', ibid., p. 207. The subjectivist, pre-sociological character of Rousseau's politics casts doubt on Lucio Colletti's claim that Rousseau developed a political theory to which 'Marx and Lenin have added nothing . . . except for the analysis . . . of the "economic bases" of the withering away of the State', *From Rousseau to Lenin*, London, 1972, p. 185. Colletti focuses on Rousseau's conception of popular sovereignty and critique of the representative state. See further Colletti's answer to a critical question about the importance of Rousseau's political theory in 'A Political and Philosophical Interview', *New Left Review* 86 (July–August, 1974), pp. 14–15.

and Sparta.[26] The most influential work of Mably, in his time a highly respected French radical, is likewise cast in the form of a dialogue in which the correct answers are those of Phoicon, an Athenian admirer of Sparta.[27]

This inclination to civic moralism coexisted with strong utilitarian tendencies in the Enlightenment – evident in the work of Locke, Helvétius, Voltaire, and many others who had little regard for Spartan virtues.[28] But it was Rousseau, Mably and their ilk who were the inspirers of the radical revolutionaries of 1789 and therefore the *philosophes* most hated by later counter-revolutionary thinkers.[29] Robespierre, who broke a bust of Helvétius at the Jacobin club, declared himself a disciple of Rousseau and Mably. 'The fundamental principle of democratic and popular government,' Robespierre said in February 1794, 'is virtue. I am speaking of public virtue, which worked such prodigies in Greece and Rome.'[30] Thus sociology can not be adequately portrayed as a reaction against the radical individualism of the Enlightenment.

2. The New Politics of a New World

Before sociology there existed two rather specialized types of discourses on society, political economy and political theory (philosophy). The former, which had a rather unspectacular existence in 19th century France, did not loom large in the first generation of sociological writings. In no case was sociology seen as especially related to political economy, either positively or negatively.

Comte and Saint-Simon knew and appreciated Adam Smith's economic work, and they were considerably influenced by the 'vulgar economist' (Marx's term), Jean-Baptiste Say, who had

[26] J.-J. Rousseau, *The Social Contract*, book II, ch. 4; book IV, chs. 4–8.

[27] Mably, *Entretiens de Phoicon sur le rapport de la morale avec la politique*, Paris, 1792. A brief sketch of Mably is given in C. Vereker, *Eighteenth Century Optimism*, Liverpool, 1967, p. 250f.

[28] Crocker, op. cit., ch. 5, gives an exposition of 18th century utilitarianism, from the point of view of ethical theory.

[29] In his introduction to a current French edition of *The Social Contract* (Paris, 1963) Henri Guillemin has put together a whole bouquet of poisonous tributes to Rousseau from French conservative thinkers (p. 32f), including a belated one from the Archbishop of Paris, who in 1924 condemned Rousseau as 'born vicious and died mad' and as one who brought 'more evil to France than the blasphemies of Voltaire and all the *Encyclopédistes*' (p. 38).

[30] A. Soboul, *Histoire de la révolution française*, Paris, 1962, vol. 2, p. 168f.

polemically emphasized the importance of the industrial entrepreneurs as against the agricultural capitalists praised by the
physiocrats. Saint-Simon could write: 'Mr. Say has taken a step
forward from Smith's philosophy: he establishes that political
economy is distinct from and independent of politics; he says that
the former science has a base of its own, a base completely different
from that of the science which deals with the organization of nations.'[31] Saint-Simon went on to advocate the propagation of
political economy, but he never bothered to master the independent
system of political economy or to pursue any economic analysis
himself. The argument just quoted in fact ushers in a number of
political considerations: the *industriels* constitute the real social
force in contemporary society, therefore they ought to possess
political power, and the problem is how is this to be achieved. In
Saint-Simon's economic studies his secretary Comte – who unlike
his master had an academic training (cut short, though, when the
whole Ecole Polytechnique was dismissed for having rallied to
Napoleon during the hundred days) – seems to have played a
strategic role. According to Comte's letters part of his job was to
'do political economy' for Saint-Simon.[32] In his own works Comte
acknowledged that political economy had contributed some 'useful
preliminary elucidations' and had directed his attention to industrial
affairs. However, Comte was very hostile to the 'supposed science'
of economics for its narrow view of social organization and its
laissez-faire bias.[33]

Spencer defended the laws of political economy against those
who attacked them.[34] But he did not regard them as being of
particular importance. In the enormous corpus of Spencer's
'synthetic philosophy' no space is allotted to a systematic exposition
or treatment of economics.[35] He made use of the economists'

[31] H. Saint-Simon, 'L'Industrie', in *Oeuvres*, vol. II, Paris, 1966, p. 156. (As
the *Oeuvres* edition, a reprint of the 1869 edition, has no continuous pagination,
the page refers to the original publication by Saint-Simon.)

[32] F. Manuel, *The New World of Henri Saint-Simon*, Cambridge, Mass., 1956,
p. 206. Comte's statement is corroborated in the acknowledgement by Saint-
Simon, op. cit., p. 157 n.

[33] A. Comte, *Cours de philosophie positive*, Paris, 1908, IV, pp. 138–46. *The
Positive Philosophy of Comte*, II, pp. 203–8.

[34] E.g. H. Spencer, *The Study of Sociology*, London, 1881, p. 150f.

[35] This is also the case with his exposition of economic, or as Spencer calls them,
industrial institutions in part VIII of his *Principles of Sociology*.

emphasis on the division of labour – and on exchange – in his own evolutionary scheme. He believed he had taken this emphasis from physiology, which in turn had borrowed it from political economy, but Spencer did not regard the ideas of biologists as having been taken from economics as a distinct science of society.[36]

Sociology's relationship to political economy does not, then, appear to provide a very fruitful theoretical starting-point for an analysis of its emergence. Embarking upon their new intellectual enterprise, the first generation of sociologists did not see it as primarily consisting in either a critique or a continuation of political economy. This is most conspicuous of all in Tocqueville, from whose work such considerations are virtually completely absent. Early sociological discourse was thus not even implicitly tied to a discourse on the market.

The situation with regard to political theory or political philosophy was different. The development of a political science and a political system corresponding to the demands of the new century was a central and explicit aim of Saint-Simon. In this perspective economists were seen as theorists of the industrial state, their main object being to 'consider a national association as an industrial enterprise, whose object is to procure for every member of society, in proportion to his contribution, as much comfort and welfare as possible.'[37]

The objective of Comte, set out systematically for the first time in his *Plan des travaux scientifiques nécessaires pour réorganiser la société*, was a positive science of politics.[38] Comte used the expressions social science, sociology, political philosophy and political science interchangeably,[39] and one of his most important works is entitled *Système de politique positive*. His contemporary Tocqueville, the student of *Democracy in America* and *The Ancien Regime and the*

---

[36] Spencer, *The Study of Sociology*, p. 334f.

[37] It is developed in his periodicals *L'Industrie* and *L'organisateur* in *Oeuvres*, vol. II. The quote is from *L'Industrie*, p. 153 (italics omitted).

[38] First published in 1824 under the title 'Système de politique positive' in Saint-Simon's *Catéchisme des industriels*, and as such included in the latter's *Oeuvres*, vol. IV. The mode of publication of Comte's essay led to a break between Comte and Saint-Simon. The story is told by Manuel, op. cit., ch. 29, and from a different angle by Comte's biographer Henri Gouhier, *La vie d'Auguste Comte*, Paris, 1965, p. 106f. Comte appended the essay, under the title of a draft from 1822, given above in the text, to his *Système de politique positive*, vol. IV.

[39] E.g. Comte, *Cours de philosophie positive*, IV, pp. 127, 132, 271.

French Revolution, concluded from his studies that 'a new political science is needed for a new world'.[40] Though he did not adopt Comte's neologism 'sociology', Tocqueville clearly belongs to the first generation of sociologists, because of his basically similar conception of a new political science.

Spencer, however, did not define his own sociology as a science of politics. For him it was part of a philosophy of universal evolution and of a search for a scientific basis for ethics. But in a very immediate sense his sociology was also an expression of the 'anti-political' politics of English middle-class provincial radicalism in the mid 19th century, which took its stand on nonconformism (the religious component of which had now faded), naturalism, and laissez-faire.[41] A strategic concern of his social theory was indicated by the telling title of his first published book, a collection of letters to the dissident Protestant paper *The Nonconformist*. It was called *The Proper Sphere of Government*. (In Spencer's opinion that sphere was tiny indeed.) He stuck to the world sociology, in spite of its by now embarrassing associations with Comte.[42] In the preface to his *Principles of Sociology*, 'politics' was considered as an alternative, but was dismissed as 'too narrow in its meaning, as well as misleading in its connotations'.[43] It was when discussing political institutions in *Principles of Sociology* and in earlier essays, that he made his central theoretical distinction between militant and industrial societies.

Political theory thus seems to be the real intellectual background against which sociology's claim to represent a new science of society should be analyzed – more particularly, the background of previous attempts at a scientific discourse on politics. In the present framework there is no room for a systematic historical survey of the development of political theory. An *a priori* choice of noteworthy theorists must therefore be made, which it is hoped will not be unduly arbitrary. The chosen few selected here will be Macchiavelli, Hobbes, Locke, and Montesquieu. Some special attention will be paid to the 'proto-sociological' Scots, Adam Ferguson and John Millar. In order to deal with the 'Conservative Thesis' of the origins

[40] A. de Tocqueville, *De la démocratie en Amérique*, Paris, 1951, vol. I, p. 5.

[41] Peel, op. cit., esp. ch. 3.

[42] For the uneasy relationship of Spencer to Comte see R. A. Jones, 'Comte and Spencer: A Priority Dispute in Social Science', *Journal of the History of the Behavioral Sciences*, 6, 1970, pp. 241–54.

[43] H. Spencer, *Principles of Sociology*, New York, 1897, vol. I: 1, p. ix.

of sociology, the principal philosophers of counter-revolutionary reaction, de Maistre and de Bonald, to whose intellectual powers both Comte and Saint-Simon paid generous tribute, will be taken into consideration too.[44] No detailed presentation of these theorists will be given. Our concern here is simply to explore the question of whether there is any critical difference – with reference to the definition of science set out earlier – between the conception of politics in the early sociologists and in these political philosophers. If so, in what does it consist? Sociology will be seen to emerge as a study of *politics after the bourgeois revolution*.

3. The Working Class and the Socialist Thesis

So far, however, we have only dealt with the start of the age of sociology. Sociology is still with us, and in spite of the increasing frequency with which the word 'crisis' has been attached to it, no end is in sight. Nevertheless, there is a limited set of problems with which sociology has been pre-eminently concerned, and which give us the possibility of delimiting an 'age of sociology'. To discern it we must define what sociology strove towards from the outset.

Central to its preoccupations were problems of politics and political reconstruction; but there was also 'the social question', or as it was often put in the USA, 'social problems'. The social question was part of the sociological tradition from the beginning, and it was of paramount importance in its establishment as an institutionalized discipline.

A characteristic concern of sociology throughout its development has been the condition of the lower classes of society: their poverty, their work or lack of work, their leisure, their housing, their health, their morality, their delinquency, and so on. This was no less the case in the establishment of American sociology, in spite of the

---

[44] Comte, *Cours de philosophie positive*, IV, p. 14 (English ed., II, p. 145f): *Système de politique positive*, p. 614f (English ed., III, p. 527f). Saint-Simon had more appreciation of de Bonald ('Introduction to the Scientific Studies of the 19th Century', in F. Markham, ed., Henri de Saint-Simon, *Social Organization, the Science of Man and other Writings*, New York, 1964, pp. 14–18; *Oeuvres*, VI, pp. 167f). In the reference above, Manuel's way of quoting Saint-Simon's enthusiastic admiration for the theoretical powers of de Bonald (Manuel, op. cit., p. 389) does not adequately convey to the reader that Saint-Simon's objective in the chapter in question is to refute de Bonald's view of the role of religion (*Oeuvres*, VI, p. 158).

laissez-faire influence of Spencer.

'The only early department of sociology that did not originate in connection with charities, philanthropy and reform, was at Yale because of Sumner's negative views on these matters', writes Anthony Oberschall in a penetrating essay on the early history of American sociology. Oberschall also makes it clear that philanthropic sociology was not absent at Yale either. 'Philanthropy, social economics, and social reform were offered in the Yale Divinity School's Department of Christian Sociology.'[45]

The investigation of the situation of the proletariat and of other impoverished social strata has always been a major subject of empirical social research and of sociology, although its lengthy history was generally forgotten until recently. There were important early works in this tradition apart from Charles Booth's survey of the London poor at the turn of the last century, and Le Play's studies of European workers of about half century before. There existed, for example, the work of the British statistical societies of the 1830's, along with Parent-Duchatelet's study of prostitution in Paris and Villermé's study of workers during the French July Monarchy, and even Sir Frederick Morton Eden's *The State of the Poor* of 1797.[46]

Only later did this tradition of empirical investigation effect a juncture with the development of sociological theory. However, they shared from the beginning a common interest and concern. The social question became the main problem for Saint-Simon in his later years. He announced that his aim was 'to ameliorate the lot of this class [the working-class] not only in France, but in England . . . in the rest of Europe and the whole world'.[47] He wrote an open letter to 'Messieurs les Ouvriers',[48] and in his last work, *Le Nouveau Christianisme*, he asserted: 'The whole of society should work to

---

[45] A. Oberschall, 'The institutionalization of American sociology', in Oberschall, op. cit., p. 212. The general American intellectual background is portrayed by R. Hofstadter, *The Age of Reform*, New York, 1960.

[46] An overview of this tradition of empirical social research is given in the article 'Sociology: Early History of Social Research', by B. Lécuyer and A. Oberschall, in *International Encyclopedia of the Social Sciences*, New York, 1968. Cf. P. Lazarsfeld, 'Notes on the History of Quantification in Sociology', *ISIS* 52, 2, June 1961. Lazarsfeld is directing a large-scale research project on the history and development of empirical sociology.

[47] H. Saint-Simon, 'Du système industriel II', p. 81, *Oeuvres*, vol. III.

[48] In *Oeuvres*, vol. VI.

ameliorate the moral and physical existence of the poorest class; society should be organized in a manner most suited to attaining this great end.'[49] In the *Communist Manifesto* he is included, with respect, among the critical-utopian socialists, and much later Engels was even to write that 'nearly all the ideas of later socialists that are not strictly economic are found in him in embryo'.[50]

Comte, for his part, also came to notice that 'the growth of industry . . . naturally brought to the front the great question of modern times, the incorporation of the proletariat into society, which had been ignored so long as the anomalous interval of warfare [*anomalie guerrière*] had lasted'.[51] He professed sympathy with some of the aims of socialism and communism and stated that his positivism adhered to 'the spontaneous principle of communism; namely that property is in its nature social, and that it needs control'. He criticized the economists for their interdiction of the regulation of property.[52]

Spencer, of course, as a laissez-faire ultra was an odd man out in the company of such social reformers, though in his writings on state and society he had to deal with the actual existence of the social question, if only to develop a more and more extreme reaction against the solutions suggested to it.[53] The Marquis de Tocqueville, a large number of whose relatives had been guillotined during the French Revolution, was for all his perspicacity too obsessed with the anti-aristocratic revolution to be able to devote any systematic attention to what Comte called 'the modern question'.[54]

[49] Saint-Simon, 'Le Nouveau Christianisme', p. 173, *Oeuvres*, vol. III.

[50] F. Engels, 'Socialism; Utopian and Scientific', Marx and Engels, *Selected Works*, Moscow n.d., p. 400; *MEW* 19, p. 196. The context, where Engels talks of the limitations imposed upon Saint-Simon, strongly qualifies this well-known statement.

[51] Comte, *Système de politique positive*, III, p. 610 (English ed., III, p. 523).

[52] Ibid., I, p. 154f.

[53] In certain late writings there is however, even in Spencer, a clear and sad awareness of the social problems of capitalism, absent from the simple models of competitive commodity production. See below ch. 5.

[54] In his introduction to *Democracy in America* (pp. 6–7), Tocqueville says à propos this revolution: 'The whole book that is here offered to the public has been written under the influence of a kind of religious awe produced in the author's mind by the view of that irresistible revolution which has advanced for centuries in spite of every obstacle and which is still advancing in the midst of the ruins it has caused.' During the 1848 revolution Tocqueville witnessed the new class struggle, as his vivid *Recollections* (London, 1970) show. But its effect on his

Durkheim, on the other hand, the key figure in the later French institutionalization of sociology, was acutely aware of the social problems involved in the 'abnormal forms' of the contemporary capitalist division of labour. The last part of his first major work, *The Division of Labour in Society*, was to be devoted to a critical exposure of these aberrant forms, whose negative effects on the situation of workers endangered and undermined social solidarity. In his preface to the second edition, Durkheim – for all his avowed scientism – went so far as to advocate a concrete (albeit utopian) solution to the social problem, in the form of a corporatist arrangement of occupational groups.

In Germany the focal organization of the period in which sociology was established was the *Verein für Sozialpolitik* (Social Policy Association), founded in 1873. It sponsored a large number of studies on economic and social matters and acted as an intellectual, later an overwhelmingly academic, forum of social reform. The German Society for Sociology developed out of it in 1909 as an exclusively scientific society, but not as a hostile or competing organization. Leading German sociologists such as Ferdinand Tönnies and Max Weber were members of both.[55]

4. The Social Question in the New Society

The social concerns of these sociologists betray a difference between them and even the more radical thinkers of the Enlightenment which is rarely noticed. The scale of human misery was in significant respects larger in the new period, its causes and its forms in many ways distinct and novel. But poverty, of course, was an old phenomenon, and so was philanthropy. Nevertheless, there now occurred an interesting shift of perspective in the application of social theory to the traditional problems of inequality.

scholarship seems very limited, as can be seen from the foreword of his second major work, *The Ancien Regime and The French Revolution*, London, 1971, esp. p. 29.

[55] About the *Verein* see D. Lindenlaub, *Richtungskämpfe im Verein für Sozialpolitik*, Wiesbaden, 1967. Albion Small, the chief organizer among the classical American sociologists and the head of the then leading sociology department in Chicago, was among the admirers of the *Verein* and presented it as a model to be emulated. See A. Small, *The Meaning of Social Science*, Chicago 1910, p. 269f. There is a monograph on early social research in Germany, as part of Lazarsfeld's project, in A. Oberschall, *Empirical Social Research in Germany, 1848–1914*, The Hague, 1965.

The intellectuals of the Enlightenment were by and large theorists of the bourgeois revolution, and it is in that perspective that they examined inequality and class. They had two predominant preoccupations. One of them related to what has been aptly called 'formally free labour': in other words the campaign for the abolition of slavery, and the attack on serfdom, whose result was, in the words of the congenial historian of the *philosophes* Peter Gay – that 'even the labouring poor came to be regarded as human beings with real feelings and a right to subsistence'.[56]

The final chapter of one of the most important proto-sociological treatises of the eighteenth century, John Millar's *The Origin of the Distinction of Ranks*, is called 'Masters and Servants' and is devoted to contemporary problems of class. In his time and context Millar was relatively radical, but he shows no awareness of what was to become 'the social question' even for conservative Prussian scholars a century later, and in the end even for a liberal ultra like Herbert Spencer. Millar attacks slavery in American colonies and also, with a courage lacking in Adam Smith, in Scottish collieries, proclaiming: 'In the history of mankind, there is no revolution of greater importance to the happiness of society than this which we have now had occasion to contemplate (i.e., the abolition of slavery). The laws and customs of the modern European nations have carried the advantages of liberty to a height, which was never known in any other age or country. In the ancient states, so celebrated upon account of their free government, the bulk of their mechanics and labouring people were denied the common principles of men and treated upon the footing of inferior animals.'[57] So far, so good; but that is all.

The second and more radical main idea of the time is to be found in another famous Enlightenment discourse on inequality, that of Rousseau. Rousseau was a democrat, a social critic living in an absolutist monarchy, with no Glorious Revolution to defend. He saw glaring inequality before him, and denounced it. 'It is plainly

[56] Gay, op. cit., II, p. 39. On the abolitionist campaign, see p. 407f. As a whole, the *philosophes* were less concerned with serfdom, the mode of economic organization in the countries of the 'enlightened despots', Catherine of Russia and Frederick II of Prussia.

[57] The full text of Millar's *The Origin of the Distinction of Ranks*, as well as other selections, is included in W. Lehmann, *John Millar of Glasgow*, Cambridge, 1960 (quotation, p. 315).

contrary to the law of nature . . . that the privileged few should gorge themselves with superfluities, while the starving multitude are in want of the bare necessities of life.' That certainly has a modern ring. But for the reference to the law of nature, it might have been written in the age of reform in the late 19th century. The point is, however, that in Rousseau as well as in his contemporaries and co-thinkers, the political stress is on the first term of the inequality, the luxury and overabundance of the rich, not on the misery or vicious effects of poverty. Rousseau's discourse on inequality is structured by the contrast between the virtuous simplicity of a state of nature and the vicious opulence of civil society. 'Luxury is a remedy much worse than the disease it sets up to cure; or rather it is in itself the greatest of all evils, for every state, great or small: for in order to maintain all the servants and vagabonds it creates, it brings oppression and ruin on the citizen and the labourer.'[58] Luxury corrupts rich and poor alike, 'one by possession, the other by desire (*convoitise*)'. Hence Rousseau emphasizes in *The Social Contract* that a democratic state must be small, egalitarian and poor.[59]

This concentration on the opulent and luxurious side of inequality is also evident in the social criticism of the worldly *salon* host Baron d'Holbach, who lashed out in the third part of his *Système Social* against wealth, ostentation, and idleness. The same focus is to be found in the most radical – even more or less socialist – tracts of the time, in Mably's *Entretiens de Phoicon*, in Morelly's *Code de la Nature*, and in Meslier's *Testament*.[60]

The argument was based on moral philosophy. To Meslier

[58] *Discourse on the Origin of Inequality*, Rousseau, op. cit., p. 227; cf. p. 202f. The same theme is developed much more emphatically in Rousseau's first Discourse, *Discourse on the Arts and Sciences*. But within his particular scheme, Rousseau could have a sharp eye for the situation of the common people, noting, for example, the dangerous working conditions in the preparation of materials (loc. cit.).

[59] Rousseau, op. cit., pp. 37–8, 42–3. This specifically 18th century egalitarianism seems to undermine another claim for the modernity of Rousseau, in terms of a socialist, non-levelling egalitarianism, made by another Italian Marxist philosopher, Galvano Della Volpe, *Rousseau et Marx et autres essais de critique matérialiste*, Paris, 1974, pp. 55–195.

[60] The revolutionary priest Meslier, whose Testament was divulged in extracts long after his death by Voltaire and d'Holbach, is the subject of an interesting monographic study by M. Dommanget, *Le curé Meslier*, Paris, 1965.

inequality was odious 'because, on the one hand, it inspires and sustains ostentation, vainglory, ambition, vanity, arrogance and pride, while, on the other hand, it engenders hatred, envy, anger, desire for vengeance, complaints and murmurs, all passions which become source and cause of an infinitude of evil and wickedness committed in the world'.[61]

The historical situation was thus one in which what seemed to be the 'social question' was not the misery and exploitation of a proletariat but the corrupt rule of a rakish court and aristocracy. 'Before the Revolution, the social question did not exist in the sense in which we understand it today [this was written in 1899]; the reforms demanded by the States-General make no allusion to it.'[62]

There is, in fact, also a 'Socialist Thesis' of the origins of sociology, that presents it as a close relative of socialism. Belief in a relationship between sociology (or social science in general) and socialism has a long history, among friends as well as foes of the pair in question. Already Lorenz Stein, the young German academic who in the early 1840's made a remarkable study of the social question and the socialist movement in France, and was strongly impressed by Saint-Simonism, considered that socialism 'belonged to the field of the social sciences'.[63] The *Verein für Sozialpolitik* housed a *Kathedersozialismus*, and in France in the same period a *socialisme universitaire*, which even included members of actual socialist parties, was part of Durkheim's milieu.[64] Among modern friends the Socialist Thesis has been put forward by Alvin Gouldner, pointing to the founding role of Saint-Simon.[65]

[61] Ibid., p. 275.

[62] These words are from André Lichtenberger, the French historian of socialistic ideas before and during the French Revolution, *Le socialisme et la révolution française*, Paris, 1899, p. 291.

[63] L. Stein, *The Social Movement in France*, Totowa, N.J., 1964, p. 278.

[64] On French university socialism there are two interesting inside accounts, mixing poisonous polemic with personal recollections, by Hubert Bourgin (a disciple of Durkheim, in turn socialist and later chauvinist, anti-semitic rightwinger and finally Nazi collaborator), *De Jaurès à Léon Blum, L'Ecole Normale et la politique*, Paris, 1970 (1st ed. 1938); *Le socialisme universitaire*, Paris, 1942. See now the recent full-scale biography of Durkheim, S. Lukes, *Emile Durkheim, His Life and Work*, London, 1973, esp. ch. 17.

[65] In Gouldner's introduction to the 1958 Antioch Press edition of Durkheim's *Socialism*, reprinted in his collection of essays, *For Sociology*, London, 1973, pp. 369–91. The thesis is restated, in considerably more complicated and attenuated form, in *The Coming Crisis of Western Sociology*, pp. 88–111: Saint-Simon is

In the ranks of the powerful and the privileged, there have been many adherents of the Socialist Thesis. Lester Ward's *Dynamic Sociology* was burnt in Russia by the Tsarist censors, reportedly because they read the title as Dynamite Socialism.[66] To avoid the risk of any similar fate, when anti-communist persecution was intensifying in the United States towards 1950, certain American scholars – Bernard Berelson, Ralph Tyler and others – and – certain foundations such as those of Ford and Russel Sage replaced the embarrassing term 'social science' with the safer 'behavioral science'.[67]

5. The Sociologists and the Class Struggle

'Socialism' is an extremely loose designation, which can cover a whole panorama of social systems, from monarchical paternalism and fascism, through capitalist welfare-states to more or less proletarian dictatorships attempting to build a classless society. A century and a quarter ago Marx and Engels, in *The Communist Manifesto*, distinguished six different and opposed types of 'socialism', and new uses and abuses of the word have been added to the list since then. Below we will try to trace the location of early and classical sociologists and the development of their ideas in the social struggles of their time.

However, the nature of sociology's concern with the condition of the lower classes and strata in society indicates the common boundaries of the sociological vista, the unsurpassable limits of sociological commitment: the proletarian revolution. The age of sociology can thus be delimited between two poles – after the bourgeois revolution and before the proletarian revolution.

Whatever one's view of the class struggle or the proletarian revolution, whatever one's opinion of the desirability or actuality of the latter today, the fact is indisputable that in the development of

---

presented as the founding father of both socialism and Western sociology, after whose death there followed a 'binary fission' of sociology into Academic Sociology and Marxism.

[66] The story is told by Ward himself, with excerpts from his Russian correspondence, in the preface to the 2nd ed. of his *Dynamic Sociology*, p. xiif.

[67] This piece of sociological history has been treated in a fitting context, the *Journal of the History of the Behavioral Sciences*, by P. Seen, 'What is "Behavioral Sciences"?', 2 (1966), pp. 107–22.

the social concerns of sociology the 'red' revolution was a very real historical spectre. It could be seen in broad daylight in Paris in 1848 and 1871, in Saint Petersburg in 1905, in the Russian October revolution, in Germany in 1918–19, in Italy in 1920–21. It could be heard from the tribunes and in the programme of the working-class movement throughout Europe.

The revolutionary proletariat haunted even the American sociologists of the classical era. Today this may sound incredible, but in the period of the Haymarket and Homestead massacres, the Pullman strike and other violent class struggles, when the American labour movement was rapidly developing, it was only natural. In the *American Journal of Sociology* Albion Small assimilated militant America trade unions to 'Russian Nihilism' and 'German Social-ism',[68] while Charles Ellwood warned against the possibility of a new civil war, between 'the capitalistic and the wage-earning classes'.[69] The American Sociological Society devoted a session in 1907 to discussing class conflict in the United States.[70]

The decade of the rise of classical sociology, the 1890's, was at the same time the decade of the rapid rise of the labour movement. In 1889 the Second International had been formed. The proletarian revolution cast different shadows over different sociologists and different sociologies, but when the die were cast all sociologists knew which side of the barricades they were on.

In June 1848, when the national workshops were dissolved, the Parisian workers rebelled against the bourgeois government that had emerged from the February Revolution. Tocqueville the politician-cum-sociologist, the Legitimist who had turned Orleanist after the July Revolution and Republican after the overthrow of the July Monarchy, was among the main organizers of the violent suppression of the workers.[71] The more plebeian Comte, with his aspirations for social reconstruction, had some sympathy for the workers against the bourgeois politicians and their generals, but he

[68] A. Small, 'The Scope of Sociology VI', *American Journal of Sociology*, vol. VI (1900–1), p. 366.

[69] C. Ellwood, 'A Psychological Study of Revolutions', *American Journal of Sociology*, vol. XI (1905–6), pp. 58–9.

[70] *American Journal of Sociology*, vol. XIII (1907–8), p. 756f.

[71] Tocqueville, *Recollections*, p. 136. Tocqueville self-critically confides to his memoirs, not intended for publication, that he did not distinguish himself by any military resoluteness in the suppression of the insurrectionary proletariat.

condemned the 'reds', 'the monkeys of the great revolution'. The full meaning of his stand – he was completely detached from the actual events – became clear somewhat later when he rallied to Louis Bonaparte. Comte was for the republic and against parliamentary politicians, but in the final analysis everything, even the Bourbon pretender, was preferable to red tyranny.[72]

No sociologists were at hand during the Paris Commune in 1871, though one can hear echoes of it in Durkheim's *Division of Labour in Society*, where the author refers to 'class wars', civil wars which occur 'due to the manner in which labour is distributed'.[73] We can probably catch a glimpse of what Durkheim thought were its lessons in his account of the tasks of a teacher of philosophy, which is what Durkheim himself was when he wrote it: 'To the teacher of philosophy also belongs the task of awakening in the minds that are entrusted to his care the concept of law; of making them understand that mental and social phenomena are like any other phenomena, subject to laws that the human will cannot upset simply by willing, and therefore that *revolutions*, taking the word literally, *are as*

[72] Gouhier, op. cit., p. 218f. Comte's opinions on the threat of a communist revolution are expounded in *Système de politique positive*, I, pp. 128–203 (English ed., pp. 101–63) and in the preface to vol. III.

[73] E. Durkheim, *The Division of Labor in Society*, New York, 1964, p. 374. Though they have left little imprint upon the history of sociology, it might be added that the defenders of the Commune included a few Comteans. The best-known of them are two Englishmen, Edward Beesly, a professor of ancient history, and the left-wing publicist Frederic Harrison. In a letter to Tönnies, Engels wrote about them in 1895: 'Professor E. Beesly deserves great credit for his defence of the International in the press at the time of the Commune against the vehement attacks of that day. Frederick Harrison too publicly took up the cudgels for the Commune. But a few years later the Comtists cooled off considerably toward the labour movement. The workers had become too powerful and it was a question of maintaining a proper balance between capitalists and workers (both producers, after all, according to Saint-Simon) and to that end of once more supporting the former. Ever since then the Comtists have wrapped themselves in complete silence as regards the labour question.' Marx and Engels, *Selected Correspondence*, Moscow, n.d., p. 560; *MEW* 39, p. 395. Marx too had a high opinion of Beesly personally. Just after the fall of the Commune he wrote to him: 'Permit me to observe by the way that as a Party man I entertain a thoroughly hostile attitude towards Comtism, while as a scientific man I have a very poor opinion of it, but I regard you as the only Comtist, in England as well as in France, who deals with historical turning-points (crises) not as a sectarian but as an historian in the best sense of the word.' Ibid., p. 322; *MEW* 33, p. 228.

impossible as miracles.[74]

Those disciples of Durkheim, who in contrast to their un-affiliated master and to Durkheim's closest lieutenant, Bouglé (who eventually entered the liberal so-called Radical-Socialist party)[75] joined the French Socialist Party, belonged to its right wing and tried to form a reformist group within the (not very revolutionary) tendency of Jean Jaurès.[76] In 1914 all of them, with Durkheim at their head, zealously rallied to the national cause.[77] In doing so they were, of course, far from being alone.

The German sociologists were, naturally, equally convinced that the cause of their nation was the only just one, and Simmel, Sombart, Tönnies, Weber and others enthusiastically contributed to the war effort of the Reich.[78] When revolution threatened in 1918–19

[74] E. Durkheim, 'La Philosophie dans les universités allemandes', *Revue Internationale de l'enseignement*, vol. XIII (1887), p. 440, quoted from Lukes, op. cit., p. 88.

[75] Paul Honigsheim, a fine sociological memoirist from the Weber circle in Heidelberg, has written of Bouglé and the French radical socialists: 'The term is a misnomer, for the members of the party were neither radical nor socialist. . . . "Socialist" connoted opposition to laissez-faire and unrestricted competition. The radical socialist party was made up of middle-class farmers in the South who hated Catholicism and practised birth control, and of lower middle-class people in the towns. There and in the villages, the radical socialists were led by the primary-school teacher.' P. Honigsheim, 'Reminiscences of the Durkheim School', in K. Wolff (ed.), *Essays on Sociology and Philosophy by Emile Durkheim et al.*, New York, 1964, p. 312.

[76] Bourgin, *Le socialisme universitaire*, p. 127f. The animator of the group was Robert Hertz, and its most prominent figure was the Durkheimian economist François Simiand. The Durkheimians were connected with the socialist paper *L'Humanité*, édited by Jaurès, a connection pointed out by Lukes (p. 327) and by Clark Terry ('Emile Durkheim and the French University: the Institutionalization of Sociology', in Oberschall (ed.), *The Establishment of Empirical Sociology*, pp. 171, 182). It should be noted that in contrast to the German *Vorwärts* or the Swedish *Social-Demokraten*, *L'Humanité* at that time was not a working-class party organ but a project launched by the intellectual entourage of Jaurès as a both intellectual and popular paper and financed by private (mainly Jewish) capital. H. Goldberg, *The Life of Jean Jaurès*, Madison, 1962, pp. 319–20.

[77] Bourgin, op. cit., has no quarrel with the behaviour of the Durkheimians during World War I.

[78] Ringer, op. cit., pp. 180–99, gives a brief overview of the German academic community and the war. Several sociologists made important intellectual contributions to the war effort, theorizing the positive features of Germany in comparison to the enemy countries. The most famous example of the genre was Werner Sombart's *Händler und Helden*, Munich, 1915, and even Tönnies, for

Simmel was dead, and Sombart had definitely abandoned his sympathies for proletarian socialism, heading instead for national socialism.[79] Leopold von Wiese in Cologne and Franz Oppenheimer in Frankfurt, who were to be the first two professors of sociology in the Weimar Republic, were both liberals and published liberal political pamphlets.[80] Tönnies belonged to the far left among German sociologists and in that capacity sympathized (without being a member) with the far right of the Social Democrats. In December 1918 he sent an article to the social democratic theoretical journal *Die neue Zeit*, praising the loyalty of the traditional state officials towards the new republican regime. The gist of the argument was that the old bureaucracy should be preserved and gradually developed into a socially-minded *Verwaltungsstaat*.[81]

Max Weber seems to have been even more anxious than Tönnies at the danger threatening traditional Prussian institutions in those days. He was especially worried about the prospect of a dissolution of the army, which was necessary to maintain order – above all against 'the mad Liebknecht gang" (*die verrückte Liebknecht-Bande*), in other words against the proletarian revolution.[82] As so many other 'nationalists' of the 20th century were later to do, Weber held that if insurrectionary workers could not be put down by domestic

example, contributed a piece on *Der englische Staat und der deutsche Staat*, Berlin, 1917. The sociologists did not, however, belong to the extreme annexationists.

[79] See W. Krause, *Werner Sombarts Weg vom Kathedersozialismus zum Fascismus*, Berlin, 1962.

[80] Oppenheimer presented his idea of a liberal land reform as *Der Ausweg*, Berlin, 1919. Von Wiese expounded his dissenting liberalism in *Staatssozialismus*, Berlin, 1916.

[81] F. Tönnies, 'Gegenwarts- und Zukunftsstaat', *Die neue Zeit*, 20.12.1918. In his preface to the third edition of *Gemeinschaft und Gesellschaft*, which appeared in the spring of 1919, Tönnies suggested an 'extended state and community (municipality [*Gemeinde*]) capitalism' as the German road to socialism, between Russian communism and Anglo-American individualist capitalism. The prefaces to the three editions of Tönnies' famous work are all included in vol. I of his *Soziologische Studien und Kritiken*, I–III, Jena, 1925; citation from p. 65.

[82] See, for example, the letters to Friedrich Crusius of 24.11 and 26.12.1918, in M. Weber, *Politische Schriften*, München, 1921, p. 482f. These letters are not included in the otherwise more comprehensive edition by Johannes Winckelmann: Max Weber, *Gesammelte politische Schriften* (3rd ed.), Tübingen, 1971. On Weber's politics in general, there is the first-class work by W. Mommsen, *Max Weber und die deutsche Politik*, Tübingen, 1959. See also D. Beetham, *Max Weber and the Theory of Modern Politics*, London, 1974.

forces of repression, then American troops would have to be called in to do so. On the 18th of November 1918 Weber wrote to his mother: 'If things go badly, we'll have to let the Americans restore order, whether we like it or not.'[83]

In Russia Mikhailovsky, the author of the subjective sociology attacked by Lenin in his polemics with populism, had died in 1904, long before the October Revolution.[84] Young and active in 1917, however, were three other sociologists of later renown, two of whom had already started their intellectual careers: Nicholas Timasheff, Pitirim Sorokin, and George Gurvitch. They came from very different backgrounds (though none from the urban working-class), but all of them turned their backs on the revolution and went into exile in 1920–22.[85] Neither could the short-lived Hungarian Soviet Republic count upon the support of the Hungarian sociologists who were organized in the Society for the Social Sciences.[86] When working-class revolution threatened in Czechoslovakia in the summer and autumn of 1920, with a wave of strikes and with the revolutionaries gaining control of the Social Democratic Party, Thomas Masaryk revealed himself to be not only a sociological scholar and his nation's intellectual leader, but also as President of the Republic a resolute inspirer and organizer of Czech counter-revolution.[87] When the moment of truth came in Italy, Pareto and Mosca rallied to Fascism, Pareto invoking Mussolini as the providential man of sociology.[88] From Switzerland, Robert Michels,

[83] Weber, op. cit., p. 482.

[84] V. I. Lenin, *Who Are the Friends of the People?*, in *Collected Works*, Moscow, 1960, vol. 1. Mikhailovsky was also the 'chief adversary' of George Plekhanov in the latter's great work, *The Development of the Monist View of History*, in *Selected Philosophical Works*, vol. I, London, 1961. Novikov and Kovalevsky were also dead by 1917.

[85] A. Simirenko, 'Social origin, revolution and sociology: the work of Timasheff, Sorokin and Gurvitch', *British Journal of Sociology*, XXIV, 1 (March 1973). There was no institutionalized sociology in Russia.

[86] L. Coser, *Masters of Sociological Thought*, New York, 1971, p. 445. There was at the time another group of Hungarian intellectuals interested in social affairs, among them Georg Lukács, who approved the revolution and joined the Communist Party. A few of them did not, one of the latter becoming a well-known sociologist in Weimar Germany: Karl Mannheim.

[87] V. Mamatey, 'The Development of Czechoslovak Democracy, 1920–1938', in V. Mamatey and R. Luža (eds.), *A History of the Czechoslovak Republic 1918–1938*, Princeton, 1973, p. 102f.

[88] Pareto and Mosca both gave Mussolini's Fascist coup their support, but

the analyst of oligarchical tendencies in working-class organizations, rushed to join the Italian Fascist party.[89] Even the most radical of the American Fathers of sociology, Edward Ross, was a critic of

both shrank back from the plebeian demagogy and brutality of Fascism and wanted to preserve some liberties for the old political and cultural elite. Pareto wrote in January and March 1923: 'Mussolini has really revealed himself as the man whom sociology can invoke . . . France will only save herself if she finds her Mussolini.' The quotation is taken from what seems to be the best biography of Pareto to date, that of his disciple G. H. Bousquet, from the new edition, *Pareto*, Lausanne, 1960, p. 193 n. Fascism had been able to do what weak bourgeois democratic governments in Italy had not: to crush the revolutionaries during the factory occupations of 1920–1 (p. 195). On the other hand, whereas primary and to some extent secondary education might be put under surveillance, university education ought to be quite free from control, and parliament should be preserved (p. 196). For Mosca, see the substantial intellectual biography by James Meisel, *The Myth of the Ruling Class*, Ann Arbor, 1958. Unfortunately, Meisel is very evasive on the subject of Mosca and fascism, presumably because he does not see clearly the class character of Mosca's 'rejection of authoritarianism'. Meisel says of Mosca: 'The Mussolini who made war on socialists had Mosca's plaudits, but his schemes of corporate representation threw our author into a confusion which he was not able to resolve' (p. 231). Much the same could be said of Meisel. Mosca was obsessed with the 'syndicalist peril', once an important tendency in the early Italian labour movement, and he was against the corporate schemas of the new state. But that hardly makes him an 'anti-Fascist' and an 'anti-authoritarian', as Meisel goes on to claim in the passage quoted above. He was hardly an anti-authoritarian in his hostility to the working classes, lamenting that 'the ruling classes in a number of European countries were stupid and *cowardly* enough to accept the eight-hour day after the World War' (p. 229, emphasis added). On the other hand, in 1925 during the Matteotti crisis (after the Fascist murder of the socialist MP Matteotti), Mosca stood up in the Senate, not to condemn the murder, but at least to oppose the proposal of greatly increased powers for the Prime Minister (Mussolini) and in defence of parliament and the prerogatives of the king (p. 224f).

[89] On Robert Michels and his road from syndicalist opposition in the labour movement to Fascism, there is an excellent study by W. Röhrich, *Robert Michels, vom sozialistischen-syndikalistischen zum fascistischen Credo*, Berlin, 1972, p. 10. Michels was later called to a chair at the militant Fascist university of Perugia. The Polish-Austrian Ludwig Gumplowicz, the fourth member of the group of elite theorists, along with Michels, Mosca, and Pareto, had committed suicide, for private reasons, in 1909. Other distinguished Italian social scientists and participants in the sociological movement also rallied to Mussolini's régime, among them the economist Achille Loria and the criminologist Enrico Ferri (once a socialist leader). Cf. A. Gramsci, *Gli Intellettuali, Quaderni del Carcere*, Turin, 1964, vol. 2, p. 169f; B. Gustafsson, *Marxism och revisionism. Edvard Bernsteins kritik av marxismen: dess idéhistoriska förutsättningar*, Stockholm, 1969, p. 231 n. (on Ferri).

revolutionary socialism. But even before the socialist movement suffered the massive repression of the so-called Palmer Raids in 1919, socialist revolution had become a far-off threat in the USA, so that among American sociologists there were a few friends of foreign revolutions.[90]

Sociology's position in the world is well symbolized by the composition of the praesidium of the *Institut International de Sociologie*, elected in 1920 to sit for the following year. In that time of turmoil the Institute elected for president Thomas Masaryk, President of Czechoslovakia, and as vice-presidents 'in alphabetical order': B. Machado, ex-President of Portugal (and future Prime Minister), Raymond Poincaré, ex-president of France (1913-20), Woodrow Wilson, ex-President of the United States (elected when President of USA).[91] The political eminence of the praesidium was exceptional, but the ideological configuration represented by these distinguished men of state – all notable academics as well, though only Masaryk was a sociologist in the contemporary sense[92] – was on the

[90] Thorstein Veblen, the theorist and critic of *The Leisure Class* and the spokesman of productive engineers, was one (Coser, op. cit., p. 286). In an interesting journalistic reportage, *Russia In Upheaval*, London, 1919 (original American edition 1918), Ross displayed both a sympathetic understanding of the foreign revolution and a concern with the need to 'insure ourselves against a disastrous reverberation from the Russian Revolution' (p. 348). Such a reverberation was not a direct revolutionary threat but 'anti-capitalist agitation' and working-class restiveness expressed in 'concerted "slacking", restriction of output, sabotage, and sudden capricious strikes' (p. 345). Thus, American capitalists should treat their workers better, and conflicts should be settled by joint boards of employers and employees. But capitalism should remain.

[91] *Revue Internationale de Sociologie*, vol. 29 (1921), p. 100. Among the earlier presidents of the *Institut* had been John Lubbock (1893-94), Albert Schäffle (1895), Achille Loria (1899), Carl Menger (1901), Lester Ward (1904), Gustav v. Schmoller (1905), Maxim Kovalevsky (1907). Masaryk was succeeded by Albion Small (among the vice-presidents that year were a prince Bonaparte and a former Prime Minister of Spain). The *Institut* functioned as the international sociological association till World War II. It also tried, with some success, to enlist distinguished representatives from the older, established disciplines, like economics and law, as well as prominent public personalities. Its organizing spirit and general secretary during its first three decades was the French organicist René Worms, who also was a high civil servant.

[92] Masaryk's first major sociological work, *Suicide and the Meaning of Civilization* (from 1881) has recently been issued in an English edition with an introduction by Anthony Giddens (Chicago, 1970). Among Masaryk's other sociological contributions is a critique of Marxism, *Die philosophischen und sociologischen*

contrary very typical. It extended from the moderate republican liberalism of the vice-presidents to the moderate social-democratic sympathies of the president. Such were the social forces sponsoring the academic institutionalization of sociology in the liberal republics of the USA, France, and (after 1918) Czechoslovakia (Edvard Benes was also a member of the International Institute and a national promoter of sociology). The same was true of official support for sociology in Weimar Germany.[93] Sociology in Sweden emerged, during and just after World War II, in a very similar ideological milieu.[94] When the bourgeois revolution and capitalist rationalization finally penetrated the mediaeval defences of academia, sociology came – after a delay which varied in length from one country to another – to be accepted as an official discipline.

The social questions which were the focus of the anxieties, enquiries and remedies of sociologists, were obviously economic in nature. They evidently concerned problems of industrial enterprise, unemployment, poverty, inequality, division of labour, capitalism. The sociologists thus had great interest in phenomena which were also within the domain of economics – the science of the market. The *emergence* of sociology cannot be fruitfully analyzed from the point of view of its relationship to economics. An analysis of its *development*, however – its establishment as a new discourse on society with scientific pretensions – will have to focus on that relationship.

It is in its relationship to *politics after the bourgeois revolution* and to *economics before the proletarian revolution* that we will try to grasp sociology as a social phenomenon, and as a possibly scientific body of thought. Sociology emerged as a new approach to politics after the upheavals of the French Revolution. It developed and became decisively established as an attempt to deal with the social, moral and cultural problems of the capitalist economic order, under the shadow of a militant working-class movement and a more or less immediate threat of revolutionary socialism. The sociological

Grundlagen des Marxismus. Studien zur sozialen Frage, Vienna, 1899. Cf. J. Roucek, 'Czechoslovak Sociology', in G. Gurvitch and W. Moore (eds.), *Twentieth Century Sociology*, New York, 1945, pp. 717–31.

[93] Carl Heinrich Becker, the secretary for higher education in Prussia who promoted the academic introduction of sociology, adhered to the Democratic party (Ringer, op. cit., p. 69).

[94] A. Gullberg, *Till den svenska sociologins historia*, Stockholm, 1972.

approach to politics and economics alike was rooted in a bourgeois point of view, the product of an intelligentsia attached to the bourgeoisie. However, in this case the relationship between the bourgeoisie and the intelligentsia was hardly ever as congenial and harmonious as in the case of economics. The sociologists were usually not directly related to the hegemonic fraction of the bourgeoisie. Their basic class allegiance was as a rule either mediated through links to the lower and petty bourgeoisie or combined with aristocratic and other pre-bourgeois attachments. Sociologists, therefore, were typically part of an alienated bourgeois intelligentsia within a bourgois society.

The age of sociology is the era between the bourgeois and the proletarian revolutions. Sociology is a social intellectual activity, upon which the tensions, contradictions and struggles of a society poised between a painful break with its feudal and patriarchal past and the threat of an even more painful break with its bourgeois present, have set their decisive imprint. In the next two chapters we will see how this historical context has shaped the formation of sociological theory.

Chapter Four

Politics after the Bourgeois Revolution: the New Society and the Masses

I. The Political Theory of a New Society

One thing that sociology urgently wanted to introduce into the consideration of politics was a certain determinism. The first sociologists emphasized the wider social context of forms of government, disregard of which rendered political theory superficial and much political initiative and legislation futile. The new theorists argued that principles of government should be seen as related to and determined by the laws of social organization in general, which should themselves be studied by the methods of natural science. In particular, the contemporary breakthroughs in biology, in the physiological and anatomical works of Bichat, Cabanis, and Vicq d'Azyr, were a great scientific inspiration to Saint-Simon and Comte. The influence of biology was very important for Spencer's work and has ever since, indeed, been pervasive in sociology.[1]

[1] Saint-Simon was the first to draw attention to developments in physiology. He at first attached enormous importance to these, though this was gradually attenuated. See 'Essay on the Science of Man', abridged in H. de Saint-Simon, *Social Organization* (ed. Markham); full text in *Oeuvres*, V. While Comte gave the physiologists their due, he asserted the specificity of social science, on the basis of the social law of evolution. *Plan des travaux scientifiques nécessaires pour réorganiser la société*, appended to *Système*, IV, p. 125f. (English ed., p. 527f). Spencer gives an overview of sociology's dependence on biology in *The Study of Sociology*, op. cit., ch. XIV. Biological influence on sociology reached its apex in the late 19th century, with the elaboration of detailed, now long forgotten analogies between societies and organisms (by Paul von Lilienfeld, Albert Schäffle, René Worms and others). But it has been significant even in more recent times. At Harvard in the 1930's the biochemist Lawrence Henderson was an important inspirer of the up and coming sociologists there – of Talcott Parsons, George Homans and others. See the autobiographical articles by Parsons, 'On

Political conceptions, Comte argued in his first elaboration of a 'positive politics', had previously been based on imagination instead of upon observation. Politics had been arbitrary and vainly voluntarist. 'Down to the present time man has had faith in the unlimited power of his political combinations to perfect social order. In other words, the human race has hitherto been regarded politically as unmoved by inherent forces, and always disposed passively to receive whatever impulse the legislator, armed with a competent authority, wished to give.'[2] Comte had compelling arguments to hand, when he alluded to 'the production, within a period of thirty years, of [ten] constitutions, each in succession proclaimed eternal and irrevocable, several of which contain more than two hundred very circumstantial articles'.[3]

Saint-Simon had already criticized the classification of societies in terms of governmental forms as superficial, and had insisted on the derivative character of politics.[4] In spite of some carping at his disciple for not having included the 'sentimental and religious part' of the Saint-Simonian doctrine in his essay, Saint-Simon called it 'the best writing that has ever been published about general politics'.[5] Similarly, when Tocqueville demanded a new political science, he did so because he believed it necessary to take into account those omnipresent social dimensions of politics whose overwhelming importance his encounter with American society had brought home to him.[6] When Spencer in the first chapter of *The Study of Sociology* set out to explain (in the words of the title of the chapter), 'Our Need of It', he argued that the great merit and purpose of sociology was its ability to show that social conditions, good and bad, were scarcely malleable by governmental action.

In their anti-voluntarist emphasis the sociologists of this epoch were far from alone. The same theme can be found in the counter-revolutionary writings of Burke, de Bonald, de Maistre and their comrades-in-arms. It was also a central idea of the Historical School

---

Building Social Systems Theory', *Daedalus*, Fall 1970, and Homans, *Sentiments and Activities*, New York, 1962, ch. 1.

[2] A. Comte, *Système de politique positive*, p. 84 (English ed., p. 552).

[3] Ibid., p. 61 (English ed., p. 536).

[4] See, for example, Saint-Simon, *l'Industrie*, pp. 30f, 80f, *Oeuvres*, II.

[5] H. Saint-Simon, *Catéchisme des industriels, Troisème Cahier*, p. 5, in *Oeuvres*, IV.

[6] Tocqueville, *Democracy in America*, vol. 1, p. 14.

of Jurisprudence in Germany. In itself, this emphasis did not constitute a total break with the grand tradition of political philosophy, but it did represent a rupture with the theories of philosophers like Macchiavelli, Hobbes and Locke. Macchiavelli was an admirer of strong-willed founders of states and of lawgivers, mythical and historical – men like Moses, Cyrus, Theseus, Romulus and Lycurgus.[7] He told Lorenzo di Medici, whom he wished to propel into action as a leader of Italian unification and 'redemption', that 'nothing does so much honour to a man newly risen to power as do the new laws and institutions he devises. . . . In Italy there is no lack of matter on which to impose any form.'[8]

In Hobbesian society everything is ultimately reducible to the will of the sovereign (as a rule the king). Even property and its distribution is 'the act only of the Soveraign'.[9] Custom, too, gains its authority ultimately from the will of the sovereign, explicit or implicit: 'When long Use obtaineth the authority of Law it is not the Length of Time that maketh the Authority, but the Will of the Soveraign signified by his silence'.[10]

As a Whig, Locke did not plead the cause of arbitrary absolutism, and he regarded property not as a political institution but as one derived from the state of nature.[11] On the other hand, it was neither the immoral caprice nor the social inefficacy of arbitrary power to which he objected, so much as its illegitimacy in terms of natural law. 'A Man, as has been proved, cannot subject himself to the Arbitrary Power of another; and having in the State of Nature no Arbitrary Power over the Life, Liberty, or Possessions of another, but only so much as the Law of Nature gave him for the preservation of himself, and the rest of Mankind; this is all he doth, or can give up to the Commonwealth, and by it to the *Legislative Power*, so that the Legislative can have no more than this'.[12] The legislative focus of Locke's social theory is summarized in his classification of societies: 'According as the Power of making Laws is placed, such

---

[7] Macchiavelli, *The Prince, selections from The Discourses and other writings*, London, 1972; *The Prince*, p. 72, *Discourses on the First Decade of Titius Livius*, p. 161f.

[8] Macchiavelli, *The Prince*, p. 133.

[9] Hobbes, *Leviathan*, p. 296.

[10] Ibid., p. 313.

[11] J. Locke, *Two Treatises of Government*, Cambridge, 1960: Second Treatise, ch. v.

[12] Ibid., p. 375 (italics original).

is the Form of Common-wealth.'[13]

These writers did not, of course, see politics as completely indeterminate. Political institutions and actions were regarded as determined by man's nature. This premise is most explicit in Hobbes, who devotes Part I of *Leviathan* to an exposition 'Of Man'. But between human nature and the will of the ruler there was not so much a social space as a theoretical void.

Montesquieu, however, set out to fill that void, and he explicitly propounded a determinist view of politics. 'I have first of all considered mankind; and the result of my thoughts has been, that amidst such an infinite diversity of laws and manners, they were not solely contributed by the caprice of fancy.'[14] Montesquieu asserted that laws must be related to the people for whom they are designed, and to the nature and principle of government. 'They should be related to the climate of each country, to the quality of its soil, to its situation and extent, to the principal occupation of the natives, whether husbandmen, huntsmen, or shepherds; they should have relation to the degree of liberty which the constitution will bear; to the religion of the inhabitants, to their inclinations, riches, numbers, commerce, manners and customs . . . These relations I shall examine, since all these together constitute what I call the Spirit of Laws.'[15]

Of particular importance, in Montesquieu's own view[16] as well as in our comparative perspective here, was his distinction between the nature and the principle of government. Governments he classified according to their different natures into three categories: republics (of which there are two subtypes, aristocracies and democracies), monarchies, and despotisms, The criterion of this classification was the location of sovereignty.

Montesquieu gives an intrapolitical exposition of the relationship between political institutions within the different types of government (Book II). On the other hand, he also argues the dependence of the system of political institutions on the *principle* of government, or 'the human passions which set it in motion'.[17] The principles

[13] Ibid., p. 373 (italics omitted).
[14] Montesquieu, *De l'esprit des lois*, Preface, p. 33; *The Spirit of Laws*, Preface, p. xxi.
[15] Ibid., Book I, ch. 3, p. 44 (English ed., p. 3).
[16] Ibid., Book III, ch. I, p. 60 n (English ed., p. 9 n).
[17] Ibid., Book III, ch. I, p. 60 (English ed., p. 9).

which correspond to his types of government are, respectively: virtue (meaning political virtue, 'the love of one's country, that is, the love of equality'),[18] moderation, honour and fear. These are not just aspects of man's psychological composition, but form ideological ensembles present in some societies and absent in others, for specific reasons including the size and climate of a society, which delimit the possibilities of any political system. The absence of the necessary 'principle' in a given society makes it futile to attempt to establish a political system in it corresponding to the absent principle. Montesquieu points to the unsuccessful attempts of the English to establish a republic in the 17th century, which were doomed because virtue was lacking. Conversely, when the principle of a government for one reason or another changes, the nature of government becomes corrupted and changes too.[19]

Thus in asserting a social determination of politics, governmental institutions and legislation, the early sociologists did not break entirely new ground. Comte, and Durkheim after him, acknowledged Montesquieu as an important forerunner in the development of their science.[20] But *what* was it that determined politics?

After all, Comte concluded, 'his [Montesquieu's] labours are far from having raised politics to the rank of a positive science'.[21] For him, this meant that Montesquieu had not been sufficiently far-reaching in his determinism. '[His principal conception] has a double fault. Instead of being historical it is dogmatic; in other words it does not sufficiently regard the necessary succession of the different political states. In the second place it attributes an exaggerated importance to a fact, which is altogether secondary – the form of government.' The essence of Comte's objections was that Montesquieu had not discovered the evolutionary principle underlying the development of humanity. 'Montesquieu did not

---

[18] In French 'amour de la patrie, c'est-à-dire l'amour de l'égalité', 'Advertisement', ibid., p. 31 (English ed., p. xxii).

[19] Ibid., Book III, p. 61f (English ed., p. 9f).

[20] Comte, *Plan*, op. cit., p. 166f (English ed., p. 563f); *Cours de philosophie positive*, IV, p. 127 f (198f in English ed.). Durkheim wrote his subsidiary doctoral thesis on 'What Secondat [Montesquieu's family name, Montesquieu being the name of his barony] contributed to the constitution of political science'. It is published in Durkheim, *Montesquieu and Rousseau, Forerunners of sociology*, Ann Arbor, 1960.

[21] Comte, *Plan*, p. 167 (English ed., p. 568).

perceive that great fact which regulates all political phenomena, the natural development of civilization.'[22]

1. Politics in Social Evolution

The sociologists thus brought to the tradition of political theory an evolutionary principle, a conception of politics as determined by evolution. Their decisive contribution, in other words, was not to situate politics in a wider social context. It was to identify *a new and evolving social reality, to which the polity must be adapted*. In Saint-Simon, Comte and Spencer social theory was part of an all-embracing evolutionary schema of a rationalist-utilitarian type. To Spencer, sociology was 'the study of evolution in its most complex form',[23] the final product of a cosmic system of inorganic, organic and super-organic evolution.[24] Tocqueville was much less ambitious, concentrating on one great social tendency which constituted, in his view, an irresistible revolution advancing through the centuries. Common to all four, however, were two fundamental themes: a focus on vast processes of social change, within which a decisive moment was held to have occurred, and an insistence that political theory and political action must adapt themselves to these developments.

An important forerunner of Saint-Simon and Comte in this respect was Condorcet and his *Esquisse d'un tableau historique du progrès de l'esprit humain*, written during the French Revolution. This work was a rationalistic and utilitarian philosophy of history, interpreted as mankind's progress in rationality and felicity. This

[22] Idem, cf. *Cours de philosophie*, IV, p. 127f (English ed., p. 198f). That Montesquieu did not adequately present the social determination of politics was also Durkheim's main criticism. Basically, Durkheim says, Montesquieu classifies societies in terms of their political forms, and instead of showing how different societies engender different social institutions, focuses on the legislator, relating the institutions necessary for societies of different nature. Durkheim, op. cit., p. 136 f. Durkheim, for his part, indicated social mores as the most direct societal determinant, from which laws derive (p. 61f). It was in his principal *thèse, The Division of Labor in Society*, which we will take up in the next chapter, that Durkheim developed his view of the newly evolved society.

[23] Spencer, *The Study of Sociology*, p. 385.

[24] The overall conception of Spencer's 'synthetic philosophy' is set forth in *First Principles* (1st ed. London, 1862). It is briefly recapitulated at the beginning of *Principles of Sociology*.

progress was seen by Condorcet as the consequence of a fundamental utilitarian drive in man, realized by the struggle of men of
science and invention against the forces of ignorance and prejudice.[25]
Saint-Simon acknowledged his debt to Condorcet, together with
the physiologists, in the earliest of his social writings.[26] But Saint-
Simon came increasingly to dwell upon the specific characteristics,
interests and problems of the new industrial society that had
emerged in the 19th century.

To Comte, basing himself on the ideas of Condorcet, evolution
was essentially a development of the human mind. Social organization was determined by the current stage of civilization, which was
subject to law-bound development. In its turn, 'Civilization,
properly so-called, consists on one hand in the development of the
human mind, on the other in the result of this, namely the increasing
power of man over nature.' The stage of civilization determined
social organization thus: 'In the first place it determines its nature
by fixing the aim of social action; in the next place it prescribes its
essential form by creating and developing the social forces, temporal
and spiritual, destined to guide this general action.'[27] In the
development of civilization there are three main stages – the
theological-military, the transitional-metaphysical, and the positive-
scientific. The 'law of three stages', which is Comte's first sociological law, is explicitly a law of 'intellectual evolution', stating the
three stages through which all human theories necessarily pass.[28]
In Comte's view, 'the main element of Sociology is Mental Science
in the widest sense'.[29] The intellectual stages are connected with
certain types of human activity, and Comte's third sociological law
states that there is an evolution of human activity from military to
industrial. The two fundamental stages, then, are the theological-

---

[25] A brief introduction to Condorcet is the chapter on him in F. Manuel, *The
Prophets of Paris*, Cambridge, Mass., 1962.

[26] Saint-Simon, "Essay on the Science of Man', op. cit. Cf. also the first of
Saint-Simon's periodical publications, *L'Industrie, Oeuvres*, I–II.

[27] Comte, *Plan*, p. 86f (English ed., p. 554).

[28] Like most of the ideas in Comte's bulky and repetitive *oeuvre*, the law of the
three stages is adumbrated in the *Plan*. A mature systematization is to be found in
the third volume of the *Système*, devoted to social dynamics, p. 28 (English ed.,
p. 23).

[29] *Système de politique positive*, III, p. 48 (English ed., p. 40). On the same page
Comte says that 'Mental science [*la science de l'esprit*] must needs form far the
largest part of sociology'.

military and the scientific-industrial.[30]

Spencer's evolutionary principle was more conducive to a science of society in that its basic unit was not humanity and the human mind, but social organization. Social evolution, in Spencer's conception, meant 'changes from societies which are small, loose, uniform and vague in structure, to societies which are large, compact, multiform, and distinct in structure'.[31] It also meant increasing consensus of functions and mutual dependence of parts.[32] In this way societies were to be classified as simple, compound, doubly-compound and trebly-compound.[33]

More crucial to Spencer, however, because of more direct relevance to the political and social questions of his age, was another classification, based on predominant social activity. Spencer distinguishes two main types of such activity, one concerned with war, the other with material sustenance. The corresponding types of society are the militant and the industrial. Though the second classification cuts across the first, Spencer tended on the whole to view the trend of evolution as proceeding from societies of the militant type to those of the industrial. The latter construction, however, is an uneasy and shaky evolutionism both because it is not, like the first, fitted into the laws of evolution of the universe as a whole, and because Spencer, writing his *Principles of Sociology* in the last quarter of the nineteenth century, was painfully aware of the retreat of contemporary liberalism.[34] In the end his evolutionary optimism broke down – at least in the short and intermediate run – and the final chapter of the final volume of *Principles of Sociology*, which appeared in 1896, twenty years after the first edition of the

[30] Ibid., p. 55f (English ed., p. 46f). The second law holds that human theories go through the three stages in a definite order, beginning with mathematics and ending with morality, after sociology (p. 41f; English ed., p. 34f).

[31] Spencer, *Principles of Sociology*, II, 2, p. 646. The evolutionary scheme is systematically developed in part II of this work, vol. I: 2. There Spencer summarizes his argument thus: 'Like evolving aggregates in general, societies show *integration*, both by simple increase of mass and by coalescence and re-coalescence of masses. The change from *homogeneity* to *heterogeneity* is multitudinously exemplified . . . With progressing integration and heterogenity goes increasing coherence . . . Simultaneously comes increasing definiteness.' (I: 2, p. 596. Italics original.)

[32] *Principles of Sociology*, I: 2, p. 485f.

[33] Ibid., p. 550f.

[34] Ibid., pp. 556–96; II: 2, pp. 568–667.

first volume, ended with a gloomy prediction of a socialistically regimented society 'in the near future'.

It was, of course, the evolutionary perspective which set a chasm between the sociologists proper and the theorists of counter-revolution. To de Maistre the French Revolution was not a transitional period in the evolution of mankind. It was the incarnation of pure evil, and as such a totally destructive non-reality. 'Evil has nothing in common with life; it cannot create, since its power is purely negative. *Evil is a fissure in being; it has no reality.* What distinguishes the French Revolution and what makes it an event unique in history is that it is radically *evil*'.[35] De Maistre was one of the most ferocious deriders of deliberative constitutions and voluntarist politics. But his determinism was providential, not in any derived and abstruse way but in the most immediate and palpable sense. The divine character of political constitutions was for him manifest. 'When Providence has decreed the more rapid formation of a political constitution, a man appears invested with indefinable powers: he speaks and exacts obedience.' Without exception such men are always 'kings or high nobles'. They bring together in a new way elements to be found in existing customs, and they always act in the name of Divinity and in roles in which the priest and the legislator can only be separated with difficulty.[36] The decisive role of divinely-inspired will was the lesson that de Maistre, in an oft-quoted and scientific-sounding dictum, drew from 'history, which is experimental politics'.[37]

The real import of such scientific and scholarly rhetoric was much the same in de Bonald, de Maistre's comrade-in-arms. De Bonald could write, for example: 'Others have defended the religion of Man, I defend the religion of Society; they have proved the truth of religion by religion itself, I wish to prove it by history.'[38] For: 'In all questions concerning man and society, the answers must be deduced from the facts.'[39] But his conclusion was already foregone:

---

[35] J. de Maistre, *Considerations on France*, in *The Works of Joseph de Maistre*, London, 1965, p. 69. Italics in original.

[36] Ibid., p. 78. *The Generative Principle of Political Constitutions*, also in op. cit., p. 162 and passim.

[37] Ibid., p. 162.

[38] L.-A.-G. de Bonald, *Théorie du Pouvoir, Oeuvres*, vol. 3, Bruxelles, 1845, p. 406.

[39] Ibid., p. 560.

there was one social constitution and one only, which derived from the nature of man and God. Other social forms were mere temporary aberrations.[40] 'I have sought to prove that, assuming the existence of social beings, God, and intelligent physical man . . . royal monarchical government [an aristocratic social order] and the Catholic Christian religion are *necessary* . . .'[41]

It is therefore quite logical that Comte in his two general expositions of the major steps towards a science of politics and society, the *Plan* of 1822–24 and the *Cours* of 1838, did not mention de Maistre or any other of the counter-revolutionary philosophers. Later, in the *Système*, he was to put de Maistre alongside Condorcet, but in a special capacity, as the man who brought out the positive lessons of the spiritual life of the Middle Ages. Even here de Maistre has only supplied 'the essential supplement' to the 'principal thought' of Condorcet.[42] To Comte, the 'positive' was the real as against the imaginary, but to de Bonald and de Maistre, the new positive stage for which Comte and his sociology spoke was – strictly speaking – unreal.

Common to both the early sociologists and the emigré philosophers of counter-revolution was an anti-Jacobin background. In the France of this period all writers on society wrote in the shadow of the guillotine and the unprecedented radicalism of the Revolution. (In its official terror, the French Revolution was more violent than the Russian.) To the three French pioneers of sociology this shadow had a tangibly personal aspect. Saint-Simon and Tocqueville both came from the aristocracy; the father of each was imprisoned during the height of the Terror. Many of the latter's relatives perished on the scaffold, among them his maternal grandfather, Malesherbes, the benevolent censor of the encyclopaedists and defence counsel of

[40] The thesis is summarized in ibid., p. 9f.

[41] De Bonald, *Oeuvres*, vol. 4, p. 154. 'Necessary' here meant approximately what it meant for Montesquieu, expressing a scientific law. De Bonald's criticisms of Montesquieu (basically two) were quite different from Comte's. One took up Rousseau's criticism from *Emile*, that Montesquieu had been exclusively interested in what exists, and not in 'the principles of that which must exist'. The second criticism was that Montesquieu did not acknowledge that it is the passions of men that cause the temporary differences and aberrations in social forms, and instead pointed to climatic influences (op. cit., vol. 3, p. 17). De Bonald's main work also contains a supplement condemning the hero of Saint-Simon and Comte, Condorcet, and his belief in scientific progress (vol. 4, pp. 159–83).

[42] Comte, *Système de politique positive*, III, p. 615 (English ed., pp. 258–9).

the ex-king at his trial. Comte's family managed to avoid falling under suspicion, but secretly remained vehemently anti-Jacobin, devoutly Catholic, and solidly bourgeois. The Marquis de Condorcet was less fortunate, hunted down as a suspect moderate, finally captured and dying in jail.[43]

The sociologists wanted to prevent the *new* society of their time from sharing the fate of the old regime before it. It was therefore natural for them to look to traditional forms of social integration and to search for new mechanisms that would correspond to them. Saint-Simon and Comte focused on novel forms of 'spiritual power' to replace the old doctrines of the church, and ended up founding new religions. Tocqueville, for his part, emphasized the role of the aristocracy as mediator between the central royal power and the people in Europe, and commented on the corresponding role in new societies such as America, of political, cultural and other associations.

The rise of sociology was, moreover, congruent and contemporary with the German discovery of national culture (see below) and the distinction between state and civil society. It seems that Hegel, in his *Philosophy of Right*, was the first major thinker who explicitly formulated the latter. Hegel defined civil scoiety very precisely: 'Civil society is the [order of] difference which intervenes between the family and the state . . .'. He added that 'the creation of civil society is the achievement of the modern world'.[44]

To Hobbes and to Locke civil society was contrasted with a state of nature and was synonymous with a politically organized society.[45]

---

[43] Biographical data can be found in Gouhier, op. cit. (Comte); Manuel, *The New World of Henri Saint-Simon* and *The Prophets of Paris* (Condorcet, but also briefer overviews of Comte and Saint-Simon). For Tocqueville, I have relied on Hugh Brogan's introduction to the Fontana edition of *The Ancien Regime and the French Revolution*. Spencer, the pacifist Victorian liberal, was of course no Jacobin either.

[44] G. W. F. Hegel, *Philosophy of Right* (ed. Knox), Oxford, 1942, 182 & Addition (p. 266). The quotation is taken from the somewhat later Additions compiled from lecture notes, but the distinction is already made in the main text, in the paragraph in question. The first edition of the *Philosophy of Right* appeared in 1821. Hegel's claim to priority has been cogently argued by the West German Hegel scholar Manfred Riedel, *Studien zu Hegels Rechtsphilosophie*, Frankfurt, 1969, pp. 135–66.

[45] On Hobbes, see the discussion of Civitas, Commonwealth, and Civil Society in *Leviathan*, chs. XVII, and XXXVII, pp. 223–8, 478. For Locke, see *Second Treatise*, ch. VII, significantly called 'Of political *or* civil Society' (emphasis

In the first of his *Two Treatises on Government*, attacking Filmer's *Patriarcha* which had derived the divine right of kings from divinely instituted paternal authority, Locke set out to distinguish the family and the state. But what might intervene between the two did not bother him. Montesquieu's distinction between *état politique* and *état civil*, taken from the Neapolitan *philosophe* Gravina, refers in fact to two aspects of the political organization of the state: respectively its governmental structure, and the union of wills which must of necessity underpin it.[46]

De Bonald's chief work is called *Theory of political and religious power in civil society*, but de Bonald's concept of civil society, like his work as a whole, belongs to pre-bourgeois and pre-sociological political thought. Civil society is defined as the union of political and religious society.[47] De Bonald continues the tradition of Bossuet, who in the preface to his *Discours sur l'histoire universelle* (of 1681) told the French Dauphin, to whom the book was dedicated, that 'religion and political government are the two hinges on which all human affairs turn'. The new idea of civil society was to become a third hinge in this perspective on human affairs.

2. Proto-Sociology: the Scottish Enlightenment between Man's Nature and Morality

Before considering the rise of sociology as a distinct system of thought, it is necessary to look back at the greatest achievements of its prehistory. These are to be found above all in the work of Adam Ferguson and John Millar in the Scottish Enlightenment – a movement enigmatic both in its sudden flowering in a small, subordinate and peripheral nation in the latter half of the 18th century, and in its rapid demise in the second quarter of the 19th century. The social thought of Ferguson and Millar belonged to an intellectual culture unrivalled in its age outside France. The Scotland of this epoch

---

added). The full title of *Leviathan* is significant in the same respect: 'Leviathan or the Matter, Forme & Power of a Commonwealth Ecclesiastical and Civill' Edmund Burke, op. cit., p. 150, uses 'civil society' in the same traditional and undifferentiated sense.

[46] Montesquieu, op. cit., Book I, ch. 3, pp. 43–4 (English ed., p. 2f).

[47] De Bonald, op. cit., vol. 3, pp. 9f, 58f. The family is included in the conception of political society, as its partial and particular rather than general aspect; there is nothing in between (vol. 4, p. 145).

included the philosopher David Hume, the central figure of classical economics Adam Smith, the historian William Robertson, the chemist Joseph Black, the Edinburgh Medical School, the poet Robert Burns and the novelist Walter Scott, to mention only a few names.[48]

In this period there was a fantastic capitalist boom in Scotland. Linen production quadrupled in value between 1736–40 and 1768–72. Glasgow prospered mightily as a result of its dominant position in the British tobacco trade, its population increasing from 13,000 in 1707 to 40,000 in 1780, and (with the new cotton boom) to 200,000 in 1830. Agriculture, too, underwent a rapid process of commercialization and expansion.[49] The suppression of the last Stuart uprising at Culloden in 1746 had, in effect, been a decisive defeat for feudal and clan institutions in Scotland.[50]

The cultural boom had a firm academic base at the universities of Edinburgh and Glasgow. It also flourished in a host of urban clubs, such as we noted above in surveying Adam Smith's milieu. The Scottish universities were not primarily geared to provide a general 'gentlemanly' culture as were Oxford and Cambridge, but catered rather to the needs of the Scottish bourgeoisie. 'By the time William Robertson became principal of Edinburgh [University] in 1762 . . . Scottish universities were famous throughout Britain and Europe for the breadth of their intake from the middle class, for the relative cheapness of their fees, for the excellence and relevance of their instruction, and for the toleration by the university authorities of diverse opinions among the lecturers.'[51] Not only the universities

[48] For an overview, see the excellent study by T. S. Smout, *A History of the Scottish People 1560–1830*, London, 1969, ch. XIX.

[49] Ibid., chs. X–XII. The population of Glasgow is given on p. 380, linen output on p. 244.

[50] W. Ferguson, *Scotland: 1689 to the Present*, Edinburgh, 1969, p. 154f; Smout, op. cit., p. 225f. Heritable jurisdiction and military tenure, for instance, were abolished. For a brief Marxist discussion of the bourgeois revolution in Scotland and the development of capitalism prior to the union with England in 1707, see J. Foster, 'Capitalism and the Scottish Nation', G. Brown (ed.), *The Red Paper on Scotland*, Edinburgh, 1975, p. 143f.

[51] Smout, op. cit., p. 507. On winning an Oxford scholarship (one that had originally been set up for the promotion of the Episcopalian Church in Scotland), Smith was obliged to discontinue the mathematical studies that he had pursued in Glasgow and instead took up Latin and Greek (Rae, *Life of Adam Smith*, pp. 20–3).

but also the church (the two were closely interrelated), was uniquely adapted to bourgeois society. Under the control of the Moderate party led by Robertson, the historian and principal of Edinburgh University, the Puritan zealotry of the Scottish kirk had considerably mellowed, in keeping with the more circumspect views of the mercantile bourgeoisie and commercialized estate-owners who were the patrons of the Moderates.[52] It was in this ambience that Adam Ferguson (1723–1816), professor of pneumatics (the study of man's mental nature) and moral philosophy at Edinburgh, and John Millar (1735–1801), professor of law at Glasgow, respectively, wrote *An Essay on the History of Civil Society* (1766) and *The Origin of the Distinction of Ranks* (1st ed. 1771). No overall exposition of these works is possible here, let alone a comprehensive analysis.[53] An attempt can, however, be made to locate the specific advance over previous political and social philosophy achieved by these Scottish writers, and – no less important – the specific barrier which prevented them from developing a new science of society. Though little explicit attention has been paid to the latter problem, it is the more intriguing of the two. The moral philosophy of Francis Hutcheson was a starting-point for both Adam Smith and Ferguson and Millar. However, out of moral philosophy Smith created a new scientific discipline – political economy; while there is no similar rupture in the works of Ferguson and Millar.

To appreciate the achievement of the Scotsmen, the obvious point of reference and comparison is the work of Montesquieu, the commanding figure of 18th century political thought, of whom Ferguson was an ardent admirer: 'When I recollect what the President Montesquieu has written, I am at a loss to tell, why I

[52] Smout, op. cit., pp. 229–39.

[53] The reader is referred to the existing literature, which though not very extensive, is generally of high quality. On Millar, the best study is that by Lehmann, already cited, which includes Millar's main works and other selections. For Ferguson, see David Kettler, *The Social and Political Thought of Adam Ferguson*, Ohio, 1965. Although marred by its author's eagerness to identify sociological anticipations, Lehmann's early study, *Adam Ferguson and the Beginnings of Modern Sociology*, New York, 1930, remains valuable. Gladys Bryson, *Man and Society*, Princeton, 1945, is a good and, although it neglects even to mention Millar, comprehensive presentation of the social thought of the Scottish Enlightenment. See also Ronald Meek's very interesting essay on 'the Scottish Historical School' of Ferguson, Millar, Robertson and Smith: 'The Scottish Contribution to Marxist Sociology', *Economics and Ideology and Other Essays*, London, 1967, pp. 34–50.

should treat of human affairs.'[54] Ferguson and Millar shared Montesquieu's conception of man as a social animal and his deterministic view of law and politics. The variety of human governments derived from the different circumstances in which men lived. This approach to politics contrasted with that of their countryman David Hume, whose idea of a 'science' of politics was quite the opposite: 'So great is the force of laws, and of particular forms of government, and so little dependence have they on the humours and tempers of men, that consequences almost as general and certain may sometimes be deduced from them, as any which the mathematical sciences afford.'[55] Like their French master, Ferguson and Millar developed a broad comparative and empirical framework, drawing upon many sources, including travellers' reports from non-European societies.

Ferguson and Millar, however, took two important steps beyond Montesquieu towards a science of society. First of all, whereas *The Spirit of Laws* revolved around forms of government, the works of Ferguson and Millar were focused on social pursuits and social relations in general: on ways of procuring subsistence, forms of property, division of labour, and non-political distinctions and subordinations. Millar's main opus, for instance, which grew out of a social conception of the study of law, dealt equally with the position of women, and with father-child and master-servant relations in different ages, as well as with forms of government and political authority. Millar explicitly criticized previous political historiography: 'Historians of reputation . . . have been more solicitous to give an exact account of battles, and public negotiations, than of the interior police and government of a country.'[56] The rationale, for this extra-political focus is evident from the following statement by Ferguson: 'In every society there is a casual subordination, independent of its formal establishment, and frequently adverse to its constitution . . . this casual subordination, possibly arising from the distribution of property, or from some other circumstance that bestows unequal degree of influence, gives the state its tone, and fixes its character.'[57]

[54] A. Ferguson, *An Essay on the History of Civil Society*, p. 65.
[55] David Hume, 'That Politics may be reduced to a Science', *Essays Moral, Political and Literary*, London, 1875, vol. I, p. 99.
[56] Millar, *The Origin of the Distinction of Ranks*, p. 180.
[57] Ferguson, op. cit., p. 133; cf. Millar, *An Historical View of the English*

The second important step beyond Montesquieu lay in a much more clear and explicit conception of social determination. Millar made short shrift of the importance attributed to climate, in other words of a non-social determination of society: 'National character depends very little upon the immediate operation of climate. . . . The modern Italians live under the country of the ancient Romans.'[58] Both very explicitly repudiated the idea of a legislator-founder of states: 'No constitution is formed by concert, no government is copied from a plan. . . . We are therefore to receive, with caution, the traditional histories of ancient legislators, and founders of states.'[59]

Montesquieu could still counterpose a state of nature to society.[60] But Ferguson stated bluntly: 'If we are asked therefore, Where the state of nature is to be found? we may answer, It is here; . . . While this active being is in the train of employing his talents, and of operating on the subjects around him, all situations are equally natural.'[61]

The core of the new Scottish social determinism was a technico-economic interpretation of history, which Ferguson and Millar shared with Adam Smith and William Robertson.[62] This view was stated squarely by Millar in his own introduction: 'In searching for the causes of these peculiar systems of law and government which have appeared in the world, we must undoubtedly resort, first of all, to the differences of situation, which have suggested different views and motives of action to the inhabitants of particular countries. Of this kind, are the fertility or barrenness of the soil, the nature of its productions, the species of labour requisite for procuring subsistence, the number of individuals collected together in one community, their proficiency in arts, the advantages which they

---

Government, in Lehmann, op. cit., p. 131.

[58] Millar, *The Origin of the Distinction of Ranks*, p. 180. Ferguson paid more attention to the impact of climate (op. cit., p. 108f). It should be added that Montesquieu's estimate of the importance of climate varied from one society to the next: in the case of ancient Sparta, for instance, he thought it secondary (*De l'esprit des lois*, p. 212).

[59] Ferguson, op. cit., p. 123. Millar was even more critical (*Origin*, pp. 177–8), whereas Montesquieu, for example, made a number of uncritical passing references to Lycurgus, the 'founder' of Sparta, *De l'esprit des lois*, pp. 91 n, 93.

[60] Montesquieu, op. cit., Bk. I, ch. II.

[61] Ferguson, op. cit., p. 8.

[62] Meek, op. cit., p. 37. See Smith, *Wealth of Nations*, Bk. V, ch. I.

enjoy for entering into mutual transactions, and for maintaining an intimate correspondence. The variety that frequently occurs in these, and such other particulars, must have a prodigious influence upon the great body of a people; as, by giving a peculiar direction to their inclinations and pursuits, it must be productive of correspondent habits, dispositions and ways of thinking.'[63] There is no equally eloquent methodological statement in Ferguson. But his work too is organized, not round philosophical principles of government, but the technical-economic evolution of mankind – the emergence of agriculture, the introduction of property (which for Ferguson separated the barbarian from the savage stage of the rude era of mankind[64]), the 'improvement of arts and manufactures', the development of the division of labour and of commerce. For both, it was above all the last – the division of labour and commerce – which characterized modern societies, which in their view were 'commercial societies' or 'commercial states'.[65]

This Scottish perspective also included an awareness of a new type of social question. Unlike later sociologists, Ferguson and Millar scarcely glimpsed the new misery of the industrial proletariat, not to speak of its exploitation. But they were highly sensitive to the fact that the blessings of the division of labour also brought with them curses, in the mental degradation of those who had to specialize in menial tasks. Marx paid tribute to Ferguson for this perspicacity.[66] Whereas Ferguson mainly took note of this phenomenon and therein saw the 'absurdity of pretensions to equal influence and consideration after the characters of men have ceased to be similar',[67] Millar in a later work suggested a measure to counteract it – education, the classical bourgeois remedy to social ills. 'As the circumstances of commercial society are unfavourable to the mental improvements of the populace, it ought to be the great aim of the public to counteract, in this respect, the natural tendency of mechanical employments, and by the institution of schools and seminaries of education, to communicate, as far as possible, to the most useful, but humble class of citizens, that knowledge which their way of life has, in some

[63] Millar, *The Origin of the Distinction of Ranks*, p. 175.
[64] Ferguson, op. cit., p. 98.
[65] Ibid., p. 180f; Millar, *Origin of the Distinction of Ranks*, p. 290f.
[66] Marx, *The Poverty of Philosophy, MEW* 4, pp. 145–7; English ed., pp. 128–130; *Capital*, vol. 1, *MEW* 23, pp. 382–4 n; English ed., pp. 354, 361, 362.
[67] Ferguson, op. cit., p. 188.

degree, prevented them from acquiring.'[68] In contrast to Durkheim, neither Millar nor Ferguson saw the division of labour as a bond of interdependence, but rather as something which presented a threat to social union.

However, Ferguson and Millar never broke through to a discourse on society emancipated from moral philosophy, a philosophical history of man or political philosophy. Society never became an object of discourse for them distinct from man and the state. Ferguson's *Essay on the History of Civil Society* significantly did not arrive at a concept of civil society as something different and separate from the state. The word occurs sparsely in the essay and is approximately synonymous with 'polished society', of which political government was a crucial aspect. Civil society remains in Ferguson the pre-sociological concept to be found Hobbes and Locke, though the Scot contrasts it, not with a mythical state of nature, but with 'rude society'.[69]

The technico-economic conception of history did not include any social dynamic to drive mankind from one mode of subsistence to another. No evolutionary theory of economic systems was developed. Particularly striking, perhaps, is the fact that Ferguson and Millar, for all their attention to rank and extra-political subordination, never hit upon any conception of class struggle. Technico-economic evolution was instead interpreted as the unfolding of man's natural and inherent capacity for progress and improvement.[70]

Characteristically, even Adam Smith saw the division of labour, market and modern commercial society in the same terms: 'This division of labour ... is the necessary, though very slow and gradual consequence of a certain propensity in human nature ... the propensity to truck, barter and exchange one thing for another.'[71]

There followed, then, no sociology of politics, no conception of different sociological forms of government, based on different social forces. Ferguson stayed within the classical politico-philosophical discourse of democracy, aristocracy and monarchy.[72] In

[68] Millar, *An Historical View of the English Government*, p. 382. Adam Smith shared Millar's opinion.

[69] Cf. the valuable introduction by Duncan Forbes to Ferguson's *Essay* (ed. cit.), p. xx.

[70] See, for instance, Ferguson, op. cit., pp. 96–7; Millar, *Origin of the Distinction of Ranks*, pp. 198, 203f.

[71] Smith, *Wealth of Nations* (Penguin ed.), p. 117.

[72] Ferguson, op. cit., p. 71f.

spite of his awareness of the impact of social changes upon political history, Millar's discussion of the evolution of British politics remained confined within the traditional problematic of king and people, and his presentation of religious and political parties concentrated on the principles they advocated, rather than the social interests they represented.[73]

The invisible hand of the capitalist market could manifestly be discerned in the business community of Glasgow. But even in the booming Scottish Lowlands, bourgeois civil society as a whole – with its own contradictory forces – was not yet clearly enough developed to permit a distinctly new discourse on it. At least it was not clear enough to a trusted tutor of the sons of Lord Bute and the Earl of Chesterfield (Ferguson)[74] or a protegé of Lord Kames and friend of the Earl of Lauderdale (Millar).[75] Ferguson's last work, a retrospect of his lectures published under the title *Principles of Moral and Political Science*, dealt with the 'history of man's progressive nature' and with the 'Principles of Rights'. Rather than heralding a new science of politics and society, Ferguson belonged to the close of an epoch in which political theory was basically a branch of moral philosophy.

II. The Politics of a New Society

Whatever their evolutionary principle, the new systems of sociology presented a newly emergent society, as yet insufficiently acknowledged by theorists, politicians and the public at large. The rise of capitalism had left its traces in the individualist theories of natural law, as Marx noted in his Introduction to the *Grundrisse* and as the Canadian political scientist C. B. McPherson has since perceptively analyzed.[76] But here we are concerned with theorists whose objective was to make explicit and conscious the decisive social changes that had occurred by the early 19th century.

[73] *The Origin of the Distinction of Ranks*, pp. 289–95; *An Historical View of the English Government*, pp. 337f, 352f, 370f, 378–9.

[74] Kettler, op. cit., pp. 49, 55, 62.

[75] Lehmann, *op. cit.*, pp. 17–18, 28.

[76] C. B. McPherson, *The Political Theory of Possessive Individualism*, Oxford, 1964.

1. The Polity of Industrial Society

To Saint-Simon and, by and large, to Comte and Spencer the new society was *industrial society*. (Spencer's other classification, in terms of structural complexity, stopped short with the ancient Egyptian and Assyrian empires – both, in common with late nineteenth century Britain, France, or Germany being trebly-compound societies.)[77] To none of these writers did 'industrial society' have the meaning or connotation of its usage today. Industrial society was not contrasted with, say, agricultural society or a society of handicraft technology. The term was an anti-feudal one, related to the distinction in early political economy between productive and non-productive labour. Industrial society was counterposed to military society. Industry included all economic activities, and in Saint-Simon often scientific and artistic activities as well.

'Suppose that France suddenly lost fifty of her best physicists, chemists, physiologists, mathematicians, poets, painters . . . fifty of her best mechanical engineers, civil and military engineers . . . fifty of her best bankers, two hundred of her best business men, two hundred of her best farmers, fifty of her best ironmasters, arms manufacturers . . . her fifty best masons, carpenters . . . making in all the three thousand leading scientists, artists and artisans (i.e. the farmers, manufacturers, merchants, bankers and all the clerks and men employed by them) of France.' What would happen? Indeed what would happen if, on the other hand, all the above-mentioned were to remain but France were to lose 'in the same day Monsieur the king's brother, Monseigneur le Duc d'Angoulême, Monseigneur le Duc de Berry' and so on up to thirty thousand individuals 'considered to be the most important in the State', including all ministers and councillors of state and all employees of ministries, all judges, prefects and marshals, all higher clergy from cardinals to canons, and 'ten thousand of the richest proprietors who live in the style of nobles'. The latter eventuality would distress the French, 'because they [the French] are kind-hearted', but no political evil would come of it. The former, on the other hand, would be a national disaster, which it would take a generation to repair.[78]

---

[77] Spencer, *Principles of Sociology*, I: 2, p. 554.

[78] Saint-Simon, *L'Organisateur*, p. 17f, *Oeuvres*, II (English ed., pp. 72–3). In political tactics, Saint-Simon nevertheless hoped and pleaded for an alliance

Such was Saint-Simon's famous parable. Hardly ever before had the claims of the new bourgeois society been set forth with such explicit assertiveness – further underlined by Saint-Simon's con-descending benevolence towards an amiable but futile royalty and a nobility that lacked any particular competence. Aggressive anti-feudalism was, of course, nothing new in the France of 1819. Thirty years earlier already, Abbé Sieyès had answered his own question *What is the Third Estate?* with the reply 'Everything'. He had even said: 'If the privileged orders were removed, the nation would not be something less but something more.'[79] As a revolutionary politician, Sieyès was primarily interested in the establishment of (bourgeois) state power. Saint-Simon, in a period of reaction and restoration, was above all concerned to elucidate the new type of society to which the political system must adapt itself. This type of society could not be adequately conceptualized in terms of the 'third estate' or, as with Robespierre and the Jacobins, 'the people'.

The new society for Saint-Simon is industrial society, the society of the *industriels*. 'The crisis which has gripped the body politic for the past thirty years has as its fundamental cause the total change in the social system; it is this which has produced, among the most civilized nations, all the modifications that the old political order has successively experienced to this day. In more precise terms, this crisis consists essentially in the transition from the feudal and theological to the industrial and scientific system. It will inevitably last until the formation of the new system is fully complete.'[80] In Saint-Simon's usage, industrial activity is contrasted to military activity, which had been the main temporal practice and power of feudal society.[81] War was formally then the best means to riches, or was at least so regarded. The temporal powers of the military aristocracy were connected to the spiritual powers of the clergy with its theology, while those of the *industriels* were connected with science and the arts. However, Saint-Simon's emphasis was definitely more on the industrial than on the scientific aspect of the new society. In direct criticism of Comte, Saint-Simon wrote: 'In the system which we have conceived, industrial talent should take

---

between the house of Bourbon and the industrials, above all in *Du système industriel, Oeuvres*, III; cf. *L'Organisateur*, p. 173.

[79] Sieyès, *What Is the Third Estate?*, London, 1963, p. 56f.

[80] Saint-Simon, *Du système industriel*, p. 3.

[81] Ibid., p. 72; *L'Industrie*, p. 156f; *L'Organisateur*, p. 81.

first place; it is this which should judge the value of all the other talents, and make them work for its greatest advantage.'[82]

In one important respect, at least, Saint-Simon's conception of the industrial society differed from Spencer's. In both cases industrial is roughly synonymous with producer and productive (an expression also used by Saint-Simon) and includes all economic activities. The critical difference is that whereas Spencer thinks of economic life primarily in terms of exchange, Saint-Simon puts the emphasis on economic enterprise. Political power should be placed in the hands of the 'farmers, traders and manufacturers', 'because the industrials are the most capable administrators, and above all the most economical'.[83]

In this perspective it is clear that the section of the industrial class to whom command of the state should be entrusted was what Marxists and others with them would call the bourgeoisie. Saint-Simon is very explicitly not referring to a technocratic stratum, but to a class of capitalist owner-managers.[84] As their admirer and protegé he could even mention the administrators he commended by name – such leading bankers-cum-industrialists and capitalists-cum-politicians as Jacques Laffitte, Casimir Périer and Ternaux, of whom the two former were to be Prime Ministers during the July Monarchy.[85]

On the other hand, Saint-Simon himself was anxious to distinguish his industrial class from the 'bourgeoisie'. This was part of a general operation designed to dissociate himself from the Revolution, probably both for tactical reasons (Saint-Simon made appeals to the king) and for reasons of principle. The Revolution was bourgeois and as such only a transitional stage in the development

---

[82] Saint-Simon, *Preface au troisième cahier*, *Le catéchisme des industriels*, *Oeuvres*, IV.

[83] Saint-Simon, *Du système industriel*, I, pp. 48f, 117. Cf. *Le Parti National ou Industriel Comparé au Parti Anti-National*, *Oeuvres*, II, p. 201.

[84] *Le Parti National*, p. 195f.

[85] *Du système industriel*, I, p. 118. The most faithful of Saint-Simon's protectors were Laffitte and Ternaux, who refused to dissociate themselves from him when the storm broke: shortly after Saint-Simon's parable appeared, one of those who was listed as dispensable, the Duke of Berry, successor to the monarchy, was assassinated. *Oeuvres*, II, p. 9; cf. Manuel, *The New World of Henri Saint-Simon*, ch. 17. The economic role of Ternaux and Laffitte as pioneering entrepreneurs and men of 'la haute banque' can be glimpsed in historical surveys like G. Dupeux, *La société française, 1789–1960*, Paris, 1964, pp. 37, 41.

of industrial society. The 'bourgeoisie', for Saint-Simon, were the non-noble auxiliaries of the feudal regime: 'the military officers who were not noblemen, the plebeian lawyers, and those rentiers who were not privileged'.[86] In contrast to such violent and disorderly bourgeois, 'industrials' – Saint-Simon was eager to stress – were solid, peace-loving and respectable citizens.

In spite of his intellectualist scheme of evolution, Comte treated the development of industrial society as parallel and not subordinate to the evolution from the theological to the scientific stage, a process implying the transfer of spiritual power from the Catholic clergy to positivist scientists.[87] Comte portrayed, very sketchily, science and industry, and theology and war, as functionally related to each other.[88]

Like Saint-Simon, Comte thought of economic activity basically in terms of entrepreneurial organization and not in terms of exchange or technology. In his mature works, however, Comte definitely distinguished entrepreneurs from workers in his analysis of the development of industrial society. Saint-Simon had once written: '*Industry* is one; all its members are united by the general interests of production, by the need they all have of security in work and freedom in exchange.'[89] But Comte could write: 'To display clearly the continuous effect of the growth of Industry upon the general organization of the Modern Movement, I will now separately examine, first the influence of the employers, and then that of the workmen.'[90] Comte's analysis led him to allot a decisive role to directors of machine industry and, increasingly, to bankers.[91]

Both when he presented himself as 'former student of the Ecole Polytechnique' and in his capacity as the High Priest of Humanity, Comte held fast to a political model taken from economic organization, and maintained that temporal power in the positive age duly belonged to the 'leaders of industry'. 'In a settled state of society, government, strictly so called, is a mere extension of civil influence. Ultimately, therefore, political power will fall into the hands of the

---

[86] *Catéchisme des industriels*, p. 11; cf. p. 35f.
[87] Comte, *Système de politique positive*, III, ch. 7. See esp. p. 522f (English ed., p. 441f).
[88] Ibid., p. 64f (English ed., p. 53f).
[89] Saint-Simon, *L'Industrie*, p. 47.
[90] Comte, *Système de politique positive*, III, p. 520 (English ed., p. 439).
[91] Ibid., p. 521, 594 (English ed., pp. 440, 508–9).

great leaders of industry.'[92] Comte used the term industrial in the same sense as Saint-Simon. In fact, Saint-Simon attributed the exclusive classification of societies into industrial and military to Comte.[93]

Spencer's distinction between militant and industrial societies starts from a systems-theory type of distinction between the internal processes of a system and the processes concerned with the system's relation to other systems.[94] This contrast Spencer conceives, in the case of social systems, as fundamentally one between economic activity and war. The two types of activity give rise to two different types of social organization and co-operation among men. One of them is voluntary, unconsciously social, essentially constituted by the mutual dependence of individuals exchanging services in a system of division of labour. The other is compulsory, conscious, centrally commanded organization.

The feat of making economic organization in general look like mid-nineteenth century English competitive capitalism is accomplished by classifying other economic systems as forms of subordination of the economy to military aims. Slavery and serfdom as 'industrial institutions' have military roots.[95] Socialism and communism likewise have a warrior basis: 'Communistic forms of organization existed in early societies which were predominantly warlike, and . . . at the present time communistic projects chiefly originate among, and are most favoured by, the more warlike societies.'[96]

The general trend of evolution – at least up to about 1850 – was seen as one of decreasing warfare and increasing peaceful economic activity. As a rule, political institutions had their origin in organization for war. By now, however, the evolutionary benefits of war had

[92] Comte, *Système de politique positive*, I, p. 199 (English ed., p. 161). At that time Comte was of the opinion that the industrial leaders needed a temporary moral re-education, in order to 'attain . . . to greater purity of feeling and greater breadth of view' (English ed., p. 162), under the guidance of a transitional régime of a group of positivist proletarians. Comte actually nominated a triumvirate of positivist dictators, a worker, a banker, and a landowner (Gouhier, op. cit., p. 219).

[93] Saint-Simon, *L'Industrie*, p. 157.

[94] Spencer, *Principles of Sociology*, Part II, ch. IX; part V, esp. chs. II, XVII–XIX.

[95] Ibid., Part VIII, chs. XVI–XVII.

[96] Ibid., vol. II: 2, p. 605.

been fully reaped. 'From war has been gained all that it had to give. The peopling of the Earth by the more powerful and intelligent races, is a benefit in great measure achieved; and what remains to be done, calls for no other agency than the quiet pressure of a spreading industrial civilization on a barbarism which slowly dwindles.'[97]

A polity adapted to an industrial society, in which economic activities are predominant, is a polity with severely limited functions. Since economic organization is by nature individualist and of market character, the decline of military and increase of economic activities mean that there is less need for conscious social action and concerted organization. The evolutionary differentiation of functions had divested the state of more and more activities, which were now taken over by the voluntary associations of civil society. The Spencerian state, like its Lockean predecessor, was mainly concerned with maintaining security of life and property, though it did not bow to the dictates of natural law governing the intrinsic limits of political government, but rather adapted itself to an evolved type of society. In both cases it was in fact a state appropriate to competitive capitalism.[98] In sociology, however, this result of the bourgeois revolution was – by whatever name it was known – explicitly taken into account as the central determinant of politics. In Spencer's England, as well as in the France of Comte and Saint-Simon, industrial society and the industrial classes (the bourgeoisie and the working-class) were assertive terms explicitly directed against the old aristocracy and the social order it represented – against what Bentham once called 'priest-ridden, lawyer-ridden, squire-ridden, soldier-ridden England', against Tory England.[99]

In spite of his stress on exchange, Spencer too could sometimes present entrepreneurial organization and economic associations as models of government. 'Combinations of workmen and counter-combinations of employers, no less than political societies and leagues for carrying on this or that agitation, show us the representative mode of government; which characterizes also every joint-stock company, for mining, banking, railway-making, or other commercial enterprise.'[100]

---

[97] Ibid., vol. II: 2, p. 664. The rationalization of the state apparatus had also gone as far as it could by organization for war purposes.

[98] Cf. McPherson, op. cit., ch. V.

[99] Peel, op. cit., ch. 8. Bentham is quoted from p. 51.

[100] Spencer, *Principles of Sociology*, I: 2, p. 567.

Economic organization as a direct model of political organization was a conception unknown even to John Millar, in spite of his economic determinism.[101] To Burke, a Whig with powerful if suppressed Jacobite inclinations, the idea would have been abominable: 'The state ought not to be considered as nothing better than a partnership agreement in a trade of pepper and coffee, calico or tobacco, or some other such low concern.'[102] Burke's intention in this passage had been to stress the obligatory character of social organization, but the sociologists now discovered that the new commercial economy itself created new social obligations.

In Renaissance Italy Macchiavelli had written, from another world: 'A wise prince, then, has no other object and no other interest and takes as his profession nothing else than war and its laws and discipline.'[103]

Science as a guiding light of politics was not a new idea in the tradition of political theory; it is present in Hobbes, and discernible also in Macchiavelli. But the vision of scientists as the true spiritual leaders of society, to be found in the schemes of Saint-Simon and Comte, was a novel one. Though the English Royal Society and the French Académie des Sciences had been established as early as the 17th century, such ideas were unthinkable in the age of the wars of religion, at least in public. The new conception was first developed by Condorcet during the French Revolution, during the epoch in which institutions like the Ecole Polytechnique, the Ecole Normale Supérieure, and the Institut were established in France.

2. The New Social Relations

The new society, which the early sociologists believed necessarily determined the political system, was above all a society in which people were *doing* something other than in the past, where economic activities had replaced war as the dominant preoccupation. Another way of interpreting the new society, however, was to emphasize that people *were related to each other* in a novel way. This was what Tocqueville had in mind, when he called for a new political science in his *Democracy in America*. Aristocratic and bourgeois social

[101] Cf. Millar, *Origins of the Distinction of Ranks*, ch. V.
[102] Burke, op. cit., p. 194.
[103] Macchiavelli, *The Prince*, p. 98.

relationships here constituted the focus of contrast, instead of aristocratic and bourgeois activities.

Tocqueville's key concept was '*état social*', usually translated as 'social condition'. 'Social condition is commonly the result of circumstances, sometimes of laws, oftener still of these two causes united; but when once established, it may justly be considered as itself the source of almost all the laws, the usages, and the ideas which regulate the conduct of nations: whatever it does not produce, it modifies. If we would become acquainted with the legislation and the manners of a nation, therefore, we must begin by the study of its social condition.'[104] The term 'social condition' here refers to the dimension of equality-inequality in a society, sometimes expressed as its democratic-aristocratic characteristics. It comprises a whole series of aspects: income and wealth, social mobility, legal status, education, intermarriage and social intercourse.[105] The process of social evolution and change to which Tocqueville's term drew attention was the egalitarian or democratic revolution. More concretely, this process was explicitly presented by the Marquis de Tocqueville as the decline of the aristocracy and the rise of the commoners. It was an inexorable, predetermined evolution: 'The gradual development of the principle of equality is, therefore, a providential fact. It has all the chief characteristics of such a fact: it is universal, it is lasting, it constantly eludes all human interference, and all events as well as all men contribute to its progress.'[106]

The basic fact about American society was its democratic social condition – the aspects, implications and consequences of which Tocqueville studied in his book.[107] The basic fact about the French Revolution, whose historical background Tocqueville analyzed in the second of his two major works, was its suppression of feudalism and its creation of a social and political order 'based on the concept of equality of all men'.[108] The basic cause of the Revolution was an explosive combination of increasing equality and increasing inequality. The French nobility had become steadily impoverished while commoners prospered economically, improving their educa-

---

[104] Tocqueville, *Democracy in America*, vol. 1, p. 46.

[105] Ibid., Introduction, Part I, ch. III, *The Ancien Régime*, chs. 8–9.

[106] Tocqueville, *Democracy in America*, Introduction, p. 6.

[107] Other aspects are also taken account of, for example, the physical size and wealth of the country (vol. 1, pp. 288–98).

[108] Tocqueville, *The Ancien Régime*, p. 50.

tion and style of life, so there occurred a gradual process of equalization. Yet at the same time the nobility had become more socially
exclusive in other respects: it preserved caste-like intermarriage
patterns, it increasingly monopolized higher administrative positions, it enjoyed ever larger tax exemptions. Moreover, it did not as
a rule live in the country, in contact with the peasantry and able to
guide it; while a centralized and top-heavy absolute monarchy
provided no institutions for class collaboration.

The central problem of modern politics, in Tocqueville's view,
was how to regulate and curb the irresistible pressure of the
democratic revolution. This could only be done by creating new
institutions to replace the role of the defunct aristocracy in ensuring
particular loyalties between the masses and the state.[109]

In his discovery of the determinant role of a social order beneath
the letter of constitutions, laws and decrees, Tocqueville was not
unique among his contemporaries. Interestingly enough, attempts
at sociological history have been overwhelmingly interested in
relating early sociology to the philosophers of reaction – which is,
as we have seen, gravely misleading – whereas they have generally
neglected other strands of the development of thought of which
sociology was a part. The most important line of parallel development in this respect was French historiography.

Few have expressed the enormous effect of the Revolution upon
historians with such eloquence as Augustine Thierry, Comte's
predecessor as secretary to Saint-Simon: 'There is not one amongst
us children of the 19th century, who does not know more on the
score of rebellion and conquests, of the dismemberment of empires,
of the fall and restoration of monarchies, of popular revolution and
the consequent reactions, than did Velly, Mably, or even Voltaire
himself.'[110] Thus 'the events of the last fifty years, events hitherto
unheard of, have taught us to understand the revolutions of the
Middle Ages, to perceive the spirit beneath the letter of the
chronicler, to draw from the writings of the Benedictines that which
those learned men never saw, or saw only partially, without suspect-
ing its significance. They lacked the comprehension and sentiment

---

[109] Tocqueville, *Democracy in America*, p. 8f; vol. 2, p. 332f; *The Ancien Régime*,
p. 29.
[110] A. Thierry, *Lettres sur l'histoire de France*, Paris, 1827, p. 3, quoted from
D. Johnson, *Guizot*, London, 1963, p. 325.

of great social transformations. They have studied with curiosity the laws, public acts, judicial formulae, private contracts, etc.; . . . but the political sense, all that was living beneath the dead letter, the perception of society and its various elements, whether young or old, whether barbarian or civilized, escapes them. . . . This perception, we have acquired through our experience; we owe it to the prodigious changes of power and society, which have taken place before us.'[111]

The social determination of politics was also a tenet of Tocqueville's contemporary and political colleague in the July Monarchy, the more conservative liberal Guizot, one of the foremost French historians of his time: 'The political order is necessarily the expression and the reflection of the social order.'[112] In his *Histoire de la Civilization en France* Guizot's key analytical concepts are 'état social' and 'état intellectual'.

For Guizot as well as for Tocqueville the 'social condition' developed through a struggle between *classes*. 'The struggle of the diverse classes of our society has filled our history', Guizot found in his study *De la Démocratie en France*, though he held that the Revolution had brought the class struggle to its final halt and created social harmony.[113] Tocqueville was more perspicacious: 'Seen as a whole from a distance, our history from 1789 to 1830 appears to be forty-one years of deadly struggle between the Ancien Regime with its traditions, memories, hopes and men (i.e. the aristocrats), and the new France led by the middle class.'[114] He distanced himself from Guizot (who said that the February Revolution was an accident) and emphasized the importance of the industrial revolution, and the rise of the working class, and the struggle of the latter against the bourgeoisie that had gained decisive power in 1830.[115] In contrast to Marx, neither Guizot nor Tocqueville founded their concept of class on any developed socio-economic theory.[116] But in a loose commense sense manner they

---

[111] Thierry, *Considérations sur l'histoire de France*, Johnson, loc. cit.

[112] P.-G. Guizot, *Mélanges politiques*, vol. II, p. 296, from Johnson, p. 74.

[113] Johnson summarizes the argument on pp. 74, 338.

[114] Tocqueville, *Recollections*, p. 4f.

[115] Ibid., pp. 61–3.

[116] Class, in the view of the French historians, in the end derived from conquest. Cf. the critical analysis by Plekhanov in *The Development of the Monist View of History, Selected Philosophical Works*, vol. I, pp. 558–71.

clearly discerned the economic foundation of classes; the land-owning aristocracy, the capital-owning bourgeoisie, the peasantry, and the industrial working-class. A class view of politics was not, of course, confined to sociologists and historians (-cum-politicians). It was widespread in post-revolutionary France, and is broadly diffused throughout the novels of Balzac and Stendhal. The former's *Les Paysans* and *Le Cabinet des Antiques*, for example, and the latter's *Le Rouge et Le Noir*, can also be seen as integral to the rise of a new discourse on society.

Another way of illuminating men's different relationships to one another in different societies, which was also to be pertinent to the development of sociology, was pioneered in legal history. Of particular importance in this context was Sir Henry Maine's *Ancient Law*. This work, written in 1861, originated one of the main dichotomies of sociological analysis, between social relationships based on status and on contract. History to Maine was above all the history of the decreasing importance of kinship. In a revolution both 'startling and . . . complete' kinship was succeeded as the basis of political action by some other principle, 'such as that for instance, of *local contiguity*'.[117] Summarizing the development of the law of persons, and the social changes it indicated, Maine stated: 'The movement of progressive societies has been uniform in one respect. Through all its course it has been distinguished by the gradual dissolution of family dependency and the growth of individual obligation has taken its place.'[118] 'If we employ Status . . . to signify these personal conditions only, and avoid applying them to such conditions as are the immediate or remote cause of agreement, we may say that the movement of the progressive societies has hitherto been a movement *from Status to Contract*.'[119]

By progressive societies, which he held to constitute an exception among human societies, Maine meant approximately Western Europe,[120] and the legal development he studied was mainly that of Roman law. Legal development, in turn, was a more or less slow adaptation to societal progress, the spearhead of which appeared to be 'material civilization' or 'the activity of man in discovery, in

[117] H. S. Maine, *Ancient Law*, London, 1863 (2nd ed.), p. 129.
[118] Ibid., p. 168.
[119] Ibid., p. 170. Emphasis in original.
[120] Ibid., p. 22f.

invention, and in the manipulation of accumulated wealth'.[121]

Maine's distinction was applied by Spencer to his own categories of militant and industrial societies. Tönnies, in the preface to the first edition of his *Gemeinschaft und Gesellschaft* (1887), mentioned Maine as one of the three principal influences on his theories. (The other two were Otto Gierke, another legal historian, and Karl Marx.)[122] Tönnies' enormously influential book, which can be said to have been the first major work of classical sociology, dealt with social relations. But Tönnies' strong romantic inclinations led him to confer a different connotation on his social categories from those of the English liberal Maine. The warmth and harmony of family and village *Gemeinschaft* were contrasted favourably with the calculating egotism of businesslike *Gesellschaft*. The state, Tönnies held, 'can only derive its adequate explanation from the underlying contrast to the *Gemeinschaft* of the people'.[123]

Durkheim's *The Division of Labour in Society* is also in important respects a study of law, which distinguishes legal systems by the prevalence of repressive or restitutive sanctions in them. But Durkheim was interested in explaining the differences in legal systems by referring them to two different kinds of social solidarity – one mechanical and based on common sentiments and beliefs among an undifferentiated population, another organic and contractual, deriving from the interdependence created by an extended division of labour.[124] (In a century of biological metaphors, Durkheim's reversal of the usage of the words 'mechanical' and 'organic' expresses his reversal of Tönnies' evaluation.)[125] From this point of view Durkheim criticized Maine for deriving the system of

[121] Ibid., pp. 305, 24f.

[122] F. Tönnies, Preface to the First Edition of *Gemeinschaft und Gesellschaft*, *Soziologische Studien und Kritiken*, vol. 1, p. 43; also in F. Tönnies, *On Sociology*, Chicago and London, 1971.

[123] F. Tönnies, *Community and Association*, London, 1955, p. 39.

[124] E. Durkheim, *The Division of Labor in Society*, New York, 1964, p. 129f.

[125] Tönnies pointed out in a review of Durkheim that the *Gemeinschaft-Gesellschaft* dichotomy is essentially quite different from Durkheim's types of social solidarity. Tönnies' distinction derives from a kind of philosophical anthropology, a distinction of human wills. *Gemeinschaft* is a social relationship characterized by the men involved seeing it as an end in itself, while *Gesellschaft* is one that is seen as a means to something else. *Soziologische Studien und Kritiken*, vol. 3, p. 216. Tönnies's review, together with Durkheim's review of his book, is reprinted in the *American Journal of Sociology*, vol. 77 (1972), pp. 1191–1200,

repressive sanctions from the frequency of violence in such societies, an explanation consonant with the distinction of societies on the basis of their predominant activity made by Saint-Simon, Comte and Spencer.[126]

The criteria of dominant activities and dominant social relationships in fact yielded interlocking conceptualizations of society. The role of classes and their struggle in the emergence of the industrial and scientific society was clear both to Comte and Saint-Simon, neither of whom, on the other hand, had much regard for the egalitarian aspect of social evolution. Spencer's specification of the meaning of his militant and industrial societies was mainly in terms of modes of social co-operation, which was the reason he could make ample use of Maine. Conversely, Tocqueville stressed that democracy was dysfunctional for military ambitions, but was the government best adapted to a concentration of men's activities on 'the promotion of general well-being' (literally 'on the necessities of material life').[127]

In relation to the whole natural law tradition of 17th and 18th century political theory, Maine's distinction between status and contract constitutes a break. Contract is now no longer a logical device to legitimate the establishment of society as such and to justify the existence of government, but a concept designating one of two empirical patterns of social relationships. Maine sharply criticized the theorists of social contract, particularly Rousseau and French 18th century lawyers in general, for ignoring the Historical Method.[128] The area in which he traced the movement from status to contract – the position of slaves, women, and children – is reminiscent of the work of Millar, whose treatment of it was less legalistic but also less rigorous. However, Millar is not mentioned in Maine's work. The general importance of Maine's theory has been formulated in this way by a recent biographer: 'In putting forth the theory, Maine, perhaps more than any other scholar of his generation, provided an authoritative legal rationale and the guiding

---

under the rubric 'An Exchange between Durkheim and Tönnies on the Nature of Social Relations, with an Introduction by Jane Aldous. Durkheim criticized Tönnies for regarding *Gesellschaft* as a non-natural, transient society.

[126] Durkheim, op. cit., p. 146.

[127] Tocqueville, *Democracy in America*, vol. 1, p. 252.

[128] Maine, op. cit., p. 85f.

academic spirit of the entrepreneurial attitude.'[129]

The idea that there was a social order bearing upon the political order was not unknown in the tradition of political philosophy. Macchiavelli, for example, had spoken of 'the people and the rich', who could each aid princes to power or bring them down, and had commented that 'in every city these two opposing parties exist'.[130] But he did not see this opposition as the basis of politics. The sociological view brought to light new mechanisms by which societies were maintained over time and space, undreamt of by the great political theorists.

In Tocqueville's perspective there was one single evolving social process, and one constant constellation of opposed social forces, throughout the different political regimes from 1789 to 1830. To Hobbes, on the other hand, society as such was dissolved and individuals brought back to the state of nature when the sovereign was finally defeated. 'Lastly, when in a warre (forraign or intestine) the enemies get a final Victory; so as (the forces of the Common-wealth keeping the field no longer) there is no protection of Subjects in their loyalty; then is the Common-wealth *DISSOLVED*, and every man at liberty to protect himself by such courses as his own discretion shall suggest unto him.'[131]

The democratic republic in America, Tocqueville often and rightly pointed out, was established in a vast and rich country. To Montesquieu this was impossible. A republic could only be small and relatively poor. A moderately large country demanded a monarchy and a vast country could only be held together by a despotic government. 'A large empire supposes a despotic authority in the person who governs. It is necessary that the quickness of the prince's resolutions should supply the distance of the places they are sent to; that fear (the principle of despotic government) should prevent the remissness of the distant governor or magistrate; that the law should be derived from a single person, and should shift continually, according to the accidents which necessarily multiply in a state in proportion to its extent.'[132]

---

[129] G. Feaver, *From Status to Contract*, London, 1969, p. xvii. In spite of its title this is an overwhelmingly personal biography.

[130] Macchiavelli, *The Prince*, pp. 84, 128.

[131] Hobbes, *Leviathan*, p. 375.

[132] Montesquieu, *De l'esprit des lois*, p. 152 (English ed., p. 56f, quote from p. 57, Book VIII, ch. 19).

3. National Culture: the Volksgeist

The French and English contributions to a new science of politics all explicitly pointed to a new social reality, which necessarily affected the system of government. They directly expressed the claims to political power of a new society and a new class.

In economically underdeveloped Germany, however, the defeat of the *ancien régime* – with the shattering of the obsolete Holy Roman Empire and its 300 or so more or less feudal principalities by the armed forces of the French Revolution – did not liberate any significant forces of industry or democracy. Outright serfdom was abolished, but otherwise political changes in post-revolutionary Germany were by and large concentrated in the juridical-administrative aspects of the state apparatus. The corresponding political theories within progressive German thought were Kant's idea of the *Rechtsstaat* and Hegel's idea of the post-feudal Prussian monarchy governed by a bureaucratic sense of duty.[133]

However, the impact of the French Revolution in Germany exposed a social reality which, though certainly not new – to many its ancient age was precisely the most important aspect of it – had earlier been concealed under the hard crust of princely and priestly power. This reality was national culture – the *Volksgeist* expressed in language, folk-songs and folklore, in all the customs and traditions of a people. With the juridico-political superstructures of petty absolutism breaking apart and no new strong social forces ready to replace them, national culture became all-important for social reconstruction.

The discovery of the national spirit was not a feat of German sociology, which hardly existed at this time. But the focus on cultural determination which it betokened had a critical significance for the establishment of sociology and its later development. This significance lay in its contribution to the formation of a particular tradition of thought, that of German Idealism, rather than in any direct line of influence. So far as theories of the national spirit and of the cultural determination of politics (politics as the expression

---

[133] An excellent overview of the impact on Germany of the French Revolution, especially the ideological impact, is provided by the works of Jacques Droz, *L'Allemagne et la Révolution Française*, Paris, 1949, *Le romantisme allemand et l'état*, Paris, 1966. The latter book can also be seen as an important contribution to a study of counter-revolution and its mechanisms.

of a particular culture) were concerned, there were two important elements in this idealist tradition, one Romantic and the other Hegelian.

German romanticism did not contain any self-consciously sociological tendencies. Yet it has, however, been presented as *the* origin of sociology, in a theory of sociology which was developed with particular reference to the German classics Simmel, Tönnies and Weber. The theory in question was propounded by the conservative German historian Georg von Below, in an academic feud towards 1920 over the establishment of sociology as a university subject in Germany. 'What later appears as "sociology" is in its usable elements nothing more than a continuation of these old romantic studies.'[134]

Von Below was apparently to a large extent grinding his own Greater-German axe, anxious to provide a conservative German pedigree for social studies as against the claims of Western positivism and even Marxism.[135] On the other hand, Below had a precise conception of what he meant by the romantic contribution,[136] and this contribution was noted by others too, from quite different viewpoints.[137] The names Below cited were those of Savigny, Eichhorn, the Grimm brothers, Ranke and Niebuhr – two jurists and legal historians, two philologists and pioneer students of folk

[134] G. Von Below, 'Zur Geschichte der deutschen Geschichtswissenschaft I–II', *Historische Blätter*, 1 (1921), pp. 5–30, 173–217; p. 173. Cf. idem, 'Soziologie als Lehrfach', *Schmollers Jahrbuch*, 43 (1919), pp. 59–110.

[135] This is particularly clear in Von Below's reference to his agreement with Othmar Spann ('Zur Geschichte der deutschen Geschichtswissenschaft I–II', p. 173 n). Von Below's role among the German 'Mandarins', that of an extreme right-wing imperialist, is described by Ringer, op. cit., pp. 191, 196, 218. Ringer's presentation of von Below's position in the sociology debate (pp. 228ff) is oversimplified.

[136] The recent discussion of sociology and Romanticism by Alvin Gouldner ('Romanticism and Classicism', in *For Sociology*, pp. 323–66), is more literary and analogical in orientation. The key figures in Gouldner's gallery of Romanticists are the Schlegel brothers. Gouldner's intention is to focus on two broad modes of thought in sociology: one 'romantic' stressing 'the relativity, the uniqueness or historical character of the standards or morals of any society or group', another 'classic', emphasizing 'the *universality* of the governing standards, norms, or values, or of the functional requisites of society'.

[137] For example, by Droz, *Le romantisme allemand et l'état*, ch. VIII; A Small, *The Origins of Sociology*, Chicago, 1924, ch. II. Small's stress differed considerably from the present one. To Small, Savigny was the representative of 'the principle of historical continuity'.

tales, and two historians, all from the early nineteenth century.[138] Their common contribution was above all their emphasis on the *Volksgeist* as the cultural determinant of history, politics, and legislation, and their focus on the collective relationships among men.

Von Below was against the establishment of sociology as a university subject of its own, and he was especially opposed to the proposal of the liberal secretary for higher education in the Prussian Ministry of Culture, Becker, to set sociology up as the basis for a vast cultural 'synthesis'. He had, however, a considerable regard for the formal sociology of Simmel as a sub-discipline of philosophy, and for the sociology of Tönnies and Max Weber, whose most fertile thought Below saw as romantic in origin.[139]

The central figure of this group of Romantic contributors to social science was probably Friedrich Carl von Savigny, the leader of the Historical School of Law – leaving aside the younger Ranke, whose major influence came later and was more specifically historiographic.[140] Like all German intellectuals Savigny was strongly affected by the disintegration of the Holy Roman Empire, a hopelessly decadent body politic, a 'polished grave', as Savigny called it. The task ahead was one of spiritual regeneration, the only possible basis for a new society.[141]

Savigny, like the French and English sociologists, was an incisive critic of natural law and of social contract theories, of voluntarist legislation and ambitious constitution-making. He stressed 'that the common consciousness of the people is the peculiar seat of law'.[142] Together with language, custom and constitution it forms a unique

[138] Von Below, 'Zur Geschichte der deutschen Geschichtswissenschaft I–II', pp. 14, 25.

[139] Ibid., p. 201f; 'Soziologie als Lehrfach', pp. 61, 106. Tönnies and Von Wiese, who pleaded the cause of sociology, denied any synthetic claims: F. Tönnies, 'Soziologie und Hochschulreform', *Weltwirtschafiliches Archiv*, 16 (1920–1), pp. 212–45; L. Von Wiese, 'Die Soziologie als Einzelwissenschaft', *Schmollers Jahrbuch*, 44 (1920), pp. 347–67. Von Wiese later developed a particular anti-synthetic 'formal sociology'.

[140] An introductory overview of Savigny and his work is given by D. Strauch, *Recht, Gesetz und Staat bei Friedrich Carl von Savigny*, Bonn, 1963.

[141] Ibid., p. 57f.

[142] F. C. Von Savigny, *Vom Beruf unserer Zeist für Gesetzgebung*, J. Stern (ed.), *Thibaut und Savigny*, Berlin, 1914 (1st ed. 1814), p. 78; *Of the Vocation of Our Age for Legislation* (English Translation n.d.), p. 28.

totality. 'These phenomena have no separate existence, they are but the particular faculties and tendencies of an individual people, inseparably united in nature, and only wearing the semblance of distinct attributes to our view. That which binds them into one whole is the common conviction of the people, the kindred consciousness of an inward necessity, excluding all notion of an accidental and arbitrary origin.'[143] Conceived in this way, law 'is first developed by custom and popular faith, next by jurisprudence – everywhere, therefore, by internal silently-operating powers, not by the arbitrary will of a law-giver.'[144] Laws and constitutions are part of a particular cultural community, historically handed down. Politics is an expression of this community: 'we call . . . the connection of law with the general existence of the people – the political element; and the distinct scientific existence of law – the technical element.'[145]

Savigny explicitly compared law with language,[146] an indication of the influence of another remarkable German thinker, Johann Gottfried Herder.[147] In the three last decades of the 18th century, before the French Revolution, Herder had developed the idea of a *Volk* community, characterized above all by a common language, as the necessary basis of political activity, and of a unique *Volksgeist* for each people, manifested at any historical stage in a specific *Kultur*.[148]

Herder was a progressive bourgeois intellectual in a Germany

[143] Ibid., p. 76 (English ed., p. 24).
[144] Ibid., p. 79 (English ed., p. 30).
[145] Ibid., p. 78 (English ed., p. 29).
[146] Ibid., p. 77 (English ed., p. 27).
[147] For Herder I have made use of F. M. Barnard, *Herder's Social and Political Thought*, Oxford, 1965, and G. A. Wells, *Herder and After*, The Hague, 1959. Herder's thought contained both cultural and naturalistic elements (stressing the role of man's physical habitat and the physiological bases of psychology). The uneasy mixture of different strands of thought was one of the reasons for the rather chilly reception of Herder's large-scale philosophy of history, *Ideen zur Philosophie der Geschichte der Menschheit* (1784). Wells, an admirer of the naturalistic historiography of Buckle, largely concentrates on the naturalistic tendencies in Herder, least influential in Germany, whereas Barnard skilfully analyses Herder's conceptions of *Kultur, Volk* and so on.
[148] The critical role of Herder in the development of the concept of *Kultur*, a central concept in German discourse on society and history ever since, is illuminated in J. Niedermann, *Kultur, Werden und Wandlungen des Begriffes und seiner Ersatzbegriffe*, Bibliotheca dell' 'Archivum Romanicum', vol. 28, Florence, 1941.

ruled by despots, whose 'enlightenment' was perhaps above all admiration for a culture other than that of their own subjects, largely serfs, whom they sometimes sold as mercenaries to the highest bidder.[149] Herder put forward his ideas of the *Volk*, its language and culture, in a country where princes called their castles Sans Souci and La Solitude, ruled with 'Frenchified nobles and cour-tiers' and could set up, in Berlin, the *Académie des sciences et des belles lettres de Prussie.*[150]

Herder constitutes a link between the Enlightenment and Romanticism. It was among the Romantics, after the French Revolution and Napoleon had smashed the political structure of the old Germany, that Herder's conception of society – never presented very systematically, and containing both positivist and idealist tendencies in an unstable mixture – gained a wide influence. Because of the weakness of the German bourgeoisie, these elements were then inserted into a much more conservative context, with strong mystical and irrationalist tendencies.[151] Herder was essentially a literary intellectual – a pastor and a friend of Goethe, at his best as a writer on the origin of language and as an early collector and student of folksongs. Both Herder and the Romantics tended towards a cultural sublimation of politics – a dissolution of political questions into cultural problems, instead of a study of the concrete relationships between culture and politics. An example of this tendency was Savigny's famous polemical theme that 'organic jurisprudence' was still too immature to make possible the creation of a new legislative code for the new Germany.[152]

Savigny, Eichhorn and Gustav Hugo of the Historical School appear to have been conscientious historians of Roman law,[153] but in their theories the *Volksgeist* remained an essentially mystical phenomenon, graspable by intuition rather than by systematic empirical investigation. 'Law is not produced by the arbitrary will

[149] Barnard, op. cit., p. 4 n.

[150] Gay, op. cit., vol. II, p. 245.

[151] On Herder in German Romanticism, see Barnard, p. 152f, Wells, p. 191f. Savigny was a noble landowner, strongly religious and conservative but not a militant reactionary.

[152] Savigny, op. cit. Later on, Savigny was to take a leading part in Prussian legislation, in which capacity he became a target of Marxian criticism. See below.

[153] Writing as a non-historian and non-jurist, I am relying on the judgment of G. P. Gooch, *History and Historians of the Nineteenth Century*, Boston, 1963 (1st ed. 1913), ch. IV, and of Droz, *Le romantisme allemand et l'état*, p. 217f.

of the individual members of a nation: for the wills of individuals could perhaps by chance choose the same law, but they are more likely to choose something far more manifold. Rather it is the spirit of the people, active in all its members alike, that produces positive law, so that it is no contingency but necessity that this law is one and the same for the consciousness of each individual.'[154] It was for this reason that Tönnies, for example, rejected the Romantic legacy, preferring the more rationalist heritage of Hegel.[155] Max Weber, for his part, broke with the intuitionist tendencies of the much more articulate historicist school of his day.[156]

The concept of *Volksgeist* also figures very early on in Hegel's thought. Under the influence of Herder and Montesquieu it can be found before the emergence of Hegelian philosophy proper, for example in the essay 'Religion is One', which dates from 1793: 'The spirit of the people [is] its history, the level of its political freedom – [these things] cannot be treated separately either with respect to their mutual influence, or in characterizing them [each by itself] – they are woven together in a single bond . . . to form the moral character of the individual men is a matter of private religion, of parental teaching, of personal effort, of particular circumstances – to form the spirit of the people is in part again a matter of the folk-religion, in part of political relations.'[157]

In Hegel's political philosophy the *Volksgeist* is one concept in a vast metaphysical system. It is part of a conception of the world and its history as a spiritual reality, in which mind realizes itself and becomes conscious of itself in the same process. The concept of *Volksgeist* is directly subordinate to concrete manifestations of the world spirit, 'around [whose] throne they [the *Volksgeister*] stand as the executors of its actualization and as signs and ornaments of its grandeur'.[158] The state is an expression of the spirit of the people

[154] F. C. Von Savigny, *System des heutigen Romischen Rechts*, Berlin, 1840, p. 14, quoted from Wells, op. cit., p. 199.

[155] Tönnies, 'Soziologie und Hochschulreform', p. 223.

[156] See, for example, M. Weber, 'Roscher und Knies und die logischen Probleme der historischen Nationalökonomie', in *Gesammelte Aufsätze fur Wissenschaftslehre*, Tübingen, 1951, pp. 1–145.

[157] G. W. F. Hegel, 'Religion ist eine', appended in English translation to H. S. Harris, *Hegel's Development*, I, Oxford, 1972, p. 506. Herder's influence on the young Hegel has not been firmly ascertained, but Harris, who knows more than most, suspects 'that it was great', op. cit., p. 271 n.

[158] G. W. F. Hegel, *Philosophy of Right*, 352. A recent perceptive analysis of

and its consciousness of itself, a manifestation of the manners (*Sittlichkeit*) and consciousness of a nation.[159]

But in Hegel's conception peoples are not unrelated, each in their own particular uniqueness. On the contrary, peoples and their minds are linked together in the chain of world history. At different stages in the development of the world spirit, different peoples are the agents of the historical process, become a 'world historical nation'.[160] History is the development of Reason; the *Volksgeister* constitute different moments of this development, but it is the unfolding of Reason that Hegel is concerned to grasp, not the unfolding of the mind of a particular people.[161] A rationalist metaphysics replaces the intuitionist empiricism of the Romantics. This allowed Hegel to construct a rationalist critique of historical development, distinguishing '*origin in external circumstances*' from '*origin in the concept*'. The result was that he could combine a historical view of law, as determined by the development of the national character of a people, with formal, rationalist criteria of valid law.[162] Whereas the Romantics dethroned the Reason of natural law in favour of empirical tradition, Hegel's philosophy represented a historicization of Reason. But in both cases society was seen as a cultural totality expressing the collective consciousness of a particular people.

Montesquieu had a great impact upon German intellectuals of the late eighteenth and early nineteenth century, as well as on thinkers of other countries. Hegel appreciated him highly and wrote in his *Philosophy of Right* that Montesquieu 'proclaimed the true historical view, the genuinely philosophical position, namely that legislation both in general and in its particular provisions is to be treated not as something isolated and abstract but rather as a subordinate moment in a whole, interconnected with the other features which make up

Hegel's political thought, making use of letters and other biographical material as well as his philosophical writings, is S. Avineri, *Hegel's Theory of the Modern State*, Cambridge, 1972. *The Philosophy of Right* is the central text of Hegel's political philosophy. The historical theory to be found there, in §§341–60, is developed in his lectures on the Philosophy of History.

[159] Hegel, op. cit., §274.

[160] Ibid., §§347, 352.

[161] Ibid., §§342, 352.

[162] Ibid., §3, which also includes some critical remarks about Gustav Hugo's history of Roman law. Cf. §258 n and the very harsh criticism of the reactionary state theorist Von Haller.

the character of a nation and an epoch'.[163]

The term '*esprit de nation*' can in fact already be found, rather inconspicuously, in Montesquieu.[164] Essentially, however, the German idea of *Volksgeist* is a new idea, part of a novel conceptual system. In Montesquieu's theory, it will be remembered, the basic concepts are the forms of government (republican, monarchical, despotic) and the corresponding 'principles' or 'human passions' (virtue, honour, fear). Montesquieu then discusses the various factors affecting the tendencies of different peoples towards these principles. This schema was transformed in the German historicist tradition, Romantic and Hegelian, by the introduction of certain fundamentally new ideas. Firstly, the German tradition introduced a *subject*: the spirit of the people in place of the spirit of the laws. Secondly, it made an *idealist purification* of the concept of spirit. Montesquieu's 'spirit', as expressed in laws, is not a very spiritual entity. In fact, it is approximately synonymous with 'determining or relevant context'. The spirit of the law consists of the relationships which the laws entertain with various factors relevant to legislation, from the climate to the 'principle' of government.[165] The *Volksgeist*, on the other hand, is accurately rendered as 'mind of the people'. Thirdly, the German tradition inserted a *historical process*, the slow motion of the Romantic *Volk* or the dialectic of the World Spirit. Montesquieu set out to find the connection between the laws of man and other phenomena, social and physical. But he focused on the spatial connection and at the core of his theory there is no temporal dimension.[166]

Of these new notions, the subject is in the foreground in the Romantic tradition, whereas in the Hegelian system the dialectical process overshadows the rather nebulous ultimate subject, the

[163] Ibid., §3, p. 16.

[164] Montesquieu, op. cit., Book XIX, e.g., p. 135.

[165] Ibid., p. 3 (Book I, ch. 3). The full title of Montesquieu's work is tellingly 'On the Spirit of the Laws or on the relationship which the laws should have to the constitution of every government, the customs, the climate, the religion, the commerce, etc.'

[166] The new historical awareness included an awareness of a historical development beyond the world of Montesquieu. Hegel did not mistake him for a modern liberal and shrewdly noticed that a monarchy governed by the principle of honour was not a modern rational state machine but a 'feudal monarchy', resting upon 'privileged persons' and not on an 'objective constitution'. Hegel, op. cit., §273, p. 178.

Idea.[167] These ideas, no less than those of early sociology, reflect the explosion of the universe of classical political philosophy by the bourgeois revolution.

III. Bourgeois Politics in the Age of Imperialism: Positivism Meets the Masses

The pioneer sociologists, though they were not unaware either of conflicts between the old society and the new, or within the new society, believed that society and polity were basically unitary – co-operative rather than antagonistic entities. Society was composed of productive and intellectual organization or cooperation, mutual exchange, egalitarian or contractual relationships, manifestations of a common national culture. Politics was mainly concerned with administration. The further development of capitalism exploded these assumptions. Bourgeois society revealed new economic and social contradictions. The bourgeois polity turned out to consist not of the administration of things but of the exercise of new forms of constraint over men, and politics after the bourgeois revolution consequently involved new struggles for power. The subsequent evolution of capitalism then produced two tendencies in the development of sociology. One, which eventually yielded the major works of classical sociology, focused on the social problems posed by a matured capitalist economy. This will be the subject of the next chapter. The other continued the focus of the first sociologists on a social theory of politics. But in the post-liberal era of imperialism this was to mean a social theory of minority rule and oppression. Political life was now seen as part of and determined by a universally antagonistic and exploitative social process.

Four authors made up the core of this group: the Austrian Ludwig Gumplowicz, professor of administrative law at Graz; Gaetano Mosca, an Italian professor of constitutional law and political theory and a conservative politician; Vilfredo Pareto, whom we have already come across as one of the foremost representatives of marginalist 'pure' economics; and Robert Michels, who after

[167] L. Althusser, 'Marx's Relation to Hegel', in *Politics and History*, London, 1972.

having been blocked in his academic career in Germany because he was then a Social Democrat, became an Italian, and ended as a personal favourite of Mussolini and a professor at the militantly Fascist university of Perugia. All had a wealthy patrician background, either bourgeois or (in Pareto's case) aristocratic. They had much in common, though they did not all interact as a group. The link between them was Mosca, who was considerably influenced by Gumplowicz – whom Mosca's intellectual biographer considered Mosca's 'teacher'.[168] Mosca to a greater or lesser extent influenced Pareto, and was a kind of intellectual master to Michels. Michels believed that they formed a group with a particular sociological tendency.[169] With the partial exception of Mosca, all were explicit advocates of sociology.

Their works belong to a definite period, the late nineteenth and early twentieth century, that is to say the early period of modern imperialism. Gumplowicz's first work, *Rasse und Staat* (Race and State) appeared in 1875, his magnum opus *Der Rassenkampf* (The Racial Struggle) in 1883, while Michel's most important contribution, *Political Parties*, was published in 1911. In the interim Mosca and Pareto had developed their elite theories of politics. The most succinct way to represent the common historical experience of these authors might be to say that in their work *positivism meets the masses*, or more exactly, the working-class movement.

Such a formulation implies a rejection of the thesis advanced by Stuart Hughes in his fine intellectual history of European thought from 1890 to 1930, *Consciousness and Society*. Of these four authors, Hughes deals with Pareto, Mosca and Michels, but his panorama is much broader. Because of this breadth, and probably also because of a certain idealist or intellectualist bias, Hughes misses one very important tendency in the social thought of this period, subsuming it under another, whose real bearing cannot be evalued here. Hughes' main thesis is that the 1890's witnessed a decisive intellectual revolution, whose most important aspect was a new view of consciousness – with the discovery of the unconscious and of partially conscious motivations.

Stated thus the thesis appears persuasive, pointing as it does to Freud and psychoanalysis, to the new interest in myth and ideology

---

[168] Meisel, op. cit., p. 133.
[169] R. Michels, *Political Parties*, Glencoe, 1958, pp. 19 n, 395.

of the time. What is more questionable, however, is Hughes' depiction of this revolution as a 'revolt against positivism'.[170] Hughes uses the term 'positivism' in a broad and loose sense to mean 'the whole tendency to discuss human behaviour in terms of analysis drawn from natural science'.[171] The critics of Marxism, in Hughes' view, formed part of this revolt: 'Basically [Marxism was seen by them] as an aberrant, and peculiarly insidious, form of the reigning cult of positivism.'[172]

With respect to sociology, Hughes' thesis hardly works at all – in spite, or rather perhaps because, of his agreement with and reliance on Parsons' *The Structure of Social Action*.[173] The latter work shares to a most eminent degree Hughes' concentration on pure thought, but on the other hand operates with a much more specific and narrow definition of positivism. Committed to serious scholarship as he is, Hughes himself admits that Durkheim and Mosca 'remain essentially in the positivist tradition' and characterizes Pareto as 'a positivist, like Durkheim'.[174] Michels' position in this regard is not discussed. On the other hand, Hughes is certainly right in arguing that a drastic transformation of sociological thought occurred in this epoch, by comparison with that of earlier positivists like Comte. But this was an intellectual change, the most important reason for which was a different social experience.

Gumplowicz, Mosca, Pareto and Michels were all firmly committed to the treatment of social phenomena by analogy with and application of the methods of the natural and mathematical sciences. Behind them loomed Darwin and his theory of the struggle for existence, Buckle's and Taine's naturalistic histories of civilization, as well as the works of their sociological predecessors Comte and Spencer. Gumplowicz was a militant adherent of Häckel's 'monistic' view of the world, and presented his work as a contribution to the 'natural science of humanity'.[175] He saw human society and history as a natural process governed by physical laws. For Mosca mathe-

---

[170] H. Stuart Hughes, *Consciousness and Society*, New York n.d. (1st ed. 1958). This phrase is the second part of the title of chapter 2.

[171] Hughes, op. cit., p. 37.

[172] Ibid., p. 42.

[173] Ibid., p. 432f.

[174] Hughes, op. cit., pp. 37, 79.

[175] L. Gumplowicz, *Der Rassenkampf*, Innsbruck, 1909 (2nd ed.). Preface to 1st ed., p. vi.

matics and, secondly, physics constituted the best examples of 'truly scientific procedure', which should be applied to a systematic analysis of history. This alone would provide the necessary empirical basis for a science of politics.[176] Setting forth the 'scientific approach' in the first chapter of his monumental *Trattato di Sociologia Generale*, Pareto singled out the geometry of Lobachevsky and went on to emphasize that 'it is imperative that they [the social sciences] should follow the example set by the physical sciences'.[177]

Michels was a friend and protegé of Max Weber – who was certainly no positivist[178] – and in his *Political Parties* there is no epistemological discussion. It is thus necessary to be cautious in applying the label 'positivist' to him. On the other hand, it is clear that Michels had no objection to the reasonings of Mosca, Pareto and Gumplowicz; on the contrary. Moreover, his 'iron law of oligarchy' has the character of a natural law – an empirical universal uniformity that is the effect of basically invariant characteristics of men and organizations. It is thus fundamentally different from Weber's account of bureaucracy and his critique of socialism as in practice the bureaucratic rule of a few. Weber believed that 'the march of bureaucracy' was part of a particular cultural process, the 'rationalization' and 'disenchantment' of the world.[179] Weber's reaction to it was exactly the opposite of that of the group of authors now under consideration. Instead of seeking to affirm the inevitably oligarchic tendencies of all politics, Weber was concerned to see whether there was any possibility of rescuing some sort of political *indeterminism*, 'any remnants of "individualist" freedom in any sense'. The form this indeterminism took in Weber's thought was charismatic leadership, and to secure the latter Weber actually

[176] G. Mosca, *The Ruling Class*, New York and London, 1939, p. 4f.

[177] Pareto's treatise has been translated into English under the title *The Mind and Society*, New York, 1935, §110.

[178] The personal relationship between Weber and Michels, and the former's influence on the latter, are amply documented in Röhrich, op. cit. Weber publicly protested against the German academic authorities who refused Michels a *Habilitation* (dissertation) because he was a Social-Democrat. Weber also drew Michels' attention to the work of Moisei Ostrogorsky on oligarchic party organizations in England and USA. For this, cf. S. M. Lipset, 'Moisei Ostrogorsky and the Analytical Approach', in his *Revolution and Counter-Revolution*, London, 1969, p. 366.

[179] M. Weber, 'Bureaucracy', in H. Gerth and C. W. Mills (eds.), *From Max Weber*, London, 1970, p. 244; 'Science as a Vocation', p. 155.

argued for political processes whose credibility the elite theorists were most of all concerned to abolish, recommending a certain amount of plebiscitary politics and 'demagogy', within the bounds of parliamentary rules and stable party organizations.[180]

Weber's solution to 'the polar night of icy darkness and hardness'[181] ahead might thus possibly be described as a 'revolt against positivism', including a revolt against positivistic politics. However, in terms of Weber's own biography such a description would not be very accurate, as Weber came out of the idealist and historicist tradition. But Michels' development after he wrote *Political Parties*, when he later made use of Weber's notion of charismatic leadership in a eulogistic account of Fascism, constitutes a genuine example of a revolt against positivism.[182]

The novelty of the sociology of Pareto and his peers is to be found neither in their view that a natural science of society was possible nor in their critique of democracy and egalitarianism. The social schemes of Saint-Simon and Comte were pedantically hierarchical, and in his later years Comte supported the dictatorship of Louis Bonaparte and appealed to all the reactionary powers of the world, from the Grand Vizir of the Ottoman Empire to the General of the Jesuits. The innovation of the elite theorists was a new interpretation of the role of science in society, and of the relationship between the mass of the people and scientific knowledge.

For all his increasingly reactionary political opinions, Comte could still write in 1852 that 'proletarians and women are the best support for Positivism'.[183] Positivism, Comte argued, would win mass success primarily among those who were 'untrained in the

[180] The best document for Weber's argument is probably Appendix II to 'Parliament and Government in a Reconstructed Germany', *Economy and Society*, New York, 1968, p. 1403. Several parts of the last section of the last chapter were first published in other contexts. One important passage, where Weber suggests that the president of the Weimar Republic should not be elected by parliament but in a 'plebiscitary way' can be found in 'Politics as Vocation', in Gerth and Mills, op. cit., p. 114.

[181] M. Weber, 'Politics as Vocation', p. 128.

[182] Michels developed his conception of Fascist charisma in, among other works, his *Corso di sociologia politica*, Milano, 1927 (see Röhrich, op. cit., p. 157f). The editors of the *Encyclopedia of the Social Sciences*, New York, 1931, considered Michels the best man in the world to write the article on Authority. Michels' sociology after *Political Parties* is not treated by Hughes.

[183] A. Comte, *Système de politique positive*, III, p. xlvii (English ed., p. xli).

present worthless methods of instruction by words and entities'.[184] The problem for the second generation of sociological positivists was that these groups could no longer be considered ideologically virgin, especially not proletarians, who had fallen victim to the 'socialist religion'. (Women in any case had scarcely any role to play in the virile struggle of elites.) Common to the new elite theorists was a profound fear and contempt of the masses, deemed incurably unable to rule themselves and incurably governed by irrational sentiments.

Behind constitutions, declarations of rights and other rhetorical devices, politics – in this conception – is an eternal struggle of the few for rule over the many. It is a natural cyclical process in which ruling elites rise, degenerate, are defeated and disappear. The process has no end and exhibits no progress. Science is the detached observation of this treadmill. To the social question there is, basically, no solution. Science is not a guide to action; at most its insights may somewhat mitigate the harshest forms of the struggle for power.[185] But beyond these common themes there are considerable differences between our authors.

[184] A. Comte, *Système de politique positive*, I, p. 129. The argument is developed in parts III and IV of that volume.

[185] In these essential respects, Gumplowicz's contemporary and compatriot Gustav Ratzenhofer, who is often classed with the former as a darwinistically inspired conflict theorist, differs fundamentally. The latter, a Fieldmarshal-Lieutenant, who, after earning his spurs in the field became president of the supreme military court and began to write positivist sociology, saw sociology in a melioristic perspective and politics as culminating in a harmonious compromise of social and individual interest. See *Die Soziologische Erkenntnis*, Leipzig, 1898, esp. p. 362f. Cf, the optimistic 'Soziologische Schlusswort' (afterword) in Ratzenhofer's *Wesen und Zweck der Politik*, Leipzig, 1893, part III, p. 472f, where a 'civilizing politics' and a 'socialism' based on the sociological insight of social interdependence is set against the 'barbarian politics' and individualism of communism and the working-class movement, as the tendency of the future. Through Lester Ward, a personal friend of Gumplowicz and Albion Small, both Gumplowicz's and Ratzenhofer's ideas became fairly widely spread among the first generation of US sociologists, who were attracted to the Darwinistic conception of social processes as natural social conflicts, which they considered to be amenable to mitigation and control in the higher stages of civilization (cf. J. Lichtenberger, *Development of Social Theory*, New York, 1936, ch. XV). A more liberal and optimistic outcome to Gumplowicz's rather gloomy conception of conflict was foreseen also by his German disciple Franz Oppenheimer, who in the social process discovered 'the gradual elimination of all those institutions which have been created by political means [i.e. violence]'. *System der Soziologie*, Jena, 1922, vol. I: 2, p. 1112.

1. From Natural Law to Natural Struggle

Gumplowicz breaks with social contract theory not because of its deliberative and rationalist character, but because of its supposition of human *equality* and because of the *voluntary* character of a contract.[186] Gumplowicz's own view of the world and its history starts instead from an assumption of the 'polygenesis' of humanity, its original ethnic differentiation. The different ethnic groups or 'races' in the world all strive for their own self-preservation and the amelioration of their situation. Once in contact, they inevitably try to exploit each other, and the state has its origin in the victory and domination of one ethnic group over another. In a 'syngenetic' process the different races – the ruling and the ruled – become assimilated, and a national culture emerges. The ruling race has then fulfilled its mission, the national state begins to degenerate, and the process starts all over again with new races in the eternal roles of ruler and ruled.

Though he later attenuated the biological character of the concept, and stressed its social character, Gumplowicz's emphasis on race (much influenced by the French theorist Gobineau) was a very personal variant of the elite theory, to which Mosca took strong exception. Gumplowicz believed that social classes – nobility, bourgeoisie and peasantry – were ethnic in origin.[187]

[186] Gumplowicz's critique of previous political theory, later developed in monographic treatment, is stated in its fundamentals in *Rasse und Staat*, p. 353f. The main target for Gumplowicz, as for Mosca, is Rousseau.

[187] In a footnote in the second edition of *Der Rassenkampf*, Gumplowicz pointed to the transformation of his race concept into a sociological group concept (p. 196 n). On the other hand he kept his ethnic interpretation of classes (p. 212f), and in the preface to the 2nd ed., written a few months before he took his life, he pointed with pride to flourishing racial research, so different a situation from the first cold reception of his own emphasis on race. Post-Hitlerian readers of Gumplowicz should note that Gumplowicz did not believe in any Aryan *Herrenvolk* (*Der Rassenkampf*, p. 189f). In fact, he was a Polish patriot (born in Austrian Galicia), who is said to have taken part in the 1863 uprising in Russian Poland (see H. E. Barnes in the article on Gumplowicz in the International Encyclopedia of the Social Sciences), and who argued for the restoration of Poland as a European bulwark against Russia (*Soziologie und Politik*, Leipzig, 1892). The history of Poland provides, of course, an indispensable background to Gumplowicz's sociology. Poland was divided into three different states, its nobility living off a servile peasantry, to whom the Habsburgs (in 1856) and even the Tsar (in 1863) could appeal against aristocratic insurrections there, with a largely Jewish

Important thematic elements in Gumplowicz were his emphasis on domination – the most important difference between man and animals being that the latter 'are incapable of *domination*';[188] his insistence on cyclical conflict, 'eternal struggle without progress', in modern times evinced in 'workers' strikes and lock-outs, in cartels and trusts, in swindling enterprises, fraudulent bankruptcies and such like';[189] and his claim that society was always ruled by a minority: 'It is of the nature of all domination that it can only be practiced by a minority. The domination of a minority by a majority is unthinkable, since it is a contradiction.'[190] Gumplowicz also sported the cynical outspokenness so characteristic of the group: 'The nature of such a division of labour [is] that some work for *others*; only a division of labour allows those who benefit from it to apply their minds to higher options, to consider loftier things and strive for an existence "worthy of human beings".'[191] Characteristic of Gumplowicz's thought was his utter contempt for the masses, 'the unmovable, stagnant mass [for whom] new and autonomous cultural tendencies [*Geistesströmungen*] are without avail',[192] and his final message that contemporary nations were dissipating their energies in the insoluble project of creating a just and harmonious society.[193]

2. The Bifurcation of the Industrial Class

Though apparently well read and interested in previous sociology, Mosca refused to apply the term to his own endeavours. The same reason that induced Spencer to accept the disreputable Comte's term 'sociology' made Mosca reject it for the term 'political science';

---

bourgeoisie and petty bourgeoisie, and with rampant anti-semitism. Finally, Gumplowicz was no anti-semite: he was himself a (bourgeois) Jew. Mosca's critique of racial theories is comparatively resolute (op. cit., p. 17f). The patrician anti-democrat could even ask: 'Are Indians and Negroes on the whole inferior to whites as individuals? While most people would answer with a ready and emphatic yes, some few with equal promptness and resolve say no. As for us, we find it as hard to agree as to disagree in terms at all positive' (p. 24).

[188] Gumplowicz, *Der Rassenkampf*, p. 233 (emphasis original).
[189] Ibid., p. 342 (emphasis omitted), p. 333.
[190] Ibid., p. 220.
[191] Ibid., p. 234.
[192] Ibid., p. 340.
[193] Ibid., p. 342f.

he considered that sociology was too broad in scope.[194] His major work, *Elementi di Scienza Politica* (Elements of Political Science), is rather misleadingly translated into English as *The Ruling Class*. Mosca's concept of 'political class' is very ambiguous and often refers primarily to the leading political personnel or the 'governmental machine' discussed in his first essay on the subject – that is to say to a very narrow definition of a power elite.[195] Antonio Gramsci noted the ambiguities in Mosca's central concept: 'His political class . . . is a puzzle . . . Sometimes he seems to think of the middle class, sometimes of men of property in general, and then again of those who call themselves "the educated". But at different occasions, Mosca has apparently the "political personnel" (parliamentary stratum) of the state in mind. In various instances, he seems to exclude the bureaucracy, even its higher stratum, from the political class which is assumed to control all appointments and all policy.'[196]

Ambiguities aside, what Mosca sought to convey first of all was that despite the formal division of states (in classical political theory from Aristotle to Montesquieu) into monarchies, aristocracies, and democracies, all states are in fact always ruled by a minority. This minority was the political class, distinguished both from the head of state and from the mass of the people. For this reason, Rousseau's theory of popular sovereignty was as hollow as the formalistic categories of Aristotle. The political class rules because it is compact and organized, and because it is materially, intellectually and morally superior to the ruled.[197] 'From the point of view of scientific

[194] Mosca, op. cit., p. 3.

[195] Cf. Meisel, op. cit., p. 35f. Franz Borkenau, the translator of the German edition, *Die Herrschende Klasse*, Berne, 1950, with his ex-Marxist background, has a more discerning view of the different extensions of Mosca's class concept, and does sometimes distinguish between 'herrschende Klasse' and 'politische Klasse' ('ruling class' and 'political class').

[196] A. Gramsci, 'La classe politica', in *Quaderni del Carcere*, Turin, 1964, vol. 4, p. 140. Earlier Gramsci had come to the rather hasty conclusion that 'Mosca's so-called "political class" is nothing other than the intellectual category of the dominant social group' ('La formazione degli intellettuali' in ibid., vol. 2, p. 4 n. *Prison Notebooks*, London, 1971, p. 6 n).

[197] Mosca, op. cit., ch. II. Mosca ends his book with a lyrical hymn to the superior few. 'Every generation produces a certain number of generous spirits who are capable of loving all that is, or seems to be, noble and beautiful, and of devoting large parts of their activity to improving the society in which they live, or at least to saving it from getting worse. Such individuals make up a small moral

research the real superiority of the concept of the ruling, or political class lies in the fact that the varying structure of ruling classes has a preponderant importance in determining the political type, and also the level of civilization, of the different peoples.'[198] Human history is a struggle for power – not so much for survival, as for pre-eminence.[199] 'One might say, indeed, that the whole history of civilized mankind comes down to a conflict between the tendency of dominant elements to monopolize political power and transmit possession of it by inheritance, and the tendency toward a dislocation of old forces and an insurgence of new forces.'[200] These new forces are based on new sources of wealth, knowledge or other cultural assets.

In Mosca's reference to the emergence of new social bases of power there was a certain Saint-Simonian influence. Mosca himself, in fact, wrote that Saint-Simon was the thinker who had 'traced in a fairly definite and clear-cut fashion . . . the fundamental outlines of [our] doctrine'.[201] However, there were critical differences in the respective theories of the ruling class in the two works of the two men. These seem to be essentially four in number – relating to the extent of the ruling class, the nature of its legitimacy, the instruments of its power, and the task allotted to it.

For all the looseness of Mosca's account of the political class, it is absolutely clear that it constituted a small minority of the population. Saint-Simon, on the other hand, emphasized that the new industrial class called to rule constituted the immense majority of the people, fifty times as numerous as the feudal class and its allies.[202] The bankers and industrial entrepreneurs whom Saint-Simon invoked as the future masters of temporal power, were the leaders and representatives of an entire social class with common interests, of which workers, farmers, scientists and artists also formed part. The breadth of this industrial class brought Saint-Simon's view of

---

and intellectual aristocracy, which keeps humanity from rotting in the slough of selfishness and material appetites' (p. 493).

[198] Ibid., p. 51.
[199] Ibid., p. 29.
[200] Ibid., p. 65.
[201] Ibid., p. 329.
[202] H. Saint-Simon, 'Le parti national ou industriel', *L'Industrie, Oeuvres*, III, p. 204f. Sometimes Saint-Simon could talk of the industrial class as constituting 24/25 of the population.

the ruling class closer to the ideas of representative democracy, which Mosca was determined to attack, than to a power elite theory.

The legitimacy of the rule of the industrial class, it will be recalled, derived from the utility of its activities – productive, scientific or artistic – by contrast with the futile leisure of the aristocratic class, the *frelons*, rendered redundant once industry had succeeded war as the most important societal activity. Large employers should govern the state, because they possessed the best administrative experience, and were the fittest to draw up a budget. Mosca's political class, by contrast, is fitted to rule precisely because it is largely a leisure class. Its wealth and ease allow it to devote itself to high culture and statecraft. 'A society is best placed to develop a relatively perfect political organization when it contains a large class of people . . . who have sufficient means to be able to devote a portion of their time to perfecting their culture and acquiring an interest in the public weal – that aristocratic spirit, we are almost tempted to say – which alone can induce people to serve their country with no other satisfaction than those that come from individual pride and self-respect.'[203]

In Saint-Simon and Comte's evolutionary schema there was a relation of correspondence between temporal and spiritual powers, most fully developed in Comte's theory of the three stages. Mosca, however, claimed that such a correspondence did not resist historical scrutiny. The evidence was rather, Mosca argued, that theological, metaphysical and scientific thought existed side by side in all societies. Nor, contrary to Comte and Spencer, did the historical record warrant the conclusion that there was any evolution from military to industrial society.[204]

Instead of the notion of a corresponding spiritual power, Mosca launched the idea of a 'political formula' 'In all fairly populous societies that have attained a certain level of civilization, ruling classes do not justify their power exclusively by de facto possession of it, but try to find a moral and legal basis for it, representing it as the logical and necessary consequence of doctrines and beliefs that are generally accepted. This legal and moral basis, or principle, on which the power of the political class rests, is what we have elsewhere called, and shall continue here to call, the political formula.'[205]

[203] Mosca, op. cit., p. 144. Cf. note 197 above.
[204] Ibid., p. 87f.
[205] Ibid., p. 70.

Such a political formula was not the same thing as the idea of priestly deception to be found in the radical Enlightenment philosophers. Mosca was at pains to assert that 'political formulas are [not] mere quackeries aptly invented to trick the masses into obedience. Anyone who viewed them in that light would fall into grave error. The truth is that they answer a real need in man's social nature.' Such formulas corresponded to the cultural level of a people.[206] The difference between Mosca's more specific notion and the general evolutionary concepts of Comte and Saint-Simon was thus that whereas in the latter, political power and the dominant mode of thought and belief in a society develop as two parts of one and the same historical process, Mosca's political formula is an ideological system which the political class adapts to the historical situation in order to ensure its rule over the masses.

The philanthropic orientation of the later Saint-Simon – society should be organized for the amelioration of the moral and physical existence of the poorest class – was, of course, completely alien to Mosca. 'Between the service that an individual renders to society and the reward that he receives there is nearly always a wide, and often a glaring, discrepancy. To fight socialism by trying to deny, or merely to extenuate, that fact, is to take one's stand on a terrain on which defeat is certain.'[207] This situation could not be altered, given the truths of economics. What then was to be done in order to combat socialism? A coherent scientific system, a scientific sociology – Mosca was committed to the view that such a sociology was possible – and a science of politics, were necessary to refute 'democratic-socialist metaphysics'. For the 'cause of causes' of the tendency towards socialism was the democratic conception of politics, which was the target of Mosca's whole work.[208] But Mosca was not overly optimistic that objective science could convince partisan interests or that scientific sociology and political science would win support even 'in our governments, or in our ruling

[206] Ibid., p. 71.

[207] Ibid., p. 267.

[208] Ibid., pp. 310–28. 'It will not be necessary to linger very long on the causes of the socialist current. The cause of those causes is the thing we have been trying to combat in the whole course of our work – the intellectual attitude of our times towards doctrines that concern the organization of society, the ideas that now prevail in persons of average and sometimes of higher education as to the laws that regulate political relations' (p. 310).

classes, which nevertheless ought to support them'.[209]

There was thus a common denominator to all the differences between Mosca and Saint-Simon: the new separation of the political elite from the broad mass of the population. In the epoch of the organized working-class movement, industry could no longer be regarded as internally united.

3. The Ruling Elite and the Threat to Property

Pareto's career as a social theorist began in economics, and it is against this background that his sociology must be seen. On the other hand, Pareto differed fundamentally from that strand of sociology which sought a sociological determination of economic phenomena. Despite its economic origins, Pareto's work is essentially a political sociology.[210]

Pareto's bulky scientific oeuvre is primarily comprised of four major works: *Cours d'économie politique* (1896–97), *Les systèmes socialistes* (1901–02), *Manuale d'economia politica* (1907) and *Trattato di sociologia generale* (1915). There is a sociological orientation in all four. The second volume of the *Cours* contains two substantial sociological chapters, one on the general principles of social evolution, the other on social physiology; while the *Manuale* starts with a general introduction to social science and includes a section on the circulation of elites. More important than this parallelism of interests in his work, however, was the marked change that occurred in Pareto's political and intellectual orientation towards the turn of the century. There is a significant discontinuity between the *Cours* and his later works.

Pareto conceived sociology as a general social science, encom-

---

[209] Ibid., p. 368.

[210] There is a voluminous literature on Pareto, a fascinating subject for discussions of power and of the relationship of liberalism to democracy, fascism and to the socialist critique, but there is so far no full-scale intellectual biography, and many critical aspects of his life and work are still obscure. Of existing biographies, the one by Bousquet, op. cit., appears to be the best. An overview of the literature, up till then, is given by the editor of Pareto's *Oeuvres complètes*, Giovanni Busoni, in his preface to volume 11, Geneva, 1967. A number of extracts from works of varying value on Pareto and Mosca has been put together by James Meisel (ed.), *Pareto and Mosca*, Englewood Cliffs, 1965. The best and most accessible general introduction to Pareto's work is provided by the selection, V. Pareto, *Sociological Writings*, London, 1966, with a very competent presentation by S. E. Finer.

passing the special disciplines studying the actions of *homo economicus, homo ethicus* or *homo politicus*. He saw the relationship of sociology and economics as one in which sociology served to analyze a general social equilibrium of which economic factors and economic equilibria formed a special part. In the *Cours* this relationship was formulated within a Spencerian frame of reference, although in contrast to Spencer's predominantly biological orientation, Pareto's social model was one of mechanical equilibrium. But Pareto's basic evolutionary framework was explicitly Spencerian. Spencer had 'masterfully' developed the fundamental notion of the mutual dependence of social phenomena;[211] he had proposed the classification of societies into industrial and military;[212] he had 'comprehensively' defined the most general principles of social organization.[213] Historical development involved economic, intellectual, moral and political progress, though the march of civilization was not straight and steady but hesitant and zig-zag. An aspect of this progress was the diminishing role of force in society.[214] Comte was not explicitly invoked by Pareto at this point, but he was given his due for acknowledging the role of intellectual progress and of a rationalist 'état d'esprit'.[215]

Pareto at this stage explicitly attacked what he called 'aristocratic theory' and 'neo-aristocrats', who ascribed an exclusive influence over social phenomena to forms of government or methods of recruiting governmental personnel, and according to whom 'the whole of mankind exists only to produce a few superior beings'.[216] Such an aristocratic theory was right to argue against the early sociologists that men are not equal; but its proponents neglected to consider that, to be of utility to the led, leaders must use their authority in the interests of the former, and that their leadership should not become an obstacle to the development of faculties among the led which would eventually permit them to guide themselves.[217]

[211] V. Pareto, *Cours d'économie politique, Oeuvres complètes*, vol. 1, Geneva, 1964, §583.
[212] Ibid., §618.
[213] Ibid., §654.
[214] Ibid., §§686–92.
[215] Ibid., §688.
[216] Ibid., §§ 669 and 1067 (included in V. Pareto, *Sociological Writings*, London, 1966, pp. 110, 122).
[217] Ibid., §§ 663, 667–9 (English ed., pp. 109–10).

The contrast, then, is not between Pareto the liberal economist and Pareto the not so liberal sociologist. In his first important work of sociology, Pareto emerges as a Victorian Liberal rather than a precursor of Fascism. Curiously enough, little seems to be known about the reasons for his later change of views.[218] The effects of this change, however, are not in doubt.

The later Pareto continued to be a liberal economist and he continued to study the interdependence of social and economic phenomena. But this interdependence now took on a very special character, hammered home in a whole series of heavy tomes – the *Systèmes* comprising 900 pages, the *Manuale* nearly 500, the *Trattato* 2000 pages – as well as in a number of articles and essays. Above all, Pareto was now concerned to assert and expose the overwhelming role of sentiment (over reason) in human action and society.

In a compact little essay published in 1901, Pareto provided a preview of the sociological laws that were to be proclaimed in the treatise on which he was then working. Pareto's first law was thus: 'Let us note that the greater part of human actions have their origin not in logical reasoning but in sentiments. This is principally true for actions that are not motivated economically. The opposite may be said of economic actions, especially those connected with commerce and industry.'[219] One outcome of this orientation was his critical study of 'socialist systems', characterized by their admission of only a minimum of private property. For Pareto, socialism included a vast panorama of 'real systems' from Sparta and the Inca empire to English Chartism and the Paris Commune, from religious doctrines to theoretical ideas, from Plato to Marx and the 'socialists of the chair'. Pareto's conclusion was simply that socialism was a religion, deriving from certain sentiments.

The *Trattato*, too, is basically a gigantic *Ideologiekritik*. It asserts that human beings are mostly driven by non-scientific ('non-logico-experimental') considerations and conceptions; that these constitute various non-rational developments ('derivations') of certain underlying impulses ('residues'), which are manifestations of

[218] This is both the opinion and the impression that Bousquet (ch. V) gives. Bousquet's interpretation of available material is similar to that adopted here, based above all on a comparison of the above-mentioned major works of Pareto and the germinal essay 'Un applicazione di teorie sociologiche' (1901) (American edition, *The Rise and Fall of the Elites*, Totowa, N.J., 1968).

[219] V. Pareto, *The Rise and Fall of the Elites*, p. 27.

basic human sentiments. The residues and the derivations – 43 in six main classes and 17 in four main classes, respectively – constitute a notoriously unmanageable bundle.[220] Together with two other elements – interests and social hetereogenity, and the circulation of elites – the residues and derivations comprise the basic forces of society and social equilibrium.[221] In spite of the enormously elaborate complexity of Pareto's sociology in the 'general treatise', its essential departure from the *Cours*, in Pareto's own opinion, was a new awareness of the decisive importance of sentiments.[222]

The second novel aspect of Pareto's social theory after the *Cours* was his famous theory of elites. It is introduced innocuously as an extension of the economic concept of business cycles: 'there is a rhythm of sentiment which we can observe in ethics, in religion and in politics as waves resembling the business cycle'.[223] The first theme of Pareto's elite theory, then, was not the rule of elites but their rise and fall.

The 'rhythm of sentiment' is a primarily political phenomenon. Pareto's debunking of the unacknowledged sentiments underlying various views of the world, in the *Trattato* as well as in the *Systèmes*, amounts to a political analysis of the circulation and struggle of elites. Here the Victorian Liberal turns into a Macchiavellian. In the last quarter of the *Trattato* (chs. XII–XIII), dealing with the general form and equilibrium of society, social interdependence is treated above all as a political mechanism, as the bearing of sentiments on politics.

The circulation of elites is a process of struggle, and a process in which the competing elites make use of the sentiments of the population at large. But in contrast to Gumplowicz and Mosca, Pareto's emphasis is neither on the never-ending struggle itself nor on the political formula and the organization of the political class. It is instead on the characteristics of the ruling elite which are necessary for its rule and for a relatively orderly rise of new elements into the elite. This is the second theme which gives Pareto's elite theory its originality, and his discourse its peculiar tenor and pathos.

Pareto distinguishes between elites composed of individuals with

---

[220] V. Pareto, *The Mind and Society*, New York, 1935, §§888, 1419.

[221] The argument is summarized in §§2205–6.

[222] Ibid., §2316, n. 10. Similarly, Spencer's sociology is now dismissed brusquely, e.g. §§6, 112, 283–95.

[223] Pareto, *The Rise and Fall of the Elites*, p. 31.

residues of classes I and II. With his strong leanings to individualist instinct psychology, Pareto was little interested in cultural and social-psychological processes. For him, groups were essentially composed of individuals with specific characteristics; change in them was due to the inflow or outflow of individuals with certain predetermined sentiments. Class I residue is the 'instinct for combination', 'an inclination to combine certain things with other things'. Pareto's translator suggests that this is sometimes synonymous with 'inventive faculty'.[224] Class II residue is the 'persistence of aggregates', a tendency to make permanent aggregates of sensations. There are several subclasses of this, as of the first residue, from tendencies to generalize from single facts to familial loyalty. Of special importance and interest here is subclass II-a3: '*Relationship of social class*. Living in a given group impresses the mind with certain concepts, certain ways of thinking and doing, certain prejudices, certain beliefs, which, as is the case with so many other entities of the kind, endure in time and space and acquire a pseudo-objective individuality.'[225]

'Aristocracies do not last. Whatever the causes, it is an incontestable fact that after a certain length of time they pass away. History is a graveyard of aristocracies.'[226] This circulation has diverse reasons – among them, insufficient biological reproduction and economic changes. Its most important cause, however, is a tendency to moral degeneration and decadence among aristocracies, or more exactly 'a decline in the proportion of the residue which enabled them to win their power and hold it'.[227] This basically inevitable tendency could be counteracted in two ways, either by social mobility and incorporation of more vigorous elements from the lower classes, or by revolution. 'Revolutions come about through accumulation in the higher strata of society – either because of a slowing-down in class-circulation or from other causes – of decadent elements no longer possessing the residues suitable for keeping them in power, and shrinking from the use of force; while meantime in the lower strata of society elements of superior quality are coming to the fore, possessing residues suitable for exercising the functions of

---

[224] Pareto, *The Mind and Society*, §889.
[225] Ibid., §1043 (emphasis original).
[226] Ibid., §2053.
[227] Ibid., §2054.

government and willing enough to use force.'[228]

The suitable residues are class II, persistence of aggregates. What really matters, then, is the militant *class consciousness of the ruling elite*: 'Had Louis XVI not been a man of little sense and less courage', and if the aristocratic victims of the September massacres (in 1792) 'had not for the most part been spineless humanitarians without a particle of courage or energy, they would have annihilated their enemies instead of waiting to be annihilated', to the advantage of France and of themselves. In the end, even an ingenious elite of 'combining' entrepreneurs and cunning politicians is doomed, and ruinous to a country, if it lacks a critical amount of persistence residues.[229]

It is here that Pareto breaks with the rationalist commitment of his earlier liberalism. His enormous emphasis on the overriding importance of sentiments in society is now not primarily geared to explaining why the scientific conclusions of 'pure' economics – on the merits of laissez-faire, free competition and trade – have been so unpersuasive or why 'communism, collectivism, protectionism, socialism of the state or the chair, bourgeois socialism . . . the neo-aristocratic theories of Nietzsche, anti-semitism, nihilism, and anarchy'[230] have thriven. Pareto is out to show that if liberal society is to be preserved its ruling elite must possess certain sentiments to lend it the necessary courage and energy.

Pareto's discovery of the role of sentiment can in a loose way be related to a long tradition of learned discussion of the decline and fall of Rome, and more particularly to the work of Macchiavelli,[231] but it also had an explicit reference to the contemporary class

---

[228] Ibid., §2057.

[229] Ibid., §2191.

[230] Pareto, *Cours d'économie politique*, p. 393f.

[231] Macchiavelli had advised the prince to 'guard himself as from a shoal' against being considered 'changeable, light, effeminate, faint-hearted, irresolute' (op. cit., p. 110) and that he should not shrink from violence (p. 104f). Both the differences and the similarities between Pareto and Macchiavelli might be illustrated by referring to what in Macchiavelli's age was the main equivalent to the parliamentary 'cunning and corruption' by which liberal 'foxes' like Depretis and Giolitti governed pre-Fascist Italy – i.e. to mercenary armies, of which Macchiavelli had much the same to say as Pareto had of an elite exclusively based on its combination instinct: 'they are disunited, ambitious, without discipline, disloyal; valiant among friends, among enemies cowardly; they have no fear of God, no loyalty to men' (p. 91).

struggle. A constant theme of Pareto's elite theory is a bitter lamentation that striking workers are no longer sufficiently repressed, the right of strike-breakers to work is not protected, and other crimes against property are no longer adequately punished. It is with constant reference to these disastrous trends that Pareto develops his sociology of norms and elites. 'The crimes committed during strikes remain unpunished . . . The workers have inherited the privilege of the noblemen of the past, they are in fact above the law.' 'Our bourgeoisie spends energy and money only to aid the enemy. Societies to help the vicious, the incapable and the degenerate spring up in extraordinary numbers; and among all these societies the bourgeoisie did not have the spirit to establish one, I say a single one, to defend their own rights.'[232] An endless series of similar quotations could be marshalled, including a passionate defence of the counter-revolutionary reaction of Tsarism to the 1905 revolution: 'We have seen the bourgeois press with pious fraud, systematically and in silence pass over the crimes of the Russian revolutionaries and dwell at length on the repressive measures which these crimes made necessary.'[233]

Pareto's view of the calamitous juncture of liberal rationalism with the masses is summed up in the following excerpt from his 'exclusively' scientific *Manual of Political Economy*: 'The work of the humanitarians of the 18th century in France paved the way for the murders of the *Terror*: the work of the liberals of the first half of the 19th century has paved the way for the demagogical oppression which is now dawning. Those who demanded equality of citizens before the law certainly did not foresee the privileges which the masses now enjoy; the old special jurisdictions have been abolished, and a new one instituted, the arbitration boards favouring the workers. Those who demanded freedom to strike did not imagine that this freedom, for the strikers, would consist of beating workers who continued to work and setting fire to factories with impunity.

[232] Pareto, *The Rise and Fall of the Elites*, pp. 63, 86, resp. Cf. p. 98f. On the other hand, as a good bourgeois, Pareto was no supporter of the use of troops to preserve feudal labour relations (ibid., p. 69).

[233] V. Pareto, *Manual of Political Economy*, London, 1972, p. 357 n. For other references to the privileged status of workers and the cowardice of the bourgeoisie see, e.g. *Systèmes* II, p. 410f; *Manual*, pp. 72f, 91f; *The Mind and Society*, §§2177f, 2257f, 2480; *La transformation de la démocratie* (a series of political articles from 1921), in *Oeuvres*, Geneva, 1970, XIII, p. 30f.

Those who demanded equality of taxes to aid the poor did not imagine that there would be a progressive tax at the expense of the rich, and a system in which the taxes are voted by those who do not pay them . . . The great error of the present time is believing that men can be governed by pure reason without making use of force, which is, on the contrary, the foundation of all social organization. . . . The humanitarian religion will very probably disappear when it has accomplished its work of social dissolution and when a new elite has risen on the ruins of the old one.'[234]

The background to these political attitudes, without which Pareto's sociology can hardly be understood, was the ascent to governmental office of the Centre and Left-of-Centre Republicans and *Dreyfusards* in France in 1899, with the Waldeck-Rousseau cabinet, and of the Liberal Giolitti in Italy in 1901. In neither case do Pareto's diatribes appear very pertinent, although opinions naturally differ as to how much workers should be repressed. It is clear, however, that these governmental changes do not suffice to explain the transformation in Pareto's views, since he had also been an outspoken opponent of the previous, more repressive, regimes in France and Italy.[235] But whatever its biographical motivation, it

---

[234] Pareto, *Manual*, p. 93f. The outburst on taxation may be seen in connection with an enormous inheritance, more than a million gold francs, which Pareto received in 1898 and which made him leave Lausanne (where he was professor, in the canton of Vaud) for Céligny, in the canton of Geneva, to dodge taxation (Bousquet, op. cit., p. 87 n).

[235] In May 1898, the Italian government put Milan under martial law and moved in troops with artillery to suppress a local general strike. According to official estimates, 80 civilians and 2 policemen were killed and 450 wounded. The commanding general Bava-Beccaris was afterwards decorated by the King. At that time Pareto vigorously and publicly protested against the government atrocities, from an orthodox liberal standpoint (*La liberté économique et les évènements d'Italie* (1898), *Oeuvres*, XIV). The *Rise and Fall* and the introductory sections to *Systèmes* and *Manual* were written only one to two years later, at the same time or just after the Waldeck cabinet was formed in France, which included the right-wing Social-Democrat Millerand. Giolitti became Minister of the Interior and the strong man in the Italian government in February 1901. He was explicitly against the previous policy of repression of the working-class. This does not mean that he gave in, and even the navy was kept ready to ensure law and order. Between 1901 and 1904, 40 workers were killed and 200 wounded by the forces of order. During the factory occupations in 1920, Giolitti's tactics of patience combined with resolute preparedness to strike hard worked very successfully. The Red Week of riots in 1914, to which Pareto refers in *The Mind and Society*, §2480, began with protests against the killing of three demonstrators

is still relevant that the orientation of Paretian sociology was a direct precursor of the rise of Fascism. It was primarily as armed bands attacking strikes and trade unions that Fascism took root in Italy, growing from 870 members in December 1919 to 20,600 a year later and to 249,000 in December 1921.[236] Though the aristocratic *Maître* in his Swiss villa would hardly have felt at ease in closer contact with the Fascist *ras* and their bullies, Pareto was not wrong to believe that Mussolini was the man his sociology had been heralding.[237]

4. The Two Problems of Robert Michels

'Our age has destroyed once and for all the ancient and rigid forms of aristocracy, has destroyed them, at least, in certain important regions of political constitutional life.' This process – the advent of the bourgeois revolution – was the starting-point of Robert Michels' investigation in *Political Parties*.[238] The question was what happens thereafter; his answer was unambiguous: 'The appearance of oligarchical phenomena in the very bosom of the revolutionary parties is a conclusive proof of the existence of immanent oligarchical tendencies in every kind of human organization which strives

---

by the police. An overview of Italian politics in these years is given by C. Seton-Watson, *Italy from Fascism to Liberalism: 1870–1925*, London, 1967 (by no means a sympathizer with the labour movement). In France, Millerand's project of arbitration met with hostility from the trade-unions, but was in fact defeated by the *patrons* and their parliamentary representatives. Strikes were also vigorously repressed by the Radical governments in France – the miners' strike in 1906, the postal strike in 1909, and the railway strike in 1910, just to take the most famous (or infamous) examples. On France in this period, see, e.g., G. Lefranc, *Le mouvement syndical sous la Troisième Republique*, Paris, 1967, esp. pp. 131–7, 157–61; Ch. Tilly-E. Shorter, 'Les vagues de grèves en France 1890–1968', *Annales*, vol. 28: 4 (Juillet-Août, 1973), pp. 857–87. An important difference between Pareto and the Liberal and Radical parliamentary foxes in France and Italy was that Pareto held that the bourgeoisie had more to fear from the revisionist Socialists than from the Marxists, as all religions were bound to become less intransigent when more widespread (*Systèmes*, II, p. 433f).

[236] Seton-Watson, op. cit., p. 572.

[237] See Chapter 3 above, n. 87. The Fascist bosses were usually called *ras*, an Ethiopian noble title, one of the few tangible conquests of the hitherto rather disastrous Italian imperialist policy towards Ethiopia. (In 1896, at Adowa, the Ethiopians had inflicted a decisive defeat on the imperialist Italian army.)

[238] R. Michels, *Political Parties*, Glencoe, 1958, p. 4.

for the attainment of definite ends.' 'The socialists might conquer, but not socialism, which would perish in the moment of the adherents' triumph.'[239] It is little wonder, then, Michels' work was to be so highly admired by ex-radical and conservative sociologists of politics and organizations, such as Seymour Lipset and Philip Selznick.[240]

Michels' book contributed little to the development of general social theory; while his later more wide-ranging sociology, developed under Fascism, is now mostly forgotten. But *Political Parties* did isolate two very important problems, one explicitly, the other by implication.

Firstly, it was concerned with the relationships between leaders and masses in modern forms of organization. The empirical substance of Michels' study was the labour movement of the Second International. Michels had first-hand experience of this, as a delegate to the 1903 and 1905 congresses of German Social Democracy and as a delegate of the Italian Socialists to the Stuttgart congress of the International in 1907. (Michels had by then moved to Italy, which seems to have been the only country in the world at that time in which Marxists and Socialists could obtain university teaching posts and present doctoral theses – except perhaps France, where, however, there were hardly any Marxists.) A large part of *Political Parties* is a fascinating inside story of the International, full of scholarly and systematized material, as well as echoes of the polemics of the syndicalist tendency within the International, for which Michels had fought, with little success. Michels thus made

---

[239] Ibid., pp. 14, 408.
[240] Lipset has written an introduction to a recent American edition of Michels, *Political Parties*, in which he also dwells on the reception of Michel's book. Lipset does not treat Michels' further contributions at all. The introduction is included in Lipset's collection of essays, *Revolution and Counterrevolution*, London, 1969. That volume also contains an introduction to an edition of another party analyst, somewhat earlier than Michels, Moisei Ostrogorsky, whose *Democracy and the Organization of Political Parties* (1902) dealt with the obstacles to democracy erected by the party systems in USA and Britain. Max Weber directed Michels' attention to the work of Ostrogorsky, but, as far as I can see, Lipset greatly exaggerates Ostrogorsky's role in Michels' thought, and correspondingly underrates the importance of Michels' own direct experiences in the international labour movement, and of the Franco-Italian elitist intellectual currents. For biographical data, the excellent study by Röhrich, op. cit., has been relied upon here. Röhrich particularly pinpoints Michels' early syndicalist and anarchist inclinations.

a valuable contribution to the study of modern political organizations. The processes of estrangement between leaders and masses on which he focused remain a critical problem – analytical and practical – today.

The second problem, which Michels posed only implicitly, was this: granted the oligarchical tendencies inherent in large-scale social organization, what determined the type of leadership, and where did the oligarchs lead the masses? Here Michels' account, as it stands in *Political Parties*, founders as a specifically sociological theory and falls back on a psychological determinism, which is unable to deal with social and historical variation. Even in its own special field of labour organization, Michels' 'iron law of oligarchy' can provide no explanation of the opposite reactions of Social Democratic parties to war in August 1914, and Communist parties in September 1939.

For Michels, the masses were inherently incapable of governing themselves, for fundamentally psychological reasons. Michels was well read in the extensive contemporary literature on the inevitable incompetence of the masses; he quotes Gumplowicz, Mosca, Pareto and Sorel, as well as critics of the masses and of democracy less well-known today, such as Gustave Le Bon, Scipio Sighele, and Gabriel Tarde. Political leaders, by and large superior in every respect, are basically driven by their avarice and greed for power. 'The apathy of the masses and their need for guidance has as its counterpart in the leaders a natural greed for power. Thus the development of the democratic oligarchy is accelerated by the general characteristics of human nature. What was initiated by the need for organization, administration, and strategy is completed by psychological determinism.'[241] The great error of the socialists was thus a consequence of 'their lack of adequate psychological knowledge'. 'A realistic view of the mental condition of the masses shows beyond question that even if we admit the possibility of moral improvement in mankind, the human materials, with whose use politicians and philosophers cannot dispense in their plans of social reconstruction, are not of a character to justify excessive optimism.'[242] Differentiated from the masses, the political leaders inevitably develop their own interests.[243]

[241] Michels, op. cit., p. 217.
[242] Ibid., p. 420 (excesses of anything are, of course, seldom justified).
[243] Ibid., p. 405f.

In one sense this brings us back to Hobbes: on one hand there is human nature and the conflicts following from it, on the other hand there is the sovereign, whose power is a necessity but whose use of that power depends on him (them) alone. As a science of politics this does not get us very far, even in terms of a discussion of relations between leaders and led.

Michels was later to see the Duce as the supreme determinant of politics, but despite the experience Michels shared with Mussolini (who had also once been a radical socialist, influenced by Pareto and Sorel, before becoming a nationalist and imperialist) *Political Parties* does not point forward to the March on Rome in the way that Pareto's works do. Michels' considered position at the time when he wrote his book was a stoical acceptance of oligarchical democracy as the best that there was, contemptuous of the masses, but not without some sympathy for the utopian labour movement of his rebellious youth.[244]

Michels' second problem highlights a fundamental contrast between Marx and the elite theorists. The latter had read Marx, and Pareto and Michels claimed to have accepted and extended the Marxian theory of class struggle. They rejected Marx's economic theory but distinguished it from the scientific 'sociological part' of his work (Pareto) or his 'philosophy of history' (Michels).[245] It obviously makes a great difference to substitute class struggle by a struggle of elites, in which inherently incompetent masses become passive material for exploitation and manipulation by means of political formulas or demagogic derivations.

Even more important, however, was another difference between Marx and these writers. The Marxian concept of class is derived

[244] The democratic attachments of the Michels of *Political Parties* are illuminated by a contrast with Tocqueville. Both regarded formal organizations as an aristocratic phenomenon in a democratic society. For Tocqueville, the aristocrat, this was their positive aspect; these organizations, by creating new particular loyalties and having particular privileges and interests, succeed the old aristocracy as the barrier against egalitarian anarchy and egalitarian despotism. (Tocqueville develops this idea in his *Democracy in America*, see e.g. the two last chapters but one.) For Michels, however, the aristocratic aspect of organizations is their oligarchical character, and far from approving this as a barrier against the revolt of the masses, Michels ends his book, noting with sadness the aristocratic deformation of democratic trends: 'It is probable that this cruel game will continue without end.'

[245] Pareto, *Systèmes*, II, p. 328; and ch. XIV passim; Michels, op. cit., p. 407.

from a theory of social determination, denoted by the concepts of relations and forces of production. The elite theorists, on the other hand, interpreted class in terms of individuals striving for their material wants. The elite theorists thereby turned a social theory into a psychologistic and biologistic conception of human existence, even of the life of organisms in general. In this way Marx's theory of class struggle can, of course, be 'extended' beyond capitalism. Thus Pareto could write: 'The struggle for life or welfare is a general phenomenon for living beings.'[246] Michels referred to the struggle between organized workers and strike-breakers as 'ergomachia', a term borrowed from an Italian physiologist meaning 'struggle for feeding-ground'.[247]

IV. Sociology and the Development of Bourgeois Politics

The rise of sociology inaugurated a new discourse on politics. Political theory was made part of a discourse on society at large. Government was no longer seen primarily in terms of the number of rulers – one, few, many – and their legitimation by religious, legal or moral principles. It was now seen in relation to societies at different stages of evolution, characterized by different activities, by different sorts of social relationships and cultural patterns. Alternatively, politics was interpreted as a manifestation of general social processes.

The rise of sociology was a crucial part of the increasing prominence and the intellectual discovery of *bürgerliche Gesellschaft* – in the sense both of bourgeois and civil society. This society was brought into focus by the upheavals consequent on the French Revolution, and sociology came into being in France as one expression of a new awareness of society and social relations, manifested also in historiography and literature.

The new discourse of Saint-Simon and Comte, and on the whole also the later work of Tocqueville, presupposed a new configuration of social forces, shaped by at least four main aspects of the new revolutionary process.

---

[246] Pareto, *Systèmes*, II, p. 455.
[247] Michels, op. cit., p. 307.

Firstly, the social revolution in France had broken the lynchpin of previous political philosophy, the relationship between king and people. The successful rebellion of the French peasantry had decisively undermined the power of the aristocracy and the church in the countryside. Urban social relations, particularly in Paris, had likewise been momentously modified by the upsurge of the revolutionary crowds of *sans-culottes*. Secondly, the frequency of political vicissitudes during the revolution, and the number of its short-lived solemn constitutions, made the superficiality of legalist political philosophy patent.

Thirdly, however, everything had not been destroyed or turned into a pure negativity of chaos, terror and destruction. A new social force emerged with the onset of industrialization and the acquisition of confiscated or abandoned noble and clerical estates: the bourgeoisie. This was clear to the intellectuals of the new era, even to a maverick legitimist like Balzac, though not to the philosophers of reaction.

Saint-Simon, Comte, and Tocqueville all emphasized that the revolution was not a primarily political, but social phenomenon. But they did not simply want to press home a thesis of social determination. They also sought to point out a contradiction, and to make a critique, of prevailing political practice – pre-revolutionary, revolutionary and post-revolutionary – in its ignorance and neglect of basic social processes. The potential contradiction between political forms and social tendencies was highlighted during the Restoration, when the French aristocracy for a brief period resumed its grip on the governmental, judicial and clerical apparatus. This was the period when sociology – before it received its name – first began to be developed. The new politics of Saint-Simon and Comte was explicitly aimed at solving the contradiction between the new industrial, positive society and the aberrant, anachronistic political superstructure of the Restoration. This contradiction was the fourth element of the conjuncture that produced sociology.

The end of the *ancien régime* revealed a society and a pattern of struggle beside and beneath the traditional spheres of government and religion. In the social theory of the sociologists, in the historiography of Guizot and Thierry, and in the novels of Balzac and Stendhal, government and church were now seen as derived from and appended to different types of society and different social forces, different social classes. In this respect the Revolution constitutes a great divide separating the sociologists and their contemporaries from the legalist and constitutionalist theories of the Encyclopedists[248] and from the rationalist *Religionskritik* of the Enlightenment *philosophes* in general. Politics in conformity with the new society – industrial or, to Tocqueville, egalitarian – replaced politics in conformity with natural law and the contract between sovereign and people.

In Germany the shattering of the old polity by French invasion brought to light another social determinant moulding political and legal institutions. In contrast to the discoveries of post-revolutionary France, this determinant was not conceived as something new coming into existence through its conflict with the old, but as the rediscovery and reaffirmation of an ancient and undivided reality: national culture. Though first clearly theorized by Hegel, acknowledgment of the central role of *bürgerliche Gesellschaft* was to be won in Germany only after a long social and intellectual struggle. The importance and the difficulty of national unification, together with the manner in which it was finally achieved – in a kind of alliance between *Junkertum* and bourgeoisie – made the State the focal organization in German discourse on society. In the Wilhelmine Reich, the prominent conservative historian Dietrich Schafer ended his academic assessment of the unfitness of Georg Simmel – a sociologist and a Jew – for a chair in Heidelberg, by echoing Bossuet's dictum from the 17th century on religion and government as the two central hinges of human affairs: 'It is, in my opinion, a most perilous error to put "society" in the place of church and state as the decisive (*massgebend*) organ of human coexistence (*Zusammenleben*).'[249]

With its primarily social rather than political or religious character, the French Revolution differed sharply from the English

[248] An overall view of the political and other conceptions of the Encyclopaedists – the authors of the monumental achievement of the French Enlightenment, the Encyclopaedia edited by d'Alembert and Diderot which started to appear in 1751 – can be gained from R. Hubert, *Les sciences sociales dans l'Encyclopédie*, Paris, 1923, and E. Weis, *Geschichtsauffassung und Staatsauffassung in der französischen Enzyklopädie*, Munich, 1956.

[249] Schafer's evaluation is reprinted as 'A Contemporary Academic View of Georg Simmel', in the *American Journal of Sociology*, LXIII, 6 (May 1958), p. 640f. Like so many German academics of the early 20th century, Schafer was an anti-semite, and his official memorandum to the Baden government is full of anti-semitic sneers at this 'dyed-in-the-wool israelite'.

revolution of the 17th century. From 1640 through to 1688, the latter was lived and fought overwhelmingly in legal and religious terms. It centred on the relationship between sovereign and parliament and between Catholicism and different brands of Protestantism. It started as a conflict between monarchy and parliament and ended with an agreement between parliament and dynasty. In this process wider economic and social issues were naturally involved, but they took a more mediated form than a century later in France. The distinguished historian of the English revolution, Christopher Hill, has written: 'The division in England is not Third Estate *versus* gentry and peerage, but country *versus* court. Court and government offered economic privilege to some merchants (monopolists, common farmers, ruling oligarchies in London and other towns); and perquisites to many members of the landed class. On the other hand, those gentlemen and merchants excluded from economic privilege – and they included some of the richest and most go-ahead members of these social groups as well as the middling men – thought that greater freedom of economic development would be of advantage to themselves and the country. They looked to parliament and common lawyers to help them to get it.'[250]

The fall of the Stuarts made the British state apparatus available for the implementation of resolute capitalist policies, abroad as well as at home. But the landowning aristocracy remained, and the peasants continued to be expelled from the land. The new society evolved symbiotically with the old. A new social theory emerged only slowly. James Harrington had held, in his *Oceana* of 1656, that the politics of the English revolution were determined by changes in the distribution of landownership.[251] But it was not until a century later, in classical political economy and in the social writings of Ferguson and Millar, that bourgeois civil society received due theoretical attention. Even then, it was only the market and not civil society as a whole which emerged as a possible and worthy object of systematic intellectual treatment. Its appearance was not a properly English discovery at that, but an achievement of the Scottish Enlightenment. For in Scotland alone a rapidly expanding capitalist

---

[250] C. Hill, *The Century of Revolution, 1603–1714*, Edinburgh, 1961, p. 102.

[251] Harrington's precocious role is pointed out by Hill, op. cit., p. 182. For the role of Harrington in the tradition of political philosophy, cf. G. Sabine, *A History of Political Theory*, London, 1960, pp. 421–30.

economy was accompanied by the emergence of a bourgeois intelligentsia and a bourgeois university, in a harmonious union of clientship and patronage with an aristocracy which had successfully undergone a process of embourgeoisement.

Even after the Industrial Revolution, the close and complex relations between aristocracy and bourgeoisie made it debatable whether the overall character of British society was aristocratic or bourgeois. Tocqueville, who like so many liberal Frenchmen was a keen student of British history and current affairs, wavered on this point. At the time of his first visit to England, in the autumn of 1833, he thought that England was still basically an aristocratic country, and as such an anachronism belonging to a past epoch.[252] Gradually Tocqueville's views altered, and in _The Ancien Regime and the French Revolution_ he had come to the conclusion that 'though at first sight one might think that the ancient [feudal] European constitution still functioned there', '17th century England was already a quite modern nation'.[253]

An important difference between England and France was that in the former the aristocracy still performed vital economic, political and social functions, whereas under the French _ancien régime_ it had become an idle and isolated privileged caste. Tocqueville clearly noted that contrast.[254] The particular characteristics of the French aristocracy played a strategic role in Tocqueville's explanation of the French Revolution, and were an important target for the polemics of Saint-Simon and Comte, who were assertively aware of themselves as heralds of a new epoch and its social theory.

The French Revolution had focused the political contradictions of pre-bourgeois Europe into an unprecedented sharpness and clarity. As a theory of politics after the bourgeois revolution, sociology could thus hardly have emerged anywhere else than in France. It was only in the subsequent heyday of Liberal reform and free

[252] Tocqueville's experiences and views of England have been treated in an excellent study by Seymour Drescher, _Tocqueville and England_, Cambridge, Mass., 1964, pp. 36–53.

[253] Tocqueville, _The Ancien Régime_, p. 49. Tocqueville's problem in dealing with British society was real enough. In a recent competent survey of British nineteenth-century history the reader is told: 'Until the early twentieth century no mere businessman could compete with the greatest landlords in wealth, let alone in power and status.' D. Beadsley, _From Castlereagh to Gladstone_, London, 1967, p. 46.

[254] Drescher, op. cit., e.g. p. 119f.

trade in England, that Herbert Spencer could start to propound the social theory of the new society as part of an attack on Tory Britain. By then it was very late. Bourgeois society was no longer new, and, to the dismay of an uncomprehending Spencer, was under increasing under attack from yet newer forces.

Politics were determined by society, and society should be studied by the methods of observation and analysis pioneered in the positive natural science. Such was the main message of the sociology of the early 19th century. This message was sufficiently important for it to have left, by the mid-20th century, its mark on the academic division of labour. For today the academic discipline of politics has ceased to be largely a branch of jurisprudence or philosophy, or occasionally a study of parliamentary history; it has now generally become an attempt to construct some kind of a social science.

The labours of the first sociologists served to map out a vast terrain; but they rarely resulted in a profound analyses. They determined the orientation and direction of sociology, rather than contributing a fruitful system of substantive concepts. Tocqueville's concern with the problems of egalitarianism and centralization, and the strategic role of intermediate organizations, has inspired later writers preoccupied with the threat of revolutions in this century. Spencer's ideas on the evolution of social differentiation and integration have echoes in the recent works of Talcott Parsons, once the coroner of Spencer's thought. For Parsons, of course, the United States of his day naturally replaces mid-Victorian Britain as the apogee of social evolution.[255]

Basically, however, bourgeois politics developed in a direction contrary to that expected by the first sociologists. The central distinction – common to Saint-Simon, Comte and Spencer – between peaceful, non-coercive societies devoted to economic and scientific pursuits, on the one hand, and societies devoted to war and theology, on the other, soon became obsolete in the new age of imperialism and violent class struggles. Contemporary theorists of 'industrial society', writing in the shadow of the so-called 'military-industrial complex', characteristically no longer set 'industrial' against 'military' or 'militant' society, but against 'agricultural' or 'post-

---

[255] T. Parsons, *Societies: Evolutionary and Comparative Perspectives*, and *The System of Modern Societies*, Englewood Cliffs, 1966 and 1971 respectively. On the United States, see the latter work, ch. 6.

industrial' society.[256]

The actual development of politics after the bourgeois revolution was more adequately grasped by the theorists of elites. Instead of an overwhelmingly majoritarian industrial class of entrepreneurs and workers, they pointed to a small political elite as the rulers of the new society. Instead of a harmoniously completed revolution, they found a new cycle of social conflict. Instead of scientific enlightenment, they emphasized the importance of non-rational ideologies. Instead of peaceful administration and laissez-faire, they focused on the role of the state as an apparatus of violence.

Elite theory developed out of the reaction of a group of high bourgeois intellectuals to the ascent of the working-class in the late 19th and early 20th century. Politics after the bourgeois revolution had also turned out to be a politics of imperialism. In 1895 a sociologist of future renown had proclaimed: 'What we must pass on to our successors is not peace and human happiness, but the *eternal struggle* for the preservations and elevation [*Emporzüchtung*] of our national species.'[257] In a passage of his major sociological work, written in 1911, the same sociologist declared: 'The universal revival of "imperialist" capitalism, which has been the normal form in which capitalist interests have influenced politics, and the revival of political drives for expansion, are thus not accidental. For the predictable future, progress will work in their favour.'[258] Such was the credo of Max Weber, distinguished not only as a great sociologist but also as a great spokesman of German imperialism.[259]

The second generation of political sociologists revived something

---

[256] The mid-20th-century concept of industrial society is usually developed with a view to emphasizing the secondary importance of the distinction between capitalism and socialism, both presented as variants of industrial society. Cf. R. Aron, *18 Lectures on Industrial Society*, London, 1967, R. Dahrendorf, *Class and Class Conflict in Industrial Society*, Stanford, 1959, p. 36f. Dahrendorf has, however, since become sceptical of industrial society as a unifying concept (*Conflict After Class*, London, 1967, pp. 6, 27 n.). Aron is aware that the industrial societies 'are in theory peaceable' but that 'seldom in history have so many great wars been fought as in the twentieth century' (op. cit., p. 362).

[257] M. Weber, *Politische Schriften*, p. 20. The words are from his famous inaugural lecture as professor of economics in Freiburg. In that lecture, Weber manifested his freedom from value-freedom in the academy (op. cit., p. 7).

[258] The passage from *Wirtschaft und Gesellschaft* is included in the Gerth and Mills selection, *From Max Weber*, p. 169.

[259] W. Mommsen, *Max Weber und die deutsche Politik*, Tübingen, 1959, esp. ch. IV.

of the shrewd perspicacity of Macchiavelli in their observations on the political game of their time. They took note of the role of force and fraud, of the distinction between private and public virtues. They threw light on the oligarchic functioning of governments and organizations, and on the importance of ideology. On the whole, however, their efforts too fell short of a breakthrough to a true science of society. The most ambitious endeavour of this group, Pareto's bold attempt at conceiving society as a mechanical system of residues, derivations, interests and social heterogenity, proved sterile. Pareto himself remained a prisoner of his individualistic and (at least partly) instinctual psychology, which prevented his emphasis on the central role of non-rational sentiments in society from becoming more than a mere adumbration of a social theory.

Associated with their assumption that politics were not fully explicable in social terms, was the tendency of the elite theorists towards a biological account of politics. Always in the foreground in Gumplowicz, this drift was visible in the others too, in their comments on the struggle for 'pre-eminence' (Mosca), for 'life and welfare' (Pareto) or for 'feeding-ground' (Michels). It was also there in their common conviction of the strategic importance of the innate inequality of men.

Consideration of the elite theorists has brought us from the politics of the French Revolution to politics confronted with the threat or promise of a socialist revolution. Of the latter Robert Michels wrote: 'the problem of socialism is not merely a problem in economics . . . socialism is also an administrative problem, a problem of democracy'.[260] With the first sentence he spoke for all the elite theorists; while the others would have willingly produced individual variations on the theme of the second. The central concern of the sociologists of elites was perhaps even more clearly conveyed by one who was not properly a member of their circle. It was Max Weber who declared in the conclusion to his Freiburg address: 'It is not a question of the *economic* position of the *ruled*, but rather the *political* qualifications of the ruling and ascending classes . . .'[261]

Yet it was to be its reflection on economic problems, which produced a critique of political economy inspired by the ascent of the

---

[260] Michels, op. cit., p. 402f.
[261] Weber, *Politische Schriften*, p. 29.

working class and the shadow of the proletarian revolution, that eventually yielded the most important contribution of sociology to the study of the society which the first sociologists had discovered. That contribution will be the subject of the following chapter. There, among others, we will encounter Max Weber again – who was, it must always be remembered, a professor of economics.

The subsequent history of the 20th century provides a clue to what is probably the fundamental reason why it was from an analysis of capitalist economics rather than of capitalist politics that the classical achievements of modern sociology were made. Two world wars, fascism, imperialist intervention and sophistication of the means of political control and repression, have all been witness to the central role of violence and domination in the capitalist world. Nevertheless, the relative political success to date of the rulers of this world has been basically determined by the elasticity and capacity for growth of the advanced capitalist economies, which has rendered the mechanisms of the economic and social integration of the ruled unexpectedly pervasive and powerful. Further, the most important political institution of advanced capitalist societies has proved to be neither an efficient administration nor a skilful elite, but bourgeois democracy. Yet a true social theory of bourgeois democracy has never been developed in sociology – nor for that matter in what is today called 'political science'. Even in historical materialism there are only a few rather general and crude beginnings of one, above all in Lenin. A developed scientific theory and analysis of bourgeois democracy is still missing.

Chapter Five

The Ideological Community: the Sociological Critique of Political Economy

I. A Natural Science of an Unnatural World

Sociology, as a discourse on politics, eventually underwent a remarkable transformation. We have seen how the self-confident evolutionary determinism of the period of successful bourgeois revolution – which persisted even during the phase of Restoration – turned into a desperate elitist voluntarism in the age of imperialism. However, this was a change which occurred as one group of sociological writers gave way to another. But the formation of sociology also reveals a basic paradox within the conceptions of the majority of its proponents.

Sociology was launched, from the very beginning, as a naturalistic enterprise – as a natural history and study of society, in contrast to dynastic historiography, theology, or traditional legal and moral philosophy. The sociologists took their inspiration from the rapidly developing biological sciences – Comte and Saint-Simon from the early 19th century French physiologists, Spencer from Lamarck and from the geologist George Lyell. In the last third of the century the work of Darwin loomed above everything else.

In the perspective of the epoch, society and social institutions were seen as part of a single, law-bound natural universe. Ideas of evolution and organic analogies – with differing emphases on the specificity of society – became widely influential. The thin stream of books on sociology which started in the 1870's and 80's – by Albert Schäffle, Paul von Lilienfeld, Guillaume de Greef, Evgeni De Roberty, Ludwig Gumplowicz, Lester Ward and a few others, even more generally forgotten – was part of a much broader naturalistic movement which developed in response to the Darwinian revolution.

This period of sociology is mostly, if vaguely, remembered as an age of rapidly obsolete, all-encompassing systems. But it was also an age notable for the enthusiastic, but often rather naive, collection of the most diverse sorts of social facts. There was Spencer's colossal compilation *Descriptive Sociology*; Le Play's family monographs,[2] the Notes or similar sections in the early volumes of the *American Journal of Sociology, Revue Internationale de Sociologie* or *Rivista Italiana di Sociologia* with their international reporting of railway statistics, housing conditions, and strikes; or the more scholarly and historically oriented surveys of interdisciplinary literature in the Durkheimian *l'Année Sociologique*. The early sociologists resembled to a great extent the early devotees of natural science, the 17th and 18th century collectors of stones and plants and amateur writers on natural phenomena.

The naturalistic treatment of society and of man broke new ground, away from the well-trodden path of traditional theology and moral philosophy. Saint-Simon and Comte asserted that theology and metaphysics had been superseded by the science they claimed to represent. Durkheim sharply counterposed the new scientific treatment of *morale* to aprioristic moral philosophy, both Kantian and non-Kantian.[3] The biographies of the founders of sociology show that they had generally broken away from religious family backgrounds – devout Catholicism in the case of Comte, Methodism in that of Spencer (a process begun by Spencer Sr in his mature age), Judaism in that of Durkheim (the son of a rabbi). Max Weber too, who was no naturalist, had a Pietistic background.

[1] Apart from Gumplowicz and Ward, the most important was Albert Schäffle and his *Bau und Leben des sozialen Körpers*, 4 vols., Tübingen, 1875–9. Schäffle was an important early influence on Durkheim, whose very first publication was a highly appreciative review of the former's work, in *Revue Philosophique*, XIX, pp. 84–101 (1885).

[2] For a recent introduction to Le Play, see M. Z. Brooke, *Le Play : Engineer and Social Scientist*, London, 1970. Cf. also W. Goldfrank, 'Reappraising Le Play', in Oberschall (ed.), *The Establishment of Empirical Sociology*. Le Play belonged to the Emperor's entourage during the Second Empire in France. His major work, *Les Ouvriers Européens*, appeared in 1855, under government auspices. Le Play never regarded himself as a 'sociologist', but his work in 'social science' is definitely part of the sociological tradition in a broad sense.

[3] E. Durkheim, 'La science positive de la morale en Allemagne', *Revue Philosophique*, XXIV (juillet–décembre 1887), p. 33f. Cf. *The Division of Labor in Society*, New York, 1964, esp. Durkheim's preface and introduction to the first edition.

The foundation in 1900 of a Belgian Society of Sociology by a predominantly Catholic group of scholars was thus logically regarded by the *Revue Internationale de Sociologie* as 'a remarkable fact'.[4]

In its naturalistic emphasis sociology paralleled the efforts of Marx and Engels, who were also working towards a natural science of society, were also admirers of Darwin, and were also hostile to theology and moral philosophy.[5] Indeed, to the dismay of the Victorian ultra-liberal himself, there were some who thought of Darwin, Marx and Spencer as a new, post-theological trinity.[6]

The fourth congress of the sociological international, the *Institut Internationale de Sociologie*, in 1900, was mainly devoted to a discussion of historical materialism. There Marx was treated by the progressive organicists and positivists as, by and large, one of their own number, with a type of benevolence and respect similar to that which he was later to receive from latter-day Hegelians and phenomenologists. In other words the approach to him was eclectic, superficial, and subject to the dictates of fashion.

Yet the unexpected outcome of this sociological naturalism was,

[4] *Revue Internationale de Sociologie*, 8, 6 (1900), p. 479. The note was probably written by the director of the journal, René Worms, the organizer and secretary of the sociological international, the Institut Internationale de Sociologie.

[5] A recent illuminating study of Marx and Darwin is V. Gerratana, 'Marx and Darwin', *New Left Review* 82 (November–December 1973).

[6] This was a rather common view among early Italian sociologists, its most famous proponent at one time being Enrico Ferri, the criminologist and disciple of Cesare Lombroso (Gerratana, 'Marx and Darwin', p. 81 n; G. Fiamingo, 'Sociology in Italy', *American Journal of Sociology*, I (July 1895–May 1896), p. 344. In France the eclectic socialist Benoît Malon also put Marx and Spencer in the same company; see D. W. Brogan, *The Development of Modern France* (1870–1939), 2nd ed., London, 1967, p. 290. (It was in Malon's *Revue Socialiste* that Marx's famous *Enquête Ouvrière* was published, in 1880.)

[7] *Annales de l'Institut Internationale de Sociologie*, vol. VIII, Paris, 1902. See esp. the interventions by Novikov, Loria, de Greef, and Worms. The tenor of the event is rather well conveyed by a conclusion of de Greef: 'Posterity will be more just; it will mingle together [*confondra*] all the great socialists and sociologists, Saint-Simon, Fourier, R. Owen, Proudhon, Marx, Quetelet, A. Comte, H. Spencer, in a common admiration, extracting more and more from their immortal works not what separates them but what unites them in the same civilizing thrust' (p. 162). For a similar juxtaposition, this time of Marx, Spencer, Comte, Benjamin Kidd, Giddings, and Ward, by Achille Loria, see p. 118f. Among the few who were absolutely and explicitly hostile to historical materialism was Gabriel Tarde (pp. 283–89).

paradoxically, a reassertion of traditional idealism on a new basis. Sociologists undertook large-scale empirical studies of morality – Durkheim's *The Division of Labour in Society*, Westermarck's *The Origin and Development of the Moral Ideas*, Hobhouse's *Morals in Evolution* – and religion, Weber's *Gesammelte Aufsätze zur Religionssoziologie* or Durkheim's *The Elementary Forms of Religious Life*. At the same time, they did something more and other than this. They made community of values and norms the basic phenomenon of every society. Indeed, the first two sociologists even founded new religions, the New Christianity of Saint-Simon and Comte's Religion of Humanity.

There were, no doubt, many factors in the religious conversions of Saint-Simon and Comte, from the ideological insecurity of many non-revolutionary yet non-reactionary intellectuals during a hollow Restoration, to the very unstable and neurotic personalities of both sociologists. What is important, however, is that they both explicitly gave their religions a definite role and function in their social theories. In the work of later sociologists, another type of ideological community was to perform basically the same role and function.

The central reason for the paradoxical development of mainstream sociology, however, was that sociology came to experience itself as a natural science of an unnatural world. This world was unnatural in two senses. Firstly, it was unnatural – or abnormal, as Durkheim was to say – in the sense that it was unhealthy – a society plagued with social diseases, 'social problems'. The critical stance it adopted towards the object of its study gave the mainstream sociologists a certain common ground with the founders of historical materialism, and distanced them from the cynical aloofness of the Social Darwinists. But to the sociologists the world was unnatural also in a second sense. It contained no natural healing element. The body-social was neither self-healing, nor did it bring into life new social forces capable of providing a natural basis for a new society. New religious or moral principles had therefore to be introduced in order to make the world normal and natural (in the first sense).

This logic can be seen very clearly in Saint-Simon and Comte. They both started by proclaiming the arrival of a new society and of an age of positive science. They claimed to have demonstrated the fundamental characteristics of the new epoch and the political and ideological changes that it needed. They regarded their own work as a contribution to those changes. They then also came to see the ills of the new society: among them, poverty and unemployment.

Now, whereas in their critique of the Restoration they could rely on the promise of the industrial class and the new system of ideas associated with it, in their critique of capitalism Saint-Simon and Comte found no new forces in the world capable of solving the social problems it created. Here they had no faith in developments among the industrial leaders, in the struggles of the working class, in the spontaneous development of new ideas or in the re-establishment of old ones. It was in this context that religion was introduced as a solution from outside, from the atemporal and non-spatial realm of spiritual principles. Confronted with the new social problems, Saint-Simon and Comte reacted with moral slogans: 'Men should act toward one another as brothers' (Saint-Simon); 'Live for the other' (Comte). To underpin this morality they created their religions. 'A doctrine of the universe as its basis – this is what [Saint-Simon's] New Christianity must consist of', as Durkheim put it.[8] The new religions became the means to create the new society – which was no longer regarded as evolving naturally; and to provide its fundamental regulatory mechanism – which was no longer primarily derived from the study of actual social tendencies.[9] It should be added that there the function of religiously sanctioned morality stopped. The latter was not proposed as a substitute for social reorganization. Comte and Saint-Simon remained committed to social reform.

The later development of the views of Saint-Simon and Comte can be fitted into a more general pattern. Each theorist took note of the new 'social question' of triumphant capitalist society and committed himself to social reform. Each thereby became increasingly alienated from the bourgeois entrepreneurs and politicians who had protected and subscribed to Saint-Simon's earlier publications on 'industry'. Without repudiating the French Revolution, the two men had from the start refused to situate themselves in the existing revolutionary tradition (bourgeois or jacobin), and equally later refused to adopt a working-class position. Instead they advocated the solution of the social question by the established authorities of the existing society.[10] They thus presented their social programmes

[8] E. Durkheim, *Socialism*, New York, 1958, p. 235.

[9] Saint-Simon's *Nouveau Christianisme* is in *Oeuvres*, vol. III, pp. 101–92. Comte's religion is developed in *Système de politique positive*, vol. IV.

[10] In his famous letter 'To Messrs. Workers' Saint-Simon had told the workers

as the alternative to impending disaster. Comte emphasized that positivism was 'the only guarantee against the communist invasion'.[11]

In short, the first sociologists displayed a fundamental yet uneasy attachment to capitalist society, defending it against reactionary feudal forces as well as against revolutionary socialist forces. But they also were keenly aware of the critical problems posed by the proletariat and the working class movement, and this led them to question the existing social order. For a partial solution to the difficulties of this position, sociology resorted to a renovation of old idealist traditions of religion and morality.

It is not just the reform programmes of the sociologists that can be understood in this way. The development of the most distinctive concepts of sociology, of the central sociological contribution to a scientific discourse on society (whatever its value), reflects the same pattern. *This sociological contribution has essentially consisted in the discovery and study of the ideological community* – i.e. community of values and norms – *in human aggregates of various types and sizes.* In the practical application of its theory, sociology has characteristically demanded a commitment to the strengthening of some such sort of ideological community. Originating as a successor to traditional political philosophy, sociology thus became in many ways a modern, scientifically oriented equivalent to theology and moral

---

how they should address the 'chiefs of the principal houses of culture, manufacture, and commerce'. They should begin like this: 'You are rich, and we are poor; you work with your heads, we with our hands; it follows from those two fundamental differences which exist between us, that we are and should be your subordinates.' *Oeuvres*, VI, p. 437. (The letter then goes on to say that the workers should ask their bosses to be their spokesmen before the King.) *The New Christianity* ends with an appeal to 'princes' to listen to the voice of God and to use all their energy to better the lot of the poor (*Oeuvres*, III). Comte's scheme for the transition to positivism starts from the protection of the doctrine by an 'empirical dictatorship' (there being no other choice in a profound ideological crisis) and ends in the final transitional phase of a positivist dictatorship. *Système de politique positive*, IV, p. 395f (English ed., p. 343f).

[11] Comte, *Système de politique positive*, IV, p. 500 (English ed., p. 434). Cf. ibid., I, p. 154. 'The 'anomaly' of proletarian participation in the positivist dictatorship is connected with this guarantee. The proletarian positivists provide the best guarantee against the 'demagogues' who try to base themselves on the proletariat. The second, more positive function of the latter is that contact with them is important to the regeneration of the patriciate. Ibid., IV, p. 453 (English ed., p. 393).

philosophy – an investigatory rather than dogmatic guardian of the ideological community.

The careers of the first American sociologists serve to illustrate this continuity of function. Seven out of nineteen early presidents of the American Sociological Society started their careers as Protestant ministers.[12] They too juxtaposed natural science with an unnatural world, though they had assembled these two elements in reverse order, coming to science as a result of their experience of an anti-natural, immoral universe.[13] (The two tendencies represented by scientific naturalism and by the experience of an unnatural world, which have here been separated for analytical purposes, were of course often complexly intertwined, and by no means constituted definite temporal sequences.)

The suggestion is not intended that everything treated and traded under the label of sociology fits into this framework. On the contrary, in the next section we will indicate an important tendency which does not. Yet others may also be found. What will be argued here is that there is a specific core to all the sprawling and bewildering activities that are commonly called sociological. It will be contended that the major scientific contribution of sociology is bound up with the analysis and investigation of the ideological community.

The typical pattern in the formation of sociology can be seen in the development of Saint-Simon and Comte. It is discernible in Pareto as well, confronted not just with the spectre of a red revolution (as Comte had been), but with an increasingly organized and unruly working-class. There is, as we have noted above, more to Pareto's sociology than his emphasis on the role of sentiments in human affairs. But it is noteworthy that it was this aspect of his work that was responsible for the popularity of his views with American sociologists of the 1930's: not only with Parsons but with Homans and Henderson as well.[14] In an oft-quoted autobiographical note

[12] R. Hinkle and G. Hinkle, *The Development of Modern Sociology*, New York, 1954, p. 3. The seven include Sumner and Small.

[13] Cf. the German Lutheran pastors of the Evangelical-Social Congress who asked Max Weber and other scholars to make studies of, and give courses for them on, economic and social questions. Marianne Weber, *Max Weber, Ein Lebensbild*, Tübingen, 1926, pp. 138–45, 203. In contrast to their American brethren, however, the German pastors had little influence on the universities and their well-entrenched mandarinate.

[14] Parsons, *The Structure of Social Action*, vol. I. Parsons was at pains to disentangle normative from non-normative elements in Pareto's sentiments

Homans has reminded us 'that much modern sociology is an effort to answer the arguments of the revolutionaries'.[15]

However, the decisive period in the formation of sociology coincided with the development of a critique of political economy (generally very rudimentary in form), and with attempts to wrestle with the problems posed by the social question: not with the development of a theory of politics. In revolt against the deductive, individualist-utilitarian and laissez-faire character of orthodox (above all 'vulgar') liberal economics, new social theories developed in the last quarter of the 19th century which were inductive, social-ethical and interventionist. Sociology was part of this movement, which also included other closely related tendencies such as historical economics in Germany and institutionalist economics in the United States.

We can distinguish in this respect three critiques of political economy, each in a particular way significant for the development of the sociological project. One centred on liberal economic policies and gave rise – or, more exactly, impetus – to a kind of investigatory practice which is often labelled sociological, but which has increasingly become part of normal administrative routine. The other two were instrumental in bringing the ideological community into focus, and in constructing sociology as a distinct theoretical and empirical discipline. One of these started from a critical analysis of the epistemological basis of economics. The other was an across-the-board critique of the epistemology, the utilitarianism and the

---

(p. 200f). It is of course only to the extent that some of the former are present that Pareto fits into our pattern as a theorist of the ideological community. This point is not belaboured by Homans and Henderson, but they agreed in focusing on the role of non-logical sentiment, not on, e.g., the circulation of the elites (G. Homans and C. P. Curtis, *An Introduction to Pareto*, New York, 1934; L. Henderson, *Pareto's General Sociology*, Cambridge, Mass., 1935). In Henderson there is also a focus on Pareto's concept of system, which stressed mutual dependence instead of cause-and-effect sequences. To Henderson, a physiologist, this is an important methodological position, whose fruitfulness he illustrates by reference to physico-chemical systems. In comparison to the latter, however, Pareto's substantive sociology is far from the mark (p. 86).

[15] G. Homans, *Sentiments and Activities*, New York, 1962, p. 4. No reader of either Homans' and Curtis' or Henderson's work (though the latter is much less a *livre de combat*) would find it difficult to agree with that statement. But it should be added that the books mentioned could also give the rather extravagant impression that much modern sociology was also an answer to the arguments of liberal intellectuals and politicians like Roosevelt.

policy recommendations of liberal economics. Max Weber may be taken to represent the second and Durkheim the third type of critique.

The sociological critique of political economy also involved a critique of Spencer's work, which could in a way be seen as liberal economics writ large. Spencer's doctrine was the nearest form of naturalism against which to react – a reaction which occurred surprisingly soon, though for a time he was smothered in eclectic embraces.[16] The need for such a critique was clear to the American sociologists of the 1890's, who had been brought up in a strongly Spencerian ideological milieu. It was also clear to Durkheim, and influenced his work on social solidarity and the division of labour.

For a brief period Spencer had been the world's leading sociologist. Yet modern sociology was constituted in critical reaction against him. Some idea of the strength of the forces at work in this reaction can be gained from the fact that Spencer's dearest disciple was one of those who struck out along a new path. To the illustrious names of Weber and Durkheim, can be added a representative of the first type of critique – Beatrice Webb. Before her marriage, as Beatrice Potter, she was a close friend of Spencer and chosen by him as his literary executor. But instead of continuing his work, she became one of the Fabian reformist socialists.[17] The Fabians also regarded their studies of society as sociological, but theirs was another kind of sociology.[18]

II. Administrative Sociology and the Twilight of Competitive Capitalism

Spencer's sociology had emphatically been a natural science of a natural world. Man and society were seen as part of a cosmic process of progressive evolution, differentiation and integration, which

[16] For example, Kidd and Ward (referred to by Loria, n. 7 above), were explicit critics of Spencer.

[17] On Spencer and Beatrice Potter see the biographers, Peel, op. cit., pp. 3, 23; and K. Muggeridge and R. Adam, *Beatrice Webb. A Life*, London, 1967, pp. 38f, 80f, 128f. Beatrice Webb has herself written of Spencer in her autobiographies, *My Apprenticeship* and *Our Partnership*, London, 1926 and 1948 respectively (the latter posthumously edited by Barbara Drake and Margaret Cole).

[18] In the Fabian essays Sidney Webb, for instance, referred to the knowledge of society bequeathed by Comte, Darwin and Spencer, and to scientific

manifested an inherent, Lamarckian tendency to perfectibility. In somewhat more concrete social terms, this process involved the division of labour and the development of harmonious mutual dependence through free exchange. It had never been a very accurate account of reality, even in Spencer's early days, when Engels was writing *The Condition of the Working Class in England*, and Disraeli his *Sybil, or the Two Nations*. But it made sense to the small merchants and manufacturers of Spencer's native Derby and other new industrial cities, who were prospering with the industrial revolution and felt secure in what was indisputably the premier country of the world. Spencer's sociology had its basis in the dissenting Radicalism of the bourgeoisie and petty bourgeoisie of competitive capitalism in England in the middle third of the 19th century.

But with the on-going concentration of capital, the rise of big corporations and trusts, and the growth of poverty and misery in the city slums, the world became less and less Spencerian. The Great Depression of the 1870's, the rise of the labour movement in the 1880's in Britain and the United States (and in France), and the challenge to English world hegemony from the ascendant powers of Germany and America, dealt decisive blows to the ideas of free exchange and free trade.

A model of competitive capitalism can, however, serve as an idyllic ideology in somewhat more sordid contexts. The men who paid homage to Spencer on his triumphant visit to the United States were largely the ruthless magnates of the new monopoly stage of capitalism – the Carnegies, Rockefellers, Hills and others. But however congenial the Spencerian notion of 'the survival of the fittest' was to the victors of reckless monopolistic competition, Spencer was not truly their man.

In the last part of his *Principles of Sociology*, the old liberal wrote of the freedom of contract in relation to the 'wage-earning factory-hand': 'But this liberty amounts in practice to little more than the ability to exchange one slavery for another; since fit only for his particular occupation, he has rarely an opportunity of doing anything more than decide in what mill he will pass the greater part of

---

sociology in general. B. Shaw (ed.), *Fabian Essays in Socialism* (2nd ed.), London, 1908, pp. 31, 49. Cf. S. and B. Webb, *Industrial Democracy*, London, 1897, preface.

his dreary days. The coercion of circumstances often leans more hardly on him than the coercion of a master does on one in bondage.'[19] In spite of this rather severe verdict on a century of industrial capitalism, Spencer ends by avowing a 'relative optimism' in the long run. But his remedies were rather pitiful: cooperatives were eventually to absorb 'superior' workers and out-compete capitalist enterprise,[20] and a limited amount of private philanthropy was to alleviate the worst aspects of the workers' lot.[21] The basis of future progress was held to lie in world peace, which was to be ensured by a 'federation of the highest nations (already foreshadowed by occasional agreements among "the Powers")'.[22]

In our first chapter, we took note of Talcott Parsons' seemingly defiant challenge in his magnum opus *The Structure of Social Action*: 'Spencer is dead. But who killed him and how? This is the problem.' Parsons' answer was that the evolution of scientific theory was responsible for his fate. But he was writing in 1937, and it is interesting that Spencer had in fact been declared dead forty years before by another American sociologist, at that time very prominent as the head of the leading Chicago department of sociology and the editor of the *American Journal of Sociology*.

In a review of the last volume of Spencer's *Principles of Sociology* Albion Small wrote in 1897: 'Yet Mr. Spencer's sociology is of the past, not of the present. It has a permanent place in the development of sociological thought. Present sociology, however, is neither Spencerianism nor is it dependent upon anything Spencerian.'[23] This was stated before very much in the way of theory, scientific or not, had been produced by US sociology. Small somewhat later claimed with disarming candour, as well as with a certain amount of rhetorical exaggeration, that sociology was established in the United States before it had a distinctive intellectual content, a distinctive method or even a point of view.[24]

[19] Spencer, *Principles of Sociology*, II, 3, p. 525.

[20] Ibid., Part VIII, ch. XXI.

[21] See the Postscript to the tenth edition of *The Study of Sociology*, p. 406f, where Spencer answers reviewers who criticized his attacks on welfare policies and even unduly generous 'individual altruism' for the 'extreme cruelty' of 'fostering the good-for-nothing at the expense of the good' (op. cit., p. 344).

[22] Spencer, *Principles of Sociology*, III, 3, p. 610.

[23] *American Journal of Sociology*, vol. II, March 1897, p. 742.

[24] A. Small, '50 Years of Sociology in the United States, 1865–1915', *American Journal of Sociology*. vol. XXI (May 1916), pp. 721–864: reprinted in *American*

Of course, Spencer was not as dead in 1897 as in 1937 – even leaving aside the incidental fact that the veteran Victorian did not depart this world until 1903. Spencerians like William Graham Sumner and the more heterodox Franklin Giddings were vigorous and prominent in US sociology. Nevertheless, Small had, on the whole, caught the tune of the times.

What killed Spencer was above all the demise of small-scale competitive capitalism and the advent of the age of monopoly capital, in an economy dominated by big corporations. With the sharpening of international as well as internal contradictions in the new epoch, the old liberalism – pacifist, cosmopolitan, and wedded to free exchange – was superseded by imperialism and social reform.[25] Spencer's sociology went under with his political ideology. It was indeed assassinated twice over in this new period. It was killed by a new kind of sociological investigation as well as by a new kind of sociological theory.

The naturalistic approach to society, which was one of the most important manifestations and achievements of the earliest sociology, now led in a different direction. Emphasis on observation and amassing of data – taken predominently from history, as in Comte, or from history and ethnography, as in Spencer – no longer served to demonstrate the natural course of evolution, but to provide information about the present unnatural world. The search was now not for social laws but for the principles on which social policies should be based.

Charles Booth, a rich philanthropic shipowner, undertook his famous *Survey of London Life and Labour* to refute the claims of the socialist leader Hyndman about the scale of poverty in London. Booth found that Hyndman's allegations were in fact rather understated. His survey was published in 1889, the same year as the successful great London dock strike. One of the assistants he had engaged was Beatrice Potter, his cousin-by-marriage, and it was her experiences of outcast London and the dock-strike that turned her away from the sociological ideas of her family friend Spencer. Other surveys followed, by Booth, Rowntree and others. The Webbs and

---

Journal of Sociology Index to Volumes I–III (1895–1947), pp. 177–269, reference to p. 225.

[25] *Imperialism and Social Reform* is the title of a very valuable study of the period in Britain by B. Semmel, London, 1960.

other Fabians studied the trade unions, and the various causes of destitution and poverty.

A combination of a Spencerian (and Comtean) social scientism, and a concern with social problems similar to that of the Fabians and others of their ilk in Britain, also marked the American sociology which developed rapidly at the same time. In 1901 the Graduate Sociological League of the University of Chicago undertook a broad study of sociology in the United States. Its findings revealed that American sociology was responsive to the influence of Spencer (and to a lesser extent of Ward) and to the needs of ameliorist agencies, as well as to the theoretical instruction of the German universities.[26] Catalogues of syllabuses from a great number of colleges were assembled, and showed an enormous number of courses on 'Sphere of State Activity, the State and Industry, Socialism'; 'Sociology of the Dependent Classes, Charities'; 'Sociology of the Delinquent Classes, Criminology'; 'Sociology of the Industrial Group, Social Economics'; 'Social Reform, Practical Sociology, Social Problems'.[27]

Thus, not so long after Spencer had fulminated in his enormously influential *Study of Sociology* against 'agencies which undertake in a wholesale way to foster good-for-nothings', George Vincent of the Chicago department of sociology could write (not very cheerfully): 'To the newspapers the sociologist is the man who deals with problems of dependence, vice, and crime. Settlement residents, probation officers, investigators of housing conditions, students of penology, are all known to the reporter as "sociological workers".'[28] 'Scientific' philanthropy and social reform investigations were not, of course, anything new. English statistical societies, government commissions and the American Social Science Association had all earlier seen themselves in such terms.[29] What was new, however,

[26] F. Tolman, 'The Study of Sociology in Institutions of Learning in the United States I', *American Journal of Sociology*, VII, p. 797.

[27] Tolman, op. cit., II–IV, *American Journal of Sociology*, vol. VIII, pp. 85–121, 251–72, 531–58. See further, Oberschall, op. cit.

[28] G. Vincent, 'Varieties of Sociology', *American Journal of Sociology*, vol. XII, August 1906, p. 9.

[29] On early English social research, there are two fine articles in the cited Oberschall volume: D. Elesh, 'The Manchester Statistical Society', and S. Cole, 'Continuity and institutionalization in science: a case study of failure'. The early American Social Science Movement is the object of a thorough monograph by L. and J. Bernard, *Origins of American Sociology*, New York, 1965.

was the scale and seriousness of the new social problems. What was soon to be most important academic sociology department in the USA was established in 1893 in Chicago, a city whose population had doubled in the single decade of the 1880's.

Chicago housed the infamous stockyards, described by Upton Sinclair and Bertholt Brecht. The most left-wing tendencies in the early American labour movement centred on Chicago. In the 1880's the 8-hour-day campaign was strongest there. The city was the site of many violent class struggles in the 1880's and 1890's. The Haymarket Affair occurred in Chicago in 1886: eight labour leaders were sentenced to death for agitation, and four of them executed, after a mysterious clash between the police and demonstrators at which those condemned had not been present. Chicago was the centre of the Pullman strike in 1894, during which the city was occupied by federal troops, and 25 workers were killed.[30]

An important innovation for the future of sociology was the relationship established in America between sociology and the university. The *ad hoc* investigations of 'applied sociology' were a form of social administration and charity organization more than a scientific pursuit. On the other hand, the grand schemes of the 'general sociology' of the time – derived from Comte, Spencer, Schäffle and others – provided little theory to 'apply'. In fact, in Britain practical research did not develop as a viable independent discipline which could be identified with sociology. For a long time it remained an aspect of social administration and of academic training explicitly geared to that purpose.[31] Social research, which might have been the product of academic sociology, was also conducted on a large scale by wealthy philanthropists. In his Land and Labour study of Belgium Seebohm Rowntree employed 101 assistants for up to 19 months.[32] With no feudal past, by contrast, the United States did not have a university system strongly linked to largely

[30] On the American labour movement of this period see, for example, vol. II of Philip Foner's *History of the Labor Movement in the United States*, New York, 1955, chs. 6, 7, 18.

[31] This is a main theme of Philip Abrams' essay, *The Origins of British Sociology: 1834–1914*, Chicago, 1968. Abrams suggests (e.g. p. 149) that this absorption of possible sociologists was basically due to the tolerance and reform orientation of the British polity. Looking at the success story of the academic establishment of sociology in the US, there seems to be no basis for regarding a less interventionist polity as a factor of any importance at all in the story of American sociology.

[32] Ibid., p. 33. Rowntree's study appeared in 1913.

pre-bourgeois social forces. On the contrary, the new US universities established in the late nineteenth century were uniquely
adapted to the running of a modern, developed bourgeois society.
A system of colleges and universities which could give courses in
'marketing methods', 'principles of advertising', 'newspaper
reporting' and 'business letter-writing', or which could have (as the
university of Chicago did) a chair in 'police administration',
naturally had no qualms about according academic status and
resources to a vulgar upstart discipline like sociology.[33]

Typically enough, the European-oriented US academic just
quoted included in his list of *horreurs* a number of topics and
activities regarded as respectable sociology even today, for example
papers on 'Experimentation in Face to Face Interaction' and
'Susceptibility to Accidents'.[34] The sociological tradition curtly
dismissed here is still venerated as sound sociology: 'Surveys are
not research; sympathetic accounts of sales-ladies, stenographers,
waitresses, deans, bankrupts, litigants, school systems, happy and
unhappy students of education, matriculating students in doubt
whether they love their father more than their mother or vice versa,
with or without graphs, curves, and percentages, are not research
and would not be called research anywhere except in the United
States.'[35]

Many writers found a contradiction in Spencer's thought
between, on the one hand, his organicist view of society and
evolutionary account of its increasing integration, and on the other,
his outright ultra-individualism. This contradiction could be resolved, and was resolved, in two basic ways – granted the premise
of a sociological commitment to the study of society as a kind of
whole. Durkheim and others were to tackle it in one way, the
Fabians, Ward and others in the interventionist tradition in another
way.

Sidney Webb and Lester Ward both cited an address by the
English biologist T. H. Huxley directed against 'Administrative

---

[33] The examples are taken from a piece of American academic self-criticism,
A. Flexner, *Universities, American, English, German*, New York, 1930, pp. 52f,
133f. Flexner alludes mainly to Columbia, Chicago, and Wisconsin, all important
in the early history of sociology (Giddings was at Columbia, Small and others of
later renown at Chicago, Ross at the University of Wisconsin).

[34] Ibid., p. 127 n.

[35] Ibid., p. 126.

Nihilism'. Following Huxley, Webb and Ward (the interventionist *doyen* of the American Fathers of Sociology) turned the organicist analogy against laissez-faire theories by pointing to the vital co-ordinating functions of the nervous system, a comparison between which and the system of government Spencer himself had drawn. Their aim was to emphasize the increasing role of cerebral control, rational management and government intervention in society.[36]

Social integration, to these authors, was above all a matter of legislative regulation and administration based on utilitarian rational calculation. Ward, who had originally thought of calling his *Dynamic Sociology* 'The Great Panacea',[37] meant by dynamic sociology the rational control of social forces.[38] His goal was to substitute 'meliorism' for humanitarianism. The former, he declared, was 'humanitarianism *minus* sentiment'. Meliorism implied 'the improvement of the social condition through cold calculation'.[39]

In his essay on the historical basis of socialism Webb compiled a number of lists of enormous length designed to prove the increasing role of the state. One such list begins: 'In addition to births, marriages, deaths, and electors, the State registers all solicitors, barristers, notaries, patent agents, brokers, newspaper proprietors, playing-card makers, brewers, bankers . . . [and so on to game dealers]; all insurance companies, friendly societies, endowed schools and charities, limited companies, lands, houses . . .' and so forth for another number of lines, including dogs, books, institutions of worship, and ending with dancing-rooms.[40] Years later, in their *Methods of Social Study*, the Webbs distinguished four types of institutions: those based on animal instinct, on religious emotion, on certain abstract humanistic principles, and on deliberative planning. For the last, to which the Webbs were committed, 'efficiency is the sole object'.[41]

Ward and the Webbs represented particular tendencies of thought

[36] For Webb, see, for example, *Fabian Essays*, op. cit., p. 60. A compact statement of Ward's views is his essay 'Sociology and Biology' in *American Journal of Sociology*, vol. I, pp. 313–26 (the argument against Spencer is on p. 323f).
[37] H. S. Commager, *The American Mind*, New Haven, 1959, p. 210.
[38] L. Ward, *Dynamic Sociology*, vol. II, p. 161.
[39] Ibid., p. 468.
[40] S. Webb, 'Historic', *Fabian Essays*, p. 48f.
[41] S. and B. Webb, *Methods of Social Study*, London, 1932, p. 22f.

within a broader spectrum. But although the practitioners of administrative sociology were subject to many other influences, and many – perhaps most – of them were not as thorough-going rationalists as Ward or Webb, the latter reveal very clearly the general significance of administrative sociology. Most of these practitioners were also affected by notions of ideological community – while Ward himself was not a sociological researcher and his influence was often indirect. But many strategic individuals, above all Albion Small, the head of the Chicago department and the chief organizer of early American sociology, had an immense admiration for Ward.[42]

1. Managers and Workers: the Class Context of Administrative Sociology

The new administrative sociology corresponded closely to the problems of post-Victorian as well as post-Jeffersonian society. It also tried to tackle them directly by its social research and its guidance of social policy. But its administrative orientation meant that it did not need to question the bases of the society with whose maladministration it was concerned. Though it came into direct contact with 'the labouring and dangerous classes', it could remain basically linked to the ruling classes. The charity of the church had never by itself implied a questioning of the existing social order. Neither did the benevolence of these sociologists.

This is illustrated most clearly, perhaps, by the Fabians – who in contrast to the usual run of sociologists were socialists and so committed to a new type of society, based on collective ownership. Yet even their (socialist) administrationism was drenched in the established assumptions of the prevailing social order.

The Fabians adhered to the principles of marginalist economics – after Bernard Shaw had been rapidly convinced by Philip Wicksteed's critique of Marx.[43] They parted company with the econom-

---

[42] 'I have often said, and I freely repeat, that I would rather have written Ward's *Dynamic Sociology* than any other book that has ever been produced in America,' Small wrote in *The Meaning of Social Science*, Chicago, 1910, p. 83. Ward was originally trained in natural science, working in various institutions of botany, geology, and so on and was an immensely erudite man. He was probably rather unique in this century in daring to give, late in his life, an academic course on 'A Survey of All Knowledge' (Commager, op. cit., p. 205).

[43] For Wicksteed, see ch. 2 and n. 130 to ch. 2 above.

ists over policy and ownership, but their economic arguments start from the principles of the liberal tradition: free exchange, private ownership in land, a marginalist theory of rent, and the inevitability of demographic growth. The emergence and misery of the proletariat derive from private property in land combined with increasing population. For the Fabians, socialism meant that the situation of the proletariat could only be solved by collective ownership.[44] Critical of the doctrinaire deductivism of the Manchester school, the Webbs and their allies were nevertheless anxious to engage orthodox liberal economists in the task of organizing the London School of Economics, whose establishment had been made possible by a large private endowment.[45] The rootedness of the Fabians in the political and social structure of the old society was patent in their own formulation of their socialist mission: 'We set ourselves two definite tasks: first to provide a parliamentary programme for a Prime Minister converted to Socialism as Peel was converted to Free Trade; and second to make it as easy and matter-of-course for the ordinary respectable Englishman to be a Socialist as to be a Liberal or a Conservative', Bernard Shaw wrote in the preface to the second edition of *Fabian Essays*. A system of society was thus equated with a tariff on corn. The social order should be changed, but only by respectable people in respectable ways.

The *Fabian Essays* were written for enlightened administrators and politicians, not for a working-class public. In Shaw's preface to the second edition this aspect of them is even more marked. While treating 'the Revolutionists and Internationalists of 1848–71' with a blend of ridicule and condescending benevolence, Shaw emphasizes that a revised edition would appeal 'more than the present one to administrative experts, bankers [!], lawyers, and constructive statesmen', and even less to 'the ordinary citizen who is in these matters an amateur'. This was, of course, an administrative equivalent to the appeal to the Princes in Saint-Simon's New Christianity.

After a meeting in 1895 with Keir Hardie, the miner who was leader of the Independent Labour Party, Beatrice Webb wrote in her diary: 'There is some truth in Keir Hardie's remark that we [the

---

[44] B. Shaw, 'Economic', in *Fabian Essays*, pp. 3–29.
[45] B. Webb, *Our Partnership*, p. 86f; E. Hobsbawm, 'The Fabians Reconsidered', in idem, *Labouring Men*, London, 1964, p. 254.

Fabians] were the worst enemies of the social revolution.[46] Fabianism, the most radical variant of administrative sociology, was also a theory of economic reconstruction developed in opposition to the proletarian revolution.

The respectable classes of US society impinged in a similar way upon the views of the American sociologists. Ward's outlook was a mixture of pre-religious Comtean scientism and an American liberalism which was chiefly concerned to emphasize the vital role of education, including education of the 'dangerous classes'.[47] In contrast both to the 'artificial inequalities' of the prevailing competitive régime of individualism, and to the 'artificial equalities' of socialism, Ward propounded a vague idea of 'sociocracy', of technocratic government and regulation of private enterprise. He professed a touching belief in the contemporary state apparatus: 'But the state, as already remarked, is essentially benevolent, and all its operations, however shortsighted and fruitless, aim at least to benefit the people. In the hands of wise and humane officers, such as the present heads of these great bureaux [like the Bureau of Labour], they are certain to be productive of immense public good.'[48]

The Chicago sociologists were concerned with the regulation and management of a corporation economy. The University of Chicago was founded by a Rockefeller endowment. When the *American Journal of Sociology* was launched at this university, it received numerous angry letters protesting against sociology's involvement with 'an educational institution founded by the arch-robber of America'. The editor rose to defend the honour of Rockefeller, although cautiously stating his case in terms of another 'working hypothesis': 'We oppose to the assumption that industrial combination is robbery, the counter assumption that industrial combination is progress. The final truth doubtless lies somewhere between these two extremes: viz., perfected combination, restrained and controlled by just principles, and operated in all its departments by just men, will signalize an advanced social condition.'[49] The world of Adam Smith had disappeared into the 'industrial world

---

[46] *Our Partnership*, p. 123.

[47] Ward, *Dynamic Sociology*, vol. II, ch. XIV.

[48] L. Ward, 'Collective Telesis', *American Journal of Sociology*, II, pp. 801–22, at p. 819f.

[49] *American Journal of Sociology*, vol. I, p. 210f.

of the living Rothschilds and Morgans and Carnegies and Vander-
bilts, the world of railroad systems and clearing houses and legislative lobbies and trusts and trade unions'.[50] Albion Small now
developed in a number of articles the thesis that 'Private Business
is a Public Trust'.[51]

At the annual meeting of the American Sociological Society in
December 1907, the institutionalist economist John Commons of
Wisconsin discussed the problem: 'Is Class Conflict in America
Growing and Is It Inevitable?'. Commons thought that it might be
growing but was not inevitable, because of the importance of a fair-
minded public, constituting two-thirds of the population, inter-
posed between the parties in conflict. That public consisted of
farmers, farm labourers, professional and government classes,
servants, small employers and their employees.[52] Among the commentators – none of them leading sociologists – there was both
agreement and disagreement. Some, including Jane Addams of
Chicago (a prominent social worker of the period), thought that the
public tended to split up into two camps once the battle was on.
Addams referred to her experience of a recent teamsters' strike in
Chicago. Yet after all, she thought, with the advent of trusts in
America managers and workers were being drawn together, while
the government could and should regulate trusts.[53]

Technical managers and skilled workers, with their 'instinct of
workmanship', were contrasted by Thorstein Veblen to the 'Leisure
Class'. In the first age of industrial capitalism Saint-Simon had
pitted the bankers, the captains of industry and their workers
against the unproductive, feudal class. Now, in the age of monopoly
capital, Veblen contrasted industrial to 'pecuniary' institutions and
employments.[54]

A dedication to applied research and practical reform does not

[50] From a short review by Small in *American Journal of Sociology*, II, p. 740.

[51] A. Small, 'Private Business is a Public Trust', 'The State and Semi-Public
Corporations', 'Scholarship and Social Agitation', *American Journal of Sociology*,
vol. I. Cf. also the article 'Business Men and Social Theorists', *American Journal
of Sociology*, I, pp. 385–97, by Charles Henderson, the second professor at the
Chicago Department of Sociology, and another member of the Chicago Civic
Federation.

[52] J. Commons, 'Is Class Conflict in America Growing and Is It Inevitable?',
American Journal of Sociology, XIII, pp. 756–66.

[53] *American Journal of Sociology*, XIII, p. 771f.

[54] T. Veblen, *The Theory of the Leisure Class*, New York, 1953 (1st ed. 1899).

exclude a profound isolation from and even contempt for the masses whose conditions are the object of this concern. The socialist Fabians boasted not merely of being respectable but 'even official, eminent and titled', and of disregarding the opinions of the 'amateur, ordinary citizen'.

In American sociology there were no feudal dignities to vaunt, but there was another factor of isolation. The founding fathers of American sociology came from old Anglo-Saxon middle-class families (with the exception of Veblen, whose parents were Norwegian immigrants). The US working class was composed largely of recent immigrants, usually of non-Anglo-Saxon origin, sometimes even non-white. Between this working class and the respectable citizenry (including sociologists) of the Chicago Civic Federation, an important organization devoted to municipal reform and industrial conciliation, there was a wide gulf. That which 'scholar, priest, preacher, philanthropist, politician and financier' could there agree upon was not based on any sympathy for the problems of the mass of workers in unskilled jobs, with their 'dawning mass-consciousness, often proceeding to senseless extremes in demands for deferred payments of the dues of partially comprehended equality'.[55]

The most radical of the early American sociologists, Edward Ross, was a Populist and later adviser to the Progressive politician La Follette. He wrote a notorious racist tract against immigrant workers and immigration.[56] Ross talked of the 'pigsty style of life' of these workers, of 'their brawls and their animal pleasures', their threat to 'the American blood', against which Ross appealed to 'the pride of race'.[57]

---

[55] A. Small, 'The Civic Federation of Chicago', *American Journal of Sociology*, vol. I, pp. 79–103; A. Small, 'The Scope of Sociology VI', *American Journal of Sociology*, vol. VI, p. 366.

[56] Ward and Ross were radicals, but Ross was the more politically committed of the two. For sociological evaluations of Ross' radicalism, see the fine work of Charles Page, *Class and American Sociology: From Ward to Ross*, New York, 1940, p. 23f and ch. 7; L. Coser, *The Functions of Social Conflict*, New York, 1964, p. 16f.

[57] E. Ross, *The Old World in the New*, New York, 1914, quoted from R. Hofstadter, *The Age of Reform*, New York, 1960, p. 179f. Sidney Webb also had racial fears. In a Fabian Tract he was concerned with the decline of the birth rate, which would lead either to national deterioration or 'this country's falling to the Irish and the Jews' (S. Webb, *The Decline in the Birth Rate*, London, 1907, cited from Semmel, op. cit., p. 51). The question of racial breeding was important to

The American historian Richard Hofstadter has noted the part played by the rise of sociology in the emergence of a broader Progressive reform movement in the USA. At the same time he has shown the bourgeois nature of the leadership of the latter and the gulf between it and the immigrant workers.[58] Ross's contempt – mingled with what were in themselves pro-labour arguments, against possible strike-breakers, and so on – and the aloofness of the municipal reformers, in Chicago and elsewhere, form part of the historical failure of reformism in the United States to unite the very divided sections of the working class. While the state apparatus – neither universally nor impartially as benevolent as Ward had believed – repressed the socialist workers' movement, bourgeois political machines became the main institutions concerned with providing for at least some of the immediate needs of the broad masses of the working-class population. Thus the rise of sociology played its role in a very important phase of US social history.

III. Culture and Morality

In tracing back the critiques of economics developed within classical sociology, we can locate a common cross-roads at which they converged, before proceeding in different directions, to join again in the later march of sociological theory. This point of convergence is to be found in German so-called 'historical' economics. Though

---

many early British sociologists. Abrams, op. cit., p. 149, says that this tendency, the so-called eugenics movement, was the 'most effective of the pre-1914 sociological groupings'.

[58] Hofstadter, op. cit., chs. IV–VI. Robert Park, Small's successor as the head of the Chicago department, substituted the curiosity of the reporter for the stern moralism of the earlier generation and had for a time worked with the very moderate Negro leader Booker T. Washington at Tuskeegee College. Under him, the Chicago sociology of the 1920's made observant studies of ethnic relations and the life of the newly arrived population groups. This was a kind of metropolitan ethnography that studied immigrants but hardly the immigrant workers (i.e., their larger economic context and class situation). With the depression of the thirties the hegemony of Chicago sociology therefore crumbled, together with many other cherished American beliefs. Cf. J. Madge, *The Origins of Scientific Sociology*, New York, 1962, ch. 4; R. Faris' rather apologetic *Chicago Sociology 1920–1932*, San Francisco, 1967; W. I. Thomas and R. Park, 'Life History', *American Journal of Sociology*, vol. 79, 1973, pp. 246–60.

little noted,[59] the strategic role played by the German economists in the formation of sociology was a natural one.

1. German Historical Economics

In their *Verein für Sozialpolitik* the German critical economists tried to confront the social question in a straightforward and systematic manner. Leaving aside the revolutionary Marxist critique, theirs was the most explicit and elaborate of the critiques of liberal competitive economics. Further, these German critics were located in a national university system that was by the second half of the 19th century the major international centre of scholarship and science. The German universities taught American social scientists from the 1870's onwards, and provided the model for the new US universities. It was to Germany that French scholars such as Durkheim and Célestin Bouglé went to learn from the culture of the victor of the 1870–71 war. In Germany itself, after the unification of the Reich, the economists came to succeed historians of the type of Dahlmann, Sybel and Treitschke as the leading representatives of the German academic *Geist*. Max Weber's development from a legal historian to an economist and sociologist was a representative example of this process.

Usually called the Historical School, the German anti-classical economists might also be designated by the term preferred by the leader of their second generation, Gustav Schmoller. Schmoller, who was the driving force of the *Verein für Sozialpolitik*, called it the 'ethical' view or ethical economics.[60] Under the influence of the earlier Historical School of Jurisprudence and contemporary *Völkerpsychologie*, Schmoller was well aware of the historical and cultural relativity of ethics. He propounded an inductivist econ-

---

[59] Parsons, for example, in *The Structure of Social Action*, only very briefly mentions that the Historical School was the milieu in which Weber grew up. Though his very serious exposition of the theories of Durkheim, Weber and Marx is centred on capitalism, Giddens swiftly dismisses the common, though different, connections of Weber and Durkheim with the Historical School as irrelevant (*Capitalism and Modern Social Theory*, Cambridge, 1971, p. 120).

[60] See, for example, G. Schmoller, *Uber einige Grundfragen des Rechts und der Volkswirtschaft*, Jena, 1875, p. 31. This short work was a defence of Schmoller's economics and social concern against ultra-right-wing attacks from Treitschke. It was the work by Schmoller that Durkheim reviewed in his survey of the moral sciences in Germany in *Revue Philosophique*, XXIV, 1887, p. 36f.

omics, and for that reason one largely historical in approach. But epistemologically Schmoller, as well as the older 'historical economists' Roscher, Knies and Hildebrand, differed from the strict historicist tendency developed by Dilthey, Windelband, Rickert, and Weber. In contrast with the latter, Schmoller seems to have been influenced by the naturalistic tradition of John Stuart Mill and others.[61]

Against the liberals Schmoller asserted that there existed not only individual economies and individual capital, but also and above all national (*Volk*) economies, national capital and so on. Schmoller did not accept a purely administrative conception of the economic totality, nor a purely state-interventionist conception of the domain of economic critique. 'The common element that unites the particular economies of a nation or a state is not simply the state itself, but rather something deeper: the community of language, of history, of memories, of customs and ideas. It is a world of common feelings and ideas, a more or less harmonious tension of all psychological drives; and more than this – it is an order of life which has grown out of these harmonious psychological foundations and become an objective fact, it is the common ethos, as the Greeks called the moral and spiritual community crystallized in custom and law, which influences all human behaviour, hence including the economic.'[62] Schmoller contrasted his own conception of ethical-cultural determination with technological and utilitarian views of economic life.[63]

Prepared by two conferences the year before, the *Verein für Sozialpolitik* was formally launched in 1873,[64] some four years after the foundation of the Social-Democratic Workers' Party and two years after the Paris Commune. In his inaugural address Schmoller pointed to 'a social revolution which has up to now threatened us

[61] D. Lindenlaub, *Richtungskämpfe im Verein für Sozialpolitik*, Wiesbaden, 1967, p. 96f.

[62] Schmoller, op. cit., p. 32.

[63] Ibid., pp. 32–42.

[64] Though specifically oriented to the internal controversies in the *Verein* in the period of 1890–1914 (mainly between the generation of Schmoller and Wagner on the one hand, and that of Weber and Sombart on the other), Linden-laub's great work also gives information about the early years. A much briefer study of the *Verein* is the perceptive Marxist dissertation by Fritz Völkerling, *Der deutsche Kathedersozialismus*, Berlin, 1959.

only from afar, it is true, but none the less clearly for that'.[65] The German *Reich* had been founded. These were the *Gründer* years of the promotion of shareholding corporations and soon famous and powerful banks, such as the Deutsche Bank, Dresdner Bank and others.

Under the inspiration of a variety of social monarchist ideas and of the principles of ethical economics, the *Verein* took its stand as much against the orthodox (or 'vulgar', Bastiat-influenced) liberal economic organization *Kongress deutscher Volkswirte*, as against the working-class movement. This did not, of course, mean that the *Verein* pursued a kind of middle-of-the-road policy in German society. While the labour movement was wholly outside it, the *Verein* was fundamentally attached to the prevailing state, the Wilhelmine monarchy. From the beginning it included a number of leading industrialists and its first chairman, Professor Nasse, was co-editor of the employers' journal *Concordia*.[66] Schmoller and others supported the repressive legislation against the labour movement of the 1880's.[67] Later, however, the professors of social policy fell out with their former industrialist friends over the rights of workers to form trade unions. The chief target of the wrath of the militant employers was the very conservative Adolph Wagner, one of the most loyal Wilhelmians.[68]

German ethical economics gained a considerable influence in the United States. It largely inspired the foundation in 1885 of the American Economic Association, which from the start was strongly biased against deductivist laissez-faire. It influenced not only the institutionalist tendency of Richard Ely, Simon Patten, John Commons and others, but also the leading American marginalist John Bates Clark – who held, among other things, that the laws of economics were valid only if they met with the approval of the moral sense of the community.[69]

AEA was the parent body of the American Sociological Society,

[65] Quoted from Völkerling, p. 19.

[66] Lindenlaub, op. cit., p. 49.

[67] The *Verein* as such took no official stand. Schmoller, for his part, was of the view that the repressive legislation was justified, though 'perhaps not draconian enough' (Völkerling, p. 77).

[68] Lindenlaub, p. 55f. Wagner was, of course, of the opinion that trade-union rights served the fight against Social Democracy (Lindenlaub, p. 58).

[69] Roll, op. cit., p. 427. Cf. also Commager, op. cit., p. 234f, Oberschall, op. cit., p. 196. Austrian marginalists, von Böhm-Bawerk, von Philippovitch, von Wieser,

among whose sponsors were economists such as Ely and Patten.[70] Small was a fervent admirer of the *Verein*.[71] Small, Henderson, and other reformist sociologists wanted to bring ethical considerations to bear upon economic phenomena. With their strong utilitarian proclivities, however, this took more of an administrative-interventionist form than a theoretical one. For all his admiration of the German economists, Small was more directly influenced in his theoretical conceptions by the optimistic interest theory of Ratzenhofer.[72]

It was thus left to a young anti-utilitarian academic, sympathetic but unsatisfied with US institutionalist economics, who went to Germany in the 1920's to study 'Capitalism in Recent German Literature', fully to exploit the heritage of German ethical economics within American sociological theory. This was the achievement of Talcott Parsons. His own studies were largely of the much more sophisticated theories of Sombart and, above all, Max Weber. But his emphasis on the decisive role of common norms and values, and his polemic against utilitarian liberalism and socialism, were in the earlier German economic tradition. It is they, rather than the spirit of capitalism, which form the true subject of *The Structure of Social Action*.

2. Durkheim and German Economics

'This book is pre-eminently an attempt to treat the facts of the moral life according to the method of the positive sciences. . . . We do not wish to extract ethics from science, but to establish the science of ethics,' Durkheim wrote in the preface to his dissertation on *The Division of Labour in Society*. Some years earlier he had pointed out that, whereas in France there existed virtually only Kantian-spiritualist and utilitarian philosophies of ethics, a positive

and others, were also members of the *Verein*, in spite of the Schmoller-Menger controversy (Lindenlaub, op. cit., p. 96).

[70] On the foundation of the American Sociological Society see *American Journal of Sociology*, vol. XI, pp. 555–69. The year was 1905.

[71] See ch. 3, note 51. Cf. also A. Small, *Origins of Sociology*, Chicago, 1911, which mainly deals with German economics.

[72] A. Small, '50 Years of Sociology', op. cit., p. 239. Though highly appreciative of both Ross and Durkheim, Ward preferred the interest theories of Ratzenhofer and, in a very mild form, of Gumplowicz. (Ward, 'Contemporary Sociology', III, *American Journal of Sociology*, p. 758f.)

science of ethics was developing in Germany.[73] That enterprise had now produced Wilhelm Wundt's *Ethik*, in which ethics was based on the studies of *Völkerpsychologie* in the evolution of religion, customs, physical milieu and civilization in general.[74] But, Durkheim emphasized, 'It is from political economy that the whole movement has started'.[75]

Durkheim therefore began his study of the incipient science of ethics in Germany with the ethical economists, Schmoller and Wagner. He referred with approval to their critique of utilitarian economics, their view of society as a reality *sui generis*, their interpretation of man as determined by his historical milieu, their linking of economy and social morality as form and matter or contained and container, and their historical conception of changing social norms.[76]

Durkheim was not uncritical of the ethical economists. In particular, he criticized their excessive voluntarism and exaggerated confidence in legislative action. Though he agreed with their hostility to the economic fatalism of the liberal economists, Durkheim's sociology developed a critique of economics which led in a direction other than that of state interventionism. In this respect he found Albert Schäffle more congenial. Schäffle was also an economist of the ethical school and a biologically inspired sociologist, but for complicated political reasons he was an outsider in the German academic world and not a member of the *Verein*.[77]

---

[73] E. Durkheim, 'La science positive de la morale en Allemagne', *Revue Philosophique*, vol. XXIV (juillet–decembre, 1887), pp. 33–58, 113–42, 275–84.

[74] Ibid., pp. 33, 116.

[75] Ibid., p. 34.

[76] Ibid., pp. 34–44.

[77] Schäffle had been one of the revolutionaries of 1848 and was later active in South German anti-Prussian politics. For six months in 1870 he was Austrian Minister of Commerce. In the sixties he had had a chair of economics in Tübingen, but after his political failure in Austria was a private scholar in Stuttgart. As a federalist anti-Prussian, he was in conflict with the state attachment of the *Verein*. With his background as a revolutionary and a newspaper editor in the fifties, he was never quite *comme il faut* among the German mandarins. It is noteworthy that this outsider was one of the earliest proponents of sociology in Germany. Schäffle was one of the first German economists to study Marx, as can be seen from his widely distributed brochure *Die Quintessenz des Sozialismus*, Gotha, 1885 (1st ed. 1874). Its sober, expository tone laid its author under suspicion of Social Democratic tendencies. He hastened to repair his reputation by publishing the telling pamphlet *Die Aussichtslosigkeit der Sozialdemokratie* (Social Democ-

Durkheim sympathized with Schäffle's more naturalistic orientation and his view of the social question, which was more com-
munitarian than statist. But even Schäffle was not naturalistic
enough, in Durkheim's opinion. Schäffle held that moral and social
phenomena were characterized by their conscious and reflected
character, and conformed to the common German tendency of
regarding the human realm as something absolutely apart from
nature, governed by its own special laws.[78]

Political economy was for two reasons a strategic point of departure for Durkheim. The first was that if ethics was to become a
science it would have to be a social science – in which case its
relationship to economics was critical, as economics was the first
social science to be constituted.[79] The second reason was that the
social problems which concerned Durkheim specifically resulted
from the economic situation of his time, for he was preoccupied
with the social disequilibrium generated by egoistic economic
pursuits and by a forced and anomic division of labour. Durkheim's
major practical proposal, the formation of public occupational
groups, which he developed in *Suicide*, in the preface to the second
edition of *The Division of Labour in Society* and above all in his
course on *Professional Ethics and Civic Morals*, was thus logically
an attempt to deal with the condition of the economy.

In 1896 Durkheim wrote to his friend and colleague Bouglé:
'When I began fifteen years ago, I thought that I would find [among
the economists] the answer to the questions that preoccupied me.
I spent several years and derived nothing from them, except what
one can learn from a negative experience.'[80] What, in that case, was

---

racy's Lack of Prospects) and wrote a more explicit conclusion to later editions
of *Die Quintessenz*. After this, however, many people came to regard him as an
opportunist. An interesting portrait of Schäffle is given by G. Schmoller in his
Zur Litteraturgeschichte der Staats und Sozialwissenschaften, Leipzig, 1888, pp.
211–32.

[78] Durkheim, op. cit., pp. 45–8, 137.

[79] Durkheim stresses this point in several early texts: in the review article 'Les
Etudes de science sociale', *Revue Philosophique*, XXII, 1886, pp. 61–80: 'La
science positive de la morale,' op. cit., p. 49; in the opening lecture of his first
'Cours de science sociale' at Bordeaux in 1888. The first and the last are included
in the very good selection edited by J.-C. Filloux, E. Durkheim, *La science sociale
et l'action*, Paris, 1970, pp. 184–214, 77–110, resp.

[80] Quoted from S. Lukes, *Emile Durkheim, His Life and Work*, London, 1973,
p. 80. Though it leaves several important biographical questions somewhat

to be the nature of the new social science of sociology, as it emerged out of the sociological critique of political economy?

3. The Society of Durkheimian Sociology

The task before us in seeking to answer this question is neither biographical – to study the various threads of influence upon Durkheim's thought – nor expository, to present such classical sociological works as *The Division of Labour in Society, The Rules of Sociological Method, Suicide, The Elementary Forms of Religious Life* and the many other articles and posthumously published courses which form the corpus of the Durkheimian *oeuvre*. It is rather analytic, to delineate as succinctly as possible the central canons of classical sociological theory. We will also be interested in its practical problematic – the system of practical political questions within which it was developed and applied.

For this purpose, an analysis of Durkheim must be set within a comparative framework. Here, of course, the sociological pioneers themselves are relevant. Of these, Durkheim was clearly influenced by and indebted to Saint-Simon, Comte, and Spencer, whereas he apparently attached no significance to Tocqueville.[81] It will also be necessary to take into account the work of Marx, the founder of historical materialism and another critic of political economy, for one of our tasks is to find the point of divergence between the two critiques of economics made by historical materialism and by sociology.

Durkheim's first major work, *The Division of Labour in Society*, was cast in an evolutionary framework. It contrasted two categories of societies – a primitive type characterized by mechanical solidarity of likeness and common sentiments, and a modern type characterized by organic solidarity arising from the division of labour. Superficially this very much resembled the evolutionary framework

---

unsettled – the tangled influences, German and French, on Durkheim in the 1880's, the exact role of Espinas in Durkheim's theory of representations, his concrete political context, for example – Lukes' massive work is the major, full-scale biography of Durkheim, something which is still lacking for Max Weber.

[81] Neither in his exposition of the history of sociology in the *cours* of 1888 nor in the later article on 'Sociology in France in the 19th century' (in *La science sociale et l'action*, op. cit., pp. 111–36) did Durkheim refer to Tocqueville. He is quoted, once, in passing, in *The Division of Labour in Society*, op. cit., p. 43f. In Lukes' 650-page biography the Marquis de Tocqueville is not mentioned.

of the pioneers. But Durkheim's problematic, the system of questions governing his study, was quite different from that of his predecessors.

The pioneers were concerned with the emergence of a new type of society – industrial or democratic (in Marxist terms capitalist) – and the political problems posed by it. But for Durkheim: 'This work had its origins in the question of the relations of the individual to social solidarity. Why does the individual, while becoming more autonomous, depend more upon society? How can he be at once more individual and more solidary? Certainly, these two movements, contradictory as they appear, develop in parallel fashion. This is the problem we are raising. It appeared to us that what resolves this apparent antimony is a transformation of social solidarity due to the steadily growing development of the division of labour.'[82]

To Durkheim the basic theoretical problem was the relationship between two given entities, individual and society. This was *the* problem – moral, political and sociological – of all Durkheim's work. The moral problem for him was how to combine individual freedom and social order. The sociological problem was how to assert and demonstrate the existence of society as a reality distinct from its individual parts. The political problem was how to assure at once individual freedom and social solidarity in contemporary strife-ridden society.

The typical Durkheimian focus is thus not on different types of social organization, but on whether or to what extent societies are organized at all, and on the amount of room social organization gives to individual development. *The Division of Labour in Society*, for example, is not structured round the changes brought about by the bourgeois revolution or the contrasts between feudal and capitalist society, however conceived. Its examples of mechanical solidarity, which is contrasted with modern organic solidarity, are taken from the ancient world, from the Old Testament, from the Roman Republic, from Egyptian law, and so on.[83] But what is significant is not that the point of comparative reference is pushed much further back in time, for in France by 1893 bourgeois society had decisively and definitively defeated all recalcitrant feudal forces.

---

[82] Durkheim, *The Division of Labour in Society*, p. 37f.
[83] Ibid., ch. 2.

Much more significant is Durkheim's thesis that in the ancient mechanical societies, social life and solidarity were derived from the similarity between the members of each society. This was a very poor analysis of the social organization of the ancient Roman, Egyptian, Chinese, Indian and other empires, or of the Greek city states and the old Hebrew kingdoms. Nor is it even very appropriate to an account of the often complicated kinship organization of so-called 'primitive' peoples, for instance of the Australian aborigines studied by Claude Lévi-Strauss and others.

Yet this rather peculiar thesis becomes comprehensible within the specific Durkheimian problematic. For the latter is only superficially concerned with societal evolution. Mechanically solidary societies all presented few opportunities for the autonomous individual development of their members of the sort valorized by modern liberal ideologies. In that sense they were characterized for Durkheim by 'likeness', in spite of the fact that many of them were based on the starkest *un*likeness: between various kinds of slaves and serfs on the one hand, and free men and aristocrats on the other. The economic and social forms which this general limitation of liberal individuality took, were of little moment to the moralist-sociologist.

Durkheim was concerned to show the solidary function of the division of labour in general, not to analyze different specific forms of this division of labour. In this perspective the organization of society – which is what the division of labour amounted to for Durkheim – could actually be seen as on a par with, and an alternative to, suicide and crime! Increasing density of population and therewith intensification of the struggle for existence had accentuated the division of labour, 'because this was also the direction of least resistance. The other possible solutions were emigration, suicide and crime.'[84]

---

[84] E. Durkheim, *The Rules of Sociological Method*, Glencoe, 1958, p. 93. Cf. *The Division of Labour in Society*, p. 286. In a footnote to the second edition of *The Rules of Sociological Method* (p. 88), Durkheim expresses some surprise that contemporary sociologists, like Comte before them, were classifying societies according to their 'state of civilization'. Durkheim had, for his part, propounded a classification starting from a completely unorganized society, the 'horde', the 'protoplasm of the social realm' (ibid., p. 82f: *The Division of Labour in Society*, p. 174f) and then distinguishing different combinations of segments. In organic societies the combination would be of occupational groupings (ibid., p. 190). Durkheim did not develop this idea. His argument in the note against another

Given his curious perspective on society as a collective moral individual, Durkheim was hardly a very acute observer or analyst of societal development and contemporary social organization. From this point of view it is difficult to contend that Durkheim's contribution represented any decisive advance over the work of the sociological pioneers; while the recommendations of his applied sociology – the establishment of an industrial occupational system modelled on the army and the church – were scarcely less fanciful, though less detailed, than the schemes of Saint-Simon and Comte.

Durkheim's central role in the formation of sociology was on another plane. For Durkheim was in fact responsible for probably the single most important contribution to the construction of a specific object of sociology, and to the development of a particular sociological conception of the pattern of social determination. Durkheim's very one-sidedness, his unswerving dedication to his own particular objective, were at the same time to clarify the specificity of sociology as a distinct discipline, and its limitation.

For Durkheim, the different historical forms of society were of little interest. The object of scientific enquiry was social order as such. In this task Durkheim's ethical and scientific preoccupations with the individual and social solidarity fitted well together.

4. The Critique of Economics and the Basis of Ideas: Durkheim and Marx

The distinguishing characteristics of the Durkheimian system can best be discerned by a comparison between it and the corresponding Marxian work on historical materialism. Durkheim and Marx had

---

view of social organization is rather curious and recalls the old German Historical tradition of Savigny: 'One finds classified there, not social species, but historical phases, which is quite different. Since its origin, France has passed through very different forms of civilization; it began by being agricultural, passed to craft industry and to small commerce, then to manufacturing, and finally to large-scale industry. Now it is impossible to admit that same collective individuality can change its species three or four times. A species must define itself by more constant characteristics. The economic state, technological state, etc., present phenomena too unstable and complex to furnish the basis of a classification. It is even very probable that the same industrial, scientific, and artistic civilization can be found in societies whose hereditary constitution is very different.' Durkheim here apparently sees national societies as resembling biological organisms.

certain important traits in common. They shared a naturalistic, scientific orientation. The discourse of each started from liberal economics and from the conflicts and crises of a capitalist society confronted with the 'Question of the Workers'. Nor was this all. They also had in common three central and specific theoretical conceptions.

Firstly, against the individualist deductions of natural law, liberal economics, and – Durkheim (who was much concerned with moral philosophy) would have added – utilitarian and Kantian moralism, both asserted the historical and social determination of the individual.[85]

Secondly, both had a fundamentally materialist approach to the study of social ideas. 'We believe it is a fertile idea', Durkheim wrote of historical materialism, 'that social life should be explained not by the conceptions of those who participate in it, but by profound causes which escape consciousness'.[86] In their explanatory models can even be found an apparently term-by-term correspondence between Marx and Durkheim.

Thirdly, both emphasized that the socially determined representations (*Vorstellungen*, the corresponding German word which Marx sometimes used) current within a society were not subjective illusions maintained by fraud and interest, but were derived from the objective nature of that society.[87]

Yet by way of summary, it can be said that Durkheim and Marx part company precisely at the point where Marx left the young Hegelians to develop historical materialism. It was Karl Marx the Young Hegelian with whom Emile Durkheim the sociologist had most in common. The beginning of the divergence between the two can be located, with respect to all three common conceptions mentioned above, at exactly the point where the distinct concepts of

[85] See, e.g., Durkheim, 'La science positive de la morale', op. cit. This critique had already been set forth in the *Economic and Philosophical Manuscripts* of 1844, London, 1970, pp. 106f, 159.

[86] E. Durkheim, 'La conception matérialiste de l'histoire', in *La science sociale et l'action*, op. cit., p. 250. Durkheim's text is a review of Antonio Labriola's *Essai sur la conception matérialiste de l'histoire*, Paris, 1897.

[87] This is a thesis that runs through the whole of Marx's critique of religion, from 'Toward the Critique of Hegel's Philosophy of Law', where Marx characterizes religion as 'the opium of the people' (*MEW* 1, p. 378) (Easton and Guddat, op. cit., p. 250), onwards. It is a basic idea in Durkheim, most fully developed in *Les Formes Elémentaires de la Vie Religieuse*, Paris, 1912.

historical materialism started to emerge.[88]

Durkheim held that the economists had played a pioneer role in social science in 'proclaiming' the law-bound character of social phenomena.[89] But he apparently never took very seriously the laws which the economists claimed to have discovered. Durkheim criticized political economy, in a criticism that was strategic to the development of his sociology, but he never undertook an analytical critique of economic theory. He criticized it – and Marx's *Capital* as well – methodologically from an inductivist standpoint.[90] His main and decisive criticism, however, was that the economists isolated economic phenomena from their social context.

The fatal flaw of liberal economics, in Durkheim's opinion, was that its principles rested on an assumed egoistic individualism, in which individuals merely pursued their self-interest. On this basis, however, no stable social order was possible. In *The Division of Labour in Society* Durkheim emphasized that the organic solidarity of a division of labour and exchange, to constitute a social order, must proceed from and be regulated by a pre-existent moral community – in order to assure the non-contractual elements of contract and to maintain equilibrium of exchanges. The market alone was incapable of securing the latter.[91] Durkheim was thus an out-and-out critic of the economic policies of laissez-faire.[92]

The egoism-community problematic was also central to the Young Hegelians Marx and Engels. It was a heritage from Hegel's reception of political economy in his theory of civil society, which for Hegel represented the sphere of private needs that was transcended in the rational state. To the Young Hegelians an egoistic and individualist economy was a manifestation of the alienation of man from his species-being. They sought its transcendence, not in the

---

[88] Anthony Giddens' comparison of Durkheim and Marx, in *Capitalism and Modern Social Theory* (chs. 14–15) refers mainly to Marx's pre-Marxist writings and to certain pre-Marxist ideas in *The German Ideology*. He captures the obvious differences in emphasis and ideological tenor in Marx and Durkheim, but his frame of reference means that his comparison of sociology and historical materialism is ultimately mistaken.

[89] Durkheim, 'Cours de science sociale', in *La science sociale et l'action*, p. 80.

[90] Ibid., p. 85; 'Socialisme et science sociale', in *La science sociale et l'action*, p. 243.

[91] *The Division of Labour in Society*, Book I, ch. 7, and p. 275f.

[92] This is developed, among other passages, in the course on Saint-Simon, in *Socialism* (e.g., the concluding tenth chapter).

Prussian bureaucracy, but in an electoral reform and the abolition of private property.

The early critiques of political economy by Marx and Engels, then, resembled Durkheim's. 'Division of labour and exchange are the two phenomena which lead the political economist to boast of the social character of his science, while in the same breath he gives expression to the contradiction in his science – the establishment of society through unsocial, particular interests.'[93] This characteristic statement of the *Economic-Philosophical Manuscripts* might have been written by Durkheim.

But when Marx and Engels, in the latter half of the 1840's, started to develop their distinctive analysis of the capitalist economy, neither their analysis nor critique were any longer framed in terms of competition and egoistic individualism. They were now centred on the relations of production, which – on the basis of a given level of the forces of production – bind a class of proletarians to a class of capitalists in an exploitative relationship. In *Capital* Marx formulated the new problematic thus: 'Political economy has indeed analyzed, however incompletely, value and its magnitude, and has discovered what lies beneath these forms. But it has never once asked the question why labour is represented by the value of its product and labour-time by the magnitude of that value.'[94]

To answer this question Marx and Engels turned to an analysis of different systems of division of labour, which they sought to theorize with the new concepts of relations and forces of production.

Durkheim's sociological road was a very different one. It led not to the location and determination of the market within a series of systems of economic organization but, to an analysis of the impingement of the moral community on the laws of supply and demand, and in general to a study of how economic phenomena are determined by social norms.

'The economists have so far only a weak presentiment that economic reality imposes itself on the observer like a physical reality, that it is subject to the same necessity . . . Further, they study the facts that they deal with as if these formed an independent whole which was self-sufficient and could be explained in isolation.

---

[93] Marx, *Economic and Philosophical Manuscripts*, p. 562 (English edition, p. 163) (emphasis omitted). A similar position is expressed by Engels in *Outlines of a Critique of Political Economy*, *MEW* 1, pp. 499–524 (English ed., pp. 197–266).

[94] K. Marx, *Capital*, I, *MEW* 23, pp. 94–5 (English ed., Moscow, 1962, p. 80).

Now in reality economic functions are social functions, integrated with other collective functions; and they become inexplicable when they are violently separated from the latter. Workers' wages do not depend simply on the relation between supply and demand, but on certain moral conceptions; they rise or fall according to the idea we have of the minimum well-being that a human being can claim, that is, in the last instance, on our idea of the human personality. Examples of this could be multiplied. By becoming a branch of sociology, economic science will naturally be wrested from this isolation, while it will at the same time be further permeated by the spirit of scientific determinism.'[95]

Now it can be objected that Durkheim, at least in his first major work, *The Division of Labour in Society*, did also try to explain why labour had taken the form it assumed in modern society. Furthermore, Durkheim used his answer to this question to explain changes in the ideological community. The sociologist and the historical materialist still do not seem to have parted company for good, in this work.

Durkheim's explanation of the development of the division of labour is utterly naturalistic. It derives from the increase in the number of human animals in contact with each other within a given area. Durkheim calls this variable the 'dynamic or moral density' of a society. It is normally inextricably connected with 'material density', manifested in means of communication and transportation. Increasing density determines increasing division of labour by making the struggle for existence more acute. For a denser population to be able to coexist, the division of labour is developed. The resultant increase in the output of each individual is also, Durkheim emphasizes, necessitated by the heightening of the struggle for existence. The latter makes for greater fatigue, and therefore 'more abundant and choicer sustenance' must be produced.[96]

[95] 'Sociologie et sciences sociales,' *La science sociale et l'action*, p. 151. This is a late, programmatic text, from 1909. We can observe its principles in action, for instance, in *The Division of Labour in Society*. That the value of labour-power had a (historical) moral component was noticed also by Marx; but this component is explained in a quite different theory of society that is not centred on it.

[96] *The Division of Labour in Society*, II, 2. Durkheim makes direct references to biological authorities like Darwin and Häckel. Durkheim's use of biology is analyzed in an essay by Paul Hirst, 'Morphology and pathology: Biological analogies and metaphors in Durkheim's *The Rules of Sociological Method*', *Economy and Society*, vol. 2, no. 1, February 1973, pp. 1–34.

In his *Rules of Sociological Method* Durkheim emphasizes the decisive significance of this theory of the social base: 'This conception of the social milieu, as the determining factor of social evolution, is of the highest importance. For if we reject it, sociology cannot establish any relations of causality. . . . The principal causes of historical development would not be found, then, among the concomitant circumstances; they would all be in the past.'[97]

This involves no reductionism, however. Durkheim always conceived reality in terms of several distinct and irreducible layers. In his later works he tended to emphasize this multiplicity of levels rather than the determinant milieu itself. Once collective representations have been formed, on the basis of a particular social milieu, they became partially autonomous, with a life of their own. 'New representations consequently . . . have as their immediate causes other collective representations, and not this or that feature of the social structure.'[98] On the other hand, his account of the base remained the same: 'Society has as a substratum the ensemble of associated individuals. The system which they form in uniting and which varies according to their disposition on the surface of the territory, and according to the nature and number of ways of communication, constitutes the base upon which social life rises.'[99]

Engels was at pains to assert in his letters to Schmidt and Bloch in the 1890's that the notion of relative autonomy and the specific efficacy of systems of ideas is also underwritten by historical materialism. Does the divergence between it and Durkheimian sociology then lie only in different conceptions of the social infrastructure, whereas their causal models are otherwise much the same? The truth is the rather the opposite. Originally Marx and Engels employed a notion very similar to Durkheim's concept of density. But they abandoned it for a new notion and thereby fundamentally reformulated a mode of explanation which already differed from a materialist reading of Durkheim.

[97] Durkheim, *The Rules of Sociological Method*, p. 116f.

[98] E. Durkheim, 'Représentations individuelles et représentations collectives', in idem, *Sociologie et Philosophie*, Paris, 1951, p. 43. This very important essay dates from 1898 and belongs to the same period as *Suicide* (1897). *The Division of Labour in Society* and *The Rules of Sociological Method* (1893 and 1895) have another, somewhat different emphasis.

[99] Ibid., p. 34. Cf. 'La conception matérialiste de l'histoire', *La science sociale et l'action*, pp. 250, 253.

The concept in question is *Verkehr*, a central notion in *The German Ideology*. It refers to the contact, communication and commerce between people, and is generally translated in English as 'intercourse'.[100] Durkheim defined his dynamic density as the interactive contact between people 'and the active commerce resulting from it'.[101] *Verkehr* and density vary along the same basic dimension: from parochial narrowness to universality. To Durkheim the progression from one to the other was the basis of the development of individuality and rationality.[102]

In the construction of historical materialism by the later Marx and Engels, *Verkehr* was replaced as a central idea by 'relations of production', a notion which refers to the ways in which production is organized. On the other hand, *Verkehr* plays a different role in the discourse of *The German Ideology* from that of density in Durkheim's work. The former is 'determined by production'.[103] In other words, it is related to a technological anchorage, which anticipates the later concept of the forces of production. To the early Marx and Engels man was not like any other sort of organism. He was a tool-making animal.

What is important here, however, is not primarily that Durkheim and Marx had different conceptions of man. Much more important is that to Durkheim the social 'infrastructure' is a social substratum in the same sense that human physiology is an organic substratum of psychology.[104] It is thus an object of study for social morphology, which is strictly speaking not a part of sociology proper, any more than physiology is part of psychology.[105] It is relevant to sociology, but it is not part of the specific object of sociology.

Durkheim was very worried about idealist attacks on his first works and defended himself vehemently against charges of materialism. 'Social life is constituted wholly of collective "representation"', he emphasized in his preface to the second edition of *The Rules*. In

---

[100] K. Marx and F. Engels, 'German Ideology', *MEW*, vol. 3, pp. 21, 26; English ed., *German Ideology*, London, 1965.

[101] *The Division of Labour in Society*, p. 257.

[102] Ibid., p. 287f; cf. *Les formes élémentaires de la vie réligeuse*, p. 633f. *MEW* 3, p. 35; *The German Ideology*, p. 45f.

[103] *German Ideology*, *MEW* 3, p. 21; English ed., p. 31.

[104] This is an analogy stressed by Durkheim himself. See, e.g., 'Représentations individuelles et représentations collectives', in *Sociologie et Philosophie*, op. cit.

[105] Cf. the figure in 'Sociologie et sciences sociales', *La science sociale et l'action*, p. 153.

another such defence he asserted: 'The principal social phenomena, religion, ethics, law, economy and aesthetics, are nothing else but systems of values.'[106]

Durkheim's increasing stress on the ideal character of society did not involve a fundamental reconstruction of his thought. Rather, it meant a change of emphasis. His analytical spotlight shifted from one area to another across the same theoretical edifice. Continuity of concern and change of focus were exemplified by Durkheim's view of the role of religion. In a letter of 1907 to a Catholic journal, Durkheim stressed the great modification of his views: 'It was not until 1895 that I achieved a clear view of the essential role played by religion in social life. . . . This was a revelation to me. That course [on the sociology of religion] in 1895 marked a dividing line in the development of my thought, to such an extent that all my previous studies had to be taken up afresh in order to be made to harmonize with these new insights . . .'[107] If a reading of Robertson Smith's studies of religion in ancient Arabia was a revelation to Durkheim, it was because they fitted so well into his own theory.

Durkheim after 1895 asserted: 'Religion contains in itself from the very beginning, even in an indistinct state, all the elements which in dissociating themselves from it, articulating themselves, and combining with one another in a thousand ways, have given rise to the various manifestations of collective life.'[108] But this affirmation involved no basic shift from a statement to be found in *The Division of Labour* (though little dwelt upon there) that: 'Originally it [religion] pervades everything; everything social is religious; the words are synonymous.'[109] In *The Division of Labour*, and later in *The Elementary Forms of Religious Life*, religion is seen basically as a system of common ideas expressing the solidary community of a given group of people living together. In *The Division of Labour* the all-embracing role of religion in society provides a starting-point for an exposition of social development, in which increasing material and moral density leads to more general, differentiated,

---

[106] E. Durkheim, 'Jugements de valeurs', in *Sociologie et Philosophie*, p. 140f.

[107] E. Durkheim, 'Letters to the Director of the Revue Néo-Scolastique', quoted from Lukes, op. cit., p. 237.

[108] E. Durkheim, 'Preface', *L'Année Sociologique*, vol. II (1897–8), p. v. English ed. in K. Wolff (ed.), *Essays on Sociology and Philosophy by Emile Durkheim et al.*, New York, 1964, pp. 350–1.

[109] *The Division of Labour in Society*, p. 169.

individualized, and rationalistic systems of ideas than the closely-knit systems of primitive religions. This is, on the other hand, where Durkheim ends his study of *The Elementary Forms of Religious Life*, with the transformation of elementary religious beliefs by increasing contact and communication between larger groups of people.[110]

In contrast to Marx and Engels' concept of the social base, Durkheim's concept of the social milieu was thus never theorized in opposition to idealist conceptions of society. It was located in a discourse polarized between the individual and the social environment. An alternative explanation of the development of the division of labour which Durkheim considered was 'man's unceasing desire to increase his happiness'. He found this unacceptable, and then concluded: 'But the desire to become happier is the only individual source which can take account of progress. . . . Consequently, it is in the social environment we must seek its original conditions.'[111] The function of the social milieu in *The Rules of Sociological Method* is the same: it is seen as the alternative to postulation of an innate tendency in humanity 'ceaselessly to exceed its achievements either in order to realize itself completely or to increase its happiness'.[112]

Durkheim's achievement in his early works was to delimit a theoretical space – the space later explored by sociology. On the one side, it was bounded by the social substratum of moral and material density, the field of social morphology, on the other by the individual and his non-social urges and tendencies, studied by human physiology and individual psychology. Between those two poles there was an irreducible entity – the community of values, norms, and beliefs.

Durkheim's conception of the social substratum determined a critical difference between himself and Marx in their definition of the social objectivity of ideas, the third point of departure common to Durkheim and Marx. To Durkheim the collective representations expressed the reality of men's collective existence. Such representations are all collective in the sense that they express men's common collectivity – the coexistence of a number of human beings in a given area – as well as in the sense that they are held in common.[113] This

---

[110] *Les formes élémentaires de la vie réligieuse*, pp. 634–5.

[111] *The Division of Labour in Society*, p. 251. Durkheim also briefly considered, and then dismissed, the possibility that the division of labour could have been brought about by boredom (p. 251f).

[112] *The Rules of Sociological Method*, p. 117.

[113] See, for example, *Les Formes élémentaires de la vie réligieuse*, pp. 338f, 603.

coexistence can be parochially local or it can be wide and extensive. But it is a *common* existence.

From Feuerbach the Young Hegelians had learnt – as had Durkheim too, for his part – that religion was of human and not divine origin. But already in the fourth Thesis on Feuerbach Marx asserted that religion must be explained 'by the cleavage and self-contradictions within this secular basis'.[114] In the *Communist Manifesto* this was further developed into: 'The ruling ideas of each age have ever been the ideas of its ruling class.'[115] With the conceptions of the relations and forces of production, Marx's account was given a basis in the *divided* material structure of society. For this theory too (as for that of Durkheim), religion could no longer be interpreted as a system of arbitrarily fostered illusions.[116]

5. Suicide and the Ideological Community

His work on *Suicide*, as Durkheim explained in his preface, was intended to bring the new discipline of sociology to scientific maturity. It was presented as an empirical study of a concrete problem, which demonstrated the operation of a specific sociological pattern of determination. In the sociological tradition it occupies today a venerated and central position. It has been called 'the first great modern work in sociology', an epithet which some sociologists might qualify, but which expresses the view of a very important body of sociological opinion.[117]

What then does Durkheim's *Suicide* demonstrate, or purport to demonstrate? It tries to show how even the very individual act of

[114] Marx, 'Theses on Feuerbach', *MEW* 3, p. 6; *The German Ideology*, p. 646.

[115] K. Marx and F. Engels, 'The Communist Manifesto', *MEW* 4, p. 480; English ed., K. Marx, *The Revolutions of 1848*, London, 1973, p. 85.

[116] Against Thomas Hodgskin, the radical liberal with whom Herbert Spencer worked at the *Economist*, Marx stressed: 'The *capitalist*, as capitalist, is simply the personification of capital, that creation of labour endowed with its own will and personality which stands in opposition to labour. Hodgskin regards this as a pure subjective illusion which conceals the deceit and the interests of the exploiting classes. He does not see that the way of looking at things arises out of the actual relationship itself; the latter is not an expression of the former, but vice versa.' *Theories of Surplus Value*, *MEW* 26:3, p. 290; English ed., London, 1972, vol. III, p. 296.

[117] A. Inkeles, 'Personality and Social Structure', in R. Merton, L. Broom and L. Cottrell (eds.), *Sociology Today*, New York, 1965, vol. II, p. 249. Durkheim's work has recently been the object of a thorough-going critical analysis with

taking one's life is determined by society. The central problem was then to ascertain what was the nature of society. The existence of societal suicide rates had been firmly established by moral statisticians before Durkheim. His objective was to provide a sociological theory explaining these rates of suicide.

Society for Durkheim is an ideological community of common values, norms, and beliefs. It is as such that 'society' determines how many individuals will commit suicide and why. 'If religion protects man against the desire for self-destruction, it is not that it preaches the respect for his person to him with arguments *sui generis*; but because it is a society.' 'What constitutes this society is the existence of a certain number of beliefs and practices common to all the faithful, traditional and thus obligatory.' Durkheim, as his reference here to 'practices' suggests, was always aware that ideas are and must be expressed in material forms, but he was in no doubt as to what was predominant. For he went on: 'The more numerous and strong these collective states of mind are . . .', thus subsuming practices under the category of ideas.[118] He was also quite explicit in his view of society: 'But the social environment is fundamentally one of common ideas, beliefs, customs and tendencies.'[119]

Though the frequency of suicides among different religious confessions is analyzed in *Suicide*, Durkheim's key variables are not communities of different ideologies but different communities of ideology. Four types of suicide are distinguished – altruistic, egoistic, anomic, and fatalistic. The first three of these are dealt with by Durkheim. Variations in the extent of community are determinant for them. Excessive or insufficient community both cause suicide. The extent of ideological community can determine variations in the four types of suicide, because this community pertains to two different relations – one between individuals, another between social and unsocial man.

The ideological community attaches men to each other by lending their existence and activity a collective purpose.[120] By contrast with

respect to its theory, method, and data: J. Douglas, *The Social Meanings of Suicide*, Princeton, 1967. The author argues that though he is specifically concerned with Durkheim's *Suicide*, his critique is pertinent to a whole central tradition in sociology.

[118] Durkheim, *Suicide*, London, 1970, p. 170.

[119] Ibid., p. 302; cf. p. 312.

[120] Ibid., p. 212.

later sociologists, Durkheim was little concerned with the direction of this collective purpose. At the same time the community also provides individuals with moral standards that restrain and regulate their passions and aspirations.[121]

Egoistic suicide results from an inadequate attachment of individuals to other people through common ideas of various sorts. Jewish and (to a lesser extent) Catholic religion, large families, and closed political ranks exhibit lower rates of suicide because of the intenser community of their members. In primitive societies, on the other hand, community can become excessive, so that the individual is not detached and isolated from his fellow men but is absorbed into the collectivity, and may therefore sacrifice his life for it. Durkheim also invokes the altruistic category to account for the high rate of suicide among military men.

Anomic and fatalistic suicides ensue respectively from inadequate and excessive regulation by common values and norms of man's appetites, which are in themselves insatiable. The appetites to which Durkheim alludes are the appetites for wealth and sex, anomic conditions for which are created by contemporary industry and trade – with their abrupt booms and slumps and their un-regulated market relationships – and by too easy divorce. Excessive regulation of these passions, making for fatalistic suicides, is of scant concern to Durkheim, who mentions the fourth type of suicide only in a footnote.[122]

In so far as the sociology propounded by Durkheim in *Suicide* accounts for regularities in social phenomena, in this case the phenomenon of suicide, it clearly does so through its concept of the ideological community. Other possible features of irreducible social reality (economic and political conditions – Durkheim refers to political and economic crises, group size,[123] and so on) are outside its analytical framework. They are relevant as external factors only insofar as they affect the ideological equilibrium. That is, they play the same role as do ideological and political factors in the market discourse of economics – in which ideological phenomena such as customs or political phenomena such as wars are taken into con-sideration in so far as they affect the schedules of supply or demand.

---

[121] Ibid., p. 247f.
[122] Ibid., p. 276 n.
[123] Ibid., p. 201f.

'In short, social life is nothing but the moral milieu that surrounds the individual – or to be more accurate, it is the sum of the moral milieus that surround the individual. By calling them moral we mean that they are made up of ideas. . . .'[124]

6. The Anomie of the Third Republic

The ideological community was the central concept of Durkheim's political thought as well as of his sociology. Development of sociological theory and intervention in the French class struggles of his time were inextricably interwoven. There was thus an important political aspect to the formation of Durkheimian sociology. Durkheim's concept of ideological community had political reference to a particular society at a particular political conjuncture.

Durkheimian sociology emerged in the second and third decades of the Third Republic, proclaimed on September 4th (1870) – one of the dramatic days in French history – after the defeat of the French army at Sedan and the surrender of the Emperor to the Germans.[125] The stormy history of the first decades of the Republic – with its recurrent parliamentary crises, planned coups d'état, reshuffled allegiances, and public scandals – was generated by a field of three basic forces. It is with reference to their constellation that the intervention of Durkheimian sociology should be seen.

On one side there was the anti-republican right, approved by the church and led by noble landowners and financial and industrial magnates, like the Duke de Broglie, Jacques Casimir-Périer, grandson of one of Saint-Simon's industrialists, and Léon Say of the Rothschild bank. They were split by their allegiance to different dynasties (Bourbon, Orléans, Bonaparte), a fact which saved the Republic during the period of 1871–77 when the monarchists had a parliamentary majority.

The opposite pole was constituted by the working-class move-

---

[124] E. Durkheim, 'Sociology and its scientific field', in Wolff, op. cit., p. 367.

[125] A general overview of the Third Republic and its political history may be gained from Brogan, *The Development of Modern France*, op. cit. For the history of its first decades, G. Chapman's *The Third Republic of France, Its First Phase 1871–94*, London, 1962, is valuable. Essential to an understanding of the social struggles in the Republic is Harvey Goldberg's biography, *The Life of Jean Jaurès*, Madison, 1962. On the socialist movement, there is also G. Lefranc, *Le mouvement socialiste sous la Troisième République (1875–1940)*, Paris, 1963, which contains a brief and compact treatment of the period under consideration here.

ment, which was repressed in the 1870's after the massacre of the *Communards*, when 20–30,000 workers and others from the lower strata of the Paris population were killed in the White Terror. It began to revive in the following decade. Trade-unions were formed, small socialist groups were organized, violent class struggles, such as the Décazesville mining strike in 1886, flared up. In 1889 the Socialist International held its founding congress in Paris. The number of strikes multiplied in the early 1890's, often fought with ferocious resistance by the employers and the state. One of the most violent clashes was the *fusillade de Fourmies* in 1891, when the army shot nine workers and wounded thirty-three at a May Day demonstration. In this situation of growing conflict the French trade union movement developed a revolutionary tendency, which aimed at a final and decisive general strike.

Between these two poles was the territory occupied by the force which governed the Republic after the monarchist bid for power of May 16th 1877 had failed. This was composed of the bourgeois and petty-bourgeois republicans, who stood above all for 'a society without a God and without a king', as Jules Ferry once put it, when asked for his political programme.[126] They instituted educational reform (in which Ferry played an important role) and fought a lengthy and strenuous struggle for the separation of church and state. Under their rule France pursued a vigorous and brutal policy of imperialist conquest and expansion overseas – Tunisia, large parts of West Africa, Madagascar and Indochina were all conquered and seized in this epoch.

Though the clashes between them were often violent, the boundaries between the three blocs were neither clearly delimited nor unchanging. In large part the monarchist *haute bourgeoisie* eventually rallied to a conservative republic; even the Pope in the end pronounced that the republic was a legitimate form of government. On the other hand, in the Dreyfus affair the traditional forces of the right were joined by some former moderate republicans, like Méline and the others who formed the anti-Dreyfusard cabinet of 1896–98.

Between the working-class movement and the petty-bourgeois republicans there also developed a considerable area of contact. On the one side there was the tradition of Jacobin radicalism, which

[126] Quoted by Goldberg, op. cit., p. 39.

was now combined with a new awareness of the social question, while on the other there was the craft tradition of French utopian socialism, which was still strong in a working class largely employed in the relatively small-scale enterprises of a torpid French industry.

With his naturalistic approach to social analysis and his particular conception of the ideological community, Durkheim was very distant from the partly feudalist right. In fact, his sociology was part of the secular education and civic morality which the republicans started to introduce in the 1880's.[127] Durkheimian sociology thus contributed actively to republican ideology, in opposition to the right-wing ideology of the Catholic church and the tradition of aristocratic authority. The French case, like the American, demonstrates that sociology acquired an academic foothold to the extent that the universities were adapted to a thoroughly bourgeois society, freed from the grip of pre-bourgeois forces. Given the persistence of these forces and the peculiarities of the situation of the working class in France, the function of French academic sociology in its relationship to bourgeois society was not, as in the USA, to provide a basis for philanthropy and administrative reform, but to help cement and diffuse secular and republican ideology. It was not, however, on the right flank of the republic that Durkheim made his most notable contribution. Durkheim belonged to the radical republicans, who were very conscious of the social question; and he was hostile to liberal economics. In fact, the 'conservative' Durkheim was at home on the republican left. It was in aid of the left flank of the republic that Durkheim's development of a social naturalism into a social morality and his work on ideological community most immediately intervened.

For it was here that Durkheim's critical concept of *anomie* operated. As a left-wing republican Durkheim was not a smug defender of the status quo. *The Division of Labour in Society*, after having depicted the rise of modern society, individualist and

[127] It was as part of the republican educational reforms that the state director of higher education, Liard, suggested that Durkheim should go to Germany, and that he made the sociologist a university instructor in social science and pedagogy at Bordeaux upon his return. It was in application of these reforms that Durkheim, for a number of years, at Bordeaux and later Paris, gave his courses on *L'Education morale*, Paris, 1925, and on *Professional Ethics and Civic Morals*, op. cit. On Durkheim in the educational system of the Third Republic, cf. D. La Capra, *Emile Durkheim*, Ithaca, 1972, ch. 2, and C. Terry, op. cit.

solidary, based on the division of labour, ends with a discussion of present 'abnormal forms' of the division of labour. *Suicide* is at once a vindication of sociology and a work of social criticism. This criticism focuses largely on what Durkheim calls anomic conditions.

He distinguishes three main abnormal forms of the division of labour. One is 'forced', when the division of labour does not correspond to the distribution of natural talent. Durkheim sought to solve this problem by means of a severe limitation on the right of testament and inheritance.[128] Another form, emphasized rather unexpectedly perhaps in the midst of the workers' agitation for an eight-hour day, is exemplified by the case of enterprises where workers have too little to do.[129] The third form was the anomie manifested in commercial crises, in conflicts between labour and capital, and in the isolating specialization of science.[130] This latter form was the major political problem for Durkheim, to the solution of which he devoted his preface to the second edition. The anomic division of labour had the same causes as the great increase in the rate of egoistic and anomic suicide, and it was to be solved in the same way.[131]

Anomie refers to a state with two crucial characteristics. First of all it is one of an absence or inadequacy of social organization. This meant that in focusing on anomic conditions, Durkheim was able to avoid dealing with 'bad' societies, for instance societies based on exploitation, or with social contradictions. Society was always good, but sometimes there was too little of it. There might also be too much of it, as in the pressure of collective sentiments in segmental societies of mechanical solidarity, or in the pressure towards altruistic forms of suicide. Durkheim as a moralist firmly adhered to the principle of the golden mean.[132]

Now the inherently good 'society' in Durkheim's thought is not

---

[128] *The Division of Labour in Society*, Book III, ch. 2; *Professional Ethics and Civic Morals*, ch. XVIII.

[129] *The Division of Labour in Society*, III, 3. Durkheim did not regard this form as very frequent or as constituting a major problem. To my knowledge, he made no specific proposals to ensure that the workers were sufficiently preoccupied. It should be noted that Durkheim did *not* refer to unemployment but to badly managed enterprises, in which the work-load of the employed workers was insufficient and intermittent (p. 372).

[130] Ibid., III, 1.

[131] *Suicide*, p. 378f.

[132] See e.g. *The Division of Labour in Society*, p. 237.

merely supra-individual social life in general.[133] On strategic occasions it also assumes the quite concrete contours of the Third Republic. Durkheim wanted to convey to the socialist revolutionaries of his country that they owed an allegiance to the existing society, although it was not perfect, and that no essentially new society was needed, merely a better organization of the present order.[134]

Society thus became the new divinity of this secularized rabbi's son. In a debate at the Society of Philosophy, Durkheim declared: 'The believer bows before God, because it is from God that he believes he has his existence, and particularly his mental existence, his soul. We have the same reasons to feel the same sentiment for the collectivity.' It should therefore be loved and respected, even though it is not 'ideally perfect', as the believer loves God, though the world he has created is full of imperfection. This was not a purely academic principle or discussion. Durkheim had a specific society and specific critics of that society in mind. He continued: 'It is true that it is rather common to speak disdainfully about society. People see in it only the bourgeois police and the gendarme who protects it. That is to pass by the richest and most complex moral reality which we can observe, without even perceiving it.'[135]

Anarchism – which possessed a considerable influence among French workers in Durkheim's time – and revolutionary socialism in fact stem from the same morbid lack of social attachment as suicide: 'The anarchist, the aesthete, the mystic, the socialist revolutionary, even if they do not despair of the future, have in common with the pessimist a single sentiment of hatred and disgust for the existing order, a single craving to destroy or to escape from reality. Collective melancholy would not have penetrated consciousness so far, if it had not undergone a morbid development; and so the development of suicide resulting from it is of the same nature.'[136]

Anomie is, secondly, not just inadequate social organization. It

---

[133] In his first course on social science at Bordeaux, Durkheim criticized Comte for substituting Society for societies, *La science sociale et l'action*, p. 88. He himself fell victim to the same error.

[134] See, e.g., Durkheim's debate, in 1906, with the then revolutionary syndicalist Lagardelle, 'Internationalisme et lutte de classe', in *La science sociale et l'action*, pp. 282–92.

[135] *Sociologie et philosophie*, op. cit., p. 114.

[136] *Suicide*, p. 370.

refers to a particular aspect of social insufficiency – to deficient normative regulation and moral authority, to the sad fact that the 'world is only feebly ruled by morality'.[137] Anomie is insufficient ideological community. The concept of anomie is the outcome of Durkheimian natural science's encounter with an unnatural, 'abnormal' society.

In Durkheim's treatment of the unnatural society the question of anomie and of social values and normative regulation occurs at three crucial moments. Respecting Durkheim's inclination towards medical and physiological metaphors, we may call them diagnosis, prescription, and therapy.

Durkheim's diagnosis of the malady of modern society was that it suffered from a crisis of morality,[138] not economic poverty but 'an alarming poverty of morality'.[139] This formulation was directed against the common material demands of workers and of others who were economically disadvantaged. Durkheim took pains to distinguish socialism – in France as in Germany a notion then popular in the most diverse circles – from the cause of the working class. For Durkheim 'the social question' was 'above all moral'.[140] He was sympathetic to Saint-Simon's religious development, but it was inadequate: 'If it curbs the wealthy by assigning as their goal the well-being of the poor, it does not restrain the latter – and the desires of the latter should be no less regulated than the needs of the others.'[141] From the social evil which Durkheim devoted most of his sociological energy to studying, suicide, poor people were after all more protected than others – as the sociologist pointed out.[142] So, 'if anomie is an evil, it is above all because society suffers from it, being unable to live without cohesion and regularity'.[143]

Though in *The Division of Labour in Society* Durkheim concluded that 'our first duty is to make a moral code for ourselves',[144] this

---

[137] *The Division of Labour in Society*, p. 4. For Durkheim's development and use of the concept of anomie, see ibid., pp. 1–31, 268f, and his treatment of anomic suicide, referred to above.

[138] *The Division of Labour in Society*, p. 408.

[139] *Suicide*, p. 387.

[140] Durkheim, 'Sur la définition du socialisme', *La science sociale et l'action*, p. 230. Cf. *Socialism*, p. 54f.

[141] *Socialism*, p. 245.

[142] *Suicide*, p. 253f.

[143] *The Division of Labour in Society*, p. 5.

[144] Ibid., p. 409.

moral diagnosis was not followed by the mere prescription of moral education. Durkheim's solution was the organization of morality through occupational groupings, with public juridical and ethical authority to regulate economic conditions.[145]

Similar ideas were current in France at the time, but Durkheim was probably above all inspired by Schäffle, for whom the young sociologist-to-be had a deep admiration. Given this moral diagnosis, his objective was to institutionalize a professional ethic for the industrial and commercial occupations. Durkheim referred to the adequate organization of other professions, 'such as the army, education, law, the government, and so on'[146] and to the 'professional ethic of the lawyer and the judge, the soldier and the priest'.[147] Exactly the same reference had been made by Schäffle twenty years earlier. In his major work *Bau und Leben des sozialen Körpers* Schäffle had ended his advocacy of a '*öffentlichrechtlich*' socialist organization of the economy by pointing out: 'In church, government, education and science, socialism is in this respect already present.'[148]

Thus Durkheim presented the imaginative proposal of modelling the reorganization of a capitalist economy on the army and the church, by setting up a professional organization 'comprised of representatives of employees and representatives of employers . . . in proportions corresponding to the respective importance attributed by opinion to these two factors in production'.[149] The organization of an industrial and commercial work ethic thus differed from either purely administrative intervention in the economy, or from the construction of a new system of economic roles, a new mode of production and distribution. Its function was to be two-fold: to provide moral discipline, and social attachment to a living ideological community.[150]

---

[145] Ibid., pp. 1–31 (preface to 2nd ed.); *Professional Ethics and Civic Morals*, chs. I–III.

[146] *Professional Ethics and Civic Morals*, p. 8. Cf. also 'Sur la définition du socialisme', *La science sociale et l'action*, p. 235.

[147] *The Division of Labour in Society*, p. 2.

[148] A. Schäffle, *Bau und Leben des sozialen Körpers*, Bd. 3, Tübingen, 1879, p. 544.

[149] *The Division of Labour in Society*, p. 24 n; cf. *Professional Ethics and Civic Morals*, p. 39.

[150] *The Division of Labour in Society*, pp. 24f, 372; *Professional Ethics and Civic Morals*, p. 10f.

Durkheim's natural history of human society had stopped at capitalism. Durkheim could thus discern no specific social forces driving towards any application of his prescription. The result was that upon the diagnosis of moral evil and prescription of moral medicine, there followed moral therapy – in the form of ethical exhortation, of pleas for the suffering of present society. Durkheim would address himself 'not to the sentiments of anger which the less privileged class feels against the other, but to the sentiments of pity inspired by this society which suffers in all its classes and all its institutions'.[151]

Durkheim's sociology was to a great extent concerned with the social question and with the ideological crisis of the Third Republic which lay behind the struggle for *laicité*. His characteristic conception of society – an entity always good in itself, but sometimes too much and sometimes too little present – operated in this context, as did his notions of ideological community and of anomie. With his fundamental attachment to the existing society and his simultaneous awareness of its 'abnormalities', Durkheim was naturally preoccupied with the demands and the strategy of the working-class movement. Coming from a petty-bourgeois background and living in academic seclusion, Durkheim never revealed any understanding either of the concrete issues of the organized working class – the eight-hour day, poverty, the right to strike and the repressive state apparatus – or its goal of establishing another type of society altogether.[152] The concepts of sociology functioned, indeed, to combat the positions of the class-conscious socialist movement.

Durkheim's suggested definition of socialism, and his course on it, had the double objective of including German 'socialism of the chair' in the doctrine and of divesting the latter of its proletarian

---

[151] E. Durkheim, review of S. Merlino, *Formes et essence du socialisme*, in *Revue Philosophique*, XLVIII (1899), p. 438.

[152] Durkheim was a personal friend of Jean Jaurès, the most outstanding French socialist leader, himself a *normalien* of bourgeois background and a brilliant academic intellectual. Jaurès was hardly a Marxist in any meaningful sense and was strongly influenced by a humanistic intellectual tradition. He developed into a socialist, however, under the decisive impact of his political experience of the shootings at Fourmies and his direct contact with the militant miners at Carmaux in his own constituency. (Goldberg, op. cit., p. 70f, ch. 5.) The sociologist Durkheim apparently never had any experience of the working class and its struggles.

character.[153] Politically, Durkheimian sociology functioned in France much like the *Kathedersozialismus* of the (particularly younger) historical economists in Germany. There was, however, the not insignificant difference that the existing state to which the Durkheimians gave their allegiance was a much more progressive one than its German counterpart.

7. Marginalist Economics and Historical Culture: The Sociology of Max Weber

Max Weber is undoubtedly one of the greatest western intellectuals of this century. In a rare combination he united enormous erudition, great theoretical power and subtlety of thought, and concern with some of the central political and cultural problems of his time. Weber is often regarded as a 'bourgeois Marx'. This is an apt characterization, both with regard to his intellectual stature and to his class position. Weber was a very class-conscious bourgeois. In opposing the somewhat naive social-reformist ideas of his friend Friedrich Naumann, Weber referred to his own position in terms of 'we bourgeois'.[154] At the congress of Naumann's Evangelical-Social Association – at Erfurt, five years after German Social Democracy had adopted its own Marxist 'Erfurt Programme' there in 1891 – Weber had declared: 'There only remains the choice whether to support the bourgeois class or the feudal-agrarian class. Social-Democracy in its campaign against bourgeois society has only paved the way for reaction.'[155]

Weber and Marx both devoted the main part of their scholarly energy to the study of capitalism, and both were politically concerned to raise the class-consciousness of their respective classes and to fight illusions of harmony and conciliation – while at the same time they respected outspoken representatives of the enemy class.[156]

The juxtaposition of Marx and Weber might even be taken somewhat further, by making allowance for the different times in

[153] 'Sur la définition du socialisme', *La science sociale et l'action*, p. 230; *Socialism*, pp. 56–61.

[154] Weber, in an article in *Christliche Welt*, 1894, quoted from Mommsen, op. cit., pp. 20 n, 139 n.

[155] Marianne Weber, *Max Weber, Ein Lebensbild*, Tübingen, 1926, p. 235.

[156] On Weber and the bourgeoisie, see Mommsen, esp. p. 138f; Beetham, op. cit., ch. 2 and passim. For references on Marx, see ch. 6 below.

which they lived. In contra-distinction to Ricardo as well as to Marx, Weber saw the capitalist economy as geared to the struggle for world power – *Weltmachtstellung*.[157] In contrast to Saint-Simon as well as to Marx, Weber was greatly preoccupied with the relationship of concrete political action and leadership to general tendencies of societal evolution. In these two important respects Weber can be compared to Lenin. In a way, Weber and Lenin might be said to constitute 'the bourgeois and the proletarian Marx' of the age of imperialism. To both imperialism was a central feature of their time – to Weber as a proponent of German imperialism, to Lenin as a fighter against imperialism, 'the highest stage of capitalism'.[158] The problems which Weber tried to address with his notion of charismatic leadership, Lenin tackled with his theory of the revolutionary party and the political conjuncture.[159] That the student of *The Development of Capitalism in Russia* later became the organizer of a revolution, while the student of the development of capitalism in East Prussia eventually wrote a treatise of sociology, no doubt pertains to the difference between a bourgeois and a proletarianized intellectual.

Max Weber can then be seen in a very broad comparative framework. He can be considered not only in relation to Marx and Lenin, but also in relation to (for example) German liberalism and nationalism, to contemporary *Kulturkritik*, to Nietzsche; and he has been studied from such angles.[160] In view of both the range of Weber's interests and the range of interest in him, the very limited objective

[157] The relationship between Weber and Lenin is also discernible in their common conception of a labour aristocracy as a support of imperialism. Both saw one in England: Lenin combated it as the social basis of revisionism, Weber looked forward to the appearance of one in Germany, with decreasing hope (up to the war). See Weber's inaugural lecture in Freiberg, op. cit., pp. 28–9; cf. Mommsen, op. cit., pp. 100f, 149f. On Lenin, see his *Imperialism – the Highest Stage of Capitalism*.

[158] M. Weber, 'Der Nationalstaat und die Volkswirtschaftspolitik', (Freiburg Inaugural Lecture), *Politische Schriften*, pp. 7–30.

[159] On Weber, see Mommsen, op. cit., ch. X. After the World War, Weber developed his views of a 'plebiscitary leader of democracy [*Führerdemokratie*]'. The most crucial of Lenin's works on the problem of political leadership is '*Left-Wing Communism*' – *An Infantile Disorder*.

[160] A survey of recent general interpretations of Weber and a valuable contribution to these is given by Wolfgang Mommsen, 'Universalgeschichtliches und politisches Denken bei Max Weber'. *Historische Zeitschrift*, vol. 201 (1965), pp. 557–612.

of the analysis below should be emphasized from the outset. Its aim is not to account for the formation of Weber's thought, not even of Weber's social thought. We will only be concerned here with the formation of Weber's conception of sociology. What made Weber specifically a sociologist – apart from being a brilliant historian, a distinguished intellectual in Wilhelmine Germany, and so on? Notwithstanding the immense literature on Weber and the great interest in Weber in current reappraisals and reorientations in sociology, the answer still seems far from clear. It is this question that we shall consider here.

8. Why Sociology?

Little predestined Max Weber to become, alongside Durkheim, the most important sociological classic, or even to become a sociologist at all, the proponent of a vulgar, Western parvenu discipline. He grew up in the midst of the very self-conscious and well-established German *Geisteswissenschaften* and met in his youth several of their celebrities in the house of his father, then a prosperous and prominent 'National Liberal' politician in Berlin: philosophers and historians such as Dilthey, Mommsen, Sybel and Treitschke.[161] He was trained in jurisprudence and the history of law. In the era of imperialism and social reform, the young Weber studied the transformation of East German agriculture by capitalist relations of production and the grave implications of the recruitment of Polish workers for the German Reich. Economics, in the German historical school of Roscher and Knies, had been Weber's second subject of academic study, and his agrarian studies in this field soon ensured him a meteoric university career. At thirty-one he was called to a chair of economics in Freiburg, while the powerful Prussian secretary of higher education, Althoff, manoeuvred to keep him in Berlin for a chair of jurisprudence. After only a couple of years in

[161] The basic biography of Weber is still that by his widow, Marianne Weber, *Max Weber. Ein Lebensbild.* Much valuable biographical material on Weber's later life can be found in the special issue of *Kölner Zeitschrift für Soziologie*, R. König and J. Winckelmann (eds.), *Max Weber zum Gedächtnis*, Köln und Opladen, 1963. In particular, this contains a reprint of Paul Honigsheim's reminiscences of the Weber circle in Heidelberg, pp. 161–271. An interesting attempt at a psychological-cum-intellectual biography is A. Mitzman, *The Iron Cage*, New York, 1970.

Freiburg he received a new call to a chair in economics, in Heidelberg. After a breakdown in 1897–1902, Weber gave up his professorship for reasons of health, against the protests of faculty and ministry. He received other academic invitations, and in 1918 eventually accepted one in Vienna, where he became the successor to Von Böhm-Bawerk, the marginalist economist.

From a man of Weber's position and cultural milieu we would expect a contempt for sociology, as a naturalistic enterprise of precocious grand theories and dilettante intrusions upon the old and developed disciplines of economics, history and jurisprudence. This is in fact what we find in Weber's early writings after his recovery. The references to sociology and sociologists, very brief and casual, in his methodological essays on Roscher, Knies, Eduard Meyer and Ostwald are all negative and derisive.[162] The following passage is representative of Weber's opinion of sociology in this period: 'The old laughable prejudice of naturalistic dilettantes, according to which "mass phenomena", when considered in a certain relationship as causes or effects, are "objectively" *less* "individual" than the actions of "heroes", will hopefully not be maintained for very much longer even by "sociologists".'[163]

Now sociology at this time was also used in a very loose sense to refer to the aggregate of disciplines dealing with man's collective existence, with a particular emphasis on the present. The fact that Weber was one of the founders of the German Society for Sociology, in 1909–10, does not seem to have involved a commitment to anything more specifically sociological than that. The main reason for Weber's interest in the initiation of the new society was his desire for a purely scientific association, distinct from the ethical-political objectives of the *Verein für Sozialpolitik*.[164]

However, from at least 1913 onwards Weber himself became a programmatic spokesman for sociology,[165] and when after his short sojourn in Vienna he had to choose from among a number of possible universities, he elected Munich, because there he could

---

[162] M. Weber, *Gesammelte Aufsätze zur Wissenschaftslehre* (2nd ed.), Tübingen, 1951, pp. 11, 48, 53 n, 93 n, 230 n, 402, 416.

[163] M. Weber, 'Knies und das Irrationalitätsproblem', *Gesammelte Aufsätze zur Wissenschaftslehre*, p. 48.

[164] Marianne Weber, op. cit., p. 425f.

[165] In the essay 'Uber einige Kategorien der Verstehenden Soziologie', in *Gesammelte Aufsätze zur Wissenschaftslehre*, pp. 427–74.

give mainly sociological lectures.[166] Yet there was no major transformation of Weber's thought involved in the change from disdain
for sociology to promotion of it. What had happened was that Weber
came to use the term sociology for the views he had earlier, in his
methodological essays, developed as an economist and a historian.
It is thus in relationship to economics and historiography – and also
jurisprudence – that the formation of Weber's *verstehende* sociology
must be seen and analyzed. In Anglo-Saxon discussions of Weber's
conception of sociology this necessity is often scarcely, if at all,
realized.[167] For the development of an understanding of the

[166] Marianne Weber, op. cit., p. 657. Karl Jaspers' report that Weber was
against the establishment of chairs of sociology thus seems to refer to an earlier
period. K. Jaspers, *Max Weber, Politiker – Forscher – Philosoph*, Munich, 1958,
p. 61.

[167] See e.g. Giddens, op. cit., ch. 10; W. G. Runciman, *A Critique of Max
Weber's Philosophy of Social Sciences*, Cambridge, 1972. In spite of the fact that
the relationship of sociology and economics is one of his central concerns, Parsons
deals very briefly with Weber's economic background: *The Structure of Social
Action*, vol. II. This is also the case with his introduction to the translation from
Weber's *Wirtschaft und Gesellschaft*, entitled *The Theory of Social and Economic
Organization*, New York, 1964, pp. 8–55. The relationship of Weber's sociology
to the economic theory of his day is overlooked in such standard expositions as
R. Bendix, *Max Weber, An Intellectual Portrait*, London, 1966, which concen-
trates on Weber's empirical writings, and J. Freud, *The Sociology of Max Weber*,
London, 1968. In their fine introduction to the selection *From Max Weber*,
London, 1970, Gerth and Mills mention in passing: 'The Robinson Crusoe
approach of the classical economists and the rationalist philosophers of the
contract is echoed in this emphasis [of Weber] on the individual' (p. 56). They
have nothing to say about Weber's much more direct and important link to Carl
Menger and marginalist economics. Two recent sociological writers on Weber's
methodology have managed to remain completely silent about this question:
J. Rex, 'Typology and objectivity: a comment on Weber's four sociological
methods'; A. Sahay, 'The relevance of Max Weber's methodology in sociological
explanation', both in A. Sahay (ed.), *Max Weber and Modern Sociology*, London,
1971. These Anglo-Saxon sociologists are in respectable company. Neither the
essay by the prominent West German scholar Johannes Winckelmann, 'Max
Webers Verständnis von Mensch und Gesellschaft' (in K. Engisch, B. Pfister
and J. Winckelmann, eds., *Max Weber*, Berlin, 1964) nor Guenther Roth's
magisterial 'Introduction' to the very carefully prepared English edition of
Economy and Society, New York, 1968, nor the centennial proceedings of the
German Society for Sociology (O. Stammer (ed.), *Max Weber und die Soziologie
heute*, Tübingen, 1965), tell us anything of the role of marginalist economics in
his formation. Nor is this question brought out by Alexander von Schelting,
fighting idealist intuitionism and *Wissensoziologie* in his classical treatise on Weber's

relationship between, or comparative significance, of Weber and Marx, a frequent preoccupation in contemporary discussions of Weber, this neglect is particularly damaging.

The project of the pioneer sociologists – a natural science of the evolution of humanity and society, focusing on the recent emergence of a bourgeois society – was completely alien to Weber. He was hostile both to its naturalism and to its generalism. He was at the same time equally hostile to the philosophies of history of the idealist tradition, whether Hegelian or Romantic.[168] On the other hand, Weber had much in common with the sociologists of the classical age.

Weber early abandoned the narrow, socially unconcerned liberalism of his father and joined the *Verein für Sozialpolitik*. Though he soon became a distinguished professor of economics, he never wrote a single piece of economic theory.[169] His economic studies were empirical and had a historical and 'institutionalist' character – ancient and contemporary east German agrarian relations, the stock exchange, the economic ethics of world religions, the typology of economic activities. He took an active interest in industrial social research and he himself contributed a substantial pilot study in this field.[170]

With this background, Weber might have been expected to launch an attack on orthodox liberal economic theory, on its deductive character, on its narrow-minded and misleading focus on economic man alone. That would have been consonant with German historical economics and with the sociological tradition of Durkheim – not to speak of the later industrial sociology of Elton Mayo and his

---

epistemology, *Max Webers Wissenschaftslehre*, Tübingen, 1934. There are, however, contributions to the German discussion which do take account of the economic context: F. Tenbruck, 'Die Genesis der Methodologie Max Webers', *Kölner Zeitschrift für Soziologie und Sozialpsychologie*, vol. 11, New Series, 1959, pp. 573–630; J. Habermas, 'Zur Logik der Sozialwissenschaften', *Philosophische Rundschau*, Sonderheft, 1967, pp. 13f, 49f.

[168] Cf. Mommsen, 'Universalgeschichtliches und politisches Denken bei Max Weber', p. 565f.

[169] For a list of Weber's writings, see Marianne Weber, op. cit., pp. 715–19.

[170] M. Weber, 'Zur Psychophysik der industriellen Arbeit', in *Gesammelte Aufsätze zur Soziologie und Sozialpolitik*, Tübingen, 1924, pp. 61–255. The same volume (pp. 1–60) also contains a memorandum on a study planned by the *Verein* (directed by Max Weber's brother Alfred) on the selection and adaptation of workers in big industry.

associates in the 1930's.[171] Now the point is that Weber did *not* take that road.[172] Instead of attacking liberal economic theory, he adopted it for his own purposes. Commissioned as editor of a new handbook of economic science intended to replace an old handbook of German historical and ethical economics, Weber chose the Austrian marginalist Von Wieser to write the volume on economic theory.[173]

Finally, another path that Weber – contrary to common belief – did not tread should be noted. Weber's sociology did not develop as a critique of historical materialism. This is remarkable because Weber was clearly interested in, appreciative of, and influenced by, the work of Marx. His early studies in economic and social history involve a largely Marxist frame of reference. The analyses of East German agriculture focus on the transformation of more or less feudal into capitalist relations of production. Weber discusses the distribution of the means of production, the objective of production,

[171] A survey (one of many) of these researches, as well as of some of the secondary literature on them, is given in J. Madge, *The Origins of Scientific Sociology*, New York, 1967, ch. 6.

[172] Weber's industrial research was an attempt to connect the economic concern with profitability [*Rentabilität*], to the physiology and experimental psychology of work. Weber surveyed the literature on the latter, of Kraepelin, Herkner and others. As an empirical pilot study he measured the performance of the workers in his uncle's weaving mill. (Marianne Weber, op. cit., pp. 397–8.) The specific findings and emphases of industrial sociology – group norms, morale, non-rational motivation – were lacking in Weber. He was not unaware that the workers set their own ceilings to their performance, but he did not see in this any particularly interesting group norm. It was either a rational action in a conflict with the employer over piece-rates, or an action with 'traditionalist' causes (*Gesammelte Aufsätze zur Soziologie und Sozialpolitik*, pp. 157–8). He could also point to the effect on performance of the cultural background and ideology of workers, but without indicating any important theoretical implications. (Ibid., p. 160f.)

[173] It was as the introductory volume to this handbook, *Grundriss der Sozial-ökonomik*, that Weber's own magnum opus, *Economy and Society*, was written. Friedrich von Wieser's *Theorie der gesellschaftlichen Wirtschaft* appeared as volume II. Another prominent marginalist contributor was Schumpeter, who wrote on the history of economic theories and methods. From a doctor of jurisprudence interested in economic conditions, one might have expected a focus on the legal and normative regulation of the economy. This would also have related to Durkheim's concerns, sociological and political. Again, this is a road Weber never took. Weber's perhaps most virulent essay was directed against an attempt in that direction, Rudolf Stammler's *Wirtschaft und Recht nach der materialistischen Geschichtsauffsung* (see Weber, *Gesammelte Aufsätze zur Wissenschaftslehre*, pp. 291–383).

and the relationship of the direct producers to those who dispose of the means of production. For this latter aspect of the relations of production Weber employs a special term, 'constitution of work' (*Arbeitsverfassung*). He relates changes in the relations of production to changes in the *Betriebsweise* – to development of the forces of production in the direction of a more intensive agriculture, exemplified by the threshing machine and the cultivation of sugar beet. The central question for Weber was that of the effects of these new forces and relations of production on the class structure of East Germany, on its aristocracy and working-class.[174]

Weber later continued to see his work as related to that of Marx. He presented his sociology of religion as a 'positive critique of the materialist conception of history'.[175] In a debate with Oswald Spengler, in 1920, Weber passionately defended Marx against the philosopher of 'The Decline of the West'. Afterwards Weber is said to have made the famous remark: 'The honesty of a scholar of today, and particularly of a philosopher, can be measured by where he stands in relation to Nietzsche and Marx [Spengler had sneered at both]. Anyone who does not admit that he could not have achieved very important parts of his own work without the work that these two men accomplished, deludes both himself and others. The mental world in which we ourselves exist bears to a great extent the stamp of Marx and Nietzsche.'[176]

Thus Guenther Roth's dismissive remark that 'Weber recognized historical materialism as a political force but did not take its ultimate claims seriously' is at best a distorting ellipse, that is largely reveal-

---

[174] See 'Die ländliche Arbeitsverfassung' and 'Entwicklungstendenzen in der Lage der ostelbischen Landarbeiter', in M. Weber, *Gesammelte Aufsätze zur Sozial- und Wirtschaftsgeschichte*, Tübingen, 1924, pp. 444–69 and 470–507, respectively. Weber's work on German agriculture was known and discussed among contemporary German Social Democrats; but their perspective – focused on the relationship between the peasants and the industrial proletariat in the struggle for socialism – was, of course, different from Weber's East Elbian concerns. German Social Democracy produced a major work of its own on the problems of agriculture, Karl Kautsky's *Die Agrarfrage* (2nd ed., Stuttgart, 1902), a solid and comprehensive analysis that owes little to Weber directly, and draws upon a mass of German and Austrian investigations.

[175] This was the title under which he lectured on the sociology of religion in Vienna in 1918 (Marianne Weber, op. cit., p. 617).

[176] E. Baumgarten (ed.), Max Weber, *Werk und Person*, Tübingen, 1964, pp. 554–5 n.

ing of its author's anti-Marxist animus.[177]

But despite this and other evidence, it will be argued here that Weber's sociology was constituted neither as a positive nor as a negative critique of historical materialism, but as a discourse on a quite different level. As such it does not lack pertinence to historical materialism, but there cannot be a correct basis for a discussion of their relationship until the difference between the two kinds of discourse has been clearly established.

9. The Historicist Reaction

'Sociology (in the sense in which this highly ambiguous word is used here) is a science concerning itself with the interpretative understanding of social action and thereby with a causal explanation of its course and consequences. We shall speak of "action" in so far as the acting individual attaches a subjective meaning to his behaviour – be it overt or covert, omission or acquiescence. Action is "social" in so far as its subjective meaning takes account of the behaviour of others and is thereby oriented in its course.'[178] 'Both for sociology, in the present sense, and for history, the object of cognition is the subjective meaning-complex of action.'[179] 'It has continually been assumed as obvious that the science of sociology seeks to formulate type concepts and generalized uniformities of empirical process. This distinguishes it from history, which is oriented to the causal analysis of and explanation of individual actions, structures, and personalities possessing cultural significance. Theoretical differenti-

[177] G. Roth, 'Introduction', *Economy and Society*, p. LXIV. Roth's argument is largely a rather fantastic piece of special pleading. It refers above all on a short verbal intervention which Weber made at the first congress of the German Sociological Association. Weber took part in a discussion of a *Referat* by Sombart on Technology and Culture and made a few remarks also on Marx, unprepared, and referring to a metaphor used by Marx (in *The Poverty of Philosophy*), about the relationship between the handmill and feudalism and the steam-mill and capitalism. Fifty years later, these remarks provide the main materials for an argument about Weber's view of Marx! For the context of Weber's words, see *Verhandlungen des Ersten Deutschen Soziologentages*, Tübingen, 1911, pp. 63–110. Cf. also Roth's somewhat more reasoned essay, 'The Historical Relation to Marxism', in R. Bendix and G. Roth, *Scholarship and Partisanship: Essays on Max Weber*, Berkeley, 1971.

[178] Weber, *Wirtschaft und Gesellschaft*, Cologne and Berlin, 1964, p. 3; *Economy and Society*, p. 4.

[179] *Wirtschaft und Gesellschaft*, p. 10; *Economy and Society*, p. 13.

ation [*Kasuistik*] is possible in sociology only in terms of ideal or pure types. It goes without saying that in addition it is convenient for the sociologist from time to time to employ average types of an empirical statistical character. . . . But when reference is made to "typical" cases, the term should always be understood, unless otherwise stated, as meaning *ideal* types . . . always constructed with a view to adequacy on the level of meaning.'[180]

Sociology, in Weber's conception, is a discourse constituted by four specific characteristics: interpretative understanding (*Verstehen*), social action, complex or context of meaning (*Sinnzummenhang*), ideal type. Sociology is an enterprise of 'interpretative understanding' of the complex of meaning of ideal-typical social actions. It thereby seeks to provide causal explanation, which to Weber means a determination such that according to some calculable rule of probability one event will be followed or accompanied by another.[181]

Weber's conception of sociology forms part of an endeavour to affirm the specificity of the social and historical disciplines as compared to the natural sciences and to a naturalistic approach to human affairs. This is explicitly, though very briefly, asserted in the introductory outline of *verstehende* sociology in *Economy and Society*.[182] Indeed, all that he later listed as the distinctive components of the sociological enterprise were developed by their author before he propounded an activity named sociology. Sociology, in the sense Weber used it about his own work, was in fact not a new science of society but a type of social study which applied the epistemological principles of economics and history formulated by Weber in 1903–6.[183] Weber's sociology was, in fact,

[180] Ibid., p. 14; *Economy and Society*, p. 20.

[181] Ibid., p. 9, *Economy and Society*, p. 11–12. The Henderson and Parsons translation here is inexact: it is not corrected in the complete edition of *Economy and Society*.

[182] See e.g. *Wirtschaft und Gesellschaft*, p. 9f; *Economy and Society*, p. 13f.

[183] These principles are presented in a number of long essays, 'Roscher und Knies und die logischen Probleme der historischen Nationalökonomie', I–III, 'Die Objectivität sozialwissenschaftlicher und sozialpolitischer Erkenntnis', 'Kritische Studien auf dem gebiete der kulturwissenschaftlichen Logik', I–II, in *Gesammelte Aufsätze zur Wissenschaftslehre*. The two latter are included in the English selection, *Max Weber on the Methodology of the Social Sciences*, Glencoe, 1949. Highly relevant also is the review article 'Die Grenznutzlehre und das psychophysische Grundgesetz', *Gesammelte Aufsätze zur Wissenschaftslehre*, pp. 384–99 (first published in 1908).

the offspring of an encounter between German historicism and Austrian marginalist economics.

Late 19th century historicism was an idealist tendency in Germany both corresponding to and reacting against the naturalistic evolutionism dominant in Britain and USA. At the beginning of the century a German Historical School of philosophers, jurists, and historians had asserted the role of historical tradition and historical knowledge against what they saw as the atemporal rationalism of the philosophy of natural law. In the course of the century there developed at the centre of German intellectual life a vigorous discipline of political history, founded by Leopold von Ranke. The culture of the 19th century was, however, dominated not only by history, but also by biology. Under the impact of the breakthroughs in the biological sciences, naturalism – usually in some form of evolutionism – eventually invaded even the territory of the German historians. The sociology of the pioneers, Saint-Simon, Comte and Spencer, had of course been part of this invasion. They advocated a natural history of society and had nothing but contempt for orthodox dynastic and diplomatic historiography.

It was to check this naturalistic invasion of history that there emerged, within the German idealist tradition, a group of philosophers who sought to provide a firmer basis for the specificity of the historical and non-naturalistic social disciplines. The first major intervention of this kind was Wilhelm Dilthey's *Einleitung in die Geisteswissenschaften*, published in 1883.[184] Georg Simmel made a significant contribution with a small book on the subject soon afterwards,[185] while Wilhelm Windelband's *Rektoratsrede* at the university of Strasburg in 1894 on 'History and Natural Science' was also very influential.[186] Thereafter the major development of the ideas of Simmel and Windelband was the work of Weber's personal friend Heinrich Rickert.[187] Himself a historical economist,

[184] The background to the emergence of the new historicist epistemology is given by Dilthey in his preface. In contrast to the other sociologists, Tocqueville is associated by Dilthey with the historical school in the reaction against the 'natural law, natural religion, abstract political theory and abstract political economy' of the 17th and 18th centuries. See W. Dilthey, *Einleitung in die Geisteswissenschaften*, Leipzig, 1883, p. xiv.

[185] G. Simmel, *Die Probleme der Geschichtsphilosophie*, Leipzig, 1892.

[186] It is reprinted in W. Windelband, *Präludien*, II, Tübingen, 1919.

[187] H. Rickert, *Die Grenzen der naturwissenschaftlichen Begriffsbildung*, Tübingen and Leipzig, 1902. Rickert's and Windelband's positions were rather

Weber shared the concern of these philosophers at the naturalistic invasion of history and social sciences (such as economics). 'Despite the powerful resistance to the infiltration of naturalistic dogma due to German idealism since Fichte, and the achievement of the German Historical School in law and economics, and partly because of the very work of the Historical School, the naturalistic viewpoint in certain decisive problems has not yet been overcome.'[188]

Weber's studies of the method of economics explicitly started from the tenets of Windelband and Rickert, after the 'first steps' taken by Dilthey and Simmel.[189] In his critical study of one of the leaders of the older school of historical economists, Wilhelm Roscher, Weber sharply criticized Roscher's naturalism. In particular he took issue with Roscher's belief that the economics of different nations revealed a law-bound development.[190] He argued that it was a contradiction that Roscher, the representative of a historical economics, should have admired classical naturalistic economists such as Smith and Malthus.[191] Weber also attacked the naturalistic tendency in Austrian marginal economics, to which Menger himself had fallen victim, to assume that the propositions of economic theory could be deduced from psychology and thus possessed the character of natural laws.[192]

---

similar. For Rickert on Simmel and Windelband, see p. 301f. Rickert's work is a full-size treatment of the problem, more than 700 pages long. An extensive overview and a discussion from within of the historicist movement is given by E. Troeltsch, *Der Historismus und seine Probleme*, Tübingen, 1922.

[188] *Gesammelte Aufsätze zur Wissenschaftslehre*, p. 187; English ed., pp. 86–7.

[189] *Gesammelte Aufsätze zur Wissenschaftslehre*, pp. 4 n, 12–13 n. In his study of Roscher's historical method, Weber also says that 'It is one of the aims of this study to investigate the utility of this author's [Rickert's] ideas for the methodology of our discipline.' Ibid., p. 7 n. Weber apparently found them of great utility. Cf. *Gesammelte Aufsätze zur Wissenschaftslehre*, p. 146 n, English ed., *On the Methodology of the Social Sciences*, p. 50.

[190] *Gesammelte Aufsätze zur Wissenschaftslehre*, pp. 3–42.

[191] Ibid., p. 7.

[192] Ibid., p. 186f; English ed. *On the Methodology of the Social Sciences*, p. 86f. Cf. *Gesammelte Aufsätze zur Wissenschaftslehre*, pp. 384–99. Without mentioning his name Weber refers to Menger, 'the creator of the theory', on p. 187 (English, p. 87). Menger's conception of a physiologically and psychologically based economics was to be developed in the second edition of his 'Principles of Economics', on which he worked in the last decades of his life. Apparently he was never wholly satisfied with the result and the work was published only posthumously. C. Menger, *Grundsätze der Volkswirtschaftslehre* (2nd ed.), Vienna and Leipzig, 1923.

What was then the distinctive character of the historical and social disciplines? Within the anti-naturalistic camp many different answers had been given. Weber's essays on epistemology were necessarily much preoccupied with this problem. Weber's reply was that the specificity of the historical and social sciences was that they were cultural disciplines. Presenting, on behalf of its editors, the aim of the *Archiv für Sozialwissenschaft und Sozialpolitik*, Weber wrote: 'The scientific investigation of the general *cultural significance of the social-economic structure of the human community*, and its historical forms of organization, is the central aim of our journal.'[193] This formulation might well have served as an introduction to Weber's own *oeuvre*.

Culture was a part of reality rendered meaningful and significant by a system of values. 'The concept of culture is a *value-concept*. Empirical reality becomes "culture" to us because and in so far as we relate it to value ideas. It includes those segments and only those segments of reality which have become significant to us because of this value-reference.'[194]

Weber's concept of culture essentially functioned within a discourse on the difference between natural and cultural sciences. Culture in Weber's sense denoted all these domains of reality registered by human beings in any system of thought – thus including, say, classical mechanics. The notion might therefore have become part of a general theory of knowledge, or it might have operated in a discussion of different types of cultural significance. On the whole, however, that was not the role of the concept in Weber's thought.[195] The concept of culture was employed by Weber in two main ways to distinguish the kind of historical and social studies to which he was committed from the natural sciences. The first, reiterated in his early methodological writings and

[193] *Gesammelte Aufsätze zur Wissenschaftslehre*, p. 165; *On the Methodology of the Social Sciences*, p. 67. Emphasis in original.

[194] Ibid., p. 175; *On the Methodology of the Social Sciences*, p. 76.

[195] In the late lecture on 'Science as a Vocation', there is a brief discussion of the latter kind. Weber there says that: 'Natural science gives us an answer to the question of what we must do, if we wish to master life technically', whereas the main contribution of 'sociology, history, economics [!], political science, and those types of cultural philosophy that make it their task to interpret these sciences' is their aid to 'clarity'. *Gesammelte Aufsätze zur Wissenschaftslehre*, pp. 583, 584, 591; English in Gerth and Mills (eds.), *From Max Weber*, pp. 144, 145, 151.

certainly within the historicist tradition, emphasized the decisive influence of the cultural meanings derived from historical values upon cultural scientists (historians, economists and so on), their concepts and analyses. The second, prominent in the conception of sociology within the historicist tradition, but in Weber largely derived from an interpretation of marginalist economics, focused on the determination of the objects of study of cultural scientists – social actions – by the complexes of meaning conferred by historical values.

Following Rickert, Weber pits the historical mutability of cultural significance against the naturalistic interest in generic concepts and search for laws. 'The "points of view", which are oriented towards "values", from which we consider cultural objects and from which they become "objects" of historical research, change. Because, and as long as they do, new "facts" will always be becoming historically "important" (*wesentlich*), and they will always become so in a new way – for in logical discussions such as these we assume once and for all that the "source materials" will remain unchanged. This way of being conditioned by "subjective values" is, however, entirely alien in any case to those natural sciences which take mechanics as a model, and it constitutes, indeed, the distinctive *contrast* between the historical sciences and them.'[196] 'The focus of attention on reality under the guidance of values which lend it significance and the selection and ordering of the phenomena which are thus affected in the light of their cultural significance is entirely different from the analysis in terms of laws and general concepts.'[197]

That the cultural sciences are guided by what is culturally significant means above all that they are interested in the unique, in what Rickert and Weber called 'the historical individual', not in law-bound recurrences.[198] This was what distinguished them from

---

[196] *Gesammelte Aufsätze zur Wissenschaftslehre*, p. 261f; *On the Methodology of the Social Sciences*, p. 159f. The English translation, by Edward Shils and Henry Finch, is not quite exact here, in that it substitutes 'the natural sciences' for the German '*sie*' (them) at the end of the passage quoted. This is not un-important, for both Rickert and Weber could envisage studies of nature with a historical character. Therefore it is not correct to suppress the distinction implied by Weber's reference to natural sciences that take mechanics as their model.

[197] *Gesammelte Aufsätze zur Wissenschaftslehre*, p. 176; *On the Methodology of the Social Sciences*, p. 77.

[198] To counterpose historical-cultural significance to law and general concepts

the classical naturalistic conception of science. Dilthey had counter-posed the *Geisteswissenschaften* (the sciences of the mind) to the natural sciences. Simmel, Windelband, Rickert and Weber form-ulated the distinction in other terms, distinguishing between not spirit and nature but the unique and the recurrent. This was some-times expressed as the contrast between 'sciences of reality' and 'sciences of laws' – a politely polemical formulation reversing the usual hierarchy of the sciences.[199] The sciences of reality could achieve something more than the nomothetic sciences. They could grasp reality in its characteristic uniqueness, in which endeavour they could use nomothetic knowledge as a first step. 'The knowledge of social laws is not knowledge of social reality but is rather one of the various aids used by our minds for attaining this end.'[200]

Having thus defined the specific cognitive goal of the cultural sciences Weber devoted considerable energy not only to refuting naturalism, but also to combatting other conceptions of the distinc-tive character of the studies of society and history. Thus he criticized theories of the irrationality of human action (Knies), the creativity of man (Wundt), the availability of cultural reality to intuition (Lipp, Croce), the role of free will and of chance (E. Meyer).[201]

By cultural sciences as sciences of reality Weber did not mean

---

has far-reaching implications, which Weber by and large bypassed or evaded. He was little interested in the problem of the historical relativity of cultural signifi-cance. (See *Gesammelte Aufsätze zur Wissenschaftslehre*, p. 213f; *On the Method-ology of the Social Sciences*, p. 111f.) Nor was he concerned with differences in cultural significance to different sorts of people – to different classes, for instance. The 'us' in the phrase 'significant to us' is not problematic to him, and as a theorist of *Verstehen* Weber never really bothered with the question: understand-able to whom? To the generation of Rickert and Weber cultural values were, in fact if not in principle, stable in time as well as social space, in a way that they emphatically were not to the generation of historicists marked by the cataclysm of war and revolution – that of Lukács and Mannheim. Weber was concerned with one particular aspect of the problem of cultural significance: the question of the relationship between cultural values, themselves accepted as unproblematic, to scientific knowledge. Throughout his methodological writings he took pains to emphasize the difference between value relevance and cultural significance, on one hand, and positive or negative evaluation and value judgment, on the other.

[199] The distinction was used already by Simmel, op. cit., p. 42f; cf. Weber, *Gesammelte Aufsätze zur Wissenschaftslehre*, p. 3, and see further below.

[200] *Gesammelte Aufsätze zur Wissenschaftslehre*, p. 180; *On the Methodology of the Social Sciences*, p. 80.

[201] The critique of Meyer, *Gesammelte Aufsätze zur Wissenschaftslehre*, pp.

only descriptive historiography. Outlining the programme of the editors of the *Archiv für Sozialwissenschaft* Weber wrote: 'The type of social science in which we are interested is a *science of reality* [*Wirklichkeitswissenschaft*]. Our aim is the understanding of the characteristic uniqueness of the reality in which we move. We wish to understand on the one hand the relationships and the cultural significance of individual events in their contemporary manifestations, and on the other the causes of their being historically *so* and not *otherwise*.'[202] The consequence, Weber contended, was the necessity for a specific type of concept formation in the cultural sciences. 'Meaningfulness ...turally does not coincide with laws as such, and the more general the laws the less the coincidence. For the specific meaning which a phenomenon has for us is naturally *not* to be found in those relationships which it shares with other phenomena.'[203] Therefore, the concepts of the cultural sciences must be other than generic.

It was in this context that Weber's famous notion of the ideal type was launched. Several themes and theses mingle in Weber's discussion of it.[204] Weber took a stand in the traditional debate between realism or nominalism – a debate still relevant because of the influence of Hegelian 'panlogism' in Germany and the traces of scholastic realism which Weber noted among the old school of historical economists. Weber adopted a firm nominalist position,

---

215–90, is translated in *On the Methodology of the Social Sciences*, pp. 88–113, but not the critique of Knies and others, *Gesammelte Aufsätze zur Wissenschaftslehre*, pp. 42–145.

[202] *Gesammelte Aufsätze zur Wissenschaftslehre*, p. 170f; *On the Methodology of the Social Sciences*, p. 72. In Shils' and Finch's translation the specific connotation of reality conveyed by the term 'science of reality' (*Wirklichkeitswissenschaft*) is attenuated into 'an empirical science of concrete reality'. In the same way, the translators attenuate Weber's identification of the real with the individually unique by rendering the German phrase: 'Ausgangspunkt des sozialwissenschaftlichen Interesses ist nun zweifellos die wirkliche, also individuelle Gestaltung des uns umgebenden Kulturlebens . . .' as 'The social-scientific has its point of departure, of course, in the *real*, i.e., concrete, individually-structured configuration of our cultural life . . .' (*Gesammelte Aufsätze zur Wissenschaftslehre*, p. 172, *On the Methodology of the Social Sciences*, p. 74. Emphasis in the original.

[203] *Gesammelte Aufsätze zur Wissenschaftslehre*, p. 176; *On the Methodology of the Social Sciences*, p. 76f.

[204] Weber develops his concept of the ideal type in the programmatic essay '"Objectivity" in Social Science and Social Policy', *Gesammelte Aufsätze zur Wissenschaftslehre*, p. 189f; *On the Methodology of the Social Sciences*, p. 89f.

sharply distinguishing reality from concepts about reality.[205] He also commented on the *ceteris paribus* assumptions of theoretical propositions, which were inevitably 'ideal' for that reason. These, however, were side issues. Weber's discussion of ideal types was not mainly concerned with concept formation in science in general. For not all fertile and methodologically acceptable concepts in science were ideal types. On the contrary, Weber's principal thesis was that there are fundamentally two types of scientific concepts, of which the ideal type is one that is particularly important to the cultural sciences as he defined them.

Weber had dismissed the claims of a naturalistic science of society. The exact natural sciences characteristically sought law-bound regularities, whereas the cultural sciences were interested in 'reality', in the individually unique. It was this that made necessary the formation of ideal-typical concepts. 'The goal of ideal-typical concept-construction is always to make clearly explicit not the class or average character but rather the unique individual character of cultural phenomena.'[206] The ideal type was a specific kind of concept designed for a specific task. The opposite to ideal-type concepts were generic concepts (*Gattungsbegriffe*) designating a class of phenomena. Generic concepts function in deductive theories. They are part of explanations of a covering-law type, in which the explanandum is explained by subsuming it as a member of the class of phenomena about which the theory states certain regularities, either of a universal or of a probabilistic sort.

By contrast with generic concepts, ideal-typical concepts, or ideal types, do not designate what characterizes a class of phenomena, but an aspect that these phenomena manifest to a greater or lesser extent. The ideal type is not 'fitted to serve as a scheme under which a real situation or action is to be subsumed as one *instance*. It has the significance of a purely ideal *limiting* concept with which the real situation or action is *compared* and surveyed for the explication of certain of its significant components. Such concepts are constructs in terms of which we formulate relationships by the application of

[205] From his materialist standpoint, Marx was also concerned with the distinction between concepts and reality, particularly in relation to his break with Hegel. Cf. 'Introduction', *Grundrisse*, Berlin, 1953, p. 21f, English ed., *Grundrisse*, London, 1973, p. 100f.

[206] *Gesammelte Aufsätze zur Wissenschaftslehre*, p. 202; *On the Methodology of the Social Sciences*, p. 101.

the category of objective possibility. By means of this category, the adequacy of our imagination, oriented and disciplined by reality, is *judged*.'[207]

The ideal type does not operate in an explanation of the covering-law type. Its onesidedness is deliberate. For its objective is to function as a standard by which to compare the historical individual studied – for example, to highlight to what extent a given economy is capitalist or a given organization is bureaucratic. If that extent turns out to be small, then the ideal type should stimulate research into other aspects of the objects in question, aspects brought into focus precisely because of the delimitation by the ideal type of what it has proved not to be. In this way, Weber pointed out, not merely static relationships but also developmental sequences could be constructed and used as ideal types.[208]

The result of his emphasis on understanding the unique was that Weber was interested in concept formation and in ideal types, but not in *theory* formation – the construction of systems of concepts and propositions. The need for such construction was obviated by re-emphasis on the role of cultural significance in the cultural sciences. The ideal types were related (though unproblematically) to changing cultural values – but not to each other.[209] Weber's magnum opus, *Economy and Society*, is to be construed in this light, not as a 'theory of social and economic organization' – as an English selection once presented it – but as a typology and a *Kasuistik*,[210] whose value derives largely from its enormous historical erudition.

His theory of ideal types illuminates Weber's relation to historical materialism after his recovery from his breakdown. Weber never undertook a methodological critique of Marx or historical materialism. In his programmatic essay for the *Archiv* he wrote: 'We have

[207] *Gesammelte Aufsätze zur Wissenschaftslehre*, p. 194; *On the Methodology of the Social Sciences*, p. 93. It should be noted that Weber argues for an ideal-typical conceptualization of ideal-typical concept formation. 'Every *individual* ideal type comprises both generic and ideal-typically constructed conceptual elements.' *Gesammelte Aufsätze zur Wissenschaftslehre*, p. 201; *On the Methodology of the Social Sciences*, p. 100.

[208] *Gesammelte Aufsätze zur Wissenschaftslehre*, p. 203; *On the Methodology of the Social Sciences*, p. 104.

[209] See *Gesammelte Aufsätze zur Wissenschaftslehre*, pp. 206f, 105f.

[210] This point is emphasized by the German editor of Weber's work, Johannes Winckelmann, 'Max Webers Verständnis von Mensch und Gesellschaft', op. cit., p. 220.

intentionally avoided a demonstration with respect to that ideal-typical construct which is the most important one from our point of view; namely, the Marxian theory. This was done in order not to complicate the exposition any further through the introduction of an interpretation of Marx and in order not to anticipate the discussions in our journal which will make a regular practice of presenting critical analyses of the literature concerning and following the great thinker.'[211] To those discussions, however, no contribution was made by Weber. The biographical reasons for this silence are unknown, it seems. But it should be emphasized that Weber's selection of theories for critical analysis was quite logical and anything but peculiar. Within the historicist problematic and the academic context of the Reich it was much more urgent to deal with the ideas of men like Wilhelm Roscher, Karl Knies, Eduard Meyer, Rudolf Stammler, and Lujo Brentano than with historical materialism.

Marx and Engels and historical materialism stood apart from the most important epistemological problems with which Weber was wrestling. They had surpassed the problems of idealism and naturalism, which emerged in Germany in the wake of Darwin. For they had long ago broken with German idealism; and while they welcomed Darwin's work as a great achievement by a fellow-scientist, they never even considered an importation of biology into the study of history and society.[212] Whereas Weber as a historian sought to explain the logic of singular events and the advent of unique cultural configurations, Marx and Engels as social scientists were concerned to develop a theory of social regularities, which could then be applied to historiography. (An example of the latter pro-

---

[211] *Gesammelte Aufsätze zur Wissenschaftslehre*, p. 204; *On the Methodology of the Social Sciences*, p. 103. Weber continues: 'We will only point out here that naturally all specifically Marxian "laws" and developmental constructs – insofar as they are theoretically sound – are ideal types. The eminent, indeed unique, *heuristic* significance of these ideal types when they are used for the *assessment* of reality is known to everyone who has ever employed Marxian concepts and hypotheses. Similarly, their perniciousness, as soon as they are thought of as empirically valid or as real (i.e., truly metaphysical) "effective forces", "tendencies", etc. is likewise known to those who have used them.'

[212] See, for instance, Engels' defence of Darwin against Dühring, and his complementary scorn for attempts to import biological and physical conceptions into social theory, in *Anti-Dühring* and *Dialektik der Natur*, *MEW* 20, p. 62f and 565f, respectively.

cedure was Marx's *Eighteenth Brumaire*.) In contrast to Weber's concern with cultural values and unique events or institutions – and later with typologies, Marx and Engels worked on the construction of a systematic theory, with inter-related concepts, designed to formulate a new pattern of determination.[213]

The most revealing aspect of the quotation above is thus not Weber's avoidance of any discussion of historical materialism. It is his superficially flattering references to it as 'the most important' 'ideal-typical construct' 'from our point of view'. Since historical materialism is not, in fact, a construction of ideal types, Weber's remark proves that in fact he knew and cared little about Marxism.

For the central concepts of historial materialism, such as forces and relations of production, are not formed by 'the one-sided *accentuation* of one or more points of view and by the synthesis of a great many diffuse, discrete, more or less present and occasionally absent *individual* phenomena . . .'. Their function is not to constitute 'purely ideal *limiting* concept[s] with which the real situation or action is *compared* and surveyed . . .'[214]. Weber's exposition of the construction of ideal-types hinges on a distinction between the average and the accentuated ideal. But in constructing the concepts of historical materialism Marx and Engels were concerned with

---

[213] A famous illustration of the Marxist epistemological problematic is provided by Engels' preface to the second volume of *Capital*. Engels there refers to the revolution in chemistry effected by Lavoisier's discovery-production of oxygen and his break with Priestley's and Scheele's concept of phlogiston. Engels seeks here to elucidate the problems involved in the construction of Marxist economic theory. The enormous distance of this epistemological universe from that of historicism is highlighted by a comment by Werner Sombart on these passages of Engels. (Sombart was rather close to Weber, personally as well as in intellectual interests, but neither their interpretations of the spirit of capitalism nor their epistemologies were identical.) 'My reason for taking exception to this comparison between Lavoisier and Marx is not just that it appears to me false in content – for neither is the importance of Lavoisier for the science of chemistry justly recognized (this lay in particular in the basic quantification of all chemical processes and all natural processes in general), nor is the "law of value" correctly appreciated in its methodological significance – but rather that it is fundamentally misplaced. This is because it is in general not admissible to compare in any way the scientific work of a social scientist with the achievements of a natural scientist.' W. Sombart, 'Karl Marx und die soziale Wissenschaft', *Archiv für Sozialwissenschaft und Sozialpolitik*, New Series, vol. 8, 1908, p. 431. For a modern Marxist discussion of Engels' preface, cf. Althusser and Balibar, *Reading Capital*, p. 145f.

[214] *Gesammelte Aufsätze zur Wissenschaftslehre*, pp. 191, 194; *On the Methodology of the Social Sciences*, pp. 90, 93.

neither. The relations of production are neither to be compared with empirical reality, nor do they express the average of it. They are constructed as part of a theoretical discourse that seeks to discover a pattern of regularities in the real world. In this respect, the concept construction of historical materialism is outside Weber's empiricist problematic, in which concepts are abstracted out of reality, either as accentuated ideals or as averages – instead of produced through theoretical work.[215]

10. Marginalist Economics and Interpretative Sociology

Weber's assertion that the specificity of the cultural sciences was their concern with what is culturally significant was based on a historicist philosophy. Compared to the latter, marginalist economics was in this respect of subsidiary moment. On the other hand, this does not mean that it was unimportant to Weber. The most significant of Weber's early methodological essays, '"Objectivity" in Social Science', is not a general discussion of science, values and objectivity. It is a specific attempt to find a way out of the *Methodenstreit* between German historical economics and Austrian marginalism. It was this conflict – not, as far as Weber was concerned, the Marxist critique of political economy – that had created the paradox of 'two sciences of economics'. Thus Weber wrote: 'What is the meaning of "objectivity" in this context? The following discussion will be devoted to this question.'[216] The ideal-typical construction which Weber discusses later in the same essay, is the marginalist model of economic action.

An established Central European intellectual, educated in German culture, Carl Menger could speak to a historian and economist such as Weber in a way that Jevons or Walras could not. The adjective 'Austrian' therefore seems appropriate in considering

[215] In another respect the basic concepts of historical materialism provide an example of what Weber's ideal types were designed to oppose. Though not expressing any average character, they are generic or class concepts. That is, a question such as: 'Is Sweden in 1976 a capitalist country?' is concerned with the problem of whether and to what extent capitalist relations of production are dominant over other relations of production. Capitalism, in the Marxist sense, is not a 'historical individual', a unique cultural configuration, but one member of the class of modes of production.

[216] *Gesammelte Aufsätze zur Wissenschaftslehre*, p. 161; *On the Methodology of the Social Sciences*, p. 63.

Weber's relationship to marginalism. (Weber was apparently never interested in the technicalities of marginalist economic theory.) Weber had a high opinion of Menger as a methodologist, for Menger's *Untersuchugen über die Methode der Sozialwissenschaften* had foreshadowed (in 1883) the distinction later developed by Windelband and Rickert, and employed by Weber. Referring to Menger, Weber wrote of 'the fundamental methodological distinction between historical knowledge and the knowledge of "laws" which the creator of the [marginalist] theory drew as the *first* and *only* one.'[217] Menger had distinguished between historical and theoretical sciences, which dealt with the same materials but from different points of view. He had also anticipated Weber's ideal-typical discussion by distinguishing within 'theoretical research' an 'empirical-realist tendency' concerned with relating its analysis to the 'full empirical reality'. The empirical-realist tendency worked with 'real types' (*Realtypen*) instead of generic concepts and strove for 'empirical' instead of universal laws.[218]

Weber's resolution of the *Methodenstreit* between Menger and Schmoller was to be a vindication of the theoretical sciences – but one applied to the historical analysis of unique cultural configurations. The concepts of economics should therefore be considered as ideal types. The result of his affirmation of interest in the historical individual was that economic theory inevitably occupied a subsidiary role in methodological argument and in historical analysis.

Weber also argued the specificity of the cultural sciences from another angle. Of the four basic components of Weber's conception of sociology, we have so far dealt directly with two: the cultural complex of meaning and significance derived from historical values; and the ideal type. The other two were interpretative understanding and social action. In Weber's usage, these concepts came to have special meanings; and in the development of these meanings, his response to marginalist economics played a critical role.

When he first presented the categories of his interpretative sociology (and again in *Economy and Society*), Weber had already formulated the difference between it and the natural sciences – the constant preoccupation of the German idealist tradition – in terms

[217] *Gesammelte Aufsätze zur Wissenschaftslehre*, p. 187; *On the Methodology of the Social Sciences*, p. 87.
[218] C. Menger, *Untersuchungen über die Methode der Sozialwissenschaften und der Politischen Oekonomie insbesondere*, Leipzig, 1883, p. 34f.

of *Verstehen*. 'Human behaviour (whether "external" or "internal") displays relationships and regularities just as all events do. But what is peculiar only to human behaviour, at least in the full sense of this term, are relationships and regularities whose occurrence is clearly understandable.'[219] This conception is, so to speak, the other side of the cultural meaning-complex. It is this that now defines the central object of study (of interpretative sociology): human behaviour that is understandable in terms of the cultural significance attached to it by the behaving human. The emphasis is no longer on cultural significance as a guide in the choice among possible objects of study (which need not be meaningful human behaviour but can also be unique natural events and objects).

In German historicist discussion before Weber, *Verstehen* was considered to be active principally in two types of thought process. These processes are exemplified in Simmel's *Die Probleme der Geschichtsphilosophie*, which Weber himself named as the most important treatment of the concept.[220] One is what Weber termed 'direct observational understanding' (*aktuelles Verstehen*), which Simmel reserved for the understanding of the strictly theoretical contents of thought,[221] but which Weber extended to the understanding of emotional reactions also.[222] This is a type of uncomplicated, immediate inter-human communication, in which an act or verbal utterance is directly understood. But *Verstehen* was also involved in a more complex type of thought process, in which it was necessary to take account of the broader context of the phenomenon to be understood. This was the main problem for epistemological and methodological discussion of the role of *Verstehen* in historical and social analysis. 'Explanatory understanding', as Weber was to call it, was considered by Simmel and others to involve an emphatic grasp of a largely intuitive, artistic nature. The understanding historian was, and could only be, a kind of artist.[223]

---

[219] *Gesammelte Aufsätze zur Wissenschaftslehre*, p. 427f. Cf. *Economy and Society*: 'We can accomplish something which is never attainable in the natural sciences, namely the subjective understanding [*Verstehen*] of the action of the component individuals. . . . subjective understanding is the specific characteristic of sociological knowledge.' *Wirtschaft und Gesellschaft*, p. 11, *Economy and Society*, p. 15.

[220] *Wirtschaft und Gesellschaft*, p. 3; *Economy and Society*, p. 3.

[221] G. Simmel, *Die Probleme der Geschichtsphilosophie*, p. 14.

[222] *Wirtschaft und Gesellschaft*, p. 6; *Economy and Society*, p. 8.

[223] Simmel, *Die Probleme*, pp. 18–19.

We have already noticed that Weber was very hostile to this sort of aesthetic conception of history; it should be added that this hostility was a starting-point for the development of his idea of sociology. In opposition to intuitionist and aestheticist conceptions of history, Weber emphasized the role of conceptualization, i.e. ideal-typical conceptualization, and increasingly became more interested in typologies of such concepts than in their historiographical employment. Weber's development of an interpretative sociology meant that *Verstehen* was released from all connection with artistic empathy, and instead became linked to the concept of social action, to ideal-typical means-ends schemas.

Weber developed his logic of interpretative understanding in a reading of political and military history. The political and military historian is concerned with the explanatory understanding of events. He formulates goals for the actor – say Bismarck or Moltke – and then investigates whether the actual course of events can be explained as the means whereby the actor strove to realize his goals in the given situation.[224] In this respect, Weber's idea of *Verstehen* was part of his reaffirmation of traditional historiography. At the same time, however, it was also part of his clarification of marginalist economics as an ideal-typical construction of a cultural meaning-complex. Marginalist economics starts from the individual actor calculating how to realize his goals with a scarcity of means, and therein seeks what can be called an explanatory understanding of the regularities of the market. Weber asserted that this economic analysis was similar in kind to that of the political historian trying to explain the actions of Friedrich Wilhelm IV (with the help of an individual and not a general means-ends schema).[225]

Weber's interpretative sociology, devoted to the understanding of social action, was thus not conceived as an imaginative art. It is a generalization of marginalist economics. When in later works he describes his own project as 'sociology', he is referring to interpretative social science in general, of which marginalist economics constitutes, so to speak, the exemplary instance.[226] In *Economy and*

---

[224] See *Gesammelte Aufsätze zur Wissenschaftslehre*, p. 122f.

[225] *Gesammelte Aufsätze zur Wissenschaftslehre*, p. 130.

[226] In *Wirtschaft und Gesellschaft*, p. 14; *Economy and Society*, p. 19, Weber talks, for instance, of 'the laws of sociology, including those of economics'. In his report as treasurer to the first conference of the German Sociological Society, Weber considered the establishment of special sections within it, for instance of

Society, Weber speaks of sociology and history as 'the empirical sciences of action', as distinguished from 'the dogmatic disciplines in that area, such as jurisprudence, logic, ethics, aesthetics'.[227] Sociology and history, then, differ in that the former deals primarily with types of action. Weber clarifies the nature of interpretative sociology by referring to marginalist economics, which, in its study of the economy from the subjective point of view of the individual actor, provides a model for explanatory understanding. 'Sociology, just like history, at first explains things "pragmatically" from the rational relationships of behaviour. This is for example how economic science [*die Sozialökonomik*] proceeds, with its rational construction of "economic man". Interpretative sociology does just the same.'[228] 'The concepts and the "laws" of pure economic theory' illustrate the achievements and potential of an interpretative sociology.[229]

In keeping with his reliance on subjectivist economics, Weber's concept of 'action' deviates from the everyday sense of the word. The opposite of action in Weber's sense is not passivity, or failure to act. On the contrary, 'failure to act and passive acquiescence' are explicitly included in 'action', which encompasses any instance of behaviour to which the individual 'attaches a subjective meaning'.[230] In so far as this subjective meaning takes into account the behaviour of other people and orients itself accordingly, 'action' is 'social'. The study of social action, therefore, is not primarily concerned with actual, ongoing behaviour but rather with actors' 'orientations' and subjective meanings.[231] Thus Weber maintains that 'the definition of economic action . . . must bring out the fact that all "economic processes" and objects are characterized as such entirely by the *meaning* they have for human action in such roles as ends, means, obstacles, and by-products. . . . The production of goods, prices, or even the "subjective valuation" of goods, if they are empirical processes, are far from being merely psychic phenomena. But underlying this misleading phrase is a correct insight. It is a fact

statisticians and theoretical economists. *Gesammelte Aufsätze zur Soziologie und Sozialpolitik*, p. 433.

[227] *Wirtschaft und Gesellschaft*, p. 4; *Economy and Society*, p. 4.
[228] *Gesammelte Aufsätze zur Wissenschaftslehre*, p. 429.
[229] *Wirtschaft und Gesellschaft*, pp. 7, 14, 15; *Economy and Society*, pp. 9, 19, 21.
[230] *Wirtschaft und Gesellschaft*, pp. 3, 16; *Economy and Society*, pp. 4, 22.
[231] *Wirtschaft und Gesellschaft*, pp. 17–18; *Economy and Society*, p. 24f.

that these phenomena have a peculiar type of subjective *meaning*. This alone defines the unity of the corresponding processes, and this alone makes them accessible to subjective interpretation.'[232]

The Marxist concept corresponding to Weber's 'action' is *practice*. The difference between the two can be illustrated by quotation from Marx's critique of Adolph Wagner, who, although one of the (older) German historical economists and not an adherent of the Austrian marginalist school, nonetheless held certain subjectivist conceptions of value. Wagner had written: 'It is a natural drive of man to bring the relation in which internal and external goods stand vis-à-vis his needs to a distinct consciousness and understanding. This is achieved by the estimation (evaluation) in which value is attributed to the goods, or respectively, the things of the external world . . .' Marx commented on these sentiments as follows: 'But for a professorial schoolmaster, the relations of men to nature are not initially practical, i.e., relations established by deeds, but theoretical . . . But in no sense do men begin by "standing in this theoretical relation to the things of the external world". They begin, like every animal, by eating, drinking, etc., i.e., not by "standing" in a relation, but by actively responding, by mastering certain things of the external world by deeds, and thus satisfying their needs (i.e., they begin with production).'[233] For Marx, the basic aspect of economic practice is the ongoing process of production, structured by a given combination of forces and relations of production. For Weber, and for the marginalist economists, by contrast, economic action (*Wirtschaft*) means essentially 'the prudent choice between ends'.[234]

11. Ideology in Politics and in the Age of Capitalism

So far, we have mostly observed the great differences exhibited by the formation of Weber's sociology with respect to our general

---

[232] *Wirtschaft und Gesellschaft*, p. 43; *Economy and Society*, p. 64. Emphasis in original.

[233] K. Marx, 'Marginal notes on Adolph Wagner's *Lehrbuch der politischen Ökonomie*', *MEW* 19, pp. 362–3; English translation in *Theoretical Practice*, No. 5 (1972), pp. 45–6. Emphasis omitted.

[234] *Wirtschaft und Gesellschaft*, p. 44; *Economy and Society*, p. 65. Emphasis omitted. I have commented on this very important difference in another context, 'Social Practice, Social Action, Social Magic', op. cit.

pattern. To what extent, then, can Weber be seen as a critic of political economy in terms of another pattern of social determination, the 'ideological community'? We have just seen how, far from criticizing it, he in fact modelled his sociology on liberal marginalist economics. Such qualifications as he did make of the latter seem rather to have been prompted by considerations of power and politics. In *Economy and Society*, for example, he remarks: 'For purposes of economic theory, it is the marginal *consumer* who determines the direction of production. In actual fact, given the distribution of power, this is only true in a limited sense for the modern situation. To a large degree, even though the consumer has to be in a position to buy, his wants are "awakened" and "directed" by the entrepreneur.'[235] On another occasion we are told: 'Political actions and structures, especially the state and the state-guaranteed legal system, are of primary importance among these non-economic events [which influence economic ones and which should be studied by economic sociology].'[236] The last remark, however, was made in the context of a discussion of economic policy and against the explicit background of the role of the state in the war economy.

Below we shall examine Weber's view of the context of the economy rather more closely. But first of all we should take note of the rather special character of Weber's political sociology, centred on his typology of domination in *Economy and Society*. In relation to previous political theory it is in fact very original; yet at the same time it constitutes a manifestation of our sociological pattern. Typologies of domination are part of the long tradition of political philosophy, in Europe going back at least to ancient Greek philosophy. In the classical tradition such typologies were usually based on the number of rulers, one, few, many (all citizens, the people). This distinction was often coupled with another, between legitimate,

[235] *Wirtschaft und Gesellschaft*, p. 65; *Economy and Society*, p. 92. Cf. *Wirtschaft und Gesellschaft*, pp. 69, 71; *Economy and Society*, pp. 97, 99f. It should be noted that Weber's account of the limitations of marginalist theory, emphasizing the role of advertising, does not go very far. Neither the marginal consumer nor the advertising director can explain, for instance, the recurrence of crises in a capitalist economy. No mere combination of marginalism plus comments on the distribution of power can account for the functioning of capitalism. I have dealt with this problem elsewhere, *Klasser och ekonomiska system*, Staffanstorp, 1971, p. 47f.

[236] *Gesammelte Aufsätze zur Wissenschaftslehre*, p. 524; *On the Methodology of the Social Sciences*, p. 45. Note that Weber here puts economic sociology on one side and the economic interpretation of history and society on the other.

law-bound governments, and illegitimate despotic regimes. This tradition was active in Montesquieu and the Enlightenment and it is continued today in modern liberal theory, with its distinction between democracy and dictatorship. After the French Revolution, as we saw in the fourth chapter, a new theory of politics emerged in the sociology of the pioneers. Political power and authority (if stable) were held on to derive from, and were distinguished by their basis in, the different kinds of dominant activity in the society or different sorts of social relations. In the German idealism of the time, political structures were held to be expressions of particular national cultures. Weber's typology of domination breaks sharply with all these types of conceptualization, and instead distinguishes between the different kinds of common values upon which stable domination is based.

From his point of view, the persons living under a given instance of domination can also be conceived as an ideological community. By domination (*Herrschaft*) Weber means 'the probability that a command with a given specific content will be obeyed by a given group of persons'.[237] To the interpretative sociologist, however, 'the merely external fact of the order being obeyed is not sufficient to signify domination in our sense; we cannot overlook the meaning of the fact that the command is accepted as a "valid" norm'. Therefore, the conduct of the dominated occurs 'as if the ruled had made the content of the command the maxim of their conduct for its very own sake'.[238] They may do this for a variety of reasons, ranging from expectations of material advantage to ideals, but a basic aspect of stable domination is the belief of the ruled in the legitimacy of the rule of the rulers.[239] Weber is not interested in illegitimate domination, in different degrees of legitimacy, or in different combinations of legitimacy and illegitimacy (for example where, among different groups under domination, some acknowledge its legitimacy and others deny it).[240] An analysis of domination

---

[237] *Wirtschaft und Gesellschaft*, p. 38; *Economy and Society*, p. 53.

[238] *Wirtschaft und Gesellschaft*, p. 695; *Economy and Society*, p. 946. Cf. p. 159, resp. 215, and on p. 38, resp. 53, the separation of 'discipline' as a special kind of obedience.

[239] *Wirtschaft und Gesellschaft*, p. 157; *Economy and Society*, p. 213.

[240] This possibility is obscured by Weber's decision to start his argument from the point of view of the kind of legitimacy to which the rulers appeal. However, he explains in a footnote: 'What is important is the fact that in a given case the

in terms of the beliefs of the ruled in its legitimacy can, on the other hand, be seen as a direct application of the specific, 'ideal-typical' concentration of interpretative sociology on actions based on a 'clearly self-conscious meaning':[241] one clear meaning of obedience is, presumably, belief in the legitimacy of the orders and commands obeyed. Within this framework, Weber distinguishes legal, traditional and charismatic *Herrschaft*: 'There are three pure types of legitimate domination. The validity of the claim to legitimacy may be based on:

1. Rational grounds – *resting on a belief* in the legality of enacted rules and the right of those elevated to authority under such rules to issue commands (legal authority).

2. Traditional grounds – *resting on an established belief* in the sanctity of immemorial traditions and on the legitimacy of those executing authority under them (traditional authority); or finally,

3. Charismatic grounds – *resting on devotion* to the exceptional sanctity, heroism or exemplary character of an individual person, and of the normative patterns of order revealed or ordained by him (charismatic authority).'[242]

The main characteristic weaknesses and strengths of Weber's deservedly famous sociology of *Herrschaft* may briefly be noted here.[243] One fundamental weakness is that his subjectivist orientation, together with his conception of sociology as *Kategorienlehre* (that is, as taxonomy rather than theory), precludes any analysis of the actual operation of the different systems of domination. Weber does not investigate the mechanisms and processes that ensure the production (or transformation) of particular systems of domination, but on the contrary dismisses factual regularities of submission in

---

particular claim to legitimacy is to a significant degree and according to its type treated as "valid"; that this fact confirms the position of the persons claiming authority and that it helps them to determine the choice of means of exercise' (*Wirtschaft und Gesellschaft*, p. 158; *Economy and Society*, p. 214). Cf. further below.

[241] *Wirtschaft und Gesellschaft*, p. 15; *Economy and Society*, pp. 21–22.

[242] *Wirtschaft und Gesellschaft*, p. 159; *Economy and Society*, p. 215. Emphasis added.

[243] Weber's sociology of domination is propounded in two passages in *Wirtschaft und Gesellschaft*, pp. 157–222 and 691–922; *Economy and Society*, pp. 212–499 and 941–1210. See also the exposition of social action oriented towards a conception of legitimate order, *Wirtschaft und Gesellschaft*, pp. 22–7; *Economy and Society*, pp. 31–37.

order to concentrate exclusively on legitimating beliefs. At the beginning of his chapter on types of domination, he states: 'In everyday life these relationships [of domination], like others, are governed by *custom*' – that is, 'rules devoid of any external sanction by which the actor voluntarily abides, whether his motivation lies in the fact that he merely fails to think about it, that it is more comfortable to conform, or whatever else the reason may be'[244] – and 'calculations of material advantage. But custom, personal advantage, purely affective or ideal motives of solidarity do not form a sufficiently reliable basis for a given domination. In addition there is normally a further element, the belief in legitimacy.'[245] However, it seems in fact that the maintenance of a given system of domination is based fundamentally on the maintenance of particular 'customs' among the dominated population, by means of a differential shaping of knowledge and ignorance (of alternative social orders, among other things), of visibility of performances and compensations, of self-confidence and so on.

A second noteworthy weakness in Weber's conception of domination is that legitimate domination is opposed not by illegitimate domination, but only by a particular form of non-legitimate domination. Legitimate domination is explicitly distinguished only from the 'market-type power relation' (*marktmässige Machtverhältnis*), or obedience prompted by a rational realization of the stronger market position of the other.[246] Weber fails to consider cases where, because of fear of one type or another, commands are obeyed by individuals or groups who nevertheless deny the legitimacy of the issuing authority (landowner, capitalist, military and so on). Fear of physical violence is only one kind of fear, but it is noteworthy in this context that despite his keen eye for the importance of forms of military organization in history (for instance, in his brilliant comparative analysis of Oriental and Occidental, ancient and mediaeval cities),[247] and despite his

[244] *Wirtschaft und Gesellschaft*, p. 21; *Economy and Society*, p. 29.

[245] *Wirtschaft und Gesellschaft*, p. 157; *Economy and Society*, p. 213.

[246] *Wirtschaft und Gesellschaft*, p. 695; *Economy and Society*, p. 946; cf. *Wirtschaft und Gesellschaft*, pp. 692–4, 157, and *Economy and Society*, pp. 943–5, 212f.

[247] For a summary, see *Wirtschaft und Gesellschaft*, pp. 960–1; *Economy and Society*, pp. 1260–2. See further, n. 282 below. In his survey of cities, Weber did briefly refer to illegitimate rulership, to the ancient tyrants and to the mediaeval Italian *signorie*. See *Wirtschaft und Gesellschaft*, pp. 995–8, *Economy and Society*,

imperialist politics, Weber allots no proper importance to a consideration of violence and the means of repression in his analysis of why commands are obeyed. In fact he mentions the problem only to by-pass it. This can be seen most clearly in a passage in 'Politics as a Vocation' where he writes: '"Every state is founded on force," Trotsky said at Brest-Litovsk. That is indeed right. . . . Today the relation between the state and violence is an especially intimate one.' He then goes on to dismiss the real issue: 'In the past, the most varied institutions – beginning with the sib – have known the use of physical force as quite normal. Today, however, we have to say that a state is a human community that (successfully) *claims* the monopoly of the legitimate use of physical force within a given territory.'[248] In Weber's perspective, there is really no room for an analysis of the functions and operation of the repressive apparatus of the state in modern systems of domination.

Weber would not deny the central importance of the repressive state apparatus in modern capitalist society. A passage from a late part of *Economy and Society* shows that the lessons of the German Revolution of 1918 revealed it to him very clearly: 'Willingness to work on the part of factory labour has been primarily determined by a combination of the transfer of responsibility for maintenance to the workers personally and the corresponding powerful indirect compulsion to work, as symbolized in the English workhouse system, and it has permanently remained oriented to the compulsory guarantee of the property system. This is demonstrated by the marked decline in willingness to work at the present time which resulted from the collapse of this coercive power in the [1918] revolution.'[249] Yet this insight was never incorporated into his sociology of domination. A basic reason for this seems to be the particular *class character* of Weber's sociology (see further below). His sociology of domination was a sociology 'from above', concerned nearly exclusively with one side of the domination/subordin-

---

pp. 1315–19. Interestingly enough, however, their illegitimacy, and that of the associated *popolo* of the mediaeval Italian cities, was defined in relation to previous political and religious principles and to superior – imperial and papal – powers, and *not* in relation to the experience of the ruled (*Wirtschaft und Gesellschaft*, pp. 985, 995, 998; *Economy and Society*, pp. 1302, 1316, 1319).

[248] *Politische Schriften*, p. 506; *From Max Weber*, p. 78 (emphasis ours). Cf. *Wirtschaft und Gesellschaft*, pp. 657–64; *Economy and Society*, pp. 901–10.

[249] *Wirtschaft und Gesellschaft*, p. 114; *Economy and Society*, p. 153.

ation relationship. Weber analyzed the variant forms of the organization of domination, but not the means whereby subordination was ensured. 'We are primarily interested in "domination" in so far as it is combined with "administration",'[250] he stated at the beginning of his historical survey of the main types of domination – legal-bureaucratic, traditional (patrimonial and feudal), and charismatic. His specification of the modern system of domination starts with a blunt description of 'the functioning of modern officialdom',[251] and, in general, his historical survey devotes itself to a description of the various forms of administration. It is only within these forms that he discusses the mechanisms of subordination – the subordination of bureaucratic officials, of feudal vassals, of patrimonial servants and of the unstable following of the charismatic leader. Weber's analysis is not designed to elucidate the various mechanisms of subordination whereby the working class in bourgeois democracies is led to acquiesce in the domination of the bourgeoisie, with its powers and privileges, or the means whereby the peasantries of pre-capitalist societies were effectively dominated by their 'patrimonial' or feudal lords.[252] Weber's political writings paid more attention to the utilization and satisfaction of material interests than to processes of legitimation in the exercise of domination. But here too his analysis was angled 'from above', concerning itself with the ways in which the ruling classes of Germany and Russia organized their power, or with the possibilities for the bourgeoisie to enlist the support of workers and peasants against the old feudal order, but not with the means whereby the subordina-

[250] *Wirtschaft und Gesellschaft*, p. 697; *Economy and Society*, p. 948. Cf. *Wirtschaft und Gesellschaft*, p. 160; *Economy and Society*, p. 217.

[251] *Wirtschaft und Gesellschaft*, p. 702; *Economy and Society*, p. 956. Cf. *Wirtschaft und Gesellschaft*, p. 157; *Economy and Society*, p. 212–13.

[252] This is probably most clearly admitted by Weber in a passage where he does mention instances of domination that are illegitimate from the point of view of the ruled: 'Furthermore, a system of domination may – as often occurs in practice – be so completely protected, on the one hand by the obvious community of interests between the chief and his administrative staff (bodyguards, pretorians, "red" or "white" guards) as opposed to the subjects, on the other by the helplessness of the latter, that it can afford to drop even the pretense of a claim of legitimacy. But even then *the mode of legitimation of the relation between chief and his staff* may vary widely according to the type of basis of the relation of the authority between them, and, as will be shown, this variation *is highly significant for the structure of domination.*' *Wirtschaft und Gesellschaft*, pp. 158–9; *Economy and Society*, p. 214 (emphasis added).

tion of workers and peasants was or could be ensured, under a new bourgeois order.[253]

Thus blinkered, Weber quite naturally believed that modern bureaucracy could be controlled only from above. Where Lenin relied on the revolutionary working class, Weber looked for a charismatic, plebiscitary leader.[254] David Beetham has shown very clearly how this idea was related to Weber's bourgeois class position, as the expression of a search for a forceful personality capable of integrating the 'propertyless masses' into capitalist society. and giving them 'leadership'.[255]

On the other hand, this weakness was also Weber's strength. With an established position in Wilhelmine Germany, personally connected not only with the bourgeoisie but also with the state bureaucracy and with the Prussian academic intelligentsia, Weber was much more familiar with legal and administrative structures than any Marxist. Not surprisingly, therefore, his analysis of bureaucracy and other administrative apparatuses is far superior in depth and detail to that of either Marx, Engels or Lenin. Further- more, his analysis – unlike his views of the bureaucratic fate of modern society, and his longing for a non-bureaucratic leader 'in secure [i.e. propertied] circumstances' and motivated by a 'purely personal conviction'[256] that was above the class struggle – was saved by its very one-sidedness from the likely negative effects of his class position, which would surely have been felt if he had undertaken a comprehensive analysis of the relations of domination and subord- ination and their contradictions in modern capitalist societies. The strength of Weber's *Herrschaftssoziologie* consists in its analysis of the institutions, roles and processes in which the ideological com- munity that founds them are crystallized. As a scientific sociologist, Weber treats the processes of legitimation not as 'a matter of

---

[253] Beetham, who particularly emphasizes the difference between Weber's sociological treatises and his political tracts, misses the fundamental continuity in the sociologist's analysis of domination (Beetham, op. cit., p. 256f, chs. 6–7). Weber's concern is always, strictly speaking, with the organization of persistent regimes rather than with explanations of the persistence of regimes.

[254] For an interesting juxtaposition of Weber's and Lenin's conceptions of bureaucracy on the eve of the Russian and German revolutions, see Eril Olin Wright, 'To Control or to Smash Bureaucracy: Weber and Lenin on Politics, the State, and Bureaucracy', *Berkeley Journal of Sociology*, vol. XIX (1974–5).

[255] Beetham, op. cit., p. 240f.

[256] Weber, *Politische Schriften*, p. 306.

theoretical or philosophical speculation', but as constituting 'the basis of the very real differences in the empirical structure of domination'. Weber's object of study in his sociology of domination is the ideological community of legitimating beliefs, and he undertakes the investigation of its operations in a systematic and empirically scrupulous manner, that is, as a scientific study of a scientific object.[257]

Pareto and Mosca too were concerned with the sociology of domination; the latter's notion of the 'political formula', and, rather more remotely, the former's 'derivation', have certain affinities with Weber's notion of the grounds of legitimation.[258] But compared with these, Weber's work represents a real scientific advance – over the very general reflections of Mosca, and over Pareto's preoccupation with the basic ideological situation of the members of the ruling elite. Weber's achievement was to analyze important aspects of the means whereby the domination of the 'ruling minority' over the 'ruled "masses"' was organized: that is, how the ideological community was institutionalized and how it concretely functioned as a pattern of social determination. Patriarchal and bureaucratic domination 'both ultimately find their inner support in the subjects'

---

[257] *Wirtschaft und Gesellschaft*, p. 701; *Economy and Society*, p. 953. Cf. *Wirtschaft und Gesellschaft*, pp. 158–9; *Economy and Society*, p. 214. Beetham is therefore correct to criticize the liberal apologetics of Gustav Schmidt, *Deutscher Historismus und der Übergang zur parlamentarischen Demokratie*, Lübeck and Hamburg, 1964: 'Schmidt's interpretation is mistaken in this respect, that he makes Weber out, in his theory of legitimacy, to be engaged in a philosophical rather than a sociological enterprise. Weber was nowhere concerned to give the kind of philosophical account of legitimacy that Schmidt portrays, and that is characteristic of the English sources he cites (notably Lindsay). Weber certainly wished to prescribe certain types of institution and political leadership as preferable to others, but he nowhere suggested that such institutions or leaders could only be *legitimate* if they accorded with a particular constitutional principle' (Beetham, op. cit., p. 115).

[258] Weber shared much of the elite theorists' contempt for and fear of 'emotional' masses (see, for example, *Politische Schriften*, p. 221f; English translation appended to *Economy and Society*, pp. 1459–60). His *Herrschaftssoziologie* appraised the advantages of a ruling minority in a way not unlike that of Mosca (*Wirtschaft und Gesellschaft*, p. 700; *Economy and Society*, p. 952). Weber shared Mosca's appreciation of the wealthy and leisured rentier as a political leader, though he did not hold that wealth and leisure in themselves necessarily made the true aristocrat (*Politische Schriften*, p. 305f; cf. ibid., pp. 334–5, 207–8, and *Economy and Society*, pp. 1427, 1447).

compliance with norms'.[259]

In Weber's sociology of law too, the ideological community occupies a central position. The study of its operation defines the sociological as opposed to the juridical point of view as regards to law. In contrast to the juridical question (what is intrinsically valid as law?) the sociologist asks: 'What *actually* happens in a group owing to the *probability* that persons engaged in social action [*Gemeinschaftshandeln*], especially those exerting a socially relevant amount of power, subjectively consider certain norms as valid and practically act according to them, in other words orient their conduct towards these norms [or in plainer words, belong *de facto* to a community of common norms]?'[260]

The ideological community is at the core of Weber's political and legal sociology. But what field of sociology is at the centre of Weber's interest in his historical and social studies? It is hardly politics and law, and this is noteworthy both because of Weber's original legal education and because of his political passions. In his Inaugural Address at Freiburg, Weber had stated as bluntly as possible that the state and the nation as a political entity constituted the supreme values, to which economic and other concerns should be subordinated. Wolfgang Mommsen has definitively shown in his study of Weber's politics that this commitment remained basic to the sociologist throughout his life. Thus, one might reasonably expect a predominating scholarly interest in the state, the nation, the empire, their historical formation, their modern characteristics and problems. Instead, Weber focused on *capitalism*.

When Jaffe, Sombart and Weber assumed the editorship of *Archiv für Sozialwissenschaft und Sozialpolitik* in 1904, they presented their aim as the treatment of all phenomena 'of economic and general social life from the point of view of their revolutionization by capitalism'.[261] Much later, in the foreword to his essays on the sociology of religion, Weber referred to 'the most fateful force in

[259] *Wirtschaft und Gesellschaft*, p. 739; *Economy and Society*, p. 1006.

[260] *Wirtschaft und Gesellschaft*, p. 233; *Economy and Society*, p. 311.

[261] 'Geleitwort der Herausgeber', *Archiv für Sozialwissenschaft und Sozialpolitik* (New Series), vol. 1 (1904), p. II. This meant a broadening of the previous central concern of the journal, which had been the 'Workers' Question'. Lindenlaub, op. cit., p. 281 n. judges the editorial foreword to have been written by Weber.

our modern life, *capitalism*'.[262] His comparative studies of religion, of 'the economic ethic of the world religions', were concerned with preconditions of the rise of modern Western capitalism.

This concentration on capitalism should be taken in a strong and strictly economic sense. Weber regarded capitalism as related to a vast cultural process of 'rationalization', which included not only the modern bureaucratic state but also 'rational harmonious music' and 'the rational use of the Gothic vault' in architecture.[263] But he was himself primarily interested in the emergence of rational capitalism, and, in opposition to Sombart, emphasized that this was not simply an aspect of a general process of rationalization. Paying respect to the 'judicious and effective observations' of Sombart, he wrote: 'It might thus seem that the development of the spirit of capitalism is best understood as part of the development of rationalism as a whole, and could be deduced from the fundamental position of rationalism on the basic problems of life. . . . But any serious attempt to carry this thesis through makes it evident that such a simple way of putting the question will not work, simply because of the fact that the history of rationalism shows a development which by no means follows parallel lines in the various departments of life.'[264] It is therefore rather misleading to characterize Weber as a student and critic of 'the age of bureaucracy': what he dealt with was the age of capitalism.

Weber's definition of capitalism was a particular blend of elements taken from Marx, marginalism, historicism, and from the aristocratic tincture of the German academic intelligentsia. The interest in capitalism as a particular, historical economic system is of Marxian inspiration. The notion of capitalism played virtually no role in the characterizations by the older generation of German historical economists – Durkheim's teachers – of economic systems

[262] M. Weber, *Gesammelte Aufsätze zur Religionssoziologie*, Tübingen, 1920, vol. I, p. 4. Unlike other collections of his essays, this one was put together by Max Weber himself. The author's foreword to the collection and the essay *The Protestant Ethic and the Spirit of Capitalism* are translated into English under the latter title (London, 1967; 1st ed. 1930). The above reference is on p. 17 of this edition.

[263] *Gesammelte Aufsätze zur Religionssoziologie*, p. 2; *The Protestant Ethic and the Spirit of Capitalism*, pp. 14–15.

[264] *Gesammelte Aufsätze zur Religionssoziologie*, p. 61; English ed. pp. 76–7. Emphasis omitted. Cf. p. 10f; English ed. p. 24f.

and epochs.[265] The reception of the Marxian concept of capitalism by Weber's and Sombart's generation of historical economists and sociologists was part of their emancipation from the confused amalgam of emanationist idealism and naturalistic organicism, of extreme empiricism and bureaucratic moralism, typical of the earlier historical economists from Roscher and Hildebrand to Schmoller. Marx had, in the words of Sombart, combined the achievements of classical economics with those of the historical school and 'made it possible to deal systematically with economic life on a historical basis by taking the economic system as the object of investigation . . . he was the first to acknowledge the prevailing economic system of our time in its specificity . . . and thus became the discoverer of capitalism (as has justly been said).'[266]

Towards the turn of the century, capitalism became a major theme of German intellectual debate. Weber's friend, the Christian social reform politician Friedrich Naumann, wrote in 1911: 'Just as the French have their theme: what was the great Revolution?, so our national destiny has given us our theme for a long time to come: what is capitalism?'[267] The study of capitalism did not mean an acceptance or even necessarily an understanding of Marx's concept. Capitalism, in German historicist thought, became the most significant 'historical individual', or unique cultural configuration, of the epoch. From the very beginning of its employment outside the Marxist fold, capitalism was approached from the point of view of the 'spirit' it expressed. Best read in Marx and at the time least distant from the labour movement was Werner Sombart, whose *Der moderne Kapitalismus* first appeared in 1902. There Sombart maintained that economic systems should be explained and analyzed in terms of the particular 'motive complexes' (*Motivreihen*) prevailing in them, and consequently posited a 'historical psychology' as the basis of historical economic studies.[268] Even earlier, Simmel had

[265] This is one of the main theses of Lindenlaub's study, op. cit., p. 285f.

[266] Sombart, 'Karl Marx und die soziale Wissenschaft', p. 446.

[267] Quoted from Lindenlaub, p. 280 n.

[268] W. Sombart, *Der moderne Kapitalismus*, Leipzig, 1902, pp. xxi–xxii. Sombart's major study of the rise of the spirit of capitalism is *Der Bourgeois*, Leipzig, 1913. Parsons' contention that Sombart's study of capitalism constitutes a 'radically idealistic emanationist theory' (*The Structure of Social Action*, p. 722), however, is hardly correct. Sombart was an idealist, but his analysis of the rise of the capitalist spirit certainly did not mean that 'the conditional elements disappear' as they do in such a theory according to Parsons' definition (p. 82). On the

presented his cultural philosophy of capitalism, *The Philosophy of Money*, thus: 'This basic insight can be expressed from a methodological aspect as follows: to construct a foundation for historical materialism (which should more precisely be described as historical sensualism) such that economic life would still be included among the original causes of spiritual culture, but these economic forces would be acknowledged as the product of deeper evaluation and tendencies, of psychological or even metaphysical assumptions.'[269]

It was as part of this historicist reception of Marx that Weber in 1904 wrote his famous essay on *The Protestant Ethic and the Spirit of Capitalism*. He was thus in good company when he asserted: 'The question of the motive forces [*Triebkräfte*] in the expansion of modern capitalism is not in the first instance a question of the origin of the capital sums which were available for capitalistic uses, but above all, of the development of the spirit of capitalism.'[270] The idea of capitalism is, in fact, the most significant Marxian influence on Weber. Weber's historicist epistemology was, as we have seen above, completely alien to the theory of historical materialism. But he took from Marx a number of hunches and insights, and, above all, the notion of capitalism as a focus of study and concern.[271]

---

contrary, Sombart designated and actually studied what he saw as three basic conditions of capitalist development, given 'the will to capitalism': the state, particularly a military apparatus providing a market and creating discipline, technology, and thirdly, production of precious metals – W. Sombart, *Der modern Kapitalismus* (2nd revised and enlarged edition), Munich and Leipzig, 1916, vol. I, p. 332; cf. p. 25, and chs. 21–35.

[269] G. Simmel, *Die Philosophie des Geldes*, Leipzig, 1900, p. x. Simmel did not, however, assign this task to sociology, but to cultural philosophy. Simmel's sociology rather focussed on the forms of social interaction. G. Simmel, *Soziologie* (3rd ed.), Munich and Leipzig, 1923. For an English selection of Simmel's sociology see K. Wolff, ed., *The Sociology of Georg Simmel*, New York, 1964.

[270] *Gesammelte Aufsätze zur Religionssociologie*, p. 53; *The Protestant Ethic and the Spirit of Capitalism*, p. 68.

[271] The most important example of this kind of inspiration in Weber's writings after his recovery from his breakdown is probably his interest in the different 'religious propensities' of different strata. The latter are not classes in the Marxist sense, not only because they include what Marxists also call strata in distinction to classes (bureaucracy, intelligentsia), but above all because when Weber subsumes under the same concept such categories as 'peasant', 'petty-bourgeois', 'nobility' – in other words, groups from different modes of production and thus different classes in the Marxist sense. (*Wirtschaft und Gesellschaft*, pp. 368–404; *Economy and Society*, pp. 468–517. Cf. *Gesammelte Aufsätze zur Religionssoziologie*, pp. 253ff.) On the other hand, in a summary of what strata were the primary agents of

This notion was even more novel to marginalism than to the older historical economics, since it belonged to a theory and study of historical economic systems. The notion of capitalism was also part of a distinction between capitalism and commodity exchange, which is customarily glossed over in marginalism.[272] Weber's economic typology, on the other hand, distinguished sharply between 'budgetary management' (*Haushalt*) and 'profit-making' (*Erwerben*), between wealth (*Vermögen*) and capital, and between the calculation of the budgetary unit (the household) and capitalist calculation: 'As distinguished from the calculations appropriate to a budgetary unit, the capital accounting and calculations of the market entrepreneur are oriented not to marginal utility, but to profitability.'[273] Weber defined capitalism as 'the pursuit of *profit*, and forever *renewed* profit, of *profitability* [*Rentabilität*] by means of continuous, rational capitalist enterprise'.[274] It is this Marxian-inspired notion of capitalism as production for the sake of ever increasing profitable production that Weber's notion of 'calling' furnishes with a motivational basis. Labour, in the sense both of the activity of the entrepreneurs and the work of their employees, is performed 'as if it were an absolute end in itself, a calling'.[275] It is in the 'sort of life, where a man exists for the sake of his business'[276] that the Protestant ethic of worldly asceticism makes sense. This is an economy geared to the production of surplus-value, as Weber

---

the world religions, Weber was in fact not attacking Marxist theory (whatever he might have thought himself): 'To be sure, all these types must not be taken as exponents of their own occupational or material "class interest" but rather as the ideological carriers of the kind of ethical or salvation doctrine which rather readily conformed to their social position.' (*Wirtschaft und Gesellschaft*, p. 401; *Economy and Society*, p. 513.) This theoretical compatibility with historical materialism does not mean that Weber presents a very illuminating class analysis, as the notion of 'carrier' is used very narrowly. We do not, for instance, learn very much about the social basis of Buddhism, either by conceiving it as an expression of the 'class interest' of the 'mendicant monk wandering through the world' or as the doctrine which readily conforms to his 'social position'.

[272] This point is substantiated and developed in my *Klasser och ekonomiska system*, p. 44f.

[273] *Wirtschaft und Gesellschaft*, p. 65; *Economy and Society*, p. 92.

[279] *Gesammelte Aufsätze zur Religionssociologie*, p. 4; *The Protestant Ethic and the Spirit of Capitalism*, p. 17. Emphasis in original.

[275] Ibid., p. 46; English ed. p. 62. Cf. p. 50f; English ed. p. 65f.

[276] Ibid., p. 54; English ed. p. 70.

explicitly pointed out,[277] but it is hardly the economic world of the marginalist economists: the Puritan ethic would make little sense in an account of, say, Philip Wicksteed's Edwardian housewife.

Weber as a student of capitalism concentrated on its ideological preconditions, on the rise of its 'spirit'. There are indeed observations in *Economy and Society* about other aspects of it, for example, the importance of a 'rational' bureaucratic state apparatus, including a 'rational' legal system, to a modern capitalist economy and their mutual interrelation.[278] But given that *Economy and Society* was written as the first part of an encyclopaedia of economics, limited attention is in fact paid to this sort of relation. Weber's major empirical studies of the rise of capitalism concerned rather the relationship of religion and economic ideology. He even said of his study of the Protestant ethic: 'The following study may thus perhaps in a modest way form a contribution to the understanding of the manner in which ideas become effective forces in history.'[279] Weber was, however, careful to deny that he intended 'to substitute for a one-sided materialistic an equally one-sided spiritualistic causal interpretation of culture and of history. Each is equally possible, but each, if it does not serve as the preparation, but as the conclusion of an investigation, accomplishes equally little in the interest of historical truth.'[280]

Our chief interest in this context is not with the substance of Weber's statements concerning the history of capitalism, but rather with their position in the structure of his sociology. In *Economy and Society*, Weber is perfectly explicit on this point (speaking here of the necessary character of any sociological analysis of socialism): 'The real sociological investigation begins with the question: What motives determine and lead the individual members and participants in this socialistic community to behave in such a way that the community came into being in the first place and that it continues to exist? Any form of functional analysis which proceeds from the whole to the parts can accomplish only a preliminary preparation for this investigation – a preparation, the utility and indispensability of which, if properly carried out, is naturally beyond

---

[277] Ibid., p. 200 n; English ed., p. 282.

[278] For instance, *Wirtschaft und Gesellschaft*, pp. 164–82, 247–55, 814–26; *Economy and Society*, pp. 223–40, 327–37, 1090–1104.

[279] *Gesammelte Aufsätze zur Religionssociologie*, p. 82; English ed., p. 90.

[280] Ibid., pp. 205–6; English ed., p. 183. Cf. ibid., p. 83; English ed., p. 91.

question.'[281] Psychological reductionism was excluded by Weber. A sociological investigation therefore meant a study of the historical system of values, the historical ideological community determining the behaviour of individuals. Like the market, the ideological community might, of course, be more or less significantly affected by various external factors. Weber's preoccupation with the spirit of capitalism and his interpretative sociology are fully compatible.[282]

To an interpretative sociologist, with his specific objective of seeking an 'explanatory understanding' of the motives of the actors, of the subjective meaning they attach to their behaviour, the development of a capitalist ideology naturally occupies the centre of an analysis of the rise of capitalism. Since 'the magical and religious forces, and the ethical ideas of duty based upon them, have in the past always been among the most important formative influences on conduct',[283] the study of religion was Weber's main empirical interest in his later years. His preoccupation with religion rather than, say, ethical ideas or social-philosophical conceptions in general, was directly related to his keen observation of the organization and institutionalization of ideological patterns of determination. He explicitly emphasized the incomparably greater efficacy (for believers) of a religiously-based morality over ethical philosophies.[284]

[281] *Wirtschaft und Gesellschaft*, p. 13; *Economy and Society*, p. 18.

[282] On the other hand, this is hardly the case with that part of *Economy and Society* where Weber deals with quite a different aspect of the problem that concerned him in his studies of the economic ethic of religions, the problem 'of the origin of the Western bourgeois class' (*Gesammelte Aufsätze zur Religionssoziologie*, p. 10; English ed., p. 24) – the specificity and development of the Western medieval city, the city commune where the burghers ruled themselves. Weber there highlights the bureaucracy necessitated by irrigation in China, Western Asia and Egypt and its effect on the distribution of military power – its firm concentration in the hands of the central ruler, stifling the rise of autonomous cities. In his analysis of the differences between the ancient and the mediaeval city in the West, the stress is on differences in economic geography and military technology. *Wirtschaft und Gesellschaft*, pp. 960, 1011–30; *Economy and Society*, pp. 1260–2, 1339–68.

[283] *Gesammelte Aufsätze zur Religionssoziologie*, p. 12; *The Protestant Ethic and the Spirit of Capitalism*, p. 27.

[289] In a long footnote to the second edition of his essays on *The Protestant Ethic and the Spirit of Capitalism*, Weber emphasized this against Werner Sombart, who had asserted that Benjamin Franklin's Puritan ethic merely repeated ideas of the Renaissance *littérateur* Leon Battista Alberti. Weber did not agree with Sombart on the factual issue, but his main point was: 'But how can anyone

Weber was more than a sociologist. But to the extent that he conformed to his own programme for an interpretative sociology, he focused on the effects of the fact that a given number of people constitute a specific ideological community, that they have certain religious conceptions, ideas of legitimacy or other values and norms in common.

Like that of many other sociologists, Weber's predominant interest in the ideological problems of capitalism was also related to his experience of an unnatural society. Contemporary capitalist German society could be considered unnatural in a number of ways, from different points of view. From a strictly bourgeois standpoint, the continuing subordination of the bourgeoisie in Wilhelmine Germany was unnatural. From the point of view of an established, self-conscious, and in many respects pre-bourgeois intelligentsia, a thoroughly or even predominantly capitalist society was an unnatural society. Max Weber's tense personality harboured both points of view. In his Freiburg Inaugural Address, he declared proudly: 'I am a member of the bourgeois classes, I feel myself as such and I am educated in its views and ideals.'[285] His studies of East German agriculture had shown the undermining of the old ruling class of feudal junkers and the rise of capitalism. With its economic system irredeemably undermined, the traditional ruling class was on its way out. This was a Marxian schema. But for Weber the problem, as he pointed out in his Address, was that the new economically ascendant class, the bourgeoisie, lacked the self-confidence and courage to assume the falling mantle of power.[286]

---

believe that such a literary *theory* could develop into a revolutionary force at all comparable to the way in which a religious belief was able to set the sanctions of salvation and damnation on the fulfillment of a particular (in this case methodically rationalized) manner of life? . . . The essential point of difference is (to anticipate) that an ethic based on religion places certain psychological sanctions (not of an economic character) on the maintenance of the attitude prescribed by it, sanctions, which, so long as religious belief remains alive, are highly effective, and which mere worldly wisdom like that of Alberti does not have at its disposal. Only in so far as these sanctions work, and, above all, in the direction in which they work, which is often very different from the doctrine of the theologicians, does such an ethic gain an independent influence on the conduct of life and thus on the economic order. *This is*, to speak frankly, *the point of this whole essay*, which I had not expected to find so completely overlooked.' *The Protestant Ethic and the Spirit of Capitalism*, p. 197 (emphasis added).

[285] *The Protestant Ethic and the Spirit of Capitalism*, p. 26.
[286] Ibid., p. 27f.

Weber had no ready solution, but stressed the need for political education. His study of the English, American and Dutch Puritans and their successful struggles against the feudal and feudally inspired classes of their countries was, no doubt, related to that endeavour. In his study of the Protestant Ethic and the Spirit of Capitalism, Weber spoke explicitly of the distinctiveness of the German bourgeoisie in this respect: 'That, furthermore, the tendency which has existed everywhere and at all times, being quite strong in Germany today, for middle-class fortunes to be absorbed into the nobility, was necessarily checked by the Puritan antipathy to the feudal way of life, is evident.'[287] 'The resort to entailed estates and nobility, with sons whose conduct at the university and in the officers' corps tries to cover up their social origin, as has been the typical history of German capitalist parvenu families, is a product of later decadence.'[288]

Another aspect of the weakness and timidity of the German bourgeoisie was, however, the markedly non-bourgeois (that is, pre-bourgeois) character of the established intelligentsia. No real bourgeois revolution occurred in Germany with the shattering of the old empire by the effects of the French Revolution. In 1848–50, the German bourgeoisie failed again; and in the creation of the new Reich under the Hohenzollern and Bismark, it played a subordinate role. Even after 1871, the bourgeois revolution in Germany in many respects stopped half-way. But it was precisely in this period of bourgeois failures and half-measures, prior to the soaring industrialization of the last part of the 19th century, that the German intelligentsia had been formed, with the expansion of the university system, the rise of Idealist philosophy and of the Historical Schools. From Fichte's Speeches to the German Nation in crowded Berlin churches, to the agitation of Von Treitschke and other Prussian historians for a German national unification under Prussian leadership, German intellectuals had played a prominent role in the largely pre-bourgeois German politics. In this milieu, a thoroughly capitalist and bourgeois society had few advocates. Liberal economists, for instance, were very few and derogatorily known as 'Manchesterleute'. During the First World War, when Britain – then the leading capitalist state (though with strong aristocratic institu-

[287] *Gesammelte Aussätze zur Religionssoziologie*, p. 193; English ed., p. 173.
[288] Ibid., p. 55; English ed., p. 71.

tions too) – was the main enemy, anti-bourgeois tendencies grew strong among German intellectuals. It was at this time that Tönnies' distinction of *Gemeinschaft* and *Gesellschaft* gained an enormous popularity, and that Sombart, in a famous ideological war effort, set 'the hero' against 'the trader'.[289]

Weber rebelled against a great deal of this pre-bourgeois intellectual tradition. His support for the creation of a Sociological Society, for example, was part of his rebellion against the attachment of the *Verein für Sozialpolitik*, under Schmoller's leadership, to the Wilhelmine state, and he was full of contempt for the feudalistic snobbishness and arrogance of the traditional student corporations. At the same time, however, he lived his life as a member of this intellectual world, never breaking with it. His attachment to the pre-bourgois intelligentsia is manifested in a number of well-known ways – in his tragic-heroic stance, his Nietzschean inclinations, his yearning for charismatic and aristocratic leaders, his friendship with the poet Stefan George, also in his preparedness to duel.[290] Max Weber was certainly not simply a 'sober, rational bourgeois'.

From a pre-bourgeois intellectual perspective, 'capitalism' became the object of a *Kulturkritik* of a basically aristocratic character. Weber's sociology of the spirit of capitalism is part also of this: he embraced not so much the spirit of *capitalism* (as distinct from the traditional feudal and other 'spirits') as the *spirit* of capitalism, the ideological commitment to a *Weltanschauung*. Thus he stressed the heroism of the Puritans as a bourgeois exception: 'Now how does it happen that at that time those countries which were most advanced economically, and within them the rising bourgeois middle classes, not only failed to resist this unexampled tyranny of Puritanism, but even developed a heroism in its defence? For bourgeois classes as such have seldom before and never since displayed heroism. It was "the last of our heroisms", as Carlyle, not without reason, has said.'[291]

The Protestant ethic and the capitalist spirit did not instil merely a commitment to the production of surplus value. Weber's conception of capitalism also included a critical marginalist element.

---

[289] See Ringer, op. cit., p. 180f.

[290] Cf. Mitzman, op. cit., p. 256f; P. Honigsheim, 'Erinnerungen an Max Weber', in König and Winckelmann (eds.), *Max Weber zum Gedächtnis*, pp. 161–271. On the duel affair, see Marianne Weber, op. cit., p. 436.

[291] *Gesammelte Aufsätze zur Religionssoziologie*, pp. 20–1, English ed., p. 37.

'Capital' is defined by Weber in terms of entrepreneurial book-keeping,[292] and a fundamental characteristic of capitalist enterprise and capitalist action is *rational calculation*. 'Exact calculation' is 'the basis of everything else'.[293] In his epistemological analysis of marginalist economics, Weber had pointed out that 'the doctrine of marginal utility treats human behaviour, for certain processes of knowledge, as if it proceeded from A to Z under the control of *commercial calculation* . . . The mode of treatment of commercial book-keeping is thus, if anything, the starting point of its construction.'[294] On that occasion, Weber's purpose was to emphasize that this calculating rationality was not deducible from psychology, but was the ideal-typical view of a particular culture. In his later sociology of capitalism, he studied the rise of that calculating capitalist culture.

In keeping with this marginalist perspective were two important aspects of Weber's conception of capitalism. The main agents of capitalist culture were not large and daring industrialists or financiers, but small and medium, prudently calculating entrepreneurs.[295] Secondly, as Gerth and Mills have noticed, Weber paid virtually no attention to business cycles and crises of capitalism.[296] Thus, mature capitalism appeared to occasion little excitement but also few substantial economic and social problems, such as unemployment, waste, poverty, wearing-out of people and so on. Had Weber been a bourgeois through and through, this would have seemed a good society. But he was not, and his essay on the spirit of capitalism ends on a note of cultural gloom. Rational, calculating

---

[292] *Wirtschaft und Gesellschaft*, p. 64, *Economy and Society*, p. 91. Weber says in a comment: 'The concept of capital has been defined strictly with reference to the individual private enterprise and in accordance with business-accounting practice . . .' (p. 67, resp. p. 94). Cf. *Gesammelte Aufsätze zur Religionssoziologie*, p. 5; *The Protestant Ethic*, p. 18.

[293] *Gesammelte Aufsätze zur Religionssoziologie*, p. 9; *The Protestant Ethic*, p. 22.

[294] *Gesammelte Aufsätze zur Wissenschaftslehre*, p. 394.

[295] *Gesammelte Aufsätze zur Religionssoziologie*, p. 49f; *The Protestant Ethic*, p. 65f. Weber here, no doubt, draws a line of distinction between his theory and Sombart's. To the latter, the capitalist spirit had two components, of which one was Weber's rationally calculating spirit, which Sombart called 'the bourgeois spirit' (*Bürgergeist*). The other was the dynamic 'spirit of enterprise' (*Unternehmungsgeist*), manifested in modern capitalism by figures such as Cecil Rhodes, John Rockefeller, and Walther Rathenau (Sombart, *Der Bourgeois*).

[296] Gerth and Mills, op. cit., p. 68.

capitalism was once part of an intense ideological commitment, defended in heroic class struggles by the ascending bourgeoisie. In this historical perspective, capitalism could appeal at once to the bourgeois and the largely aristocratic intellectual. Mature capitalism, however, has emancipated itself from its religious support. Capitalist action is no longer guided by ideological commitment but by a self-interested calculation rationally adapting itself to the market situation. The ideological foundation of capitalism has been succeeded by purely 'mechanical foundations'. This mechanical, rationally adaptive, self-interested calculation, expressed above all in market behaviour,[297] is the reason for Weber's cultural pessimism. The threat of 'mechanized petrification' derived directly from the very victory of competitive capitalism, not from the 'march of bureaucracy', from large enterprise or from state enterprise. It was capitalism that had become the 'iron cage' of our time: no longer a living ideological community, it consigned modern men to a mechanical world where they were dominated, not primarily by bureaucracy, but by the necessity to survive in 'the economic struggle for existence'. It was this necessity that drove men to their 'acquisitive manner of life'.[298] It was of capitalism that Weber concluded: 'No one knows who will live in this cage in the future, or whether at the end of this tremendous development entirely new prophets will arise, or there will be a great rebirth of old ideas and ideals, or, if neither, mechanized petrification, embellished with a sort of convulsive self-importance.'[299] But with or without this unhappy consciousness, classical sociology remained within the capitalist cage. For the key to a new world, we must turn to an altogether different type of social analysis.

[297] Cf. *Wirtschaft und Gesellschaft*, pp. 21–2; *Economy and Society*, p. 30.

[298] *Gesammelte Aufsätze zur Religionssoziologie*, p. 56; *The Protestant Ethic*, p. 72. Cf. *Gesammelte Aufsätze zur Religionssoziologie*, p. 203–4; *The Protestant Ethic*, p. 181–2.

[299] Ibid., p. 204; English ed., p. 182. Bourgeois sociologists usually subsume Weber's critique of capitalism under his critique of bureaucracy, with the latter's less anti-capitalist than anti-socialist implications. See, for example, Parsons, *The Structure of Social Action*, p. 504f; Giddens, op. cit., pp. 235–6.

Chapter Six

Working–Class Struggles and Theoretical Breaks: the Social and Theoretical Formation of Historical Materialism

Born in the mid-1840's, historical materialism was chronologically the third major social-scientific effort. It was, however, to reach the classical maturity embodied in Marx's *Capital* (1867) much earlier than sociology, whose classical achievements were above all the work of Durkheim and Weber. Economics, sociology and historical materialism had as a common background the European experience of capitalism and the bourgeois revolution. But whereas the first two were fundamentally loyal to this experience, historical materialism developed as a scientific pursuit in frontal opposition to this capitalist world. What accounts for this unique union of science and revolution in historical materialism?

I. The Bourgeois Revolution, the Radical Intelligentsia and the Proletariat

There seem to be at least three basic components in the formation of Marxism, two social and one intellectual. First, the combined experience of underdeveloped, petty conservative and largely pre-bourgeois Germany, and of the most developed bourgeois societies of Western Europe, created a particular kind of radicalized intelligentsia, profoundly alienated from all the reigning powers of the time. The second and most critical component was the encounter and union between a part of this radicalized intelligentsia and the working class, which had just embarked on its long history of independent struggle. Third, the intellectual mediation in which Marx and Engels underwent these experiences, left-Hegelian philosophy, was much more conducive to the development of a systematic theoretical discourse on society than to the relatively ephemeral responses of, say, piecemeal agitation, journalism or belles-lettres.

1. The Radicalized Intellectuals

Historical materialism emerged in the second half of the 1840's in the homelands of industrial capitalism. It took form in the great economic centres of Brussels, London and Manchester, and in Paris, the political storm-centre of the bourgeois revolutions of 1789 and 1830. Certainly, Marx and Engels were Germans, and the German determination of Marxism cannot be ignored. But it was only outside Germany that the new theory could come into being. All but one of the formative works of historical materialism were written outside Germany, the sole exception being Engels' *The Condition of the Working Class in England*, the product of a twenty-one month stay in Manchester. After *The Holy Family*, the first product of Marx and Engels' collaboration, written in Paris but published in Frankfurt in 1845, it was not until 1859, and the appearance of *A Contribution to the Critique of Political Economy*, that an important work of historical materialism was even published in Germany. *The German Ideology* found no publisher; Marx wrote *The Poverty of Philosophy* in French and had it published in Paris and Brussels; Engels's *Principles of Communism* was not sent for publication, the *Communist Manifesto* appeared in London, and *The Eighteenth Brumaire of Louis Bonaparte* was written for a German–American periodical published in New York.

It was in Paris and Manchester respectively that Marx and Engels underwent the decisive experiences that led them to break with Left Hegelian philosophy and radical-liberal politics.[1] The latest

[1] The presentation here of the formative experiences of Marx and Engels is based, firstly, on their own writings, and, secondly, on their standard biographies. Auguste Cornu's *Karl Marx et Friedrich Engels*, Paris, 1955–70, which covers in four volumes the period up to and including *The German Ideology*, is particularly important as a basic work; Franz Mehring's *Karl Marx*, London, 1936, and

surviving text in which Marx still distances himself from communism is a letter written to Arnold Ruge in September 1843, shortly before Marx left Germany for Paris.[2] In Paris he began to study political economy and the class struggles of the French Revolution, and it was there, too, that he came into contact with revolutionary workers from the French and German secret communist societies. 'When, in the spring of 1845, we met again in Brussels', Engels wrote forty years later, 'Marx had already fully developed his materialist theory of history in its main features.' Of his own experience, Engels wrote: 'While I was in Manchester, it was tangibly brought home to me that the economic facts . . . are, at least in the modern world, a decisive historical force; that they form the basis of the origination of the present-day class antagonisms; that these class antagonisms, in the countries where they have become fully developed . . . are in their turn the basis of the formation of political parties and party struggles, and thus of all political history.'[3] Engels studied political economy in England. In London in the spring of 1843 he came to know 'the first revolutionary proletarians whom I met',[4] the leaders of the League of the Just, a secret society of German artisans. Somewhat later he made contact with the Chartists.

This first-hand experience of the most developed bourgeois societies distinguished Marx and Engels from the German Left Hegelians in general. In June 1843, Engels wrote from London in a letter-article to the *Schweizerischer Republikaner*: 'Everything here is thus living and coherent, solid ground and action, everything

---

Gustav Mayer's *Friedrich Engels*, London, 1936, are also standard books. The editorial annotations of the *Marx–Engels–Werke (MEW)* edition, Berlin, 1956–64, have been consulted. Among the immense secondary literature I have found these works particularly useful: S. Hook, *From Hegel to Marx*, Ann Arbor, 1966; P. Kägi, *Genesis des historischen Materialismus*, Vienna, 1963; M. Löwy, *La theorie de la révolution chez le jeune Marx*, Paris, 1970; D. McClellan, *The Young Hegelians and Karl Marx*, London, 1969; *Marx before Marxism*, London, 1970, *Karl Marx, His Life and Thought*, London, 1973; B. Nicolaievsky and O. Maenchen-Helfen, *Karl Marx, Man and Fighter*, London, 1936; D. Riazanov, *Karl Marx and Frederick Engels*, London, n.d. [1927].

[2] *MEW* 2, p. 344; L. D. Easton and K. H. Guddat (eds.), *Writings of the Young Marx on Philosophy and Society*, New York, 1967, pp. 212–13.

[3] 'On the History of the Communist League', *MEW* 21, p. 211; Karl Marx and Frederick Engels, *Selected Works* [one volume edition], London, 1968, p. 436. (Abbreviated as *MESW*.)

[4] *MEW* 21, p. 208; *MESW*, p. 433.

here takes on an external form, while we [i.e. the Germans] think we know something if we simply digest the wretched lifelessness of Stein's book, or think that we are something if we occasionally express an opinion softened with attar of roses.'[5] Furthermore, this experience left a decisive and lasting imprint upon their whole theoretical and political *oeuvre*. Their focus on the development of the productive forces and interest in technology; their appreciation of the importance of abstract economic theory; their clear distinction between the wage-earning proletariat and the socially and historically undifferentiated category of the poor;[6] their emphasis on the revolutionary role of the bourgeoisie and the categorical refusal to make an unholy alliance with semifeudal forces against the proletariat's immediate exploiter:[7] their ruthless hostility towards every form of romanticism, sentimentality and mysticism – all these well-known features of Marxism are witness to its relationship to

[5] F. Engels, 'Briefe aus London', *MEW* 1, p. 477. The significance for Marx and Engels of Lorenz von Stein's famous study of socialism and communism in France (op. cit.), the first edition of which appeared in 1842, is not very easy to assess. It was anyhow not central, as the decisive turns in their development occurred only after Marx and Engels had left Germany and had met in their own way the world about which von Stein had written. In Marx's writings of 1842–4 I have found no reference to von Stein, but in *The Holy Family* and, above all, in *The German Ideology*, he is mentioned as the sole and not very reliable source of knowledge of socialist literature of the German ideologists, Bruno Bauer and Karl Grun. *MEW* 2, p. 142; *MEW* 3, pp. 191, 442, 473, 480–99, 518–19, 525. *The Holy Family*, Moscow, 1956, p. 180; and *The German Ideology*, Moscow, 1964, pp. 226, 502, 534, 555–85, 590.

[6] This distinction is indicated by Marx in 'Toward the Critique of Hegel's Philosophy of Right: Introduction', *MEW* 1, p. 390; Easton and Guddat, pp. 262–3. It is more fully developed by Engels in his draft contribution to the programme of the Communist League (in its final version, known as the *Communist Manifesto*), 'Principles of Communism', *MEW* 4, p. 363f; separate English ed., London n.d., p. 5f.

[7] According to Riazanov (op. cit., p. 92f), Marx and Engels even overemphasized the revolutionary potential of the bourgeois democrats in the German revolution of 1848, though they soon rectified this error. (See 'The Bourgeoisie and the Counter-Revolution', *MEW* 6, pp. 102–24, and 'Address of the Central Committee to the Communist League (March 1850)', *MEW* 7, pp. 244–54; both in English in Karl Marx, *The Revolutions of 1848*, London, 1973.) For Marx's attack on Lassalle's overtures to German semi-feudal forces, see Marx's letters to Kugelmann of 23 February, 1865 and to Schweitzer of 13 October, 1868, *MEW* 31 and 32; in Karl Marx and Frederick Engels, *Selected Correspondence*, Moscow n.d. (abbreviated as *MESC*).

the Enlightenment, the Great French Revolution and the Industrial Revolution.

Compared with England and France, Germany in the first half of the nineteenth century was economically and politically a backward country. Industrial capitalism was in its infancy, and pre-bourgeois elements held power in the patchwork of petty states into which Germany was divided. Historical materialism could not have been born in such a country. The 'German ideology' was philosophical speculation – about freedom, reason, man, praxis, alienation, criticism, love, socialism – with no room for exploitation, revolutionary class struggle or a scientific theory of history. It is notable in this connection that both Marx and Engels came from the most developed part of Germany, the Rhineland. Annexed to France from 1797 to 1814, the Rhineland had been deeply affected by the French Revolution. Progressive Germans, including the young Hegel, had warmly welcomed French rule, and Marx's father, too, was a pro-French liberal. The Engels family, though pietist and reactionary in politics, belonged in another capacity to the most advanced section of German society. Friedrich Engels senior was a successful merchant-industrialist, whose firm had branches both in Germany and Manchester. In the distinction that Engels drew in 1847, his family belonged to the bourgeoisie, 'which now rules in the civilized countries', and represented 'world trade, the exchange of products of all zones, finance, and large-scale industry based on machinery' – not to the miserable *Kleinbürger* (petty bourgeoisie) who represented 'internal and coastal trade, handicraft production and manufacture based on handicraft', and who, as the junior partner of the nobility, were a conservative force, sharing the blame for German backwardness.[8] (It was the existence of a Manchester branch of the firm Ermen and Engels that took Engels to England.)

However, Engels later said that 'the German working-class movement is the inheritor of German classical philosophy'.[9] He even claimed while Marx was still at his side, that 'without German philosophy, particularly that of Hegel, German scientific socialism – the only scientific socialism that has ever existed – would never

---

[8] 'The Status Quo in Germany', *MEW* 4, pp. 44–5.
[9] 'Ludwig Feuerbach and the End of Classical German Philosophy', *MEW* 21, p. 307; *MESW* p. 622.

have come into being'.[10] We are not so much concerned here with the strictly theoretical relationship between Hegelian philosophy and historical materialism as with the social and historical situation of the latter, and that is also Engels' concern in the text from which we have just quoted. Engels' argument there is that the German workers have an 'important advantage' over those of the rest of Europe in that 'they belong to the most theoretical people of Europe and have retained the sense of theory which the so-called "educated" classes of Germany have almost completely lost . . . What an incalculable advantage this is may be seen, on the one hand, from the indifference to theory which is one of the main reasons why the English working-class movement crawls along so slowly . . . on the other hand, from the mischief and confusion wrought by Proudhonism in its original form among the French and Belgians, and in the form further caricatured by Bakunin among the Spaniards and Italians.'[11] (Engels wrote this in 1874, shortly after the split in the First International.)

It is this 'sense of theory' that Engels has in mind in referring to 'German philosophy', and this point is further developed in his *Ludwig Feuerbach* (1886), already cited above. 'With the Revolution of 1848, "educated" Germany said farewell to theory and went over to the field of practice . . . But to the same degree that speculation abandoned the philosopher's study in order to set up its temple in the Stock Exchange, educated Germany lost the great aptitude for theory which had been the glory of Germany in the days of its deepest political humiliation – the aptitude for purely scientific investigation, irrespective of whether the result obtained was practically applicable or not, whether likely to offend the police authorities or not . . . in the sphere of the historical sciences, philosophy included, the old fearless zeal for theory has now disappeared completely, along with classical philosophy. Inane eclecticism and an anxious concern for career and income, descending to the most vulgar job-hunting, occupy its place . . . Only among the working class does the German aptitude for theory remain unimpaired . . . Here there is no concern for careers, for profit-making, or for gracious patronage from above.'[12]

[10] 'Preface to The Peasant War in Germany' (3rd ed.), *MEW* 18, p. 516; *MESW* p. 246.

[11] *MEW* 18, p. 516; *MESW*, pp. 245–6 (italics added).

[12] *MEW* 21, p. 306; *MESW*, p. 621.

But between the 'sense of theory' and the actual working class there had to be a mediation of some kind, and in *The German Ideology* Marx and Engels refer explicitly to the mediating role of the left-wing Hegelian intelligentsia, in particular the 'true socialists' of that day. 'The formation of this hybrid sect and the attempt to reconcile communism with the ideas prevailing at the time were necessary consequences of the actually existing conditions in Germany.' It was also inevitable, they thought, that some of these German philosophers and their 'disciples' (*Philosophenschüler*) cross the threshold to the communist position, while 'others, unable to extricate themselves from this ideology, [went] on preaching true socialism to the bitter end'.[13] In the early *The German Ideology*, however, one important consideration is missing, which was so obvious to the later Engels: the scientific socialism of the former Left Hegelians Engels and Marx was the only one 'that [had] ever existed'. In other words, despite its speculative verbosity and distorted ideology, the left-wing German intelligentsia of 1843–45 contributed something positive to the formation of historical materialism.

It contributed two things, in an explosive combination. One was a dedication to abstract theory and solid scholarship. The Young Hegelians were the proud heirs of the monumental encyclopaedic system of Hegel and, beyond Hegel, of the whole German idealist tradition founded by Kant. Their works of biblical criticism – David Strauss's *Life of Jesus* (1835), the starting-point of Left Hegelianism, and Bruno Bauer's *Critique of the Synoptic Gospels* – were landmarks of scholarship. Feuerbach's *Essence of Christianity* is no mere anti-religious pamphlet, but a learned and profound investigation into what today might be called the psychology of religion.[14]

This scholarly devotion was, of course, a product of the German university culture of the early nineteenth century. The first centre

[13] Karl Marx and Frederick Engels, *The German Ideology*, *MEW* 3, p. 443; English ed., p. 503.

[14] I have borrowed this characterization from Hook, *From Hegel to Marx*, p. 243. On the Young Hegelians see Cornu, *Karl Marx et Friedrich Engels*, vol. 1, Hook, and McClellan, *The Young Hegelians and Karl Marx*. These authors' general accounts of the Young Hegelian movement are somewhat different in emphasis from my own, since they focus predominantly on the development of ideas.

of Young Hegelianism was the informal 'Doctor's Club' at the University of Berlin, of which the young Karl Marx was a highly regarded member. But if it was produced within the university, it could not rest within its confines. For this was the second element of the explosive combination; Left Hegelianism was not the work of established academicians but of a radical, alienated intelligentsia of 'free' (that is, insecure) and often harrassed publicists. The Young or Left Hegelians of the early 1840's had not compromised their ideas for the sake of their careers. On the contrary, Feuerbach's academic career had been stopped short in the mid-1830's because of a heretical theological text. Strauss was hunted from his chair in Zurich in 1839. In the same year Bruno Bauer had to move from Berlin to Bonn, and at the beginning of 1842 he was dismissed from the university there, which led Marx to give up his own academic plans. Another of Marx's closest friends, Rutenberg, later editor of the *Rheinische Zeitung*, had also been dismissed from his teaching job. Scholarly yet non-academic, socially alienated yet basically non-bohemian, the Young Hegelians were of an intellectual and social calibre that was unmatched anywhere at that time. This Young Hegelian intelligentsia was, it may be suggested, a crucially important *social* component in the formation of Marx, and, to a somewhat lesser extent, of Engels, and not merely an *ideological* component, as even their best biographers tend to suggest.

The decisive difference in the social situation of Marxism, however, compared to that of both academic sociology and later radical intellectual currents such as the Frankfurt School was, of course, the union between its founders and the revolutionary workers' movement. The earliest intellectual interests of both Marx and Engels were the same as those of many left-wing *Kulturkritiker* of the 20th century – philosophy, poetry, journalism, belles-lettres in general. But although both Marx and Engels kept these cultural interests, their great creation was not a philosophy of praxis or of alienation (two popular themes of *marxisant* cultural criticism) but 'the doctrine of the conditions of the liberation of the proletariat',[15] which of necessity concentrated on the 'critique of political economy'. For, as they wrote in the *Communist Manifesto*, their theoretical conclusions expressed 'in general terms, actual relations springing from an existing class struggle, from a historical move-

[15] F. Engels, *Principles of Communism*, MEW 4, p. 363; English ed., p. 5.

ment going on under our very eyes'.[16] It is to this historical movement proceeding under the eyes of Marx and Engels in the early
1840's that we must now turn.

The political conjuncture that Marx and Engels confronted in
the late 1830's and early 1840's combined three important moments.
Firstly, in the background, was the bourgeois revolution – the Great
French Revolution, whose light still illuminated Europe, but also
the French July revolution of 1830 and the English parliamentary
reform of 1832, both significant victories of the bourgeoisie that
broke the reign of post-Napoleonic reaction. Secondly, against this
background, the failure of the bourgeois revolution in Germany
stood out as a scandal. The pious hopes of liberal bourgeois and
Young Hegelians that the new Prussian king, Frederick William IV,
would effect a revolution from above, were stifled in the winter of
1842–43 by a wave of press censorship and academic dismissals,
and the democratic intellectuals were rapidly radicalized, one way
or the other. Thirdly, this was also the period in which the working-
class movement made its decisive appearance. In England it was the
time of Chartism, the first proletarian movement in history to reach
the level of sustained nationwide organization. In France, 1831 saw
the first proletarian insurrection, by the Lyons silkworkers. Though
suppressed, it was soon succeeded by another, and a working-class
movement established itself in France also. With the revolt of the
Silesian weavers in 1844, the German proletariat made its own
entrance onto the political stage. In short, the formative period of
scientific socialism was precisely that in which the proletariat of the
major European nations raised its coarse and demanding voice.

To the German philosophers, heirs of the Enlightenment and the
French Revolution, the petty bureaucratic and feudal regimes in
Germany were disgusting, and the German bourgeoisie effete and
cowardly. But the condition of the workers in those countries where
a strong and self-conscious bourgeoisie ruled was no less terrible, as
Marx and Engels were to learn at first hand in Paris and Manchester.
The historical combination of a combative, atrociously exploited
proletariat and an abortive bourgeois revolution was to prove
explosive in Russia in the early twentieth century. In the 1840's it
was the critical experience that pushed two German intellectuals in
their twenties out on the road to a new scientific theory of society

---

[16] *MEW* 4, p. 475; *MESW*, pp. 46–7.

and to the forging of a deadly theoretical weapon against the bourgeoisie.

2. Learning from the Proletariat

Since the union of historical materialist theory and the working-class movement is the crux of Marxism, both in its own definition of itself and in the actual historical role it has played and continues to play, we must explore it further. There is a famous passage in Karl Kautsky, the leading theorist of classical Social Democracy, concerning the role of the intelligentsia in forming socialist consciousness among the proletariat, upon which Lenin later based himself in *What is to be Done?*, his polemic against the anti-theoretical Russian reformists.[17] Lenin and Kautsky were, of course, right – from the Marxist point of view – to emphasize the necessity of rigorous scientific theory and the insufficiency of spontaneous, untheoretical working-class consciousness.

It is plain, however, that two decisive elements are missing from Kautsky's formula. Firstly, Kautsky speaks emphatically of a *bourgeois intelligentsia* as the vehicle of science. But the Young Hegelians – especially after their betrayal by the bourgeois liberals in the phase of Prussian repression – were not simply a bourgeois intelligentsia. Socially, in the strategic years of 1842 to 1845, they were a *declassé* and radicalized section of the petty bourgeoisie. The second and much more important failing is Kautsky's silence about what the founders of scientific socialism *learnt* from the working class. To Kautsky, the communication is one-way only: 'It was in the minds of individual members of this stratum [the bourgeois intelligentsia] that modern socialism originated, and it was they who communicated it to the more intellectually developed proletarians who, in their turn, introduce it into the proletarian class struggle where conditions allow that to be done.' Lenin, in contrast, perceived the moment of reciprocity in this relationship, and very soon came to emphasize the central working-class contribution to revolutionary leadership. He insisted that the revolutionary cadres should be drawn mainly from the ranks of the workers, who

---

[17] V. I. Lenin, *Collected Works*, Moscow, 1960– , vol. 5, pp. 383–4. Lenin quotes Kautsky from *Neue Zeit*, XX (1901–2), I, No. 3, p. 79, a critical comment on the draft programme of the Austrian Social Democratic Party.

possessed the necessary 'class instinct' and practical experience of class struggle.[18]

We have already stressed the significant fact that the rise of proletarian class struggle preceded the upheaval in the minds of certain Young Hegelians. The founders of scientific socialism had to learn two things from the proletariat. First of all, they had to

[18] Lenin was soon to qualify, in word and deed, this use of Kautsky. See, for example, his 'Preface to the Collection *Twelve Years*', *Collected Works*, vol. 13, pp. 101–8. The relationship between workers and revolutionary intellectuals in the early period of the Russian Social-Democratic Labour Party was complex and problematic, and caused controversy in contemporary political discussions and in later historiography. The uppermost layer of the leadership was composed of revolutionary intellectuals, often sprung from the gentry. The congress delegates were predominantly non-workers: only three of the fifty-one who attended the refounding Second Congress of 1903 are known to have been workers (the social positions of eight are unknown); at the Third (all-Bolshevik) Congress of 1905, only one out of thirty was a worker. After 1905, the proportion of workers increased: thirty-six out of one hundred and forty-five at the Fourth (1906) and one hundred and sixteen out of three hundred and thirty-six at the Fifth in 1907 (see D. Lane, *The Roots of Russian Communism*, Assen, 1969, p. 37). On the other hand, the RSDLP and the Bolshevik faction as a whole were predominantly working-class in composition: a good 60% of the 5,000-strong membership of the Bolsheviks in 1905 was working-class (Lane, p. 26), as was the same percentage of the party's 24,000 members in February 1917 (P. N. Pospelov, et al., ed., *Geschichte der kommunistischen Partei der Sowjet Union*, Moscow, 1968, vol. III, 1, p. 41). Lane's very important study also shows that the majority of RSDLP activists in the period 1898–1907 were workers (p. 49). There was little difference in the social composition of the Menshevik and Bolshevik factions, except that the rank-and-file activists of the latter were more working-class and of lower educational background (pp. 49–50). The Bolsheviks were also a proletarian party in the important sense that it was their role in actual working-class struggles, particularly in 1912–14 and 1917, that decided their victory. On the Bolsheviks in the proletarian upsurge of 1912–14, see Pospelov, vol. II, ch. 6. Cf. the Preface by L. Haimson to the Menshevik Solomon Schwartz's very interesting account, *The Russian Revolution of 1905*, Chicago, 1967. Lenin fought for a proletarian reorganization of the party committees, still dominated by revolutionary intellectuals at the all-Bolshevik Third Congress (Lane, p. 47) but was narrowly defeated by a majority of the Bolshevik committee-men (Schwartz, p. 216f). Thanks to the more developed labour movement in Western Europe, the first Marxist political organization, the League of Communists, had from the outset a more proletarian leadership, including above all the three artisan leaders of the London branch of its predecessor, the League of the Just; Schapper (a type-setter), Moll (a watchmaker) and Bauer (a boot-maker). Of sixty-five personally and socially identifiable members of the League of Communists in 1847–52, thirty-three were intellectuals and professionals and thirty-two were artisans and workers (Löwy, p. 153).

discover the real social world in its concrete materiality, beyond the problems of theology and the rational state. Secondly, they had to discover the class struggle, to learn to see the proletariat not just as the class that suffered most – as did the utopian socialists – but as 'proud, threatening and revolutionary'.[19] The *Communist Manifesto* states this condition very clearly in its negative form: 'The under-developed state of the class struggle, as well as their own surround-ings, causes socialists of this kind [utopian socialists] to consider themselves far superior to all class antagonism.'[20]

Engels, the rebellious son of a manufacturer, discovered the miserable social condition of the proletariat very early. In 1839, at the age of eighteen, he wrote 'Letters from Wuppertal' (his home district) for a liberal literary journal in Hamburg, pointing to the misery of the workers and their families and to the 'broad conscience' of the manufacturers. At that time, however, he was mostly con-cerned with the sway of pietism and mysticism.[21] It was only after his arrival in England, in the autumn of 1842, that Engels could conclude – in a series of articles for the *Rheinische Zeitung*, then edited by Marx – that a violent revolution was necessary to improve the material situation of the English proletariat, and that a social revolution was 'a certainty for England'.[22]

But that was only the first lesson. A year later Engels wrote a survey of the socialist movement on the Continent for the Owenist *New Moral World* in which he showed himself still a firm Left Hegelian. He wrote of the 'philosophical communism in Germany' as a movement on a par with the English and French working-class movements. The Young Hegelians were 'our party', and Engels mentioned Moses Hess, Arnold Ruge, Georg Herwegh, Marx and himself as representatives of the communist development of the Young Hegelians. To Engels it was strange only to the English – and not to himself – that 'a party which aims at the destruction of private property is chiefly made up by those who have property; and yet this is the case in Germany. We can recruit our ranks from those classes only which have enjoyed a pretty good education, that is, from the universities and from the commercial classes; and in either

[19] 'German Socialism in Verse and Prose', *MEW* 4, p. 207.
[20] *MEW* 4, p. 490; *MESW*, p. 60.
[21] 'Letters from Wuppertal', *MEW* 1, pp. 413–32.
[22] 'Domestic Crises', *MEW* 1, p. 460.

we have not hitherto met with any considerable difficulty.'[23] It was quite without irony that Engels, after his return from England, described his agitation in Wuppertal to his friend Marx, in a letter of February 1845: 'The whole of Elberfeld and Barmen was represented [at the meetings], the proletariat alone excepted.' He proudly concluded that in Wuppertal, at least, communism was 'a *verité*, indeed almost a power already'.[24] That Engels had not yet learnt his second lesson from the proletariat is also clear from *The Condition of the Working Class in England*, where he concluded that communism would have a mitigating effect on the violence of proletarian class struggle, since 'communism by its nature stands above the strife between bourgeoisie and proletariat'.[25]

The first text in which Engels took a clearly proletarian position, breaking decisively with Left Hegelian and Feuerbachian 'true socialism', dates from September 1845, and, fittingly, was written for a working-class paper, the Chartist *Northern Star*. Engels' depiction of German communism has by now changed considerably. 'It is from the very heart of our working people that revolutionary action in Germany will commence. It is true, there are among our middle classes a considerable number of Republicans and even Communists, and young men too, who, if a general outbreak occurred now, would be very useful in the movement; but these men are "*bourgeois*", profit-mongers, manufacturers by profession; and who will guarantee us that they will not be demoralized by their trade, by their social position, which forces them to live upon the toil of other people, to grow fat by being the leeches, the "*exploiteurs*" of the working classes [?].'[26] The article stressed the pioneering role of the Silesian weavers, who were followed in 'turn-outs' and 'partial riots' by other groups of workers. What had happened between March and September 1845 was that Engels had met Marx in Brussels (in April), and returned with him to England, where they had had discussions with the Chartists and the London branch of

---

[23] 'Progress of Social Reform on the Continent', *New Moral World*, 18 November, 1843. (English original in Goldsmiths' Library, London; German translation in *MEW* 1, p. 495.)

[24] Engels to Marx, 22–6 February, 1845, *MEW* 27, p. 20.

[25] *MEW* 2, p. 505.

[26] 'The Late Butchery in Leipzig – The German Working Men's Movement', *Northern Star*, 13 September, 1845. (English original in British Museum, London; German translation in *MEW* 2, p. 560.)

the emigré German League of the Just. Back in Brussels in the autumn of 1845, Marx and Engels started work together on *The German Ideology*.

Marx was no more born a Marxist than Engels was – though in several works on the young Marx this seems to be implied, as if in a secularized version of the immaculate conception. In his Preface to *A Contribution to the Critique of Political Economy* Marx gives a brief overview of his intellectual development. There he points to his journalistic experience on the *Rheinische Zeitung*, where he first came to study economic realities (the conditions of the Rhineland peasantry, though not yet of the proletariat), and also encountered 'a philosophically weakly tinged echo of French socialism and communism', with which he did not yet identify. He also refers to his *Critique of Hegel's Philosophy of the State* as the first work in which he tried to solve the questions to which historical materialism eventually proved the solution.[27] In the published Introduction to this *Critique*, written at the turn of 1843–44, the proletariat is invoked as the 'material basis' of the German revolution. The workers are inserted here as the solution to an ideological problem of Feuerbachian philosophy. Their vocation is to be the necessary 'passive element' of the German revolution, its 'heart', while philosophy will be the active element, 'the head'.[28] In his violent polemic in August 1844 against his former colleague Arnold Ruge, who in an article in the Paris *Vorwärts* had belittled the importance of the Silesian weavers' uprising of June that year as a local phenomenon devoid of political significance, Marx expressed himself more clearly. He painted a glowing picture of the heroic and conscious workers and continued, 'The only task of a thoughtful and truth-loving mind in regard to the first outbreak of the Silesian labour revolt was not to play the role of *schoolmaster* to the event but rather to study its *peculiar* character. For the latter some scientific insight and love of humanity is necessary . . .'[29]

The Silesian weavers' uprising made an important contribution to Marx's theoretical development in the critical year of 1844, together with his personal experience of the workers' movement in Paris and his thorough reading of both French and English socialist

[27] *MEW* 13, pp. 7–8; *MESW*, p. 180f.
[28] *MEW* 1, pp. 386 and 391. Easton and Guddat, pp. 259, 264.
[29] 'Critical Notes on The King of Prussia and Social Reform', *MEW* 1, pp. 406–7; Easton and Guddat, pp. 353–4.

literature. His admiring and enthusiastic depiction of the Silesian weavers is paralleled by a passage on the collective warmth and human nobility of the Paris workers with whom he had become acquainted – a tribute that occurs in different variants in the *Economics and Philosophic Manuscripts*, in *The Holy Family*, and in a letter to Feuerbach. In the last, he wrote: 'Only by attending one of the meetings of the French *ouvriers* could you believe in the virginal freshness, the nobility, which prevails among these work-weary men.' At that time in Paris there was also a large German artisan colony, numbering about 40,000, to which the radical journal *Vorwärts*, on which Marx collaborated, was directed.[30] Writing to a friend, Ruge expressed contempt for Marx's relationship with these often very left-wing artisans: 'Marx has flung himself into German communism here – out of sociability, because it is impossible that he can find their wretched activity politically important.'[31] Marx's political evaluation was very different: the political core of this colony was the League of the Just, which he and Engels later joined.

In Paris Marx came to know the real social world, which he contrasted to the ideological shadow world of the German 'Holy Family' in his polemic of autumn 1844 against his former philosopher friends. Whereas in the *Economic and Philosophic Manuscripts* the discussion of communism and the different communist tendencies is completely philosophical, with no reference to the class struggle of the workers,[32] *The Holy Family* accords the proletariat a much more explicit and concrete role. 'But these *massy* communist

[30] Marx to Feuerbach, 11 August, 1844, *MEW* 27, p. 426. Cf. Karl Marx, *MEW*, Ergänzungsband I, pp. 553–4; *Economic and Philosophic Manuscripts of 1844*, London, 1970, pp. 154–5; and Frederick Engels and Karl Marx, *The Holy Family*, in *MEW* 2, p. 89 (Engl, ed., p. 113). When Marx was expelled from France in January 1845, in response to the demand of the Prussian government, one of the newspapers to protest was *La Fraternité*, the French communist workers' journal. Löwy, *La théorie de la révolution chez le jeune Marx*, p. 79 n. See also J. Grandjonc, *Marx et les communistes allemands à Paris 1844*, Paris, 1974, p. 12.

[31] Ruge to Fleischer, July 9, 1844, cit. Löwy, p. 87. In preparation for the demand for his expulsion, Prussian police agents compiled a dossier on Marx, which recorded, for Berlin's use, Marx's frequent visits to workers' meetings at the rue de Vincennes (see Nicolaievsky and Maenchen-Helfen, pp. 79–80). The gravity with which the French police regarded such contacts can be gauged from the report of a secret police agent, written after the deportation order, 1 February, 1845: see Cornu, vol. III, pp. 7–8 n.

[32] *MEW*, Ergänzungsband I, pp. 534f; cited in English ed., p. 132f.

workers, working in the factories of Manchester and Lyons, do not imagine they can reason away their industrial lords and their own practical degradation by "pure thought" . . . They know that property, capital, money, wage labour and the rest are in no way ideal fancies, but very practical, very objective products of their self-alienation, which therefore must also be abolished in a practical, objective way.'[33]

One other crucial element of Marxism, which Marx and Engels distilled from their practical experience, is still missing: the organized, revolutionary struggle of the working class. This was their solution to the contentious question of strategy debated among the different communist tendencies in the early 1840's. Two rival conceptions of the road to communism had already been developed, each of them influential in the early years of the League of the Just: conspiratorial action by a secret revolutionary society (the tradition of Babeuf and Blanqui, taken over by Weitling) and simple education and propaganda (the position of Cabet and Dezamy, and of the older utopians and their adherents).[34] Only in *The German Ideology* did Marx and Engels first articulate the way out of this dilemma, though the solution is anticipated in the fragmentary *Theses on Feuerbach* which Marx penned in the spring of 1845. The third thesis concludes: 'The coincidence of the changing of circumstances and of human activity of self-changing can be conceived and rationally understood only as revolutionary practice.'[35] The meaning of this was developed in the following passage from *The German Ideology*, which summarizes one of the main theses of the new theory of history. 'Both for the production on a mass scale of this communist consciousness, and for the success of the cause itself, the alteration of men on a mass scale is necessary, an alteration which can only take place in a practical movement, a *revolution*: this revolution is necessary, therefore, not only because the *ruling* class cannot be overthrown in any other way, but also because the class *overthrowing* it can only in a revolution succeed in ridding itself of all the muck of ages and become fitted to found society anew.'[36]

The German Ideology constitutes a break with many previous

[33] *MEW* 2, p. 55f.
[34] See Löwy's excellent study, op. cit., ch. 2. For the influences on the League of the Just, see also Grandjonc, pp. 14f, 55f, 77f.
[35] *MEW* 3, p. 6; *The German Ideology*, p. 646.
[36] *MEW* 3, p. 70; *The German Ideology*, p. 86.

conceptions. Scorn is poured over the Germans who judge everything according to the 'essence of man' by the same author who only
a year and a half earlier had stated that 'The only emancipation of
Germany possible *in practice* is emancipation based on *the* theory
proclaiming that man is the highest essence of man',[37] and who
somewhat later had claimed that communism was the 'real appropriation of the human essence by and for man'.[38] With Marx,
Engels now heaped his sarcasm on the German socialists, the 'party'
of 'a few pseudo-scholars',[39] membership of which he had earlier
claimed for both Marx and himself.

However, the road travelled by Marx and Engels is perhaps best
shown by their new definition of their theoretical task. They spoke
no longer of an alliance of philosophy and the proletariat, and the
realization of a philosophy of man. Theory now had a much more
modest role: to serve the proletariat by clarifying class antagonisms.
'In reality, the actual property-owners stand on one side and the
propertyless communist proletarians on the other. This opposition
becomes keener day by day and is rapidly driving to a crisis. If, then,
the theoretical representatives of the proletariat wish their literary
activity to have any practical effect, they must first and foremost
insist that all phrases be swept aside which tend to dim the realization of the sharpness of this opposition, all phrases tending to
conceal this opposition and giving the bourgeois a chance to
approach the communists for safety's sake on the strength of their
philanthropic enthusiasm.'[40]

Having followed Marx's and Engels' years of learning from the
proletariat, we can now see Lenin's view of the role of the intellectual
bearers of theory more clearly. Marx and Engels, after having
unlearnt their 'German ideology', could contribute something to the
proletarian movement that even the best theorists from the prole-

---

[37] 'Toward the Critique of Hegel's Philosophy of Law: Introduction', *MEW*
I, p. 391; Easton and Guddat, p. 264.

[38] *Economic and Philosophic Manuscripts of 1844*, *MEW*, Ergb. I, p. 536;
English ed., p. 102.

[39] *The German Ideology*, *MEW* 3, p. 453; English ed., p. 513. It was only the
lesser minds among the Young Hegelians, the latter-day 'true socialists', that
Marx and Engels considered 'pseudo-scholars'. They always acknowledged the
solidity of the theological and philosophical writings of Strauss, Bauer and
Feuerbach. On Bauer and Strauss, for example, see Engels's 'Ludwig Feuerbach',
MEW 21, pp. 271–3; *MESW*, pp. 591–3.

[40] *The German Ideology, MEW* 3, pp. 456–7; English ed., pp. 516–17.

tariat itself, such as the German tailor Wilhelm Weitling, could not: a scientific theory of history and a revolutionary strategy based on it. It was for this reason that they were commissioned in 1847 to write both the statutes of the League of Communists and its programme, the *Communist Manifesto*.

There is a further aspect of Marx's relationship to the working class that should be emphasized. As revolutionary communists, Marx and Engels soon involved themselves in organizational activity. By way of preparation for a communist party in Germany and for a kind of communist international, they began to organize, in 1845, a network of Communist Correspondence Committees, and a year later they joined with the League of the Just in its reorganization into the League of Communists. In the event, the revolutionary expectations of 1848 were defeated, and the League was destroyed. Marx withdrew into scientific work, Engels to white-collar work as an employee in his family's firm. They both continued to write political journalism, but were otherwise absorbed in their private spheres.

This is a pattern that can also be traced in the history of sociology. Both in the United States and in France, for example, there are several prominent sociologists who in their youth – and sometimes even later – had sympathies with, and perhaps even membership of the working-class movement.[41] In disillusion they left the latter and became influential sociologists instead. The point about Marx is that he did *not* take that path. *Capital* is not simply a solid work of economic and social theory; for as its author himself remarked to a friend: 'It is certainly the most formidable missile fired so far to strike the bourgeois (landed proprietors included) on the head.'[42] Even in the years of reaction, Marx maintained his connections with the Chartists and the German Workers' Education Association in London. It was because of this that he was invited by the English trade union leaders to the meeting that founded the First International, in 1864. In the leadership of the International Marx again came to play a central, organizing role, later drawing Engels into his work also.

Marxism and sociology are both reflections on capitalism and bourgeois society. Both express in their own way a disillusion with

---

[41] S. M. Lipset and J. Duvignaud are two examples.

[42] Marx to J. Ph. Becker, 17 April, 1867, *MEW* 31, p. 541.

the bourgeois revolution, mediated through a developed intelligentsia. There, however, the similarities end and are overwhelmed by the differences. There is not a single prominent sociologist in the capitalist world who, as a sociologist, has been formed by and been part of a militant labour movement. Whatever other differences there may be among them, sociologists have this in common. It is especially important to remember this fundamental difference between Marxism and academic sociology, now that Marxist ideas are being discussed among sociologists and theories of convergence or cross-fertilization being proposed.[43] Indeed, this class difference goes to the very centre of Marxist social theory: social classes and their struggles are the bearers of the forces and relations of production, their development, contradiction and transformation.

The twentieth century has, however, already seen a group of intellectuals who, both socially and intellectually, were the legitimate heirs of Marx and Engels and their closest comrades; a group who, serious and non-bohemian, were also persecuted and exiled, whose perspective was also formed by the combined experience of advanced capitalism and an abortive bourgeois revolution, who were also dedicated both to social study and social revolution, who were part of the proletarian class struggle both in their native country and elsewhere, and who viewed struggles within and between nations from an international standpoint: Lenin and the Bolshevik intellectuals.

II. Theoretical Coordinates for the Emergence of Historical Materialism

The development of historical materialism was no more magical or straightforward than that of Marxist politics: it neither sprang fully-grown from nothing, nor emerged in a continuous linear evolution. It emerged from a definite theoretical context, and at the same time constituted itself as a distinctive body of thought by breaking with this context at decisive points. This section will examine the processes of its theoretical formation. This examination is not, therefore, a study of Marxist thought as a whole: our main interest here is in those elements in the formation of historical

[43] See, for example, A. Gouldner, *The Coming Crisis of Western Sociology.*

materialism that most clearly define its distinctive contribution to social science, to the elucidation of a pattern of social determination. No intellectual biography or general exposition of influences and predecessors is intended here. The objective is to present the basic theoretical co-ordinates delimiting the space in which the new pattern of social determination was discovered and in which the new historical materialist discourse emerged. Of these co-ordinates, one was Hegelian and the other 'mechanical materialism', Feuerbachian and Anglo-French utilitarian. The role of the dialectic will be dealt with in a later section elucidating the new mode of explanation at work in historical materialism.

1. Objective Idealism and the Process Without a Subject

In the beginning was idealism, the supreme importance of mind and ideas. This not only holds for Dr Marx, the gifted young philosopher, but also for Karl Marx the editor of the *Rheinische Zeitung*, and the political journalism to which he came to devote himself instead of writing his planned essays on religious art and on the Romantics.[44] In his articles about the debate on press freedom in the Rhineland *Landtag* (provincial assembly), for example, Marx wrote that 'the Belgian revolution is a product of the Belgian mind'.[45] On another occasion, rebutting the charge that his paper had 'coquetted' with Communism, he concluded: 'We are firmly convinced that it is not the *practical effort* but rather the *theoretical explication* of communistic ideas which is the real *danger*. Dangerous practical attempts, *even those on a large scale*, can be answered with *cannon*, but *ideas* won by our intelligence, embodied in our outlook, and forged on our conscience are chains from which we cannot tear ourselves away without breaking our hearts; they are demons we can overcome only by submitting to them [i.e. by seriously and critically studying them].[46] Attacking a new law that forbade the collection of dry wood in the forests and subjected 'thieves' to the jurisdiction of the forest owners, he spoke of 'this depraved materialism, this sin against the holy spirit of the peoples and of humanity, [which] is a direct consequence of that doctrine . . .

---

[44] Marx to A. Ruge, 20 March and 27 April, 1842, *MEW* 27, pp. 399–403.

[45] K. Marx, 'Debates on the Freedom of the Press', *MEW* 1, p. 39.

[46] K. Marx, 'Communism and the Augsburg Allgemeine Zeitung', *MEW* 1, p. 108; Easton and Guddat, p. 135.

which, in the case of a law on timber, thinks only of timber and forest and is not concerned with solving the specific material problem *politically*, i.e. in relation to the rationality and morality of the state as a whole.'[47]

These words echo an important aspect of the young Marx's thinking which, recalling Lukács' usage in his study of the young Hegel, we might call *objective idealism*.[48] Objective idealism is a kind of idealist determinism, directed against subjectivist moralism or utopian idealism. Its exact meaning in this context can be illustrated by certain passages, written by Marx in 1842–43. Commenting on the Prussian government's projected divorce bill, Marx wrote: 'The legislator, however, must consider himself a naturalist. He does not *make* laws; he does not invent them; he only formulates them. He expresses the inner principles of spiritual relationships in conscious, positive laws. . . . It is obvious that neither the arbitrariness of the legislator nor that of private persons can decide whether or not a marriage is dead . . .'[49] In the *Critique of Hegel's Philosophy of Right*, Marx states that 'The will of a people can no more exceed the laws of reason than can the will of an individual', and that 'The legislature does not make the law, it merely discovers and formulates it'.[50] In a letter written shortly before his departure for Paris in September 1843, Marx wrote: 'But that is exactly the advantage of the new

---

[47] K. Marx, 'Debates on the Law against the Theft of Wood', *MEW* 1, p. 147. In his very important study, Hook (op. cit., p. 159) says that 'this event marked the complete abandonment in Marx's thought of the Hegelian theory of the State'. It is evident from the citation from Marx that Hook confused two things here, Hegelian theory and the correspondence of the actual state to the Hegelian account of it.

[48] G. Lukács, *Der Junge Hegel*, Neuwied and Berlin, 1867, p. 332f. Cf. Engels on Hegel's critique of Kant and his 'categorical imperative in "Ludwig Feuerbach"', *MEW* 21, p. 281; *MESW*, p. 600.

[49] K. Marx, 'On a Proposed Divorce Law', *MEW* 1, pp. 149–50; Easton and Guddat, pp. 140–1.

[50] K. Marx, '*Critique of Hegel's "Philosophy of Right"*', *MEW* 1, p. 260; English translation by O'Malley, Cambridge, 1970, p. 58. Cf. Hegel's treatment of the state in the work criticized by Marx: 'In so far as this treatise comprises political science it should be nothing but the attempt to understand and present the state as something rational in itself. As far as a philosophical work it should be most remote from an attempt to construct the state as it ought to be; the information it may provide cannot be that of apprising the state of how it ought to be, but rather to give advice as to how it, the moral universe, should be cognized. It is the task of philosophy to understand what is, for what is is reason.' *Grundlinien der Philosophie des Rechts*, Preface, *Sämtliche Werke*, Leipzig, 1911, vol. 6, p. 15.

direction, namely, that we do not anticipate the world dogmatically, but rather wish to find the new world through criticism of the old . . . Even though the . . . construction of the future and its completion for all times is not our task, what we have to accomplish at this time is all the more clear: *relentless criticism of all existing conditions . . .*' 'Nothing prevents us, therefore, from starting our criticism with criticism of politics, with taking sides in politics, hence with *actual* struggles, and identifying ourselves with them. Then we do not face the world in doctrinaire fashion with a new principle . . . We do not tell the world, "cease your struggles, they are stupid; we want to give you the true watchword of the struggle." We merely show the world why it actually struggles; and the awareness of this is something the world *must* acquire even if it does not want to.'[51]

The determinism (in a rather general sense of the term) of Marx the Young Hegelian is a well known characteristic of Marxism, and is the reason for its hostility to moralism and utopian schematism. 'The theoretical conclusions of the Communists are in no way based on ideas or principles that have been invented, or discovered, by this or that would-be universal reformer. They merely express, in general terms, actual relations springing from an existing class struggle. . . .'[52] 'My standpoint, from which the evolution of the economic formation of society is viewed as a process of natural history, can less than any other make the individual responsible for relations whose creature he socially remains, however much he may subjectively raise himself above them.'[53]

Idealist determinism has known two types of expression. We have already encountered the first, in our discussion of the rise of sociology. This was the historicist reaction against the Enlightenment, natural law, and the French Revolution, with its new laws and constitutions. Against this was asserted the weight of tradition, the cultural heritage of a people: constitutions and laws, according to the view of these idealists, could not really be *made*, but rather *grew* out of a people's cultural tradition and had to be *understood* in

---

[51] Marx to Ruge, September 1843, *MEW* 1, p. 344; Easton and Guddat, pp. 212, 214.
[52] *Communist Manifesto*, *MEW* 4, p. 474; English translation in Marx, *The Revolutions of 1848*, p. 80.
[53] K. Marx, *Capital*, vol. I, Preface to the First Edition, *MEW* 23, p. 16; English ed., Moscow, 1962, p. 10.

the light of this tradition. This type of idealist determinism was represented above all by the so-called Historical School of Law. Politically, it was a conservative trend of thought, and one of Marx's teachers in Berlin, the Left Hegelian E. Gans, had been involved in a sharp polemic with Savigny, the leader of the school.[54] Himself an heir of the German philosophical Enlightenment, Marx was naturally hostile to the historical school, and his early writings include a vitriolic attack against it and one of its founders, Gustav Hugo. 'With time and culture, the *rough family tree* of the historical school was befogged by the *incense of mysticism*, fantastically carved up by *romanticism*, and engrafted with *speculation*. Much *scholarly* fruit was shaken down from the tree, dried, and ostentatiously stored away in the vast warehouse of German erudition. But only very little *criticism* is needed to recognize sordid old ideas behind all the fragrant modern phrases of our enlightener from the Ancien Regime and to recognize his slovenly triviality behind all the excessive unction.'[55] With these brusque words, Marx severed one of the possible lines of communication with sociology.[56]

The alternative idealist determinism was that of Hegel. Whereas Gustav Hugo and the Historical School had, in Marx's words, turned 'the *scepticism* of the *eighteenth century* concerning *the rationality of existing conditions*' into '*scepticism* concerning the *existence of reason*',[57] world history was to Hegel 'the image and the deed of Reason'.[58] In the passions and struggles of individuals, he saw not the irrationality of man but 'the cunning of reason',[59] and in the foreword to his *Philosophy of Right* had declared that 'what is reasonable is real, and what is real is reasonable'. The meaning of this famous and obscure dictum is explained in the *Encyclopaedia*, where, having emphasized that not every arbitrary existence is real in his sense, Hegel expounds his objective idealism: 'The actuality [*Wirklichkeit*] of the rational stands opposed by the popular fancy that Ideas and ideals are nothing but chimeras, and philosophy a

---

[54] Cornu, vol. I, p. 81f.

[55] K. Marx, 'The Philosophical Manifesto of the Historical School of Law', *MEW* 1, pp. 84–5.

[56] Savigny was, by the way, the author of the divorce bill that Marx criticized (see above), *MEW* 1, p. 602, n. 72.

[57] *MEW* 1, p. 99.

[58] Hegel, *Die Vernunft in der Geschichte. Einleitung in die Philosophie der Weltgeschichte*, *Sämtliche Werke* Bd. VIII: I, Leipzig, 1920, I, p. 5.

[59] Ibid., p. 83.

mere system of such phantasms. It is also opposed by the very different fancy that Ideas and ideals are something far too excellent to have actuality, or something too impotent to procure it for themselves. . . . The object of philosophy is the Idea; and the Idea is not so impotent as merely to have a right or an obligation to exist without actually existing.'[60]

Hegel's philosophy contains, in an objective-idealist form, a manifestly determinist view of history and society. World history is the development and coming to self-consciousness of the world spirit, which is manifested in the spirits of different peoples in different epochs. The spirit of a people constitutes a social whole. '[The spirit's consciousness] is the substance of the spirit of a people; even if individuals are not aware of it, it stands there as a fixed presupposition. It is a kind of necessity; the individual is brought up in this atmosphere, he knows nothing else. Yet it is not simply upbringing and the result of upbringing; this consciousness is developed from within the individual himself, rather than taught to him: the individual *is* in this substance . . . No individual can transcend this substance; he can certainly distinguish himself from other particular individuals, but not from the *Volksgeist* . . . The gifted are only those that understand the spirit of the people and can orient themselves to it . . . Thus individual personalities disappear from our point of view, and the only ones that are relevant are those that posit in reality the will of the *Volksgeist*. In philosophical history one must avoid such expressions as: 'a state would not have perished had there been a man who . . .'''[61]

The national mind or spirit also determined the constitution and legislation of the state – a central problem in the post-revolutionary discussions of the early 19th century. 'What is thus called "making" a "constitution", is – just because of this inseparability – a thing that has never happened in history, just as little as the making of a code of laws. A constitution only develops from the national spirit identically with that spirit's own development, and runs through at the same time with it the grades of formation and the alterations necessitated by its concept. It is the indwelling spirit and the history of the nation (and, be it added, the history is only that spirit's

[60] Hegel, *Enzyclopädie der philosophischen Wissenschaften, Sämtliche Werke* Bd, V, Leipzig, 1911, 6, pp. 37, 38. English translation by Wallace, *The Logic of Hegel*, Oxford, 1892, pp. 11–12.

[61] *Vernunft der Geschichte*, I, p. 36f.

history) by which constitutions have been and are made.'[62]

History, to Hegel, was reason and development. But it was not the story of human perfectibility, or even a source of moral lessons.[63] The history of the world was not to be grasped as the realization of conscious human aims, as the creation of a human subject either in the form of the individual or in the form of the collective based on social contract. 'However, *world history* does not begin with *any* kind of *conscious purpose* – in the way that in *particular groups* of men the simple drive for the society of their fellows has already the conscious purpose of securing their life and property, and then, once this association has been achieved, the purpose straight away extends its determination . . . World history only commences *in itself*, with its *general purpose* that is to satisfy the concept of spirit *implicitly*, i.e. as *nature* . . . and the whole business of world history is . . . the work of bringing it to consciousness.'[64] In a subtle analysis, based on a study of Hegel's *Logic* and Lenin's reading of it, Althusser has aptly called this Hegelian conception of history one of a 'process without a subject'.[65]

At a lower level of the Hegelian philosophy of history, however, there does exist a relatively concrete central social subject: the spirit of the people. Out of the national spirit the constitution, laws, morals, art, and so on of the society are developed. It is thus very clear that Marx's was not the only possible 'inversion of Hegel'. He might equally have set out to develop a sociology of the ideological community.

Marx did not take that path, but we can guess where he might have ended up had he done so. The national mind might have

---

[62] *Enzyclopädie*, 540, p. 448. English translation by Wallace, *Hegel, The Philosophy of Mind*, Oxford, 1971 (1st ed. 1894, pp. 268–9.

[63] *Vernunft der Geschichte*, I, pp. 129f (the concept of development) and 173f (moral reflection on history).

[64] Ibid., p. 64.

[65] L. Althusser, 'Marx's Relation to Hegel', in the collection *Politics and History*, London, 1972. Cf. also Althusser's essay 'Lenin before Hegel' in *Lenin and Philosophy and other essays*, London, 1971. There is, of course, as Althusser points out, a subject basic to Hegel's conception of history, but that is the highly abstract and remotely unfolding Idea. On the other hand, in asserting that the 'process without a subject' was Marx's most important borrowing from Hegel, Althusser scarcely does justice to the latter's contribution to the Marxian concept of dialectic. See V. I. Lenin, *Philosophical Notebooks* (*Collected Works*, vol. 38), pp. 85–320.

become class mind, society as a whole and in its different parts the manifestation of the class mind, or class mind conscious of itself – class consciousness. The bases of the classes might have been as remote as the world spirit, and of virtually negligible importance in the concrete analysis of society and social change. It is possible to trace this alternative path of development with some confidence, precisely because, in a certain sense, it was actually taken: not by Marx himself, but by historicist interpretations of his work. This development is perhaps best represented in the case of Karl Mannheim, according to whom Marx took 'the final and most important step in the creation of the total conception of ideology', replacing 'the concept of *Volksgeist* . . . by the concept of class consciousness, or more correctly class ideology'.[66] The young Lukács was a Young Hegelian and a historicist in the contemporary German tradition. For him, society was essentially a spiritual entity, and class consciousness the determinant of a class's historical role, of social organization and social change. In the last resort, 'the strength of every society is . . . a spiritual strength. From this we can only be liberated by knowledge.[67] . . . If from the vantage point of a particular class the totality of existing society is not visible; if a class thinks the thoughts imputable to it and which bear upon its interests right through to their logical conclusion and yet fails to strike at the heart of that totality, then such a class is doomed to play only a subordinate role. It can never influence the course of history in either a conservative or a progressive direction . . . For a class to be ripe for hegemony means that its interest and consciousness enable it to organize the whole of society in accordance with those interests.'[68]

In Marx's earliest approach to the proletariat we can find

[66] K. Mannheim, *Ideology and Utopia*, London, 1960, p. 60. Mannheim explicitly assimilates this reading of Marxism to the later historicist social theory of Sombart, Troeltsch, and Weber, ibid., p. 67.

[67] G. Lukács, *History and Class Consciousness*, London, 1971, p. 262.

[68] Ibid., p. 52. Similarly, Lukács argues that in the analysis of capitalist crises 'the great emphasis must be laid on whether the "greatest productive power" of the capitalist production system, namely the proletariat, *experiences* the crisis as object or as the subject of decision.' Ibid., p. 244. Emphasis added. Cf. the excellent analysis of Lukács by Gareth Stedman Jones, 'The Marxism of the Early Lukács: An Evaluation', *New Left Review* 70 (November–December 1971). Stedman Jones also points out Lukács' emancipation from historicism in his brilliant book on *Lenin*, London, 1970 (1st ed. 1924).

expressions that recall the *Volksgeist* conception, though not as fully developed as in Mannheim and the early Lukács. Speaking of the pre-proletarian classes in Germany, Marx says, for example, in his *Toward the Critique of Hegel's Philosophy of Law*: 'But in Germany every class lacks not only the consistency, penetration, courage, and ruthlessness which could stamp it as the negative representative of society. There is equally lacking in every class that breadth of soul which identifies itself, if only momentarily, with the soul of the people – that genius for inspiring material force toward political power . . .'[69] But this belongs to a period when Marx conceived of the proletariat as the solution to the problems of German philosophy, as Lukács did in *History and Class Consciousness*. With the new (what we now call Marxist) view of the working class and the study of society, this conception is radically altered. In *The German Ideology* Marx and Engels sharply and emphatically attack the separation of 'the ruling ideas . . . from the ruling individuals and, above all, from the relationships which result from a given stage of the mode of production', from the 'empirical reasons . . . [and the] empirical conditions [of the] actual rulers'.[70] They conclude that 'the conditions under which definite productive forces can be applied, are the condition of the rule of a definite class of society'.[71] It was to the investigation of these empirical bases and conditions that the founders of historical materialism now devoted themselves. In a later methodological manuscript Marx underscored these new theoretical priorities: 'The classes [of which the population is composed] are an empty phrase if I am not familiar with the elements on which they rest. E.g. wage labour, capital, etc.'[72]

2. Civil Society: From Egoism-Alienation to Economic Relations and Class Struggle

Another Hegelian conception that was of strategic importance in Marx's discovery of society as a law-bound empirical reality was Hegel's sharply-drawn distinction between the state and what he called civil society (*bürgerliche Gesellschaft*). This distinction is set

[69] K. Marx, 'Toward the Critique of Hegel's Philosophy of Law', *MEW* 1, p. 389; Easton and Guddat, p. 261.
[70] Marx-Engels, *The German Ideology*, *MEW* 3, pp. 48, 49; English ed., p. 63.
[71] *MEW* 3, p. 69; English ed., p. 85.
[72] Marx, *Grundrisse*, p. 21; English ed., London, 1973, p. 100.

out in the *Philosophy of Right*, where civil society is defined as 'the [stage of] difference which intervenes [*tritt*] between the family and the state'.[73] This is a very clear distinction, and a very important one in the rise of a science of society; it is related to the very sharpness with which Hegel wants to focus the state as 'the actuality of the ethical Idea. It is ethical mind *qua* the substantial will manifest and revealed to itself, knowing and thinking itself, accomplishing what it knows and in so far as it knows it.'[74] Hegel's civil society comprised three 'moments': the 'system of needs' – roughly, the economy – the 'administration of justice', and the 'police and corporation'.[75] Since Hegel discusses the state only in terms of its constitution, its relations to other states and its role in world history, the more mundane activities of the state – the judicial system and the administration ('policy') – are located in civil society.

The importance of the Hegelian distinction for the development of Marxism is acknowledged by Marx himself. 'The first work which I undertook to dispel the doubts assailing me was a critical re-examination of the Hegelian philosophy of law . . . My inquiry led me to the conclusion that neither legal relations nor political forms could be comprehended whether by themselves or on the basis of a so-called general development of the human mind, but that on the contrary they originate in the material conditions of life, the totality of which Hegel . . . embraces within the term "civil society"; that the anatomy of this civil society, however, has to be sought in political economy.'[76]

However, Marx's account passes over the complexity and the discontinuity of his development. Civil society is the world of individual ends, of self-interest and dependence based on mutual advantage. One possible materialist development of Hegel's distinction would then have carried Marx to the English and French utilitarians of the 18th century and to the liberal economists, whose view of consumption as 'the sole end and purpose of all production' (Smith)[77] was close to Hegel's 'system of needs', and from whom

---

[73] G. W. F. Hegel, *Philosophie des Rechts*, 182 Zusatz, p. 246. English edition, trans. T. M. Knox, Oxford, 1967, p. 246.

[74] Ibid., 257; English ed., p. 155.

[75] Ibid., 188.

[76] K. Marx, Preface to *A Contribution to the Critique of Political Economy*, *MEW* 13, p. 8; English ed., London, 1971, p. 20.

[77] A. Smith, *The Wealth of Nations* (Cannan ed.), London, 1904, vol. 2, p. 179.

Hegel had acquired his knowledge of the division of labour.[78] Again, as in the case of the *Volksgeist*, this is not just idle speculation. It refers to an actual course of development, which in this case was very clearly followed by the young pre-Marxist Communist named Karl Marx.

Marx wrote two critiques of Hegel's Philosophy of Right, but one was designed merely to be an introduction and the other was left unfinished.[79] The latter was intended to include the critique of Hegel's account of civil society.[80] The achievement of these two critiques, in terms of a development towards historical materialism, is rather uneven. In the Feuerbachian manner of Hegel-criticism,[81] Marx reverses the relationship between family and civil society on the one hand, and the state on the other. 'Family and civil society make *themselves* into the state. They are the active force. According to Hegel they are, on the contrary, made by the actual Idea. It is not their own life's course which unites them into the state, but rather the life's course of the Idea, which has distinguished them from itself.'[82]

Marx's discussion takes place within the problematic of alienation. The differentiation between civil society – 'the accomplished principle of individualism' – and the political monarchical state is conceived as the alienation of man from his social, generic essence.[83] The text thus culminates in an attempt to *dissolve* both civil society and the state in a democratic community: 'Within the abstract political state the reform of voting advances the dissolution of this

[78] See Riedel, op. cit., especially the essay 'Die Rezeption der Nationalökonomie'. The first to reveal and emphasize the connection between Hegel and classical economics was Lukács in his *Der junge Hegel*.

[79] K. Marx, 'Critique of Hegel's Philosophy of Right', which actually analyzes that part of the Philosophy of Right that deals with the state, and 'Toward the Critique of Hegel's Philosophy of Law', *MEW* 1, pp. 203–333, and 378–91 respectively.

[80] This intention is made clear in *MEW* 1, p. 284.

[81] In his 'Vorläufige Thesen zu Reform der Philosophie', Feuerbach formulated it thus: 'The method of reformatory criticism of speculative philosophy on the whole does not differ from that already used in the philosophy of religion. We need only make the predicate into the subject and thus reverse speculative philosophy in order to arrive at the unconcealed, pure, and naked truth.' *Sämtliche Werke*, II, p. 224.

[82] '*Critique of Hegel's Philosophy of Right*', *MEW* 1, p. 207. English ed., pp. 8–9.

[83] Ibid., p. 285 (emphasis omitted); English ed., p. 81.

political state, but also the dissolution of civil society.'[84] The same problematic also pervades the approximately contemporaneous *On the Jewish Question*. Against Bruno Bauer, who as a bourgeois radical had told the Jews not to press for equality within the present pre-liberal state but to join the struggle for human rights, Marx argued at length that political emancipation was not human emancipation. In an argument which has certain formal resemblances to Sombart's later works on the spirit of capitalism,[85] he maintained that the basis of Jewishness was self-interest and '*Schacher*' (bargaining), that Jewishness had reached its climax with civil society, the full differentiation of which, in turn, was made possible by Christianity. Marx concludes that 'the Jewish question' could only be solved by a general human emancipation from bargaining and money.[86]

The second critique of Hegel, which was primarily concerned with 'the emancipation of the Germans', contains a sentence which, so to speak, casts a long shadow forward: 'The relation of industry and the world is a major problem of modern times.' However, this is mentioned explicitly only as an illustration of German backwardness. In France and England, Marx observes, the problem is one of 'political economy or the rule of society over wealth'.[87] The economic problem is located within the egoistic-individualism vs. community problematic.

A continuous linear development from the Hegelian conception of civil society, the sphere of individual needs and self-interest, to economics would have entailed a focus on competition and the division of labour as the fundamental economic fact – that is, the discovery of the market – and on the war of all against all as a basic target of social criticism. This is, indeed, just what we find in the last pre-Marxist works of Marx and Engels. In the most famous of his pre-Marxist writings, Marx put this very explicitly. '*Society*, as

[84] Ibid., p. 327 (emphasis omitted); English ed., p. 121.

[85] Cf. W. Sombart, *Die Juden und das Wirtschaftsleben*, Leipzig, 1911. Sombart's portrait of the Jewish spirit concentrates on Jewish rationalism, its abstract-quantitative and calculating orientation. Sombart's purpose is to demonstrate that the same spirit which Weber had discovered among the Calvinistic Puritans characterized the Jews, and was, basically, Jewish: 'Puritanism *is* Judaism' (p. 293. Emphasis in original).

[86] K. Marx, 'On the Jewish Question', *MEW* 1, p. 382; Easton and Guddat, p. 254.

[87] *MEW* 1, p. 382. Easton and Guddat, p. 254.

it appears to the political economist, is *civil society*, in which every individual is a totality of needs and only exists for the other person, as the other exists for him, in so far as each becomes a means for the other. . . . *Division of labour* and *exchange* are the two *phenomena* which lead the political economist to boast of the social character of his science, while in the same breath he gives expression to the contradiction in his science – the establishment of society through unsocial, particular interests.[88]

The first explicitly economic analysis by either Marx or Engels, the latter's *Outlines of a Critique of Political Economy*, concentrates on the phenomenon of competition and egoism. Engels presents the new science thus: 'This political economy or science of enrichment born of the merchants' mutual envy and greed, bears on its brow the mark of the most loathsome selfishness.'[89] He concludes 'that in the end everything comes down to competition, so long as private property exists. It is the economist's principal category . . .'.[90] The basis of both competition and private property is individualistic self-interest. 'Competition is based on self-interest, and self-interest in turn breeds monopoly. . . . The contradiction of competition is exactly the same as that of private property. It is in the interest of each to possess everything, but in the interest of the whole that each possess an equal amount.'[91] More fundamentally still, the reason for the prevailing situation is that men have no species-consciousness. Engels exhorts the people: 'Produce with consciousness, as human beings, not as dispersed atoms without consciousness of your species, and you are beyond all these artificial and untenable antitheses.'[92] Engels is here echoing an idea which, intertwined with the notion of 'civil society', tends to obscure and complicate the progression from the latter to the critique of political economy, particularly in the case of Marx: the Feuerbachian idea of the alienation of man.[93]

[88] *Economic and Philosophical Manuscripts*, *MEW*, Ergb. I, pp. 557, 562. English ed., pp. 159, 163.

[89] *MEW* 1, p. 499; *Economic and Philosophical Manuscripts*, London, 1970, p. 197.

[90] Ibid., p. 513; English ed., p. 212.

[91] Ibid., p. 513; English ed., p. 213.

[92] Ibid., p. 515; English ed., p. 215.

[93] Feuerbach's idea of alienation is developed in his *Das Wesen des Christentums*, *Sämtliche Werke*, Bd VI, Stuttgart, 1960, and *Grundsatze der Philosophie der Zukunft*, *Sämtliche* Werke II, Stuttgart, 1959.

It is well known that the *Economical and Philosophical Manuscripts* explain private property as an expression of alienated labour: all economic categories – bargaining, competition, capital and so on – are said to issue from those of alienated labour and property.[94] What is less well-known and less often noticed is that these manuscripts also include a seemingly quite different derivation of private property, more in keeping with the conception of civil society as the world of self-interested individualism. Landed property, Marx asserts, is the 'root of private property' and 'the root of landed property [is] filthy self-interest'.[95] Now, what did Marx really mean here? Were property and economics grounded in self-interest and egoism, or in alienated labour? The pages in which Marx was to analyze the roots of alienated labour were never written, or at least not preserved. However, as it happens, there is no need to choose: for far from contradicting one another, these two propositions are logically related. The key to this hidden relationship can be found in the work of Marx's early mentor Feuerbach, who, in the Preface to the *Manuscripts* is accredited with the foundation of the critique of economics.[96]

Feuerbach's view of religion as an expression of human alienation is the basis of Marx's theory of alienation. 'Man – this is the secret of religion – objectifies his essence and then makes himself again the object of this objectified, transmuted essence, transmuted into a subject, a person; he thinks himself, is to himself, an object, but the object of an object, of another essence . . . Man is the object of God.'[97] 'Religion is the estrangement of man from himself: he confronts God as a being opposed to him.'[98] The power and love attributed to God are in fact properties of the human species

---

[94] *MEW*, Ergänzungsband I, pp. 510–22; English ed., pp. 106–19.

[95] Ibid., pp. 506; English ed., pp. 101, 102. In Erich' Fromm's selection, *Marx's Concept of Man*, New York, 1961, this part is omitted. A quite different type of omission is the exclusion *in toto* of these manuscripts by the East German *Institut für Marxismus-Leninismus* – accepting the Soviet edition – from the first volume of the *Marx-Engels-Werke* edition. They were afterwards included in a supplementary volume. The so-called Economic and Philosophical Manuscripts were four separate manuscripts, written in the spring and summer of 1844, each unfinished or incompletely preserved. One of these manuscripts is excluded by Fromm.

[96] *MEW*, Ergänzungsband I, p. 468.

[97] L. Feuerbach, *Das Wesen des Christentums*, op. cit., p. 37. Emphasis omitted.

[98] Ibid., p. 41. Emphasis omitted.

attributed to an external object. Here was the inner connection between individualism and alienation. The 'exclusive self-consciousness of the individual' which suppressed the consciousness of species provided a basis for religious alienation. 'Where, then, the species as species is not the object of man, the species becomes object to him as God.'[99] Marx worked within this problematic, first in relation to the separation of state and civil society – as the alienation of man from his true social essence – and then, like Engels, in his analysis of labour and property in civil society. Although offshoots of it may be traced in later Marxist theory, it was soon surpassed as the structuring framework of analysis by the new discourse of historical materialism.

In *The Holy Family*, Feuerbach, the philosopher of man and his alienation, and Bentham, the theorist of utility and self-interest, appear together, as providers of a theoretical basis for communism. The cause that united the utilitarian tradition of Locke, Helvétius, Holbach and Bentham with Feuerbach was 'materialism', in opposition to theology and speculative philosophy. In stressing man's dependence on the surrounding world, these thinkers implied that this world must be humanized in conformity with the essence of man, and so furnished a basis for Socialism and Communism. 'There is no need of any great penetration to see from the teaching of materialism on the original goodness and equal intellectual endowment of men, the omnipotence of experience, habit and education, and the influence of environment on man, the great significance of industry, the justification of enjoyment, etc., how necessarily materialism is connected with communism and socialism. If man draws all his knowledge, sensation, etc., from the world of the senses and the experience gained in it, the empirical world must be arranged so that in it man experiences and gets used to what is really human and that he becomes aware of himself as man. If correctly understood interest is the principle of all morals, man's private interest must be made to coincide with the interest of humanity. . . . If man is shaped by his surroundings, his surroundings must be made human.'[100]

In this perspective, the work of Feuerbach becomes the theoretical analogue of the socialist movement in France and England, which

[99] Ibid., p. 190. Emphasis omitted.
[100] Marx and Engels, *The Holy Family*, MEW 2, p. 138; English ed., pp. 175–6.

in the latter case is based on the principles of Bentham. 'As Feuerbach represented materialism in the theoretical domain, French and English socialism and communism in the practical field represent materialism which now coincides with humanism.'[101] 'The *Babouvists* were coarse, uncivilized materialists, but mature communism too comes directly from French materialism. The latter returned to its mother-country, England, in the form Helvétius gave it. Bentham based his system of correctly understood interest on Helvétius's ethic, and Owen proceeded from Bentham's system to found English communism. . . . Like Owen, the more scientific French communists, Dezamy, Gay and others, developed the teaching of materialism as the teaching of real humanism and the logical basis of communism.'[102]

Only a few months after the completion of *The Holy Family* in November 1844, Marx and Engels began to dismantle this composite edifice of humanism, utilitarianism and socialism. In the spring of 1845 Marx jotted down his Theses on Feuerbach, against 'all hitherto existing materialism', and in *The German Ideology* Feuerbach and Bentham were both attacked, while the Owenite system was dismissed as having lost 'all importance'.[103] In *Capital* Bentham was to be characterized as 'a genius in the way of bourgeois stupidity'.[104]

In the rejection of Feuerbachian and Benthamite 'mechanical materialism', two decisively important conceptions emerge simultaneously into prominence in the new Marxian discourse: the economic structure of society and the class struggle determined thereby. The new discourse did not involve the discovery of the existence of classes – as we have seen, this had been made by pre-Marxist thinkers, by the historians of the French Revolution, whom Marx studied in Paris, by Saint-Simon and the pioneers of sociology, and by the Young Hegelian Karl Marx – but of their basis in social structures, and therewith of the role of the class struggle in the

[101] Ibid., p. 132; English ed., pp. 168–9.

[102] Ibid., p. 139; English ed., pp. 176–7. Emphasis omitted. Engels pointed to Bentham's important role in the early socialist movement in England, in his *The Condition of the Working-Class in England, MEW* 2, p. 455; London, 1969, pp. 265–6. This work was written at approximately the same time as *The Holy Family*.

[103] On Owen, see *The German Ideology, MEW* 3, pp. 448–9; English ed., pp. 507–8. He is still treated with respect, though belonging to a past stage in the development of the labour movement, cf. ibid., p. 197; English ed., p. 231.

[104] *Capital*, vol. 1, *MEW* 23, p. 637 n. English ed., p. 610 n.

development and change of contemporary society. In the notes that were posthumously elevated to the status of 'Theses',[105] these developments are not yet clearly visible. There Marx merely says that 'the chief defect of all hitherto existing materialism (that of Feuerbach included) is that the thing, reality, sensuousness, is conceived only in the form of the *object of contemplation*, but not as *sensuous human activity, practice*, not subjectively . . . The materialist doctrine concerning the changing of circumstances and upbringing forgets that circumstances are changed by men and that it is essential to educate the educator himself . . . The coincidence of the changing of circumstances and of human activity or self-changing can be conceived and rationally understood only as *revolutionary practice*.'[106]

In *The German Ideology* it becomes clear what Marx means by 'activity' and 'revolutionary practice'. Feuerbach's contemplative view of the sensuous world fails to appreciate that the latter is 'the product of industry and of the state of society; and indeed, in the sense that it is a historical product, the result of the activity of a whole succession of generations . . . Even the objects of the simplest "sensuous certainty" are only given him through social development, industry and commercial intercourse.'[107] 'As far as Feuerbach is a materialist he does not deal with history, and as far as he considers history he is not a materialist. . . . History is nothing but the succession of the separate generations, each of which exploits the materials, the capital funds, the productive forces handed down to it by all preceding generations, and thus, on the one hand, continues the traditional activity in completely changed circumstances, and, on the other, modifies the old circumstances with a completely changed activity.'[108]

The revolutionary practice that was the way out of the problem of the education of the educator was understood in *The German Ideology* as revolutionary class struggle – a struggle basically determined by societal development.[109]

[105] The so-called Theses on Feuerbach originally had the less pretentious heading 'ad Feuerbach'. Editorial note, *MEW* 3, p. 547.

[106] 'Theses on Feuerbach', *MEW* 3, pp. 5–6; English ed., pp. 645–6.

[107] *The German Ideology*, *MEW* 3, p. 43; English ed., p. 57.

[108] Ibid., p. 45; English ed., p. 59.

[109] Ibid., pp. 69–70; English ed., 85–6. In *The German Ideology* the new conception of society was, however, only anticipated, as we shall see in the analysis below in ch. 7.

Feuerbach's critique of theology and idealist philosophy had drawn attention away from the heaven of abstraction to the real world, but of the structure and operation of the latter he had understood little or nothing. On similar grounds Marx and Engels now criticized Bentham and utilitarianism. The chief merit of utilitarianism was that it had pointed to the connection of all social relations with economic ones. But it had done this 'only in a restricted way': it provided no basis for a scientific study of society, and its outlook was confined within the limits of bourgeois ideology. 'When the sentimental and moral paraphrases, which for the French were the entire content of the utility theory, had been exhausted, all that remained for its further development was the question how individuals and relations were to be used, to be exploited. Meanwhile the reply to this question had already been given in political economy; the only possible step forward was by inclusion of the economic content. Bentham achieved this advance. But the idea had already been stated in political economy that the chief relations of exploitation are determined by production by and large, independently of the will of individuals who find them already in existence. Hence, no other field of speculative thought remained for the utility theory than the attitude of individuals to these important relations, the private exploitation of an already existing world by individuals. On this subject Bentham and his school indulged in lengthy moral reflections. Thereby the whole criticism of the existing world provided by the utility theory also moved within a narrow compass. Prejudiced in favour of the conditions of the bourgeoisie, it could criticize only those relations which had been handed down from a past epoch and were an obstacle to the development of the bourgeoisie.'[110]

Marx's and Engels' use of the idea of 'civil society' was centred neither on man and his essence in a world of isolating individualism and alienation, nor on utility and interest as the guide of human action. We have also noted that Marx and Engels did not substitute a conception of history in terms of class consciousness for the *Volksgeist* of German idealism. They broke with this kind of theory of society and history based on the idea of a sovereign, world-creating subject, be it man, nation, class or anything else. The new science of historical materialism focused on the ever pre-given

[110] Ibid., p. 398; English ed., p. 453.

complex social totality, the always 'already existing world', its structure, its effects on the men living in it, its 'laws of motion' and its possible transformation. 'Civil society' was something other than the world of egoistic, alienated man. First and foremost, it was 'the form of intercourse determined by the existing productive forces at all previous historical stages, and in its turn determining these . . . [which had] as its premises and basis the simple family and the multiple, the so-called tribe . . .'[111]

Marx was a great and complex personality, and we are concerned here with only a few aspects of his thought, not with a comprehensive analysis and judgment of the Marxian oeuvre. This study is no more concerned with Marx's 'conception of man', for instance, than with that of Comte, Durkheim or Weber.[112] But to the extent that Marx is seen as a contributor to social science and to the class struggle, it is clear that there occurred an important theoretical break in his conceptions between *The Holy Family* and *The German Ideology*.[113] For as we have seen, there occurred in both Marx and Engels simultaneous changes in their views of social analysis and of the working class and its struggle. These changes would of course be of equal importance in a study of broader scope, for whatever else there may be in Marxism, scientific analysis and revolutionary class struggle were certainly the primary concerns of its founders.

III. The New Pattern of Social Determination

Having broken out of their inherited theoretical world of Hegelian idealism, Feuerbachian humanism and Anglo-French utilitarianism, Marx and Engels began to develop their new theory of society. The new pattern of social determination, the system of regularities in the real world which they discovered and grasped with the production of their new conceptual system, is succinctly summarized in Marx's famous Preface to *A Contribution to the Critique of Political Economy*: 'In the social production of their existence, men inevitably enter into definite relations, which are independent of their will, namely

[111] Ibid., p. 36; English ed., 48.
[112] For a recent serious effort in this genre see B. Ollman, *Alienation. Marx's Conception of Man in Capitalist Society*, Cambridge, 1971.
[113] This is exactly where Althusser located the break in Marx, though then with little detailed reference: *For Marx*, pp. 36–8.

relations of production appropriate to a given stage in the development of their material forces of production. The totality of these relations of production constitutes the economic structure of society, the real foundation on which arises a legal and political superstructure and to which correspond definite forms of social consciousness. The mode of production of material life conditions the general process of social, political and intellectual life.'[114]

What is the meaning of these new concepts, forces and relations of production? To what do they refer? The answer is neither simple nor easy to find. Marx and Engels neither defined their concepts systematically nor used them entirely consistently, even after their new theory had matured. In a loose sense, their signification is clear. 'Forces of production' denotes the level of technological development, and 'relations of production' includes at least the distribution of the means of production. But what does Marx mean when he emphasizes that capital is a relation of production? How is the concept of the forces of production related to productivity? How is it that the forces of production can have a more or less social character, and in what way are the relations of production related to exploitation and to juridical property? To the extent that Marxism claims to be a scientific theory, questions of this sort inevitably arise, and in this section we shall try to contribute to the clarification of fundamental concepts of historical materialism and their systemic interrelation.

Although the immense secondary literature on Marx and Engels has in general paid scant attention to this problem of conceptual clarification, it has been given priority in the range of work inspired by Althusser. Apart from those of Althusser himself,[115] important contributions have been made above all by Etienne Balibar, Charles Bettelheim, Nicos Poulantzas and Pierre-Philippe Rey.[116] For all

---

[114] *A Contribution to the Critique of Political Economy*, *MEW* 13, pp. 8–9; English ed., pp. 20–1.

[115] See principally *For Marx* and *Reading Capital*.

[116] E. Balibar, 'The Fundamental Concepts of Historical Materialism', in *Reading Capital* and in *Cinq études du matérialisme historique*, Paris, 1974. The latter differs significantly from Balibar's earlier presentation. C. Bettelheim, *Calcul économique et formes de propriété*, Paris, 1970. M. Hanecker, *Los conceptos elementales del materialismo historico*, Santiago de Chile (10th ed.), 1972. This work is in the form of a manual. N. Poulantzas, *Political Power and Social Classes*, London, 1973, and *Classes in Contemporary Capitalism*, London, 1975. P.-Ph. Rey, *Les alliances de classe*, Paris, 1973.

their great importance (not least in the present study), these contributions, however, pose certain difficulties in the way of an
understanding of Marx and Engels. Most of them aim also to *develop*,
often in contexts of current controversy, the basic concepts of
historical materialism, but without distinguishing clearly between
this and the more modest task of *clarification*. Here, we will confine
ourselves to the latter. Since our focus is on the formation of
historical materialism, considerable attention will be devoted to the
emergence of the new concepts in the Marxian discourse. It is hoped
in this way to account for certain ambiguities and variations of
meaning, and to present the characteristic unity of the discourse
without abolishing problems of interpretation by decree. This
study will also differ from the works mentioned above in its frame
of analysis, which posits the search for a pattern of social determination as the object of the scientific investigations of Marx and Engels,
and in the substantive results of its conceptual clarification, above
all in the case of the relations of production. With a few exceptions,
however, we will not enter into a critique of the existing interpretative literature. The references are given; the differences are available
to comparison and criticism.

1. The Forces of Production

The term '*Produktivkräfte*' ('forces of production' or 'productive
forces' in English translations of Marx) was bequeathed to Marx by
the classical economists. In the form of 'productive powers', it
occurs in Smith and Ricardo, and in his excerpts and quotations
from them, Marx (from the *Economic and Philosophical Manuscripts*
onwards) usually translates it into German as *Produktivkräfte*.[117]
By productive powers, Smith and Ricardo meant simply productivity or productive capacities. On at least one occasion Marx used
the more literal '*produktive Fähigkeiten*' to render the phrase in
German.[118] Engels, in his *Outlines of a Critique of Political Economy*
(from 1843–44) speaks alternatively of *Produktionskraft* and

[117] *Economic-Philosophical Manuscripts*, MEW, Ergb. I, pp. 491, 495–6, 502,
English ed., pp. 87, 89–90. Marx is here excerpting from Adam Smith. For
Ricardo see his *Principles*, pp. 119, 145.
[118] *Theories of Surplus-Value*, MEW 26: 2, p. 542; English ed., London,
1969–72, p. 541.

Produktionsfähigkeit.[119] Neither Smith nor Ricardo, nor their later editors (who do not give an index entry for it), seem to have attached much value to the word, although the first book of Smith's *Wealth of Nations* is entitled 'Of the Causes of the Improvement in the Productive Powers of Labour . . .'.

Another economic author, whom Marx read at a very early stage, seems to have made rather more of the notion. This was the German radical Wilhelm Schulz, the author of *Die Bewegung der Produktion* (1843). Without at this time commenting on it, Marx cites him in the *Manuscripts* as referring, obliquely, to the *social character* of the new forces of production, a notion that was to play a central role in Marxist theory: 'More comprehensive combinations of productive forces . . . in industry and trade by uniting more numerous and more diverse, human and natural powers in larger-scale enterprises. Already here and there, closer association of the chief branches of production.'[120]

So far, Marx and Engels' discovery of the forces of production was simply part of their discovery and reading of classical economics, as a point of entry into the anatomy of civil society. It was just a phrase used in passing. In Marx's critiques of Hegel, and in Engels' report on *The Condition of the Working Class in England*, it is absent altogether. In Engels' *Outlines* and Marx's *Economic and Philosophical Manuscripts*, and in *The Holy Family*, *Produktivkräfte* (or in Engels, *Produktionskraft*) is merely one word among thousands. In *The German Ideology*, however, it emerges as a strategic concept in a new historical and social theory. Before trying to define it in a more precise way, we shall locate the concept in the new theoretical system.

2. The Technological Anchorage of Society: Structures or Inventions?

'Forces of production' is a concept in a historical theory of society which asserts that social relations have a technological foundation or anchorage. It plays a part in a polemic against idealist theories

---

[119] Engels, *Outlines of a Critique of Political Economy*, *MEW* 1, p. 516f; English ed., p. 216f.

[120] *MEW*, Ergb. I, p. 496; English ed., p. 90. Long afterwards, in the first volume of *Capital*, Marx praised Schulz' book: 'In many respects a book to be recommended.' *MEW* 23, p. 392 n; English ed., p. 372 n.

that see society as constituted by a certain 'spirit' or culture: 'Men are the producers of their conceptions, ideas, etc. – real, active men, as they are conditioned by a definite development of their productive forces and of the intercourse corresponding to these . . .'[121]. The new concept of forces of production succeeds the illusions of alienated egoistic man as the basis of competitive capitalism, as can be shown by a comparison of quotations from Marx's and Engels' works before and after *The German Ideology*. 'Judaism reaches its height with the perfection of civil society, but civil society achieves perfection only in the *Christian* world. Only under the reign of Christianity, which makes *all* national, moral, and theoretical relations *external* to man, was civil society able to separate itself completely from political life, sever all man's species-ties, substitute egoism and selfish need for those ties, and dissolve the human world into a world of atomistic, mutually hostile individuals.'[122] 'The abolition of religion as people's *illusory* happiness is the demand for their *real* happiness. The demand to abandon illusions about their condition is a *demand to abandon a condition which requires illusions.*'[123] In contrast to this, *The German Ideology* states, by way of introduction: 'Since, according to their fantasy, the relationships of men . . . their chains and their limitations are products of their consciousness, the Young Hegelians logically put to men the moral postulate of exchanging their present consciousness for human, critical or egoistic consciousness (the last refers to Max Stirner), and thus of removing their limitations. This demand to change consciousness amounts to a demand to interpret reality in another way . . . They forget, however, that to these phrases they themselves are only opposing other phrases, and that they are in no way combating the real existing world when they are merely combating the phrases of this world.'[124] 'Civil society' now comprises 'the whole material intercourse of individuals within a definite stage of the development of [the] productive forces'.[125] In the *Communist*

---

[121] *German Ideology*, *MEW* 3, p. 26; English ed., p. 37.

[122] Marx, 'On the Jewish Question', *MEW* 1, p. 376; Easton and Guddat, p. 247.

[123] Marx, 'Toward the Critique of Hegel's Philosophy of Law', *MEW* 1, p. 379; English ed., p. 250. The emphasis here is original, but other emphases in the original have been omitted.

[124] *The German Ideology*, *MEW* 3, p. 20; English ed., p. 30.

[125] Ibid., p. 36; English ed., p. 48.

Manifesto the basis of competitive capitalism is characterized explicitly in terms of the new theory: 'The means of production and exchange, on whose foundation the bourgeoisie built itself up, were generated in feudal society. At a certain stage in the development of these means of production and of exchange, the conditions under which feudal society produced and exchanged, the feudal organization of agriculture and manufacturing industry, in one word, the feudal relations of property became no longer compatible with the already developed productive forces. ... They had to be burst asunder; they were burst asunder. Into their place stepped free competition, accompanied by a social and political constitution adapted to it, and by the economical and political sway of the bourgeois class.'[126]

The concept of forces of production is part of a conceptual couple, the forces and relations of production. The latter either correspond to the former, or are in contradiction with them. The forces of production are thus not seen as directly related to social relations in general, but primarily to the economic relations of production, to which Marx's studies were mainly devoted. The concept denotes the objective – not arbitrarily subjective or voluntaristic – basis of certain relations of production, and of certain transformations of the prevailing relations of production. We have seen already that Marx conceived the relations of production as anchored in their correspondence to a certain level of development of the forces of production. The emergence of a contradiction between the two provides the basis for changes in the fundamental structure of society. In the words of the famous Preface again: 'At a certain stage of development, the material productive forces of society come into conflict with the existing relations of production ... From forms of development of the productive forces these relations turn into their fetters. Then begins an era of social revolution.'[127]

Since this study concerns both sociology and historical materialism, it might be noted at this point that this theory of the technological foundation of social relationships and fundamental social

[126] *Communist Manifesto, MEW* 4, p. 467; English ed., p. 72.
[127] *MEW* 13, p. 9; English ed., p. 21. In *The German Ideology*, Marx and Engels even claim that 'All collisions in history have their origin, according to our view, in the contradiction between the productive forces and the form of intercourse.' *MEW* 3, p. 73; English ed., p. 90.

change is completely different in nature from the sociological theory of 'cultural lag'. The latter has been developed by the American sociologist William Ogburn over a number of decades.[128] Ogburn had read Marx, and has himself said that his theory developed out of what might be termed a utilitarian-cum-Freudian reading of Marx. In his interpretation, the driving force of history was disguised economic interest, but to Ogburn 'the disguise factor in social causation . . . [soon came to appear] less important than the time factor.'[129] Thus, he came to focus upon the different tempos of change, and on the maladjustments that they caused among the different parts of the man-made world of 'culture'. In modern society, technological inventions usually occur before changes in other parts of culture, which lag behind, and this leads to increasing cultural maladjustment – until the latter are adapted to the technological change. These belated adaptations or readjustments constitute 'cultural lags'.

Cultural lag theory is concerned with the chronological order of events, and conceives of technology in terms of 'inventions'. Marxist theory, of which the concept of productive forces forms part, deals first and foremost with the interrelation of different structures and processes in human society, and treats technology primarily in terms of processes of material production, which permit and (in order to function effectively) necessitate certain economic and other relations.[130] Thus, the forces of production constitute the conditions of existence for corresponding relations of production. The economic analyses of *Capital* are directly related to analyses of the labour process. For example, Marx presents a detailed exposition of how the rule of capital is related to machine technology, as distinct from handicraft.[131] Without the worker's subordination to factory machinery, 'the subjection of labour to capital' is only 'formal', not 'real'.[132]

[128] An introduction to Ogburn is furnished by his selected papers, edited by Otis Dudley Duncan, W. Ogburn, *On Culture and Social Change*, Chicago, 1964.

[129] Ibid., p. 88.

[130] The difference between cultural lag theory and historical materialism in these fundamental respects corresponds to the distinction uncovered by Althusser between a mechanistic conception of causality and the 'structural causality' peculiar to historical materialism. *Reading Capital*, 186f.

[131] *Capital* I, chs. 5, 11–14, *MEW* 23 (chs. 7, 13–16, in English editions).

[132] Ibid., pp. 510, 737.

The forces of production do not have an independent and faster tempo of development of their own that makes them the spearhead of historical development. On the contrary, one of the critical points of the Marxian analysis is that the rhythm of the forces of production is dependent on the relations of production. Capitalist relations of production are distinguished by driving forward the development of the productive forces.[133] Contradictions between the forces and the relations of production, their increasing mutual maladjustment, do not emerge because of the more rapid development of the former, but because beyond a certain point the specific development of the productive forces induced by the prevailing relations of production becomes self-destructive. In capitalism, periodic crises of over-production ensue. The further development of the productive forces becomes increasingly dependent on conditions external to the individual capitalist enterprise, and the scale of production increasingly demands resources exceeding those of private capitalists, though the elasticity of capitalism is extended by the development of the credit system and corporations, and by state support to private enterprise.[134]

There is, finally, a third decisive difference between the cultural lag theory, framed in terms of 'linear causality' and concerned with the chronological order of inventions, and historical materialism with its 'structural causality', which highlights, in this case, the ways in which technological and economic structures determine each other. Ogburn has summarized his theory of evolution in this way: 'What are the factors that explain cultural evolution? They are four: invention, accumulation, diffusion and adjustment.' In a footnote, he adds: 'Of these four factors, the central one is invention . . .'[135] The laconic Marxist rejoinder to this is: 'the history of all hitherto existing society is the history of class struggles'.[136] That is, the level and development of the productive forces are effective in that, together with the relations of production, they provide the stage and the cast of the drama of social life– in class societies, a

---

[133] Ibid., ch. 10, p. 378f; English ed., ch. 14, p. 353f. In Marx's view this was, for all its cost in suffering, 'one of the civilizing aspects of capital'. *MEW* 25, p. 827; English ed., p. 799.

[134] *Capital, MEW* 23, p. 789f; English ed., p. 761f; vol. III, chs. 15, 27, *MEW* 25.

[135] Ogburn, op. cit., p. 23.

[136] *MEW* 4, p. 462; English ed., p. 67.

theatre of the class struggle. Marx's distinction between base and superstructure does not involve an autonomously advancing base to which the superstructure is belatedly adjusted, but rather on the one hand, structural contradiction or lack of fit *within* the base – between the relations and the forces of production – and, on the other hand, the ways in which men become conscious of this and fight it out: 'In studying such transformations it is always necessary to distinguish between the material transformation of the economic conditions of production, which can be determined with the precision of natural science, and the legal, political, religious, artistic or philosophic – in short, ideological forms – in which men become conscious of this conflict and fight it out.'[137]

The specific development of the forces of production by capitalist relations of production, for instance, affects the relations of strength and power, ideological as well as material, between the bourgeoisie and the proletariat. Against a capitalist class that increases in wealth as it diminishes in numbers, stands the exploited 'working-class, a class always increasing in numbers, and disciplined, united, organized by the very mechanism of the process of capitalist production itself'.[138]

The importance that Marx attached to technology and technical relations was, as he himself pointed out, connected with his 'conception of man': 'Technology discloses man's mode of dealing with Nature, the process of production by which he sustains his life, and thereby also lays bare the mode of formation of his social relations, and of the mental conceptions that flow from them.'[139] The abyss between Marxism and Ogburn's technocratic conception of evolution, which also expresses 'man's active behaviour towards nature', is a reminder of the limitations and hazards of analyzing social theory in such general terms.

[137] Marx, *A Contribution to the Critique of Political Economy*, *MEW* 13, p. 9; English ed., p. 21. This formulation, however, leaves out the problem of the polity as an objective structure, determined 'in the last instance' by the economic. Anticipated in *The Eighteenth Brumaire*, this notion of the state was developed by Marx in his analysis of the Paris Commune, *The Civil War in France*, *MEW* 17; English original in *The First International and After*, London, 1974. The important conclusion is this: 'But the working class cannot simply lay hold of the ready-made state machinery, and wield it for its own purposes.' The old repressive state apparatus must be smashed. *MEW* 17, p. 336; English ed., p. 206.

[138] *Capital* I, *MEW* 23, pp. 790–1; English ed., p. 763.

[139] Ibid., p. 393 n; English ed., p. 372 n.

3. The Transformation of a Concept

Marx took the expression 'forces of production' from classical political economy. He could have used not only the expression but also the concept in a historical theory of society, which would then have been a theory of the relationship between productivity and social arrangements, most directly, between productivity and exploitation. Marx actually drew attention to this relationship in a critical comment on Ricardo: 'Ricardo never concerns himself about the origin of surplus-value. . . . Whenever he discusses the productiveness of labour, he seeks in it, not the cause of surplus-value, but the cause that determines the magnitude of that value. On the other hand, his school has openly proclaimed the productiveness of labour to be the originating cause of profit . . . [that is, the productivity and the productive force of labour are here synonymous].'[140] Integrated with a utilitarian 'conflict perspective', this conception might well have produced conclusions similar to those of the American sociologist, Gerhard Lenski: 'With technological advance, an increasing proportion of the goods and services available to a society will be distributed on the basis of power'.[141] The chasm between such ideas and historical materialism will emerge even more strikingly when we turn to examine the concept of relations of production; but in this section, we are concerned with the specificity of the Marxian concept of the forces of production.

In Marx's theory, 'forces of production' was transformed into a new concept. Not only is its role in Marxist theory quite distinctive, and vastly more important (in relation to other concepts) than in classical economics; it also acquires a wholly new referent. The Marxist concept refers to the connection between different types of technical organization of labour and different types of economic and social system. This connection is absent from the theories of Smith and Ricardo. Marx did not criticize the liberal economists very explicitly for this. But this early quotation (from *The German Ideology*) shows his point of departure. 'The relations of different nations among themselves depend upon the extent to which each has developed its productive forces, the division of labour and internal intercourse. This statement is generally recognized. But

[140] Ibid., p. 539; English ed., pp. 515–16.
[141] G. Lenski, *Power and Privilege*, New York, 1966, p. 46. Emphasis omitted.

not only the relation of one nation to others, but also the whole internal structure of the nation itself depends on the stage of development reached by its production and its internal and external intercourse. How far the productive forces of a nation are developed is shown most manifestly by the degree to which the division of labour has been carried. . . . The various stages of development in the division of labour are just so many different forms of ownership, i.e. the existing stage in the division of labour determines also the relations of individuals to one another with reference to the material, instrument, and product of labour.'[142]

The concept of forces of production has no doubt something to do with productivity. But it refers not, as with Smith and Ricardo, simply or even primarily to productivity or productive capacity as such. Its primary reference is rather to the *different ways in which productivity is ensured.* Productive capacity is no longer merely a quantitative phenomenon: the dominant concern is no longer with its quantitative improvement, but with the qualitatively different technical forms of labour. This change of focus is conveyed by the following formulation, from a very important summary in *Capital* of the core of historical materialism: the relations of production are here said to correspond to 'a definite stage in the development of the methods of labour [*die Art und Weise der Arbeit*] and thereby its social productivity'.[143] Marx views the means of labour in the same perspective: 'It is not the articles made, but how they are made, and by what instruments, that enables us to distinguish different economic epochs.'[144]

Marx formulates the conception that the type of organization of labour, through which a given productivity is manifested, affects the economic and social organization, in a number of phrases. Sometimes he writes of the 'mode of production', sometimes of 'the real process of appropriation', and at others (often in *Capital*, for example) of the 'labour-process'; the word *Produktivkraft* is used both in singular and plural, the former meaning simply productivity, the latter often meaning factors of production or skills.[145] But beneath all these bewildering lexical shifts, there stands an enduring conceptual structure, denoting a technical organization and labour

[142] *MEW* 3, pp. 21–2; English ed., pp. 32–3
[143] *Capital* III, *MEW* 25, p. 799; English ed., Moscow, 1962, p. 722.
[144] *Capital* I, *MEW* 23, pp. 194–5; English ed., p. 180.
[145] See, for instance, *Grundrisse*, p. 393f; English ed., p. 493f.

process, distinguished from the economic forms of production (usually designated in terms of different relations of production), but related to the latter in that it provides their conditions of existence and is developed in a particular rhythm by them. In Marxian formulations where the relations of production are said to correspond to or to be in contradiction with the forces of production, the latter refers to this technical organization and labour process. In a systematization of Marxist concepts, it should be used only in this sense.

'Forces of production' in this sense is an indivisible concept. It is pointless to try to enumerate forces of production or to dispute whether this or that is 'a force of production'. Marx speaks instead of their 'development' and of the level of their development. The forces of production have a quantitative referent, productivity, which explains the evolutionary overtones in the expression 'level of development'. But in Marx's theory the degree of productivity – as distinguished from the manner in which it is ensured and the tempo of its change – is of secondary interest. At two critical points in history, however, it is central: a certain minimum level of productivity is necessary to make possible a differentiation between producers and non-producers who appropriate part of the fruits of the producers' labour: and a certain rise in productivity is necessary to make possible a communist society, governed by the principle of 'from each according to his capacity, to each according to his needs'. In other words, the rise and the final abolition of exploitation and classes presuppose a certain quantitative level of productivity. But it is with the long intervening history that historical materialism and Marxist politics are concerned.

The relationship between the forces and the relations of production, then, centres on the problem of their structural compatibility. For example, the manner in which the forces of production come into contradiction with capitalist relations of production and provide the basis for new relations is summarized in this way in *Capital*:

'Hand in hand with this centralization, or this expropriation of many capitalists by few, develop, on an ever-extending scale, the co-operative form of the labour-process, the conscious technical application of science, the methodical cultivation of the soil, the transformation of the instruments of labour into instruments of labour only usable in common, the economizing of all means of production by their use as the means of production of combined, socialized labour, the entanglement of all peoples in the net of the world-market . . . Centralization of the means of production and socialization of labour at last reach a point where they become incompatible with their capitalist integument.'[146]

4. The Relations of Production

The single most important concept of historical materialism is 'the relations of production'. When a Marxist investigates the character of a particular society (say, England or Sweden in 1976) he is in the first instance concerned with the dominant relations of production. Social classes are derived from the relations of production, as the 'bearers' of the latter. 'Relations of production' is a very complex concept, and its interpretation continues to provoke controversy. Unlike the concept of the forces of production, it was not developed by Marx out of classical political economy. It occurs neither in Smith's *Wealth of Nations* nor in Ricardo's *Principles* (at least, using the *Marx-Engels-Werke* edition, it has not been possible to find it anywhere among Marx's many excerpts from and commentaries on other economists, including the radical post-Ricardians).

By conceptualizing economic phenomena in terms of *relations* of production, Marx is concerned primarily to stress that these phenomena denote social relations among men. Economic phenomena are not properties of nature. Political economy should not be primarily concerned with things, with natural factors of production and the natural products of production. Equally, it should avoid the complementary, idealist error of treating economic phenomena as the expression of eternal ideas or principles. It was in opposition to both of these errors – the first represented, in Marx's view, by classical political economy, and the second, by Proudhon's *Philosophie de la Misère* – that the concept of the relations of production was formulated.

In a very broad sense this relational view of the economy and economics forms a fundamental continuity in Marx's work. The reason is that for Marx the social is always historical and therefore transitory, while the properties of nature and the principles of metaphysics are, in contrast, non-historical. Already in the Paris

---

[146] *Capital* I, *MEW* 23, p. 790; English ed., p. 763.

Manuscripts of 1844, Marx presents a kind of relational critique of political economy. 'Political economy conceals the estrangement inherent in the nature of labour by not considering the direct relationship between the worker (labour) and production.'[147] In the language of the 'German ideology', Marx also hints here at the historically limited scope of political economy: 'political economy starts from labour as the real soul of production', but in fact 'political economy has merely formulated the laws of alienated labour'.[148]

The first work in which Marx explicitly employs the concept of relations of production is *The Poverty of Philosophy* (1847).[149] There it is used mainly with a historical emphasis. 'Economists express the relations of bourgeois production, the division of labour, credit, money, etc., as fixed, immutable, eternal categories. . . . Economists explain how production occurs in the above-mentioned relations, but what they do not explain is how these relations themselves are produced, that is, the historical movement which gave them birth. M. Proudhon [takes] these relations for principles, categories, abstract thoughts, . . . But the moment we cease to pursue the historical movement of production relations, of which the categories are but the theoretical expression, the moment we want to see in these categories no more than ideas, spontaneous thoughts, independent of real relations, we are forced to attribute the origin of these thoughts to the movement of pure reason.'[150] Comparing this quotation with the words of the 1844 *Manuscripts*, the reader will note that in the critique of the economists the concept of relations of production has succeeded that of alienated labour. From *Wage-Labour and Capital* (written in 1848 and first published in 1849) onwards, the concept of relations of production is very clearly directed against analyses of economic phenomena in terms of non-historical qualities instead of historical relations. In a famous quotation from the work just mentioned, cited by the author

---

[147] *MEW*, Ergb. I, p. 513; English ed., pp. 109–10.

[148] Ibid., p. 520; English ed., p. 117.

[149] The phrase 'relations of production' occurs in *The German Ideology*, but referring there to what is designated by the concept of forces of production. Marx and Engels speak of the 'bornierten Produktionsverhältnisse' ('restricted relations of production') in the feudal era, thereby referring to 'the small-scale and primitive cultivation of the land, and the craft type of industry'. *MEW* 3, p. 25; English ed., p. 36.

[150] *MEW* 4, p. 126; *The Poverty of Philosophy*, New York, 1971, pp. 104–5.

himself in *Capital*, Marx says: 'A Negro is a Negro. In certain circumstances he becomes a slave. A mule is a machine for spinning cotton. Only under certain circumstances does it become capital . . . Capital is a social relation of production. It is a historical relation of production.'[151]

Capital, to Marx, was not a thing; it was not identical with the means of production. Capital is a definite social relationship and one has to distinguish between the '*stoffliche*' (material) conditions of production and their historical–social determination. To confuse these is to reify social relationships. It is in this specific context that Marx's argument concerning reification and the fetishism of commodities belongs. This argument is not part of a cultural criticism of the 'mechanized petrification' or the 'iron cage' that concerned Max Weber. The much more material and tangible social criticism of the mature Marx was directed against the exploitation of the workers, their use as a means for the accumulation of capital with all that implied: dangerous and degrading working conditions, miserable housing, constant risk of unemployment, wages subordinated to the needs of capital accumulation and so on. These features of proletarian existence are illustrated at length and in concrete empirical form in the first volume of *Capital*.

Commodity fetishism consists in the perception of market exchange simply as an exchange of things with certain values, and not as a manifestation of certain relationships. To reify social relationships is, for example, to treat capital as a natural factor of production with its natural factor income, profit, and not as a specific relation of production, a specific way of exploiting labour. These views are part of the ideology prevailing in bourgeois society, an ideology which more or less imprisons bourgeois economists, and from which science must escape. The legitimate Marxist context of the concepts of reification and commodity fetishism is thus not *Kulturkritik*, but the rupture of science from ideology.

The social relations that Marx indicated were not social relations in general. They were relations of a particular kind, relations of production. It was some time before Marx himself specified these

[151] *MEW* 23, pp. 793–4 n; English ed., p. 766 n.
[152] *Capital* I, *MEW* 23, pp. 85–98; English ed., pp. 71–83; III, *MEW*, p. 835; English ed., p. 806.
[153] *The German Ideology*, *MEW* 3, pp. 21, 26, 71; English ed., pp. 32, 37, 87, for example.

relations clearly. In *The German Ideology*, for example, where Marx and Engels drew the first sketch of historical materialism, the concept that accompanies the forces of production is *Verkehr* or *Verkehrsform*, a much broader term meaning approximately communication, commerce or intercourse. Here, it seems to refer to social relations in general; indeed it sometimes becomes 'social relations'.[154] The sole reference to production is seemingly in the concept of forces of production; as is indeed explicit when the authors speak of the 'three moments, the forces of production, the state of society, and consciousness'.[155] It is therefore logical that both machinery and money are here regarded as forces of production.[156]

We have seen above how *The German Ideology* constitutes an important break with earlier ideas of Marx and Engels. But that work is only a beginning. Contrary to widespread belief, the first part of *The German Ideology* cannot be regarded as a summary of historical materialism. The concept of the relations of production is not present in the idea of *Verkehr*. It is absent. *Verkehr* is, in fact, a pre-Marxist concept. An approach that selects the *commercial* aspect of capitalism in preference to labour and production, and generalizes it as the central concept of *Verkehr*,[157] is quite evidently not that of the mature Marx. In fact, the concept is less an anticipation of historical materialism than an echo of Hegel and Adam Smith. What Marx and Engels have in mind when they discuss the prevailing *Verkehrsform* is Hegel's civil society.[158] The submersion of social relations in the concept of *Verkehr* also recalls Adam Smith,

[154] Ibid., pp. 31–2; English ed., p. 43.

[155] Ibid., p. 32, cf. p. 71; English ed., p. 43, cf. p. 87.

[156] Ibid., p. 69; English ed., p. 85. Correspondingly, *Verkehr* is also used in the more restricted sense of commerce, as distinguished from production. 'The next extension of the division of labour was the separation of production and commerce [*Verkehr*], the formation of a special class of merchants . . .' *MEW* 3, p. 52; see further p. 53f; English ed., p. 67.

[157] We shall see below that a long letter to a Russian intellectual, P. V. Annenkov, in December 1846, constitutes the last major example of this first stage in the development of the idea of relations of production. There Marx says, writing in French: 'I am using the word "commerce" here in its widest sense, as we use *Verkehr* in German.' *MEW* 27, p. 453; Marx-Engels, *Selected Correspondence*, p. 41. In fact, as we have seen, Marx used *Verkehr* in both the wide and narrow senses, without distinguishing between them.

[158] *The German Ideology*, *MEW* 3, p. 36; English ed., p. 48.

who wrote: 'Every man thus lives by exchanging, or becomes in some sense a merchant, and the society itself grows to be what is properly called a commercial society.'[159] The constant pre-occupation with the division of labour in *The German Ideology* is another probable indication of Smith's influence.

Now if this is true, the determinant contradiction of productive forces and *Verkehr* should have a different meaning from that of productive forces and relations of production. This is in fact the case. In *The German Ideology* there is no contradiction between the social character of the forces of production and private *Verkehr*. On the contrary, it is stressed that a 'universal' *Verkehr* develops, manifested above all in the world market. The contradiction is that the universal *Verkehr* makes the oppressions of the prevailing *Verkehr* intolerable (*unerträglich*) for the masses.[160] Within the given *Verkehrsform* the development of the productive forces involves wealth, civilization and universal human interaction on the one side, and on the other propertylessness and misery. The universality of the capitalist form of *Verkehr* makes it universally intolerable, and the revolutionary negation of the negation follows. The forces of production and the *Verkehrsform* do not form a structural contradiction, resulting in crises of the economic system.

It is not quite correct, however, to say that the idea of relations of production is absent in *The German Ideology*. Its outlines can be discerned, somewhat to one side of the main argument about productive forces and forms of *Verkehr*, in a discussion of forms of property, which together with the 'instruments of production' form a conceptual pair designed to play the role for which that of the forces and relations of production was later to be developed. The following passage makes this clear: 'Our investigation hitherto started from the instruments of production, and it has already shown that private property was a necessity for certain industrial stages. In *industrie extractive* private property still coincides with

[159] Smith, *The Wealth of Nations*, London, 1970, p. 126.

[160] *MEW* 3, pp. 34–5; English ed., pp. 46–7. 'This "estrangement" [*Entfremdung*] (to use a term which will be comprehensible to the philosophers) can, of course, only be abolished given two practical premises. For a revolution, it must necessarily have rendered the great mass of humanity "propertyless", and produced, at the same time, the contradiction of an existing world of wealth and culture, both of which conditions presuppose a great increase in productive power, a high degree of its development' (p. 34; English ed., p. 46).

labour; in small industry and all agriculture up till now property is the necessary consequence of the existing instruments of production; in big industry the contradiction between the instruments of production and private property appears for the first time and is the product of big industry; moreover, big industry must be highly developed to produce this contradiction. Thus only with big industry does the abolition of private property become possible.'[161] In this section, *Verkehr* is related not to the later concept of relations of production but to that of the productive forces. Here Marx and Engels briefly discuss the relationship between appropriation and property on the one hand, and on the other, the instruments and forces of production, which exist in a particular type of *Verkehr*, restricted or universal, only among individuals.[162]

The central importance of property had long been acknowledged. For the socialist movement, to which Marx and Engels belonged, it was a natural central target. In 1840 Proudhon had denounced it, answering the question *What Is Property?* with the famous reply: It is theft! We will leave for later consideration the relationship between the relations of production and property in the normative juridical sense. In this context we will simply note that Marx emphasizes that property is not a simple concept, that it refers at a very early stage to an *ensemble* of social relationships. This is stressed in the critique of Proudhon, first outlined in the letter to Annenkov: 'In the real world, on the other hand, the division of labour and all M. Proudhon's other categories are social relations forming in their entirety what is today known as property; outside these relations bourgeois property is nothing but a metaphysical or juristic illusion.'[163] In the published critique of Proudhon, *The Poverty of Philosophy*, this thesis is nearly exactly reproduced: 'In each historical epoch, property has developed differently and under a set of entirely different social relations. Thus to define bourgeois property is nothing else than to give an exposition of all the social relations of bourgeois production. To try to give a definition of property as of an independent relation, a category apart, an abstract and eternal idea, can be nothing but an illusion of metaphysics or jurisprudence.'[164] The significant change is from 'social relations'

---

[161] Ibid., p. 66; English ed., p. 81.
[162] Ibid., pp. 66–7; English ed., pp. 81–2.
[163] *MEW* 27, p. 456; *Selected Correspondence*, p. 44.
[164] *Poverty of Philosophy*, *MEW* 4, p. 165; English ed., p. 154. The phrase

to 'social relations of . . . production'. Here, I think, we can locate the emergence of the concept of relations of production. The concept emerges in *The Poverty of Philosophy*, in close relation with the concept of property, to denote a specific totality of economic relationships. Wider, strictly speaking, than property, it is also more limited than the extended concept of *Verkehr*.

The formal emergence of a concept, however, is not of course the same as its scientific development. In all these works of the 1840's something central is still missing. The concept of surplus-value, for example, first appears only in the *Grundrisse*.[165] What, indeed, would a Marxist concept of capitalist relations of production be without the concept of surplus-value? The concept of surplus-value is in turn directly related to the development of the general concept of relations of production, which, in significant aspects, is not covered by the enumerations of socio-economic characteristics in the works of the 1840's.

The phenomenon of surplus labour and surplus product – a surplus above the labour necessary to keep the direct producers alive, provided by the working population to maintain the unproductive classes – was not discovered by Marx. Marx himself carefully demonstrated in *Theories of Surplus Value* that it was known not only to the left-wing economic critics of the 1820's, but to the physiocrats and the classical liberal economists as well. However, it had not been clearly worked out theoretically: no scientific concept of surplus labour and surplus-value had been produced. A few significant remarks by Marx and Engels highlight the issue. 'Important as it was to reduce *value* to labour, it was equally important [to present] *surplus-value*, which manifests itself in *surplus*

'relation of production' occurs in *The Poverty of Philosophy*: 'Machinery is no more an economic category than the bullock that drags the plough. Machinery is merely a productive force. The modern workshop, which depends on the application of machinery, is a social production relation, an economic category' (*MEW* 4, p. 149; English ed., p. 133). In another critique, written a few months later and directed against the German republican writer Karl Heinzen, Marx is more explicit: 'Private property for example is not a simple relation, let alone an abstract concept, a principle, but consists rather in the totality of bourgeois production relations.' 'Die moralisierende Kritik und die kritisierende Moral', *MEW* 4, p. 356.

[165] For the development of Marx's theory of value and surplus-value, see the important study by the Soviet scholar V. S. Vygodsky, *Die Geschichte einer grossen Entdeckung*, Berlin, 1967.

product, as *surplus labour*. This was in fact already stated by Adam Smith and constitutes one of the main elements in Ricardo's argumentation. But nowhere did he clearly express it and record it in *absolute form*.'[166] This omission betrayed a great limitation in Smith: 'Yet he does not range surplus-value as such in a category of its own, separated from the particular forms contained in profit and rent. Therefore his investigation, as even more so Ricardo's, remains in many ways erroneous and lacking.'[167]

These comments are critical to our discussion of the relations of production, because the concept of surplus labour in its 'absolute form', distinguished from its different, concrete historical forms, is part of the concept of relations of production. In the chapter on capital in the *Grundrisse*, the analysis of capital is directly and explicitly related to the concept of surplus labour. This mode of *Darstellung* (presentation) is in clear contrast with the exposition in *Wage-Labour and Capital*, where the concept of surplus labour is absent, and the analysis is presented in terms of accumulated versus living labour.[168] This is taken further in part II of *Capital*, in which the analysis of the transformation of money into capital is systematically based on the distinction between necessary labour – necessary, that is, for the worker to sustain and reproduce himself – which is

[166] *Theories of Surplus Value*, vol. III, *MEW* 26: 3, p. 235 (emphasis in original); English ed., pp. 238–9.

[167] Ibid., vol. I, *MEW* 26: 1, p. 53. A concrete analysis of these errors and lacunae is provided by Marx in the first and the second volumes of *Theories of Surplus Value*, *MEW* 26: 1, p. 57f (Smith); English ed., p. 84f; and *MEW* 26: 2, p. 375f (Ricardo); English ed., p. 373f. See also Engels' preface to the second volume of *Capital*. What Marx and Engels say about classical economists and their relationship to the concept of surplus-value is pertinent, as far as the relations of production are concerned, to their own works of the 1840's, as well as to those of their later commentators who have not comprehended the meaning of this strategic concept – and there seem to be enough of them.

[168] *MEW* 6, p. 409; *MESW*, p. 81. The lack of a definite theory of surplus labour created difficulties for the early Marxian analysis of capitalism. In the *Communist Manifesto* there is still an echo of the old egoistic individualism-alienation problematic, which seems to make capitalism rest on competition among the workers: 'The essential condition for the existence, and for the sway of the bourgeois class, is the formation and augmentation of capital; the condition for capital is wage labour. Wage labour rests exclusively on competition between the labourers.' (*MEW* 4, p. 473; English ed., p. 79.) In later analyses this sort of argument was succeeded by references to different forms of surplus labour and their connections with different characteristics of the forces of production.

the value of his labour-power and for which he is paid a wage, and surplus labour. The unpaid surplus labour of the workers gives the capitalists their profits. The value of the product of surplus labour is surplus-value, which is manifested in profit and in payments out of entrepreneurial profit, such as interest and ground rent. Marx then deals with the ways in which surplus-value can be augmented: either by lengthening the working day (absolute surplus-value), which, Marx pointed out, was common in the early history of industrialization, or by increasing productivity and work-intensity (relative surplus-value).

The general concept of surplus labour, and with it the concept of relations of production, is not nearly as systematically developed by Marx as the concepts of value and surplus-value.[169] The concept is, however, *present* in Marx's mature economic works. In the chapter on the working day in the first volume of *Capital*, for example, there is a general survey of different historic types of surplus labour, of which the capitalist is only one. 'Capital has not invented surplus-labour. Wherever a part of society possesses the monopoly of the means of production, the labourer, free or not free, must add to the working-time necessary for his own maintenance an extra working-time in order to produce the means of subsistence for the owners of the means of production, whether this proprietor be the Athenian [aristocrat], Etruscan theocrat, civis Romanus, Norman baron, American slave-owner, Wallachian boyard, modern landlord or capitalist.'[170]

In Marx's investigation of the genesis of capitalist ground rent, in the third volume of *Capital*, we find the most systematic formulation of the core of historical materialism, which may be summarized in this quotation: 'The specific economic form, in which unpaid surplus-labour is pumped out of direct producers, determines the

---

[169] Give that *Capital* was not only left unfinished in itself, but that it was also intended to be part of a much broader study, there seem to be two main reasons for this. One is that Marx, both as a Marxist scientist and as a Communist revolutionary, was primarily concerned to discover the laws of motion of the capitalist economy in order to provide a guide for future social development and the base for revolutionary action. The second reason seems to have been that in Marx's time economics was the only developed science of society. For these reasons Marx gave priority to a detailed economic analysis and to very acute and subtle discussions of the value theory of classical political economy, over a systematic exposition of the basic general concepts of historical materialism.

[170] *MEW* 23, pp. 249–50; English ed., p. 235.

relationship of rulers and ruled, as it grows directly out of production itself and, in turn, reacts upon it as a determining element. Upon this, however, is founded the entire formation of the economic community which grows up out of the production relations themselves, thereby simultaneously its specific political form. It is always the direct relationship of the owners of the conditions of production to the direct producers – a relation always naturally corresponding to a definite stage in the development of the methods of labour and thereby its social productivity – which reveals the innermost secret, the hidden basis of the entire social structure, and with it the political form of the relation of sovereignty and dependence, in short, the corresponding specific form of the state. This does not prevent the same economic basis – the same from the standpoint of its main conditions – due to innumerable different empirical circumstances, natural environment, racial relations, external historical influences, etc., from showing infinite variations and gradations in appearance, which can be ascertained only by analysis of the empirically given circumstances.'[171] This is not one of the most common quotations from Marx. It is, however, extraordinarily lucid and comprehensive, encompassing the *differentia specifica* of types of society – the way in which surplus labour is extracted, the relations of production, the forces of production, the relationship between the economic base and the political structure. There is also the distinction between theoretical analysis and empirical description. Classes are not explicitly introduced, but we can easily perceive them in the owners of the conditions of production and the immediate producers. The basis of their antagonism and struggle is clearly visible, in the extraction and appropriation of surplus labour.

In the chapter quoted here, and in the *Grundrisse*, it becomes manifest that even if the analysis of capitalism and of capitalist starts from the concepts of commodity and value, Marxist social theory starts from the distinction between necessary and surplus labour.[172]

---

[171] *MEW* 25, pp. 799–800; English ed., p. 772. In the first volume of *Capital* there is a similar, shorter formulation: 'The essential difference between the various economic forms of society, between, for instance, a society based on slave-labour, and one based on wage-labour, lies only in the mode in which this surplus-labour is in each case extracted from the actual producer, the labourer.' *MEW* 23, p. 231; English ed., p. 217.

[172] *Grundrisse*, pp. 363–415; English ed., pp. 459–514. This is also the starting-point of Ernest Mandel's treatise, *Marxist Economic Theory*, London, 1968 (two vols.).

A certain minimum development of the productive forces makes it possible to sustain not only familial reproduction with temporarily non-productive family members but a distinct, non-productive section of the population: shamans, chieftains, warriors, landlords, imperial courts and administrations, capitalists, and so forth, throughout history. These social categories are maintained by the surplus labour and surplus product of the immediate producers, the peasants and the workers of various kinds who provide shares of their harvests and certain workdays a year, or, as slaves or free proletarians, their labour.[173]

5. The Three Aspects of the Relations of Production

For a more precise elucidation of the Marxian concept of relations of production there are three basic sources: the discussion of different modes of production in the *Grundrisse*[174]; the survey of different types of rent in the third volume of *Capital*;[175] and all those passages in the major mature works where Marx analyses capital as a relation of production, the 'determining production

---

[173] The distinction between necessary and surplus labour is an abstract analytical one, only approximately measurable, and moreover only *ex post facto*. The latter is the case because the necessary sustenance of the direct producers is determined not only physiologically but also historically. Marx says: 'On the other hand, the number and extent of so-called necessary wants, as also the modes of satisfying them, are themselves the product of historical development, and depend therefore to a great extent on the degree of civilization of a country, more particularly on the conditions under which, and consequently on the habits and degree of comfort in which, the class of free labourers has been formed.' (*Capital*, vol. I, *MEW* 23, p. 185; English ed., p. 171.) This would be dangerously tautological if Marxist historical analysis was primarily concerned with the magnitude of exploitation and/or if it was held that surplus labour would disappear in a socialist society. In fact, however, neither is the case. A socialist mode of production in the Marxist sense does not imply the abolition of surplus labour – though the working day can be radically shortened because of increased productivity – but the collective direction of surplus labour. 'Surplus-labour in general, as labour performed over and above the given requirements, must always remain. In the capitalist as well as in the slave system, it merely assumes an antagonistic form and is supplemented by complete idleness of a stratum of society.' (*Capital*, III, *MEW* 25, p. 827; English ed., p. 799.) In historical social analysis, Marxism is concerned with different types of exploitation, capitalist and others, and how they function.

[174] *Grundrisse*, pp. 363–415; English ed., pp. 459–514.

[175] *MEW* 25, pp. 790–821; English ed., pp. 763–93.

relation of the capitalist mode of production'.[176] It emerges quite clearly from a close reading of Marx's exposition of different relations of production that the concept has three basic aspects: the *distribution of the means of production* and the means of subsistence; the *objective of production*; and thirdly, the *structured social relations of production*, involving the immediate producers (or workers), the non-workers (those who appropriate surplus labour), and the means of production.

The first aspect refers to the union (*Vereinigung*) with or separation from the immediate producers of the raw materials (the object of labour), the instruments of production, and the means of subsistence (*Lebensmittel*).[177] Where they possess the land, the producers are united either with all three or, at least, with the first and the third. The handicraft worker exemplifies, for Marx, union with the instruments of production (tools) together with separation from the rest. Serfs and slaves – as well as the Roman plebs in the time of bread and circuses – have certain means of subsistence, but are separated from the objects and instruments of their labour. Modern proletarians are separated from all three.[178]

Marx here uses the words 'property' and 'property-owner' (*Eigentümer*) and also the expression 'sich als Eigentümer verhalten'. It is evident in this reference to slaves as 'owners' of their means of subsistence, that property and ownership are not used in their ordinary senses. They denote, rather, factual possession or non-possession.

It should be emphasized that Marx distinguished very sharply between relations of production (or 'property relations') and juridical property. In the metaphor of the 1859 Preface, juridical relations

[176] *MEW* 25, pp. 835; English ed., p. 806. Capital is, of course, an ever-present object of analysis in Marx's major economic works. The concept is defined above all in Part II (English ed., part II) of the first volume of *Capital*..

[177] *Grundrisse*, p. 396f; English ed., p. 491f.

[178] Marx also distinguishes forms of unity and separation. One such distinction views the relations of slavery and serfdom from a different angle, seeing slaves and serfs as an unseparated *part of* the objects and instruments of work. (*Grundrisse*, pp. 389, 399–400; English ed., pp. 489–90, 499–500.) Another, more important distinction treats different combinations of 'property': communal property alone, private property with and subordinated to state property, private property supplemented with communal. All this refers primarily to land and is employed to distinguish Asian, Ancient, and Germanic forms, respectively. (*Grundrisse*, p. 375f; English ed., p. 472f.)

and statutes belong to the 'superstructure'. The distinction between relations of production and juridical property relations is also formulated there: Marx speaks of the contradiction between the forces of production and 'the existing relations of production or – this merely expresses the same thing in legal terms – with the property relations'.[179] The analysis, in the third volume of *Capital*, of the transformation of feudal into capitalist agriculture, explicitly differentiates changes in the relations of production from changes in their subsidiary juridical forms.[180] In *Anti-Dühring* Engels indicated the difference between socialist relations of production and juridical property of the capitalist state: 'But the transformation, either into joint-stock companies and trusts or into state ownership, does not do away with the capitalist nature of the productive forces.'[181] Against the demand for a normative regulation of economic relationships, Marx had exclaimed rhetorically, in his *Critique of the Gotha Programme*: 'Are economic relations regulated by legal concepts of right or is the opposite not the case, that legal relations spring from economic ones?'[182] The first aspect of the concept of the relations of production does not denote only the union or separation of the immediate producers and the means of production. It also distinguishes different modes of union and separation. One such distinction is between individual and collective modes of union of the immediate producers with their means of production. Simple commodity production and socialism are modern examples of the one and the other, respectively. Marx noted that pre-modern modes of production often combined individual and collective union in complex ways:[183] part of the land might be held in common, and part individually; herds might be individually owned, while land was for all; land might be utilized by individual families, while remaining subject to communal allocation and occasional redistribution. Marx also implied an important distinction between individual and collective modes of separation, and between individual and collective appropriation of the means of production by the non-producers. The distribution of the means of production may, then, involve intricate combinations of union and

[179] *MEW* 13, p. 9; English ed., p. 21.
[180] *MEW* 25, p. 627f; English ed., p. 600f.
[181] *MEW* 19, p. 222; *MESW*, p. 422.
[182] *MEW* 19, p. 18; *The First International and After*, p. 344.
[183] *Grundrisse*, p. 375f; English ed., p. 471f.

separation. Feudal peasants, for instance, typically had to till both their own tenancies and the demesnes (personal lands) of their lord. At the same time, the principle of *nulle terre sans seigneur* (no land without a lord) meant that to the extent that the feudal mode of production prevailed, the peasants were in a sense separated from all land, which was distributed among the individual members of the aristocratic class. Here, despite the devolved and conditional character of individual distribution under the system of vassalages and fiefs of classical feudalism, the fact of individual separation of the peasants from the land by noble landlords was critical. In this respect, as Marx clearly perceived and tried unsuccessfully to conceptualize by contrast with the 'Asiatic mode of production',[184] feudalism differed significantly from modes of production where the mode of separation of the immediate producers was basically collective (in various ways and to varying extents).[185] If the rigour of historical materialism is to be upheld, it is important that these differences be formulated in terms of factual distribution and not of legal codifications. Although the latter certainly affect the functioning of the relations of production, a moment's reflection on situations where the law becomes a 'dead letter' should give some idea of the relative importance of the two in the life of society.[186]

[184] This notion's claims to scientific status have been effectively demolished by Perry Anderson, *Lineages of the Absolutist State*, London, 1975, pp. 462–549. Anderson shows both the factual inaccuracies on which Marx built his notion of 'the Asiatic mode of production' and the theoretical inadequacy of the attempt to span the fundamental differences between two major Asiatic civilizations, the Islamic and the Chinese.

[185] In the Islamic empires, from Ottoman Turkey to Mughal India, land was appropriated with varying degrees of effectiveness by the sovereign, whereas private landownership developed in China from the Sung era, between the 10th and 13th centuries, albeit together with a state apparatus that provided the main economic base of the highest magnates (see Anderson, ibid.).

[186] Such situations do occur, as for instance in Sung China. Anderson writes: 'State ownership in land was nominally retained in Sung legal theory but was in practice from now on a dead letter.' Ibid., p. 527. Anderson seems nevertheless to be a strong opponent of the distinction between relations of production and juridical property as developed here. In his conclusion (p. 401f), where he gives special attention to this theoretical and methodological problem, he summarizes his position thus: 'For historical materialism, on the contrary, juridical property can never be separated either from economic production or politico-ideological power: its absolutely central position within any mode of production derives from its linkage of the two, which in pre-capitalist social formations becomes an outright and official fusion' (p. 405). I neither intend nor am competent to criticize Ander-

Thus, as their designation suggests, the most significant aspect of 'capitalist' relations of production is not private property (even in a non-juridical sense) but the rule of capital, the 'determinant pro-

---

son's remarkable work. However, his conclusions raise several issues which should be distinguished if we are to see clearly where the possible differences lie. In this respect, there appear to be at least three distinct problems, of which two refer directly to the object of Anderson's study, and concern the conceptualization and analysis of feudalism. The first has to do with his attack on studies that analyze feudalism as an exclusively economic phenomenon dissociated from politico-juridical superstructures, which are dismissed as secondary and insubstantial. Here, there is no disagreement. Historical materialism is not synonymous with economic theory and history: it is rather a science of historical social totalities comprising economic bases and politico-juridical and ideological superstructures. A second problem relates to the definition of feudalism. Anderson polemicizes convincingly against the common, very general definition of feudalism as a 'combination of large-scale agrarian property controlled by an exploiting class, with small-scale production by a tied peasantry, in which surplus labour was pressed out of the latter by *corvées* or dues in kind' (p. 408, cf. p. 401), which, he maintains, obscures the enormous differences between mediaeval Europe and the great Asiatic civilizations, for instance. The question then is whether it is possible to formulate these differences and to explain their respective specific dynamics, at the level of the relations of production. The whole tenor of Anderson's argument implies – but does not actually state – that it is not. Yet it seems to follow from his own profound historical analyses that it is indeed possible. A central difference between feudalism proper and other post-tribal, pre-capitalist agrarian modes of production, brilliantly illuminated by Anderson, is that between what might be termed individual and collective modes of separation of the peasantry from the land. Under feudalism, the entire basis of the ruling class was the individually distributed lands of its members, whereas in the Asiatic empires this basis was mainly or at least partly a collective imperial appropriation. This difference, grounded in different factual distributions of the means of production, is obviously statable in non-juridical terms. But what about the *Lehenswesen*, the vassalage system? 'This parcellization of sovereignty was constitutive of the whole feudal mode of production' (*Passages from Antiquity to Feudalism*, London, 1974, p. 148). Anderson is of course absolutely right to treat this political structure as essential to classical feudal Europe. However, he does not seem ultimately to regard it as *constitutive* of feudalism, for the principal conclusion of his analysis of the absolutist state, with its markedly non–parcellized sovereignty, is that it is a *feudal* state: 'Absolutism was essentially just this: a *redeployed and recharged apparatus and recharged apparatus of feudal domination*' (*Lineages of the Absolutist State*, p. 18, emphasis in original). It was a feudal state because it was another political form for the maintenance of the class power of the feudal lords, whose position, I would add, is defined basically by feudal relations of production.

The third issue raised by Anderson's conclusions is that of the status of the politico-juridical superstructure in the general theoretical system of historical materialism. This issue raises a whole series of questions, including the difficult

duction relation' of the capitalist mode of production.[187] In his development of the concept of capital and the distinctive character of capitalist relations of production, Marx concentrates mainly on the second aspect of the relations of production, *the objective of production*. What then is capital? 'We know that the means of production and subsistence, while they remain the property of the

---

and still not satisfactorily solved question of 'determination in the last instance' by the economic base. The most pertinent question in this context is that of the meaning of the 'economic' in pre-market societies. Here Anderson is too elliptical, pointing only to the 'outright and official fusion' of economic production, juridical property and politico-ideological power in pre-capitalist social formations. For if the analysis above is correct, the constitutive pattern of social determination of historical materialism as a science is the combination of forces and relations of production, and in order to uphold the possibility of its application in scientific practice, of testing its explanatory power, it is essential not to blur from the very outset the distinction between the economic base and the juridical superstructure. The economic, in the sense of historical materialism, is constituted by the combination of the forces and the relations of production, which always operate in ideological and (some very primitive societies apart) in juridical and political forms. The empirical fusion of different structures and relations does not preclude their analytic distinction. Confronted with the intricate social web of pre-capitalist societies, it seems necessary precisely to emphasize this analytic distinction, which in these cases is not immediately visible.

The treatment here of the distribution of the means of production by way of combinations of modes of union and separation of the immediate producers with them, is legible in the discussions by Marx and Engels of feudalism and the 'Asiatic mode of production' but, to my knowledge, never made quite explicit. It can be related to Bettelheim's distinction between detention, possession and property.

[187] 'Capital' and 'capitalist' (as a noun) were concepts first produced by classical political economy, but 'capitalism' emerged only later. According to the *Oxford Universal Dictionary Illustrated* it did not occur in English until 1854. Only in *Capital* does Marx speak generally of *capitalist relations* of production, capitalist mode of production, capitalist production etc. Earlier, in the *Communist Manifesto* (see for example, *MEW* 4, pp. 467–8, 477, 481, 489; English ed., pp. 72–3, 83, 86, 95) and, for instance, in the programmatic Preface to *A Contribution to the Critique of Political Economy* (*MEW* 13, p. 9; English ed., p. 21) the expression 'bourgeois' (*bürgerlich*) is used instead of capitalist, and in the *Grundrisse* Marx correspondingly talks of the dissolution of 'pre-bourgeois' relations of production (German ed., pp. 373, 388; English ed., pp. 471, 487). The change of formulation is no doubt one sign of the emergence of the specifically Marxist analysis of modern society as it emancipated itself from the Hegelian and Left-Hegelian conception of *bürgerliche Gesellschaft*. But the critical role of capital was clear to Marx before *Capital*, and its relation to surplus-labour is demonstrated in the *Grundrisse*.

immediate producer, are not capital. They become capital, only under circumstances in which they serve as means of exploitation and subjection of the labourer.'[188] 'Capital is not a thing, but rather a definite social production relation, belonging to a definite historical formation of society, which is manifested in a thing and lends this thing a specific social character.'[189] Nor is capital the same thing as money, as Marx demonstrates in the fourth chapter of *Capital*. It is money, or more generally a certain sum of exchange values, which functions in a specific process, and which is used for a specific objective. 'The simplest form of the circulation of commodities is C-M-C, the transformation of commodities into money, and the change of the money back again into commodities; or selling in order to buy. But alongside of this form we find another specifically different form: M-C-M, the transformation of money into commodities, and the change of commodities back again into money; or buying in order to sell. Money that circulates in the latter manner is thereby transformed into, becomes capital, and is already potentially capital.'[190] 'The exact form of this process is therefore $M-C-M'$, where $M'=M+\Delta M=$ the original sum advanced, plus an increment. This increment or excess over the original value I call "surplus-value". The value originally advanced, therefore, not only remains intact while in circulation, but adds to itself a surplus-value or expands itself. It is this movement that converts it into capital.'[191]

Capital is a quantity of exchange-values which is injected into the economic process for the purposes of its own '*Verwertung*' (literally 'valorization') and augmentation – that is, in order to gain a surplus-value. Marx goes on to show that an economy geared to the production of surplus-value must be based on the exploitation of labour, since a surplus derived by some from buying cheap and selling dear would be cancelled out by the losses of others. Therefore, the capitalist objective of production also involves a specific distribution of the means of production,[192] and specific relations between the immediate producers and those who appropriate their surplus

[188] *Capital*, I, *MEW* 23, p. 794; English ed., p. 767.

[189] *Capital*, III, *MEW* 25, p. 822; English ed., p. 794.

[190] *Capital*, I, *MEW* 23, p. 162; English ed., pp. 146–7.

[191] Ibid., p. 165; English ed., p. 150.

[192] The means of production become capital in so far as they are used for the appropriation of surplus-value.

product as surplus-value. As a social mechanism, production for the accumulation of surplus-value necessitates the distribution of the means of production among individuals (though these 'individuals' may be collectives of various sizes) and the availability of labour-power as a commodity. The pursuit of this objective further pre-supposes competition among the different productive units. State capitalism, then, can only refer either to state-controlled capitalist enterprises, state enterprises geared to profit and competing with other, private capitalist enterprises, or, as a limiting case, a state economy that operates as a corporation competing with other corporations on the world market.[193]

In this way the different aspects of the relations of production are connected with each other. But the important point in this context is that the Marxist concept of the relations of production includes, as a specific aspect, the objective of production. It is as 'the unity of the labour-process and the process of creating value' that the production process is capitalist.[194] Besides the commodity relation-ships and their effect on the distribution of the means of production and the relationship between the agents of production, 'the second distinctive feature of the capitalist mode of production is the production of surplus-value as the direct aim and determining motive of production'.[195]

[193] Descriptions of the Soviet Union as 'capitalist' or 'state capitalist' are therefore fundamentally foreign to Marxist analysis; and to term industrialization of the Stalinist type 'capital accumulation' is merely to revert to the pre-Marxist confusion between means of production and capital as a sum of exchange-values deployed to yield more exchange-value. The Soviet industrialization of Russia was a production of use-values, predominantly in the form of more and better means of production rather than consumer goods. Charles Bettelheim, who is perhaps the foremost contemporary theorist of Soviet 'capitalism', typically neglects Marx's analysis of capital and does not even attempt to show that pro-duction in the Soviet Union is geared to the accumulation of surplus exchange-value. Bettelheim thereby implies that Marx's life work, *Capital*, is superfluous in a scientific study of capitalism. Many economists would agree, of course, but it seems difficult to substantiate any Marxist claims for such a position. See Charles Bettelheim, *Calcul économique et formes de propriété*, p. 79f. In the introduction to the first volume of his ongoing work on the Soviet Union, *Les luttes de classes en URSS*, Paris, 1974, Bettelheim characteristically opposes the erroneous 'problematic of the productive forces' to one of 'social relations', referring to the 'division of labour' and to 'ideological and political relations' – in other words, *not* a problematic of the relations of production (p. 12f).

[194] *Capital*, I, *MEW* 23, p. 211; English ed., p. 197.

[195] *Capital*, III, *MEW* 25, p. 887; English ed., p. 858.

Among different objectives of production, Marx – mostly concerned with the specificity of capitalism – distinguishes in particular between production for use (for direct consumption), production of commodities for sale on a market (the C – M – C process above), and production for the accumulation of capital (which involves production of commodities). Within the first of these he also makes the very important distinction between production directed by 'relations of dominion and servitude', that is, production undertaken primarily for the consumption of the masters, and production for the reproduction of the *Gemeinwesen* [communal society]'.[196]

The objective of production is a social mechanism, whose existence must be established by analysis. The objective of the capitalist, according to Marx, is 'the effect of the social mechanism, of which he is but one of the wheels'.[197] It is derived neither from self-interest (or some other basic human drive), nor from a normative community. It is part of the ever pre-given totality of relations of production into which men enter, and its changes are related to changes in the forces of production, equally in the cases of the dissolution of the primitive communities and of the epoch of socialist revolution against capitalism.[198] The men who live these relations of production, who constitute their 'personifications', as Marx called the capitalist in relation to capital, express the objective of production in subjective motives. Marx refers in passing to the 'passion for accumulation' of the capitalist and to its conflict with a 'desire for enjoyment' in the later development of capitalism, and of the individual capitalist *parvenu*.[199] But this is merely an aside in his analysis of the capitalist system. Moreover, if the objective of production is a social mechanism, it also follows, contrary to the belief of sophisticated liberal economics, that the appropriation by

[196] *Capital*, III, *MEW* 25, p. 839; English ed., p. 810. See further *Capital*, I, chs. 1, 5 (1, 7 in English edition). This very crude and rudimentary distinction must, of course, be much further refined in historical materialist studies of pre-capitalist modes of production. One such further distinction which is prompted by a survey of the Islamic empires is between surplus labour mainly for the consumption of the lords and surplus labour designed mainly to supply a war machine, as appears to have been the case in these empires at their height, due undoubtedly to the nomadic origins of their ruling classes. See Anderson, *Lineages of the Absolutist State*, pp. 361–94, 496–520.

[197] *Capital*, I, *MEW* 23, p. 618; English ed., p. 592.

[198] See, for instance, *Grundrisse*, pp. 394–400; English ed., pp. 493–9.

[199] *Capital*, I, *MEW* 23, p. 620; English ed., pp. 593–4

the capitalist of part of the total product is not a *deduction*, made possible by his monopoly of the means of production. Rather, in the social relations of production characteristic of capitalism, the workers are compelled to produce surplus-value. Exploitation is not a monopoly profit, but a social process of production.[200]

In the summary, in the third volume of *Capital*, of the basic propositions of historical materialism we are told that: 'It is always the direct relationship of the owners of the conditions of production to the direct producers . . . which reveals the innermost secret . . . of the entire social structure.'[201] This relation involves something more than the distribution of the means of production (and subsistence) and the objective of production. Marx also specifies *the social relationship of the production agents to each other in the economic process*. For example, he distinguishes the pre-individuated primitive community or *Gemeinwesen*, which may take on a despotic character if subjugated by a despotic superior regime (for instance, 'Oriental despotism'),[202] personal relations of domination and subordination, exchange relations,[203] exchange relations coupled with a specifically capitalist command of the labour process, and, in socialism, a differentiated community of individuals.[204]

In the first volume of *Capital* Marx gives us a rapid survey of the most important social relationships contained within the relations of production. 'Co-operation, such as we find it at the dawn of human development, among races who live by the chase, or, say, in the agriculture of Indian communities, is based, on the one hand,

[200] This point, which exposes the falsity of treating the distribution of the means of production as the sole aspect of the relations of production, is very well made by Bob Rowthorn, op. cit., p. 82f.

[201] *MEW* 25, pp. 799–800; English ed., p. 772.

[202] *Grundrisse*, pp. 376–7; English ed., pp. 475–6.

[203] Exchange relations are the social relationships of production underlying the production of commodities: 'Articles of utility become commodities, only because they are products of the labour of private individuals or groups of individuals who carry on their work independently of each other. The sum total of the labour of all these private individuals forms the aggregate labour of society. Since the producers do not come into social contact with each other until they exchange their products, the specific social character of each producer's labour does not show itself except in the act of exchange . . . To the [producers], therefore, the relations connecting the labour of one individual with that of the rest appear . . . as . . . material relations between persons and social relations between things.' (*Capital*, I, *MEW* 23, p. 87; English ed., p. 73.)

[204] *Capital*, I, *MEW* 23, pp. 92–3; English ed., pp. 77–8.

on ownership in common of the means of production, and on the other hand, on the fact, that in those cases, each individual has no more torn himself off from the navel-string of his tribe or community, than each bee has freed itself from connection with the hive. Such co-operation is distinguished from capitalistic co-operation by both of the above characteristics. The sporadic application of co-operation on a larger scale in ancient times, in the middle ages, and in modern colonies, reposes on relations of dominion and servitude, principally on slavery. The capitalistic form, on the contrary, presupposes from first to last, the free wage-labourer, who sells his labour power to capital.'[205]

The emancipation of labour from serfdom and other such forms of personal dependence is one of the preconditions of capitalism. But capitalist relations of production are not simply exchange relations between capitalist buyers and proletarian sellers of labour power. They also involve the capitalist command of labour, that is, a specific form of control of the labour process: 'The authority assumed by the capitalist as the personification of capital in the direct process of production, the social function performed by him in his capacity as manager and ruler of production, is essentially different from the authority exercised on the basis of production by means of slaves, serfs, etc. Whereas, on the basis of capitalist production, the mass of direct producers is confronted by the social character of their production in the form of a strictly regulating authority and a social mechanism of the labour-process organized as a complete hierarchy – this authority reaching its bearers, however, only as the personification of the conditions of labour in contrast to labour, and not as political or theocratic rulers as under earlier modes of production – among the bearers of this authority, the capitalists themselves, who confront one another only as commodity-owners, there reigns complete anarchy within which the social interrelations of production assert themselves only as an overwhelming natural law in relation to individual free will.'[206] Essentially, then, the concept of the relations of production designates the way in which men's necessary labour and surplus labour (where the latter exists) are related. This is determined by the distribution of the means of production, by the objective of

[205] Ibid., pp. 353–4; English ed., p. 334.
[206] *Capital*, III, *MEW* 25, p. 888; English ed., p. 859.

production, which most directly concerns the objective of surplus labour but also has to do with the utilization and division of men's working capacity into necessary and surplus labour (the amount and rate of exploitation), and, thirdly, by the social relationships in production between the immediate producers and those who appropriate their surplus labour.

IV. Science and Dialectics

So far we have presented only the most fundamental concepts of the new pattern of social determination. But how does it work as an explanatory theory? This raises the very complicated problem of the dialectic. Questions of philosophy are basically outside the scope of the present study. Nevertheless, it is pertinent to inquire into the role played by the dialectical method and by the understanding of the dialectical character of reality in the constitution of historical materialism. What is the relationship between dialectics and the foundation of this new science? Given its centrality in the whole Marxist tradition from Marx and Engels onwards, the question cannot be evaded, even if there is no intention here of entering into a discussion of dialectical and non-dialectical philosophy.

The question of the dialectic has been treated in a number of conflicting ways. These fall into two major classes, each containing a great number of different sub-groups and individuals. According to one, science and dialectics are, in one way or another, opposites, while for the other, historical materialism as a science is precisely an example or application of dialectics. In the first class of answers there are logically three major positions. One of them, represented above all by revisionist Social Democracy, dismisses the dialectic as a metaphysical obstacle to a science of society and history.[207] At the other pole, science is cast out and dialectics upheld. The so-called Frankfurt School has been a prominent exponent of this anti-scientific position, especially in such works as Horkheimer's and Adorno's *Dialectics of Enlightenment* and, more recently, Marcuse's *One-Dimensional Man*.[208] It is also possible, within this first class, to hold that science and dialectics are of equal value. The idea that

---

[207] See the classic work of Social-Democratic revisionism, E. Bernstein, *Die Voraussetzungen des Sozialismus und die Aufgaben der Sozialdemokratie*, Reinbek bei Hamburg, 1969, ch. 2.

[208] Marcuse has also written an interesting work on Hegel, Marx, the rise of

the Marxist theory of society comprises two different but equally important discourses, one scientific and the other dialectical, has probably been most cogently argued by the Italian Marxist philosopher, Lucio Colletti.[209] In the Marxist–Leninist tradition, on the other hand, from Lenin to Mao Tse tung, in current Soviet and Eastern European philosophy and in Western Communism, science is viewed as applied dialectics.[210] A subset of this second class, common in continental European *gauchiste* and *gauchisant* philosophy, is the position that the dialectic exists only in humanistic, historical sciences, as opposed to naturalistic studies of society or nature. This view was taken by Lukács in *History and Class Consciousness*,[211] and has more recently been adopted by Sartre,[212] among others.

So far as the explicit discourse of Marx and Engels is concerned, there can be no doubt that the second type, in its Marxist–Leninist variant, is the only correct interpretation of the founders. Marx, as he made clear in his Afterword to the Second Edition of *Capital*, regarded his scientific analysis of capitalism as instance of dialectical method. It is also evident that he did not regard this as in any way opposed to a natural-scientific analysis. Marx quoted with approval the following as a 'striking' exposition of his own dialectical method: 'Marx treats the social movement as a process of natural history, governed by laws not only independent of human will, consciousness and intelligence, but rather, on the contrary, determ-

sociology and the development and fate of the dialectic, *Reason and Revolution*, Boston, 1960. Unfortunately, most of its major theses are, so to speak, inverted in relation to reality.

[209] See Lucio Colletti, 'A Political and Philosophical Interview' in *New Left Review*, no. 86 July–August 1974, and 'Marxism and the Dialectic', in *New Left Review*, no. 93, September–October 1975.

[210] See for instance V. I. Lenin, *Philosophical Notebooks, Collected Works*, Vol. 38, esp. pp. 138f, 221f, 359f; Mao Tse tung, 'On Contradiction', *Selected Works*, Vol. 1, Peking, 1965, and *On the Correct Handling of Contradictions Among the People*, Peking, 1957. An accessible contemporary handbook in the mainstream Communist tradition is Maurice Cornforth, *The Philosophy of Marxism*, London, 1960. Althusser has dealt mainly with the specificity of the Marxist dialectic, rather than with its role in the science founded by Marx, but, as a thinker in the orthodox Marxist-Leninist tradition, he sees its specificity in relation to Marx's scientific analyses (*For Marx*, chs. III, VI).

[211] Georg Lukács, 'What is Orthodox Marxism?', *History and Class Consciousness*.

[212] Jean-Paul Sartre, *Critique de la Raison Dialectique*, pp. 115–35.

ining that will, consciousness and intelligence.'[213] This is certainly a long way from, say, Sartre's *verstehende* dialectical anthropology of the human project.

But what does it mean to say that historical materialism as a science is dialectics in operation? Hegel's dialectic was one of the theoretical coordinates for the development of historical materialism. It is noteworthy, however, that the importance of Hegel in this connection was not that he provided the starting-point from which the new materialist analysis of history set out, and thereafter increasingly distanced itself. It was not in the early anticipations of the new social theory in *The German Ideology* that Hegel's dialectic was so important, but rather in Marx's detailed development, from the later 1850s and onwards, of his novel method of scientific explanation and analysis. In January 1858 Marx wrote to Engels: 'In the *method* of treatment the fact that by mere accident I again glanced through Hegel's *Logic* has been of great service to me...'[214] But Marx's was a naturalistic dialectic, employed in the study of historical laws of motion, whereas to Hegel, 'the realm of law merely contains the simple, changeless but divergent content of the existing world', whose motion and change could only be comprehended by dialectical thought unconcerned with laws.[215]

The author of *Capital* certainly regarded 'the Hegelian contradiction [as] the source of all dialectics'.[216] The constitution of a dialectical science, however, was to be something very different from a mere application of Hegel's famous propositions: 'All things are contradictory in themselves'; 'Contradiction is . . . the root of all motion and life; only in so far as a contradiction is inherent in a thing, does it move, has it impulse and activity.'[217] The thesis of the

---

[213] *MEW* 23, p. 26; English ed., p. 18. The Swedish Marxist historian of ideas Sven-Eric Liedman is engaged in a major work on the role of the dialectic in developing a science distinct from the classical conception of science embodied in Newtonian mechanics. I have benefited greatly from discussions with him. A part of his research is presented in 'Marx, Engels och dialektens lagar' (Marx, Engels and the laws of dialectics), *Häften for Kritiska Studier* 3, 1975. Liedman demonstrates that it was Marx and not Engels who first conceived of a naturalistic kind of dialectic.

[214] *MEW* 29, p. 260; *MESC*, p. 100.

[215] Hegel, *Wissenschaft der Logik*, part II, *Werke*, Vol. 4, p. 131. Cf. ibid., p. 127f, and part I, Vol. 3, p. 6.

[216] *Capital*, Vol. 1, *MEW* 23, p. 623 n; English ed., p. 596.

[217] Hegel, *Logik*, *Werke* 4, p. 58.

universality of contradiction and motion is in itself merely an aprioristic *Weltanschauung* external to scientific investigation, which at worst is simply given the role of providing arbitrary illustrations for the dialectical philosopher. At best, it might function as fruitful heuristic advice: in scientific investigation one should look out for contradictions and change. In the latter mode, dialectics might also serve as a useful practical guide in everyday life. But the function of dialectics in the constitution of historical materialism as a science, in its system of concepts and propositions, remains to be shown. To do this, it is necessary to explain how the pattern of social determination discovered and produced by historical materialism may be said to have a dialectical character, and – if dialectics is not to be an empty generality – how historical materialism thus differs from the non-dialectical social sciences of economics and sociology.

From the Afterword to the Second Edition of *Capital*, we can obtain a minimal conception of what dialectics meant to the founder of historical materialism, as a contribution to the constitution of the new science. Let us first recall the quotation from Illarion Kaufman's[218] review of *Capital*, certified by Marx himself as an accurate presentation of his dialectical method:

'The one thing which is of moment to Marx, is to find the law of the phenomena with whose investigation he is concerned; and not only is that law of moment to him, which governs these phenomena, in so far as they have a definite form and mutual connexion within a given historical period. Of still greater moment to him is the law of their variation, of their development, i.e. of their transition from one form into another, from one series of connexions into a different one. . . . But it will be said, the general laws of economic life are one and the same, no matter whether they are applied to the present or the past. This Marx directly denies. . . . On the contrary, in his opinion every historical period has laws of its own. . . . Nay, one and the same phenomenon falls under quite different laws in consequence of the different structure of those organisms as a whole [i.e. social organisms], of the variation of their individual organs, of the different conditions in which those organs function. . . . The scientific value of such an inquiry lies in the disclosing of the special laws that regulate the origin, existence, development, death of a

<hr />

[218] The Saint Petersburg economics professor Kaufmann was one of the few established academics who understood Marx, or even bothered to try.

given social organism and its replacement by another and higher one.'[219]

Next we should notice what Marx himself says of the dialectic in its demystified and rational, that is, non-Hegelian, form: 'It includes in its comprehension and affirmative recognition of the existing state of things, at the same time also, the recognition of the negation of that state, of its inevitable breaking up . . . it regards every his-torically developed social form as in fluid movement, and therefore takes into account its transient nature. . . .' This recognition is forced on those whom it scandalizes, by 'the contradictions inherent in the movement of capitalist society . . . [the crisis which] by the universality of its theatre and the intensity of its action . . . will drum dialectics even into the heads of the mushroom-upstarts of the new, holy Prusso-German empire'.[220]

There is nothing here about man, subject-object, totalization, praxis or the other notions dear to many latter-day dialecticians. Instead, we have context or totality, contradiction and negation, motion or process, qualitative change, and also scientific procedure in general, the search for laws and the study of their operation by empirical investigation ('This law once discovered, he investigates in detail the effects in which it manifests itself in social life. Con-sequently, Marx . . . troubles himself . . . to establish, as impartially as possible, the facts that serve him for fundamental starting-points . . . [The] critical inquiry . . . will confine itself to the confrontation and the comparison of a fact, not with ideas, but with another fact.').[221] How then does dialectics in this minimal sense charac-terize the combination of relations and forces of production as a pattern of social determination?

The principle of totality means first of all that historical material-ism studies men in *society*, as an always pre-given entity, in contrast to all individualist 'Robinsonades' which try to 'found' a social theory on reflections on individual behaviour, exchange, choice, and

---

[219] *Capital, MEW* 23, p. 25f; English ed., p. 17f.

[220] Ibid., p. 28; English ed., p. 20.

[221] Ibid., p. 26; English ed., p. 18. This authorized presentation may be con-trasted with Marcuse's fulminations against 'the positivistic opposition to the principle that the matters of fact and experience have to be justified before the court of reason.' *Reason and Revolution*, p. 327; see also pp. 27, 377–8. Cf. idem, *One Dimensional Man*, London, 1968, p. 117: 'Dialectical thought is and remains unscientific.'

so forth. 'Individuals producing in society – hence socially determined individual production – is, of course, the point of departure. The individual and isolated hunter and fisherman, with whom Smith and Ricardo begin, belongs among the unimaginative conceits of the 18th century Robinsonades. . . .'[222] But 'totality' in the Marxist discourse means much more than this. Marx makes very specific use of this category, which is here designed to elucidate, not only the determination of the parts by the whole, but also and above all, the mutual determination and interaction of the different parts of the whole. 'In all forms of society there is one specific kind of production which predominates over the rest, whose relations thus assign rank and influence to the others.' Whereas in the feudal Middle Ages, for instance, capital was not only dominated by landed property but itself had a 'landed-proprietary character', the reverse is the case in bourgeois society. 'Capital is the all-dominating economic power of bourgeois society. It must form the starting-point as well as the finishing-point, and must be dealt with before landed property. After both have been examined in particular, their interrelation must be examined.'[223]

This specifically Marxist concept of totality is developed further in Marx's discussion of production, distribution, exchange and consumption as interdependent 'members of a totality' mutually affecting each other, in which production is the determining element,[224] and more generally *in the relation of base and superstructure*, that is of the forces and relations of production to the political and ideological structures of society (see below). Since the former examples of a determining totality are more clearly and explicitly developed by Marx himself, it is important to note that the kind of determination involved is the same as in the more complex problem of base and superstructure.

1. Contradiction and the Unity of Opposites

For the time being, instead of analyzing the Marxist concept of totality, we may make use of the general idea in an attempt to elucidate the dialectics of historical materialism as a specific unity of the principles of totality, process, qualitative change, and con-

---

[222] *Grundrisse*, p. 5; English ed., p. 83.
[223] Ibid., p. 27; English ed., pp. 106–7.
[224] Ibid., pp. 11–21; English ed., pp. 88–100.

tradiction. Of these four, the principle of contradiction is in a sense the determinant instance, the only one not to be found in non-Marxist or non-Hegelian social thought. On the other hand, the specificity of the Marxist contradiction (in relation to the Hegelian) derives from its relationship with the other core principles of Marxist dialectics.

As a general idea, totality – the study of social phenomena in their relationship to a social whole – is certainly not peculiar to historical materialism. In fact, it has been a characteristic effort of most of the major schools of sociology from Comte and Saint-Simon to Talcott Parsons. Neither is any attention paid to qualitative change: in a sense, qualitative change might even be said to have constituted *the* focus of both pioneer and classical sociology; the famous dichotomies of military and industrial society, theological and positive stages, *Gemeinschaft* and *Gesellschaft*, mechanical and organic solidarity, traditionalism and rationalism are witness to this. Nor have sociologists been innately unwilling to think of these changes as accomplished by revolutionary means rather than gradually or piecemeal. Weber's characteristic agents of rationalization, for instance, such as the Hebrew prophets and the Puritans, were undoubtedly agents of revolutionary forms of change, religious and political.

The study of social reality as motion and process might be said to be more central to historical materialism than to most other strands of social thought. The Marxian inquiry into 'the economic laws of motion of modern society' certainly differs from Adam Smith's inquiry into the causes of the wealth of nations, from Ricardo's interest in what governs the distribution of the product into profits, rent, and wages, or from the Parsonian quest for the reasons for social order. Not only did Marx not study capital as a thing (as means of production) but as a relation of production, he did not conceive of capital primarily as an anatomical structure of capitalist society but as a structure in process. The three volumes of *Capital* are appropriately entitled The Production Process of Capital, The Circulation Process of Capital, and The Process of Capitalist Production as a Whole. However, the study of market operations is also that of a process; the elite theorists Gumplowicz and Pareto conceived of society as a process; and what does a properly functionalist sociology analyze if not the functions of social processes?

Contradiction, on the other hand, is alien equally to economics and sociology, and the concept of contradiction provides the historical materialist study of social totalities, processes and change with its essential characteristics. But what can the concept of contradiction mean in empirical social science? Logicians would argue that contradiction can apply only to concepts and propositions, not to reality. For Hegel this was not a problem: in his philosophical system the universe of concepts and the real world were one. For historical materialism as an empirical science of the objective social world, however, the use of the concept of contradiction must correspond to a special purpose, and stands in particular need of clarification.

We will leave aside here the question whether there is, or can be, a particular dialectical logic. In this respect, we will by-pass the objections of orthodox logicians. What we will attempt to show is that the idea of contradiction, used to denote characteristics of social reality, provides a means of grasping scientifically something other and more than the mere existence of opposition, conflict, and competition.

Briefly and crudely defined, the principle of contradiction in historical materialism refers to the unity of opposites.[225] The pattern of social determination discovered by historical materialism is characterized precisely by a unity and conflict of opposites. To speak of contradictions in society is to acknowledge a basic unity between the parties to fundamental conflicts and between the parts of fundamental structural incongruities. Contradiction in this sense constitutes the relationship between social classes (in the Marxist theory) and (at a certain stage) between the relations and the forces of production. Whatever the philosophical propriety of the word, the concept of contradiction implies that the social conflicts discovered by historical materialism are fundamentally different from these studied by sociological 'conflict theorists'.

Social classes, as understood by historical materialism, are not competitors for scarce resources, where one class is in an advantaged position, having better 'life-chances' because of its ownership of means of production or privileged access to education and so on.[226]

---

[225] Cf. Lenin, *Philosophical Notebooks*: 'In brief, dialectics can be defined as the doctrine of the unity of opposites. This embodies the essence of dialectics, but it requires explanations and development' (p. 223).

[226] The classical non-Marxist view is Max Weber's definition of classes and

They are bearers of one and the same exploitative mode of production. The two classes of such a mode of production presuppose and precondition each other, and their relationship is not just logical, but material – between exploiter and exploited, oppressor and oppressed. The classes are the two necessary poles of a common, specific mode of exploitation and oppression. Their interrelationship and their struggle are therefore determined by the development of this mode of production, a development which occurs in and through the struggle between the classes, as Marx demonstrates in the first volume of *Capital* (struggles over the working-day, the introduction and use of machinery, wage levels, and the accumulation of capital). An exploitative mode of production, then, is contradictory in the sense that it is at the same time both a specific unity of opposing classes, of immediate producers and appropriators of surplus labour, and a conflict and struggle of these opposing classes.

A mode of production is a combination of particular relations and forces of production. Between these two also there is both unity and contradiction. What does it mean to say that the unity of the relations and the forces of production develops into a contradiction, if not simply that there develops a structural incongruity between them, and that it is the very development of their unity that leads to this incongruity? The contradiction between the private capitalist relations of production and the social character of the forces of production is generated, not by the uneven development of two different social structures (for instance the more rapid development of the forces of production), but by the specific tempo and form of development of the productive forces brought about by the capitalist relations of production.

It should be noted, however, that both the relationship between classes and that between the forces and the relations of production differ from the contradictions of Hegelian logic. The proletariat is not the negation of the bourgeoisie in the sense that poverty is the negation of wealth, nor are the forces and relations of production negations of each other. The proletariat has its own positive determinations, the development of which, together with the development of capitalism, is a critical precondition of a proletarian

---

strata, *Wirtschaft und Gesellschaft*, pp. 223f, 679f, and *Economy and Society*, pp. 302f, 926f.

[227] *Capital*, MEW 23, pp. 790–1, English ed., p. 763.

revolution: 'Along with the constantly diminishing number of magnates of capital, who usurp and monopolize all advantages of this process of transformation, grows the mass of misery, oppression, slavery, degradation, exploitation; but with this too grows the revolt of the working class, a class always increasing in numbers, and disciplined, united, organized by the very mechanism of the process of capitalist production itself.'[227]

This important difference underlies Lucio Colletti's refusal to accept dialectics as part of historical materialism as a science. Following Kant, Colletti distinguishes between opposition through contradiction and opposition without contradiction, the former being the object of dialectics and the latter of science.[228] A dialectical opposition, in Colletti's definition, involves a unity split into two aspects, which are the negations of each other. 'Each term, therefore, to be itself, implies a relation to the other term; the result is unity (the unity of opposites). Only *within* this unity is each term the negation of the other.'[229] What seems to slip through Colletti's

---

[228] Colletti, op. cit., pp. 66–76. On the other hand, the fundamental difference mentioned above vitiates Marcuse's view 'that Marx's dialectical conception of reality was originally motivated by the same datum as Hegel's, namely, by the negative character of reality', *Reason and Revolution*, p. 312. Whereas Colletti portrays historical materialism as a non-dialectical science, Marcuse presents it as a non-scientific social philosophy. Marcuse's anti-scientific bias may be seen in the confusions of this statement: 'The social facts that Marx analyzed (for example the alienation of labour, the fetishism of the commodity world, surplus-value, exploitation) are not akin to sociological facts, such as divorces, crimes, shifts in population, and business cycles. . . . [The former] will appear as facts only to a theory that takes them in the preview of their negation' (p. 321). Surplus-value is not a fact, but an analytic concept of a high level of abstraction – a level of abstraction not very different from that of the concept of value in classical economics. Exploitation, in the precise Marxist sense, is empirically ascertainable, and is hardly more laden with negativity than crime. Commodity-fetishism is a concept that Marx developed in a scientific critique of political economy (*Capital*, *MEW* 23, p. 90; English ed., p. 71f). There remains the philosophy of man's alienation, whose role is in an ideological rather than a scientific critique of society. Ironically enough, however, it is the only Marxian idea in Marcuse's list that has been taken up and domesticated by empirical sociology, in particular in the work of Melvin Seeman. It is characteristic of Marcuse's position that he should reverse Marx's view of Smith and Ricardo, as founders of a science of political economy, and of the ideological critics of capitalism such as Proudhon (Marcuse, *Reason and Revolution*, pp. 328, 337–8; Marx, *The Poverty of Philosophy*, *MEW* 4).

[229] Colletti, 'Marxism and the Dialectic', p. 4. Emphasis in original.

Kantian dichotomy of oppositions, however, is that one of the two conditions may be fulfilled without the other. Between the classes of historical materialism there is an essential unity. The bourgeoisie presupposes and is unthinkable without the proletariat, and vice versa. Though Colletti is right in stating that Engels and Lenin, and also Marx himself in *Capital*, did not properly clarify their differences with Hegel's dialectic, it is nevertheless the case that the essential unity of real opposites constitutes a characteristic aspect of the Marxist study of oppositions that contrasts with other ways of considering social conflicts.

In Marx and Engels, however, though usually not in the Leninist tradition, there is a further distinction, implicit and occasionally even explicit, according to which it is possible to speak of a contradiction between the forces and the relations of production, but not between classes. Though they are not *only* the negations of each other, the forces and the relations of production form a unity of mutually exclusive aspects when they enter into contradiction: the *private* character of the capitalist relations of production is the negation of the *social* character of the productive forces developed by advanced capitalism.[230] On the other hand, whereas classes constitute a conflictual unity of opposites, they certainly do not exclude each other. The opposition and struggle of classes, therefore, does not in itself point to the necessity of a solution, to a transformation of the system of classes or to their abolition. Indeed, as a matter of fact *Capital* does not speak of contradictions between classes, but of contradictions within the structure and processes of the capitalist mode of production, which develop in the course of the class struggle between the bourgeoisie and the proletariat, and which determine the mode of existence of their antagonism and the relations of strength between the classes. The relation between these systemic contradictions and the class struggle, and the corresponding distinction between contradiction and class conflict, is explicitly expressed by Engels in the following way: 'The contradiction

[230] This means that contradiction, in this stronger sense, is of the very essence of historical materialism. Colletti, however, finds the dialectic only in the philosophy of man and society which, in his view, Marx shared with Rousseau, Kant, Hegel and others. 'Modern society is a society characterized by division (alienation, contradiction). What was at one time united has now been split and separated. The "original unity" of man with nature and of man with man has been broken' (p. 28).

[*Widerspruch*] between socialized production and capitalistic appropriation manifested itself as the antagonism [*Gegensatz*] of proletariat and bourgeoisie.'[231]

Contradiction characterizes the historical social totalities, the social processes and the qualitative changes studied by historical materialism. The processes of the capitalist economy, for instance, are not simply processes of allocation and growth but a unity of opposite tendencies, temporarily reconciled by recurrent crises, and realized through a welter of class struggles. In his manuscripts for the second volume of *Capital*, Marx made a note for further work: 'Contradiction in the capitalist mode of production: the labourers as buyers of commodities are important for the market. But as sellers of their own commodity – labour-power – capitalist society tends to keep them down to the minimum price. Further contradiction: the periods in which capitalist production exerts all its forces regularly turn out to be periods of over-production, because production potentials can never be utilized to such an extent that more value may not only be produced but also realized; but the sale of commodities, the realization of commodity-capital and thus of surplus-value, is limited, not by the consumer requirements of society in general, but by the consumer requirements of a society in which the vast majority are always poor and must always remain poor.'[232]

The contradictions of a given social totality determine the possibilities and the necessity of social change: 'The historical development of the antagonisms, immanent in a given form of production, is the only way in which that form of production can be dissolved and a new form established.'[233] Such a theory may be contrasted with the rise and fall of master races and elites depicted by Gumplowicz, Pareto and others. The later process certainly occurs in and through conflicts, but between the rulers and the ruled there is no unity of opposites. The fall of one elite is viewed as the result of internal degeneration and the rise of a stronger force outside it, not of a development in the tie between rulers and ruled. Functionalist sociology, for its part, has not focused on the way in

[231] Engels, *Anti-Dühring, MEW* 20, p. 253; English ed., Moscow, 1962, p. 371; cf. ibid., pp. 240, 248, 255; English ed., pp. 351, 363, 374.

[232] *Capital*, Vol. 2, *MEW* 24, p. 318 n; English ed., p. 316 n.

[233] *Capital*, Vol. 1, *MEW* 23, p. 512; English ed., p. 488.

which a social phenomenon functional in the maintenance of the social system can at the same time develop a dysfunctional moment. Similarly, the social wholes that sociology theorized were not constituted by a unity and struggle of opposites, and the qualitative changes analyzed by the sociologists were not regarded as having been caused by the inner contradictions of theological, military, traditional, mechanical or *Gemeinschaft* society, but rather by the unfolding of certain evolutionary mechanisms, which might or might not have operated at times through abrupt and revolutionary processes.

Thus, a mode of analysis that can be called dialectical is at work in historical materialism, with visible and distinctive effects, and without involving any assumptions contrary to empirical, natural-scientific procedure. Dialectics in this sense is also clearly pertinent to Marxism as a guide to revolutionary politics. Men are determined by the circumstances in which they live, as the French 'mechanical materialists' of the 18th century already held. On the other hand, they can also change their circumstances, because these are themselves changing and contradictory, a unity of opposites in motion. The essential meaning of the socialist strategy laid out by Marx and Engels after their break with the 'Utopian Socialists' in the 1840s was that the emancipation of the exploited and degraded proletariat could not be brought about by socially indeterminate educators but only by the proletariat's own practice of class struggle, itself determined by the development of the inner contradictions of the capitalist mode of production as a unity of opposites. Dialectics, then, is central to Marxism both as science and as revolution.[234]

2. Totality: the Base and the Superstructure

The concept of totality is central to historical materialism not because the latter aims at grasping *all* social phenomena as a whole

---

[234] Bernstein was quite correct, from his own reformist point of view, to attack the dialectic explicitly for its revolutionary logic: it revealed the irreconcilable contradictions of capitalism, and therefore the inevitability of crises and antagonistic struggles. However, unless located within a science of exploitation, the dialectic ceases to be a guide to the practice of class struggle and becomes mere intellectual speculation compatible with the most diverse political notions, as the development of the Frankfurt School attests.

(a scientifically absurd intention), nor even because it claims to be the most general of the social sciences (a claim it would have to share with most sociologies, pioneer, classical and contemporary), but because of the particular kind of social determination represented by the forces and relations of production as a pattern of social determination. The latter are said by Marxists to determine not only the social (economic) processes covered by these concepts but also, 'in the last instance', *other* processes, ideological and political, as well. Historical materialism is not merely a critique of political economy – one which demonstrates how the market arises and develops in the historical modes of production of petty commodity production and capitalism. It is also a critique of historiography, political theory and social philosophy.

The market operates as a mechanical system of forces governed by supply and demand. Its range of operation is not necessarily to be conceived as restricted to what is ordinarily called the economy (there exist, for example, theories of generalized social exchange) but it is not conceived as determining anything other than itself, that is, behaviour covered by the concepts of market exchange. Similarly, the ideological community of values and norms always functions only through itself, through men who have internalized certain values and norms in their social behaviour, including political and economic behaviour. The social totality characterized by a certain system of values constitutes what has been called an *expressive totality*,[235] a totality of institutions and processes which express a certain system of values. The forces and the relations of production, on the other hand, operate not in themselves but only in a specific relationship to other processes. This is the problem of the base (of forces and relations of production) and the (ideological and politico-juridical) superstructure.

The metaphor of base and superstructure indicates a particularly structured totality and a particular social causality. The super-structure is not reducible to the base or to a common underlying principle or value system. The base does not simply pull along the superstructure (or push it forward), as in the so-called cultural lag theory discussed above. Nor are base and superstructure just inter-

---

[235] I owe this, and many other clarifications of the Marxist use of totality, to Louis Althusser (see, for example, *Reading Capital*, p. 186). However, the present exposition differs from Althusser's philosophical discourse, which is not, then, necessarily vulnerable to any criticism that may be made of my argument.

dependent. The former 'ultimately' determines the latter and the totality as a whole. What Marx and Engels wanted to convey in this metaphor was a conception according to which one part determines itself, the other parts, and the totality, at the same time as it is itself affected by these other parts. They regarded this conception as part of their dialectical method, not only because of the contextual analysis involved in the use of concept of totality but also, and above all, because of the particular kind of causality operating in the totality. Against reductionist interpretations of the principle of economic determination, Engels exclaimed: 'What all these gentlemen lack is dialectics. They always see only here cause, there effect.'[236] The kind of totality and determination in question were defined by Marx in his most comprehensive methodological text: 'The conclusion we reach is not that production, distribution, exchange and consumption are identical, but that they all form the members of a totality, distinctions within a unity. Production predominates not only over itself, in the antithetical definition of production, but over the other moments as well. The process always returns to production to begin anew. . . . A definite production thus determines a definite consumption, distribution and exchange as well as *definite relations between these different moments*. Admittedly, however, *in its one-sided form*, production is itself determined by the other moments. . . . Mutual interaction takes place between the different moments. This is the case with every organic whole.'[237]

Let us first try to formulate somewhat more concretely the relation of determination between the base and the superstructure. Between the economic base and the different instances of the superstructure there is at the same time a system of functional interrelationships and a fundamental asymmetrical efficacy. In order to function, a given combination of forces and relations of production necessitates a juridical system that fixes and formalizes the distribution of the means of production, the relations of domination and servitude, of exchange and so on: 'Such regulation and order are themselves indispensable elements of any mode of production, if it is to assume social stability and independence from mere chance and arbitrariness.'[238] Exploitative relations of production need a re-

---

[236] Engels to Schmidt, October 27, 1890, *MEW*, 37; *MESC*, p. 422.

[237] Marx, 'Introduction', *Grundrisse*, pp. 20–1; English ed., pp. 99–100.

[238] Ibid., p. 801; English ed., p. 774.

pressive political apparatus as their ultimate guarantee.[239] Marx points out, in his remarks on the capitalist passion for accumulation and in his rather more sustained reflections on the development of class-conscious proletarian ideology, that the reproduction of the economy is no less dependent on definite ideological conditions than is the antithetical aim of transforming it.[240]

This necessary functional interrelationship explains the meaning of the important Marxist distinction between the determinant instance of society (the economy) and the dominant one (which may be some other instance). Different economic modes of production need correspondingly different kinds of superstructure. These differ not only in their contents, but also in the specific relations of dominance and subordination that obtain among the instances of the superstructural ensemble. Thus, different modes of production may necessitate different degrees of religious sanction or different amounts of extra-economic power and legal subordination. The forms in which men live their lives in the specific combination of forces and relations of production uncovered by scientific analysis, may for example be as much ideological (say, religious), as economic. The appropriators of surplus labour may have religious attributes – as deities or as priests – class struggles may be fought out in predominantly religious terms, and so on. In answer to a contemporary critique of his *Contribution to the Critique of Political Economy*, Marx illustrated the distinction between determination and dominance, and specified the relation between the two: 'I seize this opportunity of shortly answering an objection taken by a German paper in America to my work, *Zur Kritik der Pol. Oekonomie*. In the estimation of that paper, my view that each special mode of production and the social relations corresponding to it, in short, that the economic structure of society, is the real basis on which the juridical and political superstructure is raised, and to which definite social

[239] This is developed by Engels in *The Origin of the Family, Private Property and the State*, MEW 21; *MESW*, pp. 449–583.

[240] For instance in the *Communist Manifesto*. In a letter of 1871 to the secretary of the German section of the International in New York, Frederic Bolte, Marx emphasized that 'Where the working-class is not yet far enough advanced in its organization to undertake a decisive campaign against the collective power, i.e., the political power of the ruling classes, it must at any rate be trained for this by continual agitation against this power and by a hostile attitude towards the policies of the ruling classes. Otherwise it remains a plaything in their hands . . .', *MEW* 33, p. 333; *Selected Correspondence*, pp. 328–9.

forms of thought correspond; that the mode of production determines the character of the social, political, and intellectual life generally, all this is very true for our own times, in which material interests preponderate, but not for the middle ages, in which Catholicism, nor for Athens and Rome, where politics, reigned supreme. In the first place it strikes one as an odd thing for anyone to suppose that these well-worn phrases about the middle ages and the ancient world are unknown to anyone else. This much, however, is clear, that the middle ages could not live on Catholicism, nor the ancient world on politics. On the contrary, it is the mode in which they gained a livelihood that explains why here politics, and there Catholicism, played the chief part. For the rest, it requires but a slight acquaintance with the history of the Roman republic, for example, to be aware that its secret history is the history of its landed property. On the other hand, Don Quixote long ago paid the penalty for wrongly imagining that knight errantry was compatible with all economic forms of society.'[241]

This quotation also stresses the asymmetrical efficacy of the different levels of society. Juridical and political forms and ideas are not reducible to economic phenomena, as Engels was at pains to emphasize in his late letters on methodology.[242] They have a relative autonomy and an efficacy of their own. But in the historical development of human society, the limits set by the economic base to that autonomy and efficacy are more important. The dynamic of capitalist society is determined by the accumulation of capital, not by functional juridical forms, such as rights to mobile individual property or the right to make contracts, nor by factory legislation and other forms of legal intervention that occur as later effects of the class struggle. The 'political form of the relation of sovereignty and dependence' is rooted in the relations of production,[243] and though the former has a potency and dynamic of its own, the possible forms of political power are in the long run determined by the character of the economic base. A socialist economy can start to be constructed as a result of a political revolution, but for the latter to be successful a certain economically-founded pattern of class relation-

---

[241] *Capital*, I, *MEW* 23, p. 96 n; English ed., p. 82 n.

[242] For instance, his letters to Bloch (September 1890), Schmidt (October 1890), Mehring (July 1893) and Starkenburg (January 1894), in *MEW*, vols. 37–9. All are included in the *Selected Correspondence*.

[243] *Capital*, III, *MEW* 25, pp. 799–800; English ed., p. 772.

ships is necessary: the character of the post-revolutionary society that results will be decided in the long run not by the programmes of the new political leadership but by the relations of production that develop.

Yet this is still rather vague and general – 'more important', 'in the long run'. These words do have a meaning that makes it possible to distinguish historical materialism from other theories of social processes and social change. But they are largely non-scientific notions, lacking the precision characteristic of a science. They indicate the extent to which something is more important than something else and what mechanisms operate in the long run. Again we are confronted with the question: is this a general guide to research or a scientific structure of concepts and propositions?

Determination by the economic base operates through two fundamental mechanisms, which are always functionally intertwined in actual social structures, but which may be distinguished analytically: the systemic processes of reproduction and the class struggle. The world that men enter is always pregiven: 'In the social production of their existence, men inevitably enter into definite relations, which are independent of their will, namely relations of production appropriate to a given stage in the development of their material forces of production.' Every such mode of production has certain specific 'laws of motion', through which its reproduction occurs and within which external forces have their impact. In his methodological discussion of the relationship between production and distribution, Marx observed that 'In all cases of conquest, three things are possible. The conquering people subjugates the conquered under its own mode of production . . .; or it leaves the old mode intact and contents itself with a tribute . . .; or a reciprocal interaction takes place whereby something new, a synthesis, arises. . . . In all cases, the mode of production, whether that of the conquering people, that of the conquered, or that emerging from the confusion of both, is decisive for the new distribution which arises.' Which of these three possibilities actually occurs is determined by the relationship between the modes of production of conqueror and conquered. Marx continues: 'It is a received opinion that in certain periods people lived from pillage alone. But, for pillage to be possible, there must be something to be pillaged, hence production. The mode of pillage is itself in turn determined by the mode of production. A stock-jobbing nation, for example, cannot be pillaged [or pillage: G.T.] in the same manner as a nation of cow-herds.'[244]

The relative autonomy of the instances of the superstructure means that they have their own laws of motion and temporalities. Of law, for example, Engels wrote: 'In a modern state, law must not only correspond to the general economic condition and be its expression, but must also be an *internally coherent* expression which does not, owing to inner contradictions, reduce itself to nought. In order to achieve this, the faithful reflection of economic conditions suffers increasingly.'[245] However, the determination by the base means that, in the reproduction of the social totality, the laws of motion of the superstructure are circumscribed by those of the latter.

Though there is a certain systemic logic in any kind of social system, this logic is only realized through men's ideas and actions. Here we come to the other basic mechanism, the class struggle. We have seen above that classes in the Marxist sense are defined by specific relations of production, of which they are bearers. Therefore, to say that the economic base is the determinant instance of the social totality is to say that 'the history of all societies hitherto is the history of class struggle'. The systemic logic of economic determination is realized not because men are basically motivated by economic interest, as Marx's early break with utilitarianism made clear, but through men's practices as members of different, antagonistic classes. Thus the rise and the abolition of class divisions are equally determined by the development of the forces and the relations of production. However, the complexity of the totality, with the reciprocal determination of the base by the relatively autonomous superstructure, means that the class struggle is not only economic but political and ideological as well.

What, then, in brief, is meant by the thesis of the determination of the political superstructure by the economy? The economy is defined as the combination of relations and forces of production, but what is 'the political' that is determined here? 'The political' refers to the polity, that is to the state. The political superstructure, in the theory of historical materialism, is the state and the practices relating to the state, interventions by the state, struggles for state

[244] *Grundrisse*, pp. 18, 19; English ed., p. 98.
[245] Engels to Schmidt, October 27, 1890, *MEW*, 37, p. 491; *MESC*, p. 422.

power and so on. Marx never lived to write the study of the state that he had planned as part of the same work as *Capital*; we have only his concrete political analyses, above all of Louis Bonaparte's coup d'etat in *The Eighteenth Brumaire*, of the Paris Commune in *The Civil War in France*, and some scattered remarks in his economic works. Engels, on the other hand, wrote *The Origin of the Family, Private Property and the State*. The concept of the state refers to the sovereign public force, supreme over a certain territory.[246] As such it is the 'concentration of civil society'.[247] In sum, then, *the state is the concentration of the class relationships of a given territory in a special organization*. Historical materialism explicitly acknowledges that a concrete society normally contains a plurality of modes of production, intertwined with each other, and that classes are not homogeneous units but consist of several fractions, and therefore pays strict attention to the resulting complex patterns of class relationships, of state structures, state power, and struggles for state power.[248] The state, as a concentration of class relationships, is determined by the economic base, but this determination works itself out in forms which cannot be proclaimed *a priori*, but have to be established by empirical analysis in each concrete case. Political leadership is exercised in a system of class relations, and the class struggle determines who will be the political leaders, and where the leaders will lead the led. State power is a concentration of class power. The determination of the political by the economic base was formulated by Marx thus in his Preface to *The Eighteenth Brumaire*: 'I show how . . . the *class struggle* created circumstances and conditions which allowed a mediocre and grotesque individual to play the hero's role.'[249]

Within the overall pattern of determination, the state is also said to be relatively autonomous. This is not merely or even mainly because of the effects of particular constitutional forms and traditions, but refers above all to the fact that the Marxist concept of the state does not encompass only the concentration of the class

---

[246] Engels, *The Origin of the Family, Private Property and the State*, *MEW* 21, pp. 165; English ed., London, 1972, pp. 229–30.

[247] *Grundrisse*, pp. 28–9; English ed., p. 108.

[248] See, for instance, Marx's *The Eighteenth Brumaire of Louis Bonaparte*, *MEW* 8; English translation in *Surveys from Exile*, London, 1973. Cf. the works of Nicos Poulantzas.

[249] *MEW* 8, p. 560; *Surveys from Exile*, p. 144.

relationships of a given territory, but also, by definition, this concentration in a special apparatus of administration and repression. Engels emphasized that the rise of the state meant the establishment of 'special detachments of armed men' and of a special state bureaucracy.[250] The relative autonomy of the state implies that the relationship of representation, between the classes and the functionaries of the state, from politicians downwards, is generally problematic.[251] The relative autonomy of the state has another aspect, which is of particular importance to Marxism as a guide to proletarian revolution. The state apparatus is a crystallization of class relations in a specific structure, which means that it is not a pliable organizational tool which can be controlled and used by different classes. This thesis is the basis of the Marxist theory of the dictatorship of the proletariat, according to which socialist construction must begin with the 'smashing' of the old repressive and administrative apparatus and the formation of a new type of state organization.[252]

The economic structure determines men's ideas in two ways. Firstly, their perceptions and ideas are determined by their material situation, which in class societies is predominantly a *class* situation. Marx gives a short description of this circumscribed 'religion of everyday life' in the third volume of *Capital*, where he refers to the perception of economic and social conditions by capitalists in the daily conduct of their enterprises.[253] In a more general formulation, he wrote: 'A whole superstructure of different and specifically formed feelings, illusions, modes of thought and views of life arises on the basis of the different forms of property, of the social condi-

---

[250] *The Origins of the Family, Private Property and the State*, MEW 21, p. 166; English ed., p. 230.

[251] See Marx's discussion in *The Eighteenth Brumaire* of the relationship between the Legitimist and Orleanist politicians on the one hand, and the respective fractions of the bourgeoisie that they represented on the other, in the last phase of the Second Republic, *MEW* 8, p. 182f; English ed., p. 221f.

[252] See Marx, 'The Civil War in France', *The First International and After*, esp. p. 206; cf. Lenin, *The State and Revolution, Collected Works*, Vol. 25, and Etienne Balibar, 'La rectification du "Manifeste Communiste",' in *Cinq études*, pp. 65–101.

[253] See, for example, *MEW* 25, pp. 235, 792, 838; English ed., pp. 220, 765, 810. This is part of a polemic against empiricism, which in contrast to the case of the 'German Ideology', criticizes not the lofty, abstract character of the ideological system but its 'crude realism' (p. 792; English ed., p. 765).

tions of existence. The whole class creates and forms these out of its material foundations and the corresponding social relations.'[254] More developed ideological conceptions are similarly determined. In the first volume of *Capital* Marx points, for instance, to utilitarianism, to Proudhon's ideas of justice, and to Protestant religion as corresponding to and as being formed by men's experience of commodity production and exchange relationships.[255]

The determination of ideology involves a differential shaping of the perspectives and the limits of variation of men's ideas in different historical classes, by the relations and forces of production in which they live. The relative autonomy of the ideological superstructure, on the other hand, refers to the irreducibility of these ideological variations to the economic base, and to the specific temporality and dynamics of ideological traditions. 'It was therefore no so-called principles which kept these fractions divided [i.e. the Legitimist and Orleanist parties], but rather their material conditions of existence, two distinct sorts of property; it was the old opposition between town and country, the old rivalry between capital and landed property. Who would deny that at the same time old memories, personal enmities, fears and hopes, prejudices and illusions, sympathies and antipathies, convictions, articles of faith and principles bound them to one or the other royal house? A whole superstructure of different and specifically formed feelings, illusions, modes of thought and views of life arises on the basis of the different forms of property, of the social conditions of existence.'[256] There may also be quite significant divisions of a purely ideological character within the perspective delimited by a common class situation. The bourgeois republicans in the France of Louis Philippe and the February Revolution, for instance, were 'not a fraction of the bourgeoisie bound together by great common interests and demarcated from the rest by conditions of production peculiar to [themselves]; [they were] a coterie of republican-minded members of the bourgeoisie, writers, lawyers, officers and officials'.[257]

The second mode of determination is conveyed by the well-known words of the *Communist Manifesto*: 'The ruling ideas of each

---

[254] *The Eighteenth Brumaire of Louis Bonaparte, MEW* 8, p. 139; English ed., p. 173.

[255] *MEW* 23, pp. 93, 99 n, 189f.

[256] *The Eighteenth Brumaire of Louis Bonaparte*, English edition, p. 173.

[257] Ibid.

age have ever been the ideas of its ruling class.' The next sentence is also worth quoting: 'When people speak of ideas that revolutionize society, they do but express the fact that within the old society, the elements of a new one have been created, and that the dissolution of the old ideas keeps even pace with the dissolution of the old conditions of existence.'[258] That is, the relations of domination involved in the relations of production (not, as is sometimes maintained by utilitarian 'conflict sociology', general and socially indeterminate possession of power by certain groups) determine which of the different perceptions and conceptions of the world will be dominant in a given society at a given point in time. The ideas of a society are formed and developed in the class struggle. The specific mechanisms of this kind of determination are various. One is the strengthening of proletarian ideology due to the concentration of the workers and facilitation of communication among them, as an effect of the accumulation of capital and the increasingly social character of the forces of production. Another relates to the activities of the specific categories of intellectuals attached to the different ruling classes (or fractions of classes). In *Capital* Marx denounced the bourgeois 'vulgar economists' who developed the 'everyday religion' of the capitalists into an apologetic system of ideological economics. In the *Eighteenth Brumaire*, this particular mechanism is thus described: 'Under the Bourbons, big landed property had ruled, with its priests and lackeys; under the July monarchy, it had been high finance, large-scale industry, large-scale trade, i.e. capital, with its retinue of advocates, professors and fine speechmakers.'[259]

Finally, the explanatory theory expressed in the metaphor of base and superstructure may be somewhat further clarified, if we indicate briefly what it would mean in relation to two important problems, religion and nationalism, or religious and national conflicts. A Marxist analysis would involve the assumption that the emergency and character of religions and nationalisms are related, but not reducible, to men's different experiences in different modes of production and particular classes, in ways that the analysis must disclose. It would imply that religions and nationalisms, where they

---

[258] *MEW* 4, p. 480; English ed., p. 85.
[259] *The Eighteenth Brumaire, MEW* 8, pp. 138–9; English ed., p. 173. Emphasis omitted.

exist (and nationalism is a very modern phenomenon), have a different character and function in different modes of production and that they play different roles for different classes. Marxists would assert, for instance, that the nationalism of the anti-imperialist liberation fronts of twentieth-century Africa, Asia, and Latin America is basically different from that of the 19th-century European bourgeoisie, but that both are determined by the development of capitalism. Further, Marxists would argue that religions and nationalisms, religious and national conflicts, develop in and through the class struggle. Religious and national struggles, then, can be understood and explained more adequately by the dynamics of the modes of production in which they occur than by themselves in isolation; and much more adequately than can class struggles by the religious or national context or form in which they may be fought out, or by equating class, national, and religious struggles as different manifestations of cleavage and conflict in general. Relatively little Marxist work has so far been done on either religion or nationalism.[260] But it is precisely because these constitute weak and underdeveloped areas of historical materialist investigation that they have been indicated here as examples of fields where the adequacy of historical materialism as a science should be examined. In contrast to the prim circumspection of ideology, science lives by exposing itself, scantily clad or unclad if need be, to critics and adherents alike.

3. A New Kind of Scientific Determination

Because of its dialectical character, historical materialism involves a new kind of scientific determination.[261] Very briefly summarized, this may be said to have at least two basic aspects. The first is a pattern of determination, no longer restricted as in classical mechanics to conveying invariant relationships between given phenomena, that focuses on the determination of qualitative change. The interest Marx and Engels revealed in chemistry and biological evolution is natural in this context. Historical materialism

---

[260] The one classical Marxist study of religion is Karl Kautsky, *The Foundations of Christianity*, London n.d. (first published in German, 1908). An excellent overview of the classical Marxist treatment of nationalism, is G. Haupt, M. Löwy and C. Weill, *Les marxistes et la question nationale 1848–1914*, Paris, 1974.

[261] See Zelený, *Die Wissenschaftslogik und 'Das Kapital'*, esp. chs. 7 and 9.

formulates its own specific version of this non-mechanical determination in 'laws of motion' expressing the inner contradictory processes of society.

The other aspect of the determination involved in Marxist dialectics is the substitution of intricate causal chains of 'mediation' and reciprocal effect for straightforward unidirectional cause-effect relationships and for the direct subsumption of phenomena under universal laws. There is an analogy here with Darwin's theory of evolution, which also diverges from classical mechanical determination in that it does not immediately subsume all variations under the law of natural selection. Here as in the former case, analogies do not signify an identity or even any far-reaching similarity between historical materialism and contemporaneous breakthroughs in natural science. But in their light, the attempts of Marx and Engels to relate their dialectical science of society to the new natural sciences become understandable and reasonable (this is not to say that they were in the end very successful and fruitful).

Mediated determination characterizes the historical materialist 'tendency laws' of development and change, and also the specifically Marxist explanation of how a given social system, for example, the capitalist economy, functions. This is most explicit and developed in Marx's economic analyses, above all in his analysis of the operation of the labour theory of value. One example is this telling criticism of Ricardo: 'Instead of *postulating* this *general rate of profit*, Ricardo should rather have examined in how far its *existence* is in fact consistent with the determination of value by labour-time, and he would have found that instead of being consistent with it, *prima facie*, it *contradicts* it, and that its existence would therefore have to be explained through a number of intermediary stages. . . .'[262] Mediated determination is also involved in the determination of the superstructure and the social totality by the economic base.

This complex totality, composed of the determinant economic base, incorporating as a rule several interlaced modes of production, and of relatively autonomous instances of the superstructure with their own specific traditions, also provides a particular setting for the basic contradiction in the Marxist dialectic. The contradiction between the forces and the relations of production never unfolds in pure isolation, and its determination of change is never simple and

---

[262] Marx, *Theories of Surplus Value*, *MEW* 26: 2, p. 165; English ed., p. 174.

straightforward. It does not form part of a *Zusammenbruchstheorie* (theory of collapse), nor does it in itself bring about a revolutionary situation. As part of a historical totality it is effective only in a concatenation of different forces, contradictions and conflicts, political and ideological as well as economic. Marx made this fundamental aspect of the historical materialist dialectic clear in a letter on perspectives for the English revolution, which he wrote as a leader of the First International to two cadres of this organization. England was obviously central to Marx's political as well as scientific preoccupations: 'England, being the metropolis of capital, the power which has hitherto ruled the world market, is for the present the most important country for the workers' revolution, and moreover the *only* country in which the material conditions for this revolution have developed up to a certain degree of maturity.'[263] England was also the country which Marx used for most of his illustrations of capitalism in *Capital*. What kind of analysis, then, did Marx make of how the laws of motion of capitalism would lead to a proletarian revolution in England? (Here it is the kind of analysis Marx made which is important, rather than the question whether the relationships which this analysis highlighted were correctly perceived and evaluated.)

What Marx set out to do was to delineate the historical totality in which English class struggles occurred, a situation in which colonial domination as well as nationalism, religion and other ideologies played pertinent roles. 'After occupying myself with the Irish question for many years I have come to the conclusion that the decisive blow against the English ruling classes (and it will be decisive for the workers' movement all over the world) *cannot* be delivered *in England* but *only in Ireland*. . . . Ireland is the bulwark of the *English landed aristocracy*. The exploitation of that country is not only one of the main sources of this aristocracy's material welfare; it is its greatest *moral* strength. It, in fact, represents the *domination of England over Ireland*. Ireland is therefore the great means by which the English aristocracy maintains *its domination in England itself*. If, on the other hand, the English army and police were to withdraw from Ireland tomorrow, you would at once have an agrarian revolution there. But the overthrow of the English aristocracy in Ireland involves as a necessary consequence its over-

---

[263] Marx to Meyer and Vogt, April 9, 1870, *MEW* 22, p. 669; *MESC*, p. 237.

throw in England. This would fulfil the preliminary condition of the proletarian revolution in England. The destruction of the English landed aristocracy in Ireland is an infinitely easier question than in England itself, because in Ireland *the land question* has hitherto been the *exclusive form* of the social question, because it is a question of existence, of *life and death*, for the immense majority of the Irish people, and because it is at the same time inseparable from the *national* question. . . . . As for the English *bourgeoisie*, it has in the first place a common interest with the English aristocracy in turning Ireland into mere pasture land which provides the English market with meat and wool at the cheapest possible prices. . . . But the English bourgeoisie has, besides, much more important interests in Ireland's present-day economy. Owing to the constantly increasing concentration of tenant-farming, Ireland steadily supplies its own surplus to the English labour market, and thus forces down wages and lowers the moral and the material condition of the English working class. Then most important of all! Every industrial and commercial centre in England now possesses a working class *divided* into two *hostile* camps, English proletarians and Irish proletarians. The ordinary English worker hates the Irish worker as a competitor who lowers his standard of life. In relation to the Irish worker he feels himself a member of the *ruling* nation and so turns himself into a tool of the aristocrats and capitalists of his country *against Ireland*, thus strengthening their domination *over himself*. He cherishes religious, social and national prejudices against the Irish worker . . . This antagonism is artificially kept alive and intensified by the press, the pulpit, the comic papers, in short by all the means at the disposal of the ruling classes. This *antagonism* is the *secret* of the *impotence of the English working class*, despite its organization. It is the secret by which the capitalist class maintains its power.'[264] In fact, as it happened, Irish and English history took a different course from that envisaged by Marx. However, his complex dialectic of revolution was taken up and applied to a new situation in this century by the organizer of the first victorious proletarian revolution.[265]

There can be no guarantee for the correctness of the propositions

[264] Ibid., p. 667f; English ed., pp. 235–6.
[265] That is, by Lenin. For a succinct analysis of the determinations of revolutionary situations, see the concluding chapter of his '*Left-wing Communism*' – *An Infantile Disorder, Collected Works*, vol. 31. Cf. the brilliant philosophical elucida-

of historical materialism outside the scientific practice of explaining the history of human societies. No philosophy of man's nature or 'basic needs' can add anything to the armour of historical materialism in the scientific battle for truth against rival modes of explanation. It should further be emphasized that the practice of a science is no guarantee against errors, misinterpretations and false predictions. These can be found in the foremost practitioners of historical materialism as well as among the greatest scientists of other disciplines. But a science itself provides the means of self-correction. What we have tried to do here, then, is not to prove the truth of historical materialism, but briefly and simply to expound its meaning, and thereby indicate the ways in which it can be tested and used, at once as a science and as a guide to revolution.

---

tion of Marx and Lenin by Althusser, 'Contradiction and Overdetermination', *For Marx*, ch. III.

Chapter Seven

Conclusions and Beyond: Historical Materialism and the Critique of Sociology

The scientific study of reality demands more than acute and systematic observation of the world. It involves a study of the regularities that determine the bewildering infinity of phenomena and events. The formation of a science, then, involves the discovery of a particular system of determinant regularities, and the reproduction of that system in thought, in a theory. For this reason, no historical analysis of aspiring sciences that itself lays claim to scientificity can be merely a history of the ideas given within the discourses selected for examination. Rather, such a history itself possesses a specific object of study: the possible discovery-production of patterns of determination. The present study has attempted an analysis of this type, a historical social-scientific study of social thought, and as such has diverged from the familiar, well-worn path taken by previous histories of the social disciplines. Whether new vistas have been revealed, or whether we have strayed into a wilderness, the reader must now judge.

Scientific enterprises do not subsist in a separate self-contained world. Neither are they related only to very broad and general values. They occur in specific societies at particular points in time, and are, therefore, part of particular historical economic, political and ideological conjunctures. These social contexts are, naturally, especially important to the emergence and formation of enterprises whose specific objective is a scientific grasp of the contexts themselves. The present study has tried to show how the formation of economics, sociology, and historical materialism is inextricably connected with the rise and development of capitalism.

Economics, in the modern sense of the word, emerged as a discourse on the new system of regularities exhibited by the concomitantly emerging post-feudal, capitalist economy: the market.

At the same time, with the rise of a new polity, a new state, and public finance, it developed as a *political economy*.

The arrival of capitalism also produced great social upheavals: the transformation of the economy itself and of the role of the economy in society, the rise of new classes and the decline and fall of old ones. It was as a social theory that explicitly took account of this social transformation that the discipline soon called sociology began to be developed. This new discipline emerged not in Britain, where the bourgeois revolution had first occurred, but in France, where the particularly radical course of the Revolution, and subsequently the glaringly aberrant episode of the Restoration, had rendered the social transformation uniquely visible.

The new theory of sociology began as a theory of politics, focusing primarily on the relationship between politics and the society at large, specifically demanding that political institutions should be adapted to the new bourgeois society and actual political power be vested in the bourgeoisie. It was in this context that Comte developed his notion of *consensus*, meaning not a concord of ideas but a structural congruence among the different parts of society, primarily between the 'stage of civilization' expressed in industry and science and the system of government.[1] Sociology, as a new discourse on politics, involved a critique of previous political philosophy, a critique in which the awareness of the new society was reflected. In this respect, sociology was akin to the Romantic and Hegelian theories of law and politics that were prompted by the destruction of the old German polity by the invading French Revolution.

Saint-Simon and Comte advanced their theory and proposals with a view to 'terminating the revolution', but the development of capitalism meant the development of a new class, the working class, and the labour movement: a new, proletarian revolution began to cast its shadow. It is this encounter with the threat of the masses,

---

[1] Comte, *Cours de philosophie positive*, IV, p. 170f. The Comtean concept thus differs from the latter-day sociological concept of consensus. Parsons' suggestion that Durkheim's *conscience collective* has its 'primary origin' in Comte's work is, therefore, misleading. (Parsons, 'Durkheim's Contribution to the Theory of Integration of Social Systems,' Wolff (ed.), *Essays on Sociology and Philosophy by Durkheim et al.*, p. 119.) It was noted above that the evolutionary interpretation of the development from feudalism to capitalism, which the post-revolutionary sociological pioneers used to deal with social integration, was absent from Durkheim's thought.

rather than a 'revolt against positivism', that explains the change within sociological theory from the concerns of the pioneers to the elite theories of Mosca, Pareto and others (Weber's late political writings also have the marks of this encounter).

To the mainstream of sociologists, however, the newly developed society and its problems were above all of an economic character. The capitalist economy and the new 'social question' that it raised, the 'workers' question', now become prominent. Herein is the pertinence of a comparison between sociology and historical materialism: both constitute critiques of liberal political economy. Sociology emerged as a discourse on politics after the bourgeois revolution and came to maturity as a discourse on economics before the threat of a proletarian revolution.

Saint-Simon and Comte had criticized liberal economics, but sociology was really developed as a critique of political economy only in its classical age. The beginning of this period, from the 1880's to about 1920, coincides with what Marxists usually regard as the beginning of the modern, monopoly stage of capitalism. The critique and rapid demise of Herbert Spencer's sociology of competitive capitalism after its brief vogue in Britain and, particularly, in the USA, was also explicitly related by the post-Spencerian sociologists to the experience of an economic epoch dominated by the big corporations and the problems in the relations between labour and capital that resulted from this. This sociological critique of the prevailing economy and the prevailing economic discipline was, however, little inspired by or related to the Marxist critique. Instead, German historical economics was an important, though differently felt influence on the development of classical sociology in France, the USA, and in Germany. A critique of competitive capitalism furthermore constituted the starting-point of Talcott Parsons' work, which for some two decades after World War II was the dominant sociological theory.[2]

The capitalist market economy had grown to maturity, and sub-

[2] See ch. 1 above. It is an interesting aspect of sociology's relation to the world that Parsons' brief but clear statements of his concern with the analysis of capitalism – he had already written his doctoral dissertation on Weber's and Sombart's treatments of the subject – have frequently been presented in much more vague and evasive terms, for example, as 'the non-rational elements in economic behaviour' (L. Coser, *The Functions of Social Conflict*, New York, 1964, p. 21; cf. J. Rex, *Key Problems in Sociological Theory*, London, 1970, p. 96f).

jected the lives of ever-increasing numbers of people to its rule. The classical economists had discovered it and begun to analyze its operations. But how was it related to other aspects of human society? How were its attendant social problems to be dealt with? These were key questions for a general social theory, of the kind that both sociology and historical materialism aimed to provide.

One answer was that the market was part of the functioning of a particular historical mode of production, which had arisen from the transformation of a previous mode of production and would some time in the future develop into another mode, which Marx and Engels predicted would be socialist. Men had always lived in certain relations of production on the basis of certain forces of production, and to these relations and forces of production certain political structures and systems of ideas were related. The scientific task, then, was to study the given mode of production, basically determined by its specific combination of forces and relations of production. Since existing relations of production divided people into opposing classes, evaluation of social problems and proposals advanced for their solution depended on the class position of the observer. The problems that were actually treated, and the manner of their treatment, depended on the struggle between the classes, whose size and strength derived from the given mode of production and its development.

Another answer was that the competitive market was in itself fundamentally not a social but a biological pattern of determination, an expression of an aggregate of human organisms struggling for their existence. Society, the object of sociology, was constituted by a 'moral milieu', a system of common values and norms restraining and integrating these human organisms. The market was related to society to the extent that it was controlled and regulated by values and norms. The social problem, then, was above all the prevalent deficiency of this relationship, and the solution to it was an increase of value-integration and normative regulation. This was the sort of answer provided by Durkheim[3] and, in a number of variations, by

---

[3] In Durkheim's view, a socially unregulated system of human organisms was, in contrast with animal systems, inherently unstable because the appetites of human beings were not instinctually limited. Man's very power of reflection made human systems incapable of equilibrium, unless normatively controlled, because it made men's desires unlimited and therefore inherently insatiable (*Socialism*, p. 239f).

a host of other contemporary French sociologists.[4]

Much inspired by Durkheim, but with a more positive regard for the factual cooperation involved in market exchange, a rather similar theory was codified in American sociology, with Park and Burgess's influential textbook *Introduction to the Science of Sociology* (first published in 1921). Park and Burgess saw the market economy as a system of 'competitive cooperation'. The 'barest abstraction' of this, the special subject matter of economics, was exhibited by the botanical 'plant community'.[5] In distinction to the botanic-economical system, society and social groups, as social systems, were characterized by *consensus*, which had three aspects, an *esprit de corps*, 'morale' or collective will, and collective representations, 'which embody the objectives of group activity'.[6] 'Consensus' was evidently not used here in the original Comtean sense, but in the latter-day sense of agreement.

A third answer that was of importance in the formation of modern social theory viewed the market as a system of individuals, each rationally calculating his needs and chances of acquiring utilities to satisfy them, and adapting his behaviour accordingly. This rational, purely self-interested calculation did not derive from human nature, physiological or psychological, but from a particular historical system of values. The task was to investigate the character and development of this system of values. The social problem was not that society was divided by this self-interested calculation: it consisted, on the one hand, in the strength (in the particular society in question) of non-capitalist values, and, on the other, in the 'mechanized petrification' ensuing from the decay of original capitalist values, leaving only a compulsive market mechanism. This was the answer produced by Max Weber's ingenious combination of German historicism and Austrian marginalism.

In the second and third answers, the polarization between

[4] Cf. for example, A. Espinas, 'Leçon d'ouverture d'un cours d'histoire d'économie sociale', *Revue Internationale de Sociologie*, vol. 2, no. 5 (1894); M. Bernes, 'Programme d'un cours de sociologie générale I–II', *Revue Internationale de Sociologie*, vol. 3, no. 12, and vol. 4, no. 1 (1895, 1896); L. Beaurin-Gressier, 'Des forces qui déterminent l'évolution du milieu social', *Revue internationale de Sociologie*, vol. 4, no. 4 (1896); R. Worms, 'L'économie sociale I–II', *Revue Internationale de Sociologie*, vol. 6, nos. 6, 7 (1898).

[5] R. Park and E. Burgess (ed.), *Introduction to the Science of Sociology*, Chicago, 1924 (2nd ed.), pp. 162, 165.

[6] Ibid., p. 166.

individual self-interest and social context furnished sociology with a specific object of empirical study. To the extent that human behaviour was socially determined – and was not simply determined by the market, which Weber regarded as a social mechanism and as such adequately studied by marginalist economics – it was determined by a system of common values and norms. This was a specific social pattern of determination, which we have called the ideological community – in a neutral sense with no implications of 'false consciousness'. Historical materialism, by contrast, was constituted outside this problematic of self-interest and ideological community.[7] It focused on men as part of a certain ever pre-given social totality, an irreducible complex of forces and relations of production, and politico-juridical structures, in which the two former are attributed a special weight as constituting the 'determinant instance' or 'base'. In embarking on their new theoretical enterprise, Marx and Engels broke with the above-mentioned type of problematic, in the forms of utilitarianism and Feuerbachian humanism. Part of this change of problematic was that the economists' and sociologists' concept of 'action' centred on the choosing subject, was succeeded by that of *practice*: by a theory of men as working in ongoing processes of transformation – economic, political and ideological.

Capitalism is a class-divided society. It is not just the development of the capitalist economy that has constituted the framework for the rise of the modern social disciplines. The latter have developed in the midst of and as part of class struggles. Thus these different systems of thought have always been related to different classes. This can be seen at a number of specific points: in the decisive differences between the bourgeois pioneer sociologists and the contemporary feudalist philosophers of reaction, in the development of Pareto's ideas of the necessities of a ruling elite, in the notion of an administrative sociology, in the 'socialism' of Durkheim and in Weber's theory of domination and bureaucracy, and in the ideal society of radical economists.

The relationship of the social theorists to the class struggle has

---

[7] This common problematic of the bourgeois social sciences might perhaps be seen as a variant of what Althusser has seen as the essential pair of bourgeois ideology, economism and humanism (see *Réponse à John Lewis*, pp. 79–80).

been central in the discovery and development of the patterns of social determination that constitute the core of the disciplines investigated here. The new determination of the 'wealth of nations' and the new principles that should govern public finance were expounded by the classical economists, the physiocrats, and their predecessors, from a bourgeois point of view in the thick of current social struggles. It was from a bourgeois and petty-bourgeois point of view that the marginalist theory of value could be understood as 'common sense'. Whatever his 'conception of man', Marx's social thought changed course decisively in 1845. This change was directly related to Marx's (and Engels') experience of the working class and its concrete struggles. Simultaneously with their discovery and development of a new pattern of social determination, Marx and Engels began to work out a new strategy for socialism that acknowledged the proletariat as the bearer of tendencies indicated by the new theory of society. Similarly, the classical sociologists worked out their theory of the social determination of human behaviour from their own quite different experiences of capitalist society and its problems and contradictions. This too was largely a critical experience of capitalism, an experience of crisis – but one undergone by intellectuals who were not related to the working class. On the contrary, they looked at the working class and the problems posed by it from the point of view of bourgeois society. But at the same time, the sociological intellectuals were alienated from the hegemonic fraction of the bourgeoisie, either because they were tinged by aristocratic attachments and traditions or because they were related to the petty or lower bourgeoisie. To these subaltern bourgeois fractions, the prevailing state of capitalist society was unnatural, and needed to be remedied by the revival of an ideological community.

The particular character of the sociological critique of 'economic individualism' is also dramatically illustrated by the effect on sociology of the American 1930's, a very important period for post-classical sociology. From one perspective that decade was a period of mass unemployment, of hunger marches, of ferocious resistance to trade-unions from employers. Martial law was proclaimed in a number of towns and the National Guard and the police were called out to break strikes; in the Memorial Day Massacre of 1937 ten steel workers were killed by the Chicago police. It was in these 'turbulent years'[8] that Talcott Parsons formulated his sociology of value-integration, and that Elton Mayo, Fritz Roethlisberger and their associates developed their theory of the critical role of non-economic 'sentiment' in industrial relations, as the framework of industrial sociology. Most striking, perhaps, is the fact that the sociological experience of the 1930's led to the virtual disappearance of the concept of class struggle from sociological language, and that the concept of class was submerged under 'stratification' and evaluational ranking. The Encyclopaedia of the Social Sciences (of 1930) had entries for Class, Class consciousness and Class struggle but no entry for Stratification. With the works of Parsons[9] and Lloyd Warner (whose Yankee City series began to appear in 1941), there developed an idea of classes and strata as grounded in a con-sensus of social values, according to which people were ranked. In the current International Encyclopaedia of the Social Sciences there is no entry for Class, and, of course, none for Class Struggle.[10] The new theory of stratification, industrial sociology, and the 'volun-taristic theory of action' were all part of a critique of the 'merely economic logic', as Mayo put it, of competitive capitalism.[11] This critique was largely the work of a group of intellectuals at the upper bourgeois University of Harvard, anxious to preserve the founda-tions of the society in whose patrician establishment it occupied a secure position.[12]

[8] This is the title of the second volume of Irving Bernstein's important work, A History of the American Worker, 1933–41. Turbulent Years, Boston, 1969.

[9] Parsons' essay, 'An Analytical Approach to the Theory of Stratification', appeared in 1940 and is included in his Essays in Sociological Theory, New York, 1964 (paperback ed.), pp. 69–88.

[10] Bernard Barber writes there on 'Stratification, Social', and says that it was adopted into general sociological use 'only since 1940', International Encyclopedia of the Social Sciences, New York, 1968, vol. 15, p. 289.

[11] E. Mayo, The Human Problems of an Industrial Civilization, New York, 1933, p. 116.

[12] Warner's survey of Newburyport, Massachusetts, grew directly out of his participation in Mayo's Hawthorne project, and was designed to study the broader social context affecting the worker in the factory. Warner, however, was not starting from a problem to be explained, but was rather searching for a solution to recommend: 'We sought above all a well-integrated community, where the various parts of society were functioning with comparative ease. We did not want a city where the ordinary daily relations were in confusion or in conflict.' (L. Warner and P. Lunt, The Social Life of A Modern Community, New Haven, 1941, p. 38, cf. pp. 4–5).

Reporting the first international congress of sociology, in 1894, its general secretary René Worms concluded with satisfaction: 'Finally, despite the independence that has been granted to the speakers, the boldness with which some of them have presented their ideas, and the free opening of the Congress to the general public, there has been no incident of a kind to give rise to the fear that the established order could suffer anything from the free development of academic sociology. On the contrary . . .'[13] Sociology has not often made a sounder prediction.

The present study started with a consideration of the discussion within sociology of the discipline's theoretical heritage and extra-theoretical formation, and with the problems raised in recent philosophies of Marxism concerning the scientificity and practical historical affiliations of historical materialism. In its contribution to a Marxism of the formation of Marxism, it has corroborated Althusser's thesis that 1845 saw a decisive break in the work of Marx and Engels, and that working-class politics played a central role in this theoretical rupture. The analysis of the decisive relationship of the sociologists with the development of the capitalist mode of production and with the class struggle, if correct, furnishes strong evidence for the view that the objective of a social-scientific study of sociology as a social phenomenon is more adequately served by a Marxism of sociology than by a sociology of sociology, that relates the discipline to a community of values (Gouldner or Friedrichs), or by an economics of sociology that relates it to a supply-and-demand mechanism (Ben-David, Oberschall and others).

The scientificity of the disciplines studied here has not been taken as self-evident, but rather as a complex historical product. The contribution of this study to sociology might be said to be an identification of its specific object, the ideological community; and to historical materialism, a systematization and clarification of the pattern of social determination discovered-produced by Marx. Its comparative approach provides a possible framework for the current debates on the interrelationships of the social disciplines. In this respect, one of the most important conclusions of our study is that economics, sociology and historical materialism are distinct disciplines. It is strictly speaking indefensible and merely confusing to

---

[13] R. Worms, 'Le premier Congrès de l'Institut internationale de Sociologie', *Revue Internationale de Sociologie*, vol. 2, no. 10 (1894), p. 722.

speak of a Marxist sociology, of Marxism as a sociology, of Ricardian Marxism, or of a convergence between Marxism and either sociology or economics. What, then, can be said of the scientificity of the three disciplines? The fact that each possesses a specific object and that each has discovered-produced a pattern of social determination, connects these fundamentally controversial disciplines with the objectives and achievements of developed science. Their patterns of determination do not invoke any mysterious forces, and generate effects that are readily amenable to empirical investigation, in the functioning of capitalist competition, in the functioning of different forms of production and in the oppositions and conflicts between men in different socio-economic roles, in the operations of institutions like the family and other formal organizations and groups. The effects of these patterns of determination must be studied empirically and systematically. The history of the social disciplines is abundantly strewn with falsified predictions, inaccuracies, ideological distortions, periods of stagnation and decay, heated polemics over fundamentals, but so too is the history of the natural sciences. There appear to be no sure grounds for denying the title of scientificity to the endeavours of the social disciplines. The real question, it appears, concerns rather their relative fertility as producers of knowledge about society, and their interrelationships – whether, for instance, the object of one discipline is an unacknowledged special case or aspect of another.

Throughout the history of economics up to the present, there has been a basic continuity of object. This is also the case with historical materialism – so much so that the science very often goes by the name of Marxism, in acknowledgment of the undiminished centrality and importance of the work of its founder, Karl Marx. Within sociology, however, no such continuity can be taken for granted. But nevertheless, as was seen in the first chapter, there is at least a continuity in the profoundly influential post-classical works of Talcott Parsons and in those of his foremost sociological critic, Alvin Gouldner. It is in fact possible, we may argue, to demonstrate more concretely that *the ideological community and the market are the twin axes of post-classical non-Marxist social science*. In the field of sociology this hypothesis implies two things: first, that the basic explanatory pattern in empirical sociological studies, in so far as these are concerned with scientific explanation and are not undertaken as *ad hoc* and mainly administrative investigations, rests on

the values and norms of different human aggregates, from civilizations and whole societies to formal organizations and informal small
groups; and second, that post-Parsonian sociology as a social theory
also remains within the confines of the ideological community. The
alternative, in both cases, is reliance on the mechanism of market
exchange – as we have seen exemplified in the current sociology of
sociology.

It seems that later developments in sociological theory exhibit
two main novel tendencies. One, concerned with the proper range
of social determination as such, is the theme of the so-called conflict
perspective developed by Lewis Coser, Ralf Dahrendorf, Dennis
Wrong, John Rex and others. The problematic of these writers is
essentially Durkheimian: non-social self-interest versus society as
a moral community, of which there may be too much or too little.
They differ from Durkheim and from Parsons in that, writing in the
period of intense internal Cold War pressure and the beginnings of
international peaceful coexistence, the main problem appeared to
them to be that there was too much 'society'. They believed that
there was undue social integration in the Western society of the
1950's, and in the social theory of Durkheim and Parsons. These
authors questioned 'the oversocialized conception of man',[14] and
pointed to men's tendency to resist sanctioned norms.[15] They also
stressed that in a society there are groups driven by different values
and norms, that these groups may be in conflict with one another,
and that they are not all equally capable of imposing their values and
norms on others.[16] The mode of operation of the ideological
community studied by these sociologists has thus been different
from that focused by Parsons. Yet another way of delimiting social
determination by the ideological community has been developed by

[14] D. Wrong, 'The Oversocialized Conception of Man in Modern Sociology',
American Sociological Review 26 (April 1961), pp. 183–93.

[15] See Dahrendorf's summary of his theory of society as a normative community, *Essays in the Theory of Society*, London, 1968, p. 173f. Cf. also the
perceptive article by David Lockwood, 'Social Integration and System Integration', in G. Zolschran and W. Hirsch (ed.), *Explorations in Social Change*, London,
1964, pp. 244–57.

[16] The basic similarity between this 'conflict' or 'constraint' theory and so-
called consensus theory, in their common problematic of non-social self-interest
and ideological community, has been noted by a British sociologist, B. Jessop,
Social Order, Reform and Revolution, London, 1972, pp. 26–33. Jessop is mistaken,
however, in assimilating historical materialism to sociological 'constraint theory'.

the schools of symbolic interactionism and ethnomethodology. Here it is emphasized that values and norms are not only *internalized* to different extents but are also interpreted differently by different people. From this point of view, an 'interpretative paradigm' is set against the 'normative paradigm'.[17]

The second novel tendency of recent developments in sociology has been the importation of the market mechanism into sociological theory. Sociology largely developed as a critique of economics, but, in a remarkable reversal, the theory of the competitive market is today often taken as a model for a theory of 'social exchange', developed by George Homans, Peter Blau and others.[18] The stone-age hunter-entrepreneur or the shopping marginalist housewife are now succeeded, however, as the starting-point of social organization by white-collar employees exchanging advice and approval.

One further implication of our hypothesis that social science is centred on the patterns of determination identified in this study, is that 'political science' does not have – or has not yet discovered and developed – any distinct scientific object comparable to those of economics, sociology, and historical materialism. This is very obvious in contemporary Western 'behavioural' political science, where the theoretical framework is either taken from sociology (largely Parsons) or, in the theories of Anthony Downs, Mancur Olson and others, from market economics.[19] Historical materialism, however, possesses its own political theory.[20]

[17] T. Wilson, 'Normative and Integrative Paradigms in Sociology', in J. Douglas (ed.), *Understanding Everyday Life*, London, 1971, pp. 57–79. There seem to be certain analogies between the relationship of this effort to sociology and that of Sartre's project in the *Critique of Dialectical Reason* to historical materialism, which seeks to base a materialistic dialectic on the praxis of the individual in his immediate, everyday experience.

[18] G. Homas, *Social Behaviour, Its Elementary Forms*, London, 1961; P. Blau, *Exchange and Power in Social Life*, New York, 1964.

[19] Cf. S. M. Lipset (ed.), *Politics and Social Science*, New York, 1969, esp. the essay by William Mitchell, with the telling title: 'The Shape of Political Theory to Come: From Political Sociology to Political Economy'; B. Barry, *Sociologists, Economists, and Democracy*, London, 1970. Within his framework of values, Parsons has also come to incorporate exchange mechanisms into his theory of politics: see the collection of Parsons' political essays, *Political and Social Structure*, New York, 1969.

[20] In historical materialism, politics is a 'regional theory', dealing with a specific level of the mode of production. Cf. Poulantzas, *Political Power and Social Classes*: R. Miliband, *The State in Capitalist Society*, London, 1969.

Social life is also significantly affected by patterns of determination other than those of the social sciences: for example, by language, by psychic forces, by natural ecology. A central problem for the development of the social sciences is therefore their articulation with the findings of the sciences of these patterns. The women's movement has also posed the question of sexuality, of sexual discrimination and oppression whose causes and possibilities of abolition no social discipline has yet been able to analyze adequately.

This book located itself at the outset in a conjuncture of crisis and controversy in the social disciplines, above all in sociology and historical materialism. Is it possible now, in conclusion, to indicate a way forward in this troubled situation? Undoubtedly, there can be no escape from crisis and controversy, which inhere in social life in general, not excluding that small part of it that is devoted to the practice of science. It may nevertheless be possible to advance beyond the present situation, to new crises and controversies. One direction was indicated in our first chapter, where we posed the question of a Marxism of Marxism, of a historical-materialist study of the history of the union of Marxist theory and the revolutionary labour movement. The contribution made here to that task, however modest, seems to indicate the importance of a Marxism of Marxism to the development of historical materialism as a science and a guide to revolutionary politics, to the liberation of Marx from the attentions of esoteric philosophizing, and from ideological exploitation, whether factionalist or more or less straightforwardly counter-revolutionary.

Another direction is suggested by the specific relations that obtain among the social sciences. Although their mutual distinctiveness renders all eclectic attempts at 'synthesis' futile and all theoretical promiscuity sterile, the three core disciplines of the social sciences are related in determinate ways. The relationship between economics and historical materialism is grounded in the historical fact that the latter developed as a critique of political economy. This was so not only because of the Marxian conception of the determinant role of the economy, but also and perhaps above all because political economy was at that time the only developed social science. Political economy had already taken up its position within the field delimited by Marx's theoretical project, and therefore had to be dislodged. Today, sociology too has developed a body of knowledge of society, of the functioning of groups, organizations and institutions.

Accordingly, the present situation of historical materialism demands a *critique of sociology*. Since the object of sociology (the ideological community) is related to that of historical materialism in the same way as that of economics (the market), a critique of sociology should be of the same type as Marx's critique of political economy. The ideological community refers to an external reality, to values and norms transmitted in empirical processes of socialization and determining men's social behaviour in ascertainable ways. We noted above that the object of sociology does not involve the assumption that society is a unitary ideological community: on the contrary, the discipline has explicitly dealt with relations of domination and conflict among groups, organizations and institutions governed by different values and norms. Like the market, the ideological community has been and continues to be utilized for bourgeois and petty-bourgeois ideological ends in the class struggle. Nevertheless, sociology does include a scientific component; and, following the example of Marx's critique of political economy, it is necessary to distinguish between scientific and vulgar sociology. The radical interventions of recent years have been concerned mainly with the latter, exposing and denouncing ideological distortion. That kind of criticism has been timely and, on the whole, appropriate. But for the further development of social science, it now seems urgently necessary to advance to a critique of scientific sociology. Like Marx's long struggle with classical political economy, this effort will indubitably enhance historical materialism. If the present study is correct in its analysis of the constitution of the different social sciences, the basis for such a critique has now been laid.

Economics and sociology allot no proper space to the object of historical materialism, which is constituted outside their common problematic of self-interest and social values. Economists may speak of capitalism and sociologists of classes and class conflicts, but the former do not see capital as a relation of production and the latter do not relate classes and class struggle to particular historical combinations of the forces and relations of production. On the other hand, in historical materialism, the market and the ideological community have a space as irreducible social determinants. Capitalist relations of production function through the competitive market mechanism, and are explicitly analyzed as such by Marx; while in every mode of production, there is a specifically effective ideological superstructure.

Summarily, Marx's transformation of the object of economics may be said to have had two aspects. First, the market was related to a broader determining social context, the mode of production. His analyses showed not only how the rise and development of the market could be explained by the dynamics of the mode of production, but also – and this was the second aspect – how certain theoretical contradictions in classical economics, such as those in the analysis of the mode of operation of the labour theory of value, could be resolved. Marx at once posed and explained problems unseen by the classical economists, and solved the riddles of political economy itself.

The tasks of a Marxist critique of sociology are similar. It is necessary first to insert systems of values and norms into a historical totality, to articulate them with the forces and relations of production, with the state and with the class struggle based on these structures, and to demonstrate how the ideological community is determined by this totality. The second duty is to demonstrate how the ideological communities incarnated in different groups, organizations, institutions and societies are structured by the class struggle, constituting different and mutable examples of the unity of opposites, contradictory unities of the values and norms of opposing classes (this would imply, for example, an analysis of organizations different from that of Max Weber, who perceived organizations of domination as expressions of the values and norms of the ruling class only).

What the present study indicates, then, is neither convergence nor synthesis, but a *transcendence of sociology*, similar to Marx's transcendence of classical economics, and the development of historical materialism as *the* science of society. To indicate a task, however, is not to accomplish it. The extent to which these possibilities prove capable of realization will not depend on intra-scientific events alone. The rise and formation of the social sciences were determined by the class struggles of particular historical societies, and so, no doubt, will be their further development or arrested development. Thus the question of a future development of social sciences in the direction of historical materialism remains open – above all to those of us who are committed to working for it.

Bibliography

Abbreviations used:
AJS = American Journal of Sociology
ASR = American Sociological Review
RIS = Revue Internationale de Sociologie
RP = Revue Philosophique

Abrahams, Ph., *The Origins of British Sociology* (Chicago: University of Chicago Press, 1968).
Althusser, L., *Montesquieu, La politique et l'histoire* (Paris: PUF, 1959).
Althusser, L., *For Marx* (London: Allen Lane and Penguin, 1970).
Althusser, L. & Balibar, E., *Reading Capital* (London: New Left Books, 1970).
Althusser, L., *Lenin and Philosophy and Other Essays* (London: New Left Books, 1971).
Althusser, *Politics and History* (London: New Left Books, 1972).
Althusser, L., 'The Conditions of Marx' Scientific Discovery'. *Theoretical Practice* no. 7/8 (1973).
Althusser, L., *Réponse à John Lewis* (Paris: Maspéro, 1973).
Althusser, L., *Philosophie et philosophie spontanée des savants (1967)* (Paris: Maspero, 1974).
Althusser, L., *Eléments d'autocritique* (Paris: Hachette, 1974).
Anderson, P., *Passages from Antiquity to Feudalism* (London: NLB 1973).
Anderson, P., *Lineages of the Absolutist State* (London: NLB 1975).
Annales de l'Institut Internationale de Sociologie vol. VIII (Paris 1902).
Aron, R., *18 Lectures on Industrial Society* (London 1967).
Aston, T. (ed.), *Crisis in Europe 1560–1660* (Garden City: Doubleday, 1967).
Avineri, S., *Hegel's Theory of the Modern State* (Cambridge: University Press, 1972).
Bachelard, G., *La formation de l'esprit scientifique* (Paris: Vrin, 5th ed. 1967).
Bachelard, G., La formation de l'esprit scientifique (Paris: Vrin, 5th ed. 1967).
Balibar, E., 'Self-Criticism', *Theoretical Practice* no. 7/8 (1973).

Barnard, F. M., *Herder's Social and Political Thought* (Oxford: Clarendon Press, 1965).

Barry, B., *Sociologists, Economists, and Democracy* (London: Collier-Macmillan, 1970).

Baumgarten, E. (ed.), *Max Weber, Werk und Person* (Tübingen: Mohr, 1964).

Beadsley, D., *From Castlereagh to Gladstone* (London: Nelson, 1969).

Beaurin-Gressier, L., 'Des forces qui déterminent l'évolution du milieu social', *RIS*, 4 no. 4 (1896).

Beetham, D., *Max Weber and the Theory of Modern Politics* (London: George Allen & Unwin, 1974).

Below, G. v., 'Soziologie als Lehrfach', *Schmollers Jahrbuch* vol. 43 (1919) pp. 59–110.

Below, G. v., '*Zur Geschichte der deutschen Geschichtswissenschaft* I–II', *Historische Blätter* I (1912) pp. 5–30, 173–217.

Ben-David, J. and Zlozcover, A., 'Universities and Academic Systems in Modern Society', *Archives Européennes de Sociologie*, vol. 3 (1962) pp. 45–84.

Ben-David, J., 'The Scientific Role: The Conditions of Its Establishment in Europe', *Minerva*, vol. 4 (1965) pp. 15–54.

Ben-David, J. and Collins, R., 'Social Factors in the Origins of A New Science', *ASR*, 31 (1966) pp. 451–66.

Bendix, R., *Max Weber. An Intellectual Portrait* (London: Methuen, 1966, paperback ed.).

Bendix, R., and Roth, G., *Scholarship and Partisanship* (Berkeley: University of California Press, 1971).

Bernard, L. and J., *Origins of American Sociology* (New York: Russel & Russel, 1965).

Bernal, J., *Science in History* 1–4 (Harmondsworth: Penguin, 1972).

Bernès, M., 'Programme d'un cours de sociologie générale I–II', *RIS*, 3 no. 12, 4 no. 1 (1895, 1896).

Bernstein, E., *Die Voraussetzungen des Sozialismus und die Aufgaben der Sozialdemokratie* (Reinbek bei Hamburg: Rowohlt, 1969).

Bernstein, I., *A History of the American Worker 1933–41. Turbulent Years* (Boston: Houghton Mifflin, 1969).

Bettelheim, Ch., *Calcue économique et formes de propriété* (Paris: Maspéro, 1970).

Bettelheim, Ch., *Les luttes de classes en URSS* vol. I (Paris: Seuil/Maspéro, 1974).

Blau, P., *Exchange and Power in Social Life* (New York: Wiley, 1964).

Blaug, M., *Economic Theory in Retrospect* (London: Heinemann, 1968).

Blaug, M., 'Was There a Marginal Revolution?', *History of Political Economy* vol. 4: 2 (Fall 1972).

Bonald, L.-A.-G. de, *Théorie du Pouvoir, Oeuvres* vols. 3–4 (Bruxelles 1845).

Bourgin, *De Jaurès à Léon Blum, L'Ecole Normale et la politique* (Paris: Gordon and Breach, 1970, 1st ed. 1938).

Bourgin, H., *Le socialisme universitaire* (Paris: Stock, 1942).

Bousquet, G. H., *Pareto* (Lausanne: Payot, 1960).

Bramson, L., *The Political Context of Sociology* (Princeton: Princeton University Press, 1961).

Brogan, D. W., *The Development of Modern France* (2nd ed. London: Hamish Hamilton, 1967).

Brooke, M. Z., *Le Play: Engineer and Social Scientist* (London: Longman, 1970).

Bryson, G., *Man and Society* (Princeton: University Press, 1945).

Bukharin, N., *The Economic Theory of the Leisure Class* (New York: Monthly Review Press, 1972).

Bunge, M., *Scientific Research* I–II (New York: Springer, 1967).

Burke, E., *Reflections on the Revolution in France* (Harmondsworth: Penguin, 1970).

Busoni, G., 'Préface', V. Pareto, *Oeuvres complètes* vol. 11 (Genève: Droz, 1967).

Calvez, J.-Y., *La Pensée de Karl Marx* (Paris: Seuil, 1956).

Cambridge Economic History of Europe vol. III (Cambridge: University Press, 1963).

Canguilhem, G., *Etudes d'histoire et de philosophie des sciences* (Paris: Vrin, 1968).

Cannan, E., *A Review of Economic Theory* (London: Frank Cass, 1964).

Capra, D. La, *Emile Durkheim* (Ithaca and London: Cornell University Press, 1972).

Cavaillès, J., *Sur la logique* (Paris: PUF, 1960).

Chapman, G., *The Third Republic of France. Its First Phase 1871–94* (London: Macmillan, 1962).

Coats, A. W. and S. E., 'The Changing Social Composition of Royal Economic Society 1890–1960 and the Professionalization of British economics', *British Journal of Sociology* vol. XXIV: 2 (June 1973).

Cole, G. D. H. and Postgate, R., *The Common People* (London: Methuen, 1963, paperback ed.).

Colletti, L., *From Rousseau to Lenin* (London: NLB, 1972).

Colletti, L., *Marxism and Hegel* (London: NLB, 1973).

Commager, H. S., *The American Mind* (New Haven: Yale Univ. Press, 1961, paperback ed.).

Commons, J., 'Is Class Conflict in America Growing and Is It Inevitable?', *AJS* XIII pp. 756–66.

Comte, A., *Système de politique positive* I–IV (Paris 1851–54).

Comte, A., *Cours de philosophie positive* I–IV (Paris 1908).

Comte, A., *The Positive Philosophy of Comte* 1–3 (H. Martineau ed., London 1896).

Comte, A., *System of Positive Polity* I–IV (London 1876).

Cooley, C. H., *Sociological Theory and Social Research* (New York: Henry Holt, 1930).

Cornforth, M., *The Philosophy of Marxism* (London: Lawrence & Wishart, 19).

Coser, L., *The Functions of Social Conflict* (New York: Free Press, 1964, paperback ed.).

Coser, L., *Masters of Sociological Thought* (New York: Harcourt, Brace, Jovanovich, 1971).

Cornu, A., *Karl Marx et Friedrich Engels* I–IV (Paris: PUF, 1955–70).

Crawford, E., 'The Sociology of the Social Sciences', *Current Sociology* vol. XIX no. 2 (1971, actually published in 1973).

Crocker, L., *Nature and Culture: Ethical thought in the Enlightenment* (Baltimore: Johns Hopkins Press, 1963).

Dahrendorf, R., 'Out of Utopia: Toward A Re-Orientation of Sociological Analysis', *AJS* 64 (1958) pp. 115–27.

Dahrendorf, R., *Class and Class Conflict in Industrial Society* (Stanford: University Press, 1959).

Dahrendorf, R., *Conflict After Class* (London: Longmans, 1967).

Dahrendorf, R., *Essays in the Theory of Society* (London: Routledge and Kegan Paul, 1968).

Della Volpe, G., *Rousseau et Marx et autres essais de critique materialiste* (Paris: Grasset, 1974).

Della Volpe, G., *Logica come scienza positiva* (Messina: D'Anna, 1956).

Dilthey, W., *Einleitung in die Geisteswissenschaften* (Leipzig 1883).

Dobb, M., *Political Economy and Capitalism* (2nd ed. London: Routledge and Kegan Paul, 1968).

Dommanget, M., *Le curé Meslier* (Paris: Juillard, 1965).

Douglas, J., *The Social Meanings of Suicide* (Princeton: University Press, 1967).

Drescher, S., *Tocqueville and England* (Cambridge Mass.: Harvard University Press, 1964).

Droz, J., *L'Allemagne et la Révolution Française* (Paris: PUF, 1949).

Droz, J., *Le romantisme allemand et l'état* (Paris: Payot, 1966).

Dupeux, G., *La société francaise 1789–1960* (Paris: Armand Colin, 1964).

Durkheim, E., 'A. Schaeffle, Bau und Leben des sozialen Körpers vol. 1', review, *RP* XIX (1885) pp. 84–101.

Durkheim, E., 'Les études de science sociale', *RP* XXII (1886) pp. 61–80.

Durkheim, E., 'La science positive de la morale en Allemagne', *RP* XXIV (Juillet–décembre 1887) pp. 33–58, 113–42, 275–84.

Durkheim, E., *Les Formes Elémentaires de la Vie Réligieuse* (Paris 1912).

Durkheim, E., *L' Education morale* (Paris: Alcan, 1925).

Durkheim, E., *Sociologie et Philosophie* (Paris: PUF, 1951).

Durkheim, E., *Professional Ethics and Civic Morals* (London: Routledge and Kegan Paul, 1957).

Durkheim, E., *Socialism* (New York: Collier Books, 1958, 1st ed. 1925).

Durkheim, E., *The Rules of Sociological Method* (Glencoe: Free Press, 1958).

Durkheim, E., *Montesquieu and Rousseau, Forerunners of Sociology* (Ann Arbor, 1960).

Durkheim, E., *The Division of Labour in Society* (New York: Free Press, 1964, paperback ed.).

Durkheim, E., 'Sociology and its scientific field', in K. Wolf (ed.) *Essays on*

Sociology and Philosophy by Emile Durkheim et al. (New York: Harper Torch-books, 1964).

Durkheim, E. *La science sociale et l'action* (J.-C. Filloux ed., Paris: PUF, 1970).

Durkheim, E., *Suicide* (London: Routledge Paperback, 1970).

Ellwood, C., 'A Psychological study of Revolutions', *AJS* XI (1905–06).

Encyclopaedia of the Social Sciences (New York: Macmillan, 1930).

Engels, F., *The Condition of the Working-Class in England* (London: Panther, 1969).

Engels, F., *Principles of Communism* (London: Pluto Press, n.d.).

Espinas, A., 'Leçon d'ouverture d'un cours d'histoire d'économie sociale', *RIS*, 2 no. 5 (1894).

Faris, R., *Chicago Sociology 1920–1932* (San Francisco: Chandler, 1967).

Feaver, G., *From Status to Contract* (London: Longman, 1969).

Ferguson, A., *An Essay on the History of Civil Society* (Edinburgh: University Press, 1966).

Ferguson, A., *Principles of Moral and Political Science I–II* (Edinburgh, 1792).

Ferguson, W., *Scotland: 1689 to the Present* (Edinburgh: Olivier & Boyd, 1969).

Feuerbach, L., 'Vorläufige Thesen zu Reform der Philosophie', *Sämtliche Werke* vol. II (Stuttgart 1959).

Feuerbach, L., 'Grundsätze der Philosophie der Zukunft', *Sämtliche Werke* vol. II (Stuttgart 1959).

Feuerbach, L., *Das Wesen der Christentums*, Sämtliche Werke vol. VI (Stuttgart 1960).

Fiamingo, G., 'Sociology in Italy', *AJS* I (1895) pp. 335–52.

Finley, M. J., *The Ancient Economy* (Berkeley and Los Angeles: University of California Press, 1973).

Flexner, A., *Universities, American, English, German* (New York: Oxford University Press, 1930).

Foner, Ph., *History of the Labor Movement in the United States* (New York, 1955) vol. II.

Foster, J., 'Capitalism and the Scottish Nation', in G. Brown (ed.), *The Red Paper on Scotland* (Edinburgh: EUSPD, 1975) pp. 141–52.

Frank, A. G., *Sociology of Development and Underdevelopment of sociology* (Lund: Zenit, 1968).

Freund, J., *The Sociology of Max Weber* (London: Allen Lane, 1968).

Friedrichs, R., *A Sociology of Sociology* (New York: The Free Press, 1970).

Fromm, E., *Marx's Concept of Man* (New York: Frederick Ungar, 1961).

Galbraith, J. K., *The New Industrial State* (New York: Houghton-Mifflin, 1967).

Gay, P., *The Enlightenment I: The Rise of Modern Paganism* (London: Widenfeld & Nicholson, 1967).

Gay, P., *The Enlightenment* vol. II (New York: Alfred Knopf, 1969).

Gerratana, V., 'Marx and Darwin', *New Left Review* 82 (November–December, 1973).

Gibbon, E., *The History of the Decline and Fall of the Roman Empire* I–VII (Bury ed. London 1896–1900).

Giddens, A., *Capitalism and Modern Social Theory* (Cambridge: University Press, 1971).

Gillespie, Ch., *The Architecture of Matter* (New York: Harper & Row, 1962).

Godelier, M., *Horizons, trajets marxistes en anthropologie* (Paris: Maspéro, 1973).

Goldberg, H., *The Life of Jean Jaurès* (Madison: The University of Wisconsin Press, 1962).

Goldfrank, W., 'Reappraising Le Play', in Oberschall (ed.) *The Establishment of Empirical Sociology* (New York: Harper & Row, 1972).

Gooch, G. P., *History and Historians of the Nineteenth Century* (Boston: Beacon Press, 1965, 1st ed. 1913).

Gouhier, H., *La vie d'Auguste Comte* (Paris: Vrin, 1965).

Gouldner, A., *The Coming Crisis of Western Sociology* (London: Heineman, 1971).

Gouldner, A., 'For Sociology: "Varieties of Political Experience" Revisited', *AJS* 78 (1973) pp. 1083–93.

Gouldner, A., *For Sociology* (London: Heineman, 1973).

Gramsci, A., *Quaderni del Carcere* I–VI (Torino: Einaudi, 1964).

Gramsci, A., *Prison Notebooks* (London: Lawrence and Wishart, 1971).

Grandjonc, J., *Marx et les communistes à Paris* (Paris: Maspéro, 1974).

Grundriss der Sozialökonomik (2nd ed. Tübingen: Mohr, 1924–30).

Gullberg, A., *Till den svenska sociologins historia* (Stockholm: Unga Filosofers förlag, 1972).

Gumplowicz, L., *Rasse und Staat* (appended to 2nd ed. of *Der Rassenkampf*, Innsbruck 1909, 1st ed. Innsbruck 1875).

Gumplowicz, L., *Sociologie und Politik* (Leipzig, 1892).

Gumplowicz, L., *Der Rassenkampf* (Innsbruck 1909, 2nd ed.).

Gustafsson, B., *Marxism och revisionism. Eduard Bernsteins kritik av marxismen: dess idéhistoriska förutsättninger* (Stockholm: Scandinavian University Books, 1969).

Gardlung, T., *Knut Wicksell* (Stockholm: Bonniers, 1956).

Habermas, 'Zur Logik der Sozialwissenschaften', *Philosophische Rundschau* Sonderheft (1967).

Hanecker, M., *Los conceptos elementales del materialismo histórico* (Santiago de Chile: Siglo XX, 1972).

Harcourt, G. C. & Laing, N. F. (eds.), *Capital and Growth* (Harmondsworth: Penguin, 1971).

Harrod, R. F., *The Life of John Maynard Keynes* (London: Macmillan, 1951).

Haupt, G., Lowry, M. & Weill, L., *Les marxistes et la question nationale* (Paris: Maspéro, 1974).

Hayek, F. A. v. (ed.), *Collectivist Economic Planning* (London: George Routledge & Sons, 1935).

Heaton, H., *Economic History of Europe* (New York: Harper & Brothers, 1948).

Hegel, G. W. F., *Phänomenologie des Geistes*, Sämtliche Werke II (G. Lasson ed. Leipzig 1911).

Hegel, G. W. F., *Grundlinien der Philosophie des Rechts*, Sämtliche Werke IV (G. Lasson ed. Leipzig 1911).

Hegel, G. W. F., *Enzyclopädie der philosophischen Wissenschaften*, Sämtliche Werke Bd. V (G. Lasson ed. Leipzig 1911).

Hegel, G. W. F., *Die Vernunft in der Geschichte. Einleitung in die Philosophie der Weltgeschichte*, Sämtliche Werke Bd. VIII: 1 (G. Lasson ed. Leipzig 1920).

Hegel, G. W. F., *The Logic of Hegel* (Wallace trans. Oxford 1892).

Hegel, G. W. F., *The Philosophy of Mind* (Wallace trans. Oxford: University Press, 1971, 1st ed. 1894).

Hegel, G. W. F., *Philosophy of Right* (Knox ed. Oxford: University Press, 1942).

Hegel, G. W. F., 'Religion ist eine', in H. S. Harris, *Hegel's Development* (Oxford: Clarendon Press, 1972).

Henderson, Ch., 'Business Men and Social Theoritsts', *AJS* I (1895–96) pp. 385–97.

Henderson, L., *Pareto's General Sociology* (Cambridge Mass.: Harvard University Press, 1935).

Hill, C., *The Century of Revolution, 1603–1714*. (Edinburgh: Thomas Nelson, 1961).

Hinkle, R. and Hinkle, G., *The Development of Modern Sociology* (New York: Random House, 1954).

Hirst, P., 'Morphology and pathology: Biological analogies and metaphors in E. Durkheim, The Rules of Sociological Method', *Economy and Society* vol. 2 no. 1 (Febr. 1973).

Hobbes, T., *Leviathan* (Harmondsworth: Penguin, 1972).

Hobsbawm, E., *Labouring Men* (London: Weidenfeld & Nicholson, 1964, paperback ed.).

Hofstadter, R., *Social Darwinism in American Thought* (Boston: Beacon Press, 1955).

Hofstadter, R., *The Age of Reform* (New York: Vintage Books, 1960).

Hollander, J., 'The Dawn of Economic Science', in *Adam Smith 1776–1926* (Chicago: University Press, 1928).

Homans, G. and Curtis, C. P., *An Introduction to Pareto* (New York: Knopf, 1934).

Homans, G., *Social Behaviour. Its Elementary Forms* (London: Routledge and Kegan Paul, 1961).

Homans, G., *Sentiments and Activities* (New York: Free Press, 1962).

Honigsheim, P., 'Reminiscences of the Durkheim School', in K. Wolff (ed.) *Essays on Sociology and Philosophy by Emile Durkheim et al.* (New York: Harper Torchbooks, 1964).

Hook, S., *From Hegel to Marx* (Ann Arbor: The University of Michigan Press, 1966).

Horkheimer, M. and Adorno, T., *Dialektik der Aufklärung* (Amsterdam, 1947).

Hubert, R., *Les sciences sociales dans l'Encyclopédie* (Paris: Félix Alcan, 1923).

Hume, D., *Essays. Moral, Political and Literary* I–II n.d. (London, 1875).

Hughes, S., *Consciousness and Society* (New York: Vintage Books n.d.).

Hunt, E. & Schwartz, J. (eds.), *A Critique of Economic Theory* (London, 1974).

Hutchison, T. W., *A Review of Economic Doctrines 1870–1929* (2nd ed. Oxford: Clarendon Press, 1962).

Inkeles, A., 'Personality and Social Structure', in R. Merton, L. Broom and L. Cottrell (eds.) *Sociology Today* (New York: Harper Torchbooks, 1965).

International Encyclopedia of the Social Sciences (New York: Macmillan & Free Press, 1968).

Jaspers, K., *Max Weber. Politiker–Forscher–Philosoph* (München: Piper, 1958).

Jessop, B., *Social Order, Reform and Revolution* (London: Macmillan, 1972).

Jevons, S., *Principles of Political Economy* (London 1871).

Jevons, S., *The State in Relation to Labour* (London, 1882).

Johansson, I., *Kritik av den popperianska metodologin* (Göteborg: Dept. of Theoretical Philosophy, mimeo, 1973).

Johnson, D., *Guizot* (London: Routledge and Kegan Paul, 1963).

Jones, R. A., 'Comte and Spencer: A Priority Dispute in Social Science', *J. of the Hist. of the Behavioral Sciences*, vol. 6 (1970) pp. 241–54.

Jones, G. S., 'The Marxism of the Early Lukács: An Evaluation', *New Left Review* 70 (November–December, 1971).

Kamenka, E., *The Ethical Foundations of Marxism* (London: Routledge and Kegan Paul, 1962).

Kaufmann, W., *Hegel* (London: Weidenfeld & Nicholson, 1966).

Kautsky, K., *Die Agrarfrage* (3rd ed., Stuttgart, 1902).

Kautsky, K., *Foundations of Christianity* (London: Orbach and Chambers, 1972).

Kettler, D., *The Social and Political Thought of Adam Ferguson* (n.p.: Ohio State University Press, 1965).

Keynes, J. M., *General Theory of Employment, Interest and Money* (London: Macmillan, 1936).

Klein, L., *The Keynesian Revolution* (2nd ed. London: Macmillan, 1968).

Knight, F., *Risk, Uncertainty and Profit* (Boston and New York, 1921).

Knight, F., *The Ethics of Competition and Other Essays* (London: George Allen & Unwin, 1935).

Krause, W., *Werner Sombarts Weg vom Kathedersozialismus zum Fascismus* (Berlin: Rütten & Loening, 1962).

Kuhn, T., *The Structure of Scientific Revolution* (Chicago: University Press, 1962).

Kuhn, T., 'Logic of Discovery or Psychology of Research?', in I. Lakatos and A. Musgrave (eds.) *Criticism and the Growth of Knowledge* (Cambridge: University Press, 1970).

Kuznets, S., *Modern Economic Growth* (New Haven: Yale University Press, 1966).

Kägi, P., *Genesis des historischen Materialismus* (Wien: Europa, 1963).

Lakatos, I. and Musgrave, A. (eds.) *Criticism and the Growth of Knowledge* (Cambridge: University Press, 1970).

Lane, D., *The Roots of Russian Communism* (Assen: van Gorcum, 1969).

Lange, O., 'Marxian Economics and Modern Economic Theory', in D. Horowitz (ed.), *Marx and Modern Economics* (New York: Monthly Review Press, 1968).

Lazarsfeld, P., 'Notes on the History of Quantification in Sociology', *ISIS* 52: 2 (June, 1961).

Lecourt, D., *L'épistemologie historique de Gaston Bachelard* (Paris: Vrin, 1969).

Lecourt, D., *Pour une critique de l'épistemologie* (Paris: Maspéro, 1972).

Lécuyer, B. and Oberschall, A., 'Sociology: Early History of Social Research', *International Encyclopedia of the Social Sciences* (New York: Macmillan and Free Press, 1968).

Lefranc, G., *Le mouvement socialiste sous la Troisième République (1875–1940)* (Paris: Payot, 1963).

Lefranc, G., *Le mouvement syndical sous la Troisième République* (Paris: Payot, 1967).

Lehmann, W., *Adam Ferguson and the Beginnings of Modern Sociology* (New York: Columbia University Press, 1930).

Lehmann, W., *John Millar of Glasgow* (Cambridge: University Press, 1960).

Lenin, V. I., *Collected Works*, 45 vols. (Moscow: Progress Publishers, 1960–).

Lenski, G., *Power and Privilege* (New York: McGraw-Hill, 1966).

Lentini, O., 'Storiografia della sociologia italiana (1860–1925)', *La Critica Sociologica* no. 20 (Inverno 1971–72).

Lichtenberger, A. *Le socialisme et la révolution française* (Paris 1899). *K*

Lichenberger, J., *Development of Social Theory* (New York: D. Appleton-Century, 1936) ch. XV.

Liedman, S. E., 'Marx, Engels och dialektikens lagar', *Häften för Kritiska Studier* no. 3, 1975.

Lindenlaub, D., *Richtungskämpfe im Verein für Sozialpolitik* (Wiesbaden: Franz Steiner, 1967).

Lipset, S. M. (ed.), *Politics and Social Science* (New York: Oxford University Press, 1969).

Lipset, S. M., *Revolution and Counterrevolution* (London: Heineman, 1969).

Locke, J., *Two Treatises of Government* (Cambridge: University Press, 1960).

Lockwood, D., 'Social Integration and System Integration', in G. Zolschnan and W. Hirsch (eds.) *Explorations in Social Chamge* (London 1964).

Löwy, M., *La théorie de la révolution chez le jeune Marx* (Paris: Maspéro, 1970).

Lukács, G., *Der Junge Hegel* (Neuwied and Berlin: Luchterhand, 1967).

Lukács, G., *Lenin* (London: NLB, 1970).

Lukács, G., *History and Class Consciousness* (London: Merlin Press, 1971).

Lukes, S., *Emile Durkheim. His Life and Work* (London: Allen Lane, 1973).

Mably, *Entretiens de Phoicon sur le rapport de la morale avec la politique* (Paris, 1792).

Macchiavelli, N., *The Prince, selections from The Discourses and other writings* (London: Fontana, 1972).

McClellan, D., *The Young Hegelians and Karl Marx* (London: Macmillan, 1969).

McClellan, D., *Marx Before Marxism* (London: Macmillan, 1970).

McClellan, D., *Karl Marx, His Life and Thought* (London: Macmillan, 1973).

Machlup, F., *Essays on Economic Semantics* (Englewood Cliffs: Prentice-Hall, 1963).

McPherson, C. B., *The Political Theory of Possessive Individualism* (Oxford: University Press, 1964, paperback ed.).

Madge, J., *The Origins of Scientific Sociology* (New York: Free Press, 1962).

Maine, H. S., *Ancient Law* (2nd ed. London 1863).

Maistre, J. de, *The Works of Joseph de Maistre* (London: George Allen & Unwin, 1965).

Mamatey, V., 'The Development of Czechoslovak Democracy, 1920–1938', in V. Mamatey and R. Luza (eds.), *A History of the Czechoslovak Republic 1918–1948* (Princeton: University Press, 1973).

Mandel, E., *Marxist Economic Theory* I–II (London: Merlin Press, 1968).

Mannheim, K., 'Der Historismus', *Archiv für Sozialwissenschaft und Sozialpolitik*, vol. 54 (1924) pp. 1–66.

Mannheim, K., *Ideology and Utopia* (London: Routledge Paperback, 1960).

Manuel, F., *The New World of Henri Saint-Simon* (Cambridge Mass.: Harvard University Press, 1956).

Manuel, F., *The Prophets of Paris* (Cambridge Mass.: Harvard University Press, 1962).

Mao Tse tung, *Selected Works*, 4 vols. (Peking: Foreign Language Press, 1965–67).

Marcuse, H., *Reason and Revolution* (Boston: Beacon Press, 1960).

Marcuse, H., *One-dimensional Man* (London: RKP, 1967).

Marshall, A., *Memorials of Alfred Marshall* (A. C. Pigou ed., London: Macmillan, 1925).

Marx, K., *Grundrisse* (Berlin: Dietz, 1953).

Marx, K. and Engels, F., *Werke* 41 vols. (Berlin: Dietz, 1956–).

Marx, K. and Engels, F., *Selected Correspondence* (Moscow: Progress Publishers, n.d.).

Marx, K. and Engels, F., *Selected Works* 1 vol. (Moscow: Progress Publishers, 1970).

Marx, K. and Engels, F., *The Holy Family* (Moscow: FLPH, 1956).

Marx, K., *Capital* I–III (Moscow: Progress Publishers, 1962).

Marx, K. and Engels, F., *The German Ideology* (Moscow: Progress Publishers, 1964).

Marx, K., *Writings of the Young Marx on Philosophy and Society* (L. D. Easton and K. H. Guddat eds. New York: Anchor Books, 1967).

Marx, K., *Theories of Surplus Value* I–III (London: Lawrence and Wishart, 1969–72).

Marx, K., *Critique of Hegel's 'Philosophy of Right'* (O'Malley trans. Cambridge: University Press, 1970).

Marx, K., *Economic and Philosophic Manuscripts of 1844* (London: Lawrence & Wishart, 1970).

Marx, K., *The Poverty of Philosophy* (New York: International Publishers, 1971).

Marx, K., *A Contribution to the Critique of Political Economy* (London: Lawrence & Wishart, 1971).

Marx, K., 'Marginal Notes on Adolph Wagner's Lehrbuch der politischen Okonomie', in *Theoretical Practice* No. 5 (1972).

Marx, K., *Grundrisse* (Harmondsworth: Penguin, 1973).

Marx, K., *The Revolution of 1848* (Harmondsworth: Penguin, 1973).

Marx, K., 'The Eighteenth Brumaire of Louis Bonaparte', in *Surveys from Exile* (Harmondsworth: Penguin, 1973).

Marx, K., *The First International and After* (Harmondsworth: Penguin, 1974).

Masaryk, T., *Suicide and the Meaning of Civilization* (Chicago: University Press, 1970).

Mayo, E., *The Human Problems of an Industrial Civilization* (New York: Macmillan, 1933).

Maus, H., 'Bericht über die Soziologie in Deutschland 1933 bis 1945', *Kölner Zeitschrift für Soziologie* vol. 11 (1959).

Mayer, G., *Friedrich Engels* (London: Chapman & Hall, 1936).

Meek, R., 'The Scottish Contribution to Marxist Sociology', in *Economics and Ideology and Other Essays* (London: Chapman & Hall, 1967), pp. 34–50.

Mehring, F., *Karl Marx* (London: Allen & Unwin, 1936).

Meisel, J., *The Myth of the Ruling Class* (Ann Arbor: The University of Michigan Press, 1958).

Meisel, J., (ed.), *Pareto and Mosca* (Englewood Cliffs: Prentice-Hall, 1965).

Menger, C., *Untersuchungen über die Methode der Sozialwissenschaften und der Politischen Oekonomie insbesondere* (Leipzig, 1883).

Menger, C., *Grundsätze der Volkswirtschaftslehre* (2nd ed. Wien and Leipzig: Hölder-Pichler-Tempsky, 1923).

Michels, R., *Political Parties* (Glencoe: The Free Press, 1958).

Miliband, R., *The State in Capitalist Society* (London: Weidenfeld and Nicholson, 1969).

Mill, J. S., *The Earlier Letters of J. S. Mill* (Toronto and London: Toronto University Press and Routledge and Kegan Paul, 1963).

Mill, J. S., *Principles of Political Economy* (Harmondsworth: Penguin, 1970).

Mills, C. W., *The Sociological Imagination* (London: Oxford University Press, 1967, paperback ed.).

Mises, L. v., *Human Action* (New Haven: Yale University Press, 1949).

Mitzman, A., *The Iron Cage* (New York: Knopf, 1970).

Mommsen, W., *Max Weber und die deutsche Politik* (Tübingen: J. C. B. Mohr, 1959).

Mommsen, W., 'Universalgeschichte und politisches Denken bei Max Weber',

Historische Zeitschrift vol. 201 (1965) pp. 557–612.

Montesquieu, *L'esprit des lois* (Paris: Gallimard Idées, 1970).

Montesquieu, *The Spirit of Laws* (Chicago and London: Encyclopaedia Britannica, 1952).

Moore, B., *Social Origins of Dictatorship and Democracy* (Boston: Beacon Press, 1967).

Mosca, G., *The Ruling Class* (New York and London: McGraw, 1939).

Mosca, G., *Die herrschende Klasse* (Bern: Francke, 1950).

Muggeridge, K. and Adam, R., *Beatrice Webb. A Life* (London: Secker & Warburg, 1967).

Nicolaievsky, B. and Maenchen-Helfen, O., *Karl Marx. Man and Fighter* (London: Methuen, 1936).

Niedermann, J., *Kultur, Werden und Wandlungen des Begriffes und seiner Ersatzbegriffe*, Bibliotheca dell' 'Archivum Romanum' vol. 28 (Florence, 1941).

Nisbet, R., *The Sociological Tradition* (London: Heineman, 1967).

Oberschall, A. *Empirical Social Research in Germany, 1848–1914* (The Hague: Mouton, 1965).

Oberschall, A. (ed.), *The Establishment of Empirical Sociology* (New York: Harper & Row, 1972).

Odaka, K., 'Sociology in Japan: Accommodation of Western Orientations', in H. Becker and A. Boskoff (eds.) *Modern Sociological Theory* (New York: Holt, Rinehart and Winston, 1957) pp. 711–30.

Ogburn, W., *On Culture and Social Change* (O. D. Duncan ed. Chicago: University Press, 1964).

Ollman, B., *Alienation, Marx's Conception of Man in Capitalist Society* (Cambridge: University Press, 1971).

Oppenheimer, F., *Der Ausweg* (Berlin, 1919).

Oppenheimer, F., *System der Soziologie* (Jena: Fischer, 1922).

Oxford Universal Dictionary Illustrated (Oxford: Clarendon Press, 1964).

Page, C., *Class and American Sociology: From Ward to Ross* (New York: The Dial Press, 1940).

Pareto, V., *The Mind and Society* (New York: Harcourt, Brace, 1935).

Pareto, V., *Cours d'économie politique*. Oeuvres complètes vol. 1 (Genève: Droz, 1964).

Pareto, V., *Sociological Writings* (S. E. Finer ed. London: Pall Mall, 1966).

Pareto, V., *The Rise and Fall of the Elites* (Totowa, N.J.: Bedminster Press, 1968).

Pareto, V., *La transformation de la démocratie*, Oeuvres complètes vol. 13 (Genève: Droz, 1970).

Pareto, V., *Les systèmes socialistes* I–II (Paris, 1926).

Pareto, V., *La liberté économique et des événements d'Italie*, Oeuvres complètes vol. 14 (Genève: Droz, 1971).

Pareto, V., *Manual of Political Economy* (London: Heineman, 1972).

Park, R. and Burgess, E. (eds.), *Introduction to the Science of Sociology* (Chicago: University Press, 1924, 2nd ed.).

Parsons, T., *Essays in Sociological Theory* (New York: Free Press, 1964, paperback ed.).

Parsons, T., 'Durkheim's Contribution to the Theory of Integration of Social Systems', in K. Wolff (ed.) *Essays on Sociology and Philosophy by Durkheim et al.* (New York: Harper Torchbooks, 1964).

Parsons, T., *Societies: Evolutionary and Comparative Perspectives* (Englewood Cliffs: Prentice-Hall, 1966).

Parsons, T., *The Structure of Social Action* (New York: Free Press, 1968, paperback ed.).

Parsons, T., *Politics and Social Structure* (New York: Free Press, 1969).

Parsons, T., 'On Building Social Systems Theory', *Daedalus*, Fall 1970.

Parsons, T., *The System of Modern Societies* (Englewood Cliffs: Prentice-Hall, 1971).

Pécheux, M. and Balibar, E., 'Définitions', in M. Fichant and M. Pécheux, *Sur l'histoire des sciences* (Paris: Maspéro, 1969).

Peel, J. D. Y., *Herbert Spencer. The Evolution of a Sociologist.* (New York: Basic Books, 1971).

Petridis, A., 'Alfred Marshall's Attitudes to the Economic Analysis of Trade Unions', *History of Political Economy* vol. V: 1 (Spring 1973).

Plekhanov, G., *The Development of the Monist View of History*, Selected Philosophical Works vol. I (London: Lawrence & Wishart, 1961).

Political Economy Club. Centenary Volume (London: Macmillan, 1921).

Polanyi, K., Arensberg, C. and Pearson, H. (eds.), *Trade and Market in the Early Empires* (New York: Free Press, 1957).

Polanyi, K., *Primitive and Modern Economies* (M. Dalton ed. Garden City: Doubleday, 1968).

Popper, K., *The Logic of Scientific Discovery* (London: Hutchinson, 1959, 1st ed., in German, 1934).

Popper, K., *The Poverty of Historicism* (London: Routledge Paperback, 1961, 1st ed. 1957).

Popper, K., *The Open Society and Its Enemies* I–II (5th ed. London: Routledge and Kegan Paul, 1966).

Popper, K., *Conjectures and Refutations* (4th ed. London: Routledge & Kegan Paul, 1972).

Popper, K., *Objective Knowledge* (Oxford: Clarendon Press, 1972).

Pospelor, P. N. et al. (ed.), *Geschichte der Kommunistischen partei der Sowjetunion* (Moscow: Progress, 1968– 6 vols.).

Poulantzas, N., *Political Power and Social Classes* (London: New Left Books, 1973).

Poulantzas, N., *Classes in Contemporary Capitalism* (London: NLB, 1975).

Quesnay, F., *Tableau économique des physiocrates* (M. Lutfalla ed. Paris: Calmann-Lévy, 1969).

Rae, J., *Life of Adam Smith* (2nd New York: Augustus Kelly, 1965).

Ratzenhofer, G., *Wesen und Zweck der Politik* (Leipzig, 1893).

Ratzenhofer, G., *Die sociologische Erkenntnis* (Leipzig, 1898).

Recktenwald, H. C. (ed.), *Lebensbilder grosser Nationalökonomen* (Köln-Berlin: Kiepenheuer & Witsch, 1965).

Revolution oder Reform? Herbert Marcuse und Karl Popper, Eine Konfrontation (München: Kösel, 1971).

Rex, J., *Key Problems in Sociological Theory* (London: Routledge and Kegan Paul, 1970, paperback ed.).

Rex, J., 'Typology and objectivity: a comment on Weber's four sociological methods', in A. Sahay (ed.), *Max Weber and Modern Sociology* (London: Routledge and Kegan Paul, 1971).

Rey, P.-P., *Les alliances de classes* (Paris: Maspéro, 1973).

Reynolds, L. and Reynolds, J., *The Sociology of Sociology* (New York: David McKay, 1970).

Riazanov, D., *Karl Marx and Frederick Engels* (London: Martin Lawrence, 1927).

Ricardo, D., *Principles of Political Economy and Taxation* (Harmondsworth: Penguin, 1971).

Rickert, H., *Die Grenzen der naturwissenschaftlichen Begriffsbildung* (Tübingen and Leipzig, 1902).

Riedel, M., *Studien zu Hegel's Rechtsphilosophie* (Frankfurt: Suhrkamp, 1969).

Ringer, F., *The Decline of the German Mandarins* (Cambridge Mass.: Harvard University Press, 1969).

Robbins, L., *Essay on the Nature and Significance of Economic Science* (2nd ed. London: Macmillan, 1952).

Robbins, L., *The Theory of Economic Policy in English Classical Political Economy* (London: Macmillan, 1952).

Rogin, L., *The Meaning and Validity of Economic Theory* (New York: Harper & Brothers, 1956).

Röhrich, W., *Robert Michels, vom sozialistischen-syndikalistischen zum fascistischen Credo* (Berlin: Duncker & Humblot, 1972).

Roll, E., *A History of Economic Thought* (London: Faber, 1961, 2nd ed.).

Ross, E., *Russia in Upheaval* (London: Fisher-Unwin, 1919).

Roth, G., 'Introduction', in M. Weber, *Economy and Society* (New York: Bedminster Press, 1968).

Roucek, J., 'Czechoslovak Sociology', in G. Gurvitch and W. Moore (eds.), *Twentieth Century Sociology* (New York: The Philosophical Library, 1945) pp. 717–31.

Rousseau, J.-J., *Du contrat social* (Paris: 10/18, 1963).

Rousseau, J.-J., *The Social Contract* (including other discourses, London: J. M. Dent, 1955).

Rowthorn, B., 'Neo-Classicism, Neo-Ricardianism and Marxism', *NLR* no. 86 (July–August, 1974).

Rumney, J., *Herbert Spencer's Sociology* (London: Williams and Norgate, 1934).

Runciman, W. G., *A Critique of Max Weber's Philosophy of Social Science* (Cambridge: University Press, 1972).

Sabine, G., *A History of Political Theory* (London: George Harrap, 1960).

Sahay, A., 'The relevance of Max Weber's methodology in sociological explanation', in A. Sahay (ed.), *Max Weber and Modern Sociology* (London: Routledge and Kegan Paul, 1971).

Saint-Simon, H. de, *Oeuvres* 6 vols. (Paris: Anthropos, 1966).

Saint-Simon, Henri de, *Social Organization, the Science of Man and Other Writings* (F. Markham ed. New York, 1964).

Samuelson, P., *Economics* (6th ed. New York: McGraw-Hill, 1961).

Sartre, J. P., *Critique de la raison dialectique* (Paris: Gallimard, 1960).

Sartre, J. P., *The Question of Method* (London, 1963).

Savigny, F. C. v., 'Vom Beruf unserer Zeit für Gesetzgebung', in J. Stern (ed.), *Thibaut und Savigny* (Berlin, 1914).

Savigny, F. C. v., *Of the Vocation of Our Age for Legislation* (English trans. n.d.).

Schäfer, D., 'A Contemporary Academic View of Georg Simmel', *AJS* 63: 6 (May, 1958) pp. 640–41.

Schäffle, A., *Bau und Leben des sozialen Körpers* 1–4 (Tübingen, 1875–79).

Schäffle, A., *Die Quintessenz des Sozialismus* (Gotha, 1885, 1st ed. 1874).

Schelting, A. v., *Max Webers Wissenschaftslehre* (Tübingen: Mohr, 1934).

Schwartz, S., *The Russian Revolution of 1905* (Chicago: University of Chicago Press, 1967).

Schmidt, A., *Geschichte und Struktur* (München: Hauser, 1971).

Schmidt, G., *Deutscher Historismus und der Ubergang zur parlamentarischen Demokratie* (Lübeck und Hamburg, 1964).

Schmoller, G., *Uber einige Grundfragen des Rechts und der Volkswirtschaft* (Jena, 1875).

Schmoller, G., *Zur Literaturgeschichte der Staats- und Sozialwissenschaften* (Leipzig, 1888).

Schumpeter, J., *Ten Great Economists* (New York: Oxford University Press, 1951).

Schumpeter, J., *History of Economic Analysis* (New York: Oxford University Press, 1954).

Schumpeter, J., *Economic Doctrine and Method* (London: Allen & Unwin, 1954).

Schumpeter, J., *Capitalism, Socialism and Democracy* (4th ed. London: Allen & Unwin, 1961).

Schwendinger, H. and H., *The Sociologists of the Chair* (New York: Basic Books, 1974).

Second International Conference of Economic History, vol. I: Trade and Politics in the Ancient World (Paris: Mouton, 1965).

Seen, P., 'What is "Behavioral Science"?', *J. of Hist. of the Behavioral Sciences* vol. 2 (1966) pp. 107–22.

Semmel, B., *Imperialism and Social Reform* (London: George Allen & Unwin, 1960).

Seton-Watson, C., *Italy from Fascism to Liberalism: 1870–1925* (London: Methuen, 1967).

Shackleton, R., *Montesquieu* (Oxford: University Press, 1961).

Shaw, B. (ed.), *Fabian Essays in Socialism* (2nd ed. London 1908).

Sièyes, *What Is the Third Estate?* (London: Pall Mall Press, 1963).

Simmel, G., *Die Probleme der Geschichtsphilosophie* (Leipzig, 1892).

Simmel, G., *Die Philosophie des Geldes* (Leipzig, 1900).

Simmel, G., *Soziologie* (3rd ed. München and Leipzig: Duncker und Humblot, 1923).

Small, A., 'The Civic Federation of Chicago', *AJS* I (1895–95) pp. 79–103.

Small, A., 'Private Business Is a Public Trust', *AJS* I (1895–96) pp. 276–89.

Small, A., 'The State and Semi-Public Corporations', *AJS* I pp. 398–410.

Small, A., 'Scholarship and Social Agitation', *AJS* I pp. 564–82.

Small, A., 'The Scope of Sociology I–IX', *AJS* V–X (1899–1900–1904–05).

Small, A., '50 Years of Sociology in the United States, 1865–1915', *AJS Index to Volumes I–LII* (1947) pp. 177–269.

Small, A., *The Cameralists* (Chicago, 1909).

Small, A., *The Meaning of Social Science* (Chicago, 1910).

Small, A., *Origins of Sociology* (Chicago 1911).

Small, A., *The Origins of Sociology* (Chicago: University Press, 1924).

Smith, A., *The Wealth of Nations* I–II (E. Cannan ed. London: Methuen, University Paperbacks, 1970).

Smith, A., *The Wealth of Nations* (Harmondsworth: Penguin, 1970).

Smout, T. S., *A History of the Scottish People 1560–1830* (London: Collins, 1969).

Soboul, A., *Histoire de la révolution française* I–II (Paris: Gallimard, 1962).

Sombart, W., *Der moderne Kapitalismus* (Leipzig, 1902).

Sombart, W., 'Karl Marx und die soziale Wissenschaft', *Archiv für Sozialwissenschaft und Sozialpolitik*, New Series vol. 8 (1908).

Sombart, W., *Die Juden und das Wirtschaftsleben* (Leipzig 1911).

Sombart, W., *Der Bourgeois* (München and Leipzig, 1913).

Sombart, W., *Händler und Helden* (München 1915).

Sombart, W., *Der moderne Kapitalismus* (2nd revised and enlarged edition, München and Leipzig, 1916).

Spencer, H., *Social Statics* (London, 1850).

Spencer, H., *The Study of Sociology* (10th ed. London, 1882).

Spencer, H., *Principles of Sociology* (New York, 1897).

Herbert Spencer (S. Andreski ed. London: Nelson, 1971).

Sraffa, P., *Production of Commodities by Means of Commodities* (Cambridge: University Press, 1960).

Stammer, O. (ed.), *Max Weber und die Soziologie heute* (Tübingen: Mohr, 1965).

Stein, L., *The Social Movement in France* (Totowa N.J.: Bedminster Press, 1964).

Stigler, G., *Essays in the History of Economics* (Chicago: University Press, 1965).

Strauch, D., *Recht, Gesetz und Staat bei Friedrich Carl von Savigny* (Bonn: Bouvier, 1963).

Strauss, L., *Natural Right and History* (Chicago: University Press, 1953).

Struik, D., *Matematikens historia* (Stockholm: Prisma, 1966).

Sweezy, P., *The Theory of Capitalist Development* (New York: Monthly Review Press, 1964).

Tenbruck, F., 'Die Genesis der Methodologie Max Webers', *Kölner Zeitschrift f. Soziologie u. Sozialpsychologie* vol. II (New Series) (1959) pp. 573–630.

Terray, *Le marxisme devant les sociétés primitives* (Paris: Maspéro, 1969).

Terry, C., 'Emile Durkheim and the French University: the Institutionalization of Sociology', in A. Oberschall (ed.), *The Establishment of Empirical Sociology* (New York: Harper & Row, 1972).

Therborn, G., 'Frankfurt Marxism', *New Left Review* no. 63 (September–October, 1970).

Therborn, G., 'Habermas: A New Eclectic', *New Left Review* no. 67 (May–June 1971).

Therborn, G., *Klasser och ekonomiska system* (Staffanstorp: Cavefors, 1971).

Therborn, G., *Critica e rivoluzione* (Bari: Laterza, 1972).

Therborn, G., *Om klasserna i Sverige 1930–70* (2nd ed. Lund: Zenit, 1973).

Therborn, G., 'Social Practice, Social Action, Social Magic', *Acta Sociologica* vol. 16 no. 3 (1973).

Therborn, G., *Vad är bra värderingar värda?* (Staffanstorp: Cavefors, 1973).

Thier, E., *Das Menschenbild des jungen Marx* (Göttingen, 1957).

Thomas, W. I. and Park, R., 'Life History', *AJS* vol. 79 (1973) pp. 246–60.

Tilly, Ch. and Shorter, E., *Strikes in France 1830–1968* (Cambridge: University Press, 1974).

Tinbergen, J., 'Do Communist and Free Economies Show A Convergent Pattern?', *Soviet Studies* vol. XII (April, 1961).

Tocqueville, A. de, *De la démocratie en Amérique*, Oeuvres complètes vol. I: 1–2 (Paris: Gallimard, 1951).

Tocqueville, A. de, *Recollections* (London: Macdonald, 1970).

Tocqueville, A. de, *The Ancien Regime and The French Revolution* (London: Fontana, 1971).

Tocqueville, A. de, *Democracy in America* I–II (New York, 1971).

Tolman, F., 'The Study of Sociology in Institutions of Learning in the United States I–IV', *AJS* VII (1901–02) pp. 797–838, VIII pp. 85–121, 251–72, 531–58.

Tönnies, F., *Der englische Staat und der deutsche Staat* (Berlin, 1917).

Tönnies, F., 'Gegenwarts- und Zukunftsstaat', *Die neue Zeit* 20. 12. 1918.

Tönnies, F., 'Soziologie und Hochschulreform', *Weltwirtschaftliches Archiv* 16 (1920–21), pp. 212–45.

Tönnies, F., *Soziologische Studien und Kritiken* I–III (Jena: Fischer, 1925).

Tönnies, F., *Community and Association* (London: Routledge and Kegan Paul, 1955).

Tönnies, F., *On Sociology* (Chicago and London 1971).

Toulmin, S., *Foresight and Understanding* (New York: Harper Torchbooks, 1963).

Toulmin, S. and Goodfield, J., *The Discovery of Time* (London: Hutchinson, 1965).

Tozzi, G., *Economisti greci e romani* (Milano: Feltrinelli, 1961).

Troeltsch, E., *Der Historismus und seine Probleme* (Tübingen: Mohr, 1922).

Tullberg, R. M., 'Marshall's "Tendency to Socialism",' *History of Political Economy* Vol. VII: 1 (Spring, 1975), pp. 75–111.

Veblen, T., *The Theory of the Leisure Class* (New York: Mentor Books, 1953).

Vereker, Ch., *Eighteenth Century Optimism* (Liverpool: Univ. Press, 1967).

Verhandlungen des ersten deutschen Soziologentages (Tübingen, 1911).

Vincent, G., 'Varieties of Sociology' *AJS* XII (1906) pp. 1–10.

Vygodsky, V. S., *Die Geschichte einer grossen Entdeckung* (Berlin: Verlag Die Wirtschaft, 1967).

Völkerling, F., *Der deutsche Kathedersozialismus* (Berlin: Verlag der Wissenschaften, 1959).

Wallerstein, I., *The Modern World System* (New York: Academic Press, 1974).

Walras, L., *Etudes d'économie appliquée* (Paris-Lausanne, 1898).

Walras, L., *Eléments d'économie politique pure* (Lausanne-Paris, 1900).

Walras, L., *The Correspondence of Léon Walras and Related Papers* (W. Jaffé ed. Amsterdam: North Holland Publishing Co., 1965).

Walton, P. and Gamble, A., *From Alienation to Surplus Value* (London: Sheed & Ward, 1972).

Ward, L., *Dynamic Sociology* I–II (2nd ed. New York, 1898).

Ward, L., 'Collective Telesis', *AJS* II (1896–97) pp. 801–22.

Ward, L., 'Contemporary Sociology I–III', *AJS* VII (1901–02) pp. 476–500, 629–58, 749–62.

Warner, L. and Lunt, P., *The Social Life of A Modern Community* (New Haven: Yale University Press, 1941).

Webb, B., *My Apprenticeship* (London: Longman Green, 1926).

Webb, B., *Our Partnership* (London: Longman Green, 1948).

Webb, S. and B., *Industrial Democracy* (London, 1897).

Webb, S. and B., *Methods of Social Study* (London: Longmans, Green, 1932).

Weber, Marianne, *Max Weber. Ein Lebensbild* (Tübingen: Mohr, 1926).

Weber, M., *Gesammelte Aufsätze zur Religionssoziologie* I–III (Tübingen: Mohr, 1920).

Weber, M., *Politische Schriften* (München: Drei Masken, 1921).

Weber, M., *Gesammelte Aufsätze zur Social- und Wirtschaftsgeschichte* (Tübingen: Mohr, 1924).

Weber, M., *Gesammelte Aufsätze zur Soziologie und Sozialpolitik* (Tübingen: Mohr, 1924).

Weber, M., *Gesammelte Aufsätze zur Wissenschaftslehre* (2nd ed. Tübingen: Mohr, 1951).

Weber, M., *Gesammelte politische Schriften* (3rd ed. Tübingen: Mohr, 1971).

Weber, M., *Wirtschaft und Gesselschaft* 2 vols. (4th ed. Studienausgabe, Berlin: Kiepenheuer and Witsch, 1964).

Weber, M., *On the Methodology of the Social Sciences* (Glencoe: Free Press, 1949).

Weber, M., *The Theory of Social and Economic Organization* (New York: Free Press, 1964, paperback ed.).

Weber, M., *Economy and Society* 3 vols. (New York: Bedminster Press, 1968).

Weber, M., *From Max Weber* (H. Gerth and C. W. Mills eds. London: Routledge paperback, 1970).

Weis, E., *Geschichtsauffassung und Staatsauffassung in der französischen Enzyklopädie* (München: Franz Steiner, 1956).

Wells, G. A., *Herder and After* (The Hague: Mouton, 1959).

Wicksell, K., *Socialiststaten och nutidssamhället* (Stockholm, 1905).

Wicksteed, Ph., *Common Sense of Political Economy* I–II (London: Routledge, 1933).

Wiese, L. v., *Staatssozialismus* (Berlin, 1916).

Wiese, L. v., 'Die Soziologie als Einzelwissenschaft', *Schmollers Jahrbuch* 44 (1920) pp. 347–67.

Wiese, L. v., 'Der internationale Entwicklungsstand der Allgemeinen Soziologie' in E. Jurkat (ed.), *Reine und angewandte Soziologie. Eine Festgabe für Ferdinand Tönnies zu seinum achtzigsten Geburtstage am 26. Juli 1935* (Leipzig: Hans Buske, 1936).

Wieser, F. v., *Gesammelte Abhandlungen* (Tübingen: Mohr, 1929).

Wilson, T., 'Normative and Interpretative Paradigms in Sociology', in J. Douglas (ed.), *Understanding Everyday Life* (London: Routledge and Kegan Paul, 1971).

Winckelmann, J., 'Max Webers Verständnis von Mensch und Gesellschaft', in K. Engisch, B. Pfister and J. Winckelmann (eds.), *Max Weber* (Berlin: Duncker and Humbolt, 1964).

Windelband, W., *Präludien* II (Tübingen, 1919).

Wolff, K. (ed.), *The Sociology of Georg Simmel* (New York: Free Press, 1964, paperback ed.).

Wolff, K. (ed.), *Essays on Sociology and Philosophy by Emile Durkheim et al.* (New York: Harper Torchbooks, 1964).

Worms, R., 'Le premier Congrès de l'Institut International de Sociologie', *RIS*, 2 no. 10 (1894).

Worms, R., 'L'économie sociale' I–II, *RIS*, 6 no. 6–7 (1896).

Wright, E. O., 'To Control or to Smash Bureaucracy: Weber and Lenin on Politics, the State, and Bureaucracy', *Berkeley Journal of Sociology* vol. XIX (1974–75).

Wrong, D., 'The Oversocialized Conception of Man in Modern Sociology', *ASR*, 26 (April 1961) pp. 183–93.

Zeleny, J., *Die Wissenschaftslogik und 'Das Kapital'* (Frankfurt: Europaische Verlagsanstalt, 1968).

Zeitlin, I., *Ideology and the Development of Sociology* (Englewood Cliffs N.J.: Prentice-Hall, 1968).

Periodicals
American Journal of Sociology
L'Année Sociologique
Archiv für Sozialwissenschaft und Sozialpolitik
Revue Internationale de Sociologie
Rivista Italiana di Sociologia

Index